"We are pleased to witness publication of the
Ancient Christian Commentary on Scripture. It is most beneficial for us to learn
how the ancient Christians, especially the saints of the church
who proved through their lives their devotion to God and his Word, interpreted
Scripture. Let us heed the witness of those who have gone before us in the faith."

METROPOLITAN THEODOSIUS
Primate, Orthodox Church in America

"Across Christendom there has emerged a widespread interest
in early Christianity, both at the popular and scholarly level. . . .
Christians of all traditions stand to benefit from this project, especially clergy
and those who study the Bible. Moreover, it will allow us to see how our traditions are
both rooted in the scriptural interpretations of the church fathers while at
the same time seeing how we have developed new perspectives."

ALBERTO FERREIRO
Professor of History, Seattle Pacific University

"The Ancient Christian Commentary on Scripture fills a long overdue need for scholars and
students of the church fathers. . . . Such information will be of immeasurable
worth to those of us who have felt inundated by contemporary interpreters and novel theories
of the biblical text. We welcome some 'new' insight from the
ancient authors in the early centuries of the church."

H. WAYNE HOUSE
Professor of Theology and Law
Trinity University School of Law

Chronological snobbery—the assumption that our ancestors working without benefit of
computers have nothing to teach us—is exposed as nonsense by this magnificent
new series. Surfeited with knowledge but starved of wisdom, many of us are
more than ready to sit at table with our ancestors and listen to their holy
conversations on Scripture. I know I am.

EUGENE H. PETERSON
Professor Emeritus of Spiritual Theology
Regent College

"Few publishing projects have encouraged me as much as the recently announced Ancient Christian Commentary on Scripture with Dr. Thomas Oden serving as general editor. . . . How is it that so many of us who are dedicated to serve the Lord received seminary educations which omitted familiarity with such incredible students of the Scriptures as St. John Chrysostom, St. Athanasius the Great and St. John of Damascus? I am greatly anticipating the publication of this Commentary."

FR. PETER E. GILLQUIST
Director, Department of Missions and Evangelism
Antiochian Orthodox Christian Archdiocese of North America

"The Scriptures have been read with love and attention for nearly two thousand years, and listening to the voice of believers from previous centuries opens us to unexpected insight and deepened faith. Those who studied Scripture in the centuries closest to its writing, the centuries during and following persecution and martyrdom, speak with particular authority. The Ancient Christian Commentary on Scripture will bring to life the truth that we are invisibly surrounded by a 'great cloud of witnesses.'"

FREDERICA MATHEWES-GREEN
Commentator, National Public Radio

"For those who think that church history began around 1941 when their pastor was born, this Commentary will be a great surprise. Christians throughout the centuries have read the biblical text, nursed their spirits with it and then applied it to their lives. These commentaries reflect that the witness of the Holy Spirit was present in his church throughout the centuries. As a result, we can profit by allowing the ancient Christians to speak to us today."

HADDON ROBINSON
Harold John Ockenga Distinguished Professor of Preaching
Gordon-Conwell Theological Seminary

"All who are interested in the interpretation of the Bible will welcome the forthcoming multivolume series Ancient Christian Commentary on Scripture. Here the insights of scores of early church fathers will be assembled and made readily available for significant passages throughout the Bible and the Apocrypha. It is hard to think of a more worthy ecumenical project to be undertaken by the publisher."

BRUCE M. METZGER
Professor of New Testament, Emeritus
Princeton Theological Seminary

ANCIENT CHRISTIAN COMMENTARY ON SCRIPTURE

OLD TESTAMENT

XIV

THE TWELVE PROPHETS

EDITED BY

ALBERTO FERREIRO

GENERAL EDITOR
THOMAS C. ODEN

InterVarsity Press
Downers Grove, Illinois

InterVarsity Press
P.O. Box 1400, Downers Grove, IL 60515-1426
World Wide Web: www.ivpress.com
E-mail: mail@ivpress.com

Library of Congress Cataloging-in-Publication Data

The Twelve Prophets / edited by Alberto Ferreiro; general editor,
Thomas C. Oden.
    p. cm.—(Ancient Christian commentary on Scripture. Old
Testament; 14) Includes bibliographical references and indexes.
    ISBN 0-8308-1484-1 (alk. paper)
    1. Bible. O.T. Minor Prophets—Commentaries. I. Ferreiro, Alberto.
II. Oden, Thomas C. III. Series.
    BS 1560.T87 2003
    224'.9077'09—dc21

                                                                2003001548

P	25	24	23	22	21	20	19	18	17	16	15	14	13	12	11	10	9	8	7	6	5	4	3	2	1
Y	24	23	22	21	20	19	18	17	16	15	14	13	12	11	10	09	08	07	06	05	04	03			

ANCIENT CHRISTIAN COMMENTARY
PROJECT RESEARCH TEAM

GENERAL EDITOR
Thomas C. Oden

ASSOCIATE EDITOR
Christopher A. Hall

OPERATIONS MANAGER
Joel Elowsky

TRANSLATIONS PROJECTS DIRECTOR
Joel Scandrett

RESEARCH AND ACQUISITIONS DIRECTOR
Michael Glerup

EDITORIAL SERVICES DIRECTOR
Warren Calhoun Robertson

ORIGINAL LANGUAGE VERSION DIRECTOR
Konstantin Gavrilkin

GRADUATE RESEARCH ASSISTANTS

Chris Branstetter	*Sergey Kozin*
Jeffrey Finch	*Hsueh-Ming Liao*
Steve Finlan	*Michael Nausner*
Alexei Khamine	*Robert Paul Seesengood*
Vladimir Kharlamov	*Baek-Yong Sung*
Susan Kipper	*Elena Vishnevskaya*

ADMINISTRATIVE ASSISTANT
Judy Cox

142355

CONTENTS

GENERAL INTRODUCTION

The Ancient Christian Commentary on Scripture has as its goal the revitalization of Christian teaching based on classical Christian exegesis, the intensified study of Scripture by lay persons who wish to think with the early church about the canonical text, and the stimulation of Christian historical, biblical, theological and pastoral scholars toward further inquiry into scriptural interpretation by ancient Christian writers.

The time frame of these documents spans seven centuries of exegesis, from Clement of Rome to John of Damascus, from the end of the New Testament era to A.D. 750, including the Venerable Bede.

Lay readers are asking how they might study sacred texts under the instruction of the great minds of the ancient church. This commentary has been intentionally prepared for a general lay audience of nonprofessionals who study the Bible regularly and who earnestly wish to have classic Christian observation on the text readily available to them. The series is targeted to anyone who wants to reflect and meditate with the early church about the plain sense, theological wisdom and moral meaning of particular Scripture texts.

A commentary dedicated to allowing ancient Christian exegetes to speak for themselves will refrain from the temptation to fixate endlessly upon contemporary criticism. Rather, it will stand ready to provide textual resources from a distinguished history of exegesis that has remained massively inaccessible and shockingly disregarded during the last century. We seek to make available to our present-day audiences the multicultural, multilingual, transgenerational resources of the early ecumenical Christian tradition.

Preaching at the end of the first millennium focused primarily on the text of Scripture as understood by the earlier esteemed tradition of comment, largely converging on those writers that best reflected classic Christian consensual thinking. Preaching at the end of the second millennium has reversed that pattern. It has so forgotten most of these classic comments that they are vexing to find anywhere, and even when located they are often available only in archaic editions and inadequate translations. The preached word in our time has remained largely bereft of previously influential patristic inspiration. Recent scholarship has so focused attention upon post-Enlightenment historical and literary methods that it has left this longing largely unattended and unserviced.

This series provides the pastor, exegete, student and lay reader with convenient means to see what Athanasius or John Chrysostom or the desert fathers and mothers had to say about a particular text for preaching, for study and for meditation. There is an emerging awareness among Catholic, Protestant and Orthodox laity that vital biblical preaching and spiritual formation need deeper grounding beyond the scope of the historical-critical orientations that have governed biblical studies in our day.

Hence this work is directed toward a much broader audience than the highly technical and specialized scholarly field of patristic studies. The audience is not limited to the university scholar concentrating on the study of the history of the transmission of the text or to those with highly focused philological interests in textual morphology or historical-critical issues. Though these are crucial concerns for specialists, they are not the paramount interests of this series.

This work is a Christian Talmud. The Talmud is a Jewish collection of rabbinic arguments and comments on the Mishnah, which epitomized the laws of the Torah. The Talmud originated in approximately the same period that the patristic writers were commenting on texts of the Christian tradition. Christians from the late patristic age through the medieval period had documents analogous to the Jewish Talmud and Midrash (Jewish commentaries) available to them in the *glossa ordinaria* and catena traditions, two forms of compiling extracts of patristic exegesis. In Talmudic fashion the sacred text of Christian Scripture was thus clarified and interpreted by the classic commentators.

The Ancient Christian Commentary on Scripture has venerable antecedents in medieval exegesis of both eastern and western traditions, as well as in the Reformation tradition. It offers for the first time in this century the earliest Christian comments and reflections on the Old and New Testaments to a modern audience. Intrinsically an ecumenical project, this series is designed to serve Protestant, Catholic and Orthodox lay, pastoral and scholarly audiences.

In cases where Greek, Latin, Syriac and Coptic texts have remained untranslated into English, we provide new translations. Wherever current English translations are already well rendered, they will be utilized, but if necessary their language will be brought up to date. We seek to present fresh dynamic equivalency translations of long-neglected texts which historically have been regarded as authoritative models of biblical interpretation.

These foundational sources are finding their way into many public libraries and into the core book collections of many pastors and lay persons. It is our intent and the publisher's commitment to keep the whole series in print for many years to come.

Thomas C. Oden
General Editor

A GUIDE TO USING THIS COMMENTARY

Several features have been incorporated into the design of this commentary. The following comments are intended to assist readers in making full use of this volume.

Pericopes of Scripture

The scriptural text has been divided into pericopes, or passages, usually several verses in length. Each of these pericopes is given a heading, which appears at the beginning of the pericope. For example, the first pericope in the commentary on Hosea is "1:1-3 God Tells Hosea to Marry a Harlot." This heading is followed by the Scripture passage quoted in the Revised Standard Version (RSV) across the full width of the page. The Scripture passage is provided for the convenience of readers, but it is also in keeping with medieval patristic commentaries, in which the citations of the Fathers were arranged around the text of Scripture.

Overviews

Following each pericope of text is an overview of the patristic comments on that pericope. The format of this overview varies within the volumes of this series, depending on the requirements of the specific book of Scripture. The function of the overview is to provide a brief summary of all the comments to follow. It tracks a reasonably cohesive thread of argument among patristic comments, even though they are derived from diverse sources and generations. Thus the summaries do not proceed chronologically or by verse sequence. Rather they seek to rehearse the overall course of the patristic comment on that pericope.

We do not assume that the commentators themselves anticipated or expressed a formally received cohesive argument but rather that the various arguments tend to flow in a plausible, recognizable pattern. Modern readers can thus glimpse aspects of continuity in the flow of diverse exegetical traditions representing various generations and geographical locations.

Topical Headings

An abundance of varied patristic comment is available for each pericope of these letters. For this reason we have broken the pericopes into two levels. First is the verse with its topical heading. The patristic comments are then focused on aspects of each verse, with topical headings summarizing the essence of the patristic comment by evoking a key phrase, metaphor or idea. This feature provides a bridge by which modern readers can enter into the heart of the patristic comment.

Identifying the Patristic Texts

Following the topical heading of each section of comment, the name of the patristic commentator is given. An English translation of the patristic comment is then provided. This is immediately followed by the title of the patristic work and the textual reference—either by book, section and subsection or by book-and-verse references.

The Footnotes

Readers who wish to pursue a deeper investigation of the patristic works cited in this commentary will find the footnotes especially valuable. A footnote number directs the reader to the notes at the bottom of the right-hand column, where in addition to other notations (clarifications or biblical cross references) one will find information on English translations (where available) and standard original-language editions of the work cited. An abbreviated citation (normally citing the book, volume and page number) of the work is provided. A key to the abbreviations is provided on page xv. Where there is any serious ambiguity or textual problem in the selection, we have tried to reflect the best available textual tradition.

Where original language texts have remained untranslated into English, we provide new translations. Wherever current English translations are already well rendered, they are utilized, but where necessary they are stylistically updated. A single asterisk (*) indicates that a previous English translation has been updated to modern English or amended for easier reading. The double asterisk (**) indicates either that a new translation has been provided or that some extant translation has been significantly amended. We have standardized spellings and made grammatical variables uniform so that our English references will not reflect the odd spelling variables of the older English translations. For ease of reading we have in some cases edited out superfluous conjunctions.

For the convenience of computer database users the digital database references are provided to either the Thesaurus Linguae Graecae (Greek texts) or to the Cetedoc (Latin texts) in the appendix found on pages 314-21.

ABBREVIATIONS

Works Cited

ACD	St. Augustine. *On Christian Doctrine.* Translated by D. W. Robertson Jr. Library of Liberal Arts. Indianaapolis: Bobbs-Merrill, 1958.
ACW	Ancient Christian Writers: The Works of the Fathers in Translation. Mahwah, N.J.: Paulist, 1946-.
ANF	A. Roberts and J. Donaldson, eds. Ante-Nicene Fathers. 10 vols. Buffalo, N.Y.: Christian Literature, 1885-1896. Reprint, Grand Rapids, Mich.: Eerdmans, 1951-1956. Reprint, Peabody, Mass.: Hendrickson, 1994.
ARL	St. Athanasius. *The Resurrection Letters.* Paraphrased and introduced by Jack N. Sparks. Nashville: Thomas Nelson, 1979.
BFG	Gregory the Great. *Be Friends of God: Spiritual Reading from Gregory the Great.* Translated by John Leinenweber. Cambridge, Mass.: Cowley Publications, 1990.
CAME	Augustine. *The Confessions of Augustine in Modern English.* Translated and abridged by Sherwood E. Wirt. Clarion Classics. Grand Rapids, Mich.: Zondervan, 1971.
CCL	Corpus Christianorum. Series Latina. Turnhout, Belgium: Brepols, 1953-.
COP	St. John Chyrsostom. *Six Books on the Priesthood.* Translated by Graham Neville. Crestwood, N.Y.: St. Vladimir's Seminary Press, 1984.
CS	Cistercian Studies. Kalamazoo, Mich.: Cistercian Publications, 1973-.
CSCO	Corpus Scriptorum Christianorum Orientalium. Louvain, Belgium: 1903-.
ECTD	C. McCarthy, trans. and ed. *Saint Ephrem's Commentary on Tatian's Diatessaron: An English Translation of Chester Beatty Syriac MS 709.* Journal of Semitic Studies Supplement 2. Oxford: Oxford University Press for the University of Manchester, 1993.
EKOG	Eznik of Kolb. *On God.* Translated by Monica J. Blanchard and Robin Darling Young. Leuven, Belgium: Peeters, 1998.
ESOO	J. S. Assemani, ed. *Sancti Patris nostri Ephraem Syri Opera omnia.* 6 vols. Rome, 1732-1746.
FC	Fathers of the Church: A New Translation. Washington, D.C.: Catholic University of America Press, 1947-.
FGFR	*Faith Gives Fullness to Reasoning: The Five Theological Orations of Gregory Nazianzen.* Introduction and commentary by F. W. Norris. Leiden and New York: E. J. Brill, 1990.
GCS	Die griechischen christlichen Schriftsteller der ersten Jahrhunderte. Berlin: Akademie-Verlag, 1897-.
GNTIP	Ronald E. Heine, trans. *Gregory of Nyssa's Treatise on the Inscriptions of the Psalms.* Oxford Early Christian Studies. Oxford: Clarendon Press, 1995.
INAL	St. Isaac of Nineveh. *On Ascetical Life.* Translated by Mary Hansbury. Crestwood, N.Y.: St. Vladimir's Seminary Press, 1989.
LCC	J. Baillie et al., eds. The Library of Christian Classics. 26 vols. Philadelphia: Westminster Press, 1953-1966.

LF	A Library of Fathers of the Holy Catholic Church Anterior to the Division of the East and West. Translated by members of the English Church. 44 vols. Oxford: John Henry Parker, 1800-1881.
LSL	Eugen J. Pentiuc. *Long-Suffering Love: A Commentary on Hosea with Patristic Annotations.* Brookline, Mass.: Holy Cross Orthodox Press, 2002.
NPNF	P. Schaff et al., eds. A Select Library of the Nicene and Post-Nicene Fathers of the Christian Church. 2 series (14 vols. each). Buffalo, N.Y.: Christian Literature, 1887-1894. Reprint, Grand Rapids, Mich.: Eerdmans, 1952-1956. Reprint, Peabody, Mass.: Hendrickson, 1994.
OSW	*Origen: An Exhortation to Martyrdom, Prayer and Selected Writings.* Translated by Rowan A. Green. New York: Paulist, 1979.
OUC	St. Cyril of Alexandria. *On the Unity of Christ.* Translated by John Anthony McGuckin. Crestwood, N.Y.: St. Vladimir's Seminary Press, 2000.
OWP	John Chrysostom. *On Wealth and Poverty.* Translated by Catharine P. Roth. Crestwood, N.Y.: St. Vladimir's Seminary Press, 1984.
PDCW	*Pseudo-Dionysius: The Complete Works.* Translated by Colm Luibheid. Classics of Western Spirituality. New York: Paulist, 1987.
PG	J.-P. Migne, ed. Patrologiae cursus completus. Series Graeca. 166 vols. Paris: Migne, 1857-1886.
PL	J.-P. Migne, ed. Patrologiae cursus completus. Series Latina. 221 vols. Paris: Migne, 1844-1864.
PMPC	E. B. Pusey. *The Minor Prophets: A Commentary.* 2 vols. Grand Rapids, Mich.: Baker, 1972.
POG	Eusebius. *The Proof of the Gospel.* Translated by W. J. Ferrar. London: SPCK, 1920. Reprint, Grand Rapids, Mich.: Baker, 1981.
PS	R. Graffin, ed. Patrologia Syriaca. 3 vols. Paris: Firmin-Didot et socii, 1894-1926.
SC	H. de Lubac, J. Daniélou et al., eds. Sources Chrétiennes. Paris: Éditions du Cerf, 1941-.
TTH	G. Clark, M. Gibson and M. Whitby, eds. Translated Texts for Historians. Liverpool: Liverpool University Press, 1985-.
WLUA	Manley, Johanna, ed. *Wisdom, Let Us Attend: Job, the Fathers and the Old Testament.* Menlo Park, Calif.: Monastery Books, 1997.
WSA	J. E. Rotelle, ed. *The Works of St. Augustine: A Translation for the Twenty-First Century.* Hyde Park, N.Y.: New City Press, 1990-.

General Abbreviations

ch., chs.	chapter, chapters
Cn	correction in RSV text made by the Standard Bible Committee where agreement was reached regarding restoration of the original text
LXX	the Septuagint, a Greek version of the Old Testament
Heb	Hebrew of the consonantal Masoretic Text of the Old Testament
Tg	Targum, any one of various Aramaic translations or expanded paraphrases of the Old Testament
Vg	Vulgate, the Latin version of the Old Testament

Introduction to the Twelve Prophets

In comparison to many other books of the sacred Scriptures, the Minor Prophets do not receive much attention in our time in either homilies or catecheses. The church fathers, however, recognized the importance of the twelve prophets. This view was already signaled by the New Testament authors in their search for prophetic oracles regarding the Messiah. For Christians, Jesus Christ was the direct subject of the prophecies. Although the New Testament writers refer to select parts of the Old Testament as prophetic revelation about Jesus Christ, which they believed he fulfilled, the church fathers took this exegetical exercise to greater heights. In the Gospel of Luke, Jesus engaged in the same exegesis with the two disciples on the road to Emmaus when he expounded to them, beginning with Moses through the Prophets and the Psalms, all manner of things concerning himself (Lk 24:27, 44).

As the postapostolic church forged its identity, the question of its relationship to the old covenant was of paramount importance. The question over the relevance of the Old Testament Scriptures regarding the new covenant became an increasingly pressing issue as discussions over the canon of Scripture unfolded. Since a consensus was quickly established that the Old Testament Scriptures were a patrimony of the church—a view that was already established in the apostolic church proper—the main goal of the exegesis of these Scriptures focused on finding the hidden Christ within them. The preservation of the new covenant in written form in the Gospels and in the rest of the corpus of the New Testament became the most tangible way of expressing the connection between the two covenants in the Old and New Testament Scriptures. A good number of the twelve prophets were given prominence in key places of the New Testament, but among the church fathers they were accorded an even more significant role in scriptural exegesis of prophecies pointing to Jesus Christ as the promised Messiah.

It is not necessary here to delve into questions of authorship, date and other such matters for each of the twelve prophets (see the introductions for each book in the commentary). One is directed to the abundant commentaries on each of these books that reveal almost as many viewpoints as there are commentators. Of fundamental importance for us is that the twelve prophets were for Jesus, the apostles, the church fathers and Jews the very word of God. Numerous Christians—Catholic, Orthodox, Protestant—and Jews still believe this today, regardless of the radical claims in certain quarters of the modern academic community.

The Major Interpreters

As might be expected, the patristic references to the twelve prophets are abundant. I have attempted to give a broad representation of both Greek and Latin fathers with a few from other traditions, such as Syriac. Also, I have given attention to many authors of complete commentaries on the twelve prophets: Jerome, Cyril of Alexandria, Theodore of Mopsuestia, Theodoret of Cyr and Isho'dad of Merv. Jerome and Cyril represent a type of exegesis representative of the Alexandrian School,[1] while Theodore, Theodoret and Isho'dad are representative of Antioch's exegesis.[2]

Jerome wrote many, although not all, of his commentaries on the twelve prophets when he was at an advanced age. For instance, he wrote two commentaries on Obadiah, the first of which was highly allegorical (374 A.D.) but is entirely lost to us. He remarks that his second commentary (396) took him only a couple of nights to complete and was based somewhat on Origen and rabbinical sources. His comments provide interesting insights into the historiography and geography of the area during his time in Bethlehem, but they are also christocentric in emphasis and allegorical analysis.

Cyril shows an interest in the historicity of events portrayed. Although also schooled in the Alexandrian allegory epitomized in Origen, who believed there was a hidden meaning behind every word, Cyril avers that some texts do not speak of Christ at all. Nonetheless, Cyril finds Christ allegorized in any number of texts.

Theodore's commentary epitomizes the Antiochene form of exegesis. It is one of the few Greek works of his that have survived in their entirety. His exegesis is largely historical-grammatical, oriented toward a literal understanding of the text although sometimes coupled with a typological interpretation[3] of the Hebrew text in order to establish a connection to the New Testament.

The commentary of Theodoret of Cyr exhibits exegesis which demonstrates typological and christocentric interpretation at many points. The twelve prophets are also quoted extensively in letters and homilies of many of the fathers, especially when they were speaking of direct prophecies of Christ's life, such as Micah 5:2 or Zechariah 9:9, but also on other issues. Gregory the Great's *Morals on the Book of Job*, for instance, refers frequently to the twelve prophets on issues of pastoral care.

As much as possible, I chose quotations from the fathers that reveal the diversity of interpretations and pastoral applications of a single biblical text. In rare cases, some church fathers engaged in abstract exegetical explanations, which likely were lost to their wider audience, save a select few theologians. I have by and large avoided this type of commentary. In any case, the reader of this volume will come away with a deeper appreciation of the twelve prophets and their central role in Christian exegesis of the Old Testament, whose primary goal has always been to proclaim that Jesus Christ is indeed the Messiah, the Son of God and Savior of all seekers of God.

Prophecy and the Hebrews

The designation of major or minor prophet reflects the length of the material only. It is not a qualitative or even hierarchical distinction of the status of the prophets. The prophetic books reflect an official canon and institution of the true Word of God that formed a nexus between God and his people either to console or to reprimand. These oracles were communicated to the prophets by way of dreams, visions, ecstasies and concrete events, which they in turn delivered in the form of sermons, writings or symbolic actions. All of the evidence points to the fact that the prophetic office was not inherited. Instead God called men and

---

[1] Alexandrian exegesis often emphasized the spiritual meaning of the text that was to be found hidden under the literal sense.

[2] Antiochene exegesis, on the whole, emphasized the literal meaning of the text and used typology to demonstrate connections between the Old and New Testaments (cf. below).

[3] Typology perceived events and utterances found in the Prophets as *typoi* (types) foreshadowing Christ and the events of the New Testament.

women to the prophetic office at distinct times and in distinct places, regardless of social rank. (A similar development occurred later with apostolic succession.) Formulaic prefaces such as "thus says the Lord," "word of the Lord" and "hear this word" demonstrate that the prophets spoke directly for God.

When the prophets spoke on moral issues, they always delivered their messages in view of the Mosaic law and people's fidelity or infidelity to it. The primary concern was to heal a rupture of the covenant with God and his people. There are also frequent references to the promised Messiah who would come to subdue all the nations, establish justice, bring all peoples under the covenant and judge their deeds. The judgment and standards of conduct are especially hard on the Hebrews precisely because they were expected to be a light to the nations. Thus they could not claim ignorance of their relation to the one true God.

Moreover, prophetic revelations do not follow any strict historical chronological order or perspective. A single prophecy may at times contain predictions about events in the immediate or distant future. We witness these same phenomena in the New Testament in prophecies attributed to Jesus. Matthew 24 is a clear example. Numerous scholars point out that immediate prophecy also served as types and figures of future events so that a single prophecy had potential application for a contemporary situation in the prophet's lifetime and the distant future. Most of the church fathers, with the exception of those who followed Theodore of Mopsuestia, who limited themselves to the prophecies singled out by the New Testament, were convinced that all of the prophecies, even the Psalter, spoke of Christ either in explicit or veiled ways.

The prophet's main ministry was to call the Hebrews back to their God (e.g., Zech 1:4). At times the prophets did not appear to have full knowledge of the meaning and purpose of what God called them to proclaim. For example, Jonah expressed his lack of understanding by initially refusing to cooperate with God. Among the Hebrews, Moses would always be regarded as the archetypal prophet, even though Elijah too would reach great prominence. That is why the prophetic books were always placed in the Old Testament after the Torah. Likewise the Gospels, which contain the words and deeds of the new Moses, have prominence in the New Testament order. In the Hebrew canon the books designated as prophetic were more broadly conceived and thus spanned from Joshua to Malachi, excluding Daniel. In the Greek canon, however, the prophetic books were restricted to Isaiah through Malachi, including Daniel.

In general terms, the emerging church and the community at Qumran read prophecy in one of two ways: as pointing to the distant future, when all secrets would be revealed, or as pointing specifically to their communities as the direct objects of prophetic fulfillment. Both groups considered many in the larger community of Jews to have fallen away from God's designs. The New Testament itself established the foundation for this approach at the outset for the postapostolic church. Thus it is clear that this was not something the church fathers invented or even forced upon the texts. However, there is no doubt that they took the prophetic texts to greater lengths of interpretation to extract from them, mainly through allegory and typology, their christological meaning.

Christians adopted the belief from Mishnaic and Talmudic Judaism that the age of formal prophecy ended with the destruction of the first temple or during the time of Haggai, Zechariah and Malachi. The extra books, not even the extended version of Daniel of the Septuagint, did not in themselves upset this scheme. Moses too was given the primacy in relation to the prophets among all Jews. In Christianity, however, the church fathers promoted building on the apostolic belief that Jesus, the new Moses, had fulfilled the law of Moses and the prophets and had established a new Israel, the church. Early medieval Jewish exegetes vigorously rejected this idea in their apologetics as a way to counter the teaching that Israel had been replaced by the church.

This transition from Israel to the church as the new chosen people, which included Jew and Gentile, revolved around the church fathers' interpretation of the significance of the destruction of the temple by the Romans in A.D. 70. The church fathers repeatedly commented on the destruction of the temple in their interpretation of virtually all of the minor prophets, and this event was deciphered at a variety of levels. It provided proof of the divinity of Christ and of his true prophetic status, since, in the Gospels, he had predicted the desolation of the temple and Jerusalem, which occurred after his ascension decades later. The silence about the actual event in the Gospels was also proof for many of the church fathers that the Gospels were written during the eyewitness period (that is, before A.D. 70 for all four Gospels). It is much harder to explain how that first generation of Jews could have written their Gospels after the fact, for they say virtually nothing about the destruction. This idea is gaining significant support again in the scholarly community (see J. A. T. Robinson, Carsten P. Thiede and Klaus Berger, among others). For a long time, New Testament scholars dismissed the issues based upon dubious assumptions and methodologies originating as far back as the Enlightenment. Furthermore, the church fathers saw the event as a punishment from God upon unbelieving Jews for their rejection of Jesus as the Messiah. Lastly, it demonstrated that the old covenant priesthood, sacrifices, rituals and symbols had been abolished for good and had been replaced by the priesthood and sacraments of the new covenant, most especially the Eucharist. The profound spiritual, sacramental and historical impact of the destruction of the temple was lost neither to the church fathers nor to contemporary Jews.

Prophecy and the Church

The belief of the church that God's revelation of his will was progressive is a major foundation for the Christian view of prophecy and did not originate with the church fathers. It was already revealed by Jesus and by the apostles, most especially by Paul in his epistles. The church fathers appropriated this theme and elaborated it with great vigor and creativity. An important qualifier, not lost to the church fathers, needs to be mentioned. The apostle Paul, while believing that Jesus had fulfilled all of the law and the prophets, maintained that the old covenant with Israel was an eternal one and had not been abolished in spite of their rejection of Christ. For this reason Paul prophesied that at some time in the future Israel would come to full belief in Jesus as the Messiah.

This statement by Paul about the conversion of the Jews proved to be a restraining hand against anti-Semitism, which would have been considerably worse without it. This explains why the forced conversion of Jews, or anyone for that matter, was consistently condemned and was never an official teaching of the church. Throughout the history of the church, the Jews have always been considered a central part of God's overall plan of salvation, even in this age. The strong language that one finds in the church fathers concerning the Jews' rejection of Jesus strikes us as strident, if not shocking, in this more ecumenical time in which we live.

We must bear several things in mind about this hard language. For centuries, even well into the early modern period, the use of sharp imagery, metaphors, allegory and other literary devices was the normal way of expression, intended to drive a major point home through striking forms of communication. In the era of the church fathers, one finds similarly shocking remarks made by Jews against Jesus and Christians. Even Jesus, who expressed himself in rather strident ways, manifests this Jewish way of teaching. What was a normal way of expression then, particularly in apologetics—Jewish or Gentile—would now be considered unacceptable, and rightly so. We must, however, let the texts speak as they were written without imposing our agendas in anachronistic ways.

The church fathers interpreted the entire Old Testament (Septuagint) as prophecy about Christ, as type pointing to Christ and antitype against the Jews for rejecting Christ. The pericopes chosen for this volume overwhelmingly demonstrate that for the church fathers, all of the ceremonies and sacrifices of the temple prefigured Christ, the church and the sacraments of the new covenant. Moreover, the fact that such types could be clearly discerned was proof for the church fathers that the Christian faith was the only true fulfillment of the prophecies. They were convinced of this also by the clear evidence that the sacraments of the old covenant were never intended to be perpetually valid. The church fathers repeatedly stress that the old Israel had been transformed into the new Israel. Prophecy and its fulfillment by Christ was also a sign that he was the anointed one. On numerous occasions, the church fathers utilized the christological interpretation of prophecy to demonstrate the inspiration of the New Testament testimony, thus giving it equal if not superior status to that of the Old Testament. The formation of the New Testament canon of Scripture was the result of not only a polemic between Catholic and Gnostic groups but also of the polemic with Judaism.

In the heated exchange between Jews and Christians regarding the messianic texts, both used metaphor to vindicate their respective claims. While the church fathers argued that Christ fulfilled a certain set of prophecies, they maintained that many future prophecies still awaited their realization and that Christ would bring them to fruition in the second advent. Jews rejected Christ as the fulfillment of the first advent, and they denied that the Messiah they still awaited had anything to do with Jesus, a position that has remained largely unchanged within Judaism.

The New Testament laid the foundation for the prophetic search for Jesus in the Old Testament with the goal of demonstrating that he had fulfilled all the necessary requisites of the Messiah. These references to the Old Testament are found in the Gospels, Acts of the Apostles, Paul's epistles, 1 Peter, 1 John and Revelation. The church fathers—as is evident from the volumes of the ACCS series, which contain representative and consensual texts—used various exegetical approaches to derive from the Old Testament what they saw were abundant christological references. In the post-New Testament era, there was considerable debate about discernment of the teachings of self-proclaimed prophets and their messages. These prophecies are distinct from those that pointed to the future Messiah in either of the two advents because they were alleged new messages regarding Jesus and his church. This discussion was distinct from the one between Jews and Christians—via the church fathers—who argued about the identity of the Messiah. The selected commentary in this volume does not delve into this internal debate in the church regarding the legitimate or illegitimate manifestations of the Holy Spirit or new messages regarding Jesus subsequent to the apostolic teaching. The church fathers were intent to show that Jesus was the Messiah, that the church was the new Israel and that the temple sacrifices were fulfilled in those of the new covenant, and replaced by the Eucharist. They also wanted to demonstrate that the Old Testament priesthood had been replaced by the new one established with the Twelve and their successors, the bishops and priests, and that there was still a second advent to take place in the future. This advent would bring about the last judgment and the establishment of a universal, eternal kingdom. For the church fathers, Old Testament prophecy had a past, present (their time) and future dimension, which collectively pointed to Jesus Christ and his church.

What follows are selected, representative quotations of the church fathers in which they focus upon Christ's fulfillment of Hebrew prophecies. There are, of course, many other applications to these specific texts, and readers will find these also within the covers of this volume. In keeping with tradition, I have chosen to present the prophets in the order in which they are found in the common Old Testament shared by Catholics, Orthodox, Protestants and Jews who, at least on this point, uphold a canonical consensus.

Hosea is one of the more extensive narratives of the Minor Prophets, and therefore the numerous christological messages the church fathers found there should not come as a surprise. Hosea 1:1-3 was typically viewed as a prophetic description of Jesus and the prostitute as recorded Matthew 26:6-13. In Hosea 2:19-23, the prediction of the salvation of the Gentiles is proclaimed. Hosea 3:4-5 contains references to Christ coming from the offspring of David and to the manner in the Eucharist. Christ's passion, descent to the dead (summarized in many early baptismal confessions) and resurrection were anticipated in Hosea 6:1-11. The temple worship of the old covenant foreshadowed the new temple of the new covenant, namely, Christ, in Hosea 6:6-9. The promise of the Holy Spirit is announced in Hosea 7. The falling away and replacement of Judas was prophetically anticipated in Hosea 8. Mainly secular opposition to the Christ by Herod, Pontius Pilate and the Roman state is alluded to in Hosea 10:1-11. In addition, the flight of the holy family to Egypt and the designation of Jesus as the new Son of Egypt is represented in Hosea 11. The gifts of the Holy Spirit manifested in the new covenant at Pentecost were announced prophetically in Hosea 12. The destruction of death through Christ's paschal mystery was anticipated in Hosea 13:13-15. Hosea 14 ends with a disturbing prophecy regarding the future apostasy of the Jews, which is associated with their rejection of Christ.

Undoubtedly Joel is the prophet most associated with the outpouring of the Holy Spirit at Pentecost, and the New Testament recognized as much. Joel 2:14-25 signals the demise of the devil by Christ, the cross of Christ as the new tree of life and the fig tree as the new vine, which is Christ, who gives the new wine of eternal life. Joel 2:28-32 promises the sending of the Holy Spirit, Christ's ascension and the day of Pentecost, which completes redemption. Joel 2:31-32 has a double message regarding martyrdom and salvation. Joel 3:1-21 speaks of the judgment of the nations, a remnant of true believers and the incarnation.

According to the Fathers, the prophet Amos predicted the rending of the veil of the temple and the earthquake at Jesus' crucifixion. The betrayal of Judas is foreseen by the prophet in Amos 2:6. Amos 4:11 warns that the destruction of Sodom and Gomorrah reveals that Christ is also a judge. In Amos 8, the passion of Christ, the rending of the temple veil, the earthquake and the darkened sun are foretold in striking detail. Within this same chapter Joseph is depicted as a type of Christ. Also, Christ is depicted as the new bread of eternal life. Amos 9 contains a prophetic reference to the ascension and to Christ as the new tabernacle that has replaced the old temple, which was destroyed by the Romans.

The briefest of all the prophets is Obadiah. The fall of Lucifer makes a contribution to New Testament diabology and its related relevance to the problem of evil and theodicy. The catastrophic consequences of the destruction of the temple, as predicted by Jesus, was foretold in the fall of the Edomites. Edom, moreover, is a type of the devil. The "Day of the Lord" is a time of punishment, but it is likewise a time for divine justice and fairness. Some church fathers applied the "Day" to the punishment of unbelievers at the last judgment. The cup of wrath that the Assyrians and Chaldeans drank foreshadowed that which the Jews experienced with the Romans in A.D. 70. Jerusalem, Mount Zion and Mount Esau are all used as types of the church.

The prophet Jonah emerged as one of the central minor prophets in relation to the new covenant. This is so mainly because Jesus likened himself to Jonah. Thus the prophet Jonah and his prophecy were singled out by the church fathers to flesh out more fully its christological meaning. They argued that Jonah 1:17 spoke of the resurrection of Christ. Jonah 1:4-17 contains a variety of later-disclosed meanings: Jesus calming the sea and the winds, Matthias replacing the apostate Judas by lot, and the whole episode reflecting Jonah as a type of the resurrection. Jonah 2:1-2 casts Jonah as being in line with the heroics of Elijah and the seven Maccabees. Not only is the whale related to Jonah, but also the belly of the beast is seen as a type of Mary's womb and of Christ's tomb. The book of Jonah also further connects Jonah's repentance with that of Peter. Jonah's three days in the whale was a type of the harrowing of hell by Christ, as professed in the Apostles' Creed. Furthermore, even as Jonah survived the whale and Elijah survived the fiery chariot, so Christ survived the tomb. The Fathers typologically connected the ship and the whale of Jonah 3:1-4 to the tree of crucifixion and the tomb respectively, as well as Jonah and the sailors to Christ at the hands of sinners. Jonah 3:5-10 images and contrasts Nineveh as an example of repentance as opposed to the unrepentant attitude of Sodom. In Jonah 4, the gourd, the vine and the worm that consumed them is Christ, who with his sacrifice consumed the old covenant.

In Micah 1, the church fathers managed to find a variety of typological and spiritual messages. Micah was a foreshadowing of Jesus, while the three men who appeared to Abraham were a type of the triune revelation. Moreover, the living waters of paradise are to be found in this chapter. Micah 2 reveals that Mount Zion as a type of the messianic hope has found fulfillment in the church, which is called the new Jerusalem. Micah 3 contains a solemn prediction of the destruction of Jerusalem fulfilled by the Romans and foretold by Jesus. Micah 4 identifies Jesus as the mountain that will judge all of the nations. Also, Jesus is symbolically represented as the vine and the Holy Spirit as the fig tree. Micah 5:1-2 contains the entire nativity: the magi, the star, Bethlehem and the virgin birth. Micah 5:3 speaks further about the birth of Jesus and the special election of Mary. Moreover, Assur-Nimrod typologically anticipates the antichrist in the Apocalypse of John and his attack upon the church. Micah 7:14-20 speaks of the removal of sin through baptism, which was foretold by the exodus. The Egyptians were a type of sin, while the Red Sea waters are Christian baptismal waters that unite one to the death and resurrection of Christ.

The brief prophetic book of Nahum did not deter the church fathers from discovering a rich depository of New Testament images. Nahum's parting of the water (Nahum 1) mirrors Jesus walking on the water, thus showing Christ's lordship. The breath of the Holy Spirit is applied to the resurrection of Christ and Christ's breath upon the twelve apostles in the Gospel of John. Furthermore, all of the Old Testament temple sacrifices and rituals have been fulfilled in the new covenant, including the exodus, which is now reflected in the eucharistic new Passover. Nahum 2—3 reemphasizes that the breath of the Holy Spirit refers to the special anointing Jesus gave to the twelve apostles to remit sin as new priests of the new covenant. This anointing they pass on through apostolic succession.

For the church fathers, Habakkuk 2:1-3 revealed a prophecy regarding the second advent of Christ, as well as a rejection of the first advent by the Jews. Habakkuk 2:4 suggests the costly perfume and Mary Magdalene's act of worship of Jesus, which is an exemplary act of almsgiving. Habakkuk 2:5-20 speaks of Mary as the one who would carry the Messiah in her womb. Habakkuk 3:1-2 shows how Christ is the one who links the two covenants, represented by the two animals. The miracle of the wine at Cana reveals God's perfect timing and provision and accentuates divine providence. Lastly, the transfiguration reveals how the old covenant has been replaced by the new covenant. Habakkuk 3:3-6 speaks of Jerusalem, the Mount of Olives, the ascension of Christ, Judea and Bethlehem. The Son of the unicorns (Ps 28:6 LXX) is a type of Christ and the cross. Habakkuk 3:7-19 contains a variety of prophetic images about Christ and priests: the sun and moon are the ascension and the priests. Emmanuel refers to God's own coming as high priest.

The book of Zephaniah was consistently interpreted by the church fathers as revealing the passage from an exclusively Jewish, old-covenant relationship with God to a universal, Gentile-inclusive new covenant. Zephaniah 1—2 reveals that the islands are the Gentiles, to whom the message of salvation is being proclaimed. The destruction of the temple was God's dramatic way of doing away with the old covenant and judging the Jews for resisting Christ as Messiah. Zephaniah 3 compares and contrasts the sacrifices of both covenants, the new being the greater because it includes the Gentiles. The new covenant has replaced the old, and the new city of God has replaced Jerusalem. The arm and shoulder in this section typify the universality of the new covenant in Christ, who alone can truly wash away sins.

Haggai 1 shows that the new temple of the Holy Spirit is no longer a fixed building like the old temple but rather the body of believers. Haggai 2:1-7 typologically speaks of Christ's second advent garments in the person of Jehozadak. Zerubbabel has a double typological meaning in that he points to Christ and the church, and anticipates the movement in revelation from idolatry to law, from law to gospel. The two advents of Christ were foretold by the prophet. Haggai 2:8-23, when speaking about the restored temple, was a prophecy about the new covenant. The comparison of David and Zerubbabel mirrors the same between Elijah and John the Baptist in the New Testament. The signet ring of Zerubbabel, which signifies kingly power, foretells Christ the king.

The prophet Zechariah is one of the longer books of the twelve and thus provided the church fathers with much material for comment. Zechariah 2 had hidden within it a foreshadowing of the Father and the Son, including the salvific message of Jesus for Jews and Gentiles. Zechariah 3:1-2 contributed to the belief that Melchizedek was a type of the eternal priesthood of Christ. Zechariah 3:3-10 speaks about the spiritual regeneration that a person who is baptized experiences, and how Jesus, who is incarnate, consumed human sin through his humanity. Zechariah 4 reveals an apocalyptic message through the two candles, which are antichrists, and the two olive trees, which are the Lord. Furthermore, the lamp of seven orifices is the old and new covenants. Zechariah 5 signals the first advent through the sign of the ax and sickle. Zechariah 6 points out that Christ resurrected is contained in a veiled way through the names *Orient* and *Sunrise*. The darkness, however, is a symbol for the betrayal of Judas. Zechariah 7—8 predicted the removal of temple worship along with its sacrifices when the Romans destroyed the temple. Zechariah 9:1-9 prophesies in detail the entry of Jesus into Jerusalem riding on a donkey. Zechariah 9:10-17 contains a wide range of types and symbols, including the resurrection. The tower is Jesus, and the wheels refer to the movement in history of God the Spirit. Zechariah 11:12 foretells the betrayal of Jesus by Judas for thirty pieces of silver, while Zechariah 12 warns about the last judgment that awaits the Jews for rejecting Jesus. It is a defense that when Jesus returns to judge the human race, he will have a human body, albeit a resurrected one. Also, Christ and the wounds of his passion will be used to judge his crucifiers at his second advent. The mourning of the tribes refers to the trials of martyrdom. Zechariah 13 speaks of Judas's betrayal and Peter's denial of Jesus. Moreover, the rock that Moses struck was Jesus. Zechariah 14 proclaims the second advent of Christ at the Mount of Olives as the final judgment. Finally, the darkness of the day and the two thieves at the crucifixion were explicitly foretold.

Malachi, the bookend for the Old Testament, closes a long phase of revealed truth for Jews. For Christians, however, it anticipates the fulfillment of all the messianic expectation of the old covenant in Christ. In general, this messianic expectation is what the church fathers gleaned from the last of the prophets. Malachi 1:1-9 reveals justice and judgment through Jacob and Esau, respectively, whereas Rachel and Leah are a type of Christ and the synagogue, respectively. Malachi 1:10 heralds the removal of the temple as a sign of the coming of the Gentiles into a covenant with God through Christ. Malachi 1:10-14 is pregnant with rich eucharistic meaning. The Eucharist replaces Aaron and Melchizedek, and the flour of the old covenant finds its fulfillment in the bread of the Eucharist. It continues the theme by stating that the Eucharist replaced the temple sacrifices, and Melchizedek was a type of the Eucharist. The fact that worship of God no longer takes place in the temple or at Mount Gerizim demonstrates the universal relevance of the Eucharist. Malachi 2:10-17 highlights that marriage is not only a civic or social union but a full sacrament before God. Malachi 3:1 once again identifies John the Baptist as the Elijah who would proclaim the Messiah. In Malachi 4:1-3 the cross is foretold symbolically in Jacob's thigh, and Jesus is the Sun of Justice who will come to judge the nations of the earth. Malachi 4:4-6 appropriately closes by once again heralding that Elijah will reveal the Messiah—which was a role fulfilled by John the Baptist.

This is only a sampling of the major themes that the church fathers emphasized in their search for christological types, symbols and prophecies in the Minor Prophets. There is much more besides that readers of this volume can feast upon as they allow the church fathers to nurture and instruct.

I owe an enormous debt of gratitude to my student assistants Joshua Adam, Michael Lucero and Jaron Kamin. Especially I owe a debt to Thomas C. Oden, Christopher Hall, Joel Elowsky, Calhoun Robertson, Alexei Khamine and Chris Branstetter. Without their expert interventions this work would have never seen the light of day. I dedicate this volume to my earliest mentors: the Rev. Dr. Bede K. Lackner, O. Cist; Dr. Douglas W. Richmond; and Dr. Edward C. Bock[†] (University of Texas-Arlington).

Alberto Ferreiro
Seattle Pacific University
Feast of John of the Cross

HOSEA

OVERVIEW: Hosea (Heb *hôšēʿa*) is probably an abbreviation of "Yahweh saves." He is listed as the first of the so-called twelve minor prophets. Hosea 1:1 dates the oracles of Hosea in the reigns of Uzziah, Jotham, Ahaz and Hezekiah of Judah and Jeroboam II of Israel. It is likely that his oracles began in the last years of the reigns of Jeroboam II (786-746 B.C.). Scholars do not agree when the last oracle was given. The tribute of Menahem of Israel to Assyria is probably reflected in Hosea 5:13, 7:11, 8:9, 10:5 and 12:2. Some scholars set the date at 725, just before the final siege of Samaria by the Assyrians, while others set it at the fall of the city in 721. There is, however, no specific evidence for this calamity in the book. Hosea was a subject of the northern kingdom, and his oracles related to that region. All we know about his life is that his father was Beeri and that he married.

Thematically the book falls into two large parts: Hosea 1—3 and Hosea 4—14. Hosea 1—3 contains the title and tells of Hosea's marriage to Gomer (Hos 1:1-9), an oracle of restoration (Hos 1:10-11 [2:1-2 Heb]), Yahweh as the husband of Israel (Hos 2:1-23 [2:3-25 Heb]) and a personal account of Hosea's marriage (Hos 3:1-5). Hosea 4—14 contains collections of oracles that display no discernable order.

While the most significant interpreters were Jerome and Theodore of Mopsuestia, many other church fathers commented on this prophet. For others, such as Didymus the Blind, we have only fragments of a commentary written at the request of Jerome. Theodore of Mopsuestia approached Hosea mainly from a historical-grammatical orientation to arrive at the literal sense as a stepping stone in making typological connections with the Old Testament. As noted earlier, he limited himself to the Old Testament texts cited specifically as prophecy about Christ in the New Testament. Among others, Cyril of Alexandria used the allegorical method extensively to connect the Old Testament with the New Testament while maintaining the historicity of the events in question at the same time. Hosea yielded much regarding prophecies about Christ, the church and the sacraments of the new covenant.

THE ESSENCE OF HOSEA'S PROPHETIC MINISTRY. THEODORE OF MOPSUESTIA: Blessed David had long foretold the disasters that would befall the people. This foretelling had its beginning at the time when Hezekiah reigned over Judah and Benjamin. It was at this time that divine grace communicated to the prophets when the events were close at hand—although it was communicated to Hosea before the other prophets. He recounted what would befall the people from God as though he were recalling what was said by David in the dim and distant past. He would show how the Israelites were responsible for the coming disasters, having set aside worship and adoration of God while showering all their attention on idols and demons. Hosea was also to make it clear that this was not happening by chance. Rather, its occurrence had been told and foreseen well in advance by God. God understood this people's wickedness and clearly realized how he needed to conduct affairs where they were concerned by way of preparing for the manifestation and coming of Christ the Lord. COMMENTARY ON HOSEA, INTRODUCTION.[1]

HOW BY THREATS GOD INTENDS TO BLESS.
THEODORET OF CYR: The divinely inspired Hosea thus received the charisma of prophecy, and on contemplating these things in retrospect with the eyes of the spirit he was bidden to make predictions to the people so that they might be frightened by the prophecies, avoid the punishments and not experience the troubles. The reason that the God of all threatens punishment, you see, is not to inflict it on those he threatens but to strike them with fear and lead them to repentance, and by ridding them of their wicked behavior extend to them salvation. After all, if he wanted to punish, he would not threaten punishment; instead, by threatening he makes clear that he longs to save and not to punish. Accordingly he sends blessed Hosea to foretell what would happen to the ten tribes and likewise to the two and to predict the salvation that would be achieved in the time of Sennacherib and to signal in advance the destruction that would be inflicted on them under the Babylonians. COMMENTARY ON HOSEA, INTRODUCTION.[2]

---

[1]PG 66:124-25. [2]PG 81:1552-53.

1:1-3 GOD TELLS HOSEA TO MARRY A HARLOT

[1]*The word of the LORD that came to Hosea the son of Beeri, in the days of Uzziah, Jotham, Ahaz, and Hezekiah, kings of Judah, and in the days of Jeroboam the son of Joash, king of Israel.*

[2]*When the LORD first spoke through* Hosea, the LORD said to Hosea, "Go, take to yourself a wife of harlotry and have children of harlotry, for the land commits great harlotry† by forsaking the LORD."*[3]*So he went and took Gomer the daughter of Diblaim, and she conceived and bore him a son.*

*LXX has *to* or *in* †LXX renders the action in the future

OVERVIEW: God often calls the prophets to undertake a difficult path in calling people to repentance (ISHO'DAD). The union between Christ and the church is symbolized by the relation between Hosea and Gomer (JEROME, IRENAEUS). The unusual choice for Hosea's wife highlights the paradox of divine election and condescension (THEODORE). Hosea's marriage is God's symbolic charge against Israel. It accuses them of lawlessness and impiety (THEODORET). Sensual people pursue false teaching as one would a prostitute. The prostitute Gomer prefigured the prostitute who washed Jesus' feet (AUGUSTINE).

1:1-3 Hosea Marries Gomer

A WIFE OF WHOREDOM. ISHO'DAD OF MERV: "Take for yourself a wife who gives herself over to whoredom." God does not say "a whore" but "who gives herself over to whoredom," that is, consorts with men and idols. Note the words "children who give themselves over to whoredom." How could they give themselves to whoredom if they were not yet born? But this means that when she has children, they too will give themselves over to whoredom in body and mind just like her. The Hebrew text says "children of harlotry." We may wonder how people knew that the prophet, by taking a woman of whoredom, was doing something different from what he seemed to be doing, since he had not made any revelation to the people yet. It is probable that the prophet himself, after taking the woman, explained to the people the reason why he had taken her. . . . It may be that the people understood this situation because the prophet had so far kept himself in a state of chastity. . . . God represented through the woman of whoredom the community of the ten tribes who openly practiced the worship of idols. They are like the woman of whoredom who prostitutes herself by leaving her room open—at the time of Jeroboam. They are like those of the house of Judah who through the adulterous woman publicly swore to God but secretly worshiped the idol Milkom.[1] In fact Gomer was famous for her whoredom, like the Egyptians Oholah and Oholibah.[2] God may order the prophet to do what is unsuitable and inconvenient, as he ordered Isaiah to walk naked and barefoot[3] and Ezekiel to bake bread on human excrement.[4] In fact, it was typical for the

hard and stubborn heart of the people of Israel to despise actively the words before their eyes, which showed the afflictions coming their way. And so, if God punishes the holy prophets because of the people, he will punish even more the people themselves, in order that, after being confronted with the outrage of these terrifying actions, they may be frightened and turn away from their crimes. COMMENTARY ON HOSEA.[5]

THE CHURCH AND ITS STRUGGLES. JEROME: If you merely regard the narrative, the words are simple enough, but if you look beneath the surface at the hidden meaning of it, you find a description of the small numbers of the church and of the wars the heretics wage against it. The twelve prophets, whose writings are compressed within the narrow limits of a single volume, have typical meanings far from their literal ones. Hosea speaks many times of Ephraim, of Samaria, of Joseph, of Jezreel, of a wife of whoredoms and of children of whoredoms, of an adulterous woman shut up within the chamber of her husband, sitting for a long time in the widowhood and in the garb of mourning, awaiting the time when her husband will return to her. LETTER 53.7.[6]

CHRIST SANCTIFIES THE CHURCH. IRENAEUS: From these [unlikely] people God will build the church, which will be made holy through its union with the Son of God, as this woman was made holy by her union with the prophet. Paul says that the unbelieving wife is made holy by her believing husband.[7] AGAINST HERESIES 4.20.12.[8]

FROM WHOREDOM TO VIRTUE. JEROME: We should not blame the prophet if he converted a prostitute to virtue, but we should rather praise him because he turned a bad woman into a good one. . . . Hence we understand that it was not the prophet who lost virtue by joining with a prosti-

---

[1]1 Kings 11:5, 33. [2]See Ezek 23. [3]Is 20. [4]Ezek 4:12. [5]CSCO 303 (128):64-65. [6]NPNF 2 6:100. [7]1 Cor 7:14. [8]SC 2:670-71; *LSL* 29.

tute, but rather the latter gained virtue that she never had before. COMMENTARY ON HOSEA.[9]

THE PARADOX OF DIVINE CONDESCENSION.
THEODORE OF MOPSUESTIA: By the law the prophet was allowed to take a woman into the marriage relationship, and on marrying her he probably brought her to chaste ways. In fact, while everyone could not but be surprised that a man who was very conscious of propriety should pass over women who enjoyed a good reputation and choose to take a prostitute into the marriage relationship, the novelty of the event provided the prophet with the occasion of telling them their duty. In addition [Hosea's marriage demonstrated] the greater marvel of God's condescending to choose such ungrateful people for special attention by the powerful example—namely, the remarkable prophet's doing his duty by entering into association with a prostitute. COMMENTARY ON HOSEA 1.2.[10]

A CHARGE OF IMPIETY AGAINST ISRAEL. THEODORET OF CYR: Likewise the Lord of all had bade Hosea also, therefore, marry a loose woman so as by the event to charge the people with impiety and give evidence of his characteristic long-suffering. If the God of all put up with the loose and adulterous synagogue, however, and the fount of holiness was not defiled by that loathsome and abominable thing, neither did the prophet incur any defilement from that licentious woman. Without being in thrall to lust, and instead carrying out a command from on high, he put up with that awful relationship. Now one must realize how judgment is made between good and bad by the purpose involved: on that basis marriage is distinguished from adultery, and though intercourse involves no difference, the difference emerges in the purpose and the law, and on the same basis what is lawful is distinguished from what is lawless. COMMENTARY ON HOSEA 1.2.[11]

THE SCENE PREFIGURES THE PROSTITUTE WITH JESUS. AUGUSTINE: Under no circumstances would any reasonable person imagine that the Lord's feet were anointed with precious ointment by the woman[12] for the same reason that was customary for sensual, dissolute men whose banquets were such that we loathe them. In that case the good odor[13] is the good reputation that each one will possess by the works of good life, as long as one follows the footsteps of Christ, and as it were, anoints his feet with very precious ointment. Hence what is frequently sinful in other persons is a symbol of some sublime truth in the person of God or a prophet. CHRISTIAN INSTRUCTION 12.18.[14]

---

[9]PL 25:863; LSL 29. [10]PG 66:128-29. [11]PG 81:1556. [12]Lk 7:37-38; Jn 12:3. [13]2 Cor 2:15. [14]ACD 90**.

1:4-11 PROPHETIC SIGNIFICANCE OF HOSEA'S FAMILY

[4]And the LORD said to him, "Call his name Jezreel; for yet a little while, and I will punish the house of Jehu* for the blood of Jezreel, and I will put an end to the kingdom of the house of Israel. [5]And on that day, I will break the bow of Israel in the valley of Jezreel."
[6]She conceived again and bore a daughter. And the LORD said to him, "Call her name Not pit-

ied, *for I will no more have pity on the house of Israel, to forgive them at all.* ⁷*But I will have pity on the house of Judah, and I will deliver them by the* LORD *their God; I will not deliver them by bow, nor by sword, nor by war, nor by horses, nor by horsemen."*

⁸*When she had weaned Not pitied, she conceived and bore a son.* ⁹*And the* LORD *said, "Call his name Not my people, for you are not my people and I am not your God."ᵃ*

¹⁰ᵇ*Yet the number of the people of Israel shall be like the sand of the sea, which can be neither measured nor numbered; and in the place where it was said to them, "You are not my people," it shall be said to them, "Sons of the living God."* ¹¹*And the people of Judah and the people of Israel shall be gathered together, and they shall appoint for themselves one head; and they shall go up from the land, for great shall be the day of Jezreel.*

a Heb *I am not yours*   b Ch 2.1 in Heb   *LXX *the house of Judah*

OVERVIEW: God in Hosea revealed that he would send salvation through his Son, although still in a veiled manner (HILARY). It is proposed here that salvation is not of this world based upon earthly wisdom but rather from God alone (NOVATIAN). The Jews were chastised for rejecting Christ, and this in turn denied them any peace with God. Moreover, peace belongs to the church, the new people, loyal servants, who have returned to God through Christ (JEROME). Jews showed they lacked wisdom having lost peace with God, since they refused to drink of the living water, which is Christ (SALVIAN). Hosea foretold the salvation of the Gentiles, who, once having been outcasts in the old covenant, are given full access to the kingdom. The apostles affirmed this prophecy by announcing the spiritual adoption of the Gentiles as sons of Abraham (AUGUSTINE). "They shall go up" is interpreted as a reference to resurrection (CYRIL OF ALEXANDRIA).

1:7 Pity for Judah

GOD REVEALS HIS ETERNAL PLAN. HILARY OF POITIERS: He says to Hosea the prophet, "I will not add any more to have mercy on the house of Israel, but as their adversary I shall oppose them. But I shall have mercy on the sons of Judah, and I shall save them by the Lord their God." The Father unmistakably gives the name of God to his Son in whom he chose us before the eternal ages.

For this reason he says "their God," because the unborn God is from no one, and God the Father has given us as an inheritance to his Son. ON THE TRINITY 4.37.[1]

CHRIST IS GOD. NOVATIAN: Why, then, should we hesitate to say what Scripture does not hesitate to say? Why should the truth of faith waver where the authority of Scripture has never faltered? For behold, the prophet Hosea says in the person of the Father, "I will not save them by bow nor horses, but I will save them by the Lord their God." If God says that he will save them by God and if God does not save except by Christ, then why should people hesitate to call Christ God when they realize that the Father declares, through the Scriptures, that he is God? In fact, if God the Father cannot save except by God, no one can be saved by God the Father, unless one has acknowledged that Christ is God, in whom and through whom the Father promises to grant salvation.[2] ON THE TRINITY 12.[3]

1:9 Not My People

GENTILES ALSO TO BE SAVED. JEROME: "For he proclaims peace to his people, and to his faithful ones, and to those who turn to him from their hearts."[4] I note here a threefold classification: his

---

¹FC 25:124. ²Acts 4:12. ³FC 67:49-50*. ⁴Ps 85:8 (84:9 LXX).

people, his loyal servants, and those who come back to him in hope. He proclaims peace to his people, not to the Jews of whom in Hosea he says, "You are not my people." Homilies on the Psalms 17.[5]

Prophetic Rejection of Jesus. Salvian the Presbyter: For this reason, our God spoke elsewhere about the Hebrew people to the prophet, saying, "Call his name Not Beloved," and again to the Jews, "You are not my people, and I am not your God." But he himself showed clearly elsewhere why he said this about them, for he said, "They have forsaken the Lord, the vein of living waters,"[6] and again, "For they have cast away the word of the Lord, and there is no wisdom in them."[7] The Governance of God 4.1.[8]

1:10 Children of the Living God

Gentile Salvation Foretold. Augustine: Because Hosea is such a profound prophet, it is no easy matter to get at his meaning. Still, I must keep my promise and quote something from him at this point. He says, "And it shall be in the place where it was said to them, 'You are not my people'; it shall be said to them, 'You are sons of the living God.'" The apostles themselves understood this text as a prophecy of the calling of the Gentiles, who were previously not God's people.[9] And because the Gentiles are spiritually sons of

Abraham and correctly therefore alluded to as Israel, Hosea goes on to say, "And the children of Judah and the children of Israel shall be gathered together, and they shall appoint themselves one head, and they shall come up out of the earth." Now to add one word of explanation to this text would be to lose the savor of Hosea's prophetic style. City of God 18.28.[10]

1:11 They Shall Go Up

The Community of Faith "Shall Come Up." Cyril of Alexandria: "They come up out of the land," namely, they will live the life of the saints as well, "for great is the day of Jezreel." Indeed, great is the day of Christ, when he will raise to life all the dead. In fact, he will descend from heaven and sit on his glorious throne. "And he will give everyone according to his works."[11] Therefore if one wishes to understand by "day" the time of the visitation—when the remission of sins is given by Christ to the Greeks, the Judaeans and those who have sinned against him—this will not deviate from the true words. For David too indicated the time of the coming of our Savior by saying, "This is the day that the Lord has made; let us be glad and rejoice in it."[12] Commentary on Hosea 1.9.[13]

---

[5]FC 57:53. [6]Jer 17:13. [7]Jer 8:9. [8]FC 3:91. [9]Rom 9:26. [10]FC 24:122. [11]Mt 16:27. [12]Ps 118:24 (117:24 LXX). [13]PG 71:57; LSL 35.

2:1-18 ISRAEL'S SIN AND RESTORATION

[1c]*Say to your brother,[d] "My people," and to your sister,[e] "She has obtained pity."*
    [2]*"Plead with your mother, plead—*
        for she is not my wife,
        and I am not her husband—

that she put away her harlotry from her face,
        and her adultery from between her breasts;
    [3]*lest I strip her naked*

and make her as in the day she was born,
and make her like a wilderness,
 and set her like a parched land,
 and slay her with thirst.
⁴Upon her children also I will have no pity,
 because they are children of harlotry.
⁵For their mother has played the harlot;
 she that conceived them has acted
  shamefully.
For she said, 'I will go after my lovers,
 who give me my bread and my water,
 my wool and my flax,* my oil and my
  drink.'†
⁶Therefore I will hedge up her^f way with
  thorns;
 and I will build a wall against her,
 so that she cannot find her paths.
⁷She shall pursue her lovers,
 but not overtake them;
and she shall seek them,
 but shall not find them.
Then she shall say, 'I will go
 and return to my first husband,
 for it was better with me then than now.'
⁸And she did not know
 that it was I who gave her
 the grain, the wine, and the oil,
and who lavished upon her silver
 and gold which they used for Baal.‡
⁹Therefore I will take back
 my grain in its time,
 and my wine in its season;
and I will take away my wool and my flax,
 which were to cover her nakedness.
¹⁰Now I will uncover her lewdness
 in the sight of her lovers,
 and no one shall rescue her out of my hand.

¹¹And I will put an end to all her mirth,
 her feasts, her new moons, her sabbaths,
 and all her appointed feasts.
¹²And I will lay waste her vines and her fig
  trees,
 of which she said,
'These are my hire,
 which my lovers have given me.'
I will make them a forest,
 and the beasts of the field shall devour them.
¹³And I will punish her for the feast days of
  the Baals
 when she burned incense to them
and decked herself with her ring and jewelry,
 and went after her lovers,
 and forgot me, says the LORD.

¹⁴"Therefore, behold, I will allure her,
 and bring her into the wilderness,
 and speak tenderly to her.
¹⁵And there I will give her her vineyards,§
 and make the Valley of Achor a door of
  hope.#
And there she shall answer as in the days of
  her youth,
 as at the time when she came out of the
  land of Egypt.
¹⁶"And in that day, says the LORD, you will
call me, 'My husband,' and no longer will you
call me, 'My Baal.' ¹⁷For I will remove the
names of the Baals from her mouth, and they
shall be mentioned by name no more. ¹⁸And I
will make for you^g a covenant on that day with
the beasts of the field, the birds of the air, and
the creeping things of the ground; and I will
abolish^h the bow, the sword, and war from the
land; and I will make you lie down in safety."

---

^c Ch 2.3 in Heb ^d Gk: Heb *brothers* ^e Gk Vg: Heb *sisters* ^f Gk Syr: Heb *your* ^g Heb *them* ^h Heb *break* *LXX *garments and linen cloth* †LXX adds *and everything that befits me.* ‡LXX *and multiplied silver to her; but she made silver and gold [images] for Baal.* §LXX *possessions* #LXX *to open her understanding*

OVERVIEW: The words of Hosea's oracle reflect the frustration of broken intimacy (CYRIL OF ALEXANDRIA). Unbelievers and schismatics are like prostitutes who have gone astray. They lead others astray as well with the falseness of their dogmas and dissensions (AUGUSTINE). Those like Israel whom an evil will perverts, adversity often corrects (GREGORY THE GREAT). Those who have been unfaithful to the Lord and have returned should be careful to avoid unfaithfulness again (ORIGEN). Jerusalem is an image of the prostitute who leaves her way of life and later returns to her first husband. This represents a prophetic image of a Christian who returns to serving the Lord faithfully (JOHN CASSIAN). True believers stay away from prostitutes and remain faithful to their first husband, the Lord. This is a call to remain faithful in total trustworthiness (ORIGEN). God guides Israel for her well-being; the wilderness protects her from harm (CYRIL OF ALEXANDRIA). God speaks to the heart through the law (JULIAN OF ECLANUM, CYRIL OF ALEXANDRIA), and grants heavenly and inner wealth to his own (CYRIL OF ALEXANDRIA, THEOPHYLACT). Israel will learn the lessons of suffering due to her apostasy in captivity (THEODORET OF CYR). Ultimately, however, she will return to God as in her days of youth (CYRIL OF ALEXANDRIA). The unfaithful are like a harlot who rejected the bridegroom, Christ, while the church was like the harlot who embraced Christ (CHRYSOSTOM).

2:2 She Is Not My Wife

RUPTURE OF INTIMACY. CYRIL OF ALEXANDRIA: She has not preserved the genuineness of love toward me, but rather she denied the intimacy and underestimated the purity of spiritual communion with me. Nor was she willing to bring forth the fruits of my will. COMMENTARY ON HOSEA 2.11.[1]

2:5 Pursuing Lovers

HERETICS AND SCHISMATICS. AUGUSTINE: Who is that adulterous woman whom the proph-

et Hosea points out, who said, "I will go after my lovers, that give me my bread and my water, my wool and my flax, and everything that befits me"? Let us grant that we may understand this also of the people of the Jews who went astray. Yet who else are false Christians (such as are all heretics and schismatics) prone to imitate, except false Israelites? ON BAPTISM 3.26.[2]

UNBELIEVERS ARE LIKE ADULTERERS. AUGUSTINE: "And she shall follow after her lovers, but she shall not overtake them: and she shall seek them, but she shall not find them. Then shall she say, 'I will go and return to my first husband; for then it was better with me than now.'" Then he adds something, in order that they may not attribute to their seducers what they have that is sound and derived from the doctrine of truth, by which they lead them astray to the falseness of their own dogmas and dissensions. And in order that they may not think that what is sound in them belongs to them, he immediately added, "And she did not know that I gave her corn and wine and oil, and multiplied her money; but she made vessels of gold and silver for Baal." ON BAPTISM 3.27.[3]

2:6-7 Seeking Lovers, Then Returning to Her First Husband

ADVERSITY OFTEN BENEFITS US SPIRITUALLY. GREGORY THE GREAT: The ways of the elect are hedged up with thorns when they find the pain of piercing in that which they desire in this world. He obstructs, as it were by interposing a wall, the ways of those whose desires the difficulty of attainment opposes. Their souls truly seek their lovers but do not find them. They follow malignant spirits but do not gain hold of those pleasures of this world that they desire. It is well added that she says immediately in consequence of this very difficulty: "I will go and return to my former husband, for then it was better

---

[1]PG 71:60; LSL 36. [2]NPNF 1 4:444. [3]NPNF 1 4:445-46*.

with me than now." For the Lord is the first husband, who united to himself the chaste soul by means of the love of the Holy Spirit. And the mind of each one then longs for him when it finds manifold bitternesses, as thorns in those delights that it desires in this world. For when the mind has begun to be stung by the adversities of the world that it loves, it then understands more fully how much better for it was its former husband. Those whom an evil will perverts, adversity frequently corrects. MORALS ON THE BOOK OF JOB 6.34.3.[4]

THE CALL TO RETURN TO GOD. ORIGEN: So, therefore, understand that there were also many lovers of your soul who have been seduced by its splendor with whom it has been a prostitute. It was also said of these, "I will go after my lovers, who give me my wine and my oil." But the soul has now come to that time that it should say, "I will return to my first husband because it was better for me than now." You have returned, therefore, to your first husband. You have doubtless displeased your lovers with whom you used to commit adultery. Unless, therefore, you now remain with your husband in total faith and are joined to him in total love, because of the many evil deeds that you committed, your every movement and look and even your walk is suspected by him, if these should be too careless. He must see nothing further in you that is playful, licentious or prodigal. But when you turn aside your eyes in the slightest from your husband, immediately he necessarily is reminded of your former conduct. Therefore, that you may destroy the former things and he henceforth may be able to have confidence in you, not only must you do nothing immodest, but also you must not even think of such. HOMILIES ON EXODUS 8.4.[5]

CALL TO RETURN. JOHN CASSIAN: Through the prophet Hosea the divine word well expressed God's concern and providence toward us. He speaks of the image of Jerusalem as a prostitute who is drawn with wicked ardor to the worship of idols. She says, "I will go after my lovers, who give me my bread and my water, my wool and my flax, my oil and my drink." The divine condescension replies, with a view to her salvation and not to her will, "Behold, I will hedge in her paths with thorns, and I will hedge her in with a wall, and she will not find her ways. And she will pursue her lovers and not lay hold of them, and she will seek them and not find them, and she will say, 'I will return to my first husband, because then it was better for me than it is now.'" CONFERENCE 13.8.1.[6]

2:9 Uncovering Her Naked Body

DO NOT YIELD TO CARELESSNESS. ORIGEN: "And if [the adulterous spirit] comes and finds the house vacant, clean, and furnished, it goes and brings with it seven other spirits more wicked than itself and enters that house and lives in it. And the last of that man is worse than the first."[7] If we give attention to these words, how can we give place to carelessness even in a small matter? For the unclean spirit dwelled in us before we believed, before we came to Christ when our soul, as I said previously, was still committing fornication against God and was with its lovers, the demons. But afterward it said, "I will return to my first husband," and it came to Christ who "created" it from the beginning "in his image." Necessarily the adulterous spirit yielded when it saw the legitimate husband. We therefore have been received by Christ, and our house has been "cleansed" from its former sins and has been "furnished" with the furnishing of the sacraments of the faithful which they who have been initiated know. But this house does not deserve to have Christ as its resident immediately unless its life and conduct are so holy, so pure and incapable of being defiled that it deserves to be called the "temple of God."[8] HOMILIES ON EXODUS 8.4.[9]

---

[4]LF 31:621**. [5]FC 71:323-24*. [6]ACW 57:473*. [7]Mt 12:43-45; Lk 11:24-26. [8]2 Cor 6:16. [9]FC 71:324*.

2:14 God Will Allure Israel

GOD GUIDES ISRAEL TO THE RIGHT PATH.
CYRIL OF ALEXANDRIA: "Behold, I will mislead
her" not from what is necessary and useful to
life . . . but from the things that are shameful
and harmful to the fulfillment of any enjoyment.
. . . And as her ways are usefully hedged around
with thorns so that she may not lay hold of her
lovers, in the same manner she believes herself—now running downhill toward ruin and
destruction—to be led astray by the mercy of
God when she is brought to desire virtue. Having received the light of the knowledge of God
in mind and heart, as I said, she is no longer able
to find her old path. COMMENTARY ON HOSEA
2.22.[10]

WILDERNESS PROTECTS HER. CYRIL OF ALEX-
ANDRIA: Since she [Israel] is accessible like a
well-watered land to the herds of demons, he
[the Lord] promises to treat her as a wilderness. . . . He will display it to their desires
as an austere, untrodden and waterless place,
so that finding no resting place they will
despise it and depart. COMMENTARY ON HOSEA
2.22.[11]

THE HEART AND THE LAW. JULIAN OF
ECLANUM: Speaking directly to the heart indicates the promulgation of the law, which shaped
the hearts of the listener. COMMENTARY ON
HOSEA 1.2.[12]

THE HEART IS AWARE OF THE LAW. CYRIL OF
ALEXANDRIA: We who have Christ, the author of
necessary things dwelling inside the heart, were
at once enriched in every kind of virtue, and in
the abundant and inalienable possession of the
spiritual gifts. . . . He promises to speak in her
heart. For the synagogue of the Judeans, exactly
as the church from the nations, will be called to
awareness by taking into mind the divine laws inscribed through the Spirit. COMMENTARY ON
HOSEA 2.23.[13]

2:15 God Gives Israel Possessions

HEAVENLY WEALTH. CYRIL OF ALEXANDRIA:
Whatever is necessary for life and understanding
of God's knowledge in Christ, through whom and
in whom we saw the Father, enriched in unfading
hope[14]—as I said, in glory, pride of adoption, of
grace and of reigning together with Christ himself—these are the possessions of the saints; this
is the heavenly wealth. COMMENTARY ON HOSEA
2.23.[15]

INNER POSSESSIONS. THEOPHYLACT: The possessions of everyone baptized in Christ are the remission of sins and the mansions above, which
someone procures through the way that leads to
each one of these. For there are as many ways as
there are different mansions. But the one who
sins ceases to hold the possessions and is deprived of them, while the divine Word becomes
silent in him. Yet whenever he [the Lord] touches
his heart, he speaks in it and then gives him those
possessions from there, that is, from the heart.
For the kingdom of heaven is inside of us. Therefore, either our heart takes these goods away
from us or he [the Lord] gives [them to us].
COMMENTARY ON HOSEA 2.[16]

THE LESSONS OF SUFFERING. THEODORET OF
CYR: Just as those at that early time have learned
through Achan's punishment how serious is the
transgression of the law,[17] in the same manner
these will come to the realization of their own
trespasses through the captivity. COMMENTARY
ON HOSEA 2.[18]

**ISRAEL'S KNOWLEDGE OF GOD WILL REGEN-
ERATE.** CYRIL OF ALEXANDRIA: [Israel] will be
humble and obedient just as in the beginning,
when she was born to the knowledge of God
through the law and gladly received the decree of

---

[10]PG 71:80-81; *LSL* 40-41. [11]PG 71:81; *LSL* 41. [12]PL 21:977-78; *LSL*
42. [13]PG 71:81-84; *LSL* 42. [14]1 Pet 5:4. [15]PG 71:84; *LSL* 42. [16]PG
126:613; *LSL* 60 n. 165. [17]Josh 7. [18]PG 81:1565; *LSL* 43*.

the divine adoption. Accordingly, he calls the regeneration to the knowledge of God through the law the "days [of her youth]." COMMENTARY ON HOSEA 2.25.[19]

2:18 A New Covenant

GOD'S ESPOUSAL OF SINNERS. CHRYSOSTOM: Therefore in a way similar to those of old who took harlots for wives, even so God too espoused to himself the nature that had played the harlot.

This the prophets from the beginning declare to have taken place with respect to the synagogue. But that spouse was ungrateful toward him who had been a husband to her, whereas the church, when once delivered from the evils received from our fathers, continued to embrace the Bridegroom. HOMILIES ON THE GOSPEL OF MATTHEW 3.5.[20]

---

[19]PG 71:88; *LSL* 43. [20]NPNF 1 10:17.

2:19-23 DIVINE MERCY ON ISRAEL

[19]*And I will betroth you to me for ever; I will betroth you to me in righteousness and in justice, in steadfast love, and in mercy.* [20]*I will betroth you to me in faithfulness; and you shall know the* LORD.
   [21]*"And in that day, says the* LORD,
     I will answer the heavens
     and they shall answer the earth;
   [22]*and the earth shall answer the grain, the wine, and the oil,*
     and they shall answer Jezreel;[i]
   [23]*and I will sow him*[j] *for myself in the land.*
   And I will have pity on Not pitied,
     and I will say to Not my people, 'You are my people';
     and he shall say, 'Thou art my God.'"

i That is *God sows*   j Cn: Heb *her*

OVERVIEW: God shows great mercy to Israel through a relationship beyond mere reconciliation. This betrothal culminates in a new covenant in faith (JEROME). God's grace is extended to the Jews who strayed from grace and to those fallen from grace regardless of age. God desires to espouse the fallen away, Jew or Gentile, just the same (AMBROSE). Prophecy of espousement was directed to the Gentiles, the church, rather than the Jews (PETER CHRYSOLOGUS). The war against the flesh, even in lustful dreams, was foretold by Hosea with the promise of victory resulting in sleeping securely (JOHN CASSIAN). The triune God prophesied that he would call the Gentiles and hence extend salvation universally to all peoples (AMBROSE). Gentiles are the not-people and not-beloved spoken of by Hosea (CHRYSOSTOM). Gentiles are recipients of a grace they could not even hope for (BEDE). Those who thought they were God's people truly were not, and those who were not God's people have been proclaimed the people of God, namely, the Gentiles (ORIGEN). The Gentiles are the new people chosen by God to replace the people of the old covenant as foretold by the prophet (APHRAHAT).

2:19-20 Betrothal of Righteousness and Faithfulness

AN UNUSUAL BETROTHAL. JEROME: How great is God's mercy! A prostitute fornicates with many lovers, and because of her offense is handed over to the beasts. After she returns to her husband, she is said not at all to be reconciled to him but rather to be betrothed. Now notice the difference between God's union and that of men. When a man marries, he turns a virgin into a woman—that is, a nonvirgin. But when God joins with prostitutes, he changes them into virgins. COMMENTARY ON HOSEA 1.2.[1]

THREE TYPES OF BETROTHAL. JEROME: First, he [God] betrothed her [Israel] in Abraham (or rather, in Egypt) so that he may have an everlasting spouse. Second, on Mount Sinai in the betrothal, he gave her the equity and judgment of the law and the compassion added to the law, so that whenever she should sin she would be given up into captivity; whenever she should show penitence, she would be brought back to [her] homeland, and she would gain compassion. . . . By his crucifixion and resurrection from the dead, he [Jesus] betroths [her] not in the equity of the law but rather in faith and the grace of the gospel. COMMENTARY ON HOSEA 1.2.[2]

MERCY AND FORGIVENESS FOR THE FALLEN. AMBROSE: You have made a wise decision to seek an answer to the question whether there is some difference in God's love of those who have had faith since childhood and of those who believed in the course of youth or later years. Holy Scripture has not failed to note this problem, nor has it left your matter untouched. Indeed, the Lord our God said meaningfully to the prophet Joel, "La-

ment with me over my spouse in sackcloth and for the husband of her youth,"[3] while he wept either for the synagogue that formerly, in her virginity, had been espoused to the Word of God, or perhaps for a soul that had fallen from grace. Her offense had led her into serious crimes so that she became hated. And, having been cast aside because of her stain of impurity and the foul marks of wickedness and the stains of unbelief, she became an object of pity and a person despised, far removed from the grace of that spouse who had been worthy to hear the words "I will espouse thee to me in faith and justice and mercy." LETTER 74.[4]

PROPHECY OF CHRIST AND BRIDEGROOM. PETER CHRYSOLOGUS: A betrothed woman was chosen, so that Christ's church might already be symbolically indicated as bride, according to the words of the prophet Hosea: "I will make you my bride in justice and right; I will make you my bride in mercy and benevolence, and I will espouse you in fidelity." Thus John says, "He who has a bride is the bridegroom."[5] And blessed Paul: "I have promised you to one bridegroom, to present you to Christ as a chaste virgin."[6] She is truly a bride who regenerates the new infancy of Christ by a virginal birth.[7] SERMON 146.[8]

WE DREAM ACCORDING TO HOW WE BEHAVE. JOHN CASSIAN: The sixth degree of chastity is that he not be deluded by the alluring images of women even when asleep. For although we do not believe that this delusion is sinful, nonetheless it is an indication of a desire that is still deeply ingrained. It is evident that this delusion can occur in a number of ways. For each person is tempted, even while asleep, according to how he behaves and thinks while awake. Those who have known sexual intercourse are led astray

---

[1]PL 25:881; LSL 45. [2]PL 25:881-82; LSL 45*. [3]Joel 1:8. [4]FC 26:420. [5]Jn 3:29. [6]2 Cor 11:2. [7]Within the church the prophetic text anticipates the regeneration of a believer in baptism, which is also an act of birth by the church, the virgin and spouse of Christ. [8]FC 17:240**.

in one way, those who have had no part in union with a woman in another way. The latter are usually disturbed by simpler and purer dreams, such that they can be cleansed more easily and with less effort. But the former are deceived by filthier and more explicit images until, gradually and according to the measure of chastity for which each is struggling, even the mind that has fallen asleep learns to hate what it used to find pleasurable, and, through the prophet, the Lord grants it what is promised to brave men as the highest reward for their labors: "I will destroy the bow and the sword and war from your land, and I will make you sleep securely." CONFERENCE 12.7.4-5.[9]

2:23 Pity on "Not Pitied"

UNIVERSAL CALLING OF ALL PEOPLE FORE-TOLD. AMBROSE: And not only is the operation of the Father, Son and Holy Spirit everywhere one, but also there is one and the same will, calling and giving of commands, which one may see in the great and saving mystery of the church. For as the Father called the Gentiles to the church, saying, "I will call her my people which was Not my people, and her beloved who was not beloved;" and elsewhere, "My house shall be called a house of prayer for all nations,"[10] so too the Lord Jesus to Ananias: "Go, for he is a chosen vessel unto me to bear my name before all nations."[11] ON THE HOLY SPIRIT 2.10.101.[12]

GENTILES ARE THE BELOVED. CHRYSOSTOM: Here to prevent their saying that you are deceiving us here with specious reasoning, he calls Hosea to witness, who cries and says, "I will call them *my people*, who were *not my people*." Who then are the not-people? Plainly, the Gentiles. And who are the not-beloved? The same again. However, he says, they shall become at once people, and beloved, and children of God.[13] "For even they shall be called," he says, "the children of the living God." But if they should assert that this was said of those of the Jews who believed, even then the argument stands. For if with those who

after so many benefits were hardhearted and estranged and had lost their being as a people, so great a change was wrought, what is there to prevent even those who were not estranged after being taken to him but were originally aliens, from being called, and, provided they obey, from being counted worthy of the same blessings? Having then done with Hosea, he does not content himself with him only, but also brings Isaiah in after him, sounding in harmony with him. HOMILIES ON ROMANS 16.[14]

CALLING OF GENTILES PREDICTED. BEDE: "You who were once not a people but now are the people of God, who did not seek after mercy but now have received mercy."[15] By these verses he indicates clearly that he has written this letter to those who had come from the Gentiles to the faith, who were once separated from the way of life of the people of God but then through the grace of faith were joined to his people[16] and obtained the mercy that they did not know how to hope for. He takes them, however, from the prophet Hosea, who predicted the calling of the Gentiles and said, "I shall call [those who were] not my people my people and [those who did] not receive mercy [a people] having received mercy. And it will be in the place where it was said, 'You are not my people,' there they will be called sons of the living God."[17] COMMENTARY ON 1 PETER 2:10.[18]

THE CHURCH FORETOLD. ORIGEN: Next the promise of God is said for those who hear; if they do what is "commanded: And you will be my people and I will be your God."[19] Not everyone who says they are a people of God are "a people" of God. Hence, that people who were proclaimed to be a people of God heard, "You are not my people," in the passage, "Therefore you are not my people." And it has been said to that people you are "not my people." Elsewhere this people was called a "peo-

---

[9]ACW 57:443-44. [10]Is 56:7. [11]Acts 9:15. [12]NPNF 2 10:127. [13]Rom 9:26. [14]NPNF 1 11:469. [15]1 Pet 2:10. [16]Eph 2:12-13. [17]Rom 9:25-26; Hos 1:9. [18]CS 82:88. [19]Jer 11:4.

ple," for "they have provoked me to jealousy with what is not God"—he speaks concerning the former—"they have provoked me with their idols. So I will provoke them to jealousy with those who are not a people, with a senseless nation I will provoke them."[20] HOMILIES ON JEREMIAH 9.4.[21]

FREE FROM EARTHLY KINGDOMS. APHRAHAT: And the holy people inherited an eternal kingdom; the holy people who were chosen instead of the people. For "he provoked them to jealousy with a people that was not a people. And with a foolish people he angered them."[22] For even if one has served the heathen, as soon as ever he draws near to the covenant of God, he is set free. The Gentiles are the new people chosen by God to replace the people of the old covenant as foretold by the prophet. DEMONSTRATIONS 5.23.[23]

---

[20]Deut 32:21. [21]FC 97:88-89. [22]Deut 32:21. [23]NPNF 2 1 3:360-61.

3:1-5 THE RESTORATION OF GOMER

[1]And the LORD said to me, "Go again, love a woman who is beloved of a paramour and is an adulteress; even as the LORD loves the people of Israel, though they turn to other gods and love cakes of raisins." [2]So I bought her* for fifteen shekels of silver and a homer and a lethech of barley.[†] [3]And I said to her, "You must dwell as mine for many days; you shall not play the harlot, or belong to another man; so will I also be to you." [4]For the children of Israel shall dwell many days without king or prince, without sacrifice or pillar, without ephod or teraphim. [5]Afterward the children of Israel shall return and seek the LORD their God, and David their king; and they shall come in fear to the LORD and to his goodness in the latter days.

*LXX I hired her   † LXX and a skin of wine

OVERVIEW: The prostitute with whom Hosea joined himself was a prophetic anticipation of the Gentiles purchased in the new covenant (AMBROSE). The Jews now suffer, deprived of their hope and their temple worship, but will be saved in the end when the time of the Gentiles is fulfilled (JEROME). Manna from heaven is given on the Christian Lord's day, not during the Jewish sabbath. This is a clear reference to the Eucharist. The prophecy that there would be no more king, altar, victory or priesthood was fulfilled with the destruction of the temple. This indicates that God intended to turn toward the Gentiles (ORI- GEN). There is promised here the future salvation of the Jews because Christ is the king David foretold to save the human race, especially the house of Israel (AUGUSTINE).

3:2 Gomer Redeemed

PURCHASE PRICE. AMBROSE: Those are the seven and eight of which Hosea says that with this number he bought and took to himself the fullness of faith, for you read, "And I went and bought her to me for fifteen pieces of silver and for a core of barley and for a half core of barley and a measure of wine." The Lord had told him previously to buy a harlot, and it is proof that he bought her, since he declares how much he paid. The fifteen pieces of silver consist of seven and eight. LETTER 50.[1]

MANY DAYS REQUIRED TO RETURN. JEROME: And how shall I speak of the whore married by the prophet? She is the figure either of the church as gathered in from the Gentiles, or—an interpretation that better suits the passage—of the synagogue. She, Israel, was first adopted from among the idolaters by Abraham and Moses. She has now denied the Savior and proved unfaithful to him. Therefore she has long been deprived of her altar, priests and prophets and has to abide many days to return to her first husband.[2] For when the faithfulness of the Gentiles shall be fulfilled, all Israel shall be saved.[3] LETTER 123.13.[4]

3:4 Without King or Sacrifice

THE LORD'S DAY AND THE SABBATH COMPARED. ORIGEN: I ask, therefore, on what day the heavenly manna began to be given. I wish to compare our Lord's day with the sabbath of the Jews. For the divine Scriptures it appears that manna was first given on earth on the Lord's day. For if, as Scripture says, it was gathered for six consecutive days, but on the seventh day, which is the sabbath, it was stopped, without doubt it began on the first day, which is the Lord's day. But if it is plain from divine Scriptures that on the Lord's day God rained manna and on the sabbath he did not, let the Jews understand that already at that time our Lord's day was preferred to the Jewish sabbath. Even then it was revealed that on their own sabbath no grace of God descended to them from the sky; no bread of heaven, which is the Word of God, came to them. For a prophet also says elsewhere, "The sons of Israel will sit for many days without a king, without a prince, without a prophet, without a victim, without a sacrifice, without a priest." On our Lord's day, however, the Lord always rains manna from the sky. HOMILIES ON EXODUS 7.[5]

THE SALVATION OF THE GENTILES PROPHESIED. ORIGEN: For the prophecy was fulfilled that had declared, "For the children of Israel shall abide many days without king and prince. There shall be no victim, nor altar, nor priesthood, nor answers." These testimonies, accordingly, we employ against those who presume to assert that what is spoken in Genesis by Jacob refers to Judah.[6] They say that there still remains a prince of the race of Judah— he, namely, who is the prince of their nation, whom they style patriarch—and that there cannot fail [a ruler] of his seed, who will remain until the advent of that Christ whom they picture themselves. But if the prophet's words are true when he says, "The children of Israel shall abide many days without a king, without prince; and there shall be no victim, nor altar, nor priesthood," and if, certainly, since the overthrow of the temple, victims are neither offered, nor any altar found, nor any priesthood exists. So it is most certain that, as it is written, princes have departed from Judah and a leader from between his thighs, until the coming of him for whom it has been reserved. It is established, then, that he has indeed come from whom it has been reserved and in whom is the expectation of the Gentiles. And this manifestly seems to be fulfilled in the multitude of those who have believed in God through Christ out of the different nations. ON FIRST PRINCIPLES 4.1.3.[7]

3:5 The Children of Israel Return

RETURNING TO THE LORD. AUGUSTINE: But let us hear what Hosea goes on to say: "And after this the children of Israel shall return and shall seek the Lord their God and David their king; and they shall fear the Lord and his goodness in the last days." You will never find a prophecy plainer than this, for the name King David means Christ, who, as Paul says, "was born according to the flesh of the offspring of David."[8] Further on still, Hosea foretold the resurrection of Christ on

---

[1]FC 26:267*. [2]Hos 2:7. [3]Rom 11:25-26. [4]NPNF 2 6:235*. [5]FC 71:308. [6]Gen 49:10. [7]ANF 4:351*. [8]Rom 1:3.

the third day, but in the mysterious way that is proper to prophecy. He says, "He shall heal us after two days, and on the third day we shall rise up again."[9] This is the theme underlying the words of Paul: "Therefore if you have risen with Christ, seek the things that are above."[10] CITY OF GOD 18.28.[11]

---

[9]Hos 6:2. [10]Col 3:1. [11]FC 24:123.

4:1-8 DIVINE ACCUSATIONS AGAINST ISRAEL

[1]*Hear the word of the* LORD, *O people of Israel;*
  for the LORD *has a controversy with the inhabitants of the land.*
There is no faithfulness or kindness,
  and no knowledge of God in the land;
[2]*there is swearing, lying, killing, stealing, and committing adultery;*
  they break all bounds* and murder follows murder.
[3]*Therefore the land mourns,*
  and all who dwell in it languish,
and also the beasts of the field,†
  and the birds of the air;
  and even the fish of the sea are taken away.

[4]*Yet let no one contend,*
  and let none accuse,
  for with you is my contention, O priest.ᵏ
[5]*You shall stumble by day,*
  the prophet also shall stumble with you by night;
  and I will destroy your mother.‡
[6]*My people are destroyed for lack of knowledge;*
  because you have rejected knowledge,
  I reject you from being a priest to me.
And since you have forgotten the law of your God,
  I also will forget your children.

[7]*The more they increased,*
  the more they sinned against me;
  I will change their glory into shame.

⁸*They feed on the sin of my people;*
they are greedy for their iniquity.

k Cn: Heb uncertain   *LXX adds *in the land*   †LXX adds *and the creeping things of the ground*   ‡LXX reads *I have likened your mother to night*

OVERVIEW: The continued hardness of heart in the covenant people was repeatedly played out among the ancient Jews. Repentance is as much a requirement in the new covenant as was expected in the old (CYRIL OF JERUSALEM). Israel is compared to a priest who has been dishonored. The stumbling of the people is like one in the darkness (THEODORE OF MOPSUESTIA). Yet their judgment is temporary (CYRIL OF ALEXANDRIA). The mother of the night was Mary, through whom Christ was born. Furthermore, Jesus was born at night and rose from the dead at night (or dawn) too. The woman and the night compared with sin, in contrast to those who live in the light (AUGUSTINE). The mother of the people is the synagogue (THEOPHYLACT). The priests used to eat the sacrifices, thereby eating sins of the people (CYRIL OF ALEXANDRIA) and approving of them (JEROME). Christ is the ultimate sacrifice who continually devours sin by his saving grace and which is now mediated through his priesthood. The cleansing sacrifice for sin is now perpetually offered up by priests in the Eucharist sacrifice (ORIGEN).

4:2 They Break All Bounds

NO REPENTANCE. CYRIL OF JERUSALEM: After Moses, prophets were sent to heal Israel. But in their exercise of healing they deplored the fact that they could not overcome evil, so that one of them says, "The faithful are gone from the earth, among men the upright are no more,"[1] and again, "All alike have gone astray; they have become perverse; there is not one who does good, not even one."[2] And again, "Cursing, and theft, and adultery, and killing have overflowed" upon the land. "They sacrificed their sons and daughters to demons."[3] They engaged themselves in auguries and enchantments and divinations; and again, "they fastened their garments with cords

and hung veils next to the altar."[4] CATECHETICAL LECTURE 12.6.[5]

4:4 Dispute with a Priest

ISRAEL IS LIKE A COMPROMISED PRIEST. THEODORE OF MOPSUESTIA: My people are like a priest who is compromised. He has fallen from his previous dignity and does not appear worthy for any reason, just as a priest who falls into controversy would be set aside and dishonored by everyone. "And he will be weak by day." To the greatest extent he will become weak because of the upcoming evils. COMMENTARY ON HOSEA 4.[6]

4:5 Stumbling During the Day

STUMBLING AS IN DARKNESS. THEODORE OF MOPSUESTIA: Of the ones who first made use of false predictions to deceive you, most will also themselves become weak because of the calamity that holds them back. As if they were wrapped up in some kind of night darkness, they see the pursuit of deceit, which was useless for them. COMMENTARY ON HOSEA 4.[7]

JUDGMENT IS TEMPORARY. CYRIL OF ALEXANDRIA: One says that Israel will be weak not forever but for days. For it has been reserved for her a time of salvation and a return to faith. COMMENTARY ON HOSEA 3.37.[8]

A STAR OF THE NIGHT. AUGUSTINE: For us too, you see, once the night of this age is done, there will be a resurrection of the flesh for the kingdom; it's the model or sample of this that has already occurred in our head. That, indeed, is why the Lord

---

[1]Mic 7:2. [2]Ps 14:3 (13:3 LXX). [3]Ps 106:37 (105:37 LXX). [4]Amos 2:8. [5]FC 61:230-31. [6]PG 66:148; *LSL* 72. [7]PG 66:148; *LSL* 73. [8]PG 71:120; *LSL* 73*.

wished to rise again at night; because, in the apostle's words, "God, who commanded the light to shine out of the darkness, has shone in our hearts."[9] So the Lord represented light shining out of darkness by being born at night and also by rising at night. Light out of darkness, in fact, is Christ out of the Jews, to whom it was said, "I have likened your mother to night." But in that nation, as it were in that night, the virgin Mary was not night but somehow or other a star of the night; which is why a star also signaled her childbearing, guiding a far distant night, that is the magi from the east, to worship the light. Thus in them too would be realized the command to "the light to shine out of darkness." SERMON 223D.2.[10]

REFERRING TO SIN. AUGUSTINE: "Day continues according to your ordinance."[11] For all these things are day: "and this is the day which the Lord has made; let us rejoice and be glad in it"[12] and "let us walk honestly as in the day."[13] "For all things serve you." He said "all things of some," "all" which belong to this day "serve you." For the ungodly, of whom it is said, "I have compared thy mother unto the night," do not serve you. EXPLANATION OF THE PSALMS 119.91.[14]

THE SYNAGOGUE IS THE "MOTHER." THEOPHYLACT: The mother of the people is the synagogue, which—since it is covered by the darkness of ignorance and did not receive the radiance of God's knowledge—may be compared to the night. COMMENTARY ON HOSEA 4.[15]

4:8 Feeding on Sin

THEY EAT THE OFFERINGS. CYRIL OF ALEXANDRIA: They used to sacrifice goats for sin; for this reason the sacrifice was called sin. By offering a goat on the altar, the priests at the right time used to bring the intestines and the lard, and they ate the rest. This was ordered by the divine law.[16] . . . "They eat the sins of my people" means they eat the offerings brought for sins. COMMENTARY ON HOSEA 3.40.[17]

PRIESTS APPROVE OF SINS. JEROME: [The priests] are feasting on the sins of my people, approving the crimes of the sinners. For when they behold them sinning, not only do they not argue but they praise and extol them, calling them fortunate. COMMENTARY ON HOSEA 1.4.[18]

CHRIST THE PRIEST DEVOURS OUR SIN. ORIGEN: The text wants you to make a more daring assertion if your hearing will still follow. What is the "sacrifice" that is offered "for sin" and is "very holy" except "the only begotten Son of God,"[19] Jesus Christ my Lord? He alone is the "sacrifice for sins," and he is "a very holy offering." But since it added that "the priest who offers it will eat it,"[20] it seems to be hard to understand. For that which it says must be eaten seems to be referring to the sin, just as in another place the prophet says concerning the priests that "they will eat the sins of my people." This also shows that the priest ought to eat the sin of the one who is offering. We frequently show from holy Scripture that Christ is also the sacrifice that is offered for the sin of the world and the priest who brings the offering. HOMILIES ON LEVITICUS 5.2.[21]

---

[9]2 Cor 4:6. [10]*WSA* 3 6:224. [11]Ps 119:91 (118:91 LXX). [12]Ps 118:24 (117:24 LXX). [13]Rom 13:13. [14]NPNF 1 8:575*. [15]PG 126:637; *LSL* 73. [16]Lev 3:3. [17]PG 71:124; *LSL* 75. [18]PG 25:890; *LSL* 75. [19]Jn 3:16, 18. [20]Lev 6:26. [21]FC 83:93-94*.

4:9-19 DIVINE PUNISHMENT FOR IDOLATRY

⁹And it shall be like people, like priest;
 I will punish them for their* ways,
 and requite them for their* deeds.
¹⁰They shall eat, but not be satisfied;
 they shall play the harlot, but not
 multiply;
because they have forsaken the Lord
 to cherish harlotry.

¹¹Wine and new wine
 take away the understanding.
¹²My people inquire of a thing of wood,
 and their staff gives them oracles.
For a spirit of harlotry has led them astray,
 and they have left their God to play the
 harlot.
¹³They sacrifice on the tops of the
 mountains,
 and make offerings upon the hills,
under oak, poplar,† and terebinth,
 because their shade is good.

Therefore your daughters play the harlot,
 and your brides commit adultery.
¹⁴I will not punish your daughters when
 they play the harlot,

nor your brides when they commit
 adultery;
for the men themselves go aside with
 harlots,
 and sacrifice with cult prostitutes,
and a people without understanding shall
 come to ruin.

¹⁵Though you play the harlot, O Israel,
 let not Judah become guilty.
Enter not into Gilgal,
 nor go up to Bethaven,
 and swear not, "As the Lord lives."
¹⁶Like a stubborn heifer,
 Israel is stubborn;
can the Lord now feed them
 like a lamb in a broad pasture?

¹⁷Ephraim is joined to idols,
 let him alone.
¹⁸A bandˡ of drunkards, they give themselves
 to harlotry;
 they love shame more than their glory.ᵐ
¹⁹A wind has wrapped themⁿ in its wings,
 and they shall be ashamed because of
 their altars.ᵒ

l Cn: Heb uncertain   m Cn Compare Gk: Heb of this line uncertain   n Heb her   o Gk Syr: Heb sacrifices   *LXX his   †LXX white poplar

Overview: Those who neglect their spiritual duties become caught up in worldly pursuits (Gregory the Great). Thoughts are subject to divine judgment just as deeds are (Cyril of Alexandria, Theophylact), and the degree of punishment that they will experience will match the degree to which they achieved their desires (Julian of Eclanum). Israel's insatiability results in captivity (Cyril of Alexandria). Desire is insatiable, but righteousness satisfies (Jerome). Israel's leaders fail the people because they promote rather than redirect error (Cyril of Alexandria). Temptation continues even among the saints (Athanasius). Recourse to astrologers is likened to spiritual fornication (John Cassian). The unfaithful synagogue is likened to the spirit of harlotry (Jerome). The next generation need not be directly punished, for it will be enough that they will reap the ill effects of their parent's sin (CYRIL OF ALEXANDRIA). The patience of God regarding idolatry has its limits. Spiritual fornication and adultery without repentance causes God to no longer show any jealousy toward unbelievers, hence leaving the idolaters to their own devices (ORIGEN). The Jews' resistance to revelation was likened to a stubborn heifer that refused to be yoked (CHRYSOSTOM). Those who have abandoned God have given themselves to spiritual prostitution (ISHO'DAD).

4:9 Punishment for Sin

LIKE PEOPLE, LIKE PRIEST. GREGORY THE GREAT: We do not seek to gain souls; we devote ourselves daily to our own pursuits, we attend to earthly matters, we strive for human praise with all our will. From being set over others we have greater freedom to do anything we like, and so we turn the ministry we have received into an occasion for display. We abandon God's cause, and we devote ourselves to earthly business; we accept a place of holiness and involve ourselves in earthly deeds. What is written in Hosea is truly fulfilled in us: "And so it will be, like people, like priest." A priest does not differ from the people when he does not surpass their deeds by any merit of his own. FORTY GOSPEL HOMILIES 19.[1]

PUNISHMENT OF DEED AND THOUGHT. CYRIL OF ALEXANDRIA: Seemingly he calls "ways" the walking in works and "counsels" the faults from outrageous thoughts. Then, he says, she [Israel] did not go rightly, having turned aside from the straight road. As if marching the footpath of all profanity, they devised the most shameful and absurd things, dishonoring the God of all while turning toward idolatry. COMMENTARY ON HOSEA 3.41.[2]

PUNISHMENT FOR DEEDS AND THOUGHTS. THEOPHYLACT: By calling the deeds "ways" he says that "I will bring over them all the judgment and punishment for their deeds. And I will pun-

ish not the deeds only but also 'his' counsels," namely, of the people. For we will suffer punishment not only for the deeds but for the outrageous thoughts. COMMENTARY ON HOSEA 4.[3]

PUNISHMENT MEETS TRANSGRESSION. JULIAN OF ECLANUM: When, he says, the avenging judgment begins to work, these measures of griefs that they [Israel] made in sins will be filled, so that they may experience in punishments what they have achieved in desires. COMMENTARY ON HOSEA 1.4.[4]

4:10 They Will Not Be Satisfied

EATING WITHOUT SATISFACTION. CYRIL OF ALEXANDRIA: A remnant from Israel has been preserved. Since the judgment does not go entirely to the priest, he adds, "They eat, but they are not satisfied." This means either emigration and captivity for those leaders of Israel or, because of Christ, desolation of Judea by the hands of Romans.... For among those Israelites brought then by Shalmaneser and Tiglath-pileser III to Assyria and Media, very few could offer to the priests the things prescribed by the law. COMMENTARY ON HOSEA 3.42.[5]

RIGHTEOUSNESS, NOT DESIRE, SATISFIES. JEROME: Desire is insatiable, and the more it is felt, the more it creates in those who enjoy it a greater hunger. On the contrary: "Blessed are the ones who hunger and thirst for righteousness, for they will be satisfied."[6] For righteousness satisfies, while wickedness—because it has no substance—deceives by fraud those who feed on vain things and leaves empty the stomachs of those who hunger. "They played the whore continually." In fornication they run out of strength, yet the ardent desire of the fornication does not make a pause. The ten tribes played the whore with the idols of Jeroboam son of Naboth. COMMENTARY ON HOSEA 1.4.[7]

---

[1]CS 123:145. [2]PG 71:125; LSL 76. [3]PG 126:641; LSL 76. [4]PL 21:985; LSL 76. [5]PG 71:125-28; LSL 76*. [6]Mt 5:6. [7]PL 25:891; LSL 76-77**.

SPIRITUAL LEADERS MUST REMAIN VIGILANT. CYRIL OF ALEXANDRIA: "They kept the whoredom" means that they [Israel's leaders] got ready to preserve the error for those who were under their authority. Yet they should rather have removed and thrown it from their midst. For it is the vigilance of the teachers which should eagerly remove what hurts the people and turn down without delay what is hateful to God. By refusing to do this, they allow the works of error to stay somehow and to keep. Yet they confirm rather the contrary, when the minds of those who teach receive nothing but wine and drunkenness. For how will the disciples keep vigil, and how will they be able to point the eye of the understanding to God in nature and in truth, if the instructors and the teachers of useful things will still encourage them to err? COMMENTARY ON HOSEA 3.43.[8]

4:12 A Spirit of Harlotry

HOW THE SPIRIT OF HARLOTRY TEMPTED ANTHONY. ATHANASIUS: Anthony then asked, "Who are you who say such things to me? And at once he [the demonic voice] uttered a contemptible speech: 'I am a lover of fornication; I have undertaken to ensnare the young and to entice them to it, and I am called the spirit of fornication. How many I have deceived who wished to be chaste! How many who practiced self-restraint have I by my seductions persuaded to change! I am he on whose account the prophet reproaches the fallen, saying, "You have been deceived by the spirit of fornication," for through me they were tripped up. I am he who often troubled you but whom you as often overthrew.'" LIFE OF ST. ANTHONY 6.[9]

THE OCCULT LIKENED TO FORNICATION. JOHN CASSIAN: "It is written in the law: 'You shall not commit fornication.'"[10] This is kept in a beneficial way according to the simple sound of the letter by the person who is still entangled in the passions of fleshly impurity. It is necessarily observed in spiritual fashion, however, by one who has already left behind this filthy behavior and

impure disposition. This person also rejects not only all idolatrous ceremonies but also every superstition of the Gentiles and the observance of auguries and omens, and of all signs and days and times, and is certainly not engaged in the divination of particular words or names. [This] befouls the wholesomeness of our faith. Jerusalem is said to have been debauched by this fornication, having fornicated "on every high hill and under every green tree."[11] And the Lord, rebuking [Jerusalem], says by the prophet: "Let the astrologers stand and save you, who gazed on the stars and counted the months, so that from them they might announce the things that are to happen to you."[12] Concerning this fornication the Lord reproaches them elsewhere when he says, "The spirit of fornication has deceived them, and they went fornicating away from their God." CONFERENCE 14.11.2-3.[13]

THE UNHOLY CANNOT ABIDE WITH THE HOLY. JEROME: The unclean spirit before had been in the synagogue and had led them into idolatry. Of him it is written, "The spirit of harlotry has led them astray." The spirit had gone out of a man and was roaming in the dry places in search of a resting place and could find none. He took with him seven other demons and returned to his former dwelling place.[14] All these spirits were in the synagogue and could not bear the presence of the Savior. Indeed, "what harmony is there between Christ and Belial?"[15] Christ and Belial could not abide in the same assembly. "Now in their synagogue there was a man with an unclean spirit, and he cried out, saying, 'What have we to do with you?'" Who is asking, "What have we to do with you?" He is only one, but he cries out the recognition of many. He is aware that in his own defeat, his devils have been vanquished with him. HOMILIES ON MARK 76.[16]

4:14 The Ruin of a People

---

[8]PG 71:128; *LSL* 77*. [9]FC 15:140. [10]Ex 20:14. [11]Jer 3:6. [12]Is 47:13. [13]ACW 57:515-16. [14]Mt 12:43-46. [15]2 Cor 6:15. [16]FC 57:140*.

ISRAEL'S CHILDREN. CYRIL OF ALEXANDRIA: And when these things occur, he says, I will remain calm, and I will not lay charges. Because of the misfortunes of the war and the troubles of the captivity, it seems right that all that will happen be predicted to the sinners. For they who once captured and overcame others will do with the captives as they like, making use of power without bridle and shamelessly attacking whomever they please, neither taking into account the law or considering what is likely or proper. But hardened and extremely wild in soul, they refuse to refrain from any kind of wretchedness. Therefore he clearly showed that the young children will be exposed to enemies because of the insult and shameless conduct of the fornicators. COMMENTARY ON HOSEA 3.46.[17]

LACK OF CORRECTION CONDEMNED. ORIGEN: Hear what he says through the prophet. When he had enumerated abominable things that the people had committed, he adds these words also: "And for this reason I will not visit your daughters when they fornicate, nor your daughters-in-law when they commit adultery." This is terrible! This is the outcome when we are no longer reproached for sins, when we offend and are no longer corrected. For then, when we have exceeded the measure of sinning "the jealous God" turns his jealousy away from us, as he said above, "For my jealousy will be removed from you, and I will no longer be angry over you."[18] I have said these things about the statement "God is jealous." HOMILIES ON EXODUS 8.[19]

4:16 Can the Lord Feed Them?

GROWN PLUMP, WE REJECT DISCIPLINE. CHRYSOSTOM: But what is the source of this hardness? It comes from gluttony and drunkenness. Who says so? Moses himself. "Israel ate and was filled, and the darling grew fat and frisky."[20] When brute animals feed from a full manger, they grow plump and become more obstinate and hard to hold in check; they endure neither the yoke,

the reins, nor the hand of the charioteer. Just so, the Jewish people were driven by their drunkenness and plumpness to ultimate evil. They kicked about and failed to accept the yoke of Christ. And they failed to pull the plow of his teaching. Another prophet hinted at this when he said, "Israel is as obstinate as a stubborn heifer." And still another called the Jews "an untamed calf."[21] DISCOURSES AGAINST JUDAIZING CHRISTIANS 1.2.5.[22]

4:19 The Shame of Their Altars

KISSING THE CALF. ISHO'DAD OF MERV: The words "I will not visit your daughters when they prostitute themselves," that is, when a woman is accused of being adulterous and there is no witness, "she will make," Scripture says, "her offering of barley flour and will not pour any oil or incense."[23] And since she is in her sorrow, the appearance of her offering will be equally sad. "And the priest," Scripture says, "will take some water from a vase of clay, and will throw some dust of the soil into the water, and will place the woman before the Lord and will make her swear."[24] If she is innocent, she will remain unscathed and will still be fertile and will conceive; otherwise she will be torn. But in the meantime God threatens, "I will ravage Jerusalem, and there will be no one of your establishments which you cared for," and so on, because everything in the temple will be bound and delivered. "A nation that does not understand has kissed the woman of whoredom," that is, these people, who are blind and do not realize who God is, who lives and abides among them, prefer to worship idols rather than God. They foolishly kiss the calves and give themselves over to the prostitution with demons. COMMENTARY ON HOSEA.[25]

---

[17]PG 71:132; *LSL* 79. [18]Ezek 16:42. [19]FC 71:328. [20]Deut 32:15. Chrysostom reads "Israel" for "Jacob" of LXX. [21]Jer 31:18 (38:18 in LXX), which reads, "Like a calf I was untamed." [22]FC 68:8*. [23]Num 5:11-31. [24]Num 5:17-19. [25]CSCO 303 (128):69.

5:1-15 IMPENDING JUDGMENT ON ISRAEL AND JUDAH

Hear this, O priests!
Give heed, O house of Israel!
Hearken, O house of the king!
For the judgment pertains to you;
for you have been a snare at Mizpah,
and a net spread upon Tabor.
2 *And they have made deep the pit of Shittim;*[p]
*but I will chastise all of them.**

3 *I know Ephraim,*
and Israel is not hid from me;
for now, O Ephraim, you have played the harlot,
Israel is defiled.
4 *Their deeds do not permit them*
to return to their God.
For the spirit of harlotry is within them,
and they know not the LORD.

5 *The pride of Israel testifies to his face;*
Ephraim [q] *shall stumble in his guilt;*
Judah also shall stumble with them.
6 *With their flocks and herds they shall go*
to seek the LORD,
but they will not find him;
he has withdrawn from them.
7 *They have dealt faithlessly with the* LORD;
for they have borne alien children.
Now the new moon shall devour them
with their fields.

8 *Blow the horn in Gibeah,*
the trumpet in Ramah.
Sound the alarm at Beth-aven;
tremble,[r] *O Benjamin!*
9 *Ephraim shall become a desolation*
in the day of punishment;
among the tribes of Israel
I declare what is sure.
10 *The princes of Judah have become*
like those who remove the landmark;
upon them I will pour out
my wrath like water.
11 *Ephraim is oppressed,*† *crushed in judgment,*
because he was determined to go after vanity.[s]
12 *Therefore I am like a moth to Ephraim,*
and like dry rot to the house of Judah.

13 *When Ephraim saw his sickness,*
and Judah his wound,
then Ephraim went to Assyria,
and sent to the great king.[t]
But he is not able to cure you
or heal your wound.
14 *For I will be like a lion to Ephraim,*
and like a young lion to the house of Judah.
I, even I, will rend and go away,
I will carry off, and none shall rescue.
15 *I will return again to my place,*
until they acknowledge their guilt and seek my face,
and in their distress they seek me.

p Cn: Heb uncertain **q** Heb *Israel and Ephraim* **r** Cn Compare Gk: Heb *after you* **s** Gk: Heb *a command* **t** Cn: Heb *a king that will contend* *LXX *I will correct you* †LXX has active form: *Ephraim has oppressed his adversary*

OVERVIEW: The shepherds by right living provide the flock with pure waters of truth. However, when they pollute the water by evil living, they jeopardize the lives of their flock (GREGORY THE GREAT). Christ is our educator who leads us to eternal life and imparts the necessary truth to save us (CLEMENT OF ALEXANDRIA). That God knows Ephraim means that God loves Ephraim, and God will correct Ephraim in love rather than anger (THEOPHYLACT). The spirit of whoredom blocks Israel's knowledge of God (JEROME). Baptism regenerates believers and leads them away from their fallen nature (THEODOTUS). God becomes like a moth, or rot, by allowing a long time for penitence. Human terms of place do not completely fit when discussing God's place (JEROME). To seek God's face is to seek Christ. Those who come to their senses will stop worshiping idols and turn to seek God (CYRIL OF ALEXANDRIA).

5:1 Israel's Judgment

HOW PRIESTS FOUL THE FLOCK'S WATER. GREGORY THE GREAT: For indeed the shepherds drink most pure water, when with a right understanding they imbibe the streams of truth. But to foul the same water with their feet is to corrupt the studies of holy meditation by evil living. And truly the sheep drink the water fouled by their feet, when any of those subject to them follow not the words that they hear but only imitate the bad examples that they see. Thirsting for things said but perverted by the works observed, they take in mud with their draughts, as from polluted fountains. Hence also it is written through the prophet, "A snare for the downfall of my people are evil spirits." PASTORAL CARE 1.2.[1]

5:2 Chastising All

THE WORD EDUCATES THE FAITHFUL. CLEMENT OF ALEXANDRIA: Therefore the Word who leads us his children to salvation is unquestionably an educator of little ones. In fact, through Hosea, the Word says plainly of himself, "I am your educator."[2] The matter he educates us in is fear of God, for this fear instructs us in the service of God, educates to the knowledge of truth, and guides by a path leading straight up to heaven. CHRIST THE EDUCATOR 1.7.53.[3]

5:3 I Know Ephraim

TO KNOW IS TO LOVE. THEOPHYLACT: That "I know" means "I loved" is seen from God's words: "I instruct them because I loved Ephraim, and I did not remove Israel from me. For though she plays the whore in idolatry, nevertheless I would not reject her, but I will be with her." This is in harmony with what the prophet was told in the beginning, when he was ordered to marry a whore. Who would not love an instructor who corrects with love rather than with anger? This is also the instruction pertaining to every leader: to chastise not for anger but for education and assistance. COMMENTARY ON HOSEA 5.[4]

5:4 They Do Not Know the Lord

THE SPIRIT OF WHOREDOM BLOCKS THEIR KNOWLEDGE. JEROME: First the king [Jeroboam I] chose to play the whore away from the worship of God, wishing to adore golden calves. And the people followed him willingly—with equal zeal they accomplished equal ungodliness.[5] They do not return to the Lord, for they found what they were looking for, and the spirit of whoredom—which according to the apostle "works in the sons of distrust"[6]—holds their hearts captive. As long as it governs, they will not know the Lord. In fact, they forgot their Creator. . . . They—whoever advances in ruin—do not have thoughts of penitence. For the spirit of whoredom, by which they played the whore in the church and by which they went away from the true marriage, dwells in

---

[1]NPNF 2 12:2*. [2]The word used is *paideutēs*. [3]FC 23:49*. [4]PG 126:657; *LSL* 84*. [5]See 1 Kings 12:1-33. [6]Eph 2:2.

their midst. That is why they did not know the Lord. Commentary on Hosea 1.5.[7]

5:8 Sound a Warning

Christ Our Teacher. Theodotus the Valentinian: The Spirit through Hosea says, "I will correct you." "Blow the trumpet upon the hills of the Lord; let it sound upon the high places."[8] And is not baptism itself, which is the sign of regeneration, a transcending of the flesh, which is a great impetuous stream, ever rushing on and bearing us along? The teaching of the Lord accordingly leads us out of disorder, illumines us by bringing us into light, beyond the shadows of unilluminated matter. Excerpts of Theodotus 5.[9]

5:12 Like a Moth, Like Dry-Rot

A Surprising Metaphor. Jerome: Just as the moth consumes clothing and decay or dry-rot consumes wooden things (which both occur over a long time), in the same manner God, giving a place of penitence over a long time to the ten tribes and then afterward to the two tribes—summoning to salvation those who treasure for themselves wrath for the day of wrath—becomes like a moth or rot. Commentary on Hosea 2.5.[10]

5:15 I Will Go Back to My Place

God's Place. Jerome: By "my place" we have to understand God's place, his splendor and majesty, so that by no means according to the dispensation does he descend to men, become angry, merciful, forgetful, become as a panther, turn into a lion, change into beasts. On the contrary, he disdains human things and allows those whom he once protected to be cast to enemies so that they may languish, disappear and be destroyed, and seek eventually the face of the Lord. . . . Others consider God's place the heaven where God re-

turns after being offended by the inhabitants of the earth, and he allows to go to ruin those who, due to the multitude of their sins, turned the mercy of the Lord into the rage of beasts toward them. Commentary on Hosea 2.5.[11]

God's Face Is Christ. Cyril of Alexandria: It seems that the saying refers very suitably to the mystery of Christ and the redemption through him, pointing to the conversion to God. For the face of God we seek signifies most certainly the Son himself, "who is the image, and the radiance, and the very seal of the Father's nature."[12] Thus the true face of God and Father is the Son, inasmuch as he is recognized in him: "And who saw him, saw the Father."[13] The psalmist thus calls him when he cries out to God of all, saying: "Cause your face to shine upon your servant."[14] Indeed, just as from the person of those who were already transformed according to the Son through the Spirit: "The light of your face, O Lord, has been marked upon us."[15] Or as the prophet says: "The light of our face, the anointed Lord."[16] Commentary on Hosea 4.61.[17]

Divine Chastisement Awakens the People to Repentance. Cyril of Alexandria: "They seek early" seems to indicate here that they, as if awakened from the sleep of thoughtlessness which was in them, and further as if brought from night and darkness to light and day, will call out to one another that it is fitting to return to the Lord. This is a return to the senses of those fallen into deception and those taken up by the worship of idols. For the fruit of vigilance is at present seeking to get out of the gloom which is demonic. Commentary on Hosea 4.62.[18]

---

[7]PL 25:899; *LSL* 84. [8]Heb. *Gibeah* ("hill of the Lord"); *Ramah* ("high place"). [9]ANF 8:43*. [10]PL 25:906; *LSL* 91. [11]PL 25:908; *LSL* 92-93. [12]Heb 1:3. [13]Jn 14:9. [14]Ps 119:135 (118:135 LXX). [15]Ps 4:6 LXX. [16]Lam 4:20. [17]PG 71:161; *LSL* 93*. [18]PG 71:161; *LSL* 93*.

6:1-11 CALL FOR REPENTANCE

[1]"Come, let us return to the LORD;
for he has torn, that he may heal us;
 he has stricken,* and he will bind us up.
[2]After two days he will revive us;
 on the third day he will raise us up,
 that we may live before him.
[3]Let us know, let us press on to know the
 LORD;
 his going forth is sure as the dawn;
he will come to us as the showers,
 as the spring rains that water the
 earth."

[4]What shall I do with you, O Ephraim?
 What shall I do with you, O Judah?
Your love is like a morning cloud,
 like the dew that goes early away.
[5]Therefore I have hewn them by the
 prophets,
 I have slain them by the words of my
 mouth,

and my judgment goes forth as the light.[u]
[6]For I desire steadfast love and not sacrifice,
 the knowledge of God, rather than burnt
 offerings.

[7]But at[v] Adam they transgressed the
 covenant;
 there they dealt faithlessly with me.
[8]Gilead is a city of evildoers,
 tracked with blood.
[9]As robbers lie in wait[w] for a man,
 so the priests are banded together;[x]
they murder on the way to Shechem,
 yea, they commit villainy.
[10]In the house of Israel I have seen a
 horrible thing;
 Ephraim's harlotry is there, Israel is
 defiled.

[11]For you also, O Judah, a harvest is
 appointed.

u Gk Syr: Heb *thy judgment goes forth*   v Cn: Heb *like*   w Cn: Heb uncertain   x Syr: Heb *a company*   *LXX *he will strike*

OVERVIEW: The Holy Spirit calls us to pray that Christ will provide us the grace of eternal light (CYPRIAN). God judges not for the sake of punishment but for repentance (THEOPHYLACT) and healing in Christ (CYRIL OF ALEXANDRIA). Jesus' resurrection was foretold by Hosea, and so will he who was raised revive us to live in his presence (CYRIL OF JERUSALEM, AUGUSTINE). We must be baptized with Christ that we may also rise with him on the third day (ORIGEN). The three days of Jesus' death represent the passion, descent and resurrection (CAESARIUS). It was Christ who came down as a shower of rain to be baptized in the Jordan (HIPPOLYTUS). Christ comes to us as both early and late rain, setting the foundation of faith and ensuring a harvest (JEROME). The early rain may also be seen as the law and prophets, whereas the late rain is the gospel (CYRIL OF ALEXANDRIA). God offers his mercy to penitents who return to him. It is a clear expression of God's mercy that he pardons those who repent (TERTULLIAN). True repentance frees one from sin and reunites one with God. The angels rejoice when a sinner repents (CLEMENT OF ALEXANDRIA). God's call for mercy was proclaimed by Moses, echoed by Israel and reiterated by Paul (AMBROSE). Both covenants demand the generosity of believers through their words, gifts and righteous deeds as outward evidences of mercy. Moses, the prophets and the apostles repeatedly stress mercy over sacrifice (CHRYSOSTOM). Worship of God displays love and knowledge of God, and both are perfected in Christ (CYRIL OF ALEXANDRIA). Love to God and to one's neighbor enables sacrifice that is acceptable to God (THEODORET).

6:1 Call to Repentance

CALL TO PRAYER. CYPRIAN: The Holy Spirit set this forth of old, when he said in the Psalms, "O my king and my God. For to you will I pray; O Lord, in the morning you shall hear my voice. In the morning I will stand before you, and will see you."[1] And again through the prophet the Lord says, "At dawn they will be on watch for me, saying, 'Let us go and return to the Lord our God.'" Likewise at the setting of the sun and at the end of the day necessarily there must again be prayer. For since Christ is the true sun and the true day, as the sun and the day of the world recede, when we pray and petition that the light come upon us again, we pray for the coming of Christ to provide us with the grace of eternal light. THE LORD'S PRAYER 35.[2]

PUNISHMENT NOT THE GOAL. THEOPHYLACT: For when God snatches away or strikes, no one can heal. Thus in the calamity they remembered God. These may refer to those among the Hebrews who afterward came to believe in Christ. In such a thirst and long captivity they will seek the face, namely, the Son. For he is the mark of the Father's hypostasis (person). Those who turn to the Son are stripped of the veil which lies on their heart. COMMENTARY ON HOSEA 6.[3]

CHRIST THE HEALER. CYRIL OF ALEXANDRIA: In the beginning he seized Adam's human nature; for he at once declared it accursed, ascribing it to death and corruption. Thus the wrath has struck, but grace plugged the wound with lint. For Christ has brought the healing. He invited [us] to know the true divine revelation; he confirmed [us] through the Spirit to observe the command-

ments. He showed us again to be zealous followers by placing us beyond corruption and freeing us from the previous infirmities, namely, sin and passions. COMMENTARY ON HOSEA 4.62.[4]

6:2 Raised on the Third Day

RESURRECTION. CYRIL OF JERUSALEM: A few of the Jews of that time were persuaded, but the world hearkened to the truth. Those who concealed the truth were buried in oblivion, but those who received it were made manifest by the power of the Savior, who rose from the dead and raised the dead himself. In the person of the risen dead the prophet Hosea says plainly, "He will revive us after two days; on the third day he will raise us up, to live in his presence." CATECHETICAL LECTURE 14.4.[5]

RESURRECTION OF CHRIST. AUGUSTINE: Further on, Hosea foretold the resurrection of Christ on the third day, but in the mysterious way that is proper to prophecy. He says, "He shall heal us after two days, and on the third day we shall rise again." This is the idea underlying the words of Paul [when he says], "Therefore if you have risen in Christ, seek the things that are above."[6] CITY OF GOD 28.[7]

RESURRECTION: CHRIST'S AND OURS. ORIGEN: Hear what the prophet says: "God will revive us after two days, and on the third day we shall arise and live in his sight." The first day is the passion of the Savior for us. The second is the day on which he descended into hell. The third day is the day of resurrection.[8] Therefore on the third day "God went before them, by day in a column of cloud, by night in a column of fire."[9] But if according to what we said above, the apostle teaches us rightly that the mysteries of baptism are contained in these words,[10] it is necessary that

---

[1]Ps 5:2-3 (5:3-4 LXX). [2]FC 36:158. [3]PG 126:673; *LSL* 94. [4]PG 71:161-64; *LSL* 94. [5]FC 64:41. [6]Col 3:1. [7]FC 24:123. [8]Mt 16:21. [9]Ex 13:21. [10]1 Cor 10:2.

"those who are baptized in Christ are baptized in his death and are buried with him." [They must] also arise from the dead with him on the third day,[11] according to what the apostle says, "He raised up together with him and at the same time made them sit in the heavenly places."[12] When, therefore, you shall have undertaken the mystery of the third day, God will begin to lead you and will himself show you the way of salvation. HOMILIES ON EXODUS 5.[13]

THREE DAYS OF RESURRECTION EXPLAINED. CAESARIUS OF ARLES: The prince of this world did not want the Lord's army to recognize the engagement of those three days, as that engagement of which the prophet said, "He will revive us after two days; on the third day he will raise us up." The first day for us is the passion of the Savior; the second day on which he descended into hell; but the third day is the day of the resurrection. So then on the third day God went before them in a pillar of cloud by day and by night in a pillar of fire, and the people were led through the Red Sea. The three days we can fittingly call the Father, Son and Holy Spirit, for the Father is a day, the Son is one, and the Holy Spirit is one, and these three are one. SERMON 97.1.[14]

6:3 How God Comes to Us

CHRIST AS RAIN. HIPPOLYTUS: Nor is this the only thing that proves the dignity of the water. But there is also that which is more honorable than all—the fact that Christ, the maker of all, came down as the rain, and was known as a spring,[15] and diffused himself as a river,[16] and was baptized in the Jordan.[17] For you have just heard how Jesus came to John and was baptized by him in the Jordan. Oh, things strange beyond compare! How should the boundless river that makes glad the city of God[18] have been dipped in a little water! ON THE HOLY THEOPHANY 2.[19]

CHRIST IS THE FOUNDATION AND FRUIT OF FAITH. JEROME: [God] is called not only at morn-

ing or dawn or daybreak; he will come to us as an early and later rain to earth. We accept Christ as an early rain when the foundations of the faith are laid within us, and we shall take him as a late rain when after the crop is ripened we grasp eternal fruits and store them up in the Master's barn. COMMENTARY ON HOSEA 2.6.[20]

LAW, PROPHETS AND GOSPEL. CYRIL OF ALEXANDRIA: For I suppose that he waters in two ways upon us who received faith and have known rightly his manifestation. On the one hand, he reveals knowledge in the spirit of the old and legal, and in addition to these, prophetic teachings. In my view, this is the early rain. On the other hand, he adds to this the late [rain], the interpretation of the gospel's teachings and the most desirable grace of the apostolic preachings. COMMENTARY ON HOSEA 4.62.[21]

6:6-7 Love Instead of Sacrifice

GOD IS MERCIFUL. TERTULLIAN: But he would not threaten the impenitent if he failed to pardon the penitent. This would be doubtful only if he had not revealed elsewhere the profusion of his mercy. Has he not said, "He who is fallen shall rise, and he who was turned away shall return"?[22] He it is, most assuredly, who "will have mercy rather than sacrifice."[23] The heavens and the angels who are there rejoice at human repentance. Look at you now, sinner, be of good heart! You see where it is that you are a cause of joy. ON PENITENCE 8.[24]

MERCY APPLIED TO REPENTANCE. CLEMENT OF ALEXANDRIA: For to every one who has turned to God in truth and with a whole heart, the doors are open, and the thrice-glad Father receives his truly repentant child. And true repentance is to

---

[11]Rom 6:3-4. [12]Eph 2:6. [13]FC 71:278-79*. [14]FC 47:74. [15]Jn 4:14. [16]Jn 7:38. [17]Mt 3:13. [18]Ps 46:4. [19]ANF 5:235. [20]PL 25:910; *LSL* 97. [21]PG 71:164; *LSL* 97-98. [22]Cf. Jer 8:4 Vulgate. [23]See also Mt 9:13; 12:7. [24]ACW 28:30**.

be no longer bound in the same sins for which he denounced death against himself, but to eradicate them completely from the soul. For on their uprooting God takes up his abode again in you. For it is said there is great and exceeding joy and festivity in the heavens with the Father and the angels when one sinner turns and repents.[25] This is why he cries, "I will have mercy, and not sacrifice."[26] WHO IS THE RICH MAN THAT SHALL BE SAVED 39.[27]

MERCY, NOT SACRIFICE. AMBROSE: God himself has said that he would rather have his commandments obeyed than sacrifice offered to him. God proclaims this, Moses declares it to the people of Israel, Paul preaches it to the nations. Do that which you see is better for the time. "I desire mercy more than sacrifice,"[28] it says. Are not those who condemn their sin truer Christians than those who think to defend it? "The just accuses himself in the beginning of his words."[29] The one who accuses himself when he sins is just, not the one who praises himself. LETTER 51.15.[30]

MERCY TO BE OBSERVED. CHRYSOSTOM: Great is the principle of mercy to God. Not only his to us, but also that issuing from us to our fellow servants. In the Old Testament and the New, God lays down innumerable laws pertaining to this matter. He orders us to be benevolent continually in all quarters, through words, money and deeds. And Moses throughout—up and down, here and there—scatters words about these matters in all his legislations. And in the person of God the prophets shout, "I desire mercy, and not sacrifice." And all the apostles act and speak in harmony with these prophetic words. Therefore let us not neglect the matter.[31] By mercy we greatly benefit ourselves, not the poor only. We receive much more than we provide. HOMILIES ON REPEN-

TANCE AND ALMSGIVING 10.5.22.[32]

WORSHIP DISPLAYS LOVE AND KNOWLEDGE OF GOD IN CHRIST. CYRIL OF ALEXANDRIA: Most of all, worship of God displays love. . . . For truly the compassion from beside the Father is Christ, as he takes away the sins, dismisses the charges and justifies by faith, and recovers the lost and makes [them] stronger than death. For what is good and he does not give? Therefore the knowledge of God is better than sacrifice and holocausts, as it is brought to perfection in Christ. For by him and in him we have known the Father, and we have become rich in the justification by faith. COMMENTARY ON HOSEA 4.65.[33]

THE DISPOSITION THAT VALIDATES SACRIFICE. THEODORET OF CYR: Whereas I [the Lord] have no need of sacrifices, I accept them out of considerateness for the limitations of your way of thinking. These two things, on the contrary, I do require: the right disposition toward me and lovingkindness toward the neighbor, these also being the first obligations I imposed, "You will love the Lord your God with your whole heart, your whole soul, your whole mind and your whole strength; and you will love your neighbor as yourself."[34] But whereas I imposed these obligations, they resembled someone breaking agreements made by him with somebody else. In similar fashion, in fact, they despised my longsuffering and trampled on the laws given them. COMMENTARY ON HOSEA 6.6-7.[35]

---

[25]See Lk 15:10. [26]See also Mt 9:13. [27]ANF 2:602*. [28]Mt 9:13. [29]Prov 18:17 LXX. [30]LCC 5:257*. Ambrose does not hesitate here to remind the emperor of his responsibility for exercising mercy in a situation in which large numbers of innocent people were killed. [31]Mt 9:13. [32]FC 96:146*. [33]PG 71:168; LSL 100*. [34]Deut 6:4; Lev 19:18. [35]PG 81:1584.

6:11—7:16 FREE REFUSAL TO REPENT

[11]*When I would restore the fortunes of my
    people,*

7   [1]*when I would heal Israel,
        the corruption of Ephraim is revealed,
    and the wicked deeds of Samaria;
for they deal falsely,
    the thief breaks in,
    and the bandits raid without.*
[2]*But they do not consider
    that I remember all their evil works.
Now their deeds encompass them,
    they are before my face.*
[3]*By their wickedness they make the king
        glad,
    and the princes by their treachery.*
[4]*They are all adulterers;
    they are like a heated oven,
whose baker ceases to stir the fire,
    from the kneading of the dough
        until it is leavened.*
[5]*On the day of our king the princes
    became sick with the heat of wine;
    he stretched out his hand with mockers.*
[6]*For like an oven their hearts burn[y] with
        intrigue;
    all night their anger smolders;
    in the morning it blazes like a flaming
        fire.*
[7]*All of them are hot as an oven,
    and they devour their rulers.
All their kings have fallen;
    and none of them calls upon me.*

[8]*Ephraim mixes himself with the
        peoples;*
Ephraim is a cake not turned.*
[9]*Aliens devour his strength,
    and he knows it not;
gray hairs are sprinkled upon him,
    and he knows it not.*
[10]*The pride of Israel witnesses against him;
    yet they do not return to the Lord their
        God,
    nor seek him, for all this.*

[11]*Ephraim is like a dove,
    silly and without sense,
    calling to Egypt, going to Assyria.*
[12]*As they go, I will spread over them my
        net;
    I will bring them down like birds of the
        air;
    I will chastise them for their wicked
        deeds.[z]*
[13]*Woe to them, for they have strayed from
        me!
    Destruction to them, for they have
        rebelled against me!
I would redeem them,
    but they speak lies against me.*

[14]*They do not cry to me from the heart,
    but they wail upon their beds;
for grain and wine they gash themselves,
    they rebel against me.*
[15]*Although I trained and strengthened their
        arms,
    yet they devise evil against me.*
[16]*They turn to Baal;[a]
    they are like a treacherous bow,*

*their princes shall fall by the sword
because of the insolence of their tongue.*

*This shall be their derision in the land of
Egypt.*

y Gk Syr: Heb *brought near*   z Cn: Heb *according to the report to their congregation*   a Cn: Heb uncertain   *Vulgate adds *under the ashes*

OVERVIEW: Hosea in harmony with Paul warned about the disclosure of all things at the last judgment (ORIGEN). A stern condemnation of adultery is set forth. Both covenants warn of the eternal consequences of living in unrepentant adultery (CAESARIUS). The oven spoken of by Hosea is a reference to the heart of adulterers that, if left unchecked, will result in their being burned up. However, another fire was promised—one that purifies the heart and leads to salvation rather than destruction (ORIGEN). Ephraim, like an unturned cake, will not repent (JEROME). To turn the cake involves turning away from earthly desires. "Strangers" signifies apostate angels, that is, malignant spirits (GREGORY THE GREAT). Being lukewarm is the most dangerous condition. Hosea referred to it as a stranger who devours the strength of the unaware (JOHN CASSIAN). The people of Ephraim offered an example of indifference (JEROME). The prophet foretold the fate of those who fall away from the faith. The blame for this condition was placed squarely upon their free choice (JOHN CASSIAN). God laments their apostasy as a father grieves for a lost child (THEODORET OF CYR).

7:2 Their Evil Deeds

ALL WILL BE REVEALED. ORIGEN: Therefore each one must keep his heart with all watchfulness,[1] for when the Lord comes in the day of judgment, "He will bring to light the hidden things of darkness and will make manifest the counsels of the hearts,"[2] "all the thoughts of men meanwhile accusing or else excusing them,"[3] "when their own devices have beset them about." But of such a nature are the evil thoughts that sometimes they make worthy of censure even those things which seem good and which, so far as the popular judgment is concerned, are indeed

worthy of praise. COMMENTARY ON THE GOSPEL OF MATTHEW 11.15.[4]

7:4-7 Like a Heated Oven

THE ADULTERER'S DOUBLE STANDARD. CAESARIUS OF ARLES: Although you might marry and in the face of the authority of all the Scriptures never commit adultery, why do you not with God's grace accept what is lawful? Instead you dare to offend God and commit what is unlawful. I would like to know whether those who have no wives, and neither fear nor blush to commit adultery before they are joined in wedlock, would want their spouses to be violated by adulterers before they come to marriage. Since there is no one who would patiently accept this, why does not each one observe toward his spouse the fidelity he wants observed by her? Why does one desire to take a virgin as his wife, when he himself is corrupted? Why does he wish to be united to a wife who is alive, when he is dead in soul because of adultery, according to what is written: "The soul that sins shall die"?[5] Moreover, the apostle exclaims in terrible words, "God will judge the immoral and adulterers,"[6] and "Adulterers will not possess the kingdom of God."[7] Furthermore, "They are all adulterers, their hearts like an oven." SERMON 43.[8]

THE DIFFERENCE BETWEEN BURNING AND BAKING. ORIGEN: But where shall I find an approach to the divine Scripture that teaches me what "an oven" is? I must call upon Jesus my Lord, that he may make me the seeker find and may open to the one knocking,[9] that I may find in Scriptures "the oven" where I can rightly bake my sacrifice that God may accept it. Indeed, I think I have

---

[1]Prov 4:23. [2]1 Cor 4:5. [3]Rom 2:15. [4]ANF 9:444*. [5]Ezek 18:20. [6]Heb 13:4. [7]1 Cor 6:9. [8]FC 31:215*. [9]Lk 11:10.

found it in Hosea the prophet, where he says, "All adulterers are as an oven ignited for burning." And again he says, "Their hearts glowed as an oven." The human heart therefore is "an oven." But this heart, if vices ignite it or the devil inflames it, will not bake, but it will burn up. But if that one who said, "I came to send fire into the earth"[10] should ignite it, the loaves of the divine Scriptures and of the words of God which I receive in my heart, I do not burn up for destruction, but I bake for sacrifice. HOMILIES ON LEVITICUS 5.2.[11]

7:8 Ephraim Is a Cake Not Turned

EPHRAIM DOES NOT REPENT. JEROME: The kingdom of the ten tribes has become like any other nation because they went away from the Lord. And he [Ephraim] is like a bread beneath the ashes that is not turned, that is, he does not repent. COMMENTARY ON HOSEA 2.7.[12]

THE TURNING OF THE CAKE SIGNIFIES CONVERSION OF THE MIND TO GOD. GREGORY THE GREAT: Ephraim is a cake under the ashes not turned. For a cake under the ashes, which has ashes on it, has its cleaner side flat to the ground and its upper side the fouler, in proportion as it carries the ashes on it. And so with the mind that harbors earthly thoughts: what else does it carry on itself but a load of ashes? But if it will be "turned," the clean surface (which it had kept downward) it brings back to the top and shakes off the ashes that it had on it. If therefore we shake off from the mind the ashes of earthly thoughts, as it were, we "turn the cake under the ashes," that this bent of our mind may henceforth go to the rear, which the ashes of groveling thought before overlaid. And the clean face may come to the top, that our right bent of mind may not henceforth be surcharged with the weight of earthly desire. MORALS ON THE BOOK OF JOB 3.6.16.[13]

7:9 He Knows It Not

"STRANGERS" SIGNIFIES EVIL SPIRITS. GREGORY THE GREAT: "Strangers have devoured his

strength, and he has known it not." "Strangers" is usually understood to be apostate angels, who devour our strength when they consume the virtue of the mind by perverting it. Ephraim endured both and did not know it, because through the temptation of malignant spirits he both lost the strength of his mind and did not understand that he had lost it. MORALS ON THE BOOK OF JOB 6.34.6.[14]

BEING UNAWARE. JOHN CASSIAN: Not content with these words, the blessed Anthony entered upon a wider field of discussion, and he said, "This way of life and this most lukewarm condition not only causes you the loss that I have spoken of, even though you yourself may not feel it now. You may even somehow say in keeping with a sentence from Proverbs:'They strike me, but I did not grieve, and they mocked me, but I was unaware.'[15] And remember what is said by the prophet Hosea: 'Aliens devoured his strength, and he himself did not even recognize it.'" CONFERENCE 24.11.3.[16]

7:11 Ephraim Is Like a Dove

EPHRAIM IS INDIFFERENT. JEROME: One may ask: Why was Ephraim compared with a dove and not with other birds? The other birds hurry to protect their offspring even at the risk of life, and when they see a bird of prey, snake, raven or crow approaching their nest, they fly to and fro, and attack with their beak, and wound with their claws, and with a crying voice show the parent's suffering. Only the dove does not grieve for or miss [its] robbed offspring. Ephraim is rightly compared with this bird because he does not suffer for his devastated people but is indifferent to its salvation. COMMENTARY ON HOSEA 2.7.[17]

7:13 They Have Strayed from Me

HOLD TO THE NARROW PATH. JOHN CASSIAN: If [birds] do not hold to the narrow path with cau-

---

[10]Lk 12:49. [11]FC 83:99. [12]PL 25:919; *LSL* 108. [13]LF 21:12*. [14]LF 31:623*. [15]Prov 23:35 LXX. [16]ACW 57:833*. [17]PL 25:921; *LSL* 109.

tious and careful restraint as they go their way, making their airy progress through the void, thanks to their marvelous skill, the earth, which is as it were the natural mooring for everyone and the most solid and safe foundation for all, becomes for them a present and manifest danger—not because its nature is changed but because they fall precipitously upon it by the weight of their body. Similarly, the unwearying goodness of God and his unchangeable substance itself certainly hurt no one, but we ourselves bring death upon ourselves by falling from the heights to the depths. For this very fall means death for the one who falls. For it is said: "Woe to them, for they have departed from

me. They shall be destroyed, for they have transgressed against me." CONFERENCE 23.9.2-3.[18]

GOD LAMENTS AS A GRIEVING FATHER. THEODORET OF CYR: "First I will educate them through the threat of sufferings. Then I will catch all of them like birds, placing around them a cloud of enemies like a net." And having said that, he does not forget his love for mankind but offers a dirge from fatherly love for them. COMMENTARY ON HOSEA 7.[19]

---

[18]ACW 57:800. [19]PG 81:1592; *LSL* 109-10.

8:1-14 SOW THE WIND, REAP THE WHIRLWIND

[1]*Set the trumpet to your lips,*
    for[b] a vulture is over the house of the LORD,
because they have broken my covenant,
    and transgressed my law.
[2]*To me they cry,*
    My God, we Israel know thee.
[3]*Israel has spurned the good;*
    the enemy shall pursue him.

[4]*They made kings, but not through me.*
    They set up princes, but without my
        knowledge.
With their silver and gold they made idols
    for their own destruction.
[5]*I have[c] spurned* your calf, O Samaria.*
    My anger burns against them.
How long will it be
    till they are pure [6]in Israel?[d]

A workman made it;

    it is not God.
The calf of Samaria
    shall be broken to pieces.[e]

[7]*For they sow the wind,*
    and they shall reap the whirlwind.
The standing grain has no heads,
    it shall yield no meal;
if it were to yield,
    aliens would devour it.[†]
[8]*Israel is swallowed up;*
    already they are among the nations
    as a useless vessel.
[9]*For they have gone up to Assyria,*
    a wild ass wandering alone;
    Ephraim has hired lovers.
[10]*Though they hire allies among the nations,*
    I will soon gather them up.
And they shall cease[f] for a little while
    from anointing[g] king and princes.

---

^{11}*Because Ephraim has multiplied altars for
    sinning,*
    *they have become to him altars for
        sinning.*
^{12}*Were I to write for him my laws by ten
    thousands,*
    they would be regarded as a strange thing.
^{13}*They love sacrifice;*^{b}
    they sacrifice flesh and eat it;

but the LORD has no delight in them.
Now he will remember their iniquity,
    and punish their sins;
    they shall return to Egypt.
^{14}*For Israel has forgotten his Maker,*
    and built palaces;
and Judah has multiplied fortified cities;
    but I will send a fire upon his cities,
    and it shall devour his strongholds.

b Cn: Heb *as*   **c** Heb *He has*   **d** Gk: Heb *for from Israel*   **e** Or *shall go up in flames*   **f** Gk: Heb *begin*   **g** Gk: Heb *burden*   **h** Cn: Heb uncertain   *LXX uses imperative:
*spurn   †LXX *A sheaf of corn that avails not to make meal, and even if it should produce it, strangers shall devour it.*

OVERVIEW: Believers are called to take refuge in God and not put full trust in earthly counsel or rulers (CHRYSOSTOM), for some hypocrites rule without God's approval (GREGORY THE GREAT). Hosea's prophecy was applied to the selection of the successor of Judas to reconstitute the Twelve. Cyprian made the argument that the process of internal election also was relevant to the selection of bishops, priests and deacons. When unworthy men were admitted, but not according to God's will, it was illegitimate (CYPRIAN). God does not give his majesty to another (NOVATIAN). Idols are empty, like wheat with no grain (THEODORET). So are the hypocrites who yield no useful fruit (GREGORY THE GREAT). One who, having received grace, has fallen from grace is like a fallen star, like gold become darkened, like a filthy vessel (BASIL).

8:4 Not Through Me

THE DESIRE TO BE INDEPENDENT. CHRYSOSTOM: Hear how he reproves the unfaithful, when he says, "You have taken counsel, but not of me, and made treaties, but not by my Spirit."[1] For this is the habit of those who love: they desire that all concerns of their beloved should be accomplished by means of themselves and that no one should do anything, or say anything, without them. On this account did God not only on that occasion, but again elsewhere, utter a reproof in the same terms: "They made kings, but not through me. They set

up princes, but they did not make it known to me." HOMILIES CONCERNING THE STATUES 3.5.[2]

THE KING WHOM GOD IGNORES, HE DISAPPROVES. GREGORY THE GREAT: How is it said in this place that the Lord makes the hypocrite to reign[3] when through the prophet he complains especially about that, saying, "They have reigned but not of me: they have become princes, and I know them not"? For who that thinks rightly can say that the Lord does that of which he knows nothing? But because God's knowledge is approval, his ignorance is disapproval. . . . In a marvelous manner then does God make hypocrites to reign and knows them not. He makes them by forbearance; by rejecting them he knows them not. Thus it is necessary, with reference to everything which is desired in this life, that the inner will should be first inquired into. And when the ear of the heart is anxious to catch its sound, let it know that it speaks not in words but in deeds. When then a post of authority is offered, it is necessary for a man first to question with himself whether his conduct is suited to the place, whether his doings are at variance with the distinction it confers, lest perhaps the just Ruler of all should afterward not regard his prayers in tribulation, because God "knows not" his very entering on that high office which is the source of all his tribulation. MORALS ON THE BOOK OF JOB 5.25.41.[4]

---

[1]Is 30:1 LXX.   [2]NPNF 1 9:356**.   [3]Job 34:30.   [4]LF 23:130-31*.

Rash Ordinations of Unworthy Ministers. Cyprian: When Peter is speaking to the people concerning the bishop to be ordained in the place of Judas, it says, "Peter stood up in the midst of the disciples, for the multitude was together."[5] But we notice that the apostles observed this, not only in the ordination of bishops and of priests but also in the ordinations of deacons. Concerning this very thing, in their Acts, it is also written, "The Twelve called together the multitude of the disciples," it says, "and spoke to them."[6]

This matter was carried on diligently and cautiously, with the whole people assembled so that no unworthy man should attain to the ministry of the altar or to the priestly rank. For the fact is that sometimes unworthy men are ordained, not according to the will of God but according to human presumption. These things that do not come from a legitimate and just ordination are displeasing to God. God himself makes this known through the prophet Hosea, saying, "They made themselves a king, but not by me." Letter 67.4.[7]

8:6 The Calf Is Not God

God Does Not Give His Majesty to Another. Novatian: We acknowledge, therefore, and know that he is God, the Creator of all things. He is our Lord, because of his power; our author, because of his creation. "He spoke, and all things were made. He commanded, and all things came forth."[8] Of him it is written, "You have made all things in wisdom."[9] Moses says of him, "God is in heaven above and on earth below,"[10] and according to Isaiah, "He has measured the heavens with a span, the earth with the width of the fist";[11] he "looks upon the earth and makes it tremble."[12] He "holds the orb of the earth and those who live on it as if they were locusts";[13] he "weighed the mountains on scales and the groves on a balance,"[14] by the exact precision of the divine plan. He laid out this weight of the earth's mass with precise equipoise, lest the huge ill-balanced mass should easily fall into ruin, if they were not balanced by providential weights.[15] It is

he who says through the prophet, "I am God, and there is none beside me."[16] He says by means of the same prophet, "I will not give my majesty to another,"[17] so that he might exclude all heathens and heretics with their images, proving that he is God who is not made by the hand of an artificer.[18] Nor is he some God whom heretical ingenuity has devised. On the Trinity 3.[19]

8:7 Like Standing Grain

The Vanity of Idolatry. Theodoret of Cyr: For you pluck no fruit from the idol's service, but their bundles are like ears of wheat destroyed by the wind, which show full stalks from the outside but which internally have no grain. Such is the nature of idolatry, for on the one hand it can take the image of a man or a woman, or a lion or a different animal from art, but on the other hand it is deprived of any strength or energy. Commentary on Hosea 8.[20]

The Sterility of Hypocrisy. Gregory the Great: The one who looks for the applause of fellow creatures in return for the good that he practices is carrying an article of great worth to be sold at a mean price. From that by which he might have earned the kingdom of heaven he seeks the coin of passing talk. His practice goes for little in that he spends a great deal and gets back but very little. Such are the hypocrites who may be compared to luxuriant and untended vines, which put forth fruit from their fertility but are never lifted from the earth by tending. All that the rich branches bud forth, stray beasts tread under foot. The more fruitful they see it is, the more greedily they devour it. . . . Hence it is well said by the prophet, "The standing stalk, there is no bud in them, and they shall yield no

---

[5]Acts 1:15. [6]Acts 6:2. [7]FC 51:234-35*. [8]Ps 148:5. [9]Ps 104:24 (103:24 LXX). [10]Deut 4:39. [11]Is 40:12. [12]Ps 104:32 (103:32 LXX). [13]Is 40:22. [14]Is 40:12. [15]Ps 104:5 (103:5 LXX). [16]Is 45:21-22; 18. [17]Is 42:8; 48:11. [18]Acts 19:26. [19]FC 67:28-29*. [20]PG 81:1596; LSL 115-16.

meal; if it happens to yield, the strangers shall swallow it up." For the stalk yields no meal when the one who thrives in this world understands nothing refined and yields no fruit of good practice. MORALS ON THE BOOK OF JOB 2.8.70.[21]

8:8 Israel Useless

ONE WHO HAS FALLEN FROM GRACE. BASIL THE GREAT: O appalling hardness! O strange cruelty! You did not fear God, nor did you reverence others or feel shame before your friends. So you have suffered shipwreck of all things at once. You have stripped yourselves of every good thing at the same time. Therefore again I grieve for you, wretched man! You who were announcing your ardor for the kingdom have fallen from the kingdom. You who were inspiring all with a reverence for the doctrine did not have the fear of God before your eyes. You who were preaching holiness are now found to be polluted. You who glory in poverty are caught stealing money. You who through your guidance point out the punishment of God have drawn down chastisement upon yourselves. How shall I bewail you? How shall I grieve for you? The morning star, which rose early, has fallen and shattered upon the earth. The two ears of everyone who hears it will ring. How did the Nazirite[22] who shone brighter than gold become darker than soot? And how did the worthy son of Zion instantly become like a polluted vessel? LETTER 44, TO A FALLEN MONK.[23]

---

[21]LF 18:472-73**. [22]Lam 4:7-8. [23]FC 13:112-13*.

9:1-17 THE DAYS OF PUNISHMENT

[1]Rejoice not, O Israel!
Exult not[i] like the peoples;
for you have played the harlot, forsaking
your God.
You have loved a harlot's hire
upon all threshing floors.
[2]Threshing floor and winevat shall not feed
them,
and the new wine shall fail them.
[3]They shall not remain in the land of the
LORD;
but Ephraim shall return to Egypt,
and they shall eat unclean food in
Assyria.

[4]They shall not pour libations of wine to the
LORD;

and they shall not please him with their
sacrifices.
Their bread[j] shall be like mourners' bread;
all who eat of it shall be defiled;
for their bread shall be for their hunger
only;
it shall not come to the house of the
LORD.

[5]What will you do on the day of appointed
festival,
and on the day of the feast of the LORD?
[6]For behold, they are going to Assyria;[k]
Egypt shall gather them,
Memphis shall bury them.
Nettles shall possess their precious things of
silver;

thorns shall be in their tents.

[7]The days of punishment have come,
    the days of recompense have come;
    Israel shall know it.
The prophet is a fool,
    the man of the spirit is mad,
because of your great iniquity
    and great hatred.
[8]The prophet is the watchman of Ephraim,
    the people of my God,
yet a fowler's snare is on all his ways,
    and hatred in the house of his God.
[9]They have deeply corrupted themselves
    as in the days of Gibeah:
he will remember their iniquity,
    he will punish their sins.

[10]Like grapes in the wilderness,
    I found Israel.
Like the first fruit on the fig tree,
    in its first season,
    I saw your fathers.*
But they came to Baal-peor,
    and consecrated themselves to Baal,[l]
    and became detestable like the thing they
    loved.
[11]Ephraim's glory shall fly away like a bird—
    no birth, no pregnancy, no conception!

[12]Even if they bring up children,
    I will bereave them till none is left.
Woe to them
    when I depart from them![†]
[13]Ephraim's sons, as I have seen, are
    destined for a prey;[m]
Ephraim must lead forth his sons to
    slaughter.
[14]Give them, O LORD—
    what wilt thou give?
Give them a miscarrying womb[‡]
    and dry breasts.

[15]Every evil of theirs is in Gilgal;
    there I began to hate them.
Because of the wickedness of their deeds
    I will drive them out of my house.
I will love them no more;
    all their princes are rebels.

[16]Ephraim is stricken,
    their root is dried up,
    they shall bear no fruit.
Even though they bring forth,
    I will slay their beloved children.
[17]My God will cast them off,
    because they have not hearkened to him;
    they shall be wanderers among the
    nations.

i Gk: Heb to exultation   j Cn: Heb to them   k Cn: Heb from destruction   l Heb shame   m Cn Compare Gk: Heb uncertain   *LXX their fathers   †LXX my flesh is from them   ‡LXX a womb that makes one childless

OVERVIEW: Israel is not to rejoice like others because she has knowledge of God yet willingly rebels (THEODORET). All who have been contaminated by the sacrifice of a blasphemous and unjust priest are not safe from the contagion of sin (CYRIL OF ALEXANDRIA, CYPRIAN). Israel stands as a sentinel to reveal the idolatry of the neighboring nations (ISHO'DAD). The patriarchs are the first figs (CAESARIUS). The flesh of human beings is good as created and is corrupted only by immoral behavior, such as adultery and wantonness. Since human flesh was created by God, it can become God's temple for the Holy Spirit (CYRIL OF JERUSALEM). The community of faith must be protected from those who are unfaithful to Christ (PACHOMIUS).

9:1 Rejoice Not, O Israel

ISRAEL WILLINGLY REBELS. THEODORE OF MOPSUESTIA: It is not fitting for you to rejoice and exult like the rest of the peoples. For they did not receive any teaching which might lead them to piety, but you, after much instruction and knowledge of God, rebelled against the knowledge which had been given to you because of the depravity of your opinion, and turned to the worship of the idols. COMMENTARY ON HOSEA 9.[1]

9:4 Mourners' Bread

THE CONTAMINATION OF BREAD FOR MOURNERS. CYRIL OF ALEXANDRIA: Having collected the fruit of the vine into the wine-vats, they offered the firstlings as a libation to the demons, and not to the God who gave them. They also offered loaves of bread as firstfruits of the harvest—except that the sacrifice will become for them defiled and impure, he says, and the offerings will be considered as mourning breads (that is, disgusting, impure and odious). For what reason? For the law considered unclean anyone who approached a dead body either by blood relationship or rather by the very touching of the body. Therefore it was easy for the relatives or friends of the dead person to become unclean during mourning, since they handled the dead body and since they were willing to do for him what was customary. And whatever they touched became unclean. Therefore the mourning bread is that bread which was at hand as food for those who were mourning for the dead; for those who strive to avoid contamination with a dead body it is considered terrible even to taste this bread. Wherefore the breads themselves are defiled and rejected, even though they may have been offered as firstfruits of the harvest. "Those who eat them will become unclean." They will be useful only to their souls, that is, as a food for them. COMMENTARY ON HOSEA 4.96.[2]

CONTAGION BY SINFUL LEADERS. CYPRIAN: Let not the people flatter themselves as if they could be safe from contagion of sin, communicating with a sinful priest and yielding their obedience to the unjust and unlawful episcopacy of their leader, when the divine censure threatens through the prophet Hosea and says, "Their sacrifices shall be like the bread of mourning: all who eat them shall be defiled." [This] teaching obviously [shows] that all are indeed involved in sin who have been contaminated by the sacrifice of a blasphemous and unjust priest. LETTER 67.3.[3]

9:8 The Watchman and a Snare

THE FALL OF THE PROPHET. ISHO'DAD OF MERV: "Ephraim is a sentinel with my God," that is, Israel was established by God, he says, so that he might receive the truth and watch over honorable feasts, and that he might be, as is the true prophet, with the help of God, the teacher of the others. But Israel, like a false prophet, has dissuaded others from the truth. The Greek [says], "The sentinel of Ephraim was with God, [yet] the prophet has become a deceptive trap in every path." In fact, the prophet was a sentinel with a god in this manner: each of the gods with a false name had his own false diviner, and those, through their heresies, differed from each other in many ways. Some worshiped Baal, some others Chemosh or Baal-Peor; and there was an idol in each temple, and by each of them an appointed false prophet sat. And finally, the ways of worship and divination differed among them. COMMENTARY ON HOSEA.[4]

9:10 The Fig Tree

FIRSTFRUITS FROM THE FIG TREE. CAESARIUS OF ARLES: Similarly, the law of the Old Testament, which we said the image of the fig tree represented, threw away the first Jewish people who were useless, that is, sinful and wicked. When these syco-

---

[1]PG 66:176; *LSL* 120. [2]PG 71:216; *LSL* 122. [3]FC 51:233. [4]CSCO 303 (128):73-74.

phants, to use the Greek word, had been rejected, that is, the conceited and worthless Israelites, there created for Christ through grace as its mother, the rich and fruitful Christian people who were further brought to perfect knowledge of the gospel. Although there is a genus of fig trees that brings its first fruits to maturity, called double bearing, it may signify those of whom it is said, "The Lord loved those figs as his precursors." The patriarchs are the precursors. SERMON 106.[5]

9:12 My Flesh Is from Them

GOD IS NOT ASHAMED OF THE HUMAN BODY. CYRIL OF JERUSALEM: God is not ashamed to take flesh from such members, for he framed these very members. Who tells us this? The Lord said to Jeremiah, "Before I formed you in the womb I knew you. Before you were born I dedicated you."[6] If in fashioning me, therefore, he touched them and was not ashamed, was he ashamed in forming for himself the holy flesh, the veil of his Godhead? It is God who even now creates the babes in the womb, as it is written in Job, "Did you not pour me out as milk, and thicken me like cheese? With skin and flesh you clothed me, with bones and sinews knit me together."[7] There is nothing corrupt in the human bodily frame unless one defiles it with adulteries and wantonness. He who formed Adam formed Eve also; and male and female were fashioned by the divine hands. None of the members of the body, as fashioned from the beginning, is corrupt. Let all heretics be silent who slander their bodies, or rather him who formed them. But let us be mindful of Paul's words: "Do you not know that your members are the temple of the Holy Spirit, who is in you?"[8] Again, the prophet has foretold in the person of Jesus, "my flesh is from them." CATECHETICAL LECTURE 12.26.[9]

9:15 Driven Out of God's House

SENDING AWAY THE UNFAITHFUL. PACHOMIUS: While he was still praying, an angel of the Lord, very terrifying, appeared to him, having in his hand a fiery sword unsheathed. He said to our father Pachomius, "Just as God has blotted out his name from the 'Book of Life,'[10] just so do you drive them out from the midst of the brothers, for they are not ignorant. Indeed, even to the ignorant, impurities of this sort seem like abominations before God." When it was morning he put them in worldly clothing and told them, "Go and do as is fitting to the clothes whose practices you have made your own." And he expelled them from among the brothers. The words of the prophet were fulfilled about them, "I will drive them out of my house, and I will love them no longer." LIFE OF PACHOMIUS (BOHAIRIC) 108.[11]

---

[5]FC 47:128. [6]Jer 1:5. [7]Job 10:10-11. [8]1 Cor 6:19. [9]FC 61:243-44. [10]Ex 32:32-33; Ps 69:28 (68:29 LXX). [11]CS 45:160.

10:1-11 JUDGMENT OF CAPTIVITY

[1]*Israel is a luxuriant vine*
that yields its fruit.
The more his fruit increased
the more altars he built;
as his country improved
he improved his pillars.

[2]*Their heart is false;*
now they must bear their guilt.
The LORD[n] will break down their altars,
and destroy their pillars.

[3]*For now they will say:*

"We have no king,
for we fear not the LORD,
    and a king, what could he do for us?"
[4]They utter mere words;
    with empty oaths they make covenants;
so judgment springs up like poisonous weeds
    in the furrows of the field.
[5]The inhabitants of Samaria tremble
    for the calf[o] of Beth-aven.
Its people shall mourn for it,
    and its idolatrous priests shall wail[p]
        over it,
    over its glory which has departed from it.
[6]Yea, the thing itself shall be carried to
        Assyria,
    as tribute to the great king.[q][*]
Ephraim shall be put to shame,
    and Israel shall be ashamed of his idol.[r]

[7]Samaria's king shall perish,
    like a chip on the face of the waters.
[8]The high places of Aven, the sin of Israel,
    shall be destroyed.

Thorn and thistle shall grow up
    on their altars;
and they shall say to the mountains, Cover
        us,
    and to the hills, Fall upon us.

[9]From the days of Gibeah, you have sinned,
        O Israel,[†]
    there they have continued.
    Shall not war overtake them in Gibeah?
[10]I will come[s] against the wayward people to
        chastise them;
    and nations shall be gathered against
        them
    when they are chastised[t] for their double
        iniquity.

[11]Ephraim was a trained heifer
    that loved to thresh,
    and I spared her fair neck;
but I will put Ephraim to the yoke,
    Judah must plow,
    Jacob must harrow for himself.

n Heb he   o Gk Syr: Heb calves   p Cn: Heb exult   q Cn: Heb a king that will contend   r Cn: Heb counsel   s Cn Compare Gk: Heb in my desire   t Gk: Heb bound   *Vulgate And they shall carry him bound as a present to the king.   †LXX Israel sinned

OVERVIEW: Israel overmatched her abundance of land with a proliferation of idols (JEROME). Pilate's sending of Jesus to Herod for trial was foretold. Herod was the Assyrian, and the gift was Christ (JUSTIN MARTYR). When Jesus was sent to Herod by Pilate, the Scriptures in Hosea were fulfilled (TERTULLIAN).

10:1 Israel Is a Luxuriant Vine

PROLIFERATION OF IDOLS. JEROME: Having good shoots and fruit-bearing branches, she [Israel] produced many clusters, and the abundance of the grapes equaled the great number of the branches. But she who before was of such a kind offended God afterward, turning the abundance of the fruits into a great number of offenses. The more people she had, the more altars she built, and she overmatched the abundance of the land by the number of the idols. COMMENTARY ON HOSEA 2.10.[1]

10:5-6 The Calf of Beth-aven

PROPHECY ABOUT JESUS. JUSTIN MARTYR: And after their departure they stayed there until

[1]PL 25:945-46; LSL 129-30.

the death of Herod, the assassin of the babes of Bethlehem. Archelaus, who succeeded him, also died before Christ fulfilled by his crucifixion the Father's plan of our redemption. And when Herod succeeded Archelaus and received what had fallen to his share, Pilate favored him by sending Jesus bound to him,[2] which God in his foreknowledge foretold in these words: "And they brought him to the Assyrian, a present to the king." DIALOGUE WITH TRYPHO 103.[3]

PILATE TO HEROD. TERTULLIAN: The Lord himself comes to a trial with "the elders and rulers of the people," as Isaiah predicted.[4] And then he fulfilled all that had been written of his pas-

sion. At that time "the heathen raged, and the people imagined vain things; the kings of the earth set themselves, and the rulers gathered themselves together against the Lord and against his Christ."[5] The heathen were Pilate and the Romans; the people were the tribes of Israel; the kings were represented in Herod and the rulers in the chief priests. When, indeed, he was sent to Herod gratuitously by Pilate,[6] the words of Hosea were accomplished, for he had prophesied of Christ, "And they shall carry him bound as a present to the king." AGAINST MARCION 4.42.[7]

---

[2]Lk 23:7. [3]FC 6:309. [4]Is 3:13-14 LXX. [5]Ps 2:1-2. [6]Lk 23:7. [7]ANF 3:420.

10:12-15 THE FRUIT OF RIGHTEOUSNESS AND THE FRUIT OF INIQUITY

[12]*Sow for yourselves righteousness,*
reap the fruit[u] of steadfast love;[*]
break up your fallow ground,[†]
for it is the time to seek the LORD,
that he may come and rain salvation
upon you.

[13]*You have plowed iniquity,*
you have reaped injustice,[‡]
you have eaten the fruit of lies.
Because you have trusted in your chariots[v]
and in the multitude of your warriors,

[14]*therefore the tumult of war shall arise*
among your people,
and all your fortresses shall be destroyed,
as Shalman destroyed Beth-arbel on the day
of battle;
mothers were dashed in pieces with their
children.
[15]*Thus it shall be done to you,[§] O house of*
Israel,[w]
because of your great wickedness.
In the storm[x] the king of Israel
shall be utterly cut off.

u Gk: Heb *according to* v Gk: Heb *way* w Gk: Heb *O Bethel* x Cn: Heb *dawn* *LXX *the fruit of life* †LXX *illuminate yourselves with the light of knowledge* ‡LXX *Why have you held your peace at impiety?* §LXX *I will do*

OVERVIEW: This light is best understood when applied so as to put faith in action (ORIGEN). The call to bear the fruit of justice and virtue was foretold in the Old Testament (BASIL). Leaders are admonished to study diligently so as to effectively

impart the faith to catechumens and believers (APOSTOLIC CONSTITUTIONS). Let the light of the knowledge of righteousness shine upon others (JOHN CASSIAN). By exhortation, through the example of personal righteousness and by warning about the day of judgment, the leader must discourage sin. A bishop is not to be reticent in condemning unrighteousness (Apostolic Constitutions). Israel's impiety gave them a false and senseless hope (Cyril of Alexandria).

10:12 *Sowing Righteousness to Reap Salvation*

First Sow Righteousness, Then Reap Fruit. Origen: Observe how holy and how marvelous is the sequence of things. Do not imagine that wisdom will come before its enactment in deeds. The deeds ought to come first, and wisdom sought afterwards.... We ought not teach others before we ourselves are instructed and rational. After these things, however, "truth" is added because "truth" is the highest wisdom. The prophet also preserves this same order when he says, "Sow for yourselves righteousness and reap the fruit of life; illuminate yourselves with the light of knowledge." See how he does not first say, "Illuminate yourselves with the light of knowledge," but first, "Sow for yourselves righteousness." It is not sufficient just to sow, but he says, "reap the fruit of life" so that after these you can fulfill what follows, "illuminate yourselves with the light of knowledge." Homilies on Leviticus 6.4.4.[1]

The Call to Bear Fruit. Basil the Great: So that we may know clearly what is meant by not having a share in the works which do not bear fruit, let us first inquire as to what sort of actions merit the attribute *unfruitful*—whether those only that are forbidden or such also are commendable but are not performed in good dispositions. In the Old Testament, the prophet, comparing the saints with the tree, says, "which shall bring forth its fruit in due season." Solomon declares, "The work of the just is unto life, but the fruit of the wicked is sin"[2]; and Hosea, "Sow for yourselves in justice, reap the fruit of life." On Baptism 2.9.[3]

Study the Word. Apostolic Constitutions: Be careful, therefore, O bishop, to study the Word, that you may be able to explain everything exactly and that you may copiously nourish your people with much doctrine and enlighten them with the light of the law. For God says, "Enlighten yourselves with the light of knowledge, while we have yet opportunity." Constitutions of the Holy Apostles 2.2.5.[4]

Purity of Heart as Ground of Knowing. John Cassian: Therefore, if you are concerned to attain to the light of spiritual knowledge not by the vice of empty boastfulness but by the grace of correction, you are first inflamed with desire for that blessedness about which it is said, "Blessed are the pure of heart, for they shall see God."[5] [Thus] you may also attain to that about which the angel said to Daniel: "Those who are learned shall shine like the splendor of the firmament, and those who instruct many in righteousness like the stars forever."[6] And in another prophet: "Enlighten yourselves with the light of knowledge while there is time." Conference 14.9.1.[7]

10:13 *The Fruit of Iniquity*

The Call to Admonition. Apostolic Constitutions: It is the bishop's duty not to be silent in the case of offenders but to admonish them, to exhort them, to wrestle them down, to afflict them with fastings, that so he may strike a pious dread into the rest. For he is called to bring up the children of Israel in piety.[8] For the bishop must be one who discourages sin by exhortations, who sets a pattern of righteousness, who proclaims those good things that are prepared by God, and who declares that wrath which will come at the day of judgment, lest he neglect the field of God and increase its condemnation. To avoid this carelessness, hear that which is said by Hosea: "Why have you held your peace at impiety? You have reaped the fruit of lies." Constitutions of the Holy Apostles 2.3.17.[9]

---

[1]FC 83:124*. [2]Prov 10:16. [3]FC 9:418. [4]ANF 7:397. [5]Mt 5:8. [6]Dan 12:3. [7]ACW 57:511-12. [8]Lev 15:31. [9]ANF 7:403*.

THE FRUIT OF DECEPTION IS IMPIETY. CYRIL OF ALEXANDRIA: "They ate the fruit of deception," namely, they had a useless and senseless hope. For the true fruit is the one that can save and help, the love toward God and the glory of righteousness. On the contrary, the false fruit would reasonably be considered impiety, for in the end it altogether descends to what is abominable. COMMENTARY ON HOSEA 6.122.[10]

---

[10]PG 71:257; LSL 137.

11:1-12 UNCONDITIONAL FATHERLY LOVE

[1]When Israel was a child, I loved him,
  and out of Egypt I called my son.
[2]The more I[y] called them,
  the more they went from me;[z]
they kept sacrificing to the Baals,
  and burning incense to idols.

[3]Yet it was I who taught Ephraim to walk,
  I took them up in my[a] arms;
  but they did not know that I healed them.
[4]I led them with cords of compassion,[b]
  with the bands of love,
and I became to them as one
  who eases the yoke on their jaws,
  and I bent down to them and fed them.

[5]They shall return to the land of Egypt,
  and Assyria shall be their king,
  because they have refused to return to me.
[6]The sword shall rage against their cities,
  consume the bars of their gates,
  and devour them in their fortresses.[c]
[7]My people are bent on turning away from
  me;[d]
so they are appointed to the yoke,
  and none shall remove it.

[8]How can I give you up, O Ephraim!
  How can I hand you over, O Israel!
How can I make you like Admah!
  How can I treat you like Zeboiim!
My heart recoils within me,
  my compassion grows warm and tender.
[9]I will not execute my fierce anger,
  I will not again destroy Ephraim;
for I am God and not man,
  the Holy One in your midst,
  and I will not come to destroy.[e]

[10]They shall go after the LORD,
  he will roar like a lion;
yea, he will roar,
  and his sons shall come trembling from
  the west;
[11]they shall come trembling like birds from
  Egypt,
  and like doves from the land of Assyria;
  and I will return them to their homes,
  says the LORD.
[12f]Ephraim has encompassed me with lies,
  and the house of Israel with deceit;
but Judah is still known by[g] God,
  and is faithful to the Holy One.

y Gk: Heb *they*   z Gk: Heb *them*   a Gk Syr Vg: Heb *his*   b Heb *man*   c Cn: Heb *counsels*   d The meaning of the Hebrew is uncertain   e Cn: Heb *into the city*   f Ch 12.1 in Heb   g Cn Compare Gk: Heb *roams with*

OVERVIEW: The ancient Christian writers thought that the calling of the holy family to Egypt was foretold by the prophets (CHRYSOSTOM). In spite of Israel's folly, God loves Israel like a father loves his wayward child. It is because of that love that God disciplines Israel (THEODORET). The fathers viewed Jesus as the son out of Egypt, alluded to by the prophet Hosea (EPHREM). The one who is called the bread of heaven is the son out of Egypt (GREGORY OF NAZIANZUS). God shows fatherly love toward Israel by binding her feet (CYRIL OF ALEXANDRIA) and drawing her toward him with cords of love (JEROME). God will not abandon Ephraim, although God's heart is metaphorically troubled with regret (CHRYSOSTOM). God expresses parental love in various ways (THEODORET). God does not dwell where sin is present (JEROME).

11:1 The Son Called Out of Egypt

WHO IS "MY SON"? CHRYSOSTOM: Herod sought him after his birth. He was going to kill all the children in that place. And the prophet revealed this too, foretelling it long beforehand when he said, "A voice was heard in Ramah, lamentation, mourning and much weeping, of Rachel weeping for her children and refusing to be comforted, because they are not."[1] The Scriptures also predicted that he would come to Egypt when they said, "Out of Egypt I called my son." DEMONSTRATION AGAINST THE PAGANS 3.7.[2]

CHASTISEMENT OF THE DIVINE LOVE. THEODORET OF CYR: It is as a result of folly and a childish attitude that they suffer this punishment. I recalled them from Egypt and freed them from that harsh servitude, but they proved ungrateful to me and opted for the worship of the idols (referring to them as "Baals"). Though I was the one who taught them to walk, who cured them of their awkward gait, showed them paternal affection and applied all kinds of healing to them, they refused to acknowledge me, even though I protected them from manifold destruc-

tion at the hands of the invaders as if clutching them to me in love like a kind of bond. It is in love that even now I care for them and invest them in these chastisements, acting in the manner of someone striking a forward child on the cheek. COMMENTARY ON HOSEA 11.1-4.[3]

HE WILL BE CALLED A NAZARENE. EPHREM THE SYRIAN: Because Israel, symbolically called "son" since Egypt,[4] had lost its sonship through having worshiped Baal and offered incense to idols, John gave them a name which suited them: race of vipers.[5] Because these had lost that title of sonship, which had been poured over them through grace in the days of Moses, they received from John a name congruent with their deeds. After the Lord went down into the land of the Egyptians and had returned from there, the Evangelist said, "Now the true word spoken by the prophet is accomplished." He said, "I will call my son out of Egypt."[6] He also said, "He will be called a Nazarene,"[7] because in Hebrew *nezer* means a "scepter,"[8] and the prophet calls him a "Nazarene" because he is the Son of the scepter. COMMENTARY ON TATIAN'S DIATESSARON 3.8-9.[9]

THE LORD WORKED IN EGYPT. GREGORY OF NAZIANZUS: I will address myself as is right to those who have come from Egypt. They have come here eagerly, having overcome ill will by zeal. They come from that Egypt which is enriched by the river who is Christ, raining out of the earth and like the sea in its season—if I too may follow in my small measure those who have so eloquently spoken of these matters. They too are enriched by Christ my Lord. He too was once fugitive in Egypt; the first, when he fled from Herod's massacre of the children,[10] and now by the love of the fathers for their children, by Christ the new food of those who hunger af-

---

[1]Jer 31:15; Mt 2:18. [2]FC 73:199. [3]PG 81:1609-12. [4]Mt 2:15. [5]Mt 3:7. [6]Mt 2:15. [7]Is 11:1; Mt 2:23. [8]Literally "branch," "sprout," "shoot." [9]ECTD 77-78*. [10]Mt 2:13.

ter good,[11] who offers the greatest alms of corn of which history speaks and men believe. He is the bread that came down from heaven and gives life to the world, that life which is indestructible and indissoluble. It is of him that I now seem to hear the Father saying, "Out of Egypt have I called my son." ON THE ARRIVAL OF THE EGYPTIANS, ORATION 34.1.[12]

11:3 God Taught Ephraim to Walk

GOD'S FATHERLY CARE. CYRIL OF ALEXANDRIA: "Because I am kind and good, I bound the feet of Ephraim," that is, the whole Israel . . . although he was awkward. God himself declares why this is so: "I will take them in my arms." This image is from child raising. Those who take infants in their arms are those who bind their feet, bringing their feet together. For it is necessary, I think, that the thighs and knees of anyone who sits down should be drawn together. And in fact this is so. "I bound the feet" as, for instance, it was written about Abraham, who bound his son Isaac when he thought to bring him as a sacrifice to God. One must note that the Hebrew version and other versions do not have "I bound the feet" but rather "I became as one who nourishes Ephraim." COMMENTARY ON HOSEA 6.126.[13]

11:4 Cords of Compassion

LOVER OF HUMANKIND. JEROME: And as the lover of humankind I will draw them to believing in cords of love, just as that which is written in the Gospel: "No one comes to me unless the Father who sent me will have drawn him."[14] But they thought that my light yoke was very heavy; and I bent toward them, leaving the kingdom of heaven so that I may eat with them, having assumed the human form. Or rather, I gave them my body as food; I was both food and table companion. COMMENTARY ON HOSEA 3.11.[15]

11:9 Promise to Ephraim

THE LIMITS OF LANGUAGE. CHRYSOSTOM: The philanthropy of God does not tolerate [abandonment]. "What can I do for you? Shall I view you as I did Sodom and destroy you like Gomorrah? My heart is upset." Here the love of God appears to imitate the passionate human being or, better yet, the affectionate mother. "My heart is upset, just as a woman would say about her child. My heart is upset just like the mother's." However, the previous metaphor was only partially adequate. "My heart is troubled in my regret"? God is troubled! Let no one ever think it! God forbid! HOMILIES ON REPENTANCE AND ALMSGIVING 4.18.[16]

FLEXIBILITY OF THE DIVINE PEDAGOGY. THEODORET OF CYR: "My heart recoils within me, my compassion grows warm and tender. I will not execute the fierceness of my anger; I will not again destroy Ephraim." God imitates a father and mother who are naturally worried and cannot turn away from their children for too long. He says that, however, not because he wills one thing now and then changes his mind. Rather, he expresses his thought in different ways, in anger and love, in threat and mercy, chastising and persuading. COMMENTARY ON HOSEA 11.[17]

GOD IS HOLY. JEROME: In the same book, it is written, "I am God and not man, the holy one in the midst of thee, and I will not enter into the city," into the den, to be sure, of vices. He himself is the only one who does not enter into the city that Cain built in the name of his son, Enoch. All of this is chanted daily by the lips of the priests: *ho monos anamartētos*, which in our language is translated as *qui solus est sine peccato*.[18] AGAINST THE PELAGIANS 2.23.[19]

---

[11]Jn 6:33. [12]NPNF 2 7:334*. [13]PG 71:265; *LSL* 141. [14]Jn 6:44. [15]PG 25:961-62; *LSL* 141. [16]FC 96:124. [17]PG 81:1612. [18]"Who alone is without sin." [19]FC 53:334.

12:1-14 GOD'S PEDAGOGICAL CARE
FOR THE REBEL

¹Ephraim herds the wind,
  and pursues the east wind all day long;
they multiply falsehood and violence;
  they make a bargain with Assyria,
  and oil is carried to Egypt.

²The LORD has an indictment against
    Judah,
  and will punish Jacob according to his
    ways,
  and requite him according to his deeds.
³In the womb he took his brother by the
    heel,
  and in his manhood he strove with God.
⁴He strove with the angel and prevailed,
  he wept and sought his favor.
He met God at Bethel,
  and there God spoke with him[b]—
⁵the LORD the God of hosts,
  the LORD is his name:
⁶"So you, by the help of your God, return,
  hold fast to love and justice,
  and wait continually for your God."

⁷A trader, in whose hands are false
    balances,
  he loves to oppress.

⁸Ephraim has said, "Ah, but I am rich,
  I have gained wealth for myself";
but all his riches can never offset[i]
  the guilt he has incurred.
⁹I am the LORD your God
  from the land of Egypt;
I will again make you dwell in tents,
  as in the days of the appointed feast.
¹⁰I spoke to* the prophets;
  it was I who multiplied visions,
  and through the prophets gave parables.
¹¹If there is iniquity in Gilead
  they shall surely come to nought;
if in Gilgal they sacrifice bulls,
  their altars also shall be like stone heaps
  on the furrows of the field.
¹² (Jacob fled to the land of Aram,
  there Israel did service for a wife,
  and for a wife he herded sheep.)
¹³By a prophet the LORD brought Israel up
    from Egypt,
  and by a prophet he was preserved.
¹⁴Ephraim has given bitter provocation;
  so his LORD will leave his bloodguilt
    upon him,
  and will turn back upon him his
    reproaches.

h Gk Syr: Heb us   i Cn Compare Gk: Heb obscure   *LXX through

---

OVERVIEW: Superstitions are compared with spiritual whoring, and our restlessness to the wind (AUGUSTINE). That Satan is able to acquire corporeality is evidenced by an experience of Emilian, whose struggle resembles that of Jacob and the angel, which seemed to acquire human form (BRAULIO). Christ's habit of teaching in the temple was foretold by Hosea (TERTULLIAN). Those who prosper materially even through honest means yet fail to tend to the poor will face the charge of robbery before God. Mercy and justice demand generosity to the poor; by this we draw closer to God (Basil). Diverse gifts of the Spirit continued to operate in the time of the apostles (Irenaeus). God condescends to meet human beings through visions and prophetic utterance. All this was in preparation for the incarnation (Chrysostom). Before his martyrdom, Stephen gave expression to the visions and messages that the prophets had announced regarding the true God who sent his Son to redeem us (Irenaeus). Prophetic visions point toward but do not directly reveal God's essence (Chrysostom).

12:1 Pursuing the Wind

The Frenetic Pursuit of Superstition. Augustine: God of my heart . . . I didn't know how to love you, because I did not know how to conceive the existence of anything—however glorious—beyond mere matter. The soul that goes puffing and wheezing after such figments of the imagination [as fortune telling] is one that goes whoring from you[1] and trusts what is phony and feeds on the wind. Yet while I wouldn't have this sorcerer sacrificing to demons on my behalf, I was actually sacrificing to them myself just by being involved in my superstition. For what else is to feed on the wind, if not to feed on error, and so to become the sport and plaything of the demonic? Confessions 4.2.[2]

12:4 God at Bethel

Wrestling with Demons. Braulio of Saragossa: It happened one day that the enemy of the human race met the wrestler of the eternal King on a journey and challenged him with these words: "If you would like to see what each of us can accomplish with his strength, let us have a contest." Barely finished speaking, he approached the saint and touched him in visible and corporeal reality, and for some time tried his wavering opponent, but the latter pressed Christ with prayers, and the divine aid strengthened his trembling steps and straightway caused the fugitive, apostate spirit to vanish into air. If it seems incredible to anyone that an invisible spirit can become substantial, save in the mystical sense, let it be explained to him how the divine pages narrate the struggle of Jacob with the angel too.[3] I have this to say: that it would require less boldness for Satan to tempt a servant than the Lord, Emilian than Christ, man than God, the creature than the Creator. Life of St. Emilian 7.[4]

God Is in His Holy Temple. Tertullian: There were places in Jerusalem where he taught and other places to which he retired.[5] "In daytime he was teaching in the temple." Just this had been foretold by Hosea: "In my house[6] did they find me, and there did I speak with them." Against Marcion 4.39.[7]

12:6 Holding to Love and Justice

Mercy and Justice to the Destitute. Basil the Great: Combine justice with mercy, spending in mercy what you possess with justice. It is written, "Keep mercy and justice, and draw near to thy God always." Because God loves mercy and justice, he who takes care to do mercy and justice draws near to God. It remains, then, for each to examine himself and for the rich person to take careful inventory of the private resources from which he is to offer gifts to God, to make sure that he has not oppressed a poor person, or used force against one weaker than himself, or cheated one dependent upon him, thus exercising license rather than justice. We are bidden to practice fairness and justice also toward those who serve us. Do not employ force because you are in command, and do not take advantage because it is within your power to do so. Homily on Mercy and Justice.[8]

12:10 Visions and Parables

The Revelation of God Foreseen by the Prophets. Irenaeus: Thus, therefore, was

---

[1]Lev 19:31. [2]CAME 51. [3]Gen 32:24. [4]FC 63:125. [5]Lk 21:37. [6]Bethel. [7]ANF 3:417*. [8]FC 9:508.

God revealed; for God the Father is shining forth through all these works, the Spirit indeed working, and the Son ministering, while the Father was approving and human salvation being accomplished. As he also declares through Hosea the prophet, "I," he says, "have multiplied visions and have used similitudes by the ministry of the prophets." But the apostle further expounded this very passage when he said, "Now there are diversities of gifts, but the same Spirit; and there are differences of ministrations, but the same Lord; and there are diversities of operations, but it is the same God who worked all in all. The manifestation of the Spirit is given to every one to profit thereby."[9] He who works all things in all is God. As to what nature he is and how great he is, God remains invisible and indescribable to all creatures that have been made by him. But he is by no means unknown. For all things learn through his Word that there is one God the Father, who contains all things, and who grants existence to all. This is written in the Gospel: "No man has seen God at any time, except the only-begotten Father, who is in the bosom of the Father; he has declared him."[10] Against Heresies 4.20.6.[11]

God Spoke to the Prophets. Chrysostom: How is it, then, that John said, "No one has at any time seen God"?[12] He was affirming that all those instances were manifestations of his humbling of himself, not the vision of pure Being itself. If they had actually seen the very nature of God, they would not have beheld it under different appearances. For that which is itself simple, and without shape, and not made up of parts, and not restricted by limits, does not sit or stand or walk about, since all these are functions of material bodies. However, he alone knows how he exists. Now, to show this, God the Father declared by one of the prophets, "I have multiplied visions, and by the hands of the prophets I have used similitudes," that is, "I reached out for the lowly. I did not appear as I was in myself." His Son was soon to appear to us in the guise of real flesh. But in the prophets he gave

them experience of this beforehand by allowing them to see something of the substance of God in the way in which it was possible for them to see him. Homilies on John 15.[13]

Stephen, Knowing the Prophets, Beheld the Son. Irenaeus: Stephen, teaching these truths, when he was yet on earth, saw the glory of God and Jesus on his right hand, and he exclaimed, "Behold, I see the heavens opened, and the Son of man standing on the right hand of God."[14] When he said these words, he was stoned. Thus did he fulfill the perfect teaching, reflecting in every respect the one who led to martyrdom and praying for those who were slaying him in these words: "Lord, lay not this sin to their charge." Thus were they made holy who came to recognize one and the same God through various dispensations, who from beginning to end was present with humanity in various dispensations, just as had been declared by the prophet Hosea: "I have multiplied visions, and used similitudes by the hands of the prophets." Against Heresies 3.12.13.[15]

God Reveals Self Gradually. Chrysostom: How is it, then, that John says, "No one has ever seen God"?[16] He says this so that you may know that he is speaking of a clear knowledge and a perfect comprehension of God. All the cases cited were instances of God's condescension and accommodation. That no one of those prophets saw God's essence in its pure state is clear from the fact that each one saw him in a different way. God is a simple being; he is not composed of parts; he is without form or figure. But all these prophets saw different forms and figures. God proved this very thing through the mouth of another prophet. And he persuaded those other prophets that they did not see his essence in its exact nature when he said, "I have multiplied visions, and by the ministries of the prophets I was represented."

[9]1 Cor 12:4-7. [10]Jn 1:18. [11]ANF 1:489*. [12]Jn 1:18. [13]FC 33:143**. [14]Acts 7:56. [15]ANF 1:435*. [16]Jn 1:18.

What God was saying was, "I did not show my very essence, but I came down in condescension and accommodated myself to the weakness of their eyes." However, John does not say only of humanity that "no one has ever seen God." This was proved by what I have said—I mean by the prophetic utterance that states, "I have multiplied visions, and by the ministries of the prophets I was represented."[17] AGAINST THE ANOMOEANS, HOMILY 4.19.[18]

---

[17]"Represented" as through parables. Cf. RSV. [18]FC 72:122.

13:1-16 SHALL I REDEEM THEM FROM DEATH?

[1]*When Ephraim spoke, men trembled;*
    he was exalted in Israel;
    but he incurred guilt through Baal and
        died.
[2]*And now they sin more and more,*
    and make for themselves molten images,
idols skilfully made of their silver,
    all of them the work of craftsmen.
Sacrifice to these, they say.[j]
    Men kiss calves!
[3]*Therefore they shall be like the morning*
        mist
    or like the dew that goes early away,
like the chaff that swirls from the threshing
        floor
    or like smoke from a window.

[4]*I am the* LORD *your God[*]*
    from the land of Egypt;
you know no God but me,
    and besides me there is no saviour.
[5]*It was I who knew you[†] in the wilderness,*
    in the land of drought;
[6]*but when they had fed[k] to the full,*
    they were filled, and their heart was
        lifted up;
    therefore they forgot me.

[7]*So I will be to them like a lion,[‡]*
    like a leopard I will lurk beside the way.
[8]*I will fall upon them like a bear robbed of*
        her cubs,
    I will tear open their breast,
and there I will devour them like a lion,
    as a wild beast would rend them.

[9]*I will destroy you, O Israel;*
    who[l] can help you?
[10]*Where[m] now is your king, to save you;*
    where are all[n] your princes,[o] to defend
        you[p]—
those of whom you said,
    "Give me a king and princes"?
[11]*I have given you kings in my anger,*
    and I have taken them away in my wrath.

[12]*The iniquity of Ephraim is bound up,*
    his sin is kept in store.
[13]*The pangs of childbirth come for him,*
    but he is an unwise son;
for now he does not present himself
    at the mouth of the womb.

[14]*Shall I ransom them from the power of*
        Sheol?

Shall I redeem them from Death?
O Death, where^q are your plagues?
  O Sheol, where^q is your destruction?§
  Compassion is hid from my eyes.

^{15}Though he may flourish as the reed plant,^{r}
  the east wind, the wind of the LORD
    shall come,
  rising from the wilderness;

and his fountain shall dry up,
  his spring shall be parched;
it shall strip his treasury
  of every precious thing.
^{16s}Samaria shall bear her guilt,
  because she has rebelled against her God;
they shall fall by the sword,
  their little ones shall be dashed in pieces,
  and their pregnant women ripped open.

j Gk:Heb to these they say sacrifices of   k Cn: Heb according to their pasture   l Gk Syr: Heb for in me   m Gk Syr Vg: Heb I will be   n Cn: Heb in all   o Cn: Heb cities
p Cn Compare Gk: Heb and your judges   q Gk Syr: Heb I will be   r Cn: Heb among brothers   s Ch 14.1 in Heb   *LXX that establishes the heaven and creates the earth, whose
hands have framed the whole host of heaven; but I did not show them to you that you should go after them; and I brought you up   †LXX I shepherded you   ‡LXX panther   §Vulgate O
death, I will be your death, O lower world, I will be your bite.

OVERVIEW: Life is a brief experience similar to a vapor, like the morning dew, like the cycle of a flower (GREGORY OF NAZIANZUS). God alone is the true Creator of all the universe (HILARY). Jesus is the lamb who suffered silently for our sins and the lion who conquered all things through his resurrection (AUGUSTINE). Evil rulers do not provide an excuse for all the evil behavior of their subjects, even in the light of the fact that governing authorities are ordained by God (GREGORY THE GREAT). Saul was a king raised up by God to punish sinners while at the same time ironically he suffered from a demon who punished him for his sins (AUGUSTINE).

John's insight into Christ's eternal existence with God was a divine revelation. It is a wisdom, which also reveals that death has been conquered (AMBROSE). Death has been conquered even though the struggle with the flesh continues to assail those who strive to live the chaste life (AUGUSTINE). Death, which separates us in this life from God and in eternity, has been conquered by Jesus (BRAULIO). Christ has rescued the lower parts of the earth and brought the souls there to paradise. The wicked and unbelievers he did not rescue, but only those whom he recognized because of their faith and deeds. Hosea prophesied the conquest of the lower world (GREGORY THE GREAT). Christ is the

brazen serpent who destroyed all of the powers of death (GREGORY OF NAZIANZUS). Christ has swallowed up sin, which resulted in death. Hence both have been consumed by the cross (PAULUS). Hosea predicted that a time of apostasy would enter, and he describes it as a burning desert wind that dried the veins—hence life-giving blood—of the perfect and godly. Hippolytus connects this prophecy with the coming of the antichrist (HIPPOLYTUS).

13:3 Like the Morning Mist

LIFE IS BRIEF. GREGORY OF NAZIANZUS: Such, brethren, is our life, we whose existence is so transitory. Such is the game we play upon earth. We do not exist, and then we are born, and being born we are soon dissolved. We are a fleeting dream,[1] an apparition without substance, the flight of a bird that passes, a ship that leaves no trace upon the sea.[2] We are dust, a vapor, the morning dew, a flower growing but a moment and withering in a moment. "Man's days are as grass: as the flower of the field, so shall he flourish."[3] How beautifully has holy David meditated on our weakness: "Declare unto me the fewness of my days."[4] ON HIS

---

[1]Job 20:8.   [2]Wis 5:10-11.   [3]Ps 103:15 (102:15 LXX).   [4]Ps 90:12 (89:12 LXX). .

BROTHER ST. CAESARIUS, ORATION 7.19.[5]

13:4 No Other God

GOD ALONE IS CREATOR. HILARY OF POITIERS: All things have been created by the Lord Christ, and therefore the proper name for him is that he is a creator. The nature and title of what he himself produced is unsuitable for him. Our witness is Melchizedek, who proclaims God as the Creator of heaven and earth in the following words: "Blessed be Abraham by the most high God, who created heaven and earth."[6] Hosea the prophet is also a witness when he says, "I am the Lord your God who strengthened the heavens and created the earth, whose hands created all the hosts of heaven." Peter also is a witness, who writes as follows: "Commending your souls as to a faithful creator."[7] Why do we attribute the name of the work to the maker? Why do we give God the same name as our own? He is our Creator, the Creator of the whole heavenly array. ON THE TRINITY 12.4.[8]

13:8 Devouring Like a Lion

THE SUFFERING LAMB AND THE VICTORIOUS LION. AUGUSTINE: In fulfillment of holy Writ, the truth has resounded through the voice of the apostles, for the psalmist has sung, "Their voice has gone forth unto all the earth, and their words unto the ends of the world."[9] So also "Christ our Passover is sacrificed,"[10] for of him the prophet had foretold: "He was led as a sheep to the slaughter, and he was mute as a lamb before its shearer, and he opened not his mouth."[11] Who is this man? He is the man of whom the prophet at once goes on to say, "In humility his judgment was taken away; who shall declare his generation?"[12] I recognize the realization of so much humility in a king of so much power, for he who is as a lamb that opens not its mouth before its shearer is also "the lion of the tribe of Judah."[13] Who is this lamb and lion? He suffered death like a lamb, and he has devoured like a lion. Who is this lamb and lion? Meek yet courageous; lovable

yet fearsome; innocent yet powerful; silent under judgment, yet roaring to pronounce judgment. Who is this lamb and lion—suffering like a lamb; rising up like a lion? Rather, is he not at the same time a lamb and lion in his suffering and his resurrection? Let us discern the lamb in the suffering. "He was," as we have just reminded you, "mute as a lamb before its shearer, and he opened not his mouth." Let us discern the lion in the suffering. SERMON 4.[14]

13:11 Kings Given and Taken

EVEN THE ELECT MAY BE UNDER THE TEMPORAL POWER OF A REPROBATE. GREGORY THE GREAT: But let no one who suffers such a ruler blame him who he suffers. His being subject to the power of a wicked ruler was no doubt of his own deserving. Let him, therefore, rather blame the fault of his own evil doings rather than the injustice of his ruler. For it is written, "I gave you a king in my anger." Why, then, do we scorn their being set over us, whose authority over us we endure from the anger of the Lord? If we receive rulers according to our deserving, from the wrath of God, we infer from their conduct how we really think in our estimate of ourselves. However, even the elect are frequently placed under the reprobate. Therefore David also for a long time endured Saul. But it is proved by a subsequent sin of adultery that he then deserved to be heavily oppressed by the cruelty of the one who was set over him. MORALS ON THE BOOK OF JOB 5.25.34.[15]

THE IRONY OF SAUL'S PUNISHMENT. AUGUSTINE: Praise wicked King Saul, because he also was a punishment for sinners, as the Lord says: "I gave you a king in my wrath." Praise the demon that king suffered, because it also was punishment for a sinner.[16] Praise the blindness of heart that has befallen Israel, and do not be silent about

---

[5]FC 22:19* [6]Gen 14:1. [7]1 Pet 4:19. [8]FC 25:503. [9]Ps 19:4 (18:5 LXX); Rom 10:18. [10]1 Cor 5:7. [11]Is 53:7. [12]Is 53:8. [13]Rev 5:5. [14]FC 11:307-8. [15]LF 23:125. [16]1 Sam 16:14.

why it is said, "Until the full number of the Gentiles should enter,"[17] although you will perhaps deny this is a punishment. If you were a lover of the inner light, you would cry out that it is not merely a punishment but a very great punishment. AGAINST JULIAN 3.8.[18]

13:14 Death's Plagues

RESURRECTION. AMBROSE: No one could have known wisdom, because "no one knows the Son except the Father, and no one knows the Father except the Son and him to whom the Son chooses to reveal him."[19] Therefore he revealed him to John, since wisdom was with the apostle, and so he spoke not his own thought but that which wisdom poured into him: "In the beginning was the Word, and the Word was with God."[20] Death indeed could not hold it, for wisdom said, "O death, where is your victory? O death, where is your sting?"[21] THE PRAYER OF JOB AND DAVID 1.9.31.[22]

LUST AND DEATH OVERCOME. AUGUSTINE: What is it the chaste person would like? That no lust at all should stir in the members against chastity. [The chaste person] wants peace but hasn't yet got it. I mean, when we get to the stage where no lusts at all rise up to be opposed, there won't be any more enemy for us to wrestle with; nor is there in that state any expectation of victory, because the triumph is being celebrated over the enemy already conquered. Listen to the apostle telling you about that victory: "The perishable must put on imperishability, and the mortal put on immortality; then will come about the saying that is written: 'Death has been swallowed up in victory.'"[23] Now listen to the song of triumph: "Where, O death, is your striving? Where, O death, is your sting?"[24] You have stabbed, you have wounded, you have knocked down; but the one who made me was wounded for me. O death, death! The one who made me was wounded for me, and by his death he conquered you. And that's when those who triumph over you are going to say, "Where, O death, is your striving? Where, O death, is your sting?" SERMON 128.[25]

LIFE VAIN WITHOUT CHRIST. BRAULIO OF SARAGOSSA: In spite of these words, we are so deeply affected that we fall into tears and the longing of desire crushes the beliefs of the mind. How miserable is the human lot! How vain is all our life without Christ! O death, that separates those who were joined, cruel and harsh in forcing apart those who were tied by friendship! Now, now your strength is destroyed. Now is that wicked yoke of yours broken by him who sternly threatened you in the words of Hosea: "O death, I will be your bite!" So let us with the apostle voice our taunt: "O death, where is your victory? O death, where is your sting?"[26] He who conquered you has redeemed us—he who betrayed his beloved soul into the hands of the wicked, that those who were once wicked he might make his beloved. LETTER 19.[27]

DEATH CONQUERED FOR THOSE WHO BELIEVE. GREGORY THE GREAT: By this solemnity the elect who, protected though they were in undisturbed rest, were yet being held within the bounds of the lower world, have been brought back to the pleasant places of paradise. By his resurrection the Lord fulfilled what he said before his passion, "If I am lifted up from the earth, I shall draw all things to myself."[28] He who left none of his elect in the lower world did indeed draw all things to himself. He took from them all the predestinate. The Lord by his rising did not restore to pardon any unbelievers or those whose wickedness had caused them to be given over to eternal punishment; he snatched away from the confines of the lower world those whom he recognized as his own as a result of their faith and deeds. Hence he says truly by the mouth of Hosea: "O death, I will be your death; O lower

---

[17]Rom 11:25. [18]FC 35:248-49. [19]Mt 11:27. [20]Jn 1:1. [21]Cf. 1 Cor 15:55. [22]FC 65:350. [23]Is 25:8. [24]Cf. 1 Cor 15:55. [25]WSA 3 4:298. [26]1 Cor 15:55. [27]FC 63:48. [28]Jn 12:32.

world, I will be your bite." What we slay we cause almost to pass out of existence, but we take some from what we bite and leave the rest. Because he completely conquered death in his elect, he became death for death; but because he took away a portion of the lower world and left part of it, he did not completely slay it but took a bite from it. Therefore he said, "O death, I will be your death," as if to say, because I am completely destroying you in my elect, "I will be your death; O lower world, I will be your bite," because by taking some away I am partially piercing through you. FORTY GOSPEL HOMILIES 14.[29]

CHRIST THE BRAZEN SERPENT. GREGORY OF NAZIANZUS: But that brazen serpent[30] was hung up as a remedy for the biting serpents, not as a type of him that suffered for us but as a contrast. And [the brazen serpent] saved those that looked upon it, not because they believed it to live but because it was killed, and killed with it were the powers that were subject to it, being destroyed as it deserved. And what is the fitting epitaph for it from us? "O death, where is your sting? O grave, where is your victory?" You are overthrown by the cross; you are slain by him who is the giver of life; you are without breath, dead, without motion, even though you keep the form of a serpent lifted up on a pole. ON HOLY EASTER, ORATION 45.22.[31]

NEW BODIES PROMISED. PAULUS OROSIUS: Thus, if the glory of incorruptibility has been hidden from all people in this time, how do you, in this very same age, boast that you are able to be clothed with that very same incorruptibility? For just as sinking into sin has become for humans the beginning of corruption, so not having sin will be the beginning of incorruption. Who, therefore, concealed this prior to the judgment of God or removed it from the bosom of Christ and

handed it over to you? Or do you perhaps think that a person would not merit this in the future from the hand of the Lord? That most distinguished man, Paul, teaches this and says, "But when this mortal thing has put on immortality, then shall come to pass the saying which is written, 'Death has been swallowed up in victory. Where, O death, is your victory? Where, O death is your sting?' Now the sting of death is sin."[32] Through this the apostle shows that by no means can anyone so scoff at death and sin, until immortality follows mortality, and incorruption, corruption, and when, with the destruction of weakness, perfect virtue succeeds it; when there will not be male and female, but when all will be similar to the angels of God. DEFENSE AGAINST THE PELAGIANS 32.[33]

13:15 *The Wind of the Lord*

PERSECUTION PREDICTED. HIPPOLYTUS: Wherefore let us direct our discourse to a second witness. And of what sort is this one? Listen to Hosea, as he speaks thus grandly: "In those days the Lord shall bring on a burning wind from the desert against them, and shall make their veins dry, and shall make their springs desolate; and all their goodly vessels shall be spoiled. Because they rose up against God, they shall fall by the sword, and their pregnant women shall be ripped up." And what else is this burning wind from the east than the antichrist that is to destroy and dry up the veins of the waters and the fruits of the trees in his times, because people set their hearts on his works? For which reason they shall serve him in his pollution. ON THE END OF THE WORLD 4.[34]

---

[29]CS 123:168-69*. [30]Num 21:9. [31]NPNF 2 7:431. [32]1 Cor 15:54-56; Is 25:8. [33]FC 99:165. [34]ANF 5:243 (spurious).

14:1-9 THE WAYS OF THE LORD ARE RIGHT

¹Return, O Israel, to the LORD your God,
  for you have stumbled because of your
    iniquity.
²Take with you words
  and return to the LORD;
say to him,
  "Take away all iniquity;
accept that which is good
  and we will render
  the fruit[t] of our lips.
³Assyria shall not save us,
  we will not ride upon horses;
and we will say no more, 'Our God,'
  to the work of our hands.
In thee the orphan finds mercy."

⁴I will heal their faithlessness;
  I will love them freely,
  for my anger has turned from them.
⁵I will be as the dew to Israel;
  he shall blossom as the lily,
  he shall strike root as the poplar;[u]

⁶his shoots shall spread out;
  his beauty shall be like the olive,
  and his fragrance like Lebanon.
⁷They shall return and dwell beneath my[v]
    shadow,
  they shall flourish as a garden;[w]
they shall blossom as the vine,
  their fragrance shall be like the wine of
    Lebanon.

⁸O Ephraim, what have I to do with idols?
  It is I who answer and look after you.[x]
I am like an evergreen cypress,
  from me comes your fruit.

⁹Whoever is wise, let him understand these
    things;
  whoever is discerning, let him know
    them;
for the ways of the LORD are right,
  and the upright walk in them,
  but transgressors stumble in them.

t Gk Syr: Heb *bulls* u Cn: Heb *Lebanon* v Heb *his* w Cn: Heb *they shall grow grain* x Heb *him*

OVERVIEW: Those of the old covenant who sit in spiritual darkness are to be pitied for having squandered the opportunity to embrace the Son of God. The Gentiles who sat in darkness have seen the light (CHRYSOSTOM). The fire, which did not harm Daniel and the three children, was a consuming fire for unbelievers, prefiguring the judgment of the triune God (AMBROSE). No holy person can claim to walk in the path of holiness through his or her efforts alone (JOHN CASSIAN). The wise search always for the spiritual meaning of the sacred Scriptures (ORIGEN). The wise and the prudent understand that God overthrew polytheism through Moses and the prophets

(CYRIL OF ALEXANDRIA). The presentation of the gospel in enigmas, dark sayings, parables and prophecies had been foretold by Hosea (ORIGEN). The wise and the righteous are those who practice virtue and avoid vice (THEODORE).

14:3 Assyria Will Not Save

IDOLATRY OF THE GENTILES REDEEMED.
CHRYSOSTOM: Do not be surprised that I view the people of the old covenant as pitiable and woeful. When so many blessings from heaven came into their hands, they thrust them aside and were at great pains to reject them. The morning

Sun of justice arose for them, but they thrust aside its rays and still sit in darkness. We [the Gentiles], who were nurtured by darkness, drew the light to ourselves and were freed from the gloom of error. They were the branches of that holy root, but those branches were broken. We had no share in the root, but we did reap the fruit of godliness. From their childhood they read the prophets, but they crucified him whom the prophets had foretold. We did not hear the divine prophecies, but we did worship him of whom they prophesied. And so they are pitiful because they rejected the blessings that were sent to them, while others seized hold of these blessings and drew them to themselves. Although they had been called to the adoption of sons, they fell to kinship with dogs; we who were dogs received the strength, through God's grace, to put aside the irrational nature that was ours and to rise to the honor of sons. DISCOURSES AGAINST JUDAIZING CHRISTIANS 1.2.1.[1]

14:5 As the Dew to Israel

GOD'S WRATH TURNS AWAY FROM ISRAEL.
AMBROSE: This is our faith. Thus did God will that he should be known by all, thus believed the three children[2] [of the fiery furnace] who did not feel the fire into which they were cast, which destroyed and burned up the unbelievers,[3] while it fell harmless as a dew upon the faithful. The flames kindled by others became cold, seeing that the torment had justly lost its power in conflict with faith. For with them there was one in the form of an angel,[4] comforting them,[5] to the end that in number of the Trinity one supreme power might be praised. God was praised; the Father of God was seen in God's angel and holy and spiritual grace in the children.[6] ON THE CHRISTIAN FAITH 1.4.33.[7]

14:8 Like an Evergreen Cypress

GOOD FRUIT ENABLED BY GOD. JOHN CASSIAN: Holy people have never testified that they

attained by their effort the right path to travel on as they made their way to the increase and perfection of virtue. Rather they would plead to the Lord and say, "Direct me in your truth,"[8] and, "Direct my way in your sight."[9] Another one declares that it is not by faith alone but also by experience and, as it were, in the very nature of things that he has seized upon this, [saying], "I have known, O Lord, that a person's way is not in him, nor is it in a man to walk and to direct his own steps."[10] And the Lord himself says to Israel, "I will direct him like a green fir tree; from me your fruit has been found." CONFERENCE 3.13.1.[11]

14:9 Let the Wise Understand

THE WISE UNDERSTAND SCRIPTURE FIGURATIVELY. ORIGEN: If any reader is "a spiritual man who judges all things and he is judged by no one,"[12] not only will he allegorize the major regions as Judea and Egypt and Babylon but also areas of the earth. And just as in Judea is Jerusalem and Bethlehem and other cities, so in Egypt when he reads, "Diospolis, Bubastis, Taphnis, Memphis, Syene," he will understand the meaning of things figuratively. "Who is wise and understands these things? Or who is understanding and will know them?"[13] HOMILIES ON JEREMIAH 28.5.[14]

DISCERNING TRUTH THROUGH THE SHADOWS. CYRIL OF ALEXANDRIA: It is only by deeply considering the matters in the divinely inspired Scriptures that we shall find the hidden truth. It would be fitting for us when looking into the dark shadows of the law to say what one of the holy prophets rightly said, "Whoever will be wise will understand these things; and whoever will be prudent will know them." "For the law is but a shadow of the good things to come, and not the

---

[1]FC 68:5*. [2]Dan 3:17. [3]Dan 3:22. [4]Dan 3:25, 28. [5]Lk 22:43. [6]Dan 3:25. [7]NPNF 2 10:206. [8]Ps 25:5 (24:5 LXX). [9]Ps 5:8 (5:9 LXX). [10]Jer 10:23. [11]ACW 57:132-33*. [12]1 Cor 2:15. [13]Hos 14:10 LXX. [14]FC 97:261-62.

exact image of the objects,"[15] as it is written. Yet the shadows bring forth the truth, even if they do not contain the whole truth in themselves. Because of this, the divinely inspired Moses placed a veil upon his face and spoke thus to the children of Israel,[16] all but shouting by this act that a person might behold the beauty of the utterances made through him, not in outwardly appearing figures but in meditations hidden within us.[17] Letter 41.7.[18]

Truth Spoken in Enigmas. Origen: And to such a degree does the gospel desire that there should be wise people among believers, that for the sake of exercising the understanding of its hearers, it has spoken certain truths in enigmas, others in what are called "dark" sayings, others in parables, and others in problems. And one of the prophets—Hosea—says at the end of his prophecy, "Who is wise, and he will understand these things? Or prudent, and he shall know them?"[19] Against Celsus 3.45.[20]

Wisdom in Practicing Good. Theodore of Mopsuestia: You could really demonstrate that a wise and understanding person is the one with knowledge of what has been said and with zeal for the things by which it is possible for people who avoid evil and zealously practice good to be established in freedom from lower things and in enjoyment of higher things. This is because everything done by God is marked by great correctness, with which he also applies punishment to the fallen and knows how to achieve their salvation when they repent. You could also demonstrate that the righteous are those of their number who also know to profit from each category and who develop greater self-control from the punishments, on the one hand, while taking the enjoyment of the good things stemming from re-pentance as a stimulus to virtue, on the other. You could also demonstrate that the impious are those who deserve troubles in every way and of every kind, gaining nothing from them, stuck fast in a downward direction, and as a result not able to understand anything of their duty. Commentary on Hosea 14.10.[21]

---

[15]Heb 10:1. [16]Ex 34:33-35; 2 Cor 3:13-17. [17]2 Cor 4:3, 18. [18]FC 76:172. [19]Hos 14:10 LXX. [20]ANF 4:482. [21]PG 66:209.

JOEL

OVERVIEW: Joel comes from the Hebrew *yôʾēl,* which means "Yahweh is El." We know nothing about the personal life of Joel. The book occupies second place in the collection of the twelve prophets. It falls into two parts: Joel 1:1—2:27 (Joel 1—2 LXX and Heb), the plague of the locusts; and Joel 2:28—3:21 (Joel 3—4 LXX and Heb), the day of Yahweh. (Chapter 3 of the book in the Septuagint and Hebrew comprises the last five verses of chapter 2 in the Vulgate, which modern English versions follow in their chapter divisions.) Joel 1:1—2:11 contains a prophetic lamentation that describes a plague of locusts, which is symbolic of judgment and recalls one of the plagues on Egypt. What follows are numerous interspersed lamentations and calls to fasting and repentance. At Joel 2:18-27 there is an oracle of deliverance. Joel 2:28—3:21 contains an apocalyptic poem comprising several short sayings. These include the outpouring of the Spirit of the Lord on Israel (Joel 2:28-29), warnings about the day of Yahweh (Joel 2:30-32), the judgment of the nations in the valley of Jehoshaphat (Joel 3:1-8, 9-15) and the deliverance of Israel from these calamities (Joel 3:16-21). On the basis of the concept of the day of Yahweh, some interpreters date the book to the postexilic period after Nehemiah.

The book of Joel figures prominently in the New Testament, as attested by its use in interpreting key events. For example, the Fathers saw the day of Pentecost in the Acts of the Apostles as the key prophecy in Joel. By extension, they found the promise of the indwelling of the Holy Spirit in Joel as in Jeremiah 31:31.[1] The powerful and unusual manifestations of the Holy Spirit through visions, dreams and prophecies signaled the unfolding of God's presence in the new covenant consistent with similar phenomena under the old covenant, but with the purpose now of revealing Jesus as the promised Messiah.

---

[1]Jn 16—17.

1:1-20 INVASION OF LOCUSTS

[1] The word of the LORD that came to Joel, the son of Pethuel:

[2] Hear this, you aged men,
    give ear, all inhabitants of the land!
Has such a thing happened in your days,
    or in the days of your fathers?
[3] Tell your children of it,
    and let your children tell their children,
    and their children another generation.

[4] What the cutting locust left,
    the swarming locust has eaten.
What the swarming locust left,
    the hopping locust has eaten,
and what the hopping locust left,
    the destroying locust has eaten.

[5] Awake, you drunkards, and weep;
    and wail, all you drinkers of wine,
because of the sweet wine,
    for it is cut off from your mouth.
[6] For a nation has come up against my land,
    powerful and without number;
its teeth are lions' teeth,
    and it has the fangs of a lioness.
[7] It has laid waste my vines,
    and splintered my fig trees;
it has stripped off their bark and thrown it
      down;
    their branches are made white.

[8] Lament* like a virgin girded with sackcloth
    for the bridegroom of her youth.
[9] The cereal offering and the drink offering
    are cut off

from the house of the LORD.
The priests mourn,
    the ministers of the LORD.
[10] The fields are laid waste,
    the ground mourns;
because the grain is destroyed,
    the wine fails,
    the oil languishes.

[11] Be confounded, O tillers of the soil,
    wail, O vinedressers,
for the wheat and the barley;
    because the harvest of the field has
      perished.
[12] The vine withers,
    the fig tree languishes.
Pomegranate, palm, and apple,
    all the trees of the field are withered;
and gladness fails
    from the sons of men.

[13] Gird on sackcloth and lament, O priests,
    wail, O ministers of the altar.
Go in, pass the night in sackcloth,
    O ministers of my God!
Because cereal offering and drink offering
    are withheld from the house of your God.

[14] Sanctify a fast,
    call a solemn assembly.†
Gather the elders
    and all the inhabitants of the land
to the house of the LORD your God;
    and cry to the LORD.

[15] Alas for the day!

For the day of the LORD is near,
    and as destruction from the Almighty it
        comes.
[16]Is not the food cut off
    before our eyes,
joy and gladness
    from the house of our God?

[17]The seed shrivels under the clods,[a‡]
    the storehouses are desolate;
the granaries are ruined
    because the grain has failed.[§]
[18#]How the beasts groan!

The herds of cattle are perplexed
because there is no pasture for them;
    even the flocks of sheep are dismayed.[**]
[19]Unto thee, O LORD, I cry.
For fire has devoured
    the pastures of the wilderness,
and flame has burned
    all the trees of the field.
[20]Even the wild beasts cry to thee
    because the water brooks are dried up,
and fire has devoured
    the pastures of the wilderness.

a Heb uncertain   *LXX to me   †LXX proclaim a time of healing   ‡Syriac The cows languish at their mangers; LXX The heifers have started in their mangers; Vulgate The heifers have putrefied in their dung.   §LXX the cows stamp by their manger   #LXX implies What shall we put in there   **LXX perish

OVERVIEW: Whether in the time of Joel or the ancient Christian writers, the persecution of innocents was shocking and called forth reflections on the restraining hand of God in history (THEODORET). The great invaders of the holy land—Tiglath-pileser, Shalmaneser, Sennacharib and Nebuchadnezzar—were represented as increasing waves of locusts (ISHO'DAD). Prophetic speech used symbolic types to convey God's purpose for the future. Joel foresaw the fall of the covenant people because of their rejection of God's mercy. He prophesied the sending forth of the Holy Spirit at Pentecost to all people (JEROME). The invaders signify the impending troubles of Israel (THEODORE). Our plans and efforts are vulnerable to loss, even in the midst of great material and spiritual prosperity (JOHN CASSIAN). The insects signify the hierarchy of the vices (GREGORY THE GREAT). Those who do not recognize what God is doing in history are likened to drunken persons (CYRIL OF ALEXANDRIA). Here we find an impassioned warning that sinful passions are demonic forces that devour a person like a lion, and once having destroyed an individual they are discarded like a fallen carcass (CHRYSOSTOM). Pride and boasting waste the fruits of one's labors (GREGORY THE GREAT). Because of the lawlessness of people, God caused the land to be infertile (THEODORET). The lament of the land of the produce is designed to call people to repentance. Joel gives us a rigorous call to fasting and repentance (GREGORY OF NAZIANZUS). True fasting is commended by the prophets (JEROME). We are to despise the dung of materialism as well (GREGORY THE GREAT).

1:2 Has Such a Thing Happened?

UNPARALLELED BRUTALITY IN PERSECUTION.
THEODORET OF CYR: But these same villains,[1] vessels of wrath fitted for destruction,[2] screwed up their noses and poured out, if I may say so, as from a well-head, foul noises through their nostrils and rent the raiment from Christ's holy virgins, whose conversation gave an exact likeness of saints. They dragged them in triumph, naked as when they were born, through all the town. They made indecent sport of them at their pleasure. Their deeds were barbarous and cruel. Anyone who interfered in pity and was urged to mercy was dismissed with wounds. Ah! Woe is me. Many a virgin underwent brutal violation. Many

[1]Theodoret here narrates the violation of a Christian church in Alexandria.   [2]Rom 9:22.

a maid beaten on the head with clubs lay dumb. Even their bodies were not allowed to be given up for burial. Their grief-stricken parents cannot find their corpses to this day. But why recount woes that seem small when compared with greater? Why linger over these and not hurry on to events more urgent? When you hear them, I know that you will wonder and will stand with us long dumb, amazed at the kindness of the Lord in not bringing all things utterly to an end. At the very altar the impious perpetrated the very things that, as Joel had prophesied, were never heard of and had never happened before in the days of our fathers. ECCLESIASTICAL HISTORY 4.19.[3]

1:4 Destruction from Locusts

INVADERS SIGNIFIED. ISHO'DAD OF MERV: The *mashota* ("cutting locust") is similar to a larva. It is black and longer than a larva; when it falls to the ground, it does not destroy completely the plant but devours just the leaves and does not touch the rest. Through it the prophet signifies Tiglath-pileser, because the troubles that he caused to the people of Israel were mild. He calls Shalmaneser the flying locust, because the destruction that he caused was more serious than that by Tiglath-pileser. He calls *zahla* the crawling locust, which does not fly and feeds on everything. He signifies through it Sennacherib, because he surpasses his predecessor in the ruin caused and brings about the annihilation of ten tribes. The *sarsoura* creeps on the ground and is only equipped with a sting; when it strikes the roots of a tree, any tree it finds, it immediately withers. And he signifies through it Nebuchadnezzar, the cause of total destruction. He calls vines the common people, fig trees the important persons, whom the Assyrians and Babylonians deported in captivity. Hanana[4] says "the vines" represent the ten tribes; "the fig trees" the house of Judah. When the Assyrians were about to come, Ezekiah sent some of the Levites to the ten tribes, before they could be destroyed. They blew the trumpet throughout the land and gathered men and women into the temple of Jerusalem, so that all prayers might be said in the temple; and a prayer more fervent than any other was said. And the prophet relating what they said through their prayer says: "Alas, alas, for the fateful day. The heifers have been roasted," that is, they have been burned by an atrocious hunger as by a fire. "The fire has devoured, that is, a fierce heat, the pastures of the wilderness." He uses [this name] for those places suitable for sowing, which many call "farms." Others say, "fertile land or places which face the south," that is, estates which are turned to the sun. COMMENTARY ON JOEL.[5]

THE PROPHETS SPOKE USING SYMBOLIC TYPES. JEROME: The twelve prophets whose writings are compressed within the narrow limits of a single volume[6] have symbolic, typical meanings far beyond their literal ones. Hosea speaks many times of Ephraim, of Samaria, of Joseph of Jezreel, of a wife of whoredoms and of children of whoredoms,[7] of an adulterous woman shut up within the chamber of her husband, sitting for a long time in widowhood and in the garb of mourning awaiting the time when her husband will return to her.[8] Joel the son of Pethuel describes the land of the twelve tribes as spoiled and devastated by the palmerworm, the cankerworm, the locust and the blight, and he predicts that after the overthrow of the former people the Holy Spirit shall be poured out upon God's servants and handmaids.[9] This is the same spirit that was to be poured out in the upper chamber at Zion upon the 120 believers.[10] LETTER 7.[11]

SIGNS OF COMING TROUBLES. THEODORE OF MOPSUESTIA: In a figurative manner he wants to convey to them the impending troubles; as always, the earlier ones are surpassed by those coming later. Tiglath-pileser, king of the Assyrians, came like

---

[3]NPNF 2 3:122. [4]Hanana of Adiabene (d. 610) was a Syriac author who wrote a now lost commentary on the twelve prophets. [5]CSCO 303 (128):78-79. [6]They are referred to as forming one book in the Hebrew Bible. [7]Hos 1:2. [8]Hos 3:1, 3-4. [9]Joel 2:29 (3:2 LXX). [10]Acts 1:13, 15. [11]NPNF 2 6:100.

a cutting locust, he is saying, and laid waste no small proportion of your possessions. After him Shalmaneser [came] like some kind of locust further ravaging your goods. After them Sennacherib [came] like a young locust wreaking general destruction on the twelve tribes of Israel. Like some kind of blight in addition to these came the attack of the Babylonian, who took the people of Judah as well and inflicted the evil of captivity on all in common. COMMENTARY ON JOEL 1.4-5.[12]

THE VULNERABILITY OF OUR PLANS AND EFFORTS. JOHN CASSIAN: For although the Lord has granted strong cattle, bodily health, a successful outcome to every activity and prosperous deeds, prayer must still be offered lest, as it is written, there be "a heaven of brass and an earth of iron"[13] and lest "the swarming locust eat what the cutting locust has left, and the caterpillar devour what the swarming locust has left, and the blight consume what the caterpillar has left." Not in this alone does the effort of the toiling farmer stand in need of divine assistance. [His effort] must also fend off unexpected accidents by which, even if a field is loaded with the desired fruitful yield, he will not only be frustrated by waiting in vain for what he has hoped for but will even be deprived of the abundant crop that has already been harvested and that is stored on the threshing floor or in the barn. CONFERENCE 13.3.4.[14]

SUCCESSION OF THE HARMFUL INSECTS SIGNIFIES THE HIERARCHY OF VICES. GREGORY THE GREAT: We certainly know that in clouds of smoke, when some are fading away above, others rise up from below. So too in carnal thoughts, though some evil desires pass away, yet others succeed. But frequently the wretched mind beholds what has already passed but does not behold where it is still detained. It rejoices in being no longer subject to some sins but neglects to be careful and to lament because others have succeeded in their place, to which perhaps it yields more sinfully. And so it is that while some sins pass away and others succeed, the heart of the

reprobate is possessed without intermission by this serpent. Therefore it is well said by the prophet Joel: "That which the palmer-worm has left, the locust has eaten; and that which the locust has left, the canker-worm has eaten; and that which the canker-worm has left, the mildew has eaten." MORALS ON THE BOOK OF JOB 6.33.65.[15]

1:5 A Warning to Drunkards

A CALL TO SOBRIETY. CYRIL OF ALEXANDRIA: What a servile mentality from a crazed brain that knows how to do nothing else but gabble. We must reply to our opponents, "You are drunken men; rouse yourselves from your cups." Why do you do such violence to the truth? Why have you twisted the sense of the divine teachings so as to have been carried off the royal road? ON THE UNITY OF CHRIST.[16]

1:6 A Powerful Nation

INORDINATE PASSIONS. CHRYSOSTOM: How shall we be enabled to mortify those inordinate affections that mar our soul? Only by the precious blood of Christ, if it is received with full assurance, for this will have power to extinguish every disease; and together with this the divine Scriptures carefully heard, and almsgiving added to our hearing. And then only shall we live; for now surely we are in no better state than the dead. For as long as we live, those passions live within us. But we must necessarily perish. And unless we first mortify them here, they will be sure to kill us in the other life. Even before death, they will exact of us, in this life, the utmost penalty. Every inordinate passion is both cruel and tyrannical and insatiable, and it never ceases to devour us every day. For "their teeth are the teeth of a lion," or rather even far more fierce. For the lion, as soon as ever he is satisfied, wants to leave the carcass that has fallen.

---

[12]PG 66:213. [13]Deut 28:23. [14]ACW 57:468. [15]LF 31:614*. [16]OUC 96.

But these passions neither are satisfied, nor do they leave the one whom they have seized, until they have set one near the devil. HOMILIES ON THE GOSPEL OF MATTHEW 4.17.[17]

1:7 Vines and Fig Trees Destroyed

PRIDE AND BOASTING DESTROY THE VINE-YARD OF ONE'S MIND. GREGORY THE GREAT: O wretched beings, who by going after the praises of men waste to themselves all the fruits of their labors, and while they aim to show themselves to the eyes of others, blast all that they do. When the evil spirits prompt them to boastfulness, taking them for a prey they strip bare their works, as we have said. Hence Truth, in setting forth by the prophet the rancor of our old enemies under the form of a particular people, says, "It has laid waste my vines and splintered my fig trees; it has stripped off their bark and thrown it down; their branches are made white." MORALS ON THE BOOK OF JOB 2.8.82.[18]

1:11-12 Crops and Trees Wither

THE LAWLESSNESS OF THE PEOPLE. THEODORET OF CYR: Describing the calamity at greater length to bring to repentance those suffering from indifference, he bids even the produce to lament the failure of the barley and the wheat and the defoliation of the vine, and in general the lack of fruit on olives and figs and the other fruit trees due to their being deprived of moisture. Now it should be understood that he instructs the land and the produce to lament, not as rational creatures but in his attempt to rouse those endowed with reason through the inanimate creatures. To emphasize this, he went on, "because human beings confounded joy," that is, the cause of the infertility is people's lawlessness—hence the end of happiness and the onset of depression. COMMENTARY ON JOEL 1.11-12.[19]

1:13 Priests Called to Lament

THE RIGOR OF EARNEST REPENTANCE. GREGORY OF NAZIANZUS: Joel again summons us wailing and will have the ministers of the altar lament under the conditions of famine. He does not allow us to revel in the misfortunes of others. After sanctifying a fast, calling a solemn assembly and gathering the old men, the children, and those of tender age, we ourselves must further haunt the temple in sackcloth and ashes,[20] prostrated humbly on the ground, because the field is wasted and the meat offering and the drink offering is cut off from the house of the Lord, till we draw down mercy by our humiliation. IN DEFENSE OF HIS FLIGHT TO PONTUS, ORATION 2.59.[21]

1:14 Fasting and Assembling

DOES GOD DESIRE FASTING? JEROME: If God does not desire fasting, how is it that in Leviticus[22] he commands the whole people in the seventh month, on the tenth day of the month, to fast until the evening, and threatens that he who does not constrain his soul shall die and be cut off from his people? How is it that the graves of lust,[23] where the people fell in their devotions to flesh, remain even to this day in the wilderness? Do we not read that the stupid people gorged themselves with quails until the wrath of God came upon them? Why was the man of God at whose prophecy the hand of King Jeroboam withered, and who ate contrary to the command of God,[24] immediately smitten? Strange that the lion which left the ass safe and sound should not spare the prophet just risen from his meal. He who, while he is fasting, had wrought miracles, no sooner ate a meal than he paid the penalty for the gratification. Joel also cries aloud: "Sanctify a fast, proclaim a time of healing." So it appears that a holy fast may avail toward the cure of sin. AGAINST JOVINIANUS 2.17.[25]

---

[17]NPNF 1 10:27-28*. [18]LF 18:484*. [19]PG 81:1632-40. [20]Is 58:5. [21]NPNF 2 7:217*. [22]Lev 16:29. [23]Num 11:34. [24]1 Kings 13:24. [25]NPNF 2 6:402*.

1:18 *The Animals Groan*

GROWTH FROM DUNG. GREGORY THE GREAT: The prophet says, "The beasts of burden have become putrid in their own dung." For beasts of burden to become putrid in their own dung means for all those who are materialistic to end their lives in the stench of dissipation. As often as we prove a materialistic heart for its sins, as often as we draw back to its memory the wrongs it has committed, it is as if we are turning a measure of dung onto a barren tree. It is to call to mind the evils it has done and grow fertile to the gift of compunction as if from the stench. FORTY GOSPEL HOMILIES 31.[26]

[26]CS 123:252.

2:1-11 THE DAY OF THE LORD

[1]*Blow the trumpet in Zion;*
  sound the alarm on my holy mountain!
Let all the inhabitants of the land tremble,
  for the day of the LORD is coming, it is near,
[2]*a day of darkness and gloom,*
  a day of clouds and thick darkness!
Like blackness there is spread upon the mountains
  a great and powerful people;
their like has never been from of old,
  nor will be again after them
  through the years of all generations.

[3]*Fire devours before them,*
  and behind them a flame burns.
The land is like the garden of Eden before them,
  but after them a desolate wilderness,
  and nothing escapes them.

[4]*Their appearance is like the appearance of horses,*
  and like war horses they run.
[5]*As with the rumbling of chariots,*
  they leap on the tops of the mountains,
like the crackling of a flame of fire
  devouring the stubble,
like a powerful army
  drawn up for battle.

[6]*Before them peoples are in anguish,*
  *all faces grow pale.**
[7]*Like warriors they charge,*
  like soldiers they scale the wall.
They march each on his way,
  they do not swerve[b] from their paths.
[8]*They do not jostle one another,*
  each marches in his path;
they burst through the weapons
  and are not halted.
[9]*They leap upon the city,*
  they run upon the walls;
they climb up into the houses,
  they enter through the windows like a thief.

[10]*The earth quakes before them,*
  the heavens tremble.
The sun and the moon are darkened,
  and the stars withdraw their shining.
[11]*The LORD utters his voice*
  before his army,
for his host is exceedingly great;

he that executes his word is powerful.[†]
For *the day of the* LORD *is great and very*

terrible;
who can endure it?

b Gk Syr Vg: Heb *take a pledge*   *LXX *every face shall be as a blackened kettle*   †LXX *the works of his words are mighty*

OVERVIEW: Compared to Christ's first advent, the second advent will be a day of judgment (GREGORY THE GREAT). The effects of the Fall were prophetically described with the words of Joel: a land desolate, scourged by famine, lost beauty and disorder (GREGORY OF NAZIANZUS). The blackened kettle of sin is cleansed by the purifying water of baptism. Believers should show forth newness of life that is more precious than jewels (BASIL). Pagans do not know God but worship the heavens (CLEMENT OF ALEXANDRIA). Jesus is the light of the spiritual world who enlightens the mind about spiritual matters (ORIGEN). Scripture does not specify the length of ages and days; hence when Joel described the Day of the Lord it is to be understood as an expanse of time (BASIL). The Word of God corrects bad behavior, makes one whole again and restores spiritual health (CHRYSOSTOM). The use of "day" in the final judgment points to a unified whole that is completed in eternal life (AMBROSE).

2:1 The Day of the Lord

THE LORD'S FIRST COMING WAS WITH MILDNESS, BUT HIS SECOND COMING WILL BE WITH JUDGMENT. GREGORY THE GREAT: The terror of the strict inquest, which Zephaniah calls "the trumpet,"[1] blessed Job designates "thundering."[2] Joel, also viewing it, says, "Let all the inhabitants of the land be troubled, for the Day of the Lord comes; for it is nigh at hand, a day of darkness and of gloominess, a day of cloud and whirlwind." For the Day of the Lord is great and very terrible, and who shall sustain it? But how incomprehensible and unimaginable that greatness with which he shall come in his second coming! In some degree we estimate correctly if we consider with heedful reflection the momentous circumstances of his first advent. Surely the Lord came

to die, and the impoverishment and punishments of our flesh he underwent in his own body that he might redeem us from death. Before he came to the stock of the cross he suffered to be bound, to be spit on, to be mocked and to be beaten with blows on his cheek. Observe to what disgraceful treatment he consented to come for our sakes, and yet, before he permitted himself to be laid hold of, he questioned his persecutors, saying, "Whom do you seek?" To that they answered, "Jesus of Nazareth." And when he said to them directly, "I am he," he only uttered a voice of the mildest answer, and at once prostrated his armed persecutors to the earth.[3] What then shall he do when he comes to judge the world, if by one utterance of his voice he struck down his enemies even when he came to be judged? What is that judgment which he exercises as immortal, that a single utterance of it could not be endured when he was about to die? Who may sustain his wrath when his very mildness even could not be sustained? So then, let the holy man consider it and say, "And while we scarcely hear a little drop of his words, who shall be able to look on the thundering of his majesty?"[4] MORALS ON THE BOOK OF JOB 3.17.54.[5]

2:3 The Land Is Like a Wilderness

EFFECTS OF THE FALL. GREGORY OF NAZIANZUS: Terrible is an unfruitful season, and the loss of the crops. It could not be otherwise, when people are already rejoicing in their hopes and counting on their all but harvested stores. Terrible again is an unseasonable harvest, when the farmers labor with heavy hearts, sitting as it were beside the grave of their crops, which the gentle rain nourished but the wild storm has rooted up, "with which the reaper does not fill his hand or the

---

[1]Zeph 1:14-16. [2]Job 26:14. [3]Jn 18:6. [4]Job 26:14. [5]LF 21:315-16*.

binder of sheaves his bosom."[6] Nor have they obtained the blessing which passers-by bestow upon the farmers. Wretched indeed is the sight of the ground devastated, cleared and shorn of its ornaments, over which the blessed Joel wails in his most tragic picture of the desolation of the land and the scourge of the famine.[7] Another prophet wails as he contrasts with its former beauty its final disorder and thus discourses on the anger of the Lord when he smites the land: before him is the Garden of Eden, behind him a desolate wilderness. ON HIS FATHER'S SILENCE, ORATION 16.6.[8]

2:6 People in Anguish

NEWNESS OF LIFE. BASIL THE GREAT: And so he will deserve to fulfill, likewise, those other words that have a bearing in this connection: "buried together with him by baptism unto death." For what purpose? "That as Christ is risen from the dead by the glory of the Father, so we also may walk in newness of life."[9] He who is dead must be buried, and he who is buried in the likeness of death must rise again by the grace of God in Christ. No longer, because of sin, should he bear about in the inner man a countenance like a blackened kettle,[10] but, after his sins have been made manifest by fire and pardon has been granted through the blood of Christ, he should shine forth in newness of life, by the justifications of Christ, more precious than any jewel. CONCERNING BAPTISM 1.2.[11]

2:10 Earth and the Heavens Shake

PAGANISM CONDEMNED. CLEMENT OF ALEXANDRIA: The holy apostle of the Lord, reprehending the Greeks, will show you, "Because that, when they know God, they glorified him not as God, neither were thankful, but [they] became vain in their imaginations, and changed the glory of God into the likeness of corruptible man, and worshiped and served the creature more than the Creator."[12] And verily this is the God who "in the beginning made the heaven and the earth."[13] But

you do not know God and worship the heaven, and how shall you escape the guilt of impiety? Hear again the prophet speaking: "The sun shall suffer eclipse, and the heaven be darkened. But the Almighty shall shine forever: while the powers of the heavens shall be shaken, and the heavens stretched out and drawn together shall be rolled as a parchment skin [for these are the prophetic expressions], and the earth shall flee away from before the face of the Lord."[14] EXHORTATION TO THE GREEKS 9.[15]

2:11 A Great and Terrible Day

JESUS IS THE LIGHT OF THE MIND. ORIGEN: But since these are light perceived by the senses, which are said in Moses to have come into existence on the fourth day, they are not the true light because they enlighten the things on the earth. The Savior, on the other hand, is the light of the spiritual world because he shines on those who are rational and intellectual, that their mind may see its proper visions. Now I mean he is the light of those rational souls which are in the sensible world, of which the Savior teaches us that he is the Maker, being, perhaps, its directing and principal artificer, and, so to speak, the sun of the great Day of the Lord.[16] COMMENTARY ON THE GOSPEL OF JOHN 1.161.[17]

THE DAY IS UNIQUE. BASIL THE GREAT: Therefore he called the beginning of time not a "first day" but "one day," in order that from the name it might have kinship with eternity. For the day that shows a character of uniqueness and nonparticipation with the rest is properly and naturally called "one." If, however, the Scripture presents to us many ages, saying in various places "age of age" and "age of ages,"[18] still in those places neither the first nor the second nor the third age is

---

[6]Ps 129:7 (128:7 LXX). [7]Joel 1:10. [8]NPNF 2 7:249. [9]Rom 6:4. [10]See also Nahum 2:10 LXX. [11]FC 9:362-63. [12]Rom 1:21, 23, 25. [13]Gen 1:1. [14]This is a compilation of verses; see Is 13:10; Ezek 32:7; Joel 2:10, 31; 3:15. [15]ANF 2:195. [16]See also Zeph 1:14; Rev 6:17; 16:14. [17]FC 80:66. [18]Ps 148:6; Jude 25.

enumerated for us. By this, differences of conditions and of various circumstances are shown to us but not limits and boundaries and successions of ages. "The Day of the Lord is great and very terrible," it is said. HOMILIES ON THE HEXAE- MERON 2.8.[19]

GOD'S WORD RESTORES SPIRITUAL AND MORAL HEALTH. CHRYSOSTOM: When a maid- servant is rebelling but then sees her master com- ing, she grows humble and returns to her good behavior. So too the paralytic's body had revolted like the maidservant, and this caused the paraly- sis. But when the body saw its master coming near, it returned to its good behavior and re- sumed its proper discipline. And the word of Christ accomplished all this. Yet the words were not mere words but the words of God, of which the prophet said, "The works of his words are mighty." For if God's words made humankind when they did not exist, much more will they make humanity whole again and restore it to health even though it has grown feeble and weak with disease? AGAINST THE ANOMOEANS, HOM- ILY 12.29.[20]

"DAY" POINTS TO ETERNAL LIFE. AMBROSE: In notable fashion has Scripture spoken of a "day," not the "first day." Because a second, then a third day, and finally the remaining days were to follow, a "first day" could have been mentioned, follow- ing in this way the natural order. But Scripture established a law that twenty-four hours, includ- ing day and night, should be given the name of day only, as if one were to say the length of one day is twenty-four hours in extent. In such fash- ion, also, is the generation of men reckoned, which is understood to include that of women al- so. Because what is secondary is bound up with what is primary, the nights in this reckoning are considered to be component parts of the days that are counted. Therefore, just as there is a single revolution of time, so there is but one day. There are many who call even a week one day, because it returns to itself, just as one day does, and one might say seven times revolves back on itself. This is the form of a circle, to begin with itself and to return to itself. Hence Scripture speaks at times of an age of the world. Although in other passages there is a mention of an age, there Scrip- ture seems to mean the diversities in public and private affairs: "For the Day of the Lord is great and glorious." And elsewhere: "What avail is it to you to seek the Day of the Lord?"[21] And here is meant darkness and not light, for it is clear that that day when innocence will gleam forth and guilt be tormented is dark to those who are con- scious of evil deeds and unworthy acts. Moreover, Scripture teaches us that the everlasting day of eternal reward is to be one in which there is no interchange or intermission of day and night. SIX DAYS OF CREATION 1.10.37.[22]

---

[19]FC 46:35. [20]FC 72:297. [21]Amos 5:18. [22]FC 42:42-43.

2:12-17 REPENTANCE AND FORGIVENESS

[12]*"Yet even now," says the* LORD,*
"return to me with all your heart,
with fasting, with weeping, and with
mourning;
[13]*and rend your hearts and not your*

garments."
Return to the LORD, *your God,*
for he is gracious and merciful,
slow to anger, and abounding in steadfast
love,

and repents of evil.

[14]Who knows whether he will not turn and
    repent,
    and leave a blessing behind him,
    a cereal offering and a drink offering
        for the LORD, your God?

[15]Blow the trumpet in Zion;
    sanctify a fast;
call a solemn assembly;
    [16]gather the people.
Sanctify the congregation;
    assemble the elders;

gather the children,
    even nursing infants.
Let the bridegroom leave his room,
    and the bride her chamber.
[17]Between the vestibule and the altar
    let the priests, the ministers of the LORD,
        weep
and say, "Spare thy people, O LORD,
    and make not thy heritage a reproach,
    a byword among the nations.
Why should they say among the peoples,
    'Where is their God?' "

*LXX the Lord your God

OVERVIEW: Service to God results in forgiveness for previous failures and power over the devil and his snares (SHEPHERD OF HERMAS). A call to prayer, fasting and penance during the holy days of Lent is enjoined which signify life in this present world. Easter prefigures eternal bliss (CAESARIUS). Cyprian gives an impassioned plea for conversion, fasting and faithfulness to God (CYPRIAN). In his compassion, God calls his people to repentance. The threats of punishment are a call to change one's heart, to repent (THEODORET). The call to rend the heart and not clothing is like watering the seeds that bear fruit. Even sinful thoughts require such repentance (FULGENTIUS). Repentance was likened to a scalpel that a doctor uses to cut away disease, in this case sin. Joel's cry for repentance was a call to allow the priest to perform spiritual surgery on the diseased patient, namely, the sinner (PACIAN OF BARCELONA). Of course, the people will not turn and must do penance in captivity (ISHO'DAD). Let us raise our voices in supplication and in mourning, that the Lord may turn and leave us a blessing (GREGORY OF NAZIANZUS). Let us fast, and when we do so, let us sanctify the fast that it may not be polluted before our God (ATHANASIUS). Bishops and priests, who are to lead the faithful to fasting and repentance, are called to

faithfulness (JEROME). Fasting and prayer were highlighted in the retelling of the life of Severin (EUGIPPIUS). The fasting and repentance of the old covenant is just as valid in the new covenant (LEO). We are called to pray like Noah, Job and Daniel, who offered prayer for peace and were heard (GREGORY OF NAZIANZUS).

2:12 Return to Me

WITH ALL YOUR HEART. SHEPHERD OF HERMAS: "I, the angel of repentance, am telling you, Do not fear the devil. For I have been sent," he said, "to be on the side of you who repent with your whole heart and to steady you in the faith. Put your faith in God, you who despair of your life because of your sins, you who add to your sins and make your life burdensome. Trust that if you turn to the Lord with your whole heart and do righteousness[1] for the rest of your life, serving him uprightly in accordance with his will, he will provide a remedy for your previous failings, and you will obtain the power of mastering the devil's snares. Do not be in the least afraid of the devil's threats, for they are as powerless as a dead man's

---

[1]Jer 24:7; Ps 14:2 (13:2 LXX); Acts 10:35.

sinews. Listen to me: Fear him who has power to save and to destroy. Keep all the mandates, and you will live to God." I said to him, "Sir, I have now gained strength in all the justifications of the Lord, because you are on my side. I know that you will break down all the devil's power and we shall have the mastery over him and overcome all his snares. Sir, I now hope, with the Lord's help, to be able to keep these mandates you have given." "You will keep them," he said, "if your heart is made pure to the Lord. All those, also, who cleanse their hearts of the vain desires of this world will keep them and will live to God." MANDATE 11.6.[2]

LENT AND EASTER. CAESARIUS OF ARLES: Our Lord and Savior exhorts us through the prophet and advises us how we ought to come to him after much negligence, saying, "Come, let us bow down in worship, let us kneel before the Lord who made us";[3] and again, "Return to me with your whole heart, with fasting and weeping and mourning." If we notice carefully, dearest brethren, the holy days of Lent signify the life of the present world, just as Easter prefigures eternal bliss. Now just as we have a kind of sadness in Lent in order that we may rightly rejoice at Easter, so as long as we live in this world we ought to do penance in order that we may be able to receive pardon for our sins in the future and arrive at eternal joy. Each one ought to sigh over his or her own sins, shed tears and give alms in such a way that with God's help he may always try to avoid the same faults as long as he lives. Just as there never has been, is not now and never will be a soul without slight sins, so with the help and assistance of God we ought to be altogether without serious sins. SERMON 198.1.[4]

2:13 Rend Your Hearts, Not Your Garments

CONFESS AND REPENT. CYPRIAN: Let each one confess his sin, I beseech you, brethren, while he who has sinned is still in this world, while his confession can be admitted, while the satisfaction and remission effected through the priest is pleasing

with the Lord. Let us turn to the Lord with our whole mind, and, expressing repentance for our sin with true grief, let us implore God's mercy. Let the soul prostrate itself before him; let sorrow give satisfaction to him; let our every hope rest upon him. He himself tells how we ought to ask. He says, "Return to me with all your hearts, in fasting and in weeping, and in mourning, and rend your hearts, not your garments." Let us return to the Lord with a whole heart; let us placate his wrath and displeasure by fastings, weepings and mournings, as he himself admonishes. THE LAPSED 29.[5]

MERCY FLOWS FROM GOD'S BEING. THEODORET OF CYR: "Rend your hearts, not your garments," that is, have recourse to thoughts of compunction, soften the obduracy of your thinking, accept beneficial advice, abandon the way of vice and travel by that way which leads directly to God. After all, many are the founts of compassion and mercy that flow from him, and in his exercise of longsuffering he is not in the custom of putting his threats into effect. In fact, he indicated as much by saying "repenting of the troubles," that is, by instilling dread by the threats of punishment, and by the changes in human beings for the better transforming the threats into something pleasant. The God of all, you see, does not intend one thing at one time and another thing at another, or like us repent of what he does. Rather, while making threats he has mercy within himself, and he offers it to those who are sorry for their sins, and while making promises of good things he knows those who are good and those who are unworthy of his gifts, extending them to the former and giving to the latter the opposite of what he promises. COMMENTARY ON JOEL 2.13.[6]

REND HEARTS IN REPENTANCE. FULGENTIUS OF RUSPE: How well does the holy prophet teach that the seeds of good works must be watered by a river of tears! No seeds germinate unless they

---

[2]FC 1:286-87. [3]Ps 95:6 (94:6 LXX). [4]FC 66:48-49*. [5]FC 36:82. [6]PG 81:1648.

are watered; nor does fruit come forth from the seed if deprived of the aid of water. Accordingly, we too, if we wish to keep the fruits of our seeds, let us not stop watering our seeds with tears that must be poured out more from the heart than from the body. Therefore it is said to us through the prophet that we rend "our hearts and not our garments," something we can do when we recall that we ourselves, even if not in deed, frequently sin at least in thought. Because the "earthly tent burdens the thoughtful mind"[7] and our land does not cease to produce thorns and thistles for us. We are unable to get to eating our bread, unless we will have been worn out by weariness and the sweat of our brow. LETTER 9.[8]

THE SURGERY OF FORGIVENESS. PACIAN OF BARCELONA: Another disease is added to the original cause and a new wound inflicted, and all that is contrary is applied, all that is dangerous is drunk. Under this evil especially does this brotherhood toil, adding new sins on top of old faults. Therefore it has burst forth into vice, and more grievously still, is now racked by a most destructive wasting disease. What then shall I now do, I who as priest am compelled to cure? It is very late in such cases. But even so, if there is any one of you who can bear to be cut and cauterized, I can still do it. Behold the scalpel of the prophet: "Return," he says, "to the Lord your God and together with fasting and weeping and mourning rend your hearts." Do not fear this incision, dearly beloved. David bore it.[9] He lay in filthy ashes and had his appearance disfigured by a covering of rough sackcloth. He who had once been accustomed to precious stones and to the purple clothed his soul in fasting. He whom the seas, the forests, the rivers used to serve, and to whom the bountiful land promised wealth, now consumed in floods of tears those eyes with which he had beheld the glory of God. This ancestor of Mary, the ruler of the Jewish kingdom, confessed that he was unhappy and wretched. ON PENITENTS 8.2.[10]

2:14 God May Turn and Leave a Blessing

CAPTIVITY AND REPENTANCE. ISHO'DAD OF MERV: The prophet in effect says what you need to do. I know, however, that you will not really repent before you are deported. But, when you would have done penance for your sins after being punished by captivity, then God will take care of you and will bring you back to your land. COMMENTARY ON JOEL.[11]

FASTING AND SELF-CONTROL. GREGORY OF NAZIANZUS: We should enter his house in sackcloth and lament night and day between the porch and the altar, in piteous array, and with more piteous voices. [We should] cry aloud without ceasing on behalf of ourselves and the people, sparing nothing, either toil or word, which may propitiate God. [We should] say, "Spare, O Lord, your people, and give not your heritage to reproach," and the rest of our prayer; surpassing the people in our sense of the affliction as much as in our rank, instructing them in our own persons in compunction and correction of wickedness, and in the consequent longsuffering of God, and cessation of the scourge. Come then, all of you, my brethren, "let us worship and fall down, and weep before the Lord our maker";[12] let us appoint a public mourning in our various ages and families; let us raise the voice of supplication. Let this, instead of the cry which he hates, enter into the ears of the Lord of Sabbaoth. Let us anticipate his anger by confession;[13] let us desire to see him appeased, after [his wrath]. Who knows, he says, if he will turn and choose again, and leave a blessing behind him? ON HIS FATHER'S SILENCE, ORATION 16.13-14.[14]

2:15 Call for Fasting

A CALL TO FAST. ATHANASIUS: Since, as I said, there are many kinds of proclamations, let us listen to the trumpet blast of the prophet: "Blow a trumpet in Zion, consecrate a fast." This is a

---

[7]Wis 9:15. [8]FC 95:338. [9]2 Sam 12:13; cf. Ps 51 (50 LXX). [10]FC 99:80*. [11]CSCO 303 (128):79. [12]Ps 95:6 (94:6 LXX). [13]Cf. Ps 94:2 LXX (variant). [14]NPNF 2 7:252*.

warning trumpet, and it earnestly commands us that when we fast, we should do it in a holy manner, for God is holy and has pleasure in his holy people.[15] Not everyone, however, who calls upon God honors him. Some defile him—although they don't actually defile *him*: that's impossible. But they do defile their own consciences concerning him. The apostle Paul tells us how it is that some people dishonor God: those who break the law dishonor God.[16] So the prophet said, in order to point out those who pollute the fast, "Sanctify a fast." Many people, though they go through the motions of a fast, are still polluted in their hearts because they do evil against their brothers and sisters or because they dare to cheat. And many, if nothing else, think more highly of themselves than of their neighbors, thereby committing a great offense. FESTAL LETTERS 1.[17]

REBUKE OF THE PRIESTS' WORLDLINESS.
JEROME: If these [vessels] were approved by the Lord it was at a time when the priests had to offer victims and when the blood of sheep was the redemption of sins. They were figures typifying things still future and were "written for our admonitions upon whom the ends of the world are come."[18] But now our Lord by his poverty has consecrated the poverty of his house. Let us, therefore, think of his cross and count riches to be but dirt. Why do we admire what Christ calls "the mammon of unrighteousness"?[19] Why do we cherish and love what it is Peter's boast not to possess?[20] Or if we insist on keeping to the letter and find the mention of gold and wealth so pleasing, let us keep to everything else as well as the gold. Let the bishops of Christ be bound to marry wives, who must be virgins.[21] Let the best-intentioned priest be deprived of his office if he bears a scar and is disfigured.[22] Let bodily leprosy be counted worse than spots on the soul. Let us be fruitful and multiply and replenish the earth,[23] but let us slay no lamb and celebrate no mystic Passover, for where there is no temple,[24] the law forbids these acts. Let us pitch tents in the seventh month[25] and noise abroad a solemn fast with

the sound of a horn. LETTER 52.10.[26]

2:16 Sanctifying the Congregation

FASTING AND REPENTANCE ENJOINED. EUGIPPIUS: He addressed them piously. "Have you not read," he said, "what divine authority has prescribed to a sinful people through the prophet: 'Be converted to me with all your heart, in fasting and in weeping,' and a little later: 'Sanctify a fast,' he says, 'call an assembly, gather the congregation,' and all that follows? Therefore, fulfill with worthy actions what you teach, that you may perhaps escape the evil of the present time. And let nobody, on any account, go out on his field as if he could ward off the locusts by human effort, lest God's wrath be provoked even more." Without delay everybody gathered in the church, and they all, each in his place, recited the psalms, as was the custom. Every age and sex, even those who could not yet speak, offered a prayer to God with tears, alms were given unceasingly, and every good work that the present emergency demanded was carried out as had been prescribed by the servant of God. THE LIFE OF ST. SEVERIN 12.[27]

A COMMENDATION OF FASTING FOR TODAY.
LEO THE GREAT: Devout fasting has a very great value for gaining the mercy of God and for strengthening human frailty. We know this from the teaching of holy prophets, dearly beloved. They insist that the arousal of divine justice—which the people of Israel frequently brought upon themselves in punishment for their wickedness—could not be placated except by fasting. Joel the prophet warns us in saying, "The Lord God says these things: 'Turn to me with all your heart, in fasting, in weeping and in mourning. Rend your hearts, and not your garments. Be converted to the Lord your God, because he is merciful and patient and magnanimous and rich

---

[15]Ps 16:3 (15:3 LXX). [16]Rom 2:23. [17]ARL 51. [18]1 Cor 10:11. [19]Lk 16:9. [20]Acts 3:6. [21]Lev 21:14. [22]Lev 21:17-23. [23]Gen 1:28. [24]Deut 26:5. [25]Lev 23:40-42. [26]NPNF 2 6:94. [27]FC 55:70-71.

in mercy.'" At another point, the same prophet says, "Make a holy fast, preach healing, call together the people, make holy the assembly." This exhortation, dearly beloved, is what we must embrace in our times also. We must of necessity preach the remedy of this healing, so that Christian devotion in the observance of that ancient means for sanctification might acquire what the Jewish transgression lost. SERMON 88.1.[28]

2:17 Spare Your People

A CALL TO PRAYER. GREGORY OF NAZIANZUS: Who will cry aloud, "Spare your people, O Lord, and do not give your heritage to reproach, that the nations should rule over them"? Noah, Job[29] and Daniel stood together as men of prayer. Who will pray for us, that we might have a slight respite from warfare and recover ourselves? IN DEFENSE OF HIS FLIGHT TO PONTUS, ORATION 2.89.[30]

---

[28]FC 93:372-73. [29]Ezek 14:14, 20. [30]NPNF 2 7:222*.

2:18-27 REDEMPTION OF THE LORD

[18]Then the LORD became jealous for his
    land,
    and had pity on his people.
[19]The LORD answered and said to his
    people,
"Behold, I am sending to you
    grain, wine, and oil,
    and you will be satisfied;
and I will no more make you
    a reproach among the nations.

[20]"I will remove the northerner far from you,
    and drive him into a parched and desolate
    land,
his front* into the eastern sea,
    and his rear into the western sea;
the stench and foul smell of him will rise,
    for he has done great things.

[21]"Fear not, O land;
    be glad and rejoice,
    for the LORD has done great things!
[22]Fear not, you beasts of the field,

for the pastures of the wilderness are
    green;
the tree bears its fruit,
    the fig tree and vine give their full yield.
[23]"Be glad, O sons of Zion,
    and rejoice in the LORD, your God;
for he has given the[†] early rain for your
    vindication,
    he has poured down for you abundant
    rain,
    the early and the latter rain, as before.[‡]

[24]"The threshing floors shall be full of grain,
    the vats shall overflow with wine and oil.
[25]I will restore to you the years
    which the swarming locust has eaten,
the hopper, the destroyer, and the cutter,
    my great army, which I sent among you.

[26]"You shall eat in plenty and be satisfied,
    and praise the name of the LORD your
    God,
    who has dealt wondrously with you.

> *And my people shall never again be put to shame.*
> [27]*You shall know that I am in the midst of Israel,*

> *and that I, the LORD, am your God and there is none else.*
> *And my people shall never again be put to shame.*

*LXX face   †LXX food   ‡LXX as at the first

OVERVIEW: Isho'dad identifies the northerners that the Lord will remove far from Israel (ISHO'DAD). Like the northerners, the devil will be removed from the people (CASSIODORUS). Christ's fruitful work on the tree will bring salvation to those who believe (TERTULLIAN). Goodness and gladness will come to those who partake of the fig tree and the vine that nourishes (METHODIUS).

2:20 Removing the Northerner

IDENTIFICATION OF THE NORTHERNER. ISHO'DAD OF MERV: "I will remove the northerner," both the Assyrian and Babylonian. Someone may ask, "Since for its position Babylon is not situated north of Jerusalem, why does God say through the prophet, 'I will remove the northerner far from you' and 'Out of the north evil shall break forth upon'[1] these people"? And we answer that first of all, these words are not said in consideration of the geographical position of Babylon and Jerusalem but of those northern nations subject to the Babylonians—the Arzanites, the Araratites[2]—who will come down to Jerusalem with the Babylonians. Second, it is because those who want to reach Jerusalem from the regions of Babylon, Persia and the east go up toward the region of the north and then come down toward Jerusalem in the south. COMMENTARY ON JOEL.[3]

THE DEVIL CAST OUT. CASSIODORUS: Joel, the prophet, offers evidence about [the devil] with these words: "And I will remove far off from you the northern one, and I will drive him into the land thirsty and desert, and I shall expel his face into the nearest sea and his hinder parts into the

utmost sea." We thank you, Lord, for this arrangement. What would the devil do if free, when he afflicts the world when bound? EXPOSITION OF THE PSALMS 36.35.[4]

2:22 The Tree Bears Fruit

THE TREE AS A TYPE FOR THE CROSS. TERTULLIAN: David said that "the Lord would reign from the tree."[5] Elsewhere too the prophet predicts the fruit of this tree, saying, "The earth has given its blessings"[6]—of course that virgin earth, not yet irrigated with rains or fertilized by showers, out of which humanity was of old first formed, out of which now Christ through the flesh has been born of a virgin. "And the tree bears its fruit"—not that tree in paradise, which yielded death to the first humans, but the tree of the passion of Christ, whence life, hanging, you did not believe! ANSWER TO THE JEWS 12.[7]

THE FIG AND VINE AS TYPES. METHODIUS: For the fig tree, on account of its sweetness and richness, represents the delights of humankind, which they had in paradise before the Fall. Indeed, not rarely, as we shall afterwards show, the Holy Spirit[8] takes the fruit of the fig tree as an emblem of goodness. But the vine, on account of the gladness produced by wine and the joy of those who were saved from wrath and from deluge, signifies the change produced from fear and anxiety into joy. Moreover, the olive, on account of the oil which it produces, indicates the com-

---

[1]Jer 1:14. [2]Two ancient peoples of Armenia. [3]CSCO 303 (128):80. [4]ACW 51:374. [5]Ps 96:10. "From the tree" is a textual variant found in other patristic texts; see ANF 3:166 n. 7. [6]Cf. Ps 67:6 (66:7 LXX); 85:12 (84:13 LXX). [7]ANF 3:169-70*. [8]Jer 8:13.

passion of God, who again, after the deluge, bore patiently when people turned aside to ungodliness, so that he gave them the law and manifested himself to some, and nourished by oil the light of

virtue, now almost extinguished. BANQUET OF THE TEN VIRGINS 10.2.[9]

[9]ANF 6:348.

2:28-32 ESCHATOLOGICAL OUTPOURING OF THE SPIRIT

[28c]*"And it shall come to pass afterward,*
    that I will pour out* my spirit on all flesh;
your sons and your daughters shall prophesy,
    your old men shall dream dreams,
    and your young men shall see visions.
[29]*Even upon the menservants and maidservants*
    in those days, I will pour out my spirit.

[30]*"And I will give portents in the heavens and on the earth, blood and fire and columns of smoke.* [31]*The sun shall be turned to darkness, and the moon to blood, before the great and terrible day of the LORD comes.* [32]*And it shall come to pass that all who call upon the name of the LORD shall be delivered; for in Mount Zion and in Jerusalem there shall be those who escape, as the LORD has said, and among the survivors shall be those whom the LORD calls."†*

c Ch 3.1 in Heb   *LXX of   †LXX and those preaching good news

OVERVIEW: The promise is of the Father (CHRYSOSTOM). The Spirit is poured out on humanity and manifested in baptism. The Spirit is power (AMBROSE), and a measure of the fullness of the Spirit is poured out on us according to the will of the Father, but not the fullness of the Spirit, for this would be too much for us (FULGENTIUS). It is not the flesh as such that is evil, but only its actions, while all flesh is to be finally ennobled by the Holy Spirit (TERTULLIAN). All flesh includes your daughters (ISHO'DAD). All this was to take place after Christ ascended (JUSTIN MARTYR). All of this should be contrasted with the Spirit's work under the old covenant, which was not as widespread as after the sending of the Spirit (ORIGEN).

The Holy Spirit is no respecter of persons, for he seeks not dignities but piety of soul (CYRIL OF JERUSALEM). Although there are dreams that are caused by demons, God has also promised bona fide visions, prophecies and dreams through his Holy Spirit (TERTULLIAN). God has taken away the power and efficacy of his Word from late Judaism and has given it to the converted of the Gentiles. Thus the devil is very angry at the holy church of God (APOSTOLIC CONSTITUTIONS). God in a well-ordered manner bestowed the Holy Spirit upon the church through Christ (NOVATIAN). The heavens and humanity can expect a resurrection. Manichaeans would do well to look to Christ instead of the stars (CYRIL OF JERUSAlem). The Lord's control of the sun and moon in Joel's prophecy demonstrates that sun and moon worshipers have their object of adoration misplaced (Eznik). Nothing is new but Christ the Lord, of whom it is written, "The Sun of justice will rise upon you" (Maximus of Turin). The end of time will be seen in the sun and in the moon (Basil). Forgiveness is promised for all those who repent and return to the Lord (Ambrose). Even the heretics may return to the Lord, who would rather heal them within the body than cut them off from the body as dead limbs (Augustine). Everyone who calls on the name of the Lord, Jew or Gentile, will be saved, even those who like Peter have fallen away (Basil, Augustine). When someone drinks of the cup of martyrdom, that person is calling on the name of the Lord and shall be saved (Origen). Joel's prophecy is fulfilled in the descent of the Holy Spirit on Pentecost, as witnessed by Peter (Theodore).

2:28-29 The Spirit Poured Out

Spirit from the Father. Chrysostom: On unessential points one must not spend many words. And besides, the sequel is enough to bear him out on this point, so now the discourse is for all in common. " 'But this is that which was spoken by the prophet Joel, and it shall come to pass in the last days,' says the Lord God."[1] Nowhere as yet the name of Christ or his promise, but the promise is that of the Father. Homilies on the Acts of the Apostles 5.[2]

No Creature Could Fill All Things. Ambrose: But of what creature can it be said that it fills all things, as it is written of the Holy Spirit: "I will pour my Spirit upon all flesh"? This cannot be said of an angel. Lastly, Gabriel himself, when sent to Mary, said, "Hail, full of grace,"[3] plainly declaring the grace of the Spirit which was in her, because the Holy Spirit had come upon her, and she was about to have her womb full of grace with the heavenly Word. On the Holy Spirit 1.7.85.[4]

Holy Spirit Given at Baptism. Ambrose: But that the Spirit is the arbiter of the divine counsel, you may know even from this. For when we showed that the Holy Spirit was the Lord of baptism and read that baptism is the counsel of God, as you read, "But the Pharisees despised the counsel of God, not being baptized of him,"[5] it is quite clear that as there can be no baptism without the Spirit, so too the counsel of God is not without the Spirit. And that we may know more completely that the Spirit is power, we ought to know that he was promised when the Lord said, "I will pour out my Spirit upon all flesh." He, then, who was promised to us is himself power, as in the Gospel the same Father of God declared when he said, "And I will send the promise of the Father upon you, but do you remain in the city until you are endued with power from on high."[6] On the Holy Spirit 2.2.21.[7]

Receiving of the Spirit's Fullness. Fulgentius of Ruspe: If we believe this, it is necessary that that proclamation of the blessed John the Baptist, which attributed to Christ a singular gift of the Spirit and one without measure, be interpreted. I refer to the statement "[God] does not ration his gift of the Spirit."[8] Since our ancestors too in us receive a measure of this gift, they profess that in Christ there abides the fullness of the Holy Spirit. For the blessed Ambrose, in the first book on the Holy Spirit, among other things, says, "I will pour out of my Spirit." He did not say "my Spirit," but "of my Spirit," for we cannot take the fullness of the Holy Spirit, but we receive so much as our master divides of his own according to his will. Therefore, Saint Ambrose, showing that we receive not the fullness but of the fullness of the Spirit, that he may show that Christ has received the entire fullness of the Spirit, a little while after this says, "So too, the Father says that he pours out of the Holy Spirit upon all flesh; for he did not pour him forth en-

---

[1]Acts 2:16-17. [2]NPNF 1 11:32. [3]Lk 1:28. [4]NPNF 2 10:104. [5]Lk 7:30. [6]Lk 24:49. [7]NPNF 2 10:117. [8]Jn 3:34.

tirely, but what he poured forth abounded for all." LETTER 14.27.[9]

ALL FLESH IS FINALLY ENNOBLED BY THE HOLY SPIRIT. TERTULLIAN: You hold to the Scriptures in which the flesh is disparaged; receive also those in which it is ennobled. You read whatever passage abases it. Now direct your eyes also to that which elevates it. "All flesh is grass."[10] Well, but Isaiah was not content to say only this; he also declared, "All flesh shall see the salvation of God."[11] Then notice what God says in Genesis: "My spirit shall not remain among these men, because they are flesh";[12] but then he is also heard saying by Joel, "I will pour out of my Spirit upon all flesh." Even the apostle ought not to be known for any one statement in which he is inclined to reproach the flesh. Admittedly he says that "in his flesh dwells no good thing"[13] and "they who are in the flesh cannot please God,"[14] because "the flesh lusts against the Spirit."[15] Yet in these and similar assertions that he makes, it is not the substance of the flesh, but its actions, which are censured. Moreover, we shall elsewhere take occasion to remark that no reproaches can fairly be cast upon the flesh without tending also to the castigation of the soul, which compels the flesh to do its bidding. However, let me meanwhile add that in the same passage Paul "carries about in his body the marks of the Lord Jesus."[16] He also forbids our body to be profaned, since it is "the temple of God."[17] He makes our bodies "the members of Christ."[18] And he exhorts us to exalt and "glorify God in our body."[19] If, therefore, the humiliations of the flesh do not prevent its resurrection, why wouldn't its high prerogatives avail to bringing it about? It better suits the character of God to restore to salvation what for a while he rejected, than to surrender to perditions what he once approved. ON THE RESURRECTION OF THE FLESH 10.[20]

PETER CONFIRMS JOEL'S PROPHECY. ISHO'DAD OF MERV: "I will pour out my spirit on all flesh." In the first instance he talks about Ezekiel, Daniel, Haggai, Zechariah and other prophets whose names are not mentioned. In addition, "your daughters"[21] will sing and intone psalms in happiness, as well as the rest of the people. This means I will openly reveal to you my fondness and will largely pour it onto you. Therefore these words follow: "My Spirit abides among you,"[22] and also, "My spirit shall not abide in man forever, for he is flesh."[23] But the truth of these words is found in Christ and in the apostles, as well as in the prophets and in the righteous ones, who were filled with the Spirit, and in the daughters of Philip.[24] Recall Peter, who testifies when he preaches to the Jews: "This is," he says, "what Joel predicted."[25] Then the words: "The sun shall be turned to darkness and the moon to blood."[26] He talks according to the state of mind of those who are plunged into their afflictions. COMMENTARY ON JOEL.[27]

ASCENSION AND HOLY SPIRIT. JUSTIN MARTYR: I have already affirmed, and I repeat, that it had been predicted that he would do this after his ascension into heaven. It was said, therefore, "He ascended on high; he led captivity captive; he gave gifts to the sons of men."[28] And in another prophecy it is said, "And it shall come to pass after this, that I will pour out my Spirit upon all flesh, and upon my servants and upon my handmaids, and they shall prophesy." DIALOGUE WITH TRYPHO 87.[29]

HOLY SPIRIT IN BOTH COVENANTS CONTRASTED. ORIGEN: Now we are of the opinion that every rational creature, without any distinction, receives a share of him in the same way as of the wisdom and of the word of God. I observe, however, that the chief advent of the Holy Spirit is declared to people after the ascension of Christ into heaven, rather than before his coming into the world. For before that, it was on the prophets

[9]FC 95:535. [10]Is 40:7. [11]Is 40:5. [12]Gen 6:3 LXX. [13]Rom 7:18. [14]Rom 8:8. [15]Gal 5:17. [16]Gal 6:17. [17]1 Cor 3:16. [18]1 Cor 6:15. [19]1 Cor 6:20. [20]ANF 3:552*. [21]Acts 21:9. [22]Hag 2:5. [23]Gen 6:3. [24]Acts 21:9. [25]Acts 2:16. [26]Joel 2:31 (3:4 LXX); Acts 2:20. [27]CSCO 303 (128):80. [28]Ps 68:18 (67:19 LXX). [29]FC 6:288.

alone, and on a few individuals, if there happened to be among the people any deserving, that the gift of the Holy Spirit was conferred. But after the advent of the Savior, it is written that the prediction of the prophet Joel was fulfilled: "In the last days it shall come to pass, and I will pour out my Spirit upon all flesh, and they shall prophesy,"[30] which is similar to the well-known statement, "All nations shall serve him."[31] By the grace, then, of the Holy Spirit, along with numerous other results, this most glorious consequence is clearly demonstrated. With regard to those things which were written in the prophets or in the law of Moses, it was only a few persons at that time, namely, the prophets themselves, and scarcely another individual out of the whole nation, who were able to look beyond the mere corporeal meaning and discover something greater, something spiritual, in the law or in the prophets. But now there are countless multitudes of believers who, although unable to unfold methodically and clearly the results of their spiritual understanding, are nevertheless most firmly persuaded that neither ought circumcision to be understood literally, nor the rest of the sabbath, nor the pouring out of the blood of an animal, nor that answers were given by God to Moses on these points. And this method of apprehension is undoubtedly suggested to the minds of all by the power of the Holy Spirit. ON FIRST PRINCIPLES 2.7.2.[32]

FOR EVERYONE, RICH AND POOR. CYRIL OF JERUSALEM: And if you would receive a testimony also, "listen," he says. "But this is that which was spoken by the prophet Joel: 'And it shall come to pass after this, says God, I will pour forth of my Spirit'"—and this word, 'I will pour forth,' implied a rich gift; 'for God gives not the Spirit by measure for the Father loves the Son, and has given all things into his hand';[33] and he has given him the power also of bestowing the grace of the all-holy Spirit on whomever he will—"I will pour forth of my Spirit upon all flesh, and your sons and your daughters shall prophesy;" and after-

ward, "Yea, and on my servants and on my handmaidens I will pour out in those days of my Spirit, and they shall prophesy."[34] The Holy Spirit is no respecter of persons, for he seeks not dignities but piety of soul. Let neither the rich be puffed up nor the poor be dejected, but only let each prepare himself for reception of the heavenly gift. CATECHETICAL LECTURE 27.19.[35]

DREAMS FROM GOD. TERTULLIAN: We declare, then, that dreams are inflicted on us mainly by demons, although they sometimes turn out true and favorable to us. When, however, with the deliberate aim after evil, of which we have just spoken, they assume a flattering and captivating style, they show themselves proportionately vain, and deceitful, and obscure, and wanton, and impure. And no wonder that the images partake of the character of the realities. But from God— who has promised, indeed, "to pour out the grace of the Holy Spirit upon all flesh, and has ordained that his servants and his handmaids should see visions as well as utter prophecies"— must all those visions be regarded as emanating. [Those visions] may be compared with the actual grace of God, as being honest, holy, prophetic, inspired, instructive, inviting to virtue, the bountiful nature of which causes them to overflow even to the profane, since God, with grand impartiality, "sends his showers and sunshine on the just and on the unjust."[36] ON THE SOUL 47.[37]

THE HOLY SPIRIT GIVEN TO THE GENTILES. APOSTOLIC CONSTITUTIONS: Since, therefore, he has forsaken his people, he has also left his temple desolate, and rent the veil of the temple, and took from them the Holy Spirit, for says he, "Behold, your house is left unto you desolate."[38] And he has bestowed upon you, the converted of the Gentiles, spiritual grace, as he says by Joel: "'And it shall come to pass after these things,' says God,

[30]Acts 2:17; cf. Joel 3:1. [31]Ps 72:11 (71:11 LXX). [32]ANF 4:285. [33]Jn 3:34. [34]The phrase "and they shall prophesy" is added in Acts 2:18. [35]NPNF 2 7:129. [36]Mt 5:45. [37]ANF 3:225-26. [38]Mt 23:38.

'that I will pour out of my Spirit upon all flesh; and your sons shall prophesy, and your daughters shall see visions, and your old men shall dream dreams.'" For God has taken away all the power and efficacy of his Word and such like visitations from that people, and he has transferred it to you, the converted of the Gentiles. For on this account the devil himself is very angry with the holy church of God. He is removed to you and has raised against you adversities, seditions, and reproaches, schisms and heresies. CONSTITUTIONS OF THE HOLY APOSTLES 6.2.5.[39]

THE OUTPOURING OF GOD THE HOLY SPIRIT PROMISED.

NOVATIAN: Next, well-ordered reason and the authority of our faith bid us (in the words and the writings of our Lord set down in orderly fashion) to believe, after these things, also in the Holy Spirit, who was in the times past promised to the church and duly bestowed at the appointed, favorable moment. He was promised by the prophet Joel but bestowed through Christ. "In the last days," says the prophet, "I will pour out from my spirit upon my servants and handmaids." And the Lord himself said, "Receive the Holy Spirit. If you forgive the sins of any, they are forgiven; if you retain the sins of any, they are retained."[40] ON THE TRINITY 29.[41]

2:30-31 Signs in the Heavens and on Earth

DO NOT MAKE THE SUN YOUR GOD.

CYRIL OF JERUSALEM: For just as man is said to perish, according to the text, "The just perishes, and no one takes it to heart,"[42] and this is said, though the resurrection is expected, so we look for a resurrection of the heavens. "The sun will be turned to darkness, and the moon to blood." Let the converts from the Manichaeans be instructed and no longer make the luminaries their gods or impiously think that this sun that is darkened is Christ. Listen to the Lord's words: "Heaven and earth will pass away, but my words will not pass away,"[43] for the master's creatures are less precious than his words. CATECHETICAL LECTURE 15.3.[44]

PAGAN MAGICIANS DO NOT CONTROL THE MOON.

EZNIK OF KOLB: True is the word of Scripture that says, "I will turn the sun into darkness and the moon into blood." It demonstrates that he is the Lord of the luminaries and of their lightening and darkening. This stands as a reproach to the sun worshipers and the moon worshipers. And there is no way for the moon to descend into the earth, as it has been claimed by magicians. It is God who commands the moon's light to appear bloody and its features demonic. The magicians prattle that they will cause the moon to descend—an impossibility! They imagine that something greater than many worlds can be contained in one little threshing floor and that one without breasts can be milked. And how many numberless thousands upon thousands of magicians are there on earth! If each one of them independently were capable of making the moon descend, it would never be allowed to ascend to the heavens. But that it never descends is clear because no one sees it descending or ascending. And if you are patient, you will become aware that right there, having become darkened, the moon becomes luminous little by little until entirely it is restored. ON GOD 315-16.[45]

CHRISTOLOGICAL MEANING OF THE SUN OF JUSTICE.

MAXIMUS OF TURIN: The people, then, call this day "the new sun," and although they say that it is new, yet they also show that it is old. This world's sun—which undergoes eclipse, is shut out by walls and is hidden by clouds—I would call old. I would call old the sun that is subject to vanity, is fearful of corruption and dreads the judgment. For it is written, "The sun will be changed into darkness and the moon into blood." Old, indeed, would I call that which is implicated in human crimes, does not flee adulteries, does not turn aside from murder and, although it does not wish to be in the midst of the human race when some offense is perpetrated,

---

[39]ANF 7:452. [40]Jn 20:23. [41]FC 67:99-100. [42]Is 57:1. [43]Mt 24:35. [44]FC 64:55-56. [45]EKOG 166-67*.

stands here alone among all the evil deeds. Therefore, inasmuch as it has been shown to be old, we have discovered that nothing is new but Christ the Lord, of whom it is written, "The Sun of justice will rise upon you"[46] and of whom the prophet also says in the person of sinners, "The sun has not risen upon us, and the light of justice has not shone upon us."[47] For when the whole world was oppressed by the darkness of the devil and the gloom brought on by sin was laying hold of the world, at the last age—that is to say, when night had already fallen—this sun deigned to bring forth the rising of his birth. At first, before the light—that is, before the Sun of justice shone—he sent the oracle of the prophets as a kind of dawning, as it is written: "I sent my prophets before the light."[48] But afterwards he himself burst forth with his rays—that is, with the brightness of his apostles—and shed upon the earth a light of truth such that no one would stumble into the devil's darkness. Sermon 62.2.[49]

End Times. Basil the Great: The Lord has already foretold that the signs of the dissolution of the universe will appear in the sun and moon and stars: "the sun shall be turned to blood, and the moon will not give its light."[50] These are the signs of the consummation of the world. Homilies on the Hexaemeron 6.4.[51]

2:32 Call on the Lord for Deliverance

Apostates Called Back. Ambrose: Return, then, to the church, those of you who have wickedly separated yourselves. For he promises forgiveness to all who are converted, since it is written, "Whosoever shall call on the name of the Lord shall be saved." And lastly, the Jewish people who said of the Lord Jesus, "He has a devil,"[52] and "He casts out devils through Beelzebub," and who crucified the Lord Jesus, are, by the preaching of Peter, called to baptism, that they may put away the guilt of so great a wickedness. Concerning Repentance 2.4.26.[53]

Warning Against Heresy. Augustine: But whether he or some partners of his error are with you—for they are too numerous to make it possible for us to hope they are not, and when they are not refuted they mislead others into their sect and increase so much that I do not know where they will break out next—we would rather see them cured in the body of the church than cut off from the body as rotten members, if necessity allows even that. We have to fear that others will be infected, if we spare their infection. But the mercy of our Lord is able rather to free them from disease, and no doubt he will do it if they note and hold faithfully to what is written: "Whoever shall call upon the name of the Lord shall be saved." Letter 157.[54]

Peter an Example of Humility. Basil the Great: Well then, someone will say, will the large number of Christians who do not keep all the commandments practice the observance of some of them in vain? In this connection, it is well to recall blessed Peter, who, after he had performed so many good actions and had been a recipient of such great blessings, was told, upon his being guilty of one lapse only: "If I do not wash you, you will have no part with me."[55] I shall not point out that his act bore no signs of indifference or contempt but was a demonstration of honor and reverence. But, someone might say, it is written, "Everyone who calls on the name of the Lord shall be saved." The Long Rules, Preface.[56]

Salvation to Jews and Gentiles. Augustine: When the holy apostle wished to show that the prophets had foretold the coming of those times when it should come to pass that all nations would believe in God, he cited the testimony that reads, "And it shall come to pass that everyone who calls on the name of the Lord shall be saved." For the name of God who has made

---

[46]Mal 4:2. [47]Wis 5:6. [48]Cf. Jer 7:25. [49]ACW 50:153. [50]An imprecise quote; cf. Joel 2:10; Mt 24:29. [51]FC 46:90. [52]Jn 7:40. [53]NPNF 2 10:348. [54]FC 20:339-40. [55]Jn 13:8. [56]FC 9:226-27.

heaven and earth used to be invoked among the Israelites only. The rest of the nations used to call upon deaf and dumb idols and were not heard by them; or they invoked demons and were heard to their own harm. "But when the fullness of time had come,"[57] then was fulfilled what had been foretold. "And it shall come to pass, that everyone who calls upon the name of the Lord shall be saved." Hence the Jews—even those of them who believed in Christ—begrudged the gospel of the Gentiles and maintained that the gospel of Christ ought not to be preached to the uncircumcised. SERMON 56.1.[58]

CUP OF MARTYRDOM. ORIGEN: Martyrdom is customarily called "the cup of salvation," as we find in the Gospel. For when those who wish to sit on Jesus' right and left in his kingdom yearn for so great an honor, the Lord says to them, "Are you able to drink the cup that I am to drink?"[59] By "cup" he means martyrdom; and the point is clear because of the verse, "Father, if it be possible, remove this cup from me; nevertheless, not as I will, but as you will."[60] We learn, moreover, that the person who drinks that cup which Jesus drank will sit with him and rule and judge with the King of kings. Thus this is the "cup of salvation," and when someone takes it, he will "call

upon the name of the Lord." For whoever calls upon the name of the Lord shall be saved.[61] EXHORTATION TO MARTYRDOM 28.[62]

2:28-32 The Coming of the Spirit

JOEL'S PROPHECY IS FULFILLED IN PENTECOST. THEODORE OF MOPSUESTIA: Blessed Peter used this text in speaking to Jews on the occasion of the descent of the Holy Spirit.[63] And rightly so, since the law contained a shadow of all things to come, whereas the people were granted care owing to the expectation of what would appear at the coming of Christ the Lord. What happened in their time was all insignificant and like a shadow, so that the account was given with use of hyperbole rather than containing facts. The reality of the account was found to be realized in the time of Christ the Lord, when everything was important and awesome, novel and really baffling, surpassing what had happened under the law to the greatest extent imaginable. COMMENTARY ON JOEL 2.28-32.[64]

---

[57]Gal 4:4; Eph 1:10. [58]FC 11:239. [59]Mt 20:22. [60]Mt 26:39; Mk 14:36. [61]See also Acts 2:21; Rom 10:13. [62]OSW 60. [63]Acts 2:16-21.

3:1-21 THE JUDGMENT OF THE LORD

[1d] "For behold, in those days and at that time, when I restore the fortunes of Judah and Jerusalem, [2]I will gather all the nations and bring them down to the valley of Jehoshaphat, and I will enter into judgment with them there, on account of my people and my heritage Israel, because they have scattered them among the nations, and have divided up my land, [3]and have cast lots for my people, and have given a boy for a harlot, and have sold a girl for wine, and have drunk it.

[4]"What are you to me, O Tyre and Sidon, and all the regions of Philistia? Are you paying me back for something? If you are paying me back, I will requite your deed upon your own head swiftly and speedily. [5]For you have taken my silver and my gold, and have carried my rich treasures into your temples.[e] [6]You have sold the people of Judah and Jerusalem to the Greeks, removing them far from

their own border. ⁷But now I will stir them up from the place to which you have sold them, and I will requite your deed upon your own head. ⁸I will sell your sons and your daughters into the hand of the sons of Judah, and they will sell them to the Sabeans,* to a nation far off; for the LORD has spoken."

⁹Proclaim this among the nations:
Prepare war,
   stir up the mighty men.
Let all the men of war draw near,
   let them come up.
¹⁰Beat your plowshares into swords,
   and your pruning hooks into spears;
   let the weak say, "I am a warrior."†

¹¹Hasten and come,
   all you nations round about,
   gather yourselves there.‡
Bring down thy warriors, O LORD.§
¹²Let the nations bestir themselves,
   and come up to the valley of Jehoshaphat;
for there I will sit to judge
   all the nations round about.

¹³Put in the sickle,
   for the harvest is ripe.
Go in, tread,
   for the wine press is full.
The vats overflow,
   for their wickedness is great.

¹⁴Multitudes, multitudes,
   in the valley of decision!
For the day of the LORD is near
   in the valley of decision.
¹⁵The sun and the moon are darkened,
   and the stars withdraw their
     shining.

¹⁶And the LORD roars from Zion,
   and utters his voice from Jerusalem,
   and the heavens and the earth shake.
But the LORD is a refuge to his people,
   a stronghold to the people of Israel.

¹⁷"So you shall know that I am the LORD
   your God,
   who dwell in Zion, my holy mountain.
And Jerusalem shall be holy
   and strangers shall never again pass
     through it.
¹⁸"And in that day
the mountains shall drip sweet wine,
   and the hills shall flow with milk,
and all the stream beds of Judah
   shall flow with water;
and a fountain shall come forth from the
     house of the LORD
   and water the valley of Shittim.#

¹⁹"Egypt shall become a desolation
   and Edom a desolate wilderness,
for the violence done to the people of
     Judah,
   because they have shed innocent blood in
     their land.
²⁰But Judah shall be inhabited for ever,
   and Jerusalem to all generations.
²¹I will avenge their blood, and I will not
     clear the guilty,ᵍ
   for the LORD dwells in Zion."

d Ch 4.1 in Heb. e Or palaces g Gk Syr: Heb I will hold innocent their blood which I have not held innocent *LXX into captivity †LXX I am strong ‡LXX gather yourselves together §LXX The one who suffers shall be a fighter #Heb. Shittim, literally acacia wood, tree; LXX schoinōn—rush, reed, cord; Vulgate thorns

OVERVIEW: A remnant shall be gathered in Jerusalem (JEROME). Those who return from captivity will know strength and peace (ISHO'DAD). God reveals consistently that his strength is made perfect through the weakness of human beings (JOHN CASSIAN). The valley of Johoshaphat will be the valley of judgment (ISHO'DAD). The cutting down of the prophet's sickle is applied to attack certain writings of Origen and his followers (THEOPHILUS). The once-sealed fountain becomes the abundant flowing waters of the river, a type of the ever-flowing consequences of the incarnation (JEROME).

3:1-2 The Fortunes of Judah

A REMNANT IN JERUSALEM. JEROME: For those who believe, salvation is in Mount Zion and Jerusalem. In the latter days, the Lord will gather the called remnant from the people of Judah, who with the apostles and through the apostles believed. He will return the captives of Judah to Jerusalem. He is the one who came to preach sight to the blind, forgiveness to the captives and freedom to those who confess the Lord and abide in the church, in which is the vision of peace. He will gather all the nations who are unwilling to believe, however, and throw them into the valley of Jehoshaphat. The Greek renders *kataxō*, which is true to the Hebrew, that is, "I will lead you downwards, and drag you down from the highest heights to the lowest depths." COMMENTARY ON JOEL 3:1.[1]

3:10-11 Implements Changed to Weapons

STRENGTH WILL RETURN. ISHO'DAD OF MERV: "Beat your plowshares," that is, change your farm implements into weapons. In fact, after coming back from captivity, they would have been poor, but then they would have acquired wealth at the expense of the house of Gog. COMMENTARY ON JOEL.[2]

STRENGTH IN WEAKNESS. JOHN CASSIAN: Whoever is protected by these weapons is always defended from the enemy's spears and devastation and will not be led as a captive and a slave, bound in the chains of the ravagers, to the territory of hostile thoughts. Nor will he hear through the prophet, "Why have you grown old in a foreign land?"[3] But he will live triumphant and victorious in that region of thoughts where he wanted to be.

Do you also want to understand the strength and fortitude of this centurion, by which he bears these weapons that we have spoken about and that are not carnal but powerful to God? Listen to the king himself and how he recruits the strong men that he gathers for his spiritual army, marking them and proving them: "Let the weak say," he says, "that I am strong." And, "The one who suffers shall be a fighter."[4] You see, then, that the Lord's battles can be fought only by the suffering and the weak. Indeed, certainly fixed in this weakness, our gospel centurion said with confidence, "When I am weak, then I am strong."[5] And again, "Strength is perfected in weakness."[6] One of the prophets says about this weakness, "The one who is weak is among them shall be as the house of David."[7] The patient sufferer shall also fight these battles with that patience of which it is said, "Patience is necessary for you so that you may do the will of God and receive a reward."[8] CONFERENCE 7.5.8-9.[9]

3:12 Judging All the Nations

THE VALLEY OF JUDGMENT. ISHO'DAD OF MERV: The words "come up to the valley of Jehoshaphat" will not gather them and bring them down, but he will let them accomplish their plan. In fact, he talks about the people over whom the house of Gog rules. "To the valley of Jehoshaphat," that is, to the valley of judgment. "Jehoshaphat" is interpreted as judgment and sentence. COMMENTARY ON JOEL.[10]

---

[1]CCL 76.1:198. [2]CSCO 303 (128):81. [3]Bar 3:10. [4]Joel 4:10, 11 LXX. [5]2 Cor 12:10. [6]2 Cor 12:9. [7]Zech 12:8 LXX. [8]Heb 10:36. [9]ACW 57:252-53. [10]CSCO 303 (128):80-81.

3:13 *The Harvest Is Ripe*

CERTAIN WRITINGS OF ORIGEN CONDEMNED.
THEOPHILUS: Theophilus, bishop, to the well-beloved and most loving brother, the presbyter Jerome. The reverend bishop Agatho with the well-beloved deacon Athanasius is accredited to you with tidings relating to the church. When you learn their import, I feel no doubt but that you will approve my resolution and will exult in the church's victory. For we have cut down with the prophet's sickle certain wicked fanatics who were eager to sow in the monasteries of Nitria the heresy of Origen. We have remembered the warning words of the apostle, "Rebuke with all authority."[11] Do you therefore on your part, as you hope to receive a share in this reward, make haste to bring back with scriptural discourses those who have been deceived. It is our desire, if possible, to guard in our days not only the Catholic faith and the rules of the church but also the people committed to our charge, and to eliminate all strange doctrines. LETTER 87.[12]

3:18 *A Fountain from the Lord's House*

THE FOUNTAIN SEALED BECOMES A TORRENT IN THE INCARNATION. JEROME: Christ himself is a virgin, and his mother is also a virgin; yes, though she is his mother, she is a virgin still. For Jesus has entered in through the closed doors,[13] and in his sepulcher—a new one hewn out of the hardest rock—no man is laid either before him or after him.[14] Mary is "a garden enclosed . . . a fountain sealed,"[15] and from that fountain flows, according to Joel, the river that waters the torrent bed either of cords or of thorns. The cords [are] those of the sins by which we were beforetime bound,[16] the thorns those which choked the seed the good man of the house had sown.[17] LETTERS 48.21.[18]

---

[11]Tit 2:15. Origen had argued that the stars have souls. [12]NPNF 2 6:183*. [13]Jn 20:19. [14]Jn 19:41. [15]Song 4:12. [16]Prov 5:22. [17]Mt 13:7. [18]NPNF 2 6:78.

A M O S

OVERVIEW: The meaning of the name Amos (Heb ʿāmôs) is unknown. The oracles were composed or delivered in Israel during the reign of Jeroboam II (786-746 B.C.), probably between 760 and 750 B.C., during a period of peace and prosperity. We know nothing of his personal life except that he is called in the book a shepherd of Tekoa in Judah (Amos 1:1), a shepherd and a dresser of figs (Amos 7:14). We also know that he was not a professional prophet or member of a guild of prophets (Amos 7:14). Rather, he seems to have answered a direct call from God. It is believed that most of the oracles were delivered at the shrine of Bethel, from which he was expelled by the priest Amaziah. The book holds the third place among the twelve prophets in the Hebrew and Latin Old Testaments and second in the Greek. Even so, the book is considered the oldest of the twelve. It is arranged into three major divisions: the judgment against the nations (Amos 1:3-2, 16), the discourses (Amos 3:1—6:13), and the visions (Amos 7:1—9:8) and conclusions (Amos 9:8-15).

The beauty and fluidity of Amos's language is captivating. This alone caused Augustine to point out that Amos, whom he believed to be but a rustic shepherd without any formal training, could have expressed himself with sophisticated human language only under the inspiration of the Holy Spirit. In Amos the church fathers were able to discover many analogies anticipating the crucifixion such as the rending of the temple veil, the subsequent earthquake, the darkening of the sun and the passion of Christ. As with the patristic interpretation of the other minor prophets, the destruction of the temple in A.D. 70 was a prophetic sign of monumental consequences, not the least of which was that it heralded the end of the old covenant and the inauguration of the new.

SUFFERINGS WOULD PREPARE THE JEWISH PEOPLE FOR SALVATION IN CHRIST. THEODORE OF MOPSUESTIA: The prophet Amos, on whom it is now our task to comment with the grace of God, speaks in almost all his prophecy of the fate that would befall the people. He reveals that the ten tribes would suffer first at the hands of the Assyrians, and this would affect Jerusalem and the tribe of Judah. Then the rest of that kingdom would suffer at the hands of the Babylonians. On the other hand, it was not without purpose that reference to this was made by the prophets. It was because God devoted complete attention to the people with a view to the manifestation of Christ the Lord, which would occur at a time of his choosing for the common salvation of all human beings. COMMENTARY ON AMOS, INTRODUCTION.[1]

AMOS WAS A CONTEMPORARY OF HOSEA AND JOEL. THEODORET OF CYR: He who by himself fashioned our hearts and understands all our doings, as the divine Scripture says,[2] and was aware of the hardness and obstinacy of the heart of Israel, does not speak to them through one prophet alone. Rather, he employs many remarkable men as ministers and thus offers exhortation and foretells the future, bringing out by the consensus of

a large number the reliability of the prophecies. Another of these is the divinely inspired Amos; he lived at the same time as the remarkable Hosea and Joel, and he prophesied the same things about both Assyrians and Babylonians, the return from there and what would happen after the return. After prophesying briefly against the neighboring races initially, he then began the prophecy about Israel. COMMENTARY ON AMOS, INTRODUCTION.[3]

---

[1]PG 66:241. [2]Ps 33:15. [3]PG 81:1663.

1:1-15 JUDGMENT ON ISRAEL'S NEIGHBORS

[1]*The words of Amos, who was among the shepherds of Tekoa, which he saw concerning Israel in the days of Uzziah king of Judah and in the days of Jeroboam the son of Joash, king of Israel, two years[a] before the earthquake.*
[2]*And he said:*
"The LORD roars from Zion,
and utters his voice from Jerusalem;
the pastures of the shepherds mourn,
and the top of Carmel withers."

[3]*Thus says the LORD:*
"For three transgressions of Damascus,
and for four, I will not revoke the
punishment;[b]
because they have threshed Gilead
with threshing sledges of iron.
[4]*So I will send a fire upon the house of*
Hazael,
and it shall devour the strongholds of
Benhadad.

[5]*I will break the bar of Damascus,*
and cut off the inhabitants from the
Valley of Aven,[c]
and him that holds the scepter from
Beth-eden;
and the people of Syria shall go into exile
to Kir,"
says the LORD.

[6]*Thus says the LORD:*
"For three transgressions of Gaza,
and for four, I will not revoke the
punishment;[b]
because they carried into exile a whole people
to deliver them up to Edom.
[7]*So I will send a fire upon the wall of Gaza,*
and it shall devour her strongholds.
[8]*I will cut off the inhabitants from Ashdod,*
and him that holds the scepter from
Ashkelon;
I will turn my hand against Ekron;

and the remnant of the Philistines shall
    perish,"
                                    says the Lord GOD.

⁹Thus says the LORD:
    "For three transgressions of Tyre,
        and for four, I will not revoke the
        punishment;ᵇ
    because they delivered up a whole people to
        Edom,
        and did not remember the covenant of
        brotherhood.
¹⁰So I will send a fire upon the wall of Tyre,
    and it shall devour her strongholds."

¹¹Thus says the LORD:
    "For three transgressions of Edom,
        and for four, I will not revoke the
        punishment;ᵇ
    because he pursued his brother with the
        sword,
        and cast off all pity,*

and his anger tore perpetually,
    and he kept his wrathᵈ for ever.
¹²So I will send a fire upon Teman,
    and it shall devour the strongholds of
    Bozrah."

¹³Thus says the LORD:
    "For three transgressions of the Ammonites,
        and for four, I will not revoke the
        punishment;ᵇ
    because they have ripped up women with
        child in Gilead,
        that they might enlarge their border.
¹⁴So I will kindle a fire in the wall of
    Rabbah,
        and it shall devour her strongholds,
    with shouting in the day of battle,
        with a tempest in the day of the
        whirlwind;
¹⁵and their king shall go into exile,
    he and his princes together,"
                                    says the LORD.

a Or *during two years* b Heb *cause it to return* c Or *On* d Gk Syr Vg: Heb *his wrath kept* *LXX *and violated his [own] womb*

OVERVIEW: The manner in which the new covenant was proclaimed through John the Baptist reveals that it was destined to Jews and Gentiles. The specific mention of Tiberius confirms the universal call of salvation (ORIGEN). The consequences of sin extend far beyond the individual person who enacts them. The text further applied to the Jews' rejection of Jesus as Messiah (JEROME). The child of Gilead is a prophetic testimony of heresies in the church. Being with child, conceiving or coming to full term is likened to the ministry of the church. It is also applied to the heretics who "rip up" the woman with child, the church, through their false teaching (GREGORY THE GREAT).

1:1 The Words of Amos

CONTEXTS OF THE PROPHETS AND THE GOSPEL. ORIGEN: When the prophetic word was sent only to the Jews, the names of Jewish kings were put in the headings of the prophecies. For example, "the vision that Isaiah, the son of Amoz, saw, against Judea and against Jerusalem, during the reign of Uzziah, Jotham, Ahaz and Hezekiah."[1] In the time of Isaiah, I see no one else named except the kings of Judah. In some prophets we also read the names of the kings of Israel, as in this instance: "And in the days of Jeroboam, the son of Joash, king of Israel." But then the mystery of the gospel was to be preached, and the gospel spread throughout the whole world. The initiator of that gospel was John, in the desert. The authority of Tiberius

[1]Is 1:1.

ruled the world. Then, "in [his] fifteenth year," it is recorded that "the word of the Lord came to John."[2] HOMILIES ON THE GOSPEL OF LUKE 21.1.[3]

1:3 Three Transgressions of Damascus

CONSEQUENCES OF HABITUAL SIN. JEROME: You must slay the allurements to vice while they are still only thoughts and dash the little ones of the daughter of Babylon against the stones[4] where the serpent can leave no trail. Be wary and lay claim to the Lord's promise: "Let them not have dominion over me: then shall I be upright and I shall be innocent from the great transgression."[5] For elsewhere also the Scripture testifies, "I will visit the iniquity of the fathers upon the children unto the third and fourth generation."[6] That is to say, God will not punish us at once for our thoughts and resolves but will send retribution upon their offspring or upon the evil deeds and habits of sin, which arise out of the offspring. As he says by the mouth of Amos, "For three transgressions of such and such a city and for four I will not turn away the punishment thereof." LETTER 8.[7]

1:13 Women with Child in Gilead

GILEAD A TYPE OF THE CHURCH AND HERETICS. GREGORY THE GREAT: The [false teachers] are also to be admonished to consider well, how sacred Scripture is set up as a kind of lantern for us in the night of this life. When the words are not rightly understood, darkness is the result. And obviously, their perverse mind would not hurry them into a false understanding unless they were first inflated with pride. For while they think themselves wiser than others, they scorn to follow others in matters which these understand better. What is more, in order that they may extort from the untutored crowd a reputation for knowledge, they make every endeavor to discredit what these rightly understand and to confirm their own perverse views. Therefore, it is well said by the prophet, "They have ripped up the women with child of Gilead to enlarge their border." Now Gilead is interpreted as meaning "a heap of testimony."[8] Since the whole congregation of the church together serves by its confession of it, as a witness to the truth, the church is not ineptly expressed as Gilead, for it witnesses to all truth concerning God by the mouth of all the faithful. But souls are said to be with child when they conceive an understanding of the Word by divine love, so that when they come to full term, they will bring forth the understanding conceived by them in showing forth their deeds. Again, "to enlarge the border" is to extend one's own reputation. Thus "they ripped up the women with child of Gilead to extend their border"—that is to say, heretics by their perverse preaching slay the minds of the faithful who have already conceived some measure of the understanding of truth, and so they extend their reputation for knowledge. The hearts of little ones, already big with conception of the Word, they cleave with the sword of error, and thereby make a reputation, as it were, for their teaching. When, therefore, we endeavor to instruct these people not to entertain perverse views, we must first admonish them not to seek their own interests. For if the root of pride is cut away, the branches of false assertions become withered. PASTORAL CARE 3.24.[9]

---

[2]Lk 3:1-2. [3]FC 94:88. [4]Ps 137:9 (136:9 LXX). [5]Ps 19:13 (18:14 LXX). [6]Num 14:18. [7]NPNF 2 6:266*. [8]Gen 31:47-48. [9]ACW 11:172-73.

AMOS 2:1-16 JUDGMENT ON ISRAEL

¹Thus says the Lord:
"For three transgressions of Moab,
     and for four, I will not revoke the
     punishment;ᵉ
because he burned to lime
     the bones of the king of Edom.
²So I will send a fire upon Moab,
     and it shall devour the strongholds of
     Kerioth,
and Moab shall die amid uproar,
     amid shouting and the sound of the
     trumpet;
³I will cut off the ruler from its midst,
     and will slay all its princes with him,"
                    says the Lord.

⁴Thus says the Lord:
"For three transgressions of Judah,
     and for four, I will not revoke the
     punishment;ᵉ
because they have rejected the law of the
     Lord,
     and have not kept his statutes,
but their lies have led them astray,
     after which their fathers walked.
⁵So I will send a fire upon Judah,
     and it shall devour the strongholds of
     Jerusalem."

⁶Thus says the Lord:
"For three transgressions of Israel,
     and for four, I will not revoke the
     punishment;ᵉ
because they sell the righteous for silver,
     and the needy for a pair of shoes—

⁷they that trample the head of the poor into
     the dust of the earth,
     and turn aside the way of the afflicted;
a man and his father go in to the same
     maiden,
     so that my holy name is profaned;
⁸they lay themselves down beside every altar
     upon garments taken in pledge;
and in the house of their God they drink
     the wine of those who have been fined.

⁹"Yet I destroyed the Amorite before them,
     whose height was like the height of the
     cedars,
     and who was as strong as the oaks;
I destroyed his fruit above,
     and his roots beneath.
¹⁰Also I brought you up out of the land of
     Egypt,
     and led you forty years in the wilderness,
     to possess the land of the Amorite.
¹¹And I raised up some of your sons for
     prophets,
     and some of your young men for
     Nazirites.
     Is it not indeed so, O people of Israel?"
                    says the Lord.

¹²"But you made the Nazirites drink wine,
     and commanded the prophets,
     saying, 'You shall not prophesy.'

¹³"Behold, I will press you down in your
     place,
     as a cart full of sheaves presses down.*

¹⁴*Flight shall perish from the swift,*
and the strong shall not retain his
strength,
nor shall the mighty save his life;
¹⁵*he who handles the bow shall not stand,*
and he who is swift of foot shall not save
himself,

nor shall he who rides the horse save his
life;
¹⁶*and he who is stout of heart among the*
mighty
shall flee away naked in that day,"
says the LORD.

e Heb *cause it to return*   *Vulgate Behold, I will shriek over you as a cart creaks laden with hay.*

OVERVIEW: Amos foretold the betrayal of Christ by Judas even in the allusion of the silver pieces (TERTULLIAN). The fact that Scripture is silent about certain sexual relations does not mean it gives license to commit them (BASIL). Religious officials betrayed justice toward the poor (THE-ODORE). The testimony of the prophets is consistent in its condemnation of idolatry and every form of divination (CYRIL OF JERUSALEM). Priests in the old covenant who did not live up to their vocation were punished more severely and serve as a warning for the priests of the new covenant (CHRYSOSTOM). Many of the chosen people of God in both covenants were those who prayed, fasted and abstained from wine and strong drink. The people are reproached for giving Nazirites wine to drink (JEROME). Metaphors of unlikely resemblances to God point to God's majesty (GREGORY THE GREAT).

2:6 Selling the Righteous for Silver

PROPHECY ABOUT JUDAS. TERTULLIAN: He might also have been betrayed by any stranger, did I not find that even here too he fulfilled a psalm: "He who did eat bread with me has lifted up his heel against me."[1] And without a price might he have been betrayed. For what need of a traitor was there in the case of one who offered himself to the people openly and might quite as easily have been captured by force as taken by treachery? This might, no doubt, have been well enough for another Christ but would not have been suitable in one who was accomplishing

prophecies. For it was written, "The righteous one did they sell for silver." The very amount and the destination of the money, which on Judas's remorse was recalled "from its first purpose of a fee" and appropriated to the purchase of a potter's field, as narrated in the Gospel of Matthew, were clearly foretold by Jeremiah: "And they took the thirty pieces of silver, the price of him who was valued, and gave them for the potter's field."[2] AGAINST MARCION 40.[3]

2:7 Forbidden Sexual Relationships

FORNICATIONS CONDEMNED. BASIL THE GREAT: The example of the patriarch seemed injurious to many who indulged their flesh so far as to live with sisters in their lifetime. What ought to be my course? To quote the Scriptures, or to work out what they leave unsaid? In the Pentateuch, it is not written that a father and son ought not to have the same concubine, but in the prophet, it is thought deserving of the most extreme condemnation. "A man and his father," it is said, "will go in unto the same maid." It makes one reflect upon how many other forms of unclean lust have been found out in the devil's school, while divine Scripture remains silent about them, not choosing to befoul its dignity with the names of filthy things and condemning their uncleanness in general terms! Recall that

[1]Ps 41:9 (40:10 LXX).   [2]Following Mt 27:9, Tertullian refers to Jeremiah, even though the passage is found in Zech 11:12-13. There is, however, a parallel in Jer 32:7-15.   [3]ANF 3:418.

the apostle Paul says, "Fornication and all uncleanness . . . let it not be one named among you as become saints."[4] This includes the unspeakable doings of both males and females under the name of uncleanness. It follows that silence certainly does not give license to voluptuaries. LETTER 3.[5]

JUSTICE AND MERCY FORSAKEN. THEODORE OF MOPSUESTIA: They so multiplied their ill-gotten gains as to betray the rights of the needy for the basest profit (the meaning of the phrase "sandals trampling the dust of the earth," which was clear proof of their setting no store by justice, especially as they easily did so for base profit). "They pummeled the heads of the poor." Of the same people he says that they not only failed to vindicate their claim on justice but even belabored them without risk—hence his going on, "and strayed from the path of the lowly." Though their behavior was correct, they changed the verdict to a negative one, scorning them for their lowliness. COMMENTARY ON AMOS 2.6-8.[6]

2:8 Laying Down Beside Every Altar

SEXUAL IMPURITIES OCCUR IN THE TEMPLE. CYRIL OF JERUSALEM: Cain was the first murderer. Afterwards a deluge engulfed the earth because of the exceeding wickedness of humanity. Fire came down from heaven upon the people of Sodom because of their corruption. Subsequently God elected Israel, but even Israel became perverse, and the chosen people were wounded. For while Moses stood on the mountain before God, the people worshiped a calf in the place of God. In the days of their lawgiver Moses, who said, "You shall not commit adultery," a man dared to enter a brothel and be wanton. After Moses, prophets were sent to heal Israel, but in their exercise of healing they deplored the fact that you could not overcome evil. One of them says, "The faithful are gone from the earth. Among men the upright are no more!"[7] and again, "All alike have gone astray; they have become perverse; there is not one who does good, not even one."[8] And

again, "Cursing and theft, and adultery, and killing have overflowed"[9] upon the land. "They sacrificed their sons and daughters to demons."[10] They engaged themselves in auguries and enchantments and divinations; and again, "They fastened their garments with cords and hung veils next to the altar." CATECHETICAL LECTURE 12.6.[11]

2:11 Sons Raised for Prophets

THE PRIEST'S WOUNDS REQUIRE GREATER HELP. CHRYSOSTOM: [This was the reason why] the Lord accused the Israelites more severely and showed that they deserved greater punishment, because they sinned after receiving the honors that he had bestowed on them. He said, "You only have I known of all the families of the earth; therefore I will visit upon you your iniquities,"[12] and again, "I took of your sons for prophets and of your young men for consecration."[13] And before the time of the prophets, when he wanted to show that sins received a much heavier penalty when they were committed by the priests than when they were committed by ordinary people, he commanded as great a sacrifice to be offered for the priests as for all the people.[14] This explicitly proves that the priest's wounds require greater help, indeed as much as those of all the people together. They would not have required greater help if they had not been more serious, and their seriousness is not increased by their own nature but by the extra weight of dignity belonging to the priest who dares to commit them. ON THE PRIESTHOOD 6.10.[15]

2:12 Nazirites Made to Drink Wine

ABSTINENCE A SIGN OF THOSE CALLED BY GOD. JEROME: Samson and Samuel drank neither wine nor strong drink, for they were children of promise and conceived in abstinence and fasting.

---

[4]Eph 5:3. [5]NPNF 2 8:213*. [6]PG 66:257. [7]Mic 7:2. [8]Ps 14:3 (13:3 LXX). [9]Hos 4:2. [10]Ps 106:37 (105:37 LXX). [11]FC 61:230-31. [12]Amos 3:2. [13]Amos 3:11 LXX. [14]Lev 4:3, 14. [15]COP 151.

Aaron and the other priests when about to enter the temple refrained from all intoxicating drink for fear they should die.[16] From this we learn that they die who minister in the church without sobriety. And hence it is a reproach against Israel: "You gave my Nazirites wine to drink." AGAINST JOVINIANUS 2.15.[17]

2:13 God Shrieks Like a Laden Cart

GOD ENDURES THE LIFE OF THE CARNAL. GREGORY THE GREAT: He sometimes compares himself with deep condescension, on account of our infirmity, to objects without sense, as he says by the prophet, "Behold, I will shriek over you as a cart creaks when laden with hay." For since the life of the carnal is hay (as it is written, all flesh is hay),[18] in that the Lord endures the life of the carnal he declares that he carries hay as a cart. And to creak under the weight of the hay is for him to bear with murmuring the burdens and iniquities of sinners. When therefore he applies to himself very unlike resemblances, we must carefully observe that some things of this kind are sometimes spoken of concerning God, on account of the effect of his doings, but sometimes to indicate the substance of his majesty. MORALS ON THE BOOK OF JOB 6.32.7.[19]

---

[16]Lev 10:9.   [17]NPNF 2 6:400*.   [18]Is 40:6.   [19]LF 31:514-15*.

3:1-15 CHARGES AGAINST ISRAEL

[1]Hear this word that the LORD has spoken against you, O people of Israel, against the whole family which I brought up out of the land of Egypt:
[2]"You only have I known
    of all the families of the earth;
therefore I will punish you
    for all your iniquities.

[3]"Do two walk together,
    unless they have made an appointment?
[4]Does a lion roar in the forest,
    when he has no prey?
Does a young lion cry out from his den,
    if he has taken nothing?
[5]Does a bird fall in a snare on the earth,
    when there is no trap for it?
Does a snare spring up from the ground,
    when it has taken nothing?

[6]Is a trumpet blown in a city,
    and the people are not afraid?
Does evil befall a city,
    unless the LORD has done it?
[7]Surely the Lord GOD does nothing,
    without revealing his secret
    to his servants the prophets.
[8]The lion has roared;
    who will not fear?
The Lord GOD has spoken;
    who can but prophesy?"

[9]Proclaim to the strongholds in Assyria,[f]
    and to the strongholds in the land of
        Egypt,
and say, "Assemble yourselves upon the
        mountains of Samaria,*
    and see the great tumults within her,
    and the oppressions in her midst."

10"They do not know how to do right," says
  the LORD,
  "those who store up violence and robbery
  in their strongholds."
11Therefore thus says the Lord GOD:
"An adversary shall surround the land,
  and bring down your defenses from you,
  and your strongholds shall be plundered."

12Thus says the LORD: "As the shepherd
rescues from the mouth of the lion two legs, or
a piece of an ear, so shall the people of Israel
who dwell in Samaria be rescued, with the
corner of a couch and part[g] of a bed."

13"Hear, and testify against the house of
  Jacob,"
  says the Lord GOD, the God of hosts,
14"that on the day I punish Israel for his
  transgressions,
  I will punish the altars of Bethel,
and the horns of the altar shall be cut off
  and fall to the ground.
15I will smite the winter house with the
  summer house;
  and the houses of ivory shall perish,
and the great houses[h] shall come to an end,"
  says the LORD.

f Gk: Heb Ashdod   g The meaning of the Hebrew word is uncertain   h Or many houses   *LXX on Mount Samaria

OVERVIEW: On the day of judgment everyone will be included (ORIGEN). God is a merciful physician who chastens those whom he loves (JEROME). No punishment or evil is imposed upon us without God's will and purpose (THEODORET). There does exist that form of evil that is harmful and leads to punishment. There is also evil that leads rather to good, holy zeal and spiritual awakening (CHRYSOSTOM). The judgment of God is not the same as that form of evil that is to us painful but may heal (JOHN OF DAMASCUS). The lion here represents the passions that try to lure a believer away from God. If human beings can tame lions, God can tame human beings (AUGUSTINE). Even if the lion appears to have devoured all but two legs and the tip of an ear, it is not too late for Christ the good Shepherd to deliver the contrite if they turn to him (BASIL). The names of God reveal his character (GREGORY OF NAZIANZUS).

3:2 Punishment for Sins

JUDGMENT DAY WILL ADDRESS ISRAEL'S INIQUITIES. ORIGEN: And each of us thinks, since he has not been an idolater, since he has not

been immoral—would that we were pure in such areas—that after he has been set free from this life, he will be saved. We do not see that "all of us must appear before the judgment seat of Christ, so that each one may receive either good or evil according to what he has done in the body."[1] We do not hear what has been said: "You especially have I known out of all the tribes on the earth. Therefore I will punish you for all"—not just some and not others—"of your iniquities." HOMILIES ON JEREMIAH 20.3.[2]

THE PAINFUL DIVINE TREATMENT. JEROME: The most merciful physician, cutting away the cancerous flesh, spares not in order to spare; he pities not in order to pity the more. For whom the Lord loves he chastens, and he scourges every son whom he receives. COMMENTARY ON EZEKIEL 7.[3]

3:3-5 Does a Lion Roar When It Has No Prey?

NO PUNISHMENT IMPOSED WITHOUT GOD'S WILL. THEODORET OF CYR: As it is impossible

[1]2 Cor 5:10. [2]FC 97:227-28. [3]PMPC 1:271*.

for two people to share a journey at the same time, he is saying, unless indicating to each other where and why they are traveling, or for a lion to roar if there is no prey, or for a bird to fall without a hunter, or for all the other things mentioned, so it is impossible for any punishment to be imposed without God willing it. He calls punishment "evil," note, by use of a general custom: we are accustomed to use "troubles" of diseases, chastisements, untimely deaths, famines, wars, and the like, not because they are troublesome by nature but because they are troublesome to human beings and the source of distress and grief. COMMENTARY ON AMOS 3.6-8.[4]

3:6 Unless the Lord Has Done It

TWO FORMS OF EVIL EXPLAINED. CHRYSOSTOM: I do not say these things in arrogance, but I have the prophet Amos standing at my side, crying and saying, "There is no evil in the city which the Lord has not done." Now evil is a many-faceted term. I wish that you shall learn the exact meaning of each expression, in order that on account of ambiguity you may not confound the nature of the things and fall into blasphemy. There is then evil, which is really evil; fornication, adultery, covetousness, and the countless dreadful things, which are worthy of the utmost reproach and punishment. Again there is evil, which rather is not evil but is called so, famine, pestilence, death, disease, and other of a similar nature. For these would not be evils. On this account I said they are called so only. Why then? Because, were they evils intended to become the sources of good to us, chastening our pride, goading our sloth and leading us on to zeal, making us more attentive. HOMILY AGAINST THOSE WHO SAY THAT DEMONS GOVERN HUMAN AFFAIRS 1.4-5.[5]

GOD NOT THE AUTHOR OF EVIL. JOHN OF DAMASCUS: It is, then, customary for sacred Scripture to speak of his permission as an action and deed, but even when it goes so far as to say that God "creates evil" and that "there is not evil in a city which the Lord has not done," it still does not show God to be the author of evil. On the contrary, since the word *evil* is ambiguous it has two meanings, for it sometimes means what is by nature evil, being the opposite of virtue and against God's will, while at other times it means what is evil and painful in relation to our sensibility, which is to say, tribulation and distress. Now while these last seem to be evil, because they cause pain, actually they are good because to such as understand them they are a source of conversion and salvation. It is these last that Scripture says are permitted by God. Moreover, one must know that we too cause them because involuntary evils spring from voluntary ones. ORTHODOX FAITH 4.20.[6]

3:8 The Lion Roars

MORE POWERFUL THAN THE LION. AUGUSTINE: "Lord, you have been our refuge."[7] Therefore we have recourse to you. Our healing shall be from you, for our evil is from ourselves. Because we have abandoned you, you have abandoned us to ourselves. May we therefore be found in you, for in ourselves we had been lost. "Lord, you have been our refuge." Why, my brethren, should we doubt that the Lord will make us gentle if we submit ourselves to be tamed by him? You have tamed the lion, which you did not create. Will your Creator be unable to tame you? What is the source of your power to tame such savage beasts? Are you their equal in bodily strength? By what power then have you been able to tame such huge beasts? The so-called beasts of burden are wild by nature, for if untamed they could not be endured. But because you are not accustomed to see them except when handled by men and under the curb and control of men, you might think that they were born tame. At any rate, consider the savage beasts. The lion roars; who does not fear? And yet, whence your knowledge of the fact that you are more powerful? Not in bodily strength but in

---

[4]PG 81:1677. [5]NPNF 1 9:182*. [6]FC 37:384-85. [7]Deut 33:27; 2 Sam 22:3; Ps 9:9 (9:10 LXX); 46:1 (45:1 LXX); 71:7 (70:7 LXX); Jer 16:19.

the inner reason of the mind. You are more powerful than a lion, because you have been made to the image of God. The image of God tames a wild beast. Is God unable to tame his own image? SERMON 55.3.[8]

3:12 Fragments Rescued

DO NOT DESPAIR OF SALVATION. BASIL THE GREAT: If, then, any hope of salvation is still left to you, if any slight remembrance of God, if any desire for future rewards, if any fear of the punishments reserved for the unrepentant come back quickly to sobriety; raise your eyes to the heavens; return to your senses; cease your wickedness; shake off the drunkenness that has drenched you; stand up against him who has overthrown you. Have the strength to rise up from the earth. Remember the good Shepherd, how he will pursue and deliver you. And if there are but "two legs, or the tip of an ear," leap back from him who has wounded you. Remember the compassion of God, how he heals with olive oil and wine. Do not despair of salvation. Recall the memory of what has been written, how he that falls rises again, and he that is turned away turns again,[9] he that has been smitten is healed, he that is caught by wild beasts escapes, and he that confesses is not rejected. The Lord does not wish the death of the sinner, but that he return and live.[10] Do not be contemptuous[11] as one who has fallen into the depths of sins. LETTER 44, TO A FALLEN MONK.[12]

3:13 The God of Hosts

NAMES OF GOD REVEAL GOD'S POWER AND ORDERING OF THE WORLD. GREGORY OF NAZIANZUS: God's other titles fall into two distinct groups. The first group belongs to his power, the second to his providential ordering of the world, a twofold providential ordering—involving, and not involving, incarnation. Clear cases of titles that belong to his power are "Almighty" and "King"—whether it be of "glory,"[13] "the ages,"[14] "of the forces,"[15] or "of the beloved" or the "rulers"[16] —"Lord Sabbaoth,"[17] which means "lord of the armies," "forces"[18] or "masters."[19] To his providential ordering belong "God"—be it "of salvation,"[20] "retribution,"[21] "peace,"[22] or "righteousness,"[23] or "of Abraham, Isaac and Jacob"[24] or all the spiritual "Israel,"[25] which has the vision of God.[26] For since we are controlled by three conditions—fear of punishment, hope for salvation and glory too, and the practice of the virtues which results in these last—the name which mentions retribution deals with fear, the one which mentions salvation with hope, and that which refers to virtues disciplines us to practice them. The intention is that by, as it were, carrying God inside one,[27] a person may have some success here and press on all the harder to perfection, toward that affinity with God which comes from the virtues. ON THE SON, THEOLOGICAL ORATION 4(30).19.[28]

---

[8]FC 11:234-35*. [9]Jer 8:4. [10]Ezek 18:32. [11]Prov 18:3. [12]FC 13:113-14. [13]Ps 24:10 (23:10 LXX). [14]1 Tim 1:17. [15]Dan 11:38. [16]1 Tim 6:15. [17]Is 1:9; Rom 9:29. [18]Dan 11:38. [19]1 Tim 6:15; Deut 10:17. [20]Ps 68:20 (67:21 LXX). [21]Ps 94:1 (93:1 LXX). [22]Rom 15:33. [23]Ps 4:1. [24]Ex 3:6. [25]Rom 9:6-8; 11:26; Gal 6:16. [26]Gen 32:30. [27]1 Cor 6:19-20. [28]FGFR 274; NPNF 2 7:316.

4:1-13 DIVINE SENTENCE

[1]"Hear this word, you cows of Bashan,
 who are in the mountain of Samaria,
 who oppress the poor, who crush the needy,

 who say to their husbands, 'Bring, that
 we may drink!'
[2]The Lord GOD* has sworn by his holiness

that, behold, the days are coming upon you,
 when they shall take you away with hooks,
  even the last of you with fishhooks.
³And you shall go out through the breaches,
 every one straight before her;
  and you shall be cast forth into Harmon,"
         says the LORD.

⁴"Come to Bethel, and transgress;
 to Gilgal, and multiply transgression;
bring your sacrifices every morning,
 your tithes every three days;
⁵offer a sacrifice of thanksgiving of that
  which is leavened,
 and proclaim freewill offerings, publish
  them;
 for so you love to do, O people of Israel!"
       says the Lord GOD.

⁶"I gave you cleanness of teeth in all your
  cities,
 and lack of bread in all your places,
yet you did not return to me,"
         says the LORD.

⁷"And I also withheld the rain from you
 when there were yet three months to the
  harvest;
I would send rain upon one city,
 and send no rain upon another city;
one field would be rained upon,
 and the field on which it did not rain
  withered;
⁸so two or three cities wandered to one city
 to drink water, and were not satisfied;
yet you did not return to me,"
         says the LORD.

⁹"I smote you with blight and mildew;
 I laid waste[i] your gardens and your
  vineyards;
 your fig trees and your olive trees the
  locust devoured;
yet you did not return to me,"
         says the LORD.

¹⁰"I sent among you a pestilence after the
  manner of Egypt;
 I slew your young men with the sword;
I carried away your horses;[j]
 and I made the stench of your camp go up
  into your nostrils;
yet you did not return to me,"
         says the LORD.

¹¹"I overthrew some of you,
 as when God overthrew Sodom and
  Gomorrah,
 and you were as a brand plucked out of
  the burning;
yet you did not return to me,"
         says the LORD.

¹²"Therefore thus I will do to you, O Israel;
 because I will do this to you,
  prepare to meet your God, O Israel!"

¹³For lo, he who forms the mountains, and
  creates the wind,
 and declares to man what is his
  thought;
who makes the morning darkness,
 and treads on the heights of the earth—
the LORD, the God of hosts, is his name![†]

---

i Cn: Heb *the multitude of* j Heb *with the captivity of your horses* *LXX omits *the Lord* †LXX *For, behold, I am he that strengthens the thunder and creates the wind, and proclaims to men his Christ, forming the morning and the darkness, and mounting on the high places of the earth, the Lord God Almighty is his name.*

OVERVIEW: Under the old covenant, unleavened bread symbolizes virtuous deeds, whereas sin corrupts the bread of a good life (GREGORY THE GREAT). One city receives rain while the other does not. These cities represent typologically a life of virtue or vice. The rain is God's Spirit. The bishop of Arles challenges believers to choose which city they would like to live in (CAESARIUS). Those who refuse to repent face the same fate as those who were destroyed by God in Sodom and Gomorrah (JOHN CASSIAN). The destruction of Sodom and Gomorrah serves as a warning to those who do not repent of sin. Moreover, it was Christ who destroyed the cities revealing his role as judge (NOVATIAN). Ambrose corrects those who use Amos's description of the spirit as wind to argue against the personhood of the Holy Spirit. Instead, it seems to be a foretelling of the incarnation (AMBROSE). The prophets foretelling the coming of Christ is in a long line of Old Testament prophetic utterances by Moses, Isaiah and Jeremiah (CYRIL OF JERUSALEM).

4:4 Multiplying Transgressions

GOD'S GIFT REQUIRES OUR RESPONSE.
GREGORY THE GREAT: It is not enough to make a true solemnity of the heart. From this must follow good works. What value is there in partaking of his body and blood with our mouths if we oppose him with our wicked practices? And so Moses required that "unleavened bread with wild herbs" is to be eaten. One who eats bread without leaven does virtuous deeds without corrupting them with vainglory, and fulfills the precepts of mercy with no addition of sin, not perversely destroying what he properly accomplishes. In reproof of some who had mingled the leaven of sin with their good deeds, the Lord spoke by the voice of the prophet: "Come to Bethel and behave wickedly," and shortly after, "And make a sacrifice of praise of that which is unleavened." A person makes a sacrifice of praise of that which is unleavened when he makes ready a sacrifice for God of his misdeeds. Wild herbs are very bitter. The flesh of the lamb is to be eaten with wild herbs, so that when we receive our Redeemer's body we humble ourselves with weeping for our sins. Thus the bitterness of repentance purges our heart's stomach of all traces of a wicked life. FORTY GOSPEL HOMILIES 22.[1]

4:7 Rain Withheld

LET THE WORD RAIN. CAESARIUS OF ARLES: If we cannot gather spiritual fruits through our own labor, it is just that we dispense with holy zeal and most fervent charity those which have been collected by others. Since the Lord threatens that, because of the sins of the people, "I will cause it to rain upon one city and cause it not to rain upon another city," we ought to strive with great care that we may not be that city upon which the rain of the Word of God either does not come at all or, at least, only late and rarely. Without any doubt, if the dew or rain of the Word of God is provided too late, the fruits of souls will be the same as earthly fruits which do not receive rain. SERMON 1.15.[2]

4:11 Overthrown Like Sodom and Gomorrah

RECALCITRANT SIN. JOHN CASSIAN: They [who refuse to repent] do not deserve to be saved by the Lord's visitation or to be healed by temporal afflictions. They are like those "who in despair have handed themselves over to lasciviousness in the working of every error, unto uncleanness."[3] In their hardness of heart and with their frequent habit of sinning, they are beyond the purgation of this very brief age and the punishment of the present life. The divine Word reproves them too through the prophet: "I have destroyed you as God destroyed Sodom and Gomorrah, and you have become like a firebrand snatched from the fire, and not even thus have you returned to me, says the Lord." CONFERENCE 6.11.6.[4]

---

[1]CS 123:170-71*. [2]FC 31:17. [3]Eph 4:19. [4]ACW 57:229*.

WHETHER THE FATHER OR THE SON OVER-THREW SODOM AND GOMORRAH. NOVATIAN: And that there might not remain any doubt that he [God the Son] had been the guest of Abraham, it is written regarding the destruction of the Sodomites that "the Lord poured down on Sodom and Gomorrah fire and sulfur from the Lord out of heaven."[5] In fact, the prophet also says in the person of God, "I destroyed you as the Lord destroyed Sodom and Gomorrah." The Lord, therefore, destroyed Sodom; that is, God destroyed Sodom. In the destruction of the Sodomites, however, it was the Lord who rained fire from the Lord. This Lord was the God seen by Abraham.[6] This God is Abraham's guest[7] and was undoubtedly seen because he was touched. Now, since the Father, inasmuch as he is invisible, was assuredly not seen at that time, he who was seen and who was hospitably received and taken in was he who was willing to be seen and touched. This one then is the Son of God, "the Lord, who rained upon Sodom and Gomorrah fire and sulfur from the Lord."[8] But he is the Word of God, and the "Word" of God "was made flesh and dwelt among us."[9] This one then is Christ. Therefore it was not the Father who was the guest of Abraham but Christ. Nor was it the Father who was seen but the Son; therefore it was Christ who was seen. Consequently Christ is both Lord and God, who could be seen by Abraham only because he was God, the Word, begotten of God the Father before Abraham even existed.[10] ON THE TRINITY 18.15-17.[11]

4:13 The Creator of Mountains and Wind

NOT REDUCIBLE TO WIND. AMBROSE: Nor does it escape my notice that heretics have been prone to object that the Holy Spirit appears to be a creature, because many of them use as an argument for establishing their impiety that passage of Amos, where he spoke of the blowing of the wind, as the words of the prophet made clear. For you read thus: "Behold, I am he that establishes the thunder and creates the wind and declare unto man his Christ, that make light and mist,

and ascend upon high places, the Lord God Almighty is his name." ON THE HOLY SPIRIT 2.6.48.[12]

THE ONE WHO ESTABLISHES THE THUNDER IS REVEALED IN CHRIST. AMBROSE: But if any one thinks that the word of the prophet is to be explained with reference to the Holy Spirit, because it is said, "declaring unto men his Christ," he will explain it more easily of the Lord's Sun of justice. For if it troubles you that he said Spirit, and therefore you think that this cannot well be explained of the mystery of the taking of human nature, read on in the Scriptures, and you will find that all agrees most excellently with Christ. Of [Christ] it is thoroughly fitting to think that he established the thunders by his coming, that is, the force and sound of the heavenly Scriptures, by the thunder, as it were, of which our minds are struck with astonishment, so that we learn to be afraid and pay respect to the heavenly oracles. ON THE HOLY SPIRIT 2.6.54.[13]

CHRIST FORESEEN BY AMOS. CYRIL OF JERUSALEM: When Christ came, the people of the old covenant denied him,[14] but the devils confessed him.[15] His forefather David was not ignorant of him when he said, "I will place a lamp for my anointed."[16] Some have interpreted "lamp" as the splendor of prophecy; others have understood by the lamp the flesh he assumed of the Virgin, according to the words of the apostle: "But we carry this treasure in vessels of clay."[17] The prophet was not ignorant of him when he said, "And declaring his Christ to men." Moses also knew him, and Isaiah and Jeremiah as well. None of the prophets was ignorant of him. Even the devils acknowledged him, for he rebuked them, and Scripture adds, "Because they knew that he was the Christ."[18] CATECHETICAL LECTURE 10.15.[19]

---

[5]Gen 19:24. [6]Gen 12:7; 18:1. [7]Gen 18:3-8. [8]Gen 19:24. [9]Jn 1:14. [10]Jn 8:58. [11]FC 67:70-71. [12]NPNF 2 10:120*. [13]NPNF 2 10:121. [14]Jn 19:5-6. [15]Lk 4:41. [16]Ps 132:17 (131:17 LXX). [17]2 Cor 4:7. [18]Lk 4:41. [19]FC 61:205.

5:1-17 LAMENT AND CALL FOR REPENTANCE

¹Hear this word which I take up over you in lamentation, O house of Israel:
²"Fallen, no more to rise,
   is the virgin Israel;
forsaken on her land,
   with none to raise her up.

³For thus says the Lord GOD:
"The city that went forth a thousand
   shall have a hundred left,
and that which went forth a hundred
   shall have ten left
   to the house of Israel."

⁴For thus says the LORD to the house of
   Israel:
"Seek me and live;
   ⁵but do not seek Bethel,
and do not enter into Gilgal
   or cross over to Beer-sheba;
for Gilgal shall surely go into exile,
   and Bethel shall come to nought."

⁶Seek the LORD and live,
   lest he break out like fire in the house of
   Joseph,
   and it devour, with none to quench it for
   Bethel,
⁷O you who turn justice to wormwood,
   and cast down righteousness to the earth!

⁸He who made the Pleiades and Orion,
   and turns deep darkness into the
   morning,
   and darkens the day into night,

who calls for the waters of the sea,
   and pours them out upon the surface of
   the earth,
the LORD is his name,
⁹who makes destruction flash forth against
   the strong,
   so that destruction comes upon the
   fortress.

¹⁰They hate him who reproves in the gate,
   and they abhor him who speaks the
   truth.
¹¹Therefore because you trample upon the
   poor
   and take from him exactions of wheat,
you have built houses of hewn stone,
   but you shall not dwell in them;
you have planted pleasant vineyards,
   but you shall not drink their wine.
¹²For I know how many are your
   transgressions,
   and how great are your sins—
you who afflict the righteous, who take a
   bribe,
   and turn aside the needy in the gate.
¹³Therefore he who is prudent will keep
   silent in such a time;
   for it is an evil time.

¹⁴Seek good, and not evil,
   that you may live;
and so the LORD, the God of hosts, will be
   with you,
   as you have said.
¹⁵Hate evil, and love good,*

and establish justice in the gate;
it may be that the LORD, the God of hosts,
    will be gracious to the remnant of Joseph.

[16]Therefore thus says the LORD, the God of
    hosts, the Lord:
"In all the squares there shall be
    wailing;

and in all the streets they shall say, 'Alas!
    alas!'
They shall call the farmers to mourning
    and to wailing those who are skilled in
    lamentation,
[17]and in all vineyards there shall be wailing,
    for I will pass through the midst of you,"
                                    says the LORD.

*LXX We have hated evil, and loved good.

OVERVIEW: Virginity serves as a type for the Christian's faithfulness (JEROME). Seek the Lord and live, for the end of the world is at hand. Believe, and you will receive the reward of eternal life (CYPRIAN). God's mercy and grace are revealed in his willingness to forgive sinners who have repented. God's creative power in creation also reveals his ability to change the hearts of humans (CHRYSOSTOM). Water is employed here metaphysically to describe the abundant grace that God pours out upon the human race (PAULUS OROSIUS). The elder and younger sons were a type of Jew and Christian, respectively. Jews resist the view that Christians have now been adopted as the new "elect" of the new covenant (TERTULLIAN). The words of the prophet admonish believers to seek God's goodness. God is the highest good that humans must seek. He is patiently awaiting the repentance of those whom he constantly calls. The prophet's cry to seek the good is in reference to Christ who is the fullness of God bodily (AMBROSE). Justice at the gate prevented quarrels inside the city (GREGORY THE GREAT).

5:2 The Virgin Israel Is Fallen

VIRGINS A TYPE OF BEING FAITHFUL. JEROME: If, then, the apostle, who was a chosen vessel[1] separated unto the gospel of Christ,[2] by reason of the pricks of the flesh and the allurements of vice keeps his body and brings it into subjection, lest when he has preached to others he may himself be a cast away;[3] and yet, for all that, sees another

law in his members warring against the law of his mind, and bringing him into captivity to the law of sin;[4] if after nakedness, fasting, hunger, imprisonment, scourging and other torments, he turns back to himself and cries, "Oh, wretched man that I am, who shall deliver me from the body of this death?"[5] do you fancy that you ought to lay aside apprehension? See to it that God say not some day of you, "The virgin of Israel is fallen, and there is none to raise her up."[6] I will say it boldly: God can do all things, but the virgin who has fallen will not be raised up. He may indeed relieve one who is defiled from the penalty of her sin, but he will not give her a crown. Let us fear lest in us also prophecy be fulfilled, "Good virgins shall faint." Notice that it is good virgins who are spoken of, for there are bad ones as well. "Whoever looks on a woman," the Lord says, "to lust after her has committed adultery with her already in his heart."[7] So that virginity may be lost even by a thought. Such are evil virgins in the flesh, not in the spirit; foolish virgins, who, having no oil, are shut out by the bridegroom.[8] LETTER 5.[9]

5:6 Seek the Lord and Live

A PLEA TO SEEK GOD IN CHRIST. CYPRIAN: Therefore, while there is time, look to the true and eternal salvation, and, since the end of the

---

[1]Acts 9:15. [2]Gal 1:15. [3]1 Cor 9:27. [4]Rom 7:23. [5]Rom 7:24. [6]Amos 5:2. [7]Mt 5:28. [8]Mt 25:3, 10. [9]NPNF 2 6:24.*

world is now at hand, out of fear of God turn your minds to God. Let not your powerless and vain dominion in the world over the just and the meek delight you. Remember that in the fields the tares and the darnel have dominion over the cultivated and fruitful corn, and you should not say that evils happen because your gods are not worshiped by us. But you should realize that this is God's anger, this is God's censure, so that he who is not recognized for his blessings may at least be recognized for his judgments. "Seek God, and your soul shall live." Acknowledge God even though it is late. For Christ advises and teaches this, saying, "Now this is everlasting life, that they may know you the only true God and him whom you have sent, Jesus Christ."[10] Believe him who by no means deceives. Believe him who has foretold that all these things would come to pass. Believe him who will give the reward of eternal life to those who believe. Believe him who by the fires of Gehenna will inflict eternal punishments on the disbelieving. To DEMETRIAN 23.[11]

5:8 Darkness Turned into Morning

THE PAST TEMPEST, THE PRESENT CALM.
CHRYSOSTOM: When I think of the past tempest and of the present calm, I do not cease to say, "Blessed be God, who makes all things and changes them; who has brought light out of darkness; who leads to the gates of hell and brings back; who chastises but does not kill." And this I desire you too to repeat constantly, and never to desist. For if he has benefited us by deeds, what pardon shall we be prepared for, if we do not requite him even by words? Therefore I exhort that we never cease to give him thanks. For if we are grateful for the former benefits, it is plain that we shall enjoy others also which are greater. Let us say, then, continually, "Blessed be God, who has permitted us to spread before you in quietness the accustomed table, while he has also granted you to hear our word with assurance of safety! Blessed be God, that we no longer run here or

there flying from the danger, but that we only have a desire to hear. Grant that we no longer meet one another with agony or trembling and anxious thoughts but with due confidence, having shaken off all our fear." Our conditions, indeed, on former days was nothing better than that of those who are tossed up and down in the midst of the deep, expecting shipwreck every hour. We were scared all day long by innumerable rumors and disturbed and agitated on every side. We were busy every day and curious to know who had come from the court. What news had he brought? And was what was reported true or false? Our nights too we passed without sleep, and while we looked upon the city we wept over it, as if it were on the eve of its destruction. HOMILIES CONCERNING THE STATUES 6.1.[12]

CREATED TO FORM OUR SOUL AFTER GOD.
CHRYSOSTOM: I made heaven and earth, he says, and to you I give the power of creation. Make your earth heaven. For it is in your power. "I am he who makes and transforms all things," says God of himself. And he has given to people a similar power, as a painter, being an affectionate father, teaches his own art to his son. I formed your body beautiful, he says, but I give you the power of forming something better. Make your soul beautiful. I said, "Let the earth bring forth grass, and every fruitful tree."[13] HOMILIES ON 1 TIMOTHY 16.[14]

GOD, SOURCE OF ALL BLESSINGS. PAULUS OROSIUS: What, then, is your opinion about that section of the statement that follows, "He brings about rain upon the just and the unjust"?[15] Surely he who gives, gives when he wishes and gives where he wishes, either by arranging the well-ordered nature or by lavishly bestowing his own munificence. And in case you contemplate also casting aside this statement, in keeping with the

---

[10]Jn 17:3. [11]FC 36:188*. [12]NPNF 1 9:412*. [13]Gen 1:11. [14]NPNF 1 13:463. [15]Mt 5:45.

madness of your impiety, listen to the prophet testifying about this truth: "He who calls for the waters of the sea and pours them out upon the face of the earth. The Lord is his name."[16] DE-FENSE AGAINST THE PELAGIANS 19.[17]

5:10 Abhoring One Who Tells the Truth

CHRISTIANS ARE THE NEW ADOPTED JEWS.
TERTULLIAN: They take the two sons as types of two peoples, the elder Jewish, the younger Christian. . . . But if I show that the Jew does not fit the type represented by the elder son, it will be admitted, in consequence, that the Christian is not typified by the younger. Admittedly, the Jew is called a "son" and an "elder son" since he is first by adoption, and although he resents the Christian's reconciliation with God his Father (this is a point which our opponents seize upon most eagerly), yet the statement "Behold, how many years I serve you and I have never transgressed your commandment"[18] cannot be one which the Jew makes to the Father. For when was Judah not a transgressor of the law? "Hearing with the ear and not hearing,[19] holding in hate him who reproves at the gates and scorning holy speech." ON PURITY 8.[20]

5:14-15 Hate Evil, Love Good

A CALL TO SEEK GOD. AMBROSE: For when a man rules his own self—and that counts for more than to govern others—his heart is in the hand of God, and God turns it where he wills. No wonder if he turns it to the good, perfect goodness is his. And so let us be in the hand of God that we may seek the good, that incorruptible and immutable good of which the prophet Amos says, "Seek good and not evil, that you may

live, and so the Lord God almighty will be with you, as you have said, 'We have hated evil and loved good.'" And so, where the good God is, there are the good things that David desired to see and believed that he would see, even as he says, "I believe I shall see the good things of the Lord in the land of the living."[21] They indeed are the good things that endure always, that cannot be destroyed by change of time or of age. FLIGHT FROM THE WORLD 6.35.[22]

THE HIGHEST GOOD. AMBROSE: Let us hurry to him in whom is that highest good, since he is goodness itself. He is the patience of Israel calling you to repentance, so you will not come to judgment but may receive the remission of sins. "Repent," he says.[23] He is the one of whom the prophet Amos cries, "Seek you good." He is the highest good, for he needs nothing and abounds in all things. Well may he abound, for in him dwells bodily the fullness of divinity.[24] Well may he abound, of whose fullness we have all received, and in whom we have been filled, as the Evangelist says.[25] LETTER 79.[26]

JUSTICE. GREGORY THE GREAT: It was the old custom that the elders should sit at the gate to make out by judicial trial the quarrels of persons at strife, in order that they should never enter the city at variance and should dwell there in harmony. And hence the Lord says by the prophet, "Establish judgment at the gate." MORALS ON THE BOOK OF JOB 4.21.32.[27]

---

[16]Amos 9:6. [17]FC 99:142. [18]Lk 15:29. [19]Cf. Is 6:9. [20]ACW 28:73*. [21]Ps 27:13 (26:13 LXX). [22]FC 65:308. [23]Mt 4:17. [24]Col 2:9. [25]Jn 1:16. [26]FC 26:441. [27]LF 21:540.

5:18-27 EXECUTION OF THE DIVINE VERDICT: THE DAY OF THE LORD

¹⁸*Woe to you who desire the day of the* LORD!
   Why would you have the day of the LORD?
It is darkness, and not light;
   ¹⁹*as if a man fled from a lion,*
   and a bear met him;
or went into the house and leaned with his hand against the wall,
   and a serpent bit him.
²⁰*Is not the day of the* LORD *darkness, and not light,*
   and gloom with no brightness in it?

²¹*"I hate, I despise your feasts,*
   and I take no delight in your solemn assemblies.
²²*Even though you offer me your burnt offerings and cereal offerings,*
   I will not accept them,
and the peace offerings of your fatted beasts
   I will not look upon.
²³*Take away from me the noise of your songs;*
   to the melody of your harps I will not listen.
²⁴*But let justice roll down like waters,*
   and righteousness like an everflowing stream.

²⁵*"Did you bring to me sacrifices and offerings the forty years in the wilderness, O house of Israel?* ²⁶*You shall take up Sakkuth your king, and Kaiwan your star-god, your images,*^k *which you made for yourselves;* ²⁷*therefore I will take you into exile beyond Damascus," says the* LORD, *whose name is the God of hosts.*

k Heb *your images, your star-god*

OVERVIEW: The day offers time to work toward righteousness. The night, however, refers to punishment, as the cry of Amos reveals. At judgment the darkness of punishment will descend upon unbelievers (ORIGEN). The judgment comes when people love darkness rather than light (THEODORET). Human grief is well expressed in the words of Amos (BRAULIO). God wants obedience rather than empty ritualism. In addition to the ineffectiveness of ritual sacrifices, even songs and musical instruments may be displeasing to the Lord if daily obedience is lacking (APOSTOLIC CONSTITUTIONS, CHRYSOSTOM). Idolatry is condemned as an abomination (GREGORY OF NAZIANZUS).

5:18 Darkness, Not Light

When the Night of Judgment Comes. Origen: Perhaps we will understand what has been written if we deal with a Gospel text spoken by the Savior, which expresses it in this way: "Work while it is day. The night comes when no one can work."[1] He has named here as this age the day—but of necessity I have added the word here, for I know that in other passages other meanings are revealed—so he has called this age the day, but the darkness and the night the consummation because of punishments. For "why do you desire the Day of the Lord? And it is darkness and not light," says the prophet Amos. If you can envision after the consummation of the world what the gloom is, a gloom that pursues nearly all of the race of humans who are punished for sins. The atmosphere will become dark at that time, and no longer can anyone ever give glory to God, since the Word has given orders to the righteous saying, go, "my people, enter into your rooms, shut the door, hide yourself for a little season, until the force of my anger has passed away."[2] Homilies on Jeremiah 12.[3]

They Loved Darkness Rather Than Light. Theodoret of Cyr: Since there were some buoyed up by audacity and temerity who resisted the prophetic oracles, raging against them, calling the divine pronouncements false and demanding the fulfillment of the prophecies, the Lord declares these people lamentable for longing to see darkness instead of light. Those who long to see the fulfillment of prophecy, he is saying, are no different from a person fleeing an attacking lion and after that running into a bear, or fearfully going into a house and, with one's soul in the grip of panic, putting a hand on the wall and being bitten by a venomous snake. In other words, as that person on that day sees darkness and not a gleam of light, so these people will be given over to deep darkness on the day of punishment. Commentary on Amos 5.18-20.[4]

5:20-24 The Day of the Lord Is Darkness

Suffering. Braulio of Saragossa: I am pierced by one wound and tortured with much grief, the bond of bitterness does not permit the tongue to perform its function, and it is easier to weep than to talk. Lo, one affliction comes upon another affliction and contrition upon contrition, "as if a man were to flee from a lion, and a bear should meet him," or howl at being struck by a scorpion, "and a snake should bite him," so completely am I dejected and afflicted with the misery of sorrow. I confess, madam, that every time I try to write to you about the passing of our lady Basilla of blessed memory, I am overcome with bitterness and experience a dullness in my mind, a heaviness in my sense and slowness in my tongue, because while I was occupied with grief, my mind was moved by death. Letter 18.[5]

Sacrifices Are Not Needed. Chrysostom: This brings us to a conclusion on another matter of great importance. The observances regarding sacrifices, sabbaths, new moons, and all such things prescribed by the Jewish way of life of that day—they are not essential. Even when they were observed they could make no great contribution to virtue; nor when neglected could they make the excellent person worthless or degrade in any way the sanctity of his soul. People of old, while still on earth, manifested by their piety a way of life that rivals the way the angels live. Yet they followed none of these observances, they slew no beasts in sacrifice, they kept no fast, they made no display of fasting. They were so pleasing to God that they surpassed this fallen human nature of ours and, by the lives they lived, drew the whole world to a knowledge of God. Discourses Against Judaizing Christians 4.6.[6]

---

[1]Jn 9:4. [2]Is 26:20. [3]FC 97:122-23. [4]PG 81:1689-92. [5]FC 63:45. [6]FC 68:86-87*.

5:23 God Rejects Their Songs

JUSTICE BETTER THAN SACRIFICE. APOSTOLIC CONSTITUTIONS: According to Jeremiah, "For in the day that I brought them out of the land of Egypt, I did not speak to you fathers or command them concerning burnt offerings and sacrifices."[7] And we hear similarly through Isaiah, "'To what purpose do you bring me a multitude of sacrifices?' says the Lord. 'I am full of the burnt offerings of rams, and I will not accept the fat of lambs and the blood of bulls and of goats. Nor do you come and appear before me; for who has required these things at your hands? Do not go on to tread my courts any more. If you bring me fine flour, it is vain; incense is an abomination unto me; your new moons, and your sabbaths, and your great day, I cannot bear them. Your fasts, and your rests, and your feasts, my soul hates them; I am overfull of them.'"[8] And he says by another: "Depart from me; the sound of your hymns, and the psalms of your musical instruments, I will not hear." And Samuel says to Saul, when he thought to sacrifice: "Obedience is better than sacrifice, and hearkening than the fat of rams. For, behold, the Lord does not so much delight in sacrifice as in obeying him."[9] CONSTITUTIONS OF THE HOLY APOSTLES 6.5.12.[10]

IDOLATRY CONDEMNED. GREGORY OF NAZIANZUS: What shall I say to those who worship Astarate or Chemosh, the abomination of the Sidions, or the likeness of a star, a god a little above them to these idolaters, but yet a creature and a piece of workmanship, when I myself either do not worship two of those into whose united name I am baptized, or else worship my fellow servants, for they are fellow servants, even if a little higher in the scale; for differences must exist among fellow servants. ORATION 40.42, ON HOLY BAPTISM.[11]

---

[7]Jer 7:22 [8]Is 1:11-14. [9]1 Sam 15:22. [10]ANF 7:460*. [11]NPNF 2 7:375.

6:1-14 CONDEMNATION OF COMPLACENCY AND LUXURIOUS LIVING

[1]"Woe to those who are at ease in Zion,
   and to those who feel secure on the
      mountain of Samaria,
the notable men of the first of the nations,
   to whom the house of Israel come!
[2]Pass over to Calneh, and see;
   and thence go to Hamath the great;
   then go down to Gath of the Philistines.
Are they better than these kingdoms?
   Or is their territory greater than your
      territory,
[3]O you who put far away the evil day,
   and bring near the seat of violence?

[4]"Woe to those who lie upon beds of ivory,
   and stretch themselves upon their
      couches,
and eat lambs from the flock,
   and calves from the midst of the stall;
[5]who sing idle songs to the sound of the
      harp,
   and like David invent for themselves
      instruments of music;
[6]who drink wine in bowls,
   and anoint themselves with the finest oils,
   but are not grieved over the ruin of
      Joseph!

⁷*Therefore they shall now be the first of*
those to go into exile,
and the revelry of those who stretch
themselves shall pass away."

⁸*The Lord God* has sworn by himself (says*
the LORD, the God of hosts):
"I abhor the pride of Jacob,
and hate his strongholds;
and I will deliver up the city and all that
is in it."

⁹*And if ten men remain in one house, they*
shall die. ¹⁰*And when a man's kinsman, he*
who burns him,ˡ shall take him up to bring the
bones out of the house, and shall say to him
who is in the innermost parts of the house, "Is
there still any one with you?" he shall say,
"No"; and he shall say, "Hush! We must not
mention the name of the LORD."

¹¹*For behold, the LORD commands,*
and the great house shall be smitten into
fragments,
and the little house into bits.
¹²*Do horses run upon rocks?*
Does one plow the sea with oxen?
But you have turned justice into poison
and the fruit of righteousness into
wormwood—
¹³*you who rejoice in Lo-debar,ⁿ*
who say, "Have we not by our own
strength
taken Karnaimᵒ for ourselves?"
¹⁴*"For behold, I will raise up against you a*
nation,
O house of Israel," says the LORD, the
God of hosts;
"and they shall oppress you from the
entrance of Hamath
to the Brook of the Arabah."

l *Or who makes a burning for him*   n *Or a thing of nought*   o *Or horns*   *LXX omits The Lord*

OVERVIEW: In his prophecy Amos had already warned against those who trust in the mountain of Samaria (TERTULLIAN). Do not treat this world as a lasting city (CHRYSOSTOM). The Jews corrupted the sabbath by engaging in gluttonous behavior in their hearts, thus nullifying the freedom it was intended to bestow upon them. The sacrifice of doves, which are sinless, gentle and guileless, are a type of the character traits believers are to have when offering themselves as living sacrifices (CLEMENT OF ALEXANDRIA). Unbridled worldliness and sensual pursuits are denounced in Scripture. Guests are to be received with great modesty when they visit the community (BASIL). Woe to those who bite and destroy one another and give those who despise piety a reason to scoff (JOHN OF ANTIOCH). They are subjected to extreme devastation (THEODORE). Amos anticipates the denunciation of Pelagian heretics for placing trust in their own merits (JEROME).

6:1 Woe to Samaria

THOSE WHO FEEL SECURE ON THE MOUNTAIN OF SAMARIA. TERTULLIAN: Jesus' miracle was performed in the district of Samaria, to which country also belonged one of the lepers.[1] Samaria, however, had revolted from Israel, carrying with it the disaffected nine tribes, which having been alienated by the prophet Ahijah,[2] Jeroboam settled in Samaria. Besides, the Samaritans were always pleased with the mountains and the wells of their ancestors. Thus, in the Gospel of John, the woman of Samaria, when conversing with the Lord at the well, says, "No doubt yours are greater," and again,

---

[1]Lk 17:17. [2]1 Kings 11:29-39; 13:15.

"Our fathers worshiped in this mountain, but you say that Jerusalem is the place where men ought to worship."[3] Accordingly, he who said "woe unto them that trust in the mountain of Samaria," promising now to restore that very region, purposely requests the men "to go and show themselves to the priests," because these were to be found only there where the temple was, submitting the Samaritan to the Jew, inasmuch as "salvation was of the Jews,"[4] whether to the Israelite or the Samaritan. AGAINST MARCION 4.35.[5]

6:4 Lying on Beds of Ivory

LUXURIOUS LIVING CONDEMNED. CHRYSOSTOM: Let us not be careless, dearly beloved, in dealing with matters concerning our salvation; recognizing instead the troubles that could come from that evil source, let us avoid the harm it produces. After all, we are warned against intemperance not only in the new dispensation by its greater attention to right thinking, its more frequent struggles and greater effort, its many rewards and ineffable consolations. Not even people living under the old law were permitted to indulge themselves in that way, even though they were sitting in the dark dependent upon tapers and were brought forward gradually into the light, like children being weaned off milk. Lest you think I am idly finding fault with intemperance in what I say, listen to what the prophet says: "Woe to those who fall on evil days in sleeping on beds of ivory, luxuriating on their couches, living on a diet of goats picked from the flocks and suckling calves from the herds, and drinking strained wines, anointed with precious unguents—like men treating this as a lasting city, and not seeking one to come." Do you see the heavy accusation the prophet levels against intemperance in charging the Jews with these faults of stupidity, sensuality and daily gluttony? I mean, note the accuracy of the words: after attacking their gluttony and their drinking to excess, he added, "like men treating this as a lasting city, and not seeking one to come," all but stating

that their satisfaction got as far as lips and palate, and they went on to nothing better. Pleasure however, is brief and fleeting, whereas pain never lets up and has no end. The truth of this comes from experience, the true meaning of lasting realities—"like men treating this as a lasting city"—and fleeting things—"not seeking one to come"—that is, not lasting for a moment. HOMILIES ON GENESIS 1.10.[6]

WHAT COMFORT IS IT TO SLEEP ON A BED OF IVORY? CHRYSOSTOM: For when he said, "Woe . . . to you who are approaching the evil day," and added, "and adopting false sabbaths," he showed by his next words how their sabbaths were false. How did they make their sabbaths false? By working wickedness, feasting, drinking, and doing a multitude of shameful and grievous deeds. To prove that this is true, hear what follows. He reveals what I am saying by saying what he adds immediately: " . . . who sleep upon beds of ivory, and live delicately on their couches, and eat kids out of the flocks, and sucking calves out of the midst of the stalls . . . who drink filtered wine, and anoint yourselves with the best ointment." You received the sabbath to free your soul from wickedness, but you have enslaved it further. For what could be worse than this frivolity, this sleeping on beds of ivory? The other sins, such as drunkenness, greed and profligacy, provide some pleasure, however small; but in sleeping on beds of ivory, what pleasure is there? What comfort? HOMILIES ON LAZARUS AND THE RICH MAN 1.[7]

BELIEVERS ARE NEW LIVING SACRIFICES. CLEMENT OF ALEXANDRIA: Again, whenever he speaks of "young suckling calves"[8] and of "the guileless and meek dove,"[9] he means us. Through Moses he orders that two young birds, a pair of pigeons or turtledoves, be offered for any sin. This means that the sinlessness of such gentle birds and

---

[3]Jn 4:12, 20. [4]Jn 4:22. [5]ANF 3:408*. [6]FC 74:26-27. [7]OWP 24. [8]1 Sam 6:7. [9]Lev 5:11; 12:8; Mt 10:16; Lk 2:24.

their guile and forgetfulness of injury is very acceptable to God. So he is instructing us to offer a sacrifice bearing the character of that which we have offended against. The plight of the poor doves, moreover, will instill into us a beginning of abhorrence for sin. Christ the Educator 5.14.[10]

6:6 Not Grieved over Joseph's Ruin

Modesty in Serving Guests. Basil the Great: Just as it is not proper to provide ourselves with worldly trappings like a silver vessel, or a curtain edged with purple, or a downy couch, or transparent draperies, so we act unfittingly in contriving menus that deviate in any important way from our usual diet. That we should run about searching for anything not demanded by real necessity but calculated to provide a wretched delight and ruinous vainglory is not only shameful and out of keeping with our avowed purpose; it also causes harm of no mean gravity when they who spend their lives in sensual gratification and measure happiness in terms of pleasure for the appetite see us also taken up with the same preoccupations that keep them enthralled. If, indeed, sensual pleasure is evil and to be avoided, we should on no occasion indulge in it, for nothing that is condemned can at any time be beneficial. They who live riotously and are anointed with the best ointments and drink filtered wine come under the denunciation of Scripture. Because she lives in pleasure, the widow is dead while she is living.[11] The rich man is debarred from paradise because he lived in luxury upon earth.[12] What then have we to do with costly appointments? Has a guest arrived? If he is a brother and follows a way of life aiming at the same objective as ours, he will recognize the fare we provide as properly his own. What he has left at home, he will find with us. Suppose he is weary from his journey. We then provide as much extra nourishment as is required to relieve his weariness. The Long Rules, Question 20.[13]

Woe to Those Who Do Not Grieve over

the Ruin of Joseph. John of Antioch: There is nothing else to see happening everywhere in the world except disorder, unheralded war, unrestrained wrath and savagery exceeding all barbaric inhumanity, and there is no one suffering "by the collapse of Joseph." We bite and we devour one another, and then we have been destroyed by one another, providing pleasure to the enemies of piety. Letter to Cyril of Alexandria 6.[14]

6:9-10 Death in the House

The Sign of Extreme Devastation. Theodore of Mopsuestia: The passage involves deep obscurity from the viewpoint of commentary. It resembles the part in Genesis where there is mention of the treaty that Laban and Jacob made with each other about ownership of the offspring of the sheep, one man owning some, the other owning others.[15] While that is obscure in its expression, the sense gains clarity in the course of comment. Now it is necessary to expound the sense of this passage as well, whose reference is not clearly expressed. His intention, in fact, is to cite a proof of the devastation affecting them in that it was very extreme. In many cases scarcely ten will be left from a large household of many members, the rest being done away with in various ways through the war. Commentary on Amos 6.9-10.[16]

6:13 Karnaim (Horns) Taken

I Abhor the Pride of Jacob. Jerome: Whence also we say that the holy men are just and that they are made pleasing to God after their sins not only through their merits but through the mercy of him to whom every creature is subject and stands in need of his mercy. Let heretics hear, who are lifted up by pride and say, "We have taken unto us horns by our own strength." Let them listen to what Moab heard

---

[10]FC 23:15. [11]1 Tim 5:6. [12]Lk 16:25. [13]FC 9:277-78*. [14]FC 77:186. [15]Gen 30:25-34. [16]PG 66:284.

said to him: "We have heard the pride of Moab, he is exceedingly proud.'His haughtiness and his arrogance and his pride and the loftiness of his heart I know,' says the Lord, 'because his strength is not according to the loftiness thereof.'"[17]AGAINST THE PELAGIANS 2.29.[18]

---

[17]Jer 48:29-30. [18]FC 53:343*.

7:1-17 THE PROPHET AND HIS PROPHECY

[1]Thus the Lord GOD* showed me: behold, he was forming locusts in the beginning of the shooting up of the latter growth; and lo, it was the latter growth after the king's mowings. [2]When they had finished eating the grass of the land, I said,
    "O Lord GOD, forgive, I beseech thee!
        How can Jacob stand?
        He is so small!"
[3]The LORD repented concerning this;
        "It shall not be," said the LORD.

[4]Thus the Lord GOD showed me: behold, the Lord GOD was calling for a judgment by fire, and it devoured the great deep and was eating up the land. [5]Then I said,
    "O Lord GOD, cease, I beseech thee!
        How can Jacob stand?
        He is so small!"
[6]The LORD repented concerning this;
        "This also shall not be," said the Lord GOD.

[7]He showed me: behold, the Lord was standing beside a wall built with a plumb line, with a plumb line in his hand.† [8]And the LORD said to me, "Amos, what do you see?" And I said, "A plumb line." Then the Lord said,
    "Behold, I am setting a plumb line
        in the midst of my people Israel;
        I will never again pass by them;
    [9]the high places of Isaac shall be made desolate,
        and the sanctuaries of Israel shall be laid waste,
        and I will rise against the house of Jeroboam with the sword."

[10]Then Amaziah the priest of Bethel sent to Jeroboam king of Israel, saying, "Amos has conspired against you in the midst of the house of Israel; the land is not able to bear all his words. [11]For thus Amos has said,
    'Jeroboam shall die by the sword,

and Israel must go into exile
away from his land.' "

¹²And Amaziah said to Amos, "O seer, go, flee away to the land of Judah, and eat bread there, and prophesy there; ¹³but never again prophesy at Bethel, for it is the king's sanctuary, and it is a temple of the kingdom."

¹⁴Then Amos answered Amaziah, "I am no prophet, nor a prophet's son;ᵖ but I am a herdsman, and a dresser of sycamore trees, ¹⁵and the LORD took me from following the flock, and the LORD said to me, 'Go, prophesy to my people Israel.'

¹⁶"Now therefore hear the word of the LORD.
You say, 'Do not prophesy against Israel,
    and do not preach against the house of Isaac.'
¹⁷Therefore thus says the LORD:
'Your wife shall be a harlot in the city,
    and your sons and your daughters shall fall by the sword,
    and your land shall be parceled out by line;
you yourself shall die in an unclean land,
    and Israel shall surely go into exile away from its land.' "

p Or one of the sons of the prophets   *LXX omits the Lord   †LXX of adamant, and in his hand was an adamant

---

OVERVIEW: God's compassion for humanity is shown through the intercession of the prophet Amos (CHRYSOSTOM). The character trait of being adamant is more powerful than the "hammer and anvil" of the devil (ORIGEN). The cornerstone of salvation, Christ, is believed to be as hard as lead, which Amos prophesied would be the plumb line in the midst of Israel (EPHREM). Amos recalls his rustic background not to boast about himself but rather to proclaim God's calling in his life (CHRYSOSTOM). The Holy Spirit calls the humble in high service. After his call, nothing is the same (GREGORY THE GREAT). In this passage a contrast is made between a divinely ordained priesthood and one that is of human origin (ISHO'DAD). Also it demonstrates that the divine Spirit is not with the prophets at all times (GREGORY THE GREAT).

7:2 O Lord God, Forgive

AMOS'S PLEA FOR GOD'S COMPASSION. CHRYSOSTOM: It is, after all, the practice of the prophets and the just to grieve not only for themselves but also for the rest of humankind. If you're inclined to check that, you will find them all giving evidence of this compassion—for example, you can listen to Jeremiah, "Who will pour water on my head, and provide a fountain of tears for my eyes?"[1] or Ezekiel, "Alas, Lord, you will destroy what remains of Israel?"[2] or Daniel lamenting in these words, "You have made us few in number by comparison with the Gentiles," or Amos, "Think better of this, Lord." HOMILIES ON GENESIS 29.7.[3]

7:7 The Lord Stands by a Wall

HOLY PEOPLE SUPERIOR TO THE EVIL ONE. ORIGEN: I will also proclaim confidently that there is someone who cannot be affected very much by the "hammer of the whole earth."[4] And since the example was offered of a perceptible "hammer," I will seek a material stronger than the "hammer" which does not feel the blows from it. In searching for it I find it too in what was writ-

---

[1]Jer 8:23 LXX. [2]Ezek 9:8. [3]FC 82:203. [4]Jer 23:29.

ten: "Behold a man standing above the adamant walls, and in his adamant." History records about "adamant"[5] that it is stronger than every "hammer" striking it, remaining unbroken and unyielding. Even if the "hammer," the devil, stands above, and the serpent, who "as an indomitable anvil,"[6] may position himself below, still "adamant" endures nothing when it is resting "in the hand of the Lord" and in his regard. Thus the two opposites to this "adamant" are the "hammer" and the immovable "anvil." Yet there is indeed among the nations a much-used proverb in the common language concerning those who are pressed by anxieties and extremely bad situations; they say, "They are 'between a hammer and an anvil.'" Still you can say that this refers to the devil and the serpent, who are always signified by names of this sort in the Scriptures for a variety of purposes. And you can say that the holy person, who is an "adamant wall" or is "adamant in the hand of the Lord," is not affected either by the "hammer" or by the "anvil," but the more one is struck, the brighter will his virtue shine. HOMILIES ON JEREMIAH 27.3.[7]

7:8 Setting a Plumb Line

CHRIST THE CORNERSTONE FORETOLD.
EPHREM THE SYRIAN: Jesus would lead his detractors to the point of judging themselves, saying, "What do the vinedressers deserve?"[8] They decided concerning themselves, saying, "Let him destroy the evil ones with evil."[9] Then he explained this, saying, "Have you not read that 'the stone which the builders rejected has become the head of the corner?'"[10] What stone? That which is known to be lead. For see, he has said, "I am setting a plumb line in the midst of the sons of Israel." To show that he himself was this stone, he said concerning it, "Whoever knocks against that stone will be broken to pieces, but it will crush and destroy whomever it falls upon."[11] The leaders of the people were gathered together against him and wanted his downfall because his teaching did not please them. But he said, "It will crush and destroy whomever it falls upon," because he had resisted idolatry, among other things. For "the stone that struck the image has become a great mountain, and the entire earth has been filled with it."[12] COMMENTARY ON TATIAN'S DIATESSARON 16.20.[13]

7:14-15 Not a Prophet or a Prophet's Son

AMOS'S HUMILITY. CHRYSOSTOM: Amos also said, "I was no prophet, nor the son of a prophet, but only a herdsman, a gatherer of sycamore fruit. And God took me." He did not say this to exalt himself but to stop their mouths that suspected him as no prophet, and to show that he is no deceiver, and what he says does not come from his own mind. HOMILIES ON 2 CORINTHIANS 24.3.[14]

GOD CALLS THE HUMBLE TO HIGH SERVICE.
GREGORY THE GREAT: How good it is to raise up eyes of faith to the power of this worker, the Holy Spirit, and to look here and there at our ancestors in the Old and New Testaments. With the eyes of my faith open, I gaze on David, on Amos, on Daniel, on Peter, on Paul, on Matthew—and I am filled with a desire to behold the nature of this worker, the Holy Spirit. But I fall short. The Spirit filled a boy who played upon the harp, and made him a psalmist; on a shepherd and herdsman who pruned sycamore trees, and made him a prophet; on a child given to abstinence, and made him a judge of his elders; on a fisherman, and made him a preacher; on one who persecuted the church, and made him the teacher of the Gentiles; on a tax collector, and made him an Evangelist. What a skilled worker this Spirit is! There is no question of delay in learning what the Spirit teaches us. No sooner does the Spirit touch our minds in regard to anything than we are taught; the Spirit's very touch is teaching. The Spirit changes the human heart in a moment, filling it

---

[5]From Greek *adamas*, a very hard metal. [6]Job 41:23. [7]FC 97:246. [8]Mt 21:40. [9]Mt 21:41. [10]Ps 118:22 (117:22 LXX); 1 Pet 2:7. [11]Lk 20:18. [12]Dan 2:35. [13]ECTD 253. [14]NPNF 1 12:392-93.

with light. Suddenly we are no longer what we were; suddenly we are something we never used to be. FORTY GOSPEL HOMILIES 30.[15]

FULL DISCLOSURE. ISHO'DAD OF MERV: "And Amaziah sends, etc." In fact, since the prophet had received the order to prophesy beside the temple of the idols, so that his words might be heard not only by the ten tribes but also by the people living around, Amaziah, the priest of the temple, thinks that if these words were addressed to the people for some time, inevitably they would have been afraid and would not have come to worship the idols anymore, and therefore he would have lost authority. So he sends his complaint to excite the reaction of the king against the prophet, asking that either he was executed or expelled from that place. But since the king was afraid to harm the prophet, Amaziah dares say to the prophet by mocking him and laughing at him—in fact, the word *seer* is used with scorn: "Go, flee away to the land of Judah." That is, there you will be treated justly by receiving the wage for your role as a prophet, because those of the house of Judah are accustomed to taking care of their prophets. This priest of the demons had believed that the prophet had taken up his task as if it was an ordinary job, that is, to make a living as he himself had done. He imagined that the motive of Amos was to stuff himself with food. But the prophet answered, according to the Greek text, "I was no prophet, nor a prophet's son." That is, I have not learned this profession as a trade nor have I inherited it from my fathers, but it is the work of divine grace that is given to those who seek after God. "I was a goat herder and dug around sycamore trees."[16] Other versions read, "I looked for the fruits of the sycamore trees,"[17] or "I scraped the wild fig trees," or "I made incisions on the fruits of the sycamores."[18] This meaning is, sometimes I pastured goats and sheep as well, sometimes I tilled the ground by digging and raking and irrigating around the trees. By mentioning the sycamore trees, which are wild fig trees, he refers to all trees. COMMENTARY ON AMOS.[19]

THE SPIRIT DOES NOT ALWAYS DWELL WITH THE PROPHETS. GREGORY THE GREAT: If the spirit of prophecy had always been present to the prophets, the prophet Amos when asked would never have said, "I am no prophet"; he even adds, "neither a prophet's son, but I am a herdsman and a gatherer of sycamore fruit." How then was he no prophet who foretold so many true things concerning the future? Or in what way was he a prophet if he at the time disowned the truth concerning himself? At the moment that he was called in question, he felt that the spirit of prophecy was not with him. He bore true testimony concerning himself in saying, "I am not a prophet." Yet he added afterward, "Now therefore hear the word of the Lord. Therefore thus said the Lord, 'Your wife shall be a harlot in the city, and your sons and your daughters shall fall by the sword, and your land shall be divided by line, and you shall die in a polluted land.'" By these words of the prophet it is plainly shown that while he was bearing that testimony about himself he was filled, and on the instant rewarded with the spirit of prophecy, because he humbly acknowledged himself to be no prophet. MORALS ON THE BOOK OF JOB 1.2.89.[20]

---

[15]BFG 160-61*; CS 123:244-45. [16]The text of LXX differs here from the Hebrew Bible. [17]Probably from Aquila, Greek translator of the Hebrew Bible. [18]Probably Theodotion's translation. [19]CSCO 303 (128):89-90*. [20]LF 18:127*.

8:1-14 THE TIME IS RIPE
FOR DIVINE PUNISHMENT

[1]Thus the Lord GOD showed me: behold, a basket of summer fruit.[q] [2]And he said, "Amos, what do you see?" And I said, "A basket of summer fruit."[q] Then the LORD said to me,
"The end[r] has come upon my people Israel;
  I will never again pass by them.
[3]The songs of the temple[s]* shall become
  wailings in that day,"
                    says the Lord GOD;
"the dead bodies shall be many;
  in every place they shall be cast out in
  silence."[t]

[4]Hear this, you who trample upon the
  needy,
  and bring the poor of the land to an end,
[5]saying, "When will the new moon be over,
  that we may sell grain?
And the sabbath,
  that we may offer wheat for sale,
that we may make the ephah small and the
  shekel great,
  and deal deceitfully with false balances,
[6]that we may buy the poor for silver
  and the needy for a pair of sandals,
  and sell the refuse of the wheat?"
[7]The LORD has sworn by the pride of Jacob:
  "Surely I will never forget any of their
  deeds.
[8]Shall not the land tremble on this account,
  and every one mourn who dwells in it,
and all of it rise like the Nile,
  and be tossed about[†] and sink again, like
the Nile of Egypt?"

[9]"And on that day," says the Lord GOD,
  "I will make the sun go down at noon,
  and darken the earth in broad daylight.
[10]I will turn your feasts into mourning,
  and all your songs into lamentation;
I will bring sackcloth upon all loins,
  and baldness on every head;
I will make it like the mourning for an only
  son,
  and the end of it like a bitter day.

[11]"Behold, the days are coming," says the
  Lord GOD,
  "when I will send a famine on the
  land;
not a famine of bread, nor a thirst for
  water,
  but of hearing the words of the LORD.
[12]They shall wander from sea to sea,
  and from north to east;
they shall run to and fro, to seek the word of
  the LORD,
  but they shall not find it.

[13]"In that day the fair virgins and the young
  men
  shall faint for thirst.
[14]Those who swear by Ashimah of Samaria,
  and say, 'As thy god lives, O Dan,'
and, 'As the way of Beer-sheba lives,'
  they shall fall, and never rise again."

q Heb qayits   r Heb qets   s Or palace   t Or be silent!   *LXX the ceiling of a room   †LXX omits this phrase

Overview: The people's inability to understand the prophecies about Christ was the result of madness and blindness. The events surrounding the passion and death of Christ—earthquake, the veil of the temple cut in two, and the sun darkened—are all foretold by Amos (Lactantius). The feast of unleavened bread was transmuted in Christianity (Gregory Thaumaturgus). By putting to death the bread of life a hunger has befallen upon those who committed the crime (Basil). We harm the body by overfeeding it and the soul by depriving it of spiritual food. Amos had predicted this state of affairs against the Jews initially, but it is now applicable to Gentiles as well (Chrysostom). Joseph and Jesus are compared and contrasted. Both were thirty years old at the inauguration of their respective ministries. Jews gathered wheat of the spiritual kind unlike the earthly type Joseph collected. Jesus has the wheat to alleviate the famine predicted by Amos. The unbelieving Jews are suffering a famine of God's Word, as predicted by Amos, because of their rejection of Jesus. Moreover, the foundation of the faith now lies in the church with Jesus Christ as the head (Origen).

8:10 Feasts Turned into Mourning

Golgotha. Lactantius: Suspended, then, and fastened to his cross Christ cried out to God the Father in a loud voice and willingly laid down his life. In that same hour there was an earthquake, and the veil of the temple that separated the two tabernacles was cut in two, and the sun was suddenly withdrawn, and from the sixth hour until the ninth hour there was darkness.[1] The prophet Amos bears witness to this. "And it shall come to pass in that day, says the Lord, that the sun shall go down at midday, and the day shall be darkened of light. And I will turn your feasts into mourning and all your songs into lamentation." Epitome of the Divine Institutes 4.19.[2]

Sadness to Joy in Christ. Gregory Thaumaturgus: Let us keep [the Feast of Annunciation] with psalms and hymns and spiritual songs.

From ancient times Israel kept their festival, but then it was with unleavened bread and bitter herbs, of which the prophet says, "I will turn their feasts into afflictions and lamentation and their joy into shame." But our afflictions our Lord has assured us he will turn into joy by the fruits of repentance.[3] On the Annunciation to the Holy Virgin Mary 2.[4]

8:11 Famine in the Land

Sin Starves People. Basil the Great: The unreliability of excessive wealth may edify even to the point of eliciting contempt of corporal riches. Wealth is unstable. It is like a wave accustomed to change back and forth due to the violence of the wind. One might suppose that the people of Israel are rich, since they have the adoption of sons and divine worship, the promises and the patriarchs. However, they have become poor because of their sin against the Lord. "But they that seek the Lord shall not be deprived of any good."[5] They have lacked nourishment in a certain way and have suffered hunger. For when they had put to death the bread of life, a hunger for the bread came upon them. A chastisement for the thirst was imposed on them, but "the hunger was not for sensible bread or the thirst for water, but a hunger to hear the Word of God." Therefore "they have wanted and have suffered hunger." Homilies on the Psalms 33.7.[6]

Feed Through Preaching. Chrysostom: We harm both soul and body if we are guilty of lack of moderation to them both by fattening one beyond need or by causing them to waste away from starvation.... The Lord of all once admonished the Jewish people ... by way of extreme indignation in the words, "I will deal you not a famine of bread nor a thirst for water, but a famine of hearing the Word of the Lord," to teach us that while one famine can torture the body, the

---

[1]Mk 15:33. [2]FC 49:296. [3]Jer 31:13. [4]ANF 6:62*. [5]Ps 34:10 (33:11 LXX). [6]FC 46:260*.

other famine affects the soul. This very thing that the Lord threatened to inflict on them by way of punishment we now of our own volition secure for ourselves despite God's show of care for us and his provision for us, through the advice of mentors, as well as the reading of Scriptures. HOMILIES ON GENESIS 54.4.[7]

JESUS THE NEW BREAD. ORIGEN: When "Joseph was about thirty years old"[8] he was released from his chains and interpreted Pharaoh's dream. He was made the governor of Egypt. During the time of plenty, he gathered in the wheat, so that during the time of famine he would have some to distribute. I think that Joseph's age of thirty came before as a type of the Savior's thirty years. For this second Joseph did not gather in the kind of wheat that first Joseph did in Egypt. He, Jesus, gathers in true and heavenly wheat, so that in the time of abundance he might gather in the wheat that he will give out when famine is sent upon Egypt, "not hunger for bread or thirst for water, but hunger to hear the word of the Lord." HOMILIES ON THE GOSPEL OF LUKE 28.5.[9]

FAMINE ON JEWS FOR REJECTING JESUS. ORIGEN: It is prophesied, "Their young men will die by the sword, and their sons and daughters will perish in famine."[10] Those who hindered Jesus from teaching have not simply perished by the sword. But now, after the advent of the Lord, a more profound famine has come upon them. It is "not a famine of bread or thirst of water, but a famine of hearing the Word of the Lord." For the "Lord almighty" no longer "speaks" with them. This famine portends that prophecy would cease. And why do I say prophecy? The Lord ceased teaching them. Even if they bear the title *sage* a thousand times with them, the Word of the Lord is still not among them, since the verse has been fulfilled: "The Lord took away from Judea and Jerusalem the strong man and strong woman, the giant and the strong man, and the soldier and judge and prophet and diviner and elder and captain of fifty and the admirable adviser and master builder and intelligent pupil."[11] For he is no longer able to say, "Like a master builder I laid a foundation."[12] The builders have passed over, have come to the church, have laid the foundation, Jesus Christ.[13] Those who came after them have also built on him. HOMILIES ON JEREMIAH 10.3.[14]

---

[7]FC 87:94*. [8]Gen 41:46. [9]FC 94:117. [10]Jer 11:22. [11]Is 3:1-3. [12]1 Cor 3:10. [13]1 Cor 3:11. [14]FC 97:98.

9:1-15 DESTRUCTION AND RESTORATION OF ISRAEL

[1]I saw the LORD standing beside[u] the altar, and
  he said:
"Smite the capitals until the thresholds shake,
    and shatter them on the heads of all the
    people;[v]
and what are left of them I will slay with
    the sword;
  not one of them shall flee away,

  not one of them shall escape.

[2]"Though they dig into Sheol,
    from there shall my hand take them;
though they climb up to heaven,
    from there I will bring them down.
[3]Though they hide themselves on the top of
    Carmel,

from there I will search out and take them;
and though they hide from my sight at the
    bottom of the sea,
      there I will command the serpent, and it
      shall bite them.
4And though they go into captivity before
    their enemies,
      there I will command the sword, and it
      shall slay them;
and I will set my eyes upon them
    for evil and not for good."

5The Lord, GOD of hosts,
he who touches the earth and it melts,
    and all who dwell in it mourn,
and all of it rises like the Nile,
    and sinks again, like the Nile of
      Egypt;
6who builds his upper chambers in the
    heavens,
    and founds his vault upon the earth;*
who calls for the waters of the sea,
    and pours them out upon the surface of
      the earth—
the LORD is his name.

7"Are you not like the Ethiopians to me,
    O people of Israel?" says the LORD.
"Did I not bring up Israel from the land of
    Egypt,
    and the Philistines from Caphtor† and
    the Syrians from Kir?
8Behold, the eyes of the Lord GOD are upon
    the sinful kingdom,
    and I will destroy it from the surface of
    the ground;
      except that I will not utterly destroy the
      house of Jacob,"
                  says the LORD.

9"For lo, I will command,
    and shake the house of Israel among all
    the nations
as one shakes with a sieve,
    but no pebble shall fall upon the
    earth.
10All the sinners of my people shall die by
    the sword,
    who say, 'Evil shall not overtake or meet
    us.'

11"In that day I will raise up
    the booth of David that is fallen
and repair its breaches,
    and raise up its ruins,
    and rebuild it as in the days of
    old;
12that they may possess the remnant of
    Edom
    and all the nations who are called by my
    name,"‡
    says the LORD who does this.

13"Behold, the days are coming," says the
    LORD,
    "when the plowman shall overtake the
    reaper
    and the treader of grapes him who sows
    the seed;
the mountains shall drip sweet wine,
    and all the hills shall flow with it.
14I will restore the fortunes of my people
    Israel,
    and they shall rebuild the ruined cities
    and inhabit them;
they shall plant vineyards and drink their
    wine,
    and they shall make gardens and eat
    their fruit.

^{15}*I will plant them upon their land,*
 and they shall never again be plucked up

out of the land which I have given them,"
 says the LORD *your God.*

u Or *upon*   v Heb *all of them*   *LXX *It is he who builds his ascent up to the heavens and establishes his promise on the earth.*   †LXX *Cappadocia*   ‡LXX *The remnant of men and all the Gentiles upon whom my name is called may earnestly seek me.*

OVERVIEW: Old Testament references to the prophets' having seen God in veiled revelations as accommodated to our eyes are not inconsistent with what the apostle John confessed later about no one ever having seen God in his essence (CHRYSOSTOM). The serpent is a type of the proud evil one who has been humbled by the great one, Christ (AUGUSTINE). The ascension of Christ was foretold by Amos, and as such points also to the end of time when we will be taken up to him (TERTULLIAN). The resurrection of Jesus is confirmed in numerous passages, including where Amos recalls that all peoples will come to know the Messiah (AUGUSTINE). The fallen tabernacle Amos talked about is a reference to the fall of humanity. Jesus Christ is the promised one sent to raise it up (CHRYSOSTOM). Now all the Gentiles can have recourse (IRENAEUS).

9:1 The Lord Stood Beside the Altar

GOD SEEN IN HIS ACCOMMODATION TO OUR EYES, NOT IN HIS ESSENCE. CHRYSOSTOM: Tell me, John, what do you mean when you say, "No one has ever seen God"?[1] What shall we think about he prophets who say that they saw God? Isaiah said, "I saw the Lord sitting on a high and exalted throne."[2] And, again, Daniel said, "I saw until the thrones were set, and the ancient of days sat."[3] And Micah said, "I saw the God of Israel sitting on his throne."[4] And again, another prophet said, "I saw the Lord standing on the altar, and he said unto me, 'Strike the mercy seat.'" And I can gather many similar passages to show you as witnesses of what I say.

How is it, then, that John says, "No one has ever seen God"? He says this so that you may know that he is speaking of a clear knowledge and

a perfect comprehension of God. All the cases cited were instances of God's condescension and accommodation. That no one of those prophets saw God's essence in its pure state is clear from the fact that each one saw him in a different way. God is a simple being; he is not composed of parts; he is without form or figure. But all these prophets saw different forms and figures. God proved this very thing through the mouth of another prophet. And he persuaded those other prophets that they did not see his essence in its exact nature when he said, "I have multiplied visions, and by the ministries of the prophets I was presented."[5] What God was saying was, "I did not show my very essence, but I came down in condescension and accommodated myself to the weakness of their eyes." AGAINST THE ANOMOEANS, HOMILY 4.18-19.[6]

9:3 Commanding the Serpent

THE DEVIL WOUNDED BY THE WOUNDED LORD. AUGUSTINE: While the little one is nourished by the example of the one who from greatness descended to humility, the devil has lost what he held: because the proud held only the proud. When such an example of humility was displayed before them, people learned to condemn their own pride and to imitate the humility of God. Thus also the devil, by losing those whom he had in his power, has even himself been humbled; not chastened, but thrown prostrate. "You have humbled the proud like one that is wounded."[7] You have been humbled and have humbled others. You have been wounded and have wounded others, for your blood as it was shed to blot the handwriting of sins[8] could not

[1]Jn 1:18. [2]Is 6:1. [3]Dan 7:9. [4]1 Kings 22:19. [5]Hos 12:11 LXX. [6]FC 72:122-23*. [7]Rev 13:3. [8]Col 2:13-14.

but wound him. For what was the ground of his pride, except the bond that he held against us? This bond, this handwriting, you have blotted out with your blood. Him therefore you have wounded, from whom you have rescued so many victims. You must understand the devil wounded, not by the piercing of the flesh, which he has not, but by the bruising of his proud heart. "You have scattered your enemies abroad with your mighty arm." EXPLANATION OF THE PSALMS 89.11.[9]

9:6 In the Heavens

ASCENSION FORETOLD. TERTULLIAN: The heavenly intelligences gazed with admiration on "the Jerusalem that is above,"[10] and by the mouth of Isaiah said long ago, "Who are these that fly as clouds, and as doves with their young ones, unto me?"[11] Now, as Christ has prepared for us this ascension into heaven, he must be the Christ of whom Amos spoke: "It is he who builds his ascent up to the heavens," even for himself and his people. AGAINST MARCION 5.15.[12]

9:11-12 Raising Up David

GOD WILL RAISE UP THE BOOTH OF DAVID WHICH IS FALLEN. AUGUSTINE: But let us hear what Hosea goes on to say: "And after this the children of Israel shall return, and shall seek the Lord their God, and David their king. And they shall fear the Lord and his goodness in the last days."[13] You will never find a prophecy plainer than this, for the name king David means Christ who, as St. Paul says, "was born according to the flesh of the offspring of David."[14] Further on still, Hosea foretold the resurrection of Christ on the third day, but in the mysterious way that is proper to prophecy. He says, "He shall heal us after two days, and on the third day we shall rise up again."[15] This is the idea underlying the words of St. Paul: "Therefore if you have risen with Christ, seek the things that are above."[16] The prophet Amos too has predictions not unlike those of Hosea. He says, "Be prepared to meet your God, O Israel, for behold, I am the one who forms the thunder, and creates the wind, and declares to men their Christ."[17] And, in another place: "'In that day I will raise up the tabernacle of David that is fallen. And I will close up the breaches of the walls thereof and repair what is fallen. And I will rebuild it as in the days of old, so that the remnant of men may seek me out, and all nations, because my name is invoked upon them,' says the Lord that does these things." CITY OF GOD 18.28.[18]

RESURRECTION FORETOLD. CHRYSOSTOM: Listen to the prophet saying, "I will raise up the tabernacle of David that has fallen." Actually, it has fallen; our human nature has had an irreparable fall and was in need of that powerful hand alone. For it was not possible to raise it up otherwise, unless he who fashioned it in the beginning stretched out a hand to it and formed it again from above by the regeneration of water and the Spirit. Behold, pray, the awesome and ineffable character of the mystery. He dwells always in this tabernacle, for he put on our flesh, not to put it off again but to have it always with him. If this were not so, he would not have deemed it worthy of his royal throne. HOMILIES ON JOHN 11.[19]

THE PROMISE TO ALL NATIONS. IRENAEUS: And thus do the words of the prophet agree, as it is written, "After this I will return, and will build again the tabernacle of David, which is fallen down; and I will build its ruins and set it up. The remnant may seek after the Lord, and all the Gentiles among whom my name has been invoked, says the Lord, doing these things." His works are known from eternity by God. Therefore I for my part give this judgment, that we do not trouble those who from among the Gentiles are turned to God. AGAINST HERESIES 3.12.14.[20]

---

[9]NPNF 1 8:432. [10]Gal 4:26. [11]Is 60:8. [12]ANF 3:462. [13]Hos 3:5. [14]Rom 1:3. [15]Hos 6:2. [16]Col 3:1. [17]Amos 4:12-13. [18]FC 24:123. [19]FC 33:109. [20]ANF 1:435*.

OBADIAH

OVERVIEW: The book of Obadiah was the subject of commentary by both Jewish and Christian exegetes. The identification of Edom as Israel's enemy was used by both Christians and Jews to refer to their own enemies—which, more often than not, they viewed as each other. There was cooperation between the two, however, with Christian exegetes using (often uncritically) many of the insights of their Jewish counterparts to gain insight into Obadiah's time and background.

One of the earliest commentators on Obadiah was Hesychius of Jerusalem (c. 300). His comments deal mostly with introductory material and thus are not included here. Jerome was the only Christian commentator to have written two commentaries on Obadiah. His first, written A.D. 374, is highly allegorical, a tendency that is much more restrained in his second commentary (A.D. 396). Much of his commentary is christological, focusing on the church as the fulfillment of the book's latter verses.

Jerome's contemporary Theodore of Mopsuestia declined to use rabbinic interpretation, even as he kept with the literal words of the text. In general, Theodore's commentaries on the Twelve Prophets follow the chronology of the Hebrew history, which he believed was emulated in the Septuagint's ordering of the prophets (which is different from the Hebrew and English ordering followed today). In the historical outline followed by Theodore, Obadiah was placed after Hosea, Amos, Micah and Joel, contemporary with Jonah and before Nahum, Habakkuk, Zephaniah, Haggai, Zechariah and Malachi. Thus, Theodore dated the prophecy of Obadiah during the Assyrian exile, among the eighth century prophets. Theodoret of Cyr, a commentator from the same exegetical school, interpreted the prophecies as types found in the New Testament.

The commentary on Obadiah by Cyril of Alexandria is similar to Jerome's in many places, focusing on the literal interpretation despite Cyril's association with the Alexandrian tradition. Cyril noted the many resemblances to the prophecy of Joel against Egypt and Edom, and thus placed Obadiah at the same time as Joel and his vision. Israel's final battle with Edom would take place in the Valley of Jehoshaphat, according to Cyril. He had in mind, however, a postexilic battle referred to in 1 Esdras 4:7-10, so it would appear that Cyril was using dubious historical resources.

Augustine commented on Obadiah only

briefly.[1] He too found the salvation of Israel prophesied in the latter verses as fulfilled in Christ and the church. Isho'dad's comments evidence his knowledge of the Hebrew text in his interpretations.

The book of Obadiah tells us little if anything about the man himself beyond his name, which means "servant of Yahweh." Obadiah most likely delivered his prophecy at the temple site in Jerusalem during the national ceremonies of lament held every year to commemorate events there during the exile.[2] The prophecy is a lament as well as a warning against Edom and its complicity in the catastrophe that befell Jerusalem at the hands of the Babylonians. The closing verses, however, offer hope to the remnant of Israel, who await salvation on Mount Zion.[3]

---

[1]Augustine *City of God* 18. [2]587 B.C.; cf. Zech 7:3, 5; 8:19. [3]This overview is adapted from Joel Elowsky, "The Annals of Obadiah: A Record of the Wars and Peace Treaties in the History of Its Interpretation" (master's thesis, Concordia Seminary, 1992), pp. 51-64.

1-21 THE VISION OF OBADIAH

[1]*The vision of Obadiah.**

Thus says the Lord GOD concerning Edom:
We have heard tidings from the LORD,
    and a messenger has been sent among the
        nations:
"Rise up! let us rise against her for battle!"
[2]*Behold, I will make you small among the*
        nations,
    you shall be utterly despised.
[3]*The pride of your heart has deceived you,*
    you who live in the clefts of the rock,[a]
    whose dwelling is high,
who say in your heart,
    "Who will bring me down to the
        ground?"
[4]*Though you soar aloft like the eagle,*
    though your nest is set among the stars,
    thence I will bring you down,
                        says the LORD.

[5]*If thieves came to you,*
    if plunderers by night—

how you have been destroyed!—
    would they not steal only enough for
        themselves?[†]
If grape gatherers came to you,
    would they not leave gleanings?
[6]*How Esau has been pillaged,*
    his treasures sought out!
[7]*All your allies have deceived you,*
    they have driven you to the border;
your confederates have prevailed against
        you;
    your trusted friends have set a trap[‡]
        under you—
    there is no understanding of it.
[8]*Will I not on that day, says the LORD,*
    destroy the wise men out of Edom,
    and understanding out of Mount Esau?
[9]*And your mighty men shall be dismayed,*
        O Teman,
    so that every man from Mount Esau will
        be cut off by slaughter.
[10]*For the violence done to your brother*
        Jacob,

shame shall cover you,
    and you shall be cut off for ever.
[11]*On the day that you stood aloof,*
    on the day that strangers carried off his
      wealth,
and foreigners entered his gates
    and cast lots for Jerusalem,
    you were like one of them.
[12]*But you should not have gloated over the*
    day of your brother
    in the day of his misfortune;
you should not have rejoiced over the people
    of Judah
    in the day of their ruin;
you should not have boasted
    in the day of distress.
[13]*You should not have entered the gate of my*
    people
    in the day of his calamity;
you should not have gloated over his disaster
    in the day of his calamity;
you should not have looted his goods
    in the day of his calamity.
[14]*You should not have stood at the parting of*
    the ways
    to cut off his fugitives;
you should not have delivered up his survivors
    in the day of distress.

[15]*For the day of the* LORD *is near upon all*
    the nations.
As you have done, it shall be done to you,
    your deeds shall return on your own
    head.

[16]*For as you have drunk upon my holy*
    mountain,
    all the nations round about shall drink;
they shall drink, and stagger,[b]
    and shall be as though they had not been.
[17]*But in Mount Zion there shall be those*
    that escape,
    and it shall be holy;[§]
and the house of Jacob shall possess their
    own possessions.
[18]*The house of Jacob shall be a fire,*
    and the house of Joseph a flame,
    and the house of Esau stubble;
they shall burn them and consume them,
    and there shall be no survivor to the
    house of Esau:
        for the LORD *has spoken.*
[19]*Those of the Negeb shall possess Mount*
    Esau,[#]
    and those of the Shephelah the land of
    the Philistines;
they shall possess the land of Ephraim and
    the land of Samaria
    and Benjamin shall possess Gilead.
[20]*The exiles in Halah[c] who are of the people*
    of Israel
    shall possess[d] Phoenicia as far as
    Zarephath;
and the exiles of Jerusalem who are in
    Sepharad
    shall possess the cities of the Negeb.
[21]*Saviors shall go up to Mount Zion*
    to rule Mount Esau;
    and the kingdom shall be the LORD'S.

a Or *Sela* **b** Cn: Heb *swallow* **c** Cn: Heb *this army* **d** Cn: Heb *which* *LXX *Obadi'ah the fifth after Joel* †Peshitta *How could you have remained silent till they had stolen enough?* ‡LXX *ambush* §LXX *There shall be deliverance, and there shall be a sanctuary.* #LXX *the men [Jews] in the Negeb will regain Mount Esau*

OVERVIEW: Obadiah from the tribe of Ephraim was a contemporary of Hosea, Joel, Amos and Isaiah. The angel sent to the nations may mystically signify Christ, the Emmanuel, who gives peace to the nations (EPHREM). Obadiah's vision is a revelation from God, which is synonymous with "word of the Lord" and is a work of the Holy Spirit (THEODORE). Those who are possessed by the demonic pride, like Edomites, are subject to humiliation, like the devil (EPHREM). The clefts of the rocks signify heresies and schisms. Obadiah gives a glimpse into the fall of Lucifer before the creation of the world. The exalted place of Lucifer was lost because of pride, and all the angels who followed him will die the same as mortals (JEROME). Nebuchadnezzar fulfilled Obadiah's prophecy by destroying Edom and taking them into captivity. Because Edomites rejoiced in the ruin and exile of the Jews, the former are punished by being subjected to the latter. The Romans, however, subdued both and thus fulfilled this prophecy (Ephrem).

While one should not despise a punished brother (THEODORET), pastors of the church are especially called to mourn with those who sin rather than deride them. In his prayer, Ambrose asks for the gift of empathy for sinners when they come to him for confession so that he weeps with them and does not judge them (AMBROSE).

The destruction of the temple by the Romans had been foretold by the prophet Obadiah (PAULINUS OF NOLA). The Day of the Lord signifies the just judgment of God (CYRIL OF ALEXANDRIA). The sufferings that heretics inflict on the church will be imposed on them on the day of the Lord's judgment (JEROME). All the nations shall drink the cup of the Assyrians and Chaldeans (EPHREM), which signifies divine judgment (THEODORET). Mount Zion is a type of the church, the most holy place and the city of God (CYRIL OF ALEXANDRIA). Salvation and holiness, realized on the eschatological Mount Zion, are the opposite of the destruction and punishment that fall on the wicked who oppose Zion (THEODORE, THEODORET). United forces of Israel and Judah will destroy the Edomites (JEROME). Yahweh is the true king of Israel, who punishes the wicked and grants salvation to his people (THEODORE). Israel's conquest of the Edomites was fulfilled

and also resulted in the conversion of the remnants of Edomites to the Lord (EPHREM).

Literally, the house of Judah is called fire, and the house of Joseph a flame (CYRIL OF ALEXANDRIA). The spiritual meaning of the fire is the consummation of the world, while salvation is granted only in the church (JEROME). Upon the return from Babylon, which is "in the south," Israel will possess a region equal to Edom (CYRIL OF ALEXANDRIA). The return of exiles from the four corners of the earth will culminate in their coming to Mount Zion and subjugation of nations under the rule of God (EPHREM, CYRIL OF ALEXANDRIA). The holy One who dwells on Zion is Christ, while Edom signifies the church of the Gentiles (AUGUSTINE). Destruction of Esau, who rejoiced over the devastation of Israel, teaches us to rejoice with those who rejoice and mourn with those who mourn (THEODORET). Jewish interpreters agree that the meaning of the prophecy is that the Lord is to send a savior and king of Israel who is to bring about the eschatological kingdom of the Lord (JEROME). The prophecy about the return of the people may also be applied to our life. Our way of returning to God and obtaining divine blessings is the way of holy life (THEODORET).

1 *The Vision of Obadiah*

OBADIAH THE PROPHET. EPHREM THE SYRIAN: Obadiah of Sichem was born in the tribe of Ephraim and prophesied against the Edomites. He seems to be a contemporary of Hosea, Joel, Amos and Isaiah. COMMENTARY ON OBADIAH.[1]

EMMANUEL THE MESSENGER OF THE LORD. EPHREM THE SYRIAN: "We have heard a report from the Lord," that is, the Lord of the world powers will do nothing if he has not first revealed his mystery to his servants, the prophets. "And a messenger has been sent among the nations." A mystical meaning is probable here, and these

---

[1]ESOO 2:269.

words may be referred to Emmanuel, the angel of the testament,[2] sent from heaven, who announced peace to the nations, and therefore was said to be the "expectation of the nations." COMMENTARY ON OBADIAH.[3]

THE REVELATION TO OBADIAH. THEODORE OF MOPSUESTIA: This differs not at all in its import from the phrase "Word of the Lord." Scripture calls God's activity "Word of the Lord" in reference to the spiritual grace by which the prophets received the revelations of the future. In the same way by "vision" he refers to the divine revelation by which in fact they received the knowledge of the unknown. They also received some insights in ineffable fashion through spiritual activity in their own soul. In response to the activity occurring within them from the Holy Spirit, they obeyed the word of instruction as though from someone speaking. Consequently Scripture calls it both "vision" and "Word of the Lord," and probably also "report" in that they receive knowledge as though by a report of some kind. COMMENTARY ON OBADIAH 1.[4]

2 A Small, Despised Nation

MADE LEAST. EPHREM THE SYRIAN: Obadiah shows here that the Edomites must be subjected to captivity because of their pride and the enmity they held against their brothers. In a different sense he says that the devil is made least, as the words that follow are extremely suitable to him as well. COMMENTARY ON OBADIAH.[5]

3 Deceived by Pride

VARIOUS MEANINGS OF "ROCK." JEROME: "The pride of your heart has deceived you." This is directed against the heretics. "You who dwell in the rock"—the rock[6] frequently refers to the Lord or standing on something solid, as the prophet says, "He has placed my feet upon a rock."[7] To Peter he said, "You are Peter, and upon this rock I will build my church."[8] Nevertheless it is also fre-

quently used in another way. Ezekiel says, "I will take the heart of stone out of your flesh."[9] In Matthew we read that God is able to raise up children of Abraham from these stones.[10] Ultimately, since here it does not say the inhabitants are on top of the rocks but rather in the fissure of the rocks, those referred to here are like heresies that split the rock of Christ and the church. COMMENTARY ON OBADIAH.[11]

4 Brought Down from Heights

THE FALL OF LUCIFER. JEROME: The Savior came not to send peace upon the earth but a sword.[12] Lucifer fell, Lucifer who used to rise at dawn;[13] and he who was bred up in a paradise of delight had the well-earned sentence passed upon him, "'Though you exalt yourself as your eagle, and though you set your nest among the stars, thence will I bring you down,' says the Lord." For Lucifer had said in his heart, "I will exalt my throne above the stars of God," and "I will be like the most high."[14] Therefore God says every day to the angels, as they descend the ladder that Jacob saw in his dream,[15] "I say, 'You are gods, sons of the most high, all of you; nevertheless you shall die like men and fall like any prince.'"[16] The devil fell first. "God has taken his place in the divine council; in the midst of the gods he holds judgment."[17] LETTER 22.4.[18]

5-6 Esau Pillaged

THE MEANING OF PLUNDERERS AND GRAPE GATHERERS. EPHREM THE SYRIAN: If thieves came to you, oh, how you would be silenced! Everything would be open for plunder because of the overwhelming fear, until [the plunderers] have stolen enough [riches] for themselves, for they are people of insatiable and consuming

---

[2]Mt 3:1. [3]ESOO 2:269. [4]PG 66:308. [5]ESOO 2:269*. [6]*Petra* in the Greek. [7]Ps 40:2 (39:3 LXX). [8]Mt 16:18. [9]Ez 36:26. [10]Mt 3:9. [11]CCL 76:358. [12]Mt 10:34. [13]Is 14:12. [14]Is 14:13-14. [15]Gen 28:12. [16]Ps 82:6-7 (81:6-7 LXX). [17]Ps 82:1 (81:1 LXX). [18]NPNF 2 6:23-24.

greed. If grape gatherers came to you—that is, if plunderers invaded you with open violence—what would you do? Would you not at least strive to have the gleanings of the vineyard remain to you? But you strive in vain against the Chaldeans, the invaders of your dominions. Therefore he refers to them [the Edomites] by adding how Esau has been pillaged, his treasures searched out. He prophesies that the people of Esau had to be pillaged by the Chaldeans with incredible zeal and then even deported to captivity. Nebuchadnezzar of Babylon fulfilled this prediction after he thouroughly destroyed Edom and moved its inhabitants elsewhere. COMMENTARY ON OBADIAH.[19]

10 Cut Off Forever

THE JEWS TO SUBJUGATE THE EDOMITES.
EPHREM THE SYRIAN: Shame shall cover you over the Jews, whose ruin you enjoyed, after they are brought back to their original power. And you shall be cut off forever. After the Jews return from Chaldea, they will subjugate you Edomites and will vex you for a long time. This will continue until the coming of a foreign people, who will defeat the Jews. Then the name and race of the Edomites will be totally obliterated. The Romans accomplished this prediction of the prophet against the Edomites by first subjugating Judea and then by scattering the Jews all over the world. COMMENTARY ON OBADIAH.[20]

12 Do Not Rejoice over Judah's Ruin

THE "DAY" AS A TIME OF PUNISHMENT. THEODORET OF CYR: "Do not despise the day of your brother in the day of his alienation." Here the time of punishment is called a "day." COMMENTARY ON OBADIAH.[21]

THE PASTOR MOURNS WITH THE SINNER.
AMBROSE: Preserve, O Lord, your work, guard the gift which you have given even to him who shrank from it. For I knew that I was not worthy to be called a bishop, because I had devoted myself to this world, but by your grace I am what I am. And I am indeed the least of all bishops, and the lowest in merit. Yet since I too have undertaken some labor for your holy church, watch over this fruit. Do not let the one who was lost before you called him to the priesthood be lost when he becomes a priest. And first grant that I may know how with inmost affection to mourn with those who sin; for this is a very great virtue, since it is written, "And you shall not rejoice over the children of Judah in the day of their destruction, and speak not proudly in the day of their trouble." Grant that so often as the sin of anyone who has fallen is made known to me I may suffer with him and not chide him proudly but mourn and weep, so that weeping over another I may mourn for myself, saying, "Tamar has been more righteous than I."[22] CONCERNING REPENTANCE 2.8.[23]

15 The Day of the Lord Nears

YOUR DEEDS SHALL RETURN ON YOUR HEAD.
PAULINUS OF NOLA: Be mindful on that day of the sons of Edom, and change their role with ours, so that they may in disarray witness the day on which your people will dwell in Jerusalem's ancient city. That nation turns its back on you and now threatens Jerusalem with cruel destruction, saying, "Level that hated city to the ground. Lay it bare by force until nothing stands and the walls are reduced to nothing." POEM 9.39.[24]

DIVINE JUSTICE IS FAIR. CYRIL OF ALEXANDRIA: Again the time of war is predicted [as in Joel][25] when the neighboring nations will join together against Edom to inflict bitter punishment. That day is truly called the Day of the Lord. For God the Lord was the one who handed them over to the Israelites in their wickedness and injustice. So that he might affirm that their divine punishment is just he says, "As you have done, so it will

---

[19]ESOO 2:270. [20]ESOO 2:270*. [21]PG 81:1713. [22]Gen 38:26. [23]NPNF 2 10:354. [24]ACW 40:56. [25]Joel 3.

be done to you." For nature is so arranged that everybody receives just treatment, and entirely equal wages are repaid to those who have undertaken similar actions. COMMENTARY ON OBADIAH.[26]

JUDGMENT IS NEAR FOR HERETICS. JEROME: Near, O heretic, is the Day of the Lord over all the nations. Near is the time of judgment in which all the nations are to be judged. As you have acted against the church, the same pain will come back upon your head, and your iniquities will descend upon the crown of your head. For as you have rejoiced in their death and as you have celebrated with a feast on my holy mountain, which is the church, you will not drink my cup, but the cup of the devil, about whom Habakkuk said, "Woe to him who gives drink to his neighbor, turning him upside down into confusion."[27] . . . Because you have worshiped in a way that causes ruin to my servants, therefore persecution will come against you and you will suffer for what you have done. And as you rejoiced against my people when you left them to the nations, likewise all the nations will rejoice against you, and they will eat and drink and continue the same persecution on you which you originally rejoiced in for my people. COMMENTARY ON OBADIAH.[28]

16 Drinking and Staggering

ALL NATIONS SHALL DRINK. EPHREM THE SYRIAN: You have drunk on my holy mountain from the cup of wrath, which David and Ahab mixed for you. All the nations around you shall drink constantly because of the Assyrians and the Chaldeans, in the days of Hezekiah and his sons. COMMENTARY ON OBADIAH.[29]

THE WINE OF REVENGE FROM THE LORD. THEODORET OF CYR: The drink of wine is called revenge, about which also blessed Jeremiah openly teaches when he says the nations will be commanded to drink even as they participated in the iniquities against my people.[30] This is also under-

stood from many other places that Edom will be given what it gave out. COMMENTARY ON OBADIAH.[31]

MOUNT ZION A TYPE OF THE CHURCH. CYRIL OF ALEXANDRIA: These words "as you have drunk" indicate, I think, that the victors insolently gloried in victory. They had a festive celebration where they got drunk with their friends, boasting in praise of their part in the victory while they got drunk. And while they were drinking and singing songs and causing all manner of damage at this party, they got drunk and began to insult the other nations. "And they will descend against you," that is, the neighboring regions will attack these parties. And so, you will want to be in a place where they are not; otherwise you too will be wiped out of existence. Mount Zion, however, by divine inspiration is called the church. For it is truly the highest and most visible, the foremost holy place. It is the house and city of the most holy God. COMMENTARY ON OBADIAH.[32]

PUNISHMENT AT HAND. THEODORE OF MOPSUESTIA: For the time when God will punish everyone who did evil against Israel is at hand. And he will impose grave punishment upon you just like the punishment you meted out against your brothers. "For as you drank on my holy mountain, so all the people will drink wine; they will drink and ascend and likewise become nothing." Because you inveighed against my holy mountain and its inhabitants, you will not escape punishment. Your thoughts and your participation indeed will mean punishment for you and your murderous, traitorous allies. In the end, there will be no difference between them and nonexistence. Already the words "you have drunk" and "they will drink" signify an observation in Edom that other enemies will be produced. For "in the hand of the Lord there is a cup, and it is fully mixed. And he has brought this cup

---

[26]PG 71:591. [27]Hab 2:15. [28]CCL 76:367. [29]ESOO 2:270. [30]Jer 25:15. [31]PG 81:1716. [32]PG 71:591.

down and will pour it out. Surely all the wicked of the earth shall drain it to the last drop and drink even the dregs."[33] But he remembered his holy mountain, recognizing the accusations of those outside against its inhabitants. Those accusers will be exposed to punishment as well as those who conspired with them, and they shall be punished with the death penalty.

In Zion, however, there will be salvation and holiness. Jacob will possess those who possessed him. To you, O Edom, therefore, and to your council of allies this will happen. But Judah will be safe and sound. Indeed there will be no adversity on Mount Zion, because they will no longer seek after wars so that my mountain will be seen as a secure place for the saints. Everyone who was so much trouble to you, Jacob, and those who plotted against you will truly be subjugated. COMMENTARY ON OBADIAH.[34]

17 Mount Zion to Be Holy

ZION'S SALVATION IS IN THE CROSS. THE-ODORET OF CYR: "On Mount Zion there will be salvation, and there will be holiness." For God is saying through the prophet, "I will bring them back from their captivity, and I will rebuild the sacred temple." And there is Obadiah, who prophesies the cause of salvation to all in Zion. From there God will disperse holiness into the entire inhabited earth through the saving cross. COMMENTARY ON OBADIAH.[35]

18 Fire and Stubble

UNITED ISRAEL AND JUDAH WILL DESTROY EDOM. JEROME: Edom is subjugated and will be devoured by the hostile nations with whom it formerly was in league against Jacob. The remnant, however, will be on Mount Zion, where there will be salvation and holiness. The interpretation here is, either it is that the Lord himself will return to the temple which he left because of sin, or there will be absolute holiness, that is, the Holy of Holies will once again be established. And the

house of Jacob will occupy it under the rule of Zerubbabel and Ezra and Nehemiah, who occupied it as Jacob's descendants. And the house of Jacob (that is, Judah) will be a fire, the house of Joseph (that is, the ten tribes of Samaria) a flame. But the house of Esau, that is, the Edomites, who nevertheless raged and cruelly stood against their brother, will be turned into stubble. And as fire and flames devour stubble, so the two kingdoms in union with one another[36] will destroy Edom and devour it. And there will be nothing left of the people of Edom that might be able to announce the destruction of the adversary to the neighboring nations. For this is why the Septuagint translates *pyrophoros*, which we interpret as "stubble," as nearest to the ancient way of speaking. COMMENTARY ON OBADIAH.[37]

THE TRUE KING BRINGS SALVATION. THE-ODORE OF MOPSUESTIA: The prosperity of Israel was made manifest as well as the punishment of their wicked enemies. . . . Yahweh proved himself as a true king to his people because he brought the very salvation they needed. COMMENTARY ON OBADIAH.[38]

HOW THE HEBREWS WILL CONSUME THE EDOMITES. EPHREM THE SYRIAN: The Hebrews, like a fire, will consume the Edomites like stubble. If anything remains, they will scatter it. What David and Amaziah had begun was accomplished by the Jews after their return, when many Israelites who came back from Persia joined them, and the Edomites were deprived of any form of domination and were forced to change their religion and to embrace the Jewish rituals. COMMENTARY ON OBADIAH.[39]

THE LITERAL MEANING OF THE FLAME. CYRIL OF ALEXANDRIA: The foolish Edomites thought that they alone were about to possess the house

---

[33]Ps 75:8 (74:9 LXX). [34]PG 66:316. [35]PG 81:1716. [36]As the rod in Ezekiel depicted a united federation; see Ezek 17:12-21. [37]CCL 76:368. [38]PG 66:317. [39]ESOO 2:271.

of Jacob. Instead the land was divided with them and with the Chaldeans. That very unforseen thing was turned against them, it says. They would be possessed by the house of Jacob and likewise be consumed like chaff or stubble by a flame. And the house of Jacob will be a fire, but the house of Joseph will be only a flame, and thus not as strong. And they will be devoured internally so that among all the tribes Jacob and Joseph will be unable to come together as one. But the other side of this fiery trope should also be seen, for the house of Jacob is called a fire and the house of Joseph a flame. It is not unreasonable to understand in the literal sense the house of Jacob as those from Judah and Benjamin. It is just as true that the house of Joseph represents Samaria, specifically, the ten tribes who were sometimes kings of the Ephraimites, since Manasseh and Ephraim were born from Joseph. Israel will possess the land of Edom and possess all of its confines to the south. They will capture no less than Mount Ephraim, Samaria, Benjamin and Gilead—which were the names of those areas when their leader, Joshua, the successor of Moses, apportioned the land to the tribes of Israel. But after Israel was devastated at the hand of Assyria and again after the attack of Nebuchadnezzar, ruled by Phua and Shalmanezer, he predicts they will once again inhabit the land after they are released from their former captivity. COMMENTARY ON OBADIAH.[40]

THE SPIRITUAL INTERPRETATION OF THE FIRE. JEROME: The spiritual interpretation is as follows: Through destruction of the works of the flesh and the desolation of earthly kingdoms, there will be salvation in the church for those who do not go out from their mother church. And the saints who die inside her—concerning whom it is said in Isaiah, "Holy, holy, holy, Lord God of Sabbaoth,"[41] because it refers to those whom he sanctifies as well as those who are sanctified—all are from one and the same church. And the house of Jacob the supplanter will occupy that which they possess by heredity

from those who persecuted the Christians. And Edom itself will be received by faith into the church. . . . The house of Esau will not survive, for when the wise men [who came from Edom] come to see Jesus, they will be turned into nothing, that is, they will be absorbed into his salvation near the same place where, in blessing, Isaac said to Esau,[42] "I have given him your master, all your sons I have given to him as servants." And there will be no remnant of the house of Esau left when all the heavens and earth bow to Christ and hell and the universe is subjected to him so that God may be all in all.[43] COMMENTARY ON OBADIAH.[44]

19 Possessing Mount Esau

ISRAELITES TO AGAIN POSSESS THE LAND. CYRIL OF ALEXANDRIA: "Those in the south" signifies the area where the Babylonians invaded Jerusalem led by Nebuchadnezzar. The entire province of Judea was laid waste, sinking back into misery so that it was reduced to absolute silence and appeared entirely deserted. However, when God will enter into the misery of the captives, he will return them to the land of their ancestors after his wrath has subsided. In their return from Babylon the entire multitude of Israel will possess the region of the nations that is equal to Edom. This is a sign of blessing from God. COMMENTARY ON OBADIAH.[45]

20-21 Possessing the Cities of the Negeb

THE PEOPLE OF GOD. EPHREM THE SYRIAN: Here he indicates the prisoners of both the kingdoms of Samaria and Jerusalem, and also those who had gone to very far regions. Therefore he recalls the transmigration to Spain, because this is the name of a province, which is extremely distant from Judea, in order to show that this is the great gathering, which God had promised to

---

[40]PG 71:593. [41]Is 6:3. [42]Gen 27:37. [43]Cf. 1 Cor 15:28. [44]CCL 76:368-69. [45]PG 71:593.

bring together again from the four corners of the world. Those who have been saved shall go up to Mount Zion to rule Mount Esau, in order to defeat and destroy the nation of the Edomites. And the kingdom shall be the Lord's. All the nations will be subjugated and subjected to the people of God, that is, to the people that God shall make. COMMENTARY ON OBADIAH.[46]

THE EXILES SHALL POSSESS THE WHOLE LAND AGAIN. CYRIL OF ALEXANDRIA: At this place in the text, the migration of Israel back to the land is mentioned, more specifically, from those Jews taken away into Babylon. . . . Perhaps here he is saying that everything that is to the south and to the north and to the east and to the west will be fully occupied by Israel as they will easily possess the whole region around them. And people will ascend, gathered on top of Zion, which sums up the goal of the prophecy. For the inhabitants of Zion, he says, are saved by God, who will burst through their chains of servitude. At that time he will ascend and take vengeance against Mount Esau. For they will fight, as I have said, against Edom after the time of captivity, and God will rule over all, although God rejected Esau long ago and withdrew from Judah because of apostasy. For they served Baal and the golden calf. But now in mercy and reconciliation he will reign again over them. COMMENTARY ON OBADIAH.[47]

MOUNT ESAU SIGNIFIES THE CHURCH OF THE GENTILES. AUGUSTINE: Obadiah, so far as his writings are concerned the briefest of all the prophets, speaks against Edom, that is, the nation of Esau, that reprobate elder of the twin sons of Isaac and of the grandsons of Abraham. Now by that form of speech in which a part is understood for the whole, we understand Edom as referring to the nations. We may understand what Christ says in the same way: "But upon Mount Zion shall be safety, and there shall be a holy one."[48] And a little further, at the end of the same prophecy, he says concerning Paul, "And the re-

deemed shall come up out of Mount Zion, that they may defend Mount Esau, and it shall be a kingdom to the Lord." It is quite evident that this was fulfilled when the redeemed out of Mount Zion (that is, the believers in Christ from Judea, of whom the apostles are chiefly to be acknowledged) went up to defend Mount Esau. How could they defend it except by making safe through the preaching of the gospel those who believed that they might be "delivered from the power of darkness and translated into the kingdom of God."[49] Consequently he expressed this by adding, "And it shall be to the Lord a kingdom." For Mount Zion signifies Judea, where it is predicted there shall be safety and a holy one, that is, Jesus Christ. But Mount Esau is Edom. It signifies the church of the Gentiles, which is defended by the redeemed from Mount Zion, so that it should become a kingdom to the Lord. This was obscure before it took place, but what believer does not understand it now that it has happened? CITY OF GOD 18.31.[50]

REJOICING AND WEEPING. THEODORET OF CYR: Ezekiel also predicts something similar at the end of his prophecy when he describes the division of the land. He too predicts the return of the people, and after they return we learn they will receive power and obtain strength from God. O that we also would obtain this from our most generous God. And we will receive this from the Lord if we do not imitate the model of Esau and his posterity [who rejoiced in Israel's destruction]. Rather, following the apostolic tradition, we should rejoice with those who rejoice and weep with those who weep, and we ought to think the same for others [as we would have them think of us]. For this reason we possess the gifts of the Lord of all life, which is the grace of our Lord Jesus Christ, to whom be glory with the Father and the Holy Spirit now and forever, world without end. Amen. COMMENTARY ON OBADIAH.[51]

---

[46]ESOO 2:271. [47]PG 71:595-96. [48]Obad 17. [49]Col 1:13. [50]PL 41:588. [51]PG 81:1717.

THE LORD WILL SEND A SAVIOR AND A KING.
JEROME: The Jewish interpreters explained this similarly that the Lord sent a Savior who would save the people from captivity and they would ascend and go to Mount Zion in order to judge and decide regarding the Mountain of Esau. And when everything is subjugated, there will be a kingdom to the Lord. COMMENTARY ON OBADIAH.[52]

---

[52]CCL 76:372.

JONAH

OVERVIEW: The writer of Jonah (Heb *yônâ*, which some scholars believe to be a personal name meaning "dove") identifies the prophet as Jonah ben ("son of") Amittai. Elsewhere a prophet named Jonah is identified as "son of Amittai . . . who was from Gath-hepher"[1] in the reign of Jeroboam II.

Jonah 1:1-16 relates his calling as a prophet, his attempt to evade his charge to preach to the inhabitants of Nineveh, and his being thrown off the boat in a storm for which he was blamed. In Jonah 1:17—2:10, Jonah is swallowed by a great fish, where he remained for three days and nights. He maintained hope by singing Psalm 2:2-9. The fish vomited him up on a shore after the prophet repented and agreed to carry out the mission given to him by Yahweh. Jonah 4 relates Jonah's despondency at the repentance of the Ninevites, whom he wished to have seen destroyed by Yahweh. It also contains the incident of the gourd tree. A worm attacked it, causing it to wither. This left Jonah exposed to the intense heat of the day. Most interpreters accept a postexilic date for the book because of its numerous Aramaisms and its use of later Hebrew prose style and grammar.

Because of the specific citations in the Gospels relating it to Jesus (Mt 12:40-41; Lk 11:29-32), Jonah was one of the principal books of exegesis for the church fathers. In the Gospels, Jesus used the conversion of the Ninevites—non-Jews—as means to chastise the Jews who were rejecting his message. In Matthew, for example, Jesus compared his three days in the tomb with Jonah's three days in the belly of the great fish. In short, it was the purpose of the church fathers to see Christ as the new Jonah who fulfilled and transcended the old covenant, which had now been entrusted to the new Ninevites, the Gentiles.

JONAH PREFIGURES CHRIST'S RESURRECTION AND THE SALVATION OF THE GENTILES. THE-ODORE OF MOPSUESTIA: What happened in the case of blessed Jonah the prophet was similar: when Jews were unbelieving and reluctant to heed his prophecies, God had him go instead to the nations. Then, after remarkably keeping him safe inside the sea monster for three days and nights, he brought him to the city that was full of countless vices and caused him to preach repentance and become a source of salvation for all in

---

[1]2 Kings 14:25.

that place, so that from the comparison we might not lack faith in Christ the Lord, who was kept incorrupt for the same number of days, rising from the dead and providing all nations in general with salvation by way of repentance and enjoying immortal life. COMMENTARY ON JONAH, INTRODUCTION.[2]

JONAH'S MISSION TO NINEVEH. THEODORET OF CYR: This is the way the God of all also appointed blessed Jonah prophet to the Ninevites. Now it was the greatest city in olden times, containing also the palace of the king of the Assyrians. When, you see, the only-begotten Word of God was due to be made manifest to human beings in his human nature and to enlighten all the nations with the light of the knowledge of God, even before his own incarnation he gives the nations a glimpse of his divine care so as to confirm what would happen from what went before, to teach everyone that he is God not only of Jews but also of nations, and to bring out the relationship of the Old and the New Testament. After all, if he had shown no care for the nations before the incarnation, Jews would have formed the impression that he was a different God in doing the opposite to the giver of the law, the former being concerned only with Jews and the latter bestowing attention on all human beings. COMMENTARY ON JONAH, INTRODUCTION.[3]

---

[2]PG 66:321. [3]PG 81:1721.

1:1-3 JONAH'S RELUCTANCE

[1]Now the word of the LORD came to Jonah the son of Amittai, saying, [2]"Arise, go to Nineveh, that great city, and cry against it; for their wickedness* has come up before me." [3]But Jonah rose to flee to Tarshish from the presence of the LORD. He went down to Joppa and found a ship going to Tarshish; so he paid the fare, and went on board, to go with them to Tarshish, away from the presence of the LORD.

*LXX for the cry of their wickedness

OVERVIEW: The story of Jonah inspires those who, like Jonah, are reluctant to accept the yoke of ministry (GREGORY OF NAZIANZUS). Perhaps Jonah was reluctant because he feared his prophecy would be proved false (GREGORY OF NAZIANZUS, THEODORE). Or perhaps he feared that Israel would perish if Nineveh was spared (JEROME). Nonetheless Jonah cannot escape God by fleeing to Tarshish (TERTULLIAN, GREGORY OF NAZIANZUS).

1:1-3 Go to Nineveh

RELUCTANCE TO ACCEPT THE YOKE OF MINISTRY. GREGORY OF NAZIANZUS: But there Jonah calls upon God, and marvelous as it is, on the third day, he, like Christ, is delivered. . . . In my own case, what could be said? What defense could be made if I remained unsettled and rejected the yoke of ministry, which, though I know not whether to call it light or heavy, had at any rate been laid upon me. . . . On this account I had much toilsome consideration to discover my duty, being set in the middle between two fears, of which the one held me back and the other urged me on. For a long while I was at a loss between them. After wavering from side to side, and, like a current driven by inconstant winds, inclining first in this direction then in that, I at last yielded to the stronger. The fear of disobedience overcame me. IN DEFENSE OF HIS FLIGHT TO PONTUS, ORATION 2.109-12.[1]

JONAH FEARS FALSE PROPHECY. GREGORY OF NAZIANZUS: What then is the story, and wherein lies its application? For, perhaps, it would not be amiss to relate it, for its general validation. Jonah also was fleeing from the face of God, or rather, thought that he was fleeing. But he was overtaken by the sea, and the storm, and the lot, and the whale's belly, and the three days' entombment. All this is a type of a greater mystery. He fled from having to announce the dread of the awful message to the Ninevites and from being subsequently, if the city was saved by repentance, convicted of falsehood. It was not that he was displeased at the salvation of the wicked, but he was ashamed of being made an instrument of falsehood and exceedingly zealous for the credit of prophecy, which was in danger of being destroyed in his own person. Indeed most would be unable to penetrate the depth of the divine dispensation in such cases. ORATION 2.106.[2]

JONAH'S FLIGHT WAS DICTATED BY HIS CONCERN OVER ISRAEL. JEROME: The prophet knows, the Holy Spirit teaching him, that the repentance of the Gentiles is the ruin of the Jews. A lover, then, of his country, he does not so much envy the deliverance of Nineveh as will that his own country should not perish. Seeing too that his fellow prophets are sent to the lost sheep of the house of Israel to excite the people to repentance, and that Balaam the soothsayer too prophesied the salvation of Israel, he grieves that he alone is chosen to be sent to the Assyrians, the enemies of Israel, and to that greatest city of the enemies where there was idolatry and ignorance of God. Even more, he feared that Israel might be wholly forsaken due to the conversion of the Ninevites

through repentance by his preaching. For he knew by the same Spirit whereby the preaching to the Gentiles was trusted to him that the house of Israel would then perish, and he feared that what was at one time to be would take place in his own time. COMMENTARY ON JONAH 1:3.[3]

GOD CANNOT BE ESCAPED. TERTULLIAN: In trying to run away from the Lord, you show up the fickleness of all who plan flight. A certain headstrong prophet also had run away from the Lord, crossing the sea from Joppa to Tarsus, as if he could escape from God. But God found him not on land or on sea but in the belly of a beast, where for three days he could not die[4] or even in that way escape from the eyes of God. Is that man not better off who, though he fears the enemy of God, does not flee from but despises him? Who trusts in the protection of God or, if you will, has an even greater fear of God, having stood the longer in his eyes? He says, "He is the Lord, he is mighty, all things are his, and wherever I shall be I am in his hands. Let him do what he will, I shall not run away. If he wishes me to die, let him destroy me, as long as I faithfully serve him. Much would I rather bring odium on him, by dying according to his will, than to live by my own cowardice." ON FLIGHT IN TIME OF PERSECUTION 10.2.[5]

THE FOLLY OF ESCAPING GOD. GREGORY OF NAZIANZUS: Jonah knew better than anyone the purpose of his message to the Ninevites and that, in planning his flight, although he changed his location, he did not escape from God. Nor is this possible for anyone else, either by concealing himself in the bosom of the earth, or in the depths of the sea, or by soaring on wings, if there be any means of doing so, and rising into the air, or by abiding in the lowest depths of hell, or by any other of the many devices for ensuring escape. For God alone of all things can-

---

[1]NPNF 2 7:226*. [2]NPNF 2 7:225*. [3]PMPC 1:398*; CCL 76:381*. [4]Jon 1:17 (2:1 LXX). [5]FC 40:296*.

not be escaped from or contended with. If he wills to seize and bring them under his hand, he outstrips the swift. He outwits the wise. He overthrows the strong. He cuts down the lofty.

He subdues rashness. He resists power. ORATION 2.108.[6]

[6]NPNF 2 7:226.

1:4-17 JONAH'S FAILED ESCAPE

[4]*But the* LORD *hurled a great wind upon the sea, and there was a mighty tempest on the sea, so that the ship threatened to break up.* [5]*Then the mariners were afraid, and each cried to his god; and they threw the wares that were in the ship into the sea, to lighten it for them. But Jonah had gone down into the inner part of the ship and had lain down, and was fast asleep.* [6]*So the captain came and said to him, "What do you mean, you sleeper? Arise, call upon your god! Perhaps the god will give a thought to us, that we do not perish."*

[7]*And they said to one another, "Come, let us cast lots, that we may know on whose account this evil has come upon us." So they cast lots, and the lot fell upon Jonah.* [8]*Then they said to him, "Tell us on whose account this evil has come upon us. What is your occupation? And whence do you come? What is your country? And of what people are you?"* [9]*And he said to them, "I am a Hebrew;* and I fear the* LORD, *the God of heaven, who made the sea and the dry land."* [10]*Then the men were exceedingly afraid, and said to him, "What is this that you have done!" For the men knew that he was fleeing from the presence of the* LORD, *because he had told them.*

[11]*Then they said to him, "What shall we do to you, that the sea may quiet down for us?" For the sea grew more and more tempestuous.* [12]*He said to them, "Take me up and throw me into the sea; then the sea will quiet down for you; for I know it is because of me that this great tempest has come upon you."* [13]*Nevertheless the men rowed hard to bring the ship back to land, but they could not, for the sea grew more and more tempestuous against them.* [14]*Therefore they cried to the* LORD, *"We beseech thee, O* LORD, *let us not perish for this man's life, and lay not on us innocent blood; for thou, O* LORD, *hast done as it pleased thee."* [15]*So they took up Jonah and threw him into the sea; and the sea ceased from its raging.* [16]*Then the men feared the* LORD *exceedingly, and they offered a sacrifice to the* LORD *and made vows.*

[17a]*And the* LORD *appointed a great fish to swallow up Jonah; and Jonah was in the belly of the fish three days and three nights.*

a Ch 2.1 in Heb   *LXX *a servant of the Lord*

OVERVIEW: The storm blew hard against the ship, its peril representing the insecurity of those who do not follow God's will (JEROME). In their attempts to lighten the ship's cargo, they proved that the weight of Jonah's disobedience was the heaviest burden (CHRYSOSTOM). Jonah was chosen by lot as the cause of the storm. This forshadowed the election of Matthias by lot to replace the fallen Judas (Bede). Knowing the God who made the sea and the dry land, it was unlikely that Jonah thought he could escape the designs of God. He is praised for being willing to sacrifice himself so that the sailors would not perish (Gregory of Nazianzus). Jonah learned that nature would not accompany him in his disobedience to God (Chrysostom, Paulinus). While Jonah would have the entire city of Nineveh destroyed, the sailors tried to spare Jonah (Chrysostom). Ultimately the sailors cast Jonah into the sea, and it becomes calm. Thus, doing God's will results in peace and tranquillity (Jerome). God's generous grace is shown by the fact that he delivered Jonah as soon as the prophet showed remorse for his disobedience (Apostolic Constitutions). God spared the Ninevites through Jonah as God spares other penitents through Christ (Tertullian). Jonah's calming the sea is likened to Christ's rebuking the wind and the sea; Jonah's three days in the belly of the whale is likened to Christ's three days in the grave (Cyril of Jerusalem). Even in Augustine's day people doubted the historicity of Jonah's story, but faithful Christians are not to fear such attacks by their critics (Augustine).

1:4 The Peril of the Ship

Nothing Is Secure When God Is Against Us. Jerome: The flight of the prophet may also be referred to that of man in general, who, despising the commands of God, departed from him and gave himself to the world, where subsequently through the storms of ill and the wreck of the whole world raging against him, he was compelled to feel the presence of God and to return to him whom he had fled. Therefore we understand that those things also which men think for their good, when against the will of God, are turned to destruction. And help not only does not benefit those to whom it is given, but those who give it are alike crushed. As we read that Egypt was con-

quered by the Assyrians because it helped Israel against the will of God, the ship is imperiled which had received the imperiled. A tempest arises in a calm; nothing is secure when God is against us. Commentary on Jonah 1:4.[1]

1:5 The Mariners Cry Out and Attempt to Lighten the Ship

Sin Is Like Heavy Cargo. Chrysostom: "They threw overboard the wares that were in the ship into the sea; but the ship was not getting any lighter," because the entire cargo still remained within it, the body of the prophet, the heavy cargo, not according to the nature of the body but from the weight of sin. For nothing is so heavy and onerous to bear as sin and disobedience. Homilies on Repentance and Almsgiving 3.8.[2]

1:7 They Cast Lots

Jonah and Matthias. Bede: And they drew lots between them, and so forth. Neither because of this example, nor because the prophet Jonah was found out by lot, are we to believe indiscriminately in lots, "since the prerogative of individuals," as Jerome says, can in no way "make a general law."[3] For in that instance pagan men were compelled by a storm to seek by lot the source of their danger. Matthias was chosen by lot so that their choice of the apostle would not appear to be out of harmony with the command of the old law, where it was ordered that the high priest be sought. Commentary on the Acts of the Apostles 1.[4]

1:9 Jonah Confesses Fear of God the Creator

Jonah Was Not Ignorant of God's Power. Gregory of Nazianzus: It was not likely that such a prophet should be ignorant of the design

---

[1]PMPC 1:398*; CCL 76:384-85. [2]FC 96:62. [3]Jerome *Commentary on Jonah* 1:7. [4]CS 117:20.

of God, which was to bring about, by means of threat, the escape of the Ninevites from the threatened doom, according to his great wisdom and unsearchable judgments and according to his ways which are beyond our tracing and finding out. . . . To imagine that Jonah hoped to hide himself at sea and escape by his flight the great eye of God is surely utterly absurd and stupid, and unworthy of credit, not only in the case of a prophet but even in the case of any sensible person, who has only a slight perception of God, whose power is over all. IN DEFENSE OF HIS FLIGHT TO PONTUS, ORATION 2.107.[5]

1:11 The Storm Intensified

THE OCEAN KNOWS JONAH. CHRYSOSTOM: Tell me, are you running away from the master? Then wait a little bit and you will learn from the state of affairs themselves that you will be unable to escape even from the hands of his servant, the ocean. For as soon as Jonah set foot on the ship, the ocean raised its waves up high and raised itself to a great height. And just as a considerate handmaid, discovering that her fellow slave has run away because he stole something of her master's, does not revolt as previously mentioned but submits the individuals who captured him to myriads of troubles until she seizes him and brings him back, likewise, the ocean found her fellow slave and recognized him. HOMILIES ON REPENTANCE AND ALMSGIVING 5.3.8.[6]

THE SEAS BELONG TO GOD. PAULINUS OF NOLA: Jonah surely teaches us that the sea and stars are moved under God's control. By vainly seeking to flee from God the controller of all things whom none can escape, he aroused the anger of both sky and sea. Nature, which belongs to the almighty Lord, realized that [Jonah] was revolting, and it was afraid to play conspirator by transporting the guilty man safely through its domain; it chained the runaway with winds and waves. POEM 22.[7]

1:12-13 "Throw Me into the Sea"; but Sailors Row Toward Land

THE SAILORS RESIST JONAH'S ENTREATY. CHRYSOSTOM: From where, my beloved, came the foresight of the prophet? From the economy of God. God made these things happen so that the prophet might learn from them to be a lover of humanity and be subdued. Only to him did he cry out and say, "Imitate the sailors, the naïve men, who neither despise a single soul nor neglect a single body, yours. And you would allow to be destroyed, on your part, an entire city with myriads of inhabitants. These sailors, when they discovered who was responsible for all the evils that confronted them, still were not eager to condemn him; but you, who have no charge brought against you by the Ninevites, would convict and annihilate them. Yet when I commanded you to go and, through preaching, summon them back to salvation, you disobeyed. They who were not accountable to anyone did all things and exerted themselves so that you, who are accountable should be punished." Although the ocean condemned him and the lot exposed him, when he implicated himself and confessed his flight, they still were not in a hurry to annihilate the prophet; rather, they demonstrated toleration and constraint and did everything possible to keep him from the fury of the ocean after such proof of his guilt. However, the ocean did not permit even this, or better yet, God did not allow this to happen, because he wanted to sober him through the sailors in the same way as through the whale. For this reason when they heard, "Take me up and cast me into the sea, and the seas will be calm to you," they strained to reach the shore, although the waves did not allow it. HOMILIES ON REPENTANCE AND ALMSGIVING 3.8.[8]

1:14 The Sailors Cry Out to the Lord

A GREATER PILOT WAS REQUIRED. CHRYSOS-

---

[5]NPNF 2 7:225-26*. [6]FC 96:61-62*. [7]ACW 40:205-6*. [8]FC 96:63-64*.

TOM: The ship's pilot . . . understood from his experience that the storm was not a usual one, but that the blow was God-sent, and that the billowy ocean was vastly superior to human skill, and that the hands of the helmsman were of no advantage. In this situation a greater pilot was required, the One who governs the whole world, and the assistance from above was critical. For this reason, they abandoned the oars, the sails, the ropes, and everything else; they drew their hands back to themselves and raised them to heaven and entreated God. HOMILIES ON REPENTANCE AND ALMSGIVING 3.8.[9]

THE SAILORS ACKNOWLEDGE THE JUST JUDGMENT OF GOD. JEROME: The sailors and the passengers in the book of Jonah say, "We beseech you, O Lord, do not destroy us on account of this man and lay not upon us innocent blood, for you, O Lord, have done as it pleased you." They do not know the reasons why the prophet, a fugitive servant, deserved to be punished. And yet they justify God and acknowledge the blood of him whose deeds they do not know to be innocent. And in conclusion, they say, "You, O Lord, have done as it pleased you." They do not question the justice of the judgment of God but acknowledge the veracity of the just Judge. AGAINST THE PELAGIANS 2.23.[10]

1:15 They Cast Jonah into the Sea

THE SEA IS CALMED. JEROME: The text does not say they seized him or that they threw him in, but that they *took* him, carrying him as one [deserving] respect and honor. They discharged him into the sea not in repugnance; rather, he submitted himself of his own volition into their hands. And the sea ceased [its turmoil] because it found what it sought. When one continues as a fugitive and keeps running away as fast as one can, sooner or later he is caught and stops his running, and whatever was chasing him stands still. It is the same way with the sea, which, absent Jonah, was irritated. But as soon as it lays hold of what is at

the center of its desire it rejoices to have it, and from that joy it returns to tranquillity. If we will give consideration to the time before the passion of Christ, [we will see that time as one disturbed by] the errors of the world and the headwinds of various opinions. The entire boat of humanity, that is, the creation of the Lord, was in peril. But then, after his passion, we see a world where there is the calm of faith, a world at peace and secure for everyone. We see a turning toward God. In this way we may understand how, after Jonah goes into the sea, the sea is alleviated of its turmoil. COMMENTARY ON JOEL 1.15.[11]

1:17 A Great Fish Swallows Jonah

THE DUTY OF ADMONITION. APOSTOLIC CONSTITUTIONS: It is also your duty, O bishop, to follow the examples of those that have gone before and to apply their judgments skillfully to the cases of those who want words of severity or of consolation. Besides, it is reasonable that in your administration of justice you should follow the will of God. As God deals with sinners and with those who return, you should act accordingly in your judging. Now did not God by Nathan admonish David for his offense? And yet as soon as he said he repented, God delivered him from death, saying, "Be of good cheer; you shall not die."[12] So also, when God had caused Jonah to be swallowed up by the sea and the whale upon his refusal to preach to the Ninevites, when yet he prayed to God out of the belly of the whale, he retrieved his life from corruption. CONSTITUTIONS OF THE HOLY APOSTLES 2.3.22.[13]

JONAH PREFIGURES CHRIST. TERTULLIAN: Did Jonah, then, on this account, think that repentance was unnecessary for the pagan Ninevites, when he tried to avoid his duty of preaching? Or was it not, rather, that he foresaw that the mercy of God would be poured out on the heathen also,

---

[9]FC 96:62-63. [10]FC 53:334. [11] CCL 76:392. [12]2 Sam 12:13. [13]ANF 7:406.

and so feared it would prove him a false prophet?[14] Actually it was because of a pagan city, which did not yet know God and which sinned in ignorance, that the prophet was almost lost. And he would have been lost, were it not for the fact that what he endured was a type of the Lord's suffering, by which pagan penitents also would be redeemed. ON PURITY 10.[15]

JONAH AND JESUS COMPARED. CYRIL OF JERUSALEM: They further object: A dead man recently deceased was raised by the living; but show us that it is possible for a man dead and buried for three days to rise again. The testimony we seek is supplied by the Lord Jesus himself in the Gospels, when he says, "For even as Jonah was in the belly of the fish three days and three nights, so will the Son of man be three days and three nights in the heart of the earth."[16] Now when we study the story of Jonah the force of the resemblance becomes striking. Jesus was sent to preach repentance. So was Jonah. Though Jonah fled, not knowing what was to come, Jesus came willingly, to grant repentance for salvation. Jonah slumbered in the ship and was fast asleep amid the stormy sea; while Jesus by God's will was sleeping, the sea was stirred up, for the purpose of manifesting thereafter the power of him who slept. They said to Jonah, "What are you doing asleep? Rise up, call upon your God, that God may save us," but the apostles say, "Lord, save us!"[17] In the first instance they said, Call upon your God, and in the second, save us. In the first Jonah said to them, "Pick me up and throw me into the sea, that it may quiet down for you"; in the other Christ himself "rebuked the wind and the sea, and there came a great calm."[18] Jonah was cast into the belly of a great fish, but Christ of his own will descended to the abode of the invisible fish of death. He went down of his own will to make death disgorge those it had swallowed up, according to the Scripture: "I shall deliver them from the power of the nether world, and I shall redeem them from death."[19] CATECHETICAL LECTURE 14.7.[20]

DO NOT FEAR CYNICISM ABOUT MIRACLES. AUGUSTINE: The last question is about Jonah, and it is not put as if it were taken from Porphyry but as if it were a laughingstock of the pagans. It is expressed thus: "Please tell me what we are to think about Jonah, who is said to have been three days in the belly of a whale. It is improbable and unbelievable that he should have been swallowed up with his clothing and should have been inside the fish. If it is figuratively said, please explain it.

...I have noticed that this sort of question is a matter of much jest and much laughter to pagans. The answer to this is that either all the divine miracles are to be disbelieved or there is no reason why they should not be believed. We should not believe in Christ himself and that he rose on the third day, if the faith of the Christians feared the laughter of the pagans. LETTER 170.6.[21]

---

[14]Cf. Jon 4:2. [15]ACW 28:80*. [16]Mt 12:40. [17]Mt 8:25. [18]Mt 8:26. [19]Hos 13:14. [20]FC 64:43. [21]FC 18:170.

2:1-10 JONAH'S PRAYER
FROM THE HEART OF THE SEA

¹Then Jonah prayed to the LORD his God
from the belly of the fish, ²saying,
"I called to the LORD, out of my distress,
    and he answered me;
out of the belly of Sheol I cried,
    and thou didst hear my voice.
³For thou didst cast me into the deep,
    into the heart of the seas,
    and the flood was round about me;
all thy waves and thy billows
    passed over me.
⁴Then I said, 'I am cast out
    from thy presence;
how shall I again look
    upon thy holy temple?'
⁵The waters closed in over me,
    the deep was round about me;
weeds were wrapped about my head

⁶at the roots of the mountains.
I went down to the land
    whose bars closed upon me for ever;
yet thou didst bring up my life from
    the Pit,
    O LORD my God.
⁷When my soul fainted within me,
    I remembered the LORD;
and my prayer came to thee,
    into thy holy temple.
⁸Those who pay regard to vain idols
    forsake their true loyalty.
⁹But I with the voice of thanksgiving
    will sacrifice to thee;
what I have vowed I will pay.
    Deliverance belongs to the LORD!"
¹⁰And the LORD spoke to the fish, and it
vomited out Jonah upon the dry land.

OVERVIEW: Reaching the uttermost limit of evil in the belly of the fish, Jonah cried out to God for help (BASIL). His endurance and prayer in the whale's belly became a pattern for Christian asceticism, which was realized, for instance, in the life of Basil the Great (GREGORY OF NAZIANZUS). The whale's belly became a house of repentant prayer for Jonah, a refuge in desperate times. Jonah prayed from the depths and gained the gifts of the highest Redeemer (CASSIODORUS). Jonah typified the Lord's three days in the tomb. He remained unharmed in the sea and waves, and though swallowed by the whale, he was not consumed by death (PAULINUS). The belly of the fish typifies Mary's womb, from whence Christ would come (AMBROSE). Also, the belly of the fish is called "the belly of hell" and is likened to the three days of Jesus' death (THEODORET). As such, Jonah typifies, Christ's descent into the nether world. Just as Jonah survived in the belly, so Christ survived the tomb (CYRIL OF JERUSALEM). Jonah cries out to the Lord like many of God's servants, is heard and is delivered (SYMEON). Christians must do as Jonah did: put their trust in Christ alone for salvation (PAULINUS). Jonah's expulsion from the whale after three days typifies resurrection (TERTULLIAN). Jonah's fate in the fish's belly was not destruction but salvation (GREGORY OF NAZIANZUS). Astrological signs at one's birth, such as natal stars, have no influence whatsoever in being chosen by God for his service (AMBROSE). Those who do not believe that Elijah was consumed by the flying chariot have also the example of Jonah, who survived unscathed from three days in the whale's belly (IRE-NAEUS).

2:1-2 Jonah Prays to God

JONAH DEMONSTRATES FAITH IN THE MIDST OF ADVERSITY. BASIL THE GREAT: Since the holy God has promised those who hope in him a means of escape from every affliction, we, even if we have been cut off in the midst of the seas of evils and are racked by the mighty waves stirred up against us by the spirits of wickedness, never-theless endure in Christ who strengthens us. We have not slackened the intensity of our zeal for the churches, nor do we, as in a storm when the waves rise high, expect destruction. We still hold fast to our earnest endeavors as much as is possi-ble, sensible of the fact that he who was swal-lowed by the whale was considered deserving of safety because he did not despair of his life but cried out to the Lord. So then, we ourselves, hav-ing reached the uttermost limit of evils, do not give up our hope in the Lord but watch and see his help on all sides. LETTER 242.[1]

JONAH'S PATTERN RECURRENT IN SCRIPTURE. GREGORY OF NAZIANZUS: Do you praise the fear-lessness of Elijah in speaking to tyrants and his translation in fire[2] and the noble heritage of Elisha, the sheepskin mantle, accompanied by the spirit of Elijah?[3] Then praise also the life of Basil passed in the midst of the fire, I mean in the multitude of temptations, and his preservation through fire which burned but did not consume, the miracle of the bush.[4] Praise also the fair garment of skin, which came to him from on high, his fleshlessness. I shall omit other parallels, as the young men be-dewed in the flames[5] and the fugitive prophet pray-ing in the belly of the fish and coming forth from the monster as from a chamber. I shall pass over the just man in the den, restraining the ferocity of lions,[6] and the struggle of the seven Maccabees,[7] who with a priest and their mother was perfected by blood and all kinds of tortures. Basil emulated their endurance and achieved their glory. ON

BASIL THE GREAT, ORATION 43.74.[8]

JONAH REPENTS THROUGH PRAYER FROM THE DEPTHS. CASSIODORUS: The word for depth (pro-fundum)[9] stands for porro fundum, the far bottom, whose lowest levels are wholly submerged. From here the prophet cried to the Lord so that he could be more easily heard. It was from this depth that Peter poured forth his glorious tears and from here that the tax collector, who had fallen so deeply into sin that he could not even raise his eyes to heaven, beat his blameworthy breast. Finally from these depths Jonah, who was set in the whale's belly and had entered hell alive, spoke to the Lord with si-lent vehemence. The whale was a house of prayer for the prophet, a harbor for him when ship-wrecked, a home amid the waves, a happy resource at a desperate time. He was not swallowed for sus-tenance but to gain rest; and by a wondrous and novel precedent the beast's belly yielded up its food unharmed, rather than consumed by the normally damaging process of digestion. Jonah bears witness to this in his book when he says, "And the Lord commanded a great fish to swallow Jonah, and Jonah was in the belly of the fish three days and three nights," and the rest. In that same passage he recounted his prayers as well with prophetic truth. What an outstandingly and wholly glorious repen-tance, a humility that experiences no fall, grief that rejoices people's hearts, tears that water the soul! Indeed this depth, which conveys us to heaven, has no inkling of hell. So observe the power of holy prayer, believing as it does that it must be heard the more quickly, the deeper the depths from which it cried to the Lord. So finally there follows, "Lord, hear my prayer," for those who have buried themselves in the bowels of holy humility are all the closer to the Highest. Thus when he prayed from the depths he quickly gained the gifts of the highest Redeemer. EXPOSITION ON THE PSALMS 129.1.[10]

---

[1]FC 28:182. [2]2 Chron 1:1. [3]2 Chron 2:9. [4]Ex 3:2-3. [5]Dan 3:5-27. [6]Dan 6:16-24. [7]2 Macc 7:1-42. [8]FC 22:92-93. [9]Ps 129:1 Vulgate. [10]ACW 53:312.

FREE FOR PRAYER BUT DETAINED IN FLIGHT.
PAULINUS OF NOLA: Now that I have made mention of the great prophet, who typifies the holy mystery, foreshadowed the death which lasted three days and the salvation it restored, I should like to retrace the footsteps of my poem and briefly hasten back to Jonah. Wondrous are the Lord's stratagems. Though plunged in the sea, he tossed on the waves unharmed. Though devoured, he lived on, and the beast that swallowed him remained unfed by the living food [of his body]. He was the booty but not the food of the whale whose belly he used as a home. What a worthy prison for God's holy runaway! He was captured on the very sea by which he had sought to flee.

Translated to the deep belly of the massive beast, he was imprisoned in a living jail. Thrown from the ship to destruction, he yet sailed upon the waters, an exile from land, a guest of the brine. He walked in the cavern of the whale's body, a prisoner both captive and free. He was free upon the waves as he floated in that whale, both within the sea and outside it. And though physically incarcerated, the prophet emerged in spirit to return to God. His body was constrained by the great body [of the whale], but the bonds of earth did not constrain the flight of his mind. Though enclosed in that belly, he broke out of his prison by prayer and reached God's ears. Free for prayer but detained from flight, he proved himself by his faith. He had attempted to escape God by sea, to hide from God in a ship, but now he believed that the Lord was with him even inside that whale submerged in the sea. POEM 24.205.[11]

THE BELLY AS A TYPE OF WOMB. AMBROSE:
Like Jonah when he was in the belly of the fish, I prayed to you on behalf of the people. Similarly, Christ was with God from his mother's womb, according to what is written, "Before the child knew good or evil, he chose the good."[12] THE PRAYER OF JOB AND DAVID 6.25.[13]

FROM THE BELLY OF HELL. THEODORET OF

CYR: "I cried out," he says, "to the Lord my God in my affliction, and he heard me. Out of the belly of hell he heard my cry." "I," says Jonah, "who previously thought that God appears to prophets only in Jerusalem, found him present even in the whale's belly. And having prayed to him, I was delivered by his love of humanity." He calls the whale's belly "the belly of hell" because the beast is deadly. In fact, Jonah was already presumed dead. He survived only by God's grace. Moreover, Jonah says that he was in the "belly of hell" because this is also a type of the Lord Jesus Christ, who was "three days and three nights in the heart of the earth."[14] It is especially surprising that the one who really tasted death said that he was three days and three nights in the belly of earth, yet the one who saw just the shadow of death called the whale's belly "the belly of hell." This was because the life of Jonah was beyond his control, while in the case of the Lord both his death and his resurrection were voluntary. That is why the Gospel calls the place of hell and death "the heart of earth," while here the belly of whale is called "the belly of hell." "He heard my voice," says Jonah, since otherwise he would not be alive to say this. COMMENTARY ON JONAH 2.3.[15]

2:6 Brought from the Depths

JONAH TYPIFIED CHRIST. CYRIL OF JERUSALEM:
Jonah fulfilled a type of our Savior when he prayed from the belly of the fish and said, "I cried for help from the midst of the netherworld." He was in fact in the fish, yet he says that he is in the netherworld. In a later verse he manifestly prophesies in the person of Christ: "My head went down into the chasms of the mountains." Yet he was still in the belly of the fish. What mountains encompass you? But I know, he says, that I am a type of him who is to be laid in the sepulcher hewn out of rock. While he was in the sea, Jonah says, "I went down into the earth," for

---

[11]ACW 40:226-27*. [12]Cf. Is 7:16 LXX. [13]FC 65:408. [14]Mt 12:40. [15]PG 81:1729.

he typified Christ, who went down into the heart of the earth. CATECHETICAL LECTURE 14.20.[16]

2:7-8 Prayers to God, Not to Idols

JONAH REMEMBERS THE LORD. SYMEON THE NEW THEOLOGIAN: When a person has completely abandoned the world, it seems to one that one is living in a remote desert, full of wild beasts.[17] One is filled with unutterable fear and indescribable trembling, and cries to God like Jonah from the whale, from the sea of this life, or like Daniel[18] from the pit of the lions and the fierce passions, or like the three children[19] from the burning furnace and the flames of innate desire, or like Manasseh[20] from the brazen statue of this earthly mortal body. The Lord hears that person and delivers him from the abyss of ignorance and love of this world, just like the prophet who came out of the whale, never to go back again. THE PRACTICAL AND THEOLOGICAL CHAPTERS 1.76.[21]

2:9 Deliverance Belongs to the Lord

PUTTING TRUST IN CHRIST ALONE. PAULINUS OF NOLA: Hoping for salvation by human resources is no salvation, for mortal means will not rout death. So those who live in a time of anxiety should be anxious to pray to the Lord of heaven, who dispenses sadness or gladness and who alone by his transcendent sway can ensure that troubles are removed and happy times restored. . . . The power of prayers and the healing efficacy of tears in the presence of God our Father is the lesson we must learn from Nineveh saved by its grief. . . . So the faith that relies on God should strengthen panicking hearts, and its trust in God should in time of sorrow anticipate untroubled days. For fear of God ensures freedom from fear, whereas the one who does not fear God alone is right to fear everything. Those who have no confidence in Christ as bearer of salvation must put their trust in legions. POEM 26.[22]

2:10 Jonah Put Out onto Dry Land

JONAH IS A TYPE OF THE RESURRECTION. TERTULLIAN: Jonah was swallowed by the monster of the deep, in whose belly whole ships were devoured, and after three days he was vomited out again safe and sound. Enoch and Elijah, who even now, without experiencing a resurrection (because they have not even encountered death), are learning to the full what it is for the flesh to be exempted from all humiliation, and all loss, and all injury and all disgrace. They have been translated from this world and from this very cause are already candidates for everlasting life.[23] To what faith do these notable events bear witness, if not to that which ought to inspire in us the belief that they are proofs and documents of our own future and our completed resurrection? To borrow the apostle's phrase, these were "figures of ourselves."[24] They are written that we may believe that the Lord is more powerful than all natural laws about the body. ON THE RESURRECTION OF THE FLESH 58.[25]

SWALLOWED BUT NOT DESTROYED. GREGORY OF NAZIANZUS: Hence he is tempest-tossed, and falls asleep, and is wrecked, and aroused from sleep, and taken by lot, and confesses his flight, and is cast into the sea, and swallowed but not destroyed by the whale. IN DEFENSE OF HIS FLIGHT TO PONTUS, ORATION 2.109.[26]

WORK OF GOD, NOT OF STARS. AMBROSE: It was not the influence of his natal star but the offense of having neglected the divine prophecy that cast Jonah into the sea. A whale received him and after three days vomited him forth, as a symbol of a future mystery, and preserved him for the service of prophecy. SIX DAYS OF CREATION 4.4.13.[27]

GOD SAVED JONAH. IRENAEUS: If, however, any

---

[16]FC 64:45. [17]Cf. Mk 1:13; Ps 63:1 (62:1 LXX). [18]Dan 6:18. [19]Dan 3:24. [20]2 Chron 33:12. [21]CS 41:54*. [22]ACW 40:257*. [23]Gen 5:24; 2 Kings 2:11. [24]1 Cor 10:6. [25]ANF 3:591*. [26]NPNF 2 7:226*. [27]FC 42:136**.

one imagines it is impossible that people should survive for such a length of time, and that Elijah was not caught up in the flesh but that flesh was consumed in the fiery chariot, let them consider that Jonah, when he had been cast into the deep and swallowed down into the whale's belly, was by the command of God again thrown out safe upon the land. AGAINST HERESIES 5.5.2.[28]

[28]ANF 1:531.

3:1-4 JONAH'S PREACHING OF REPENTANCE

[1]*Then the word of the LORD came to Jonah the second time, saying,* [2]*"Arise, go to Nineveh, that great city, and proclaim to it the message that I tell you."* [3]*So Jonah arose and went to Nineveh, according to the word of the LORD. Now Nineveh was an exceedingly great city, three days' journey in breadth.* [4]*Jonah began to go into the city, going a day's journey. And he cried, "Yet forty days,* and Nineveh shall be overthrown!"*

*LXX *three days*

OVERVIEW: As Jonah went from ship to whale, so Christ went from tree to the tomb. As Jonah's prophecy was not fulfilled until after his ordeal, so the message to the Gentiles did not take effect until after the resurrection (AUGUSTINE). We are called to repent while we have time (CAESARIUS). God's decree regarding salvation or punishment lies in the response of the hearers as to what God will do or not do (ORIGEN). God allows time for the Ninevites to repent (CHRYSOSTOM).

3:3 Jonah Went to Nineveh

PROPHECY TO GENTILES LIKE PROPHECY TO NINEVEH. AUGUSTINE: Why, then, are we asked what was prefigured by the prophet being swallowed by that monster and restored alive on the third day? Christ explained it when he said an evil and adulterous generation seeks a sign, and a sign shall not be given to it, but the sign of Jonah the prophet. For as Jonah was in the whale's belly three days and three nights, so shall the Son of man be in the heart of the earth three days and three nights.[1] . . . So then, as Jonah went from the ship into the belly of the whale,[2] so Christ went from the tree into the tomb, or into the abyss of death. And as Jonah was sacrificed for those endangered by the storm, so Christ was offered for those who are drowning in the storm of this world. And as Jonah was first commanded to preach to the Ninevites[3] but his prophecy did not come to them until after the whale had vomited him out, so the prophecy made to the Gentiles did not come to them until after the resurrection of Christ. LETTER 102.6.[4]

3:4 Time to Repent

REPENT WHILE IT IS POSSIBLE. CAESARIUS OF ARLES: We should not despair of those who are still unwilling to correct their vices and do not even blush to defend them. In a similar way hope was not abandoned for that city of which it is written, "Three days more, and Nineveh shall be destroyed"; yet in those three days it was able to be converted, pray, bewail and merit mercy from

[1]Mt 12:39-40. [2]Jon 1:15. [3]Jon 1:2. [4]FC 18:173.

the threatened punishment. Therefore let all who are such listen to God while it is possible to hear him in his silence; that is, not punishing at present. For he will come and will not be silent, and he will then reprove when there is no chance of amendment. SERMON 133.3.[5]

WHETHER GOD DECEIVES. ORIGEN: Does God for our salvation deceive and say certain things so that the sinner ceases doing what he might do if he had not heard certain of these words? Was the one who says, "Yet three days and Nineveh shall be destroyed," speaking as one who speaks truly or not? Or as one who deceives by a deceit that converts? If that kind of conversion did not happen, was what was said no longer a deceit but already truth. There would have been a destruction that followed for Nineveh. It was up to those who hear. HOMILIES ON JEREMIAH 19.7.[6]

GOD ALLOWS TIME FOR REPENTANCE. CHRYSOSTOM: If you want, let us also hear this story: "Now the word of the Lord," it says, "came to Jonah, saying, 'Rise and go to Nineveh, the great city.'" He wanted to put Jonah to shame by sending him to the great city of Nineveh, because he foresaw the prophet's escape. However, let us also listen to the preaching: "Yet three days, and Nineveh shall be overthrown." Why do you, God, foretell the sufferings that you will inflict upon Nineveh? "So that I will not do what I announced." This is why God threatened with hell—so he would not lead anyone away to hell. He says, "Fear that which is spoken to you, and do not be saddened about what has been done."[7] Why does he establish the appointed time to be only a period of three days? So that you may learn even the virtue of the barbarians—I call the Ninevites barbarians, who were able to annul in three days such anger caused by sin. I want you to marvel at the philanthropy of God, who was satisfied with three days of repentance for so many transgressions. I do not want you to sink into despair, even though you have innumerable sins. HOMILIES ON REPENTANCE AND ALMSGIVING 5.4.[8]

---

[5]FC 47:247*. [6]FC 97:218. [7]Eccles 7:21. [8]FC 96:59*.

3:5-10 THE NINEVITES REPENT

[5]*And the people of Nineveh believed God; they proclaimed a fast, and put on sackcloth, from the greatest of them to the least of them.*

[6]*Then tidings reached the king of Nineveh, and he arose from his throne, removed his robe, and covered himself with sackcloth, and sat in ashes.* [7]*And he made proclamation and published through Nineveh, "By the decree of the king and his nobles: Let neither man nor beast, herd nor flock, taste anything; let them not feed, or drink water,* [8]*but let man and beast be covered with sackcloth, and let them cry mightily to God; yea, let every one turn from his evil way and from the violence which is in his hands.* [9]*Who knows, God may yet repent and turn from his fierce anger, so that we perish not?"*

[10]*When God saw what they did, how they turned from their evil way, God repented of the evil which he had said he would do to them; and he did not do it.*

OVERVIEW: Gregory of Nazianzus pleads for Christians to imitate the repentance of Nineveh and avoid the obduracy of Sodom (GREGORY OF NAZIANZUS). True fasting is enjoined as a fitting discipline to turn away the wrath of God. Nineveh freed itself from death through penitent fasting (AMBROSE). The efficacy of fasting and repentance is remarkable in putting away even innumerable sins (CHRYSOSTOM). The fact that the Ninevites quickly accepted Jonah's preaching and his instruction highlights the seriousness of their repentance (THEODORE). The king of the Ninevites is held up as an example of repentance, which resulted in the salvation of the whole city (AUGUSTINE). He was wise also, showing humility (MAXIMUS OF TURIN). Even animals were included in the total fast. God speaks a warning through cataclysmic events (CHRYSOSTOM). The sparing of Nineveh was a certain mercy (AUGUSTINE), but the ultimate outcome is uncertain (JEROME). The Ninevites had no previous experience of God's mercy (CHRYSOSTOM). Due to their prayer of repentance they are an example of the effectiveness of prayer (CLEMENT OF ROME). In just three days all of the many sins of Nineveh were left behind. God spared the Ninevites not because of fasting only. It was their fasting along with abstaining from evil that turned God's wrath back (CHRYSOSTOM). The forgiveness of God the Father toward the Ninevites implicitly included Christ, since he has been with the Father in all eternity (TERTULLIAN).

3:5 The Ninevites Believe

NINEVEH AND SODOM CONTRASTED. GREGORY OF NAZIANZUS: Let us sow in tears, so that we may reap in joy.[1] Let us show ourselves people of Nineveh, not of Sodom.[2] Let us amend our wickedness, lest we be consumed with it. Let us listen to the preaching of Jonah, lest we be overwhelmed by fire and brimstone. And if we have departed from Sodom, let us escape to the mountain. Let us flee to Zoar. Let us enter it as the sun rises. Let us not stay in all the plain. Let us not look around us, lest we be frozen into a pillar of salt, a really immoral pillar, to accuse the soul that returns to wickedness. ON HIS FATHER'S SILENCE, ORATION 16.14.[3]

FASTING THE KEY TO REPENTANCE. AMBROSE: If the apostle said too little [about fasting], let them hear the prophet [in the psalm] saying, "I afflicted my soul with fasting."[4] One who does not fast is uncovered and naked and exposed to wounds. Finally, if Adam had uncovered himself with fasting, he would not have become naked.[5] Nineveh freed itself from death by fasting. The Lord himself said, "But this kind of demon will be cast out only by prayer and fasting."[6] LETTER 44.[7]

THE EFFICACY OF FASTING. CHRYSOSTOM: Do you see how vexed God is when fasting is treated despitefully? Learn how delighted he is when fasting is honored. When Eve was maltreated,[8] he inflicted death as a penalty upon the insolent individual. He revoked death when she was honored once again.[9] Desiring to show you the power of this thing of importance, he gave her authority over the sentence, after the arrest, to snatch the prisoners from the middle of the journey and change their course toward life. And he did this not only for two or three or twenty people but also for a whole population, in the case of the great and marvelous city of the Ninevites, which had knelt and bowed its head over this pit of perdition and was expecting to suffer the blow from above. Like a heavenly power overseeing Nineveh's charge, fasting snatched the city from these gates of death and returned Nineveh to life. HOMILIES ON REPENTANCE AND ALMSGIVING 5.4.[10]

THE NINEVITES ACCEPT ADMONITION AND

---

[1]Ps 126:5 (125:5 LXX). [2]Gen 19:17, 23. [3]NPNF 2 7:252*. [4]Ps 69:10 (68:11 LXX). [5]Gen 3:7. [6]Mt 17:21; Mk 9:29 KJV. This verse is absent in the three oldest manuscripts but present in the oldest Latin versions, including the Vulgate. [7]FC 26:229 (Benedictine Letter 42). [8]By the serpent. [9]By Mary. [10]FC 96:58-59*.

INSTRUCTION. THEODORE OF MOPSUESTIA: They could never have believed in God on the basis of this remark alone, from a completely unknown foreigner threatening them with destruction and adding nothing further, not even letting the listeners know by whom he was sent. Rather, it is obvious he also mentioned God, the Lord of all, and said he had been sent by him; and he delivered the message of destruction, calling them to repentance. When they accepted instruction in this, then, they were naturally told to believe in God; when they accepted both the sentence and the instruction from the prophet's sermon, they set their eyes on better things so as to give evidence of a decisive and serious repentance. COMMENTARY ON JONAH 3.5-9.[11]

3:6 The King Wears Sackcloth

AN EXAMPLE OF LEADERSHIP. AUGUSTINE: A sovereign serves God one way as a man, another way as a king. He serves him as man by living according to faith. He serves him as king by exerting the necessary strength to sanction laws that command goodness and prohibit its opposite. It was thus that Ezekiel served him by destroying the groves and temples of idols and the high places that had been set up contrary to the commandments of God.[12] Thus Josiah served him by performing similar acts.[13] Thus the king of the Ninevites served him by compelling the whole city to appease the Lord. LETTER 185.5.19.[14]

3:7 The King's Decree

THE WISE KING. MAXIMUS OF TURIN: The king conquered enemies with a display of valor. He conquered God, however, by humility. He is a wise king who, in order to save his people, owns himself a sinner rather than a king. He forgets that he is a king, fearing God the King of all. He does not bring to mind his own power but rather comes to possess the power of the Godhead. Marvelous! When he forgets that he is a king of men, he begins to be a king of righteousness. The prince, becom-

ing religious, did not lose his empire but changed it. Before he held a princedom of military discipline. Now he obtained a princedom in heavenly disciplines. COMMENTARY ON JONAH.[15]

3:8 People and Animals Wear Sackcloth

LET MAN AND BEAST REPENT. CHRYSOSTOM: Recall that Daniel, passionate man though he was, spent many days fasting. He received as recompense an awesome vision so that he tamed the fury of the lions and turned them into the mildest of sheep, not by changing their nature but by diverting their purpose without loss of their ferocity. The Ninevites too made use of the remedy of fasting and won from the Lord a reprieve. Animals as well as human beings were included in the fast, so that all living things would abstain from evil practices. This total response won the favor of the Lord of all. HOMILIES ON GENESIS 1.7.[16]

3:9 God May Turn from His Anger

AN OPPORTUNITY TO REPENT. CHRYSOSTOM: Consider, if God had chosen to demolish everything [in a recent earthquake], what we would have suffered. I say this, so that the fear of these events may remain sharp in you and may keep everyone's resolution firm. He shook us, but he did not destroy us. If he had wished to destroy us, he would not have shaken us. But since he did not wish to destroy us, the earthquake came in advance like a herald, forewarning everyone of the anger of God, in order that we might be improved by fear and prevent the actual retribution.

He has done this even for foreign nations. "Yet three days, and Nineveh shall be overthrown."[17] Why do you not overcome the city? You threaten to destroy it. Why do you not destroy it? "Because I do not wish to destroy, for this very reason I threaten." So what is the Lord saying? "Lest

---

[11]PG 66:340-41. [12]2 Kings 18:4. [13]2 Kings 23:4, 20. [14]NPNF 1 4:640*. [15]PMPC 1:416. [16]FC 74:24-25*. [17]Jon 3:4 LXX.

I enact my impending judgment, let my word go in advance and prevent my acting." Yet three days, and Nineveh shall be overthrown. Then the prophet spoke. Today these walls speak. I say this, and I do not cease saying it, both to the poor and to the rich: consider how great is God's anger. Consider how simple his requirement: let us abstain from evil! In a brief moment of time he shattered the mind and resolution of each one of us. He shook the foundations of our hearts. HOMILIES ON LAZARUS AND THE RICH MAN 6.[18]

3:10 God Saw Nineveh's Repentance and Spared Them

THE NINEVITES REPENT. AUGUSTINE: In uncertainty they repented and obtained certain mercy. EXPLANATION OF THE PSALMS 50.[19]

GOD'S RESPONSE. JEROME: There was no response to their repentance; rather, God met their questioning with silence. Thus [the outcome of] their repentance is left uncertain, that being doubtful of their salvation, they may repent more vehemently and know the mercy, patience and compassion of God even more. COMMENTARY ON JONAH 4.9.[20]

THE THREAT OF DEATH WAS THE PARENT OF LIFE. CHRYSOSTOM: They do not know the issue, and yet they do not neglect repentance. They are unacquainted with the method of the lovingkindness of God, and they are changed amid uncertainty. They had no other Ninevites to look to, who had repented and been saved. They had not read the prophets or heard the patriarchs, or benefited by counsel, or partaken of instruction, nor had they persuaded themselves that they should altogether propitiate God by repentance. For the threat did not contain this. But they doubted and hesitated about this, and yet they repented with all carefulness. What account then shall we give, when these, who had no good hopes held out to them as to the issue, gave evidence of such a change? [What account shall you give], who may

be of good cheer as to God's love for humanity, and have many times received pledges of his care, and have heard the prophets and apostles, and have been instructed by the events themselves, and yet you do not strive to attain the same measure of virtue as they? Great then was the virtue too of these people, but much greater was the lovingkindness of God.... That fear was the parent of salvation; the threat removed the peril; the sentence of overthrow stayed the overthrow. Now they have a new and more marvelous issue! The sentence threatening death was the parent of life. ... Was Nineveh destroyed? Quite the contrary. It arose and became more glorious, and all this intervening time has not effaced its glory. And we all yet celebrate it and marvel at it, that subsequently it has become a most safe harbor to all who sin, not allowing them to sink into despair but calling all to repentance, both by what it did and by what it gained from the providence of God, persuading us never to despair of our salvation. HOMILIES CONCERNING THE STATUES 5.5-6.[21]

LEARNING FROM NINEVEH ABOUT PRAYER. CLEMENT OF ROME: These things, dearly beloved, we are writing, not only to warn you but also to remind ourselves; for we are in the same arena, and the same contest lies before us. For this reason let us abandon empty and silly concerns and come to the glorious and holy rule of our tradition. Let us see what is good and pleasing and acceptable in the sight of our Maker. Let us fix our gaze on the blood of Christ and realize how precious it is to his Father, seeing that it was poured out for our salvation and brought the grace of conversion to the whole world. Let us look back over all the generations and learn that from generation to generation the Lord has given an opportunity of repentance[22] to all who would return to him. Noah preached penance,[23] and those who

---

[18]OWP 98*. [19]WSA 3 16:419*. [20]CCL 76:417. [21]NPNF 1 9:377-78**. [22]Wis 12:10. [23]Gen 7; Heb 11:7.

heeded were saved. Then Jonah announced destruction to the Ninevites and they repented of their sins,[24] besought God in prayer and, estranged though they were from God, obtained salvation. 1 CLEMENT 7.[25]

NINEVEH: EXAMPLE OF REPENTANCE. CHRYSOSTOM: And that these words are not a vain boast shall be made manifest to you for things that have already happened. What could be more stupid than the Ninevites? What more devoid of understanding? Yet, nevertheless, these barbarian, foolish people, who had not yet heard any one teaching them wisdom, who had never received such precepts from others, when they heard the prophet saying, "Yet three days, and Nineveh shall be overthrown,"[26] laid aside, within three days, the whole of their evil customs. The fornicator became chaste; the bold man meek; the grasping and extortionate moderate and kind; the slothful industrious. They did not, indeed, reform one or two or three or four vices by way of remedy, but the whole of their iniquity. But where does this appear, says someone? From the words of the prophet; for the same who had been their accuser and who had said that "the cry of their wickedness has ascended up even into heaven,"[27] himself again bears testimony of an opposite kind by saying, "God saw that every one departed from their own evil ways." He does not say from fornication or adultery or theft, but from their "own evil ways." And how did they depart? As God knew; not as people judged of the matter. After this are we not ashamed, must we not blush, if it turns out that in three days only the barbarians laid aside all their wickedness, but that we, who have been urged and taught during so many days, have not got the better of one bad habit? These people had moreover gone to the extreme of wickedness before; for when you hear it said, "The cry of their wickedness is come up before me," you can understand nothing else than

the excess of their wickedness. Nevertheless within three days they were capable of being transformed to a state of complete uprightness. HOMILIES CONCERNING THE STATUES 20.21.[28]

THE NINEVITES ABSTAIN FROM EVIL. CHRYSOSTOM: They applied fasting to their wounds. Yes, they even applied extreme fasting—lying prostrate on the ground, putting on sackcloth and ashes, and lamentations. More importantly, they chose a change of life. Let us then see which of these things made them whole. And how shall we know? If we come to the physician, if we seek after him earnestly, he will not hide it from us but will even eagerly disclose it. Rather, in order that no one may be ignorant or have need to ask, he has even set down in writing the medicine that restores sinners. What then is this? "God," he said, "saw that they turned every one from his evil way, and he repented of the evil that he said he would do unto them." He did not say simply that he saw their fasting and sackcloth and ashes, but their behavior. I say this not to question fasting (God forbid!) but to exhort you that with fasting you do that which is better than fasting, the abstaining from all evil. HOMILIES ON 2 CORINTHIANS 4.6.[29]

NINEVITES FORGIVEN BY THE FATHER AND THE SON. TERTULLIAN: Now, if [forgiveness of sin had not] been predicted of Christ, I should find in the Creator examples of such benignity as would hold out to me the promise of similar affections also in the Son of whom he is the Father. I see how the Ninevites obtained forgiveness of their sins from the Creator—not to say from Christ [by way of anticipation], even then, because from the beginning he was acting in the Father's name. AGAINST MARCION 4.10.[30]

---

[24]Mt 12:41. [25]FC 1:15*. [26]Jon 3:4 LXX. [27]Jon 1:2 LXX. [28]NPNF 1 9:480. [29]NPNF 1 12:299. [30]ANF 3:358*.

4:1-11 THE AMBIVALENCE OF JONAH

¹*But it displeased Jonah exceedingly, and he was angry.* ²*And he prayed to the* LORD *and said,* "*I pray thee,* LORD, *is not this what I said when I was yet in my country? That is why I made haste to flee to Tarshish; for I knew that thou art a gracious God and merciful, slow to anger, and abounding in steadfast love, and repentest of evil.* ³*Therefore now, O* LORD, *take my life from me, I beseech thee, for it is better for me to die than to live.*" ⁴*And the* LORD *said,* "*Do you do well to be angry?*" ⁵*Then Jonah went out of the city and sat to the east of the city, and made a booth for himself there. He sat under it in the shade, till he should see what would become of the city.*

⁶*And the* LORD *God appointed a plant,*ᵇ *and made it come up over Jonah, that it might be a shade over his head, to save him from his discomfort. So Jonah was exceedingly glad because of the plant.*ᵇ ⁷*But when dawn came up the next day, God appointed a worm which attacked the plant,*ᵇ *so that it withered.* ⁸*When the sun rose, God appointed a sultry east wind, and the sun** *beat upon the head of Jonah so that he was faint; and he asked that he might die, and said,* "*It is better for me to die than to live.*" ⁹*But God said to Jonah,* "*Do you do well to be angry for the plant?*"ᵇ *And he said,* "*I do well to be angry, angry enough to die.*" ¹⁰*And the* LORD *said,* "*You pity the plant,*ᵇ *for which you did not labor, nor did you make it grow, which came into being in a night, and perished in a night.* ¹¹*And should not I pity Nineveh, that great city, in which there are more than a hundred and twenty thousand persons who do not know their right hand from their left, and also much cattle?*"

b Heb *qiqayon*, probably *the castor oil plant* *LXX *burning sun*

OVERVIEW: Jonah suspected from the beginning that God would not destroy Nineveh (CHRYSOSTOM). He is indignant, therefore, because he thought he had prophesied falsely (JEROME). On the other hand, he could have truly expected destruction, for he went outside the city (CYRIL OF ALEXANDRIA). Jonah typified salvation to the Gentiles. The vine's shade symbolizes being shielded from the heat of temporal evil. The worm is Christ, who gnaws away the old covenant (AUGUSTINE). Through the metaphor of the withered vine, God teaches the prophet a lesson of divine loving-kindness (THEODORET). The book of Jonah is seen as an object lesson emphasizing the compassion the church should have toward unbelievers (AMBROSE). Children and the innocent merit God's greatest mercy (SALVIAN). The Ninevites are compared with children who cannot distinguish between good and evil. God spares them as responsible parents would care for their children (JEROME).

4:1-2 Jonah's Anger

JONAH'S FIRST THOUGHT. CHRYSOSTOM: After he preached in the midst of Nineveh, he went out of the city in order to observe if anything should happen. When he saw that three days had passed and nothing had happened anywhere near what was threatened, he then put forward his first thought and said, "Are these not my words that I was saying that God is merciful and longsuffering and repents for people's evils?" HOMILIES ON REPENTANCE AND ALMSGIVING 2.20.[1]

---

[1]FC 96:23.

JONAH'S INDIGNATION. JEROME: But God will reply by the mouth of Jeremiah, "At what instant I will speak concerning a nation, and concerning a kingdom, to pluck up, and to break down, and to destroy it; if that nation, concerning what I have spoken, turn from their evil, I will repent of the evil that I thought to do to them. And at what instant I will speak concerning a nation, and concerning a kingdom, to build and to plant it; if it does evil in my sight, that it obeys not my voice, then I will repent of the good wherewith I said I would benefit them."[2] Jonah was indignant because, at God's command, he had spoken falsely; but his sorrow was proved to be ill founded, since he would rather speak truth and have a countless multitude perish than speak falsely and have them saved. AGAINST THE PELAGIANS 3.[3]

4:5-7 Jonah Sits Outside the City

JONAH EXPECTED THE DESTRUCTION OF NINEVEH. CYRIL OF ALEXANDRIA: The days being now past, after which it was time that the things foretold should be accomplished, and his anger as yet taking no effect, Jonah understood that God had pity on Nineveh. Still he does not give up all hope, and thinks that a respite of the evil has been granted them on their willingness to repent, but that some effect of his displeasure would come, since the pains of their repentance had not equaled their offenses. So thinking in himself apparently, he departs from the city and waits to see what will become of them. He expected, apparently, that it would either fall by an earthquake or be burned with fire, like Sodom. COMMENTARY ON JONAH 4.5.[4]

THE SALVATION OF THE GENTILES GREATER THAN JONAH'S SHADE. AUGUSTINE: But when Jonah made himself a booth and sat down opposite the city of Nineveh, waiting to see what would befall it, the prophet played a part of different significance. He was a type of the carnal people of Israel, for he was sad over the preservation of the Ninevites! He was frustrated over the

redemption and salvation of the Gentiles! This is why Christ came to call "not the just but sinners to repentance."[5] But the shadow of the vine over his head was the promise of the Old Testament. Its law manifested, as the apostle says, "a shadow of things to come."[6] God was offering shade from the heat of temporal evils in the land of promise.

But the worm came in the morning. It gnawed at the vine and withered it. For when the gospel had been published by Christ's mouth, all those things withered and faded away. The shade of the vine symbolized temporal prosperity for the Israelites. And now those people have lost the kingdom of Jerusalem and their priesthood and sacrifice. All of this was a foreshadowing of the future. They were scattered abroad in captivity and afflicted with a great flood of suffering, just as Jonah—so it is written—suffered grievously from the heat of the sun. Yet the salvation of penitent nations is preferred to Jonah's suffering and the shade that he loved. LETTER 102.6.[7]

4:8 Better to Die Than to Live

THE LESSON OF DIVINE MERCY. THEODORET OF CYR: When he admitted to feeling this way to the extent of preferring death to life on this account, God said, I call you as judge. Consider, then, if it is right for you to grieve over the pumpkin vine, which you did not cultivate, neither planting it nor watering it. It came into being at dawn, and a worm and the sun proved its ruin at day's end. For my part, on the contrary, is it right for me to treat without mercy this city, which was brought into being by me, containing more than 120,000 inhabitants who do not know their right hand from their left, and many cattle? Give thought to this, then, and marvel at the lovingkindness for its reasonableness. COMMENTARY ON JONAH 4.10-11.[8]

4:11 God's Pity for Nineveh

---

[2]Jer 18:7-8. [3]NPNF 2 6:475*. [4]PMPC 1:423*. [5]Lk 5:32. [6]Col 2:17; Heb 10:1. [7]FC 18:173-74*. [8]PG 81:1740.

FOCUS MORE ON REDEMPTION THAN JUDGMENT. AMBROSE: The next day the book of Jonah was read according to custom, and when it was finished I began this sermon: Brothers, a book has been read in which it is prophesied that sinners shall return to repentance. It is understood to mean that they may hope for the future in the present. I added that the just man had been willing to receive even blame, so as not to see or prophesy destruction for the city. And because that sentence was mournful, he grew sad when the vine withered. God said to the prophet, "Are you sad over the vine?" Jonah answered, "I am sad." The Lord said that if he was grieving because the vine had withered, how much greater should his care be for the salvation of so many people! And, in fact, he did away with the destruction that had been prepared for the entire city. LETTER 60.[9]

THE PURITY OF THE INNOCENT SPARES THE GUILTY. SALVIAN THE PRESBYTER: When, at one time, God had been offended by the sins of the Ninevites, he was appeased by the crying and wailing of children. For though we read that the whole people wept, yet the lot of innocence of the little ones merited the greatest mercy. God said to Jonah, "You are greatly grieved over the vine."

And a little later, "Should I not spare Nineveh, the great city, in which there are more than 120,000 persons, who know not their left hand from their right hand?" He thereby declared that because of the purity of the innocent ones, he was also sparing the faults of the guilty ones. LETTER 4.[10]

CARING FOR THOSE UNABLE TO DISCERN GOOD FROM EVIL. JEROME: We read of Eli the priest that he became displeasing to God on account of the sins of his children.[11] And we are told that a man may not be made a bishop if his sons are loose and disorderly.[12] It is written of the woman that "she shall be saved in childbearing, if she continues in faith and charity and holiness with chastity."[13] If then parents are responsible for their children when these are of ripe age and independent, how much more must they be responsible for them when, still unweaned and weak, they cannot, in the Lord's words, "discern between their right hand and their left," when, that is to say, they cannot yet distinguish good from evil? LETTER 107.6.[14]

---

[9]FC 26:374*. [10]FC 3:247*. [11]1 Sam 1—4. [12]1 Tim 3:2-5. [13]1 Tim 2:15. [14]LCC 5:337-38.

MICAH

OVERVIEW: Micah (Heb *mîkâ*, an abbreviation of *mîkā-yĕhû*, meaning "who is like Yahweh") is given the sixth place among the twelve. Most scholars divide the book into three main sections. In Micah 1:1—3:12, the focus is on the impending judgment of God coupled with a severe censure of Judah's leaders. At Micah 4:1—5:15, the tone changes to a positive message of the restoration of Zion. Micah 5:1 is quoted by Matthew in Matthew 2:6 as fulfilled in Christ's birth in Bethlehem. Even so, in Micah 6:1—7:20, the case is made against Israel by God for their infidelity to the covenant. It ends, however, with a prayer for their restoration and a proclamation of God's mercy.

The work is dated in the reigns of Jotham, Ahaz and Hezekiah (750-687 B.C.). The absence of any utterance in the reign of Jotham leads some interpreters to question the regal chronological longevity of the prophecies. Some scholars argue that the city mentioned in Micah 6:9-16 is either Jerusalem or Samaria. Furthermore, the military disaster at Micah 1:10-16 likely refers to the invasion of Sennacherib in 701 B.C.

Micah the prophet seems to have come from Moresheth-Gath in southwest Judah. We know next to nothing about the personal life of Micah, who was a contemporary of Isaiah. Unlike Isaiah, however, Micah sees only the destruction of Jerusalem and not any hope of its immediate deliverance.

Because the book is quoted directly in all of the Gospels, Micah figured prominently in patristic exegesis. Jerome figures as one of the most prominent commentators of this prophet, although other Greek and Latin fathers accorded much attention too on account of its rich typological content. Mount Zion, for example, was viewed as a type of the church or the new Jerusalem (Rev 20—21) that had fulfilled the hope of Israel. Sacramentally, the church fathers saw in Micah a typological anticipation of Christian baptism that inaugurated one into the membership in the new covenant, thus replacing circumcision. Again the prophet Micah contained a prediction of the destruction of the temple and of the fall of Jerusalem that was accomplished by the Romans.

1:1-16 PROPHECY OF WEEPING
AND MOURNING

¹The word of the LORD that came to Micah of Moresheth in the days of Jotham, Ahaz, and Hezekiah, kings of Judah, which he saw concerning Samaria and Jerusalem.

²Hear, you peoples, all of you;
    hearken, O earth, and all that is in it;
and let the Lord GOD* be a witness against
    you,
    the Lord from his holy temple.
³For behold, the LORD is coming forth out of
    his place,
    and will come down and tread upon the
    high places of the earth.
⁴And the mountains will melt under him
    and the valleys will be cleft,
like wax before the fire,
    like waters poured down a steep place.
⁵All this is for the transgression of Jacob
    and for the sins of the house of Israel.
What is the transgression of Jacob?
    Is it not Samaria?
And what is the sin of the house[a] of Judah?
    Is it not Jerusalem?
⁶Therefore I will make Samaria a heap in
    the open country,
    a place for planting vineyards;
and I will pour down her stones into the
    valley,
    and uncover her foundations.
⁷All her images shall be beaten to pieces,
    all her hires shall be burned with fire,
    and all her idols I will lay waste;
for from the hire of a harlot she gathered

    them,
    and to the hire of a harlot they shall
    return.

⁸For this I will lament and wail;
    I will go stripped and naked;
I will make lamentation like the jackals,
    and mourning like the ostriches.
⁹For her wound[b] is incurable;
    and it has come to Judah,
it has reached to the gate of my people,
    to Jerusalem.
¹⁰Tell it not in Gath,
    weep not at all;
in Beth-leaphrah
    roll yourselves in the dust.
¹¹Pass on your way,
    inhabitants of Shaphir,
    in nakedness and shame;
the inhabitants of Zaanan
    do not come forth;
the wailing of Beth-ezel
    shall take away from you its standing place.
¹²For the inhabitants of Maroth
    wait anxiously for good,
because evil has come down from the LORD
    to the gate of Jerusalem.
¹³Harness the steeds to the chariots,
    inhabitants of Lachish;
you were[c] the beginning of sin
    to the daughter of Zion,
for in you were found
    the transgressions of Israel.
¹⁴Therefore you shall give parting gifts

to Moresheth-gath;
the houses of Achzib shall be a deceitful thing
    to the kings of Israel.
[15]I will again bring a conqueror upon you,
    inhabitants of Mareshah;
the glory of Israel

shall come to Adullam.
[16]Make yourselves bald and cut off your
    hair,
    for the children of your delight;
make yourselves as bald as the eagle,
    for they shall go from you into exile.

a Gk Tg Compare Syr: Heb *what are the high places*   b Gk Syr Vg: Heb *wounds*   c Cn: Heb *it was*   *LXX omits God

---

OVERVIEW: Micah means "one who is from God." This in a sense prefigured Jesus the Son of God, who received all things from God the Father (AMBROSE). Jesus' statements about procession from God were foretold by Micah when he talked about the coming of the Messiah (ORIGEN). God descending in the form of a human was foretold and foreshadowed when the "three men" appeared to Abraham. Micah also spoke of this divine descent when describing how God will dwell upon the earth (ORIGEN). An angel appears to Pachomius to reveal to him the meaning of the text from Micah regarding water "coming down." The water is from the river of paradise (PACHOMIUS). Others see the waters as a vehicle of divine judgment (JEROME). Like an eagle loses its feathers, Israel lost its people (GREGORY THE GREAT).

1:1 God's Word Comes to Micah

THE NAME MICAH. AMBROSE: Micah means "one who is from God," or, as we find elsewhere, "one who is the son of the Morashite," in other words son of the heir. Who is the heir but the Son of God, who says, "All things have been delivered to me by the Father,"[1] who, being the heir, wished us to be co-heirs. It is well to ask, "Who is he?" He is not one of the people but one chosen to receive the grace of God, through whom the Holy Spirit speaks. He began to prophesy in the days of Jotham, Ahaz and Hezekiah, kings of Judah. By this order the progress of the vision is signified, for it goes from the times of evil kings to those of the good king. LETTER 45.[2]

1:3 The Lord Comes Forth

HOW CHRIST PROCEEDING FROM THE FATHER IS PREFIGURED. ORIGEN: Now let us also consider Jesus' statement, "I have proceeded and come from God."[3] It seems useful to me to juxtapose to these words the following words from Micah: "Hear my words, you people, and let the earth and all who are in it pay attention; and the Lord shall be among you for a witness, the Lord from his holy house. Therefore behold, the Lord proceeds from his place and will come down and tread upon the high places of the earth, and the mountains will be shaken under him, and the valleys will be dissolved like wax, before fire and like water tumbling down in a waterfall." Now consider whether the statement, "I have proceeded from God," is equivalent to the statement, "The Lord proceeds from his place," since, when the Son is in the Father, being in the form of God before he empties himself,[4] God is his place, as it were.... Unless you understand that the Son is in the Father in a different way than he was before he proceeded from God, it will seem contradictory that he has both proceeded from God, and, after he has proceeded from God, is still in God. COMMENTARY ON THE GOSPEL OF JOHN 20.152-56.[5]

THE DESCENT OF CHRIST INCARNATE PREFIGURED. ORIGEN: "I have descended," the text says, "to see." When responses are delivered to Abraham, God is not said to descend but to stand

---

[1]Mt 11:27. [2]FC 26:231-32*. [3]Jn 8:42. [4]Phil 2:6-7. [5]FC 89:238-39*. [6]Gen 18:2.

before him, as we explained above. "Three men," the text says, "stood before him."[6] But now because sinners are involved, God is said to descend.

Beware lest you think of ascending and descending spatially. For these metaphors are frequently found in the sacred literature, as in the prophet Micah. "Behold," Scripture says, "the Lord departed from his holy place and came down and will tread upon the high places of the earth." Therefore God is said to descend when he deigns to have concern for human frailty. This should be discerned especially of our Lord and Savior, who "thought it not robbery to be equal with God but emptied himself, taking the form of a servant."[7] Therefore he descended. For "no other has ascended into heaven, but he that descended from heaven, the Son of man who is in heaven."[8] For the Lord descended not only to care for us but also to bear what things are ours. "For he took the form of a servant," and although he himself is invisible in nature, inasmuch as he is equal to the Father, nevertheless he took a visible appearance "and was found in appearance as a man."[9] HOMILIES ON GENESIS 4.5.[10]

1:4 Like Waters Poured Down

REVIEW OF PARADISE FORETOLD. PACHOMIUS: On another occasion when he[11] was sitting by himself some place reading the book of the twelve prophets, he came to the prophet Micah. An angel of the Lord appeared to him and asked him about this verse from Micah: "Like water coming down from its source." He said to him, "What do you think it means?" While he was still puzzling over it, trying to understand, the angel answered, "Theodore, why do you not perceive its meaning? Is it not obvious that it is the water of the river coming down from paradise?" As soon as the angel had said this, he ceased to see him. LIFE OF PACHOMIUS (BOHAIRIC) 1.155.[12]

THE UNGODLY SHALL BE DISSOLVED. JEROME: As wax cannot endure the nearness of the fire, and as the waters are carried headlong, so all of the ungodly, when the Lord comes, shall be dissolved and disappear. COMMENTARY ON MICAH 1.1.4.[13]

1:16 Baldness as the Eagle

NATIONS SHALL BECOME BALD. GREGORY THE GREAT: That happened which we know to have been foretold of Judea by the prophet: "enlarge your baldness like the eagle." For baldness befalls man in the head only, but the eagle in its whole body. For when it is very old, its feathers and pinions fall from all its body. She lost her feathers who lost her people. Her pinions too fell out, with which she was accustomed to fly to the prey, for all the mighty men—through which she plundered others—perished. HOMILIES ON EZEKIEL, HOMILY 18 (2.6).[14]

---

[7]Phil 2:6-7. [8]Jn 3:13. [9]Phil 2:7. [10]FC 71:108. [11]Theodore of Tabennesi, an astute and devoted disciple of Pachomius. [12]CS 45:215. [13]PMPC 2:18; CCL 76:425. [14]PMPC 2:28*.

2:1-13 REFUGE AND DELIVERANCE

¹Woe to those who devise wickedness
and work evil upon their beds!
When the morning dawns, they perform it,

because it is in the power of their hand.
²They covet fields, and seize them;
and houses, and take them away;

they oppress a man and his house,
a man and his inheritance.
³Therefore thus says the LORD:
Behold, against this family I am devising
evil,
from which you cannot remove your necks;
and you shall not walk haughtily,
for it will be an evil time.
⁴In that day they shall take up a taunt song
against you,
and wail with bitter lamentation,
and say, "We are utterly ruined;
he changes the portion of my people;
how he removes it from me!
Among our captors^d he divides our fields."
⁵Therefore you will have none to cast the
line by lot
in the assembly of the LORD.

⁶"Do not preach"—thus they preach—
"one should not preach of such things;
disgrace will not overtake us."
⁷Should this be said, O house of Jacob?
Is the Spirit of the LORD impatient?
Are these his doings?
Do not my words do good
to him who walks uprightly?
⁸But you rise against my people^e as an
enemy;

you strip the robe from the peaceful,^f
from those who pass by trustingly
with no thought of war.
⁹The women of my people you drive out
from their pleasant houses;
from their young children you take away
my glory for ever.*
¹⁰Arise and go,
for this is no place to rest;
because of uncleanness that destroys
with a grievous destruction.[†]
¹¹If a man should go about and utter wind
and lies,[‡]
saying, "I will preach to you of wine and
strong drink,"[§]
he would be the preacher for this people!

¹²I will surely gather all of you, O Jacob,
I will gather the remnant of Israel;
I will set them together
like a sheep in a fold,
like a flock in its pasture,
a noisy multitude of men.
¹³He who opens the breach will go up before
them;
they will break through and pass the gate,
going out by it.
Their king will pass on before them,
the LORD at their head.

d Cn: Heb *the rebellious*   e Cn: Heb *yesterday my people rose*   f Cn: Heb *from before a garment*   *LXX *The leaders of my people shall be cast forth from their luxurious houses; they are rejected because of their evil practices; draw near to the everlasting mountains.*   †LXX *For this is not a rest for you by reason of uncleanness. You have been corrupted with corruption.*   ‡Vulgate *Would that I were not man that had the Spirit, and that I rather spoke a lie.*   §LXX *You have fled, no one pursuing you: your spirit has framed falsehood, it has dropped on you for wine and strong drink.*

OVERVIEW: The house of Jacob provoked God's anger and is joined to the suffering of Christ in the flesh (HIPPOLYTUS). Fleeing from the world to the mountains, a symbol of where God dwells, is seen in the story of Abraham and Lot. Micah too implores the faithful to draw near to the mountains for refuge. The church is now the new Mount Zion and the new Jerusalem to which believers must flee (AMBROSE). It is in that mountain that Christians are to find refuge in the time of tribulations (JEROME). Micah is like Paul and Moses—all would have given their lives in exchange for the salvation of the Jews (JOHN CASSIAN). Christ is the shepherd at the gate (JEROME).

2:7 The Spirit of the Lord

CHRIST'S SUFFERING IN THE FLESH. HIPPOLY-TUS: "He was clothed in a vesture dipped in blood. And his name is called the Word of God."[1] See then, my brothers, how the vesture sprinkled with blood denoted in symbol the flesh, through which the impassible Word of God underwent suffering, as the prophets testify. For thus speaks the blessed Micah: "Should this be said, O house of Jacob? Is the Spirit of the Lord impatient? Are these his doings? Do not my words do well to him who walks uprightly? But you rise against my people as an enemy; you strip the robe from the peaceful." This refers to Christ's suffering in the flesh. AGAINST NOETUS 15.[2]

2:9-10 No Place to Rest

MOUNTAINS AS SYMBOLS OF GOD'S REFUGE. AMBROSE: Let him who cannot fly like an eagle fly like a sparrow. Let him who cannot fly to heaven fly to the mountains. Let him flee before the valleys that are quickly destroyed by water. Let him pass over the mountains. Abraham's nephew passed over the mountain of Segor and was saved.[3] But Lot's wife could not climb it, for she looked back in womanly fashion and lost her salvation.[4] "Draw near the everlasting mountains," the Lord says through the prophet Micah, "arise from here, for this is not a rest for you by reason of uncleanness. You have been corrupted with corruption, you have suffered pursuit."

And the Lord says, "Then let those who are in Judea flee to the mountains."[5] Mount Zion is there, and so is the city of peace, Jerusalem, built not of earthly stones but of living stones, with ten thousand angels and the church of the firstborn and the spirits of those made perfect and the God of the just, who spoke better with his blood than Abel.[6] For the one cried out for vengeance[7] but the other for pardon. The one was a reproach to

his brother's sin; the other forgave the world's sin. The one was the revelation of a crime; the other covered a crime according to what is written, "Blessed are they whose sins are covered."[8] FLIGHT FROM THE WORLD 5.31.[9]

MOUNTAIN AS REFUGE. JEROME: "In the Lord I take refuge; how can you say to me, 'Flee to the mountains like a sparrow!'"[10] Shrewd adversary; he tempted the Lord Savior in the desert, and now he wants the faithful, every one of them, to depart from the land of Judea and to dwell in a wilderness barren of virtues, that there he might crush them more easily. Even the counsel itself is crafty. It is not an exhortation to assume the wings of a dove, a gentle, simple and domestic bird—one, they say, entirely lacking in gall—which was offered in the temple in behalf of the Lord. [Instead it is an exhortation to take] the wings of a sparrow, a chattering, roving bird, one that is a stranger to its mate after hatching its young—notwithstanding that Aquila and Symmachus have usually translated "bird" in the place of "sparrow." ... The mountains, moreover, we may identify as those to which Scripture refers in another place: "Draw you near to the everlasting mountains," and in the second of the gradual psalms: "I lift up my eyes toward the mountains, whence help shall come to me."[11] They are the mountains too in which we must take refuge after the abomination of desolation shall stand in the holy place.[12] HOMILIES ON THE PSALMS 60.[13]

2:11 The Preachers of Wine and Strong Drink

THE READINESS OF THE PROPHET. JOHN CASSIAN: St. Paul wished that he could be accursed if the people of Israel be saved to God's glory.[14] The

---

[1]Rev 19:13. [2]ANF 5:229**. [3]Gen 19:12-29. [4]Gen 19:26. [5]Mt 24:16. [6]Heb 12:24. [7]Gen 4:10. [8]Ps 32:1 (31:1 LXX). [9]FC 65:305. Ambrose contrasts Cain's murder of Abel, which resulted in vengeance, with Jesus' crucifixion outside Jerusalem, which resulted in forgiveness of the sin of unbelievers. [10]Ps 11:1 (10:LXX). [11]Ps 120:1. [12]See Mt 24:15. [13]FC 57:5. [14]Rom 9:3.

man who knows that death is not the end is confident in his readiness to die for Christ. Again, "We rejoice when we are weak, but you are strong."[15] It is no wonder if St. Paul, for the glory of Christ and the conversion of his brother Jews and of the Gentiles, should be ready to be accursed of Christ. Even the prophet Micah wanted to be a liar and to lose the inspiration of the Holy Spirit if the Jews could escape the punishment and the destruction which he had prophesied: "Would that I were not man that had the Spirit, and that I rather spoke a lie." And there was the case of the lawgiver, Moses, who did not refuse to perish with his brothers who were doomed to die but said, "I beseech you, O Lord, this people have sinned a heinous sin; either forgive them this trespass, or, if you do not, blot me out of the book which you have written."[16] CONFERENCE 9.18.[17]

2:13 Passing Through the Gate

THE SHEPHERD AT THE GATE. JEROME: Whoever has entered in must not remain in the state wherein he entered but must go forth into the pasture so that entering in should be the beginning, "going forth and finding pasture,"[18] the perfecting of graces. The one who enters in is contained within the bounds of the world. The one who goes forth goes, as it were, beyond all created things and, counting as nothing all things seen, shall "find pasture" above the heavens, and shall feed upon the Word of God and say, "The Lord is my shepherd (and feeds me); I can lack nothing."[19] But this going forth can be only through Christ; as it follows, "and the Lord at the head of them." COMMENTARY ON MICAH 1.2.13.[20]

---

[15]2 Cor 13:9. [16]Ex 32:31-32. [17]LCC 12:223*. [18]Jn 10:9. [19]Ps 23:1 (22:1 LXX). [20]PMPC 2:38; CCL 76:456.

3:1-12 REBUKE OF PROPHETS AND LEADERS OF ISRAEL

[1]And I said:
Hear, you heads of Jacob
  and rulers of the house of Israel!
Is it not for you to know justice?—
  [2]you who hate the good and love the evil,
who tear the skin from off my people,
  and their flesh from off their bones;
[3]who eat the flesh of my people,
  and flay their skin from off them,
and break their bones in pieces,
  and chop them up like meat[g] in a kettle,
  like flesh in a caldron.

[4]Then they will cry to the LORD,

but he will not answer them;
he will hide his face from them at that time,
  because they have made their deeds evil.

[5]Thus says the Lord concerning the
  prophets
  who lead my people astray,
who cry "Peace"
  when they have something to eat,
but declare war against him
  who puts nothing into their mouths.
[6]Therefore it shall be night to you, without
  vision,
  and darkness to you, without divination.

The sun shall go down upon the prophets,
    and the day shall be black over them;
[7]the seers shall be disgraced,
    and the diviners put to shame;
they shall all cover their lips,
    for there is no answer from God.
[8]But as for me, I am filled with power,
    with the Spirit of the Lord,
    and with justice and might,
to declare to Jacob his transgression
    and to Israel his sin.

[9]Hear this, you heads of the house of
    Jacob
    and rulers of the house of Israel,

who abhor justice
    and pervert all equity,
[10]who build Zion with blood
    and Jerusalem with wrong.
[11]Its heads give judgment for a bribe,
    its priests teach for hire,
    its prophets divine for money;
yet they lean upon the Lord and say,
    "Is not the Lord in the midst of us?
    No evil shall come upon us."
[12]Therefore because of you
    Zion shall be plowed as a field;
Jerusalem shall become a heap of ruins,
    and the mountain of the house a wooded
    height.*

g Gk: Heb *as* *LXX be as a storehouse of fruits, and the mountain of the house as a grove of the forest*

Overview: God is not to blame for the destructive consequences of disobeying his word (Chrysostom). On the contrary, that is the fault of the leaders who forsook justice and succumbed to greed (Theodoret). Those who follow false prophets will walk in darkness (Ephrem). The inspired prophets were filled with the Holy Spirit (Cyril of Jerusalem). Cyril of Alexandria quotes Micah in reference to a forged letter that was sent under his name to Athanasius by heretics. The forger not only twists the words of Cyril but also corrupts the sacred Scriptures by misinterpreting them (Cyril of Alexandria). Priests ought to live within modest means (Jerome). Micah foretold the fall of Jerusalem (Gregory of Nazianzus). In his time Cyril of Jerusalem saw the mount of Zion become a melon patch, as predicted by the prophets (Cyril of Jerusalem).

3:1-4 Hating Good, Loving Evil

God Vindicated. Chrysostom: Indeed, the prophets repeatedly charged the people, saying, "Hear, you rulers of Sodom," and "Your princes are faithless."[1] And again Micah: "Is it not for you to know justice?" In fact, everywhere they vehemently upbraided them. What, then? Will someone on that account find fault with God? Perish the thought! The fault, in truth, is with them. Moreover, what better proof could one offer that you do not know the law, than that of your failure to obey it? Homilies on John 52.[2]

God's Accusation. Theodoret of Cyr: He delivers this address to the leaders: those entrusted with judgment trampled on justice; hence he puts it in the form of a question, Was it not you who had responsibility for judging, for punishing the guilty and letting the innocent go free without blame? How did you, then, who were entrusted with administering the laws, turn from the practice of good works and ardently support evil? You exercised such greed in regard to the needy as to strip them of all their possessions (suggesting this by saying "robbing people of their skins and the flesh from their bones"). Commentary on Micah 3.1-4.[3]

---

[1]Is 1:10, 23. [2]FC 41:45. [3]PG 81:1756.

3:5-6 Darkness and No Vision

Without Vision. Ephrem the Syrian: "The sun will go down"[4] upon those prophets who lead my people astray, dwelling in darkness. "It will be night for you, without vision, and it will be dark for you, without dawn." "For, when [the spirit] goes out of a man, it goes about wandering."[5] It does this quite by nature. [The Lord] rendered this judgment with regard to [the people]: "Thus will it be for this generation."[6] That is, in the days of the prophets the evil spirit had gone out from them, [that spirit] that was sin itself. Commentary of Tatian's Diatessaron 11.8.[7]

3:8 Filled with the Lord's Spirit

The Prophets Knew the Spirit of the Lord. Cyril of Jerusalem: If, further, one works through the twelve minor prophets, many testimonies to the Holy Spirit are to be found. Thus Micah speaks as God's mouthpiece and says, "Truly I am full of power by the Spirit of the Lord." Joel cries, "'And it shall come to pass afterwards,' says God, 'that I will pour out my Spirit upon all flesh'" and what follows.[8] Haggai said, "'For I am with you,' says the Lord of hosts ...'my Spirit remained among you.'"[9] And in like manner Zechariah says, "Receive my words and my statutes which I commanded my servants the prophets."[10] Catechetical Lecture 15.29.[11]

3:9 Those Who Abhor Justice

The Perversion of Holy Texts Continues. Cyril of Alexandria: But when some of those accustomed "to pervert what is right" turn my words aside into what seems best to them, let your holiness not wonder at this. [Know] that those involved in every heresy collect from the divinely inspired Scripture as pretexts of their own divination whatever was spoken truly through the Holy Spirit, corrupting it by their own evil ideas and pouring unquenchable fire upon their very own heads. But since we have learned that

some have published a corrupt text of the letter of our all-glorious father, Athanasius, to the blessed Epictetus, a letter which is itself orthodox, so that many are done harm from it, thinking that for this reason it would be something useful and necessary for our brothers, we have sent to your holiness copies of it made from the ancient copy which is with us and is genuine. Letter 39.8.[12]

3:11 Corruption of Israel's Leaders

Limits on the Pay of Priests. Jerome: You are permitted, O priest, to "live," not to luxuriate from the altar. "The mouth of the ox which treads out the corn is not muzzled." Yet the apostle "abused not the liberty,"[13] but "having food and raiment"[14] was "thereby content," laboring night and day that he "might not be chargeable to anybody."[15] And in his epistles he calls God to witness that he "lived reverently"[16] and without avarice in the gospel of Christ. He asserts this too not of himself alone but of his disciples, that he had sent no one who would either ask or receive anything from the churches. But if in some epistles he expresses pleasure and calls the gifts of those who sent them the grace of God,[17] he gathers not for himself but for the "poor saints at Jerusalem."[18] But these poor saints were those who of the Jews first believed in Christ and being cast out by parents, kinsmen and connections had lost their possessions and all their goods, the priests of the temple and the people destroying them. Let such poor receive. But if on plea of the poor a few houses are enriched and we eat in gold, glass and china, either let us with our wealth change our habit or let not the habit of poverty seek the riches of senators. What avails the habit of poverty while a whole crowd of poor longs for the contents of our purse? Wherefore, "for our sake" who are such, "who build up Zion with blood and Jerusalem by iniquity, who judge for

[4]Jer 15:9. [5]Mt 12:43. [6]Mt 12:45. [7]ECTD 179*. [8]Joel 2:28. [9]Hag 2:4-5. [10]Zech 1:6 LXX. [11]LCC 4:176. [12]FC 76:152. [13]1 Cor 9:13, 9, 18. [14]1 Tim 6:8. [15]1 Thess 2:6; 2 Thess 3:8. [16]1 Thess 2:10. [17]2 Cor 12:17-18, 6-7. [18]Rom 15:26.

gifts, give answers for rewards, divine for money," and thereon claiming to ourselves a fictitious sanctity say, "Evil will not come upon us," hear the sentence of the Lord which follows: "Zion and Jerusalem and the mountain of the temple"—that is, the temple of Christ—"shall" (in the consummation and the end, when "love shall grow cold"[19] and the faith shall be rare) "be plowed as a field and become heaps as the high places of a forest," so that where once were ample houses and countless ears of corn there should only be a poor cottage, keeping up the show of fruit which has no refreshment for the soul. COMMENTARY ON MICAH 1.3.11.[20]

3:12 Zion Plowed as a Field

THE DESTRUCTION OF JERUSALEM FORETOLD. GREGORY OF NAZIANZUS: Hence again the divine Micah was unable to brook the building of Zion with blood, however you interpret the phrase, and of Jerusalem with iniquity. Meanwhile, these heads of the house of Jacob abhorred justice. The priests were teaching for hire. The prophets were prophesying for money! What does Micah say will be the result of this? "Zion shall be plowed as a field, and Jerusalem shall be as a storehouse of fruit, and the mountain of the house shall be as the grove of the forest." He bewails also the scar-

city of the upright, there being scarcely a stalk or a gleaming grape left, since both the prince asks and the judge curries favor,[21] so that his language is almost the same as the mighty David's: "Save me, O Lord, for the godly man ceases."[22] Their blessings shall fail them, for "you consume like a moth what is dear to him."[23] IN DEFENSE OF HIS FLIGHT TO PONTUS, ORATION 2.58.[24]

THE PROPHECY FULFILLED. CYRIL OF JERUSALEM: Isaiah[25] lived almost a thousand years ago and saw Zion in its primitive form. The city was still standing, beautified with public squares and clothed in honor; yet he says, "Zion shall be plowed like a field." He was foretelling what has been fulfilled in our day. Observe the exactness of the prophecy; for he said, "Daughter Zion shall be left like a hut in a vineyard, like a shed in a cucumber patch."[26] Now the place is full of cucumber patches.[27] Do you see how the Holy Spirit enlightens the saints? Therefore do not be distracted by a common term but hold fast to what is exactly true. CATECHETICAL LECTURE 16.18.[28]

---

[19]Mt 24:12. [20]PMPC 2:45-46; CCL 76:465. [21]Mic 7:1-4. [22]Ps 12:1 (11:2 LXX). [23]Ps 39:11 (38:12 LXX). [24]NPNF 2 7:217*. [25]Cyril probably means Micah here rather than Isaiah. [26]Is 1:8. [27]Cyril was catechizing only a few hundred yards from Mount Zion, so he had observed these cucumber patches. This was about A.D. 350. [28]FC 64:87*.

4:1-13 THE MOUNTAIN OF THE LORD

[1]It shall come to pass in the latter days
   that the mountain of the house of the
   LORD
shall be established as the highest of the
   mountains,
   and shall be raised up above the hills;
and peoples shall flow to it,

[2]and many nations shall come, and
   say:
"Come, let us go up to the mountain of the
   LORD,
   to the house of the God of Jacob;
that he may teach us his ways
   and we may walk in his paths."

For out of Zion shall go forth the law,
   and the word of the LORD from
      Jerusalem.
³He shall judge between many peoples,
   and shall decide for strong nations afar
      off;
and they shall beat their swords into
   plowshares,
   and their spears into pruning hooks;
nation shall not lift up sword against
   nation,
      neither shall they learn war any more;
⁴but they shall sit every man under his vine
   and under his fig tree,
      and none shall make them afraid;
   for the mouth of the LORD of hosts has
      spoken.

⁵For all the peoples walk
   each in the name of its god,
but we will walk in the name of the LORD
      our God
   for ever and ever.

⁶In that day, says the LORD,
   I will assemble the lame
and gather those who have been driven
      away,
      and those whom I have afflicted;
⁷and the lame I will make the remnant;
   and those who were cast off, a strong
      nation;
and the LORD will reign over them in
      Mount Zion
   from this time forth and for
      evermore.

⁸And you, O tower of the flock,
   hill of the daughter of Zion,
to you shall it come,
   the former dominion* shall come,
      the kingdom of the daughter of Jerusalem.†

⁹Now why do you cry aloud?
   Is there no king in you?
Has your counselor perished,
      that pangs have seized you like a woman
         in travail?
¹⁰Writhe and groan,ᵇ O daughter of Zion,
   like a woman in travail;
for now you shall go forth from the city
   and dwell in the open country;
   you shall go to Babylon.
There you shall be rescued,
      there the LORD will redeem you
      from the hand of your enemies.

¹¹Now many nations
   are assembled against you,
saying, "Let her be profaned,
   and let our eyes gaze upon Zion."
¹²But they do not know
   the thoughts of the LORD,
they do not understand his plan,
      that he has gathered them as sheaves to
         the threshing floor.
¹³Arise and thresh,
   O daughter of Zion,
for I will make your horn iron
   and your hoofs bronze;
you shall beat in pieces many peoples,
      and shallⁱ devote their gain to the LORD,
      their wealth to the Lord of the whole earth.

h Heb uncertain   i Gk Syr Tg: Heb I will   *LXX adds from Babylon   †LXX And you, dark tower of the flock, daughter of Zion, on you the dominion shall come and enter in, even
the first kingdom from Babylon to the daughter of Jerusalem. Peshitta And you, O gloomy ruler of the daughter of Zion, your time has come, and the former ruler of the kingdom of the daughter
of Jerusalem is coming.

OVERVIEW: Christ is the "high mountain" about whom Micah prophesied, who will judge the nations with righteousness (AUGUSTINE). The law to be given out of Mount Zion is that which, revealed by Christ, replaced the law given to Moses on Mount Horeb (LACTANTIUS). What was prophesied in Micah was abundantly fulfilled in the apostles' worldwide witness to Christ (JUSTIN MARTYR). Micah prophesied that the mountain of God will attract pilgrims from all over the world (THEODORE). That prophecy was fulfilled in the apostolic preaching of the gospel that started in Jerusalem and reached all the nations of the world (THEODORET). The field and its trees of grapes and figs are symbolic references to the spiritual nourishment given to believers (AMBROSE). The vine is Jesus and the fig tree is the Holy Spirit, who feeds the believer (METHODIUS). The vine and the fig echo paradise (AMBROSE). Those who walk in the name of Christ give him their full obedience and make all efforts to be virtuous (CYRIL OF ALEXANDRIA). Persecution is a weaning process that allows Christians to bear more fruit as they are pruned by hardships (JUSTIN MARTYR). Zedekiah, the impious king and the cloudy shepherd, symbolizes the devil. Jesus, who ascended into heaven, will bring back the exiles. Zion will be violated and greatly despised by those who do not know that they will be thrashed by the revenging justice of God. There will be prosperity for returning captives and for the church (EPHREM).

4:1-3 Nations Come to God's House

THE MOUNTAIN OF THE PROPHETS. AUGUSTINE: The prophet Micah employed the symbol of a high mountain to speak of the gathering of the nations in Christ. He has this to say: "And it shall come to pass in the last days that the mountain of the house of the Lord shall be prepared in the top of the mountains and high above the hills; and people shall flow to it. And many nations shall come in haste, and say, 'Come, let us go up to the mountain of the Lord, and to the house of the God of Jacob; and he will teach us of his ways,

and we will walk in his paths; for the law shall go forth out of Zion, and the word of the Lord out of Jerusalem. And he shall judge among many people and rebuke strong nations afar off.' "

Further, the same prophet foretold even the place in which Christ was to be born: "But you, O Bethlehem Eph'rathah, who are little among the clans of Judah, from you shall come forth for me one who is to be ruler in Israel, whose origin is from old, from ancient days."[1] CITY OF GOD 18.30.[2]

THE PROMISED LAW. LACTANTIUS: For Micah announced that the new law would be given in this way: "The law shall go forth out of Zion, and the word of the Lord out of Jerusalem. And he shall judge among many people, and he shall vanquish and rebuke nations." For that prior law that was given through Moses was given not on Mount Zion but on Mount Horeb. And the Sibyl showed that this would be destroyed by the Son of God. "But when all these things have been fulfilled which he spoke, at that time then the whole law is destroyed."[3] EPITOME OF THE DIVINE INSTITUTES 4.17.[4]

MICAH'S PROPHECY FULFILLED BY THE APOSTLES. JUSTIN MARTYR: When the prophetic Spirit speaks as prophesying things to come, he says, "For the law will go forth from Zion, and the word of the Lord from Jerusalem, and he shall judge in the midst of the nations and rebuke many people. And they shall beat their swords into plowshares and their spears into pruning hooks, and nation will not lift up sword against nation, neither shall they learn to war anymore." We can show you that this has really happened. For a band of twelve men went forth from Jerusalem, and they were common men, not trained in speaking. But by the power of God they testified to every race of humankind that they were sent by Christ to teach to all the Word of God. And now we who once killed each other not only do

---

[1]Mic 5:2. [2]FC 24:126. [3]Sibylline Oracle 8.299-300. [4]FC 49:288.

not make war on each other, but in order not to lie or deceive our inquisitors we gladly die for the confession of Christ. For it would be possible for us to follow the saying, "The tongue has sworn, the mind remains unsworn."[5] But it would be ridiculous if the soldiers whom you[6] have recruited and enrolled remain loyal to you instead of to their own life, parents, native land and all their families. For you have nothing incorruptible to offer those who desire incorruption. Rather, endure all things in order to receive what we long for from him who is able to give it. FIRST APOLOGY 1.39.[7]

A UNIVERSAL SHRINE. THEODORE OF MOPSUESTIA: After the experience of the troubles in which they would find themselves, made captive first by the Assyrians and later by the Babylonians, such a great transformation would occur regarding this place that the mountain on which God was reputed to dwell would become famous and would be shown to be superior to all the mountains and far surpass all mountains and all hills on account of the glory enveloping it as a result of the divine compassion. Large numbers from all quarters, even from foreign peoples, would hasten to assemble to reach this mountain of God, on which God is believed to dwell, and learn how they should regulate their lives and live as they ought. COMMENTARY ON MICAH 4.1-3.[8]

APOSTOLIC PREACHING FULFILLED THIS PROPHECY. THEODORET OF CYR: The evangelical and divine preaching coursed to the ends of the earth, according to the Lord's prophecy contained in the sacred Gospels: "This good news will be preached to all the nations in witness to them." And he urged the holy apostles in the words, "Go, make disciples of all the nations, baptizing them in the name of the Father, the Son and the Holy Spirit, teaching them to observe everything I commanded you."[9] This evangelical law and apostolic preaching began with Jerusalem as with a fountain and traveled across the whole world, offering irrigation to those who made their approach with faith. It is also possible to see the divine houses situated in the middle of cities, villages, fields and remote areas, conspicuous for their size and beauty, so that they are illustrious and famous even on the highest mountains. COMMENTARY ON MICAH 4.1-3.[10]

4:4 No More Fear

FRUITS AND TREES IN THE PEACEFUL FIELD OF FAITH. AMBROSE: The Song of Songs alludes to [the vine and fig of the field] in this way: "I have adjured you, O daughters of Jerusalem, by the powers and by the virtues of the field, that you do not rouse or wake my love until he please."[11] This is the same peaceful field [of righteousness] of which the Lord also says in the psalm, "All that moves in the field is mine."[12] In this field the grape is found that was pressed and poured out blood and washed the world clean.[13] In this field is the tree, and beneath it the saints will find rest and be renewed by a good and spiritual grace. In this field is the olive tree fruitful in the overwhelming ointment of the peace of the Lord. In this field flourish the pomegranate trees[14] that shelter many fruits with the one bulwark of faith and nurture them with the warm embrace of love, so to speak. JACOB AND THE HAPPY LIFE 2.1.3.[15]

THE HEALING REST OF FAITH. METHODIUS: The vine, and that not in a few places, refers to the Lord himself,[16] and the fig tree to the Holy Spirit, as the Lord "makes glad the hearts of men,"[17] and the Spirit heals them. Hezekiah is commanded[18] to make plaster with a lump of figs—that is, the fruit of the Spirit—that he may be healed. According to the apostle this healing begins with love. For he says, "The fruit of the Spirit is love, joy, peace, longsuffering, gentleness, goodness,

---

[5]Quoted from Euripides *Hippolytus* 612. [6]Justin is addressing the authorrities and people of Rome. [7]LCC 1:266-67*. [8]PG 66:364. [9]Mt 24:14; 28:19-20. [10]PG 81:1760. [11]Song 2:7 LXX. [12]Ps 50:11 (49:11 LXX). [13]Juice produced by crushing grapes serves as a metaphor for Jesus' blood that cleansed the world from sin. [14]Song 8:2. [15]FC 65:148. [16]Jn 15:1. [17]Ps 104:5. [18]2 Kings 20:7; Is 38:21.

faith, meekness, temperance."[19] On account of their great pleasantness, the prophet calls these spiritual fruits figs. Of them Micah also says, "They shall sit every man under his vine and under his fig tree; and none shall make them afraid." Now it is certain that those who have taken refuge and rested under the Spirit and under the shadow of the Word shall not be alarmed or frightened by the one who troubles the hearts of humankind. BANQUET OF THE TEN VIRGINS 10.5.[20]

VINES AND FIGS AS ECHOES OF PARADISE. AMBROSE: We read in Genesis that God planted a garden to the east and put there the man he had formed.[21] Who had the power to create paradise, if not almighty God, who "spoke and all was made"[22] and who was never in need of that which he wished to bring into being? He planted, therefore, that paradise of which he says is his wisdom: "Every plant which my Father has not planted will be rooted up."[23] This is a goodly plantation, for angels and saints are said to lie beneath the fig tree and the vine. In this respect they are the type of the angels in that time of peace[24] which is to come. ON PARADISE 1.2.[25]

4:5 Walking in the Name of the Lord

WALKING IN THE NAME OF CHRIST. CYRIL OF ALEXANDRIA: They who are eager to go up into the mountain of the Lord and wish to learn thoroughly his ways promise a ready obedience, and they receive in themselves the glories of the life in Christ and undertake with their whole strength to be earnest in all holiness. "For let everyone," he says, "in every country and city go the way he chooses and pass his life as seems good to him, but our care is Christ, and his laws we will make our straight path; we will walk along with him; and that not for this life only, present or past, but yet more for what is beyond." It is a faithful saying. "For they who now suffer with him shall walk with him forever, and with him be glorified, and with him reign."[26] But "they" make Christ their care who prefer nothing to his love, who

cease from the vain distractions of the world and seek rather righteousness and what is pleasing to him, and to excel in virtue. Such a one was the divine Paul, for he writes, "I am crucified with Christ; and now no longer I live, but Christ lives in me."[27] And again: "I determined not to know anything among you save Jesus Christ, and him crucified."[28] COMMENTARY ON MICAH 2.4.5.[29]

4:6 Gather the Afflicted

PRUNED TO BEAR MORE FRUIT. JUSTIN MARTYR: Now it is obvious that no one can frighten or subdue us who believe in Jesus throughout the whole world. Although we are beheaded and crucified, and exposed to wild beasts and chains and flames, and every other means of torture, it is evident that we will not retract our profession of faith. The more we are persecuted, the more do others in ever-increasing numbers embrace the faith and become worshipers of God through the name of Jesus. Just as when one cuts off the fruit-bearing branches of the vine, it grows again and other blossoming and fruitful branches spring forth, so it is with us Christians. For the vine planted by God and Christ the Redeemer is his people. But the rest of the prophecy will be fulfilled at his second coming. The prophet Micah says, "In that day, says the Lord, I will gather her that is bruised, and will receive her that is cast out, and those whom I rejected." This indicates that you do not have the last word then when you and all other people, having the power, cast out every Christian not only from his own property but even from the whole world, for you allow no Christian to live. DIALOGUE WITH TRYPHO 110.[30]

4:8 The Former Dominion

THE DEVIL THE CLOUDY SHEPHERD. EPHREM THE SYRIAN: "And you, O tower, O cloudy shep-

---

[19]Gal 5:22-23. [20]ANF 6:350*. [21]Gen 2:8. [22]Ps 33:9 (32:9 LXX). [23]Mt 15:13. [24]Mk 12:25. [25]FC 42:288. [26]2 Tim 2:11-12; Rom 8:17; Rev 3:4. [27]Gal 2:19-20. [28]1 Cor 2:2. [29]PMPC 2:60. [30]FC 6:318.

herd of the daughter of Zion, your time shall come." These words refer to the impious king Zedekiah, whom the prophet calls "tower" because the people of Judea stayed under his shadow, and "shepherd" because of his administration of the kingdom, and "cloudy" because of the error of idolatry to which he adhered. Again, in the symbolic meaning of his words he calls the devil a cloudy shepherd, because in an allegorical sense he always attacks the daughter of Zion under a cloudy sky. And, after catching her, he drags her away from the light—indeed the one who acts maliciously hates the light. But later, the supreme and legitimate prince of the mystical Jerusalem destroyed this tyranny with his advent and drove the obscure shepherd away. COMMENTARY ON MICAH.[31]

4:10 Rescued from Babylon

RETURN FROM EXILE. EPHREM THE SYRIAN: "Writhe and groan, O daughter Zion, like a woman in labor, for now you shall go forth from the city and camp in the open country; you shall go to Babylon, and there you shall be rescued." The meaning is that you will go into captivity, people of Zion, to be deported to Babylon, but after years you will come back from there, not with the soldier hastening after you, but with that leader who by ascending into heaven made captivity his own prisoner. You will follow him together with Paul's brothers-in-arms and the princes of

our army, who captivate all minds to the respect of Christ. COMMENTARY ON MICAH.[32]

4:11 Nations Assemble Against Zion

ZION DESPISED. EPHREM THE SYRIAN: Now many nations are assembled against you. That is, in the meantime a mix of many different nations invades you under the command of Gog. Again there shall be profanation in Zion, and the eye shall gaze upon it, which means the holy places of Zion will be violated and greatly despised by those who did not know that they would have been thrashed by the revenging justice of God like sheaves gathered on the threshing floor. COMMENTARY ON MICAH.[33]

4:13 Horn of Iron, Hoofs of Bronze

PROSPERITY. EPHREM THE SYRIAN: "For I will make your horns, which the Babylonians broke, iron. You shall beat in pieces many people, and shall devote their grain to the Lord." This will happen when, after taking possession of their land and wealth, you pay the tithe to the Lord of the entire earth. As I have said, God showed a sign of such great prosperity to the Jews who would be coming back from captivity. He also reserved the same thing for his church. COMMENTARY ON MICAH.[34]

---

[31]ESOO 2:277. [32]ESOO 2:277. [33]ESOO 2:278. [34]ESOO 2:278.

5:1-15 THE MESSIAH FROM BETHLEHEM

[1j]Now you are walled about with a wall;[k]
   siege is laid against us;
with a rod they strike upon the cheek
   the ruler of Israel.

[2l]But you, O Bethlehem Ephrathah,
   who are little to be among the clans of
     Judah,
from you shall come forth for me

one who is to be ruler in Israel,
whose origin is from of old,
   from ancient days.
[3]Therefore he shall give them up until the
   time
   when she who is in travail has brought
   forth;
then the rest of his brethren shall return
   to the people of Israel.
[4]And he shall stand and feed his flock in the
   strength of the LORD,
   in the majesty of the name of the LORD
   his God.
And they shall dwell secure, for now he
   shall be great
   to the ends of the earth.
[5]And this shall be peace,
   when the Assyrian comes into our land
   and treads upon our soil,[m]
that we will raise against him seven
   shepherds
   and eight princes of men;
[6]they shall rule the land of Assyria with the
   sword,
   and the land of Nimrod with the drawn
   sword;[n]
and they[o] shall deliver us from the Assyrian
   when he comes into our land
   and treads within our border.

[7]Then the remnant of Jacob shall be
   in the midst of many peoples
like dew from the LORD,

like showers upon the grass,
which tarry not for men
   nor wait for the sons of men.
[8]And the remnant of Jacob shall be among
   the nations,
   in the midst of many peoples,
like a lion among the beasts of the forest,
   like a young lion among the flocks of
   sheep,
which, when it goes through, treads down
   and tears in pieces, and there is none to
   deliver.
[9]Your hand shall be lifted up over your
   adversaries,
   and all your enemies shall be cut off.

[10]And in that day, says the LORD,
   I will cut off your horses from among you
   and will destroy your chariots;
[11]and I will cut off the cities of your land
   and throw down all your strongholds;
[12]and I will cut off sorceries from your hand,
   and you shall have no more soothsayers;
[13]and I will cut off your images
   and your pillars from among you,
and you shall bow down no more
   to the work of your hands;
[14]and I will root out your Asherim from
   among you
   and destroy your cities.
[15]And in anger and wrath I will execute
   vengeance
   upon the nations that did not obey.

j Ch 4.14 in Heb   k Cn Compare Gk: Heb obscure   l Ch 5.1 in Heb   m Gk: Heb *in our palaces*   n Cn: Heb *in its entrances*   o Heb *he*

OVERVIEW: Samaria is a metaphor for those who are put to shame and dishonor (CYRIL OF ALEXANDRIA). The magi, the star and Bethlehem in Micah's prophecy were all focused upon the birth of Jesus (AUGUSTINE). Jesus fulfills all of the promises made to Abraham and David (ISHO'DAD). Christ's temporal birth at Bethlehem was not the beginning of the existence of the Son of God.

Micah indicated that the Messiah had been eternally with God in his timeless beginning (CYRIL OF JERUSALEM, THEODORET). Christ's origin is from the beginning (ISHO'DAD). Out of Bethlehem will come the Christ, who will shepherd Israel (CHRYSOSTOM). Christ was born a visible man of a virgin mother (AUGUSTINE). The pains and afflictions of Jerusalem are labor pains by which she will give birth to salvation (ISHO'DAD). The Magi, the star and the place of Christ's birth were all foretold by Micah (AUGUSTINE). Unbelieving Jews made a fundamental mistake, as did Herod, regarding the nature of Christ's announced kingdom. They erroneously thought it would be a rival earthly kingdom to bring down the Romans (LEO). The seven shepherds and eight princes represent the punishment that Assyria will receive (ISHO'DAD).

5:1 Besieged and Stricken

SAMARIA AS A TYPE OF SINFUL LIFE. CYRIL OF ALEXANDRIA: So he says that Samaria will be surrounded and encompassed by the hostile peoples. Not only will they strike her cheek with their hand, which is more bearable, but they will crush her with rods, which is especially cruel. This signifies the shameful and miserable distress of captivity, for it is unquestionable that to strike the cheek is a special dishonor. Considering that they also struck her with rods, they have caused extreme hardship and debasement. Governed by the tribe of Ephrem, Samaria is dishonored. She is in shame and suffering. However, the striking hand will stop, and we will not taste misery if only we do our best to refrain from provoking the wrath of the Lord of all by trespassing or eagerly committing sins, which are hateful to him. If we honor him with virtuousness instead, then we will enjoy prosperity and will live a joyous and commendable life. COMMENTARY ON MICAH 5.1.[1]

5:2 A Ruler from Bethlehem

WHERE CHRIST WOULD BE BORN. AUGUS-

TINE: By designating Bethlehem, they [the Jews] were like the builders of Noah's ark, providing others the means of escape, yet themselves perishing in the flood. Like milestones, they showed the way but were incapable of walking along it. They were asked where the Christ was to be born. They answered, "In Bethlehem of Judah. For thus it was written by the prophet"—they were repeating from memory, you see, what had been written about this by Micah: "And you, Bethlehem, land of Judah, are not the least among the leaders of Judah; for from you shall come forth the king who is going to be the shepherd of my people Israel."[2] SERMON 373.4.[3]

THE SMALLER MADE THE STRONGER. ISHO'DAD OF MERV: "But you, O Bethlehem, you are too little for what you are."[4] That is, even though in comparison with your enemies you are little in force and number and incapable to lead "the thousand of Judah," yet, thanks to the help that I give you, the powerful ruler will be able to make war against them. For I have destined him to that from the beginning, through the promises already made to David. This is said with the usual reference to Zerubbabel, but its true meaning has been revealed in Christ, because when he appeared, all the promises made to Abraham and David were fulfilled. COMMENTARY ON MICAH.[5]

ETERNAL BUT BORN IN A TEMPORAL PLACE. CYRIL OF JERUSALEM: It is enough for piety for you to know, as we have said, that God has one only Son, one naturally begotten, who did not begin to be when he was born in Bethlehem but is before all ages. For listen to the prophet Micah: "And you, Bethlehem, house of Ephratha, are little to be among the thousands of Judah. From you shall come forth for me a leader who shall feed my people Israel; and his goings forth are from

---

[1]PG 71:709-12. [2]Mt 2:5-6. [3]WSA 3 10:321-22. [4]The Peshitta differs from the Hebrew and is closer to the LXX: "And you, Bethlehem, are few in number to be reckoned among the thousand of Judah." [5]CSCO 303 (128):102.

the beginning, from the days of eternity."[6] Therefore do not fix your attention on him as coming from Bethlehem simply but worship him as begotten eternally of the Father. Admit no one who speaks of a beginning of the Son in time, but acknowledge his timeless beginning, the Father. CATECHETICAL LECTURE 11.20.[7]

THE INCARNATE WORD BORN IN BETHLEHEM.
THEODORET OF CYR: Now this patently resembles the prologue to the Gospel, "In the beginning was the Word, and the Word was with God, and the Word was God; he was in the beginning with God." It also resembles what was said by God through blessed David, "From the womb before the daystar I begot you."[8] This person, then, who was before time, who was in the beginning with God, who is God the Word, with his origins from that source from the beginning, receives his birth according to the flesh (the text says) in you [Bethlehem], making you famous and illustrious, even though unimportant among Judah's thousands. COMMENTARY ON MICAH 5.2.[9]

BIRTH PROMISED IN ABRAHAM FROM OLD.
ISHO'DAD OF MERV: The text says, "His origin is from the beginning," the beginning, that is, according to the promises made to Abraham and David. COMMENTARY ON MICAH.[10]

CHRIST BORN IN BETHLEHEM. CHRYSOSTOM:
It was another prophet, again, who pointed out the place where he would be born. For Micah said, "And you, Bethlehem, the land of Judah, are by no means the least among the princes of Judah. For out of you will come the leader who will shepherd my people, Israel: and his going forth is from the beginning, from the days of eternity." He revealed his existence before all ages. When he said "there will come the leader who will shepherd my people, Israel," he revealed Christ's birth in the flesh. DEMONSTRATION AGAINST THE PAGANS 3.3.[11]

CHRIST'S HUMAN BIRTH DEFENDED. AUGUSTINE: According to prophecy, Christ was born in

Bethlehem of Judah, at the time, as I said, when Herod was king in Judea. At Rome, the republic had given way to the entire empire, and the emperor Caesar Augustus had established a worldwide peace. Christ was born a visible man of a virgin mother, but he was a hidden God because God was his Father. So the prophet had foretold: "Behold, the virgin shall be with child and shall bring forth a son; and they shall call his name Emmanuel, which is interpreted, God with us."[12] To prove that he was God, Christ worked many miracles, some of which—as many as seemed necessary to establish his claim—are recorded in the Gospels. Of these miracles the very first was the marvelous manner of his birth. CITY OF GOD 18.96.[13]

5:3 When She Has Given Birth

THE TRAVAIL OF CAPTIVITY WILL END IN A BIRTH. ISHO'DAD OF MERV: "He shall give them up until the time when she who is in labor has brought forth." This is what the prophet calls Jerusalem. This means he will abandon them to the afflictions of captivity until the time of the return. This means that these predictions will not come true before they are back from their captivity. Henana of Adiabene[14] says "she who is in labor" means Jerusalem because she is in the pains of labor, which are her afflictions, and waits the birth of her salvation, until according to her expectations it sets to her return and her pains' end. But in the same manner they will endure different difficulties until the Virgin gives birth to Christ. COMMENTARY ON MICAH.[15]

THE MAGI, THE STAR AND BETHLEHEM FORETOLD. AUGUSTINE: But now, the same star which led the magi to the place where the infant God was to be found with his virgin mother could of course have led them right to the very city. But it

---

[6]Mt 2:6. [7]FC 61:222. [8]Jn 1:1-2; Ps 110:3 LXX. [9]PG 81:1768. [10]CSCO 303 (128):103. [11]FC 73:198. [12]Is 7:14; Mt 1:23. [13]FC 24:163. [14]Syriac author (d. 610) who wrote a now lost commentary on the Twelve Prophets. [15]CSCO 303 (128):103.

withdrew, and didn't appear at all to them again, until the Jews themselves had been questioned about the city where Christ was to be born. This was to oblige them to name it themselves, on the evidence of divine Scriptures, and to say themselves, "In Bethlehem of Judah. For so it is written, 'And you, Bethlehem, land of Judah, are not the least among the princes of Judah; for from you shall come forth the leader who will rule my people Israel.' "[16] What else can divine Providence have meant by this, but that among the Jews would remain only the divine Scriptures by which the nations would be instructed, they themselves being blind? This evidence they would carry about with them not as an assistance to their own salvation but as evidence of ours. Because today it may happen that when we bring forward prophecies about Christ, uttered long before and now made clear by the events that have fulfilled them, the pagans whom we wish to gain will say that they weren't foretold so long ago but have been composed by us after the event, so that what has later occurred may be thought to have been previously prophesied. Then we can cite the volumes owned by the Jews, to clear the doubts of the pagans, who were already prefigured in those magi, whom the Jews instructed from the divine books about the city in which Christ was born, without themselves either seeking or acknowledging him. SERMON 200.3.[17]

5:4 Living Secure

HEROD FEARED AN EARTHLY RIVAL. LEO THE GREAT: Evidently [the Hebrew leaders] understood [the prophecy] in a carnal manner, just as Herod did, and reckoned that Christ's kingdom would be like the powers in this world. They hoped for a temporal leader, while Herod feared an earthly rival. "Herod, you are trapped in a useless fear. In vain do you attempt to rage against the child you suspect. Your realm does not encompass Christ, nor does the Lord of the world care about the meager limits within which you wield the rod of your power. He whom you do

not wish to see reign in Judea reigns everywhere. You yourself would reign more happily if you would submit to his rule. Why not turn into honest service that which you resolve to do in falsehood and guile? Go with the wise men and worship the true king in humble adoration. But more inclined as you are toward the Jewish blindness, you do not imitate the faith of these Gentiles. You turn your perverse heart to cruel wiles. Yet you are not going to kill the one you fear, nor will you harm those whom you eliminate."[18] SERMON 34.2.[19]

5:5 When the Assyrians Invade

SEVEN SHEPHERDS AND EIGHT PRINCES. ISHO'DAD OF MERV: "We will raise against them seven shepherds and eight princes." By means of the events that happened in the days of Hezekiah, at the time of the ruin of the Assyrians, Micah provides information about those things that will happen through the agency of Zerubbabel toward the people of the house of Gog. By the numbers seven and eight he has indicated the complete and total destruction that befell the Assyrians through the intervention of the angel. The allusion is to the words of Ecclesiastes: "Cast your bread upon the waters, for you will find it after many days. Give a portion to seven, or even to eight, for you know not what evil may happen on earth."[20]

However, others suppose that he means by "seven shepherds" the prophets who lived before the invasion of the Assyrians, who prophesied their ruin, and that he means by the "eight princes of men" Hezekiah and the princes who assisted him. . . .

The phrase "seven shepherds" may indicate the fullness of the punishment that the Assyrians will undergo through the agency of the angel, while "eight bites of men" indicates what was in store for the survivors after their flight. What happened was that the Assyrian king was mur-

---

[16]Mt 2:5-6. [17]WSA 3 6:84-85. [18]Leo refers to martyrdom. [19]FC 93:145*. [20]Eccles 11:1-2.

dered by his sons and the others were exterminated by their fellow citizens. . . . From the spiritual point of view the verse applies to Satan, the abolisher of the law and the gospel, who was defeated by the prophets, the apostles and the angels. COMMENTARY ON MICAH.[21]

---

[21]CSCO 303 (128):103.

6:1-16 THE LORD'S TRIAL OVER ISRAEL

[1]*Hear what the LORD says:* *
Arise, plead your case before the mountains,
and let the hills hear your voice.
[2]*Hear, you mountains, the controversy of*
the LORD,
and you enduring foundations of the earth;
for the LORD has a controversy with his
people,
and he will contend with Israel.

[3]*"O my people, what have I done to you?*
In what have I wearied you? Answer me!
[4]*For I brought you up from the land of*
Egypt,
and redeemed you from the house of
bondage;
and I sent before you Moses,
Aaron, and Miriam.
[5]*O my people, remember what Balak king of*
Moab devised,
and what Balaam the son of Beor
answered him,
and what happened from Shittim to Gilgal,
that you may know the saving acts of the
LORD."

[6]*"With what shall I come before the LORD,*
and bow myself before God on high?
Shall I come before him with burnt
offerings,
with calves a year old?
[7]*Will the LORD be pleased with thousands*
of rams,
with ten thousands of rivers of oil?
Shall I give my first-born for my
transgression,
the fruit of my body for the sin of my
soul?"
[8]*He has showed you, O man, what is good;*
and what does the LORD require of you
but to do justice, and to love kindness,[p]
and to walk humbly with your God?
[9]*The voice of the LORD cries to the city—*
and it is sound wisdom to fear thy name:
"Hear, O tribe and assembly of the city![q]
[10]*Can I forget the[r] treasures of wickedness in*
the house of the wicked,
and the scant measure that is accursed?
[11]*Shall I acquit the man with wicked scales*
and with a bag of deceitful weights?
[12]*Your[s] rich men are full of violence;*
your[s] inhabitants speak lies,
and their tongue is deceitful in their mouth.
[13]*Therefore I have begun[t] to smite you,*
making you desolate because of your sins.
[14]*You shall eat, but not be satisfied,*
and there shall be hunger in your inward
parts;

you shall put away, but not save,
    and what you save I will give to the
        sword.
  ¹⁵You shall sow, but not reap;
    you shall tread olives, but not anoint
        yourselves with oil;
    you shall tread grapes, but not drink

    wine.
  ¹⁶For you have kept the statutes of Omri,ᵘ
    and all the works of the house of Ahab;
    and you have walked in their counsels;
    that I may make you a desolation, and yourᵛ
        inhabitants a hissing;
    so you shall bear the scorn of the peoples.ᵐʷ

p Or *steadfast love*   q Cn Compare Gk: Heb *and who has appointed it yet*   r Cn: Heb uncertain   s Heb *whose*   t Gk Syr Vg: Heb *have made sick*   u Gk Syr Vg Tg: Heb *the statutes of Omri are kept*   v Heb *its*   w Gk: Heb *my people*   *LXX *The word of the Lord, the Lord said*

OVERVIEW: "O my people, what have I done to you?" is Christ's charge and verdict against his persecutors (AMBROSE). They missed the opportunity to receive Jesus as Messiah (CASSIODORUS). Micah's words are applied against the Arians, who refuse to be conformed to the Nicaean teaching on the Trinity (GREGORY OF NAZIANZUS). Micah lamented the ingratitude of Jews of his day for God's deliverance. God is not appeased by sacrifices and rituals; rather, the Lord requires justice, mercy and love of those who profess to follow him (AMBROSE). Human beings are called to procreate and fill the earth (CLEMENT OF ALEXANDRIA). God is merciful and compassionate, and he expects the same of those who follow him (TERTULLIAN). Believers are not to delay in doing good (AMBROSE). The truth is best taught when it is embodied in actions (BEDE). The love of God and of one's neighbor, as announced by Moses, is superior to sacrifices and offerings (THEODORE). No less, however, does God ask that we give him ourselves (AUGUSTINE).

6:3 "O My People"

CHRIST'S JUDGMENT OF HIS PEOPLE.
AMBROSE: There is also a third entreaty, for although David was set in the midst of people doing evil deeds, he eagerly desires that his case be separated from contagion with them.[1] Many suppose that this sentiment should be attributed to the Lord Jesus, because it belongs to him alone not to fear judgment, as the one who overcomes

when he is judged.[2] Indeed, he has judgment from the unjust man, and into it Christ entered willingly, as you find it written, "O my people, what have I done to you? Or wherein have I grieved you?" But since the Father has given all judgment to him,[3] not indeed as if to one that was weak but as if to a Son, what judgment can he undergo? If they think that the Son must undergo the Father's judgment, surely "the Father does not judge any man, but all judgment has been given to the Son, that all men may honor the Son even as they honor the Father."[4] The Father honors the Son, and do you not put him to judgment? We have expressed this thought here, so that no one would think that we substituted the figure of the psalmist in the Lord's place out of fear of inquiry. Holy David foresees in spirit that the Jews will rise up against the Lord in his passion. Since he is not greatly afraid of the judgment upon his own faith, he beseeches that his own case be distinguished also from a nation of persecutors. Else, the stock of the entire Jewish race could be implicated with those wicked heirs of his own race and posterity. THE PRAYER OF JOB AND DAVID 4.8.29.[5]

JUDGMENT AND COMFORT.
CASSIODORUS: "For the Lord will judge his people, and he will [give] comfort among his servants."[6] The reason for the previous praise is stated: "For the Lord will judge

---

[1]Ps 43:1 (42:1 LXX).   [2]Ps 51:4 (50:6 LXX).   [3]Jn 5:22.   [4]Jn 5:22-23.   [5]FC 65:413-14.   [6]Ps 135:14 (134:14 LXX).

his people," that is, the Jewish people, to whom he revealed great miracles and assigned his prophets so that the people would not sin. He also sent to them his own Son, so that their accursed hardness could finally be melted. But because they persisted with accursed obstinacy, he will certainly judge them, because they were unwilling to be his, though he had chosen them from all nations as his possession. To them he says, "Hear, O people, and I will speak,"[7] and elsewhere, "My people, what have I done to you?" So he will judge them. But hear what follows as it concerns the faithful: "He will again have compassion upon us."[8] He means when he will render their promised rewards to those on earth afflicted with harsh contempt on account of his name. Scripture says of them, "Blessed are they that mourn, for they shall be comforted,"[9] and in another place are the words "He that believes in me is not judged but will pass from death to life. But he that does not believe is already judged."[10] EXPOSITION OF THE PSALMS 134.14.[11]

TRAGIC BROKENNESS. GREGORY OF NAZIANZUS: Would you like me to utter to you the words of God to Israel, stiff-necked and hardened? "O my people, what have I done to you, or in what way have I injured you, or wherein have I wearied you?" This language indeed is more fit from me to you who insult me. It is a sad thing that we watch for opportunities against each other and having destroyed our fellowship of spirit by diversities of opinion have become almost more inhuman and savage to one another than even the barbarians who are now engaged in war against us, banded together against us by the Trinity whom we have separated. We are not foreigners making forays and raids upon foreigners or nations of a different language, which is some little consolation in the calamity. But we are making war upon one another, and almost upon those of the same household. Or if you will, we the members of the same body are consuming and being consumed by one another. Nor is this, bad as it is, the extent of our calamity, for we even regard our diminution as a

gain. But since we are in such a condition and regulate our faith by the times, let us compare the times with one another; you your emperor, and I my sovereigns; you Ahab and I Josiah. AGAINST THE ARIANS AND ON HIMSELF, ORATION 33.2.[12]

6:5 Remember Balak

THE PEOPLE CHASTISED FOR REJECTING GOD'S MESSENGERS. AMBROSE: You see the Lord is teaching you a lesson, challenging you to goodness by his own example, teaching you even when he reproves. When accusing the Jews, for instance, he says, "O my people, what have I done to you? Or wherein have I grieved you? Or wherein have I offended you? Answer me. Is it because I brought you out of the land of Egypt, and delivered you out of the house of bondage?" adding, "And I sent before your face Moses, Aaron and Miriam. O my people, remember what Balak king of Moab devised." You were indeed oppressed, an exile in foreign lands, laden with heavy burdens. LETTER 41.24.[13]

6:6-7 Will Offerings Please the Lord?

SIN NOT REDEEMED BY OUR BURNT OFFERINGS. AMBROSE: For what is asked of you, O man? Only that you fear God: seek for him, walk after him, follow in his ways.[14] "With what shall I win over the Lord? Shall I win him over with burnt offerings?" The Lord is not reconciled, nor are sins redeemed, with tens of thousands of young goats or thousands of rams or with the fruits of unholiness, but the grace of the Lord is won with a good life. FLIGHT FROM THE WORLD 6.33.[15]

YOU CANNOT WIN GRACE. CLEMENT OF ALEXANDRIA: Is everyone who is turning from sin to faith, turning from sinful practices (as if they were his mother) to life? I shall call in evidence

---

[7]Ps 50:7. [8]Mic 7:19. [9]Mt 5:5. [10]Jn 3:18, 36. [11]ACW 53:348. [12]NPNF 2 7:329*. [13]LCC 5:247-48. [14]Deut 10:12. [15]FC 65:306.

one of the twelve prophets, who says, "Am I to make an offering of my firstborn son for my impiety? Should I offer the fruit of my womb for the sin of my soul?" Can the mother buy her way to God by giving up her firstborn? This must not be taken as an attack on the words "increase in numbers."[16] Micah is naming, by using the word *impiety*, the first impulses after birth, which do not help us to knowledge of God. If anyone misuses this as a basis for saying that that birth is evil, he should also use it as a basis for saying that it is good, in that in it we come to know the truth. "Come back to a sober and upright life and stop sinning."[17] But the sinner knows nothing of God. "We are not wrestling against flesh and blood but against spiritual beings, potent in temptation, the rulers of this dark world,"[18] so there is forbearance. This is why Paul says, "I bruise my own body and treat it as a slave, because every athlete goes into total training."[19] By "total training" we understand not that he abstains from absolutely everything but that he shows self-control in those things he has taken a deliberate decision to use. "They do it to win a crown which dies, we for one which never dies,"[20] if we win the contest. No effort, no crown! STROMATEIS 3.16.101.[21]

6:8 What Is Good

ONE WHO KNOWS GOD. TERTULLIAN: "But God,"[adulterers and fornicators say,] "is good and most kind." He is "merciful, compassionate and rich in mercy,"[22] which "he prefers to every sacrifice."[23] "He desires not so much the death as the repentance of the sinner."[24] He is "the Savior of all people, and especially of the faithful."[25] Therefore the children of God must also be "merciful"[26] and "peacemakers,"[27] "forgiving each other as Christ also forgave us,"[28] "not judging, lest we be judged."[29] For to "his master a man stands or falls; who are you to judge the servant of another?"[30] "Forgive, and you will be forgiven."[31] Yet many such things as these are only said, not done, merely bandied about, unmanning rather than strength-

ening discipline, flattering God and pandering to themselves. ON PURITY 2.[32]

WHY DELAY DOING GOOD? AMBROSE: "You have been told, O man, what is good. And what does the Lord require of you, but to do justice, to love mercy and to be prepared to walk with your Lord?" Accordingly, the gospel says to you, "Arise, let us go from here,"[33] while the law says to you, "You shall walk after the Lord your God." You have learned the method of your flight from here—why do you delay? FLIGHT FROM THE WORLD 6.33.[34]

TEACHING THE TRUTH AND DOING GOOD WORKS. BEDE: Here is a priest who serves at every hour with great fear while walking humbly with the Lord his God in accordance with the word of the prophet. Meanwhile another priest is hardly capable of having that much fear even when he is about to die and enter into the last judgment before his Lord. But the full expression of the priesthood is comprised of the combination of the teaching of truth with good works. This is in accord with blessed Luke's comment that in writing his Gospel he had composed a treatise concerning all the things that Jesus began both to do and to teach.[35] ON THE TABERNACLE 3.6.[36]

LOVE OF GOD AND NEIGHBOR. THEODORE OF MOPSUESTIA: Forget about burnt offerings, countless sacrifices and oblations of firstborn, he is saying. If you are concerned to appease the divinity, practice what God ordered you in the beginning through Moses. What in fact is that? To deliver fair judgment and decision in all cases where you have to choose better from worse, to continue giving evidence of all possible love and fellow-feeling to your neighbor, and be ready to

---

[16]Gen 1:28. [17]Tit 2:12. [18]Eph 6:12. [19]1 Cor 9:24-25. [20]1 Cor 9:25-27. [21]FC 85:319-20*. [22]Ps 145:8. [23]Hos 6:6. [24]See Ezek 18:23. [25]1 Tim 4:10. [26]Mt 5:7. [27]Mt 5:9. [28]Col 3:13. [29]Mt 7:1. [30]Rom 14:4. [31]Lk 6:37. [32]ACW 28:57*. [33]Jn 14:31. [34]FC 65:306. [35]Acts 1:1. [36]TTH 18:127*.

put into practice what is pleasing to God in every way. He means, in short, "You will love God with all your heart, all your mind and all your soul, and you will love your neighbor as yourself,"[37] as was said of old through Moses. Do this, he is saying, as something preferable to sacrifices in God's eyes. COMMENTARY ON MICAH 6.6-8.[38]

THE LORD REQUIRES THE SELF. AUGUSTINE: You ask what you should offer: offer yourself.

For what else does the Lord seek of you but you? Because of all earthly creatures he has made nothing better than you, he seeks yourself from yourself, because you have lost yourself. SERMON 48.2.[39]

---

[37]Deut 6:5; Lev 19:18. [38]PG 66:385. [39]PMPC 2:82.

7:1-13 THE SIN AND MISERY OF ISRAEL

[1]Woe is me! For I have become
  as when the summer fruit* has been
    gathered,
  as when the vintage has been gleaned:
there is no cluster to eat,
  no first-ripe fig which my soul desires.
[2]The godly man has perished from the
    earth,
  and there is none upright among men;
they all lie in wait for blood,
  and each hunts his brother with a net.
[3]Their hands are upon what is evil, to do it
    diligently;
  the prince and the judge ask for a bribe,
and the great man utters the evil desire of
    his soul;
  thus they weave it together.
[4]The best of them is like a brier,
  the most upright of them a thorn hedge.
The day of their[x] watchmen, of their[x]
    punishment, has come;
  now their confusion is at hand.
[5]Put no trust in a neighbor,
  have no confidence in a friend;

guard the doors of your mouth
  from her who lies in your bosom;
[6]for the son treats the father with contempt,
  the daughter rises up against her mother,
the daughter-in-law against her mother-in-
    law;
  a man's enemies are the men of his own
    house.
[7]But as for me, I will look to the LORD,
  I will wait for the God of my salvation;
  my God will hear me.

[8]Rejoice not over me, O my enemy;
  when I fall, I shall rise;
when I sit in darkness,
  the LORD will be a light to me.
[9]I will bear the indignation of the LORD
  because I have sinned against him,
until he pleads my cause
  and executes judgment for me.
He will bring me forth to the light;
  I shall behold his deliverance.
[10]Then my enemy will see,
  and shame will cover her who said to me,

"Where is the LORD your God?"
My eyes will gloat over her;
  now she will be trodden down
  like the mire of the streets.

[11]A day for the building of your walls!
  In that day the boundary shall be far
  extended.

[12]In that day they will come to you,
  from Assyria to[y] Egypt,
and from Egypt to the River,
  from sea to sea and from mountain to
  mountain.
[13]But the earth will be desolate
  because of[†] its inhabitants,
  for the fruit of their doings.

x Heb *your*   y Cn: Heb *and cities of*   *LXX *straw*   †LXX *along with*

OVERVIEW: Believers are challenged to ask themselves if they are the good harvest that will be gathered on the last day. The church is a mixture of clusters of fruit bearing good and bad fruit (ORIGEN). The gathering of the stubble in the harvest is a reference to the winnowing of the unjust or chaff and of the just as wheat (AMBROSE). The history of sin is unremitting, even within the history of salvation, from Cain and Abel to the unfaithfulness in Moses' time (CYRIL OF JERUSALEM). Be attentive to the secondary unintended consequences of telling the truth (JOHN CASSIAN). If one has been regenerated into a child of God, it must be reflected in the new life (GREGORY OF NYSSA). Both axe and sword are symbols of the work of the Holy Spirit, who separates good from evil (GREGORY OF NAZIANZUS). God assists those who have fallen in infirmity (AMBROSE). The consequences of sin, even repented of, must be borne with humility. Repentance is the way to persevere in heroic patience while the Lord joins in the battle against the devil (BASIL).

7:1 Like Summer Gleanings

WHO IS READY FOR HARVEST? ORIGEN: Who is speaking when the prophet says, "Woe is me, soul, for I have become one as gathering straw in harvest?" For did the prophet literally "gather" or even want to "gather"? Does the prophet have a farm? Anyway, the only one who rightly gathers from what has been planted for harvest is not the prophet but the Lord and Savior Jesus Christ.

Since there are many faults among the pagan nations but also among those who are supposed to be from the church, the prophet laments and mourns for our sins when he says, "Woe is me, for I have become as one who gathers straw." Let each of us scrutinize himself. Is he an ear of corn? Will the Son of God discover something in him to pick or harvest? Do we find that some of us are those swept by the wind? Even as we have still a little in ourselves, two or three kernels, our sins are many against us. Seeing that the churches, or those so-called, are filled with sinners, he says, "Woe is me, for I have come as one who gathers straw in the harvest and as one gathering grape gleanings in the vintage." [The Lord] comes seeking fruit on the vine, for each of us is planted also as a vine "in a fertile place"[1] or as a vine "transplanted out of Egypt,"[2] yet planted to bear fruit.[3] He comes, he seeks in what way to pick, he discovers some "grape gleanings" and a few "clusters," neither flourishing nor plentiful. Who among us has "clusters" of virtue? HOMILIES ON JEREMIAH 15.3.2.[4]

A METAPHOR OF GLEANING. AMBROSE: The unjust are winnowed away as lightweight chaff, while the just are saved as heavier wheat. Therefore heed the Lord as he says to Peter, "Behold, Satan has desired to winnow you as wheat, but I have prayed for you, that your faith may not fail."[5] Those who are winnowed as chaff fail, but that

---

[1]Is 5:1. [2]Ps 80:8 (79:9 LXX). [3]Jer 2:21. [4]FC 97:160-61**. [5]Lk 22:31-32.

one does not fail who is like the seed that fell and sprang up, augmented and increased by very many fruits.[6] And so the prophet says, "Woe is me! For I am become as one who gathers the stubble in the harvest." Thus wickedness is compared with the stubble, which is quickly burned, and with the dust. And so, Job said subsequently, "They will be like chaff driven by the wind,"[7] and at once he added a brief line and said, "or like dust that the wind has carried off." Indeed, so that you may know that the wicked person swiftly crumbles and vanishes like dust, you find it said in the first psalm, "Not so the wicked, not so,"[8] that is, not like the just, "but like the dust, which the wind drives from the face of the earth." THE PRAYER OF JOB AND DAVID 2.5.18.[9]

7:2 The Godly Perish

THE UNREMITTING HISTORY OF SIN. CYRIL OF JERUSALEM: Cain and Abel followed in the generation of humankind, and Cain was the first murderer. Afterwards a deluge engulfed the earth because of exceeding wickedness of humanity. Fire came down from heaven upon the people of Sodom because of their corruption. Subsequently God chose out Israel, but even Israel became perverse and the chosen race was wounded. For, while Moses stood on the mountain before God, the people worshiped a calf in place of God. In the days of their lawgiver Moses, who said, "You shall not commit adultery,"[10] a man dared to enter a brothel and be wanton. After Moses, prophets were sent to heal Israel, but in their exercise of healing they deplored the fact that they could not overcome evil, so that one of them [Micah] says, "The faithful are gone from the earth, among men the upright are no more!" The psalmist says, "All alike have gone astray; they have become perverse; there is not one who does good, not even one."[11] And again, "Cursing, and theft, and adultery, and killing have overflowed"[12] upon the land. "They sacrificed their sons and daughters to demons."[13] They engaged themselves in auguries and enchantments and divinations; and again, "They fastened their garments

with cords and hung veils next to the altar."[14] CATECHETICAL LECTURE 12.6.[15]

7:5 Guard Your Speech

UNINTENDED CONSEQUENCES OF TRUTH TELLING. JOHN CASSIAN: [In spiritual discipline], the disposition of the doer is given more weight than the thing that is done. Even the truth at times is found to have harmed some people and a lie to have helped them. For one time King Saul was complaining in the presence of his retainers about David's flight, saying, "Will the son of Jesse give all of you fields and vineyards and make all of you tribunes and centurions, since you have all conspired against me, and there is no one to inform me?"[16] What but the truth did Doeg the Edomite tell him when he said, "I saw the son of Jesse in Nob, with Ahimilech the son of Ahitub the priest. He consulted the Lord on his behalf and gave him provisions and he gave him the sword of Goliath the Philistines as well"?[17] For this truth he deserved to be uprooted from the land of the living, and of him it is said by the prophet, "Therefore God shall destroy you forever, pluck you up and remove you from your tent and uproot you from the land of the living."[18] For indicating the truth, then, he was everlastingly uprooted from the land in which Rahab the harlot was planted, along with her family, because of her lie. In the same way we remember that Samson in most ruinous fashion delivered over to his wicked wife a truth that had long been concealed by a lie. Therefore the truth that he had very heedlessly disclosed to her brought about his own undoing, because he failed to keep that prophetic command: "Keep the doors of your mouth from her who sleeps at your breast." CONFERENCE 17.20.10-11.[19]

7:6 Enemies in One's House

---

[6]Lk 8:8. [7]Job 21:18. [8]Ps 1:4. [9]FC 65:364. [10]Ex 20:14. [11]Ps 14:3 (13:3 LXX). [12]Hos 4:2. [13]Ps 106:37 (105:37 LXX). [14]Amos 2:8 LXX. [15]FC 61:230-31. [16]1 Sam 22:7-8. [17]1 Sam 22:9-10. [18]Ps 52:5 (51:7 LXX). [19]ACW 57:602-3*.

MAKE CLEAR WHO YOUR FATHER IS. GREGORY OF NYSSA: A man, then, who remains the same and yet prattles to himself about the change for the better that he has undergone in baptism should attend to what Paul says: "If anyone thinks he is something when he is nothing, he deceives himself."[20] For you are not what you have not yet become. The Gospel says of the regenerate, however, that "he gave all those who received him the power to become God's children."[21] Now the child born of someone certainly shares his parent's nature. If then you have received God and have become his child, let your way of life testify to the God within you. Make it clear who your father is! The marks by which we recognize God are the very ones by which a son must show his relation to him. "He opens his hand and fills everything living with joy."[22] "He overlooks iniquity."[23] "He relents of his evil purpose."[24] "The Lord is kind to all and is not angry with us every day."[25] "God is straightforward, and there is no unrighteousness in him."[26] This is what fathers do for children. Similar sayings are scattered through Scripture for our instruction. If you are like this, you have genuinely become a child of God. But if you persist in displaying the marks of evil, it is useless to babble to yourself about the birth from above. ADDRESS ON RELIGIOUS INSTRUCTION 40.[27]

DIVINE JUDGMENT SEPARATES GOOD FROM EVIL. GREGORY OF NAZIANZUS: Just what is the work of the axe? The excision of the soul that is incurably fruitless, like the tree even after the dung has been applied.[28] And what does the sword do? The sword of the Word cuts through defenses. It does the work of separating the worse from the better.[29] It actually creates a division between the faithful and the unbeliever.[30] It may even stir up the son and the daughter and the bride against the father and the mother and the mother-in-law, the young and fresh against the old and shadowy. Accordingly, what is the latchet of the shoe, which you, John, who baptized Jesus, may not let loose?[31] You who are of the desert, without food, you, the new Elijah,[32] you who are more than a prophet, inasmuch as you saw him of whom you did prophesy, you the mediator of the Old and New Testaments. What is this latchet? It is precisely the message of the advent, the incarnation. No one can make it happen—neither those yet carnal and babes in Christ nor those who are akin to John in spirit. ON THE HOLY LIGHTS, ORATION 39.15.[33]

7:8 I Shall Arise

THE WILL TO RISE. AMBROSE: The fall of infirmity is not grave if free from the desire of the will. Have the will to rise. He is at hand who will cause you to rise. EXPOSITION ON THE PSALMS 37.15.[34]

7:9 The Lord's Indignation

BEARING DIVINE JUDGMENT OF OUR SINS. BASIL THE GREAT: We sometimes bear illness as a punishment for sin intended for our conversion, "for whom the Lord loves," says the Scripture, "he chastises."[35] Again Scripture teaches, "Therefore are there many infirm and weak among you, and some have died. But if we would judge ourselves, we should not be judged, we are chastised by the Lord that we be not condemned with the world."[36] Consequently, when we who belong to this class have recognized our transgressions, it may be fitting that we should simply bear in silence and without recourse to medicine all the afflictions which come to us, remembering the words of the prophet: "I will bear the wrath of the Lord because I have sinned against him." We should, moreover, give proof of our amendment by bringing forth fruits worthy of penance, remembering the words of the Lord: "Behold, you are made whole; sin no more, lest some worse thing happen to you."[37] Sometimes also, when sickness afflicts us at the request of the evil one, our benevolent master may

---

[20]Gal 6:3. [21]Jn 1:12. [22]Ps 145:16 (144:16 LXX). [23]Mic 7:18 LXX. [24]Joel 2:13. [25]Ps 145:9 (144:9 LXX). [26]Ps 92:15 (91:16 LXX). [27]LCC 3:324-25. [28]Lk 13:8. [29]Heb 4:12. [30]Mt 10:35. [31]Jn 1:27. [32]Lk 7:26. [33]NPNF 2 7:358*. [34]PMPC 2:93. [35]Prov 3:12. [36]1 Cor 11:30-32. [37]Jn 5:14.

condescend to enter combat with him, treating him as if he were a mighty adversary and confounding his boasts by the heroic patience of his

servants. THE LONG RULES 55.[38]

[38]FC 9:334-35*.

7:14-20 SALVATION OF ISRAEL

[14]*Shepherd thy people with thy staff,*
 the flock of thy inheritance,
who dwell alone in a forest
 in the midst of a garden land;
let them feed in Bashan and Gilead
 as in the days of old.
[15]*As in the days when you came out of the*
  land of Egypt
 I will show them[z] marvelous things.

[16]*The nations shall see and be ashamed*
 of all their might;
they shall lay their hands on their mouths;
 their ears shall be deaf;
[17]*they shall lick the dust like a serpent,*
 like the crawling things of the earth;
they shall come trembling out of their

 strongholds,
 they shall turn in dread to the LORD our
  God,
 and they shall fear because of thee.
[18]*Who is a God like thee, pardoning iniquity*
 and passing over transgression
 for the remnant of his inheritance?
He does not retain his anger for ever
 because he delights in steadfast love.
[19]*He will again have compassion upon us,*
 he will tread our iniquities under foot.
Thou wilt cast all our[a] sins
 into the depths of the sea.
[20]*Thou wilt show faithfulness to Jacob*
 and steadfast love to Abraham,
as thou hast sworn to our fathers
 from the days of old.

z Heb *him*   a Gk Syr Vg Tg: Heb *their*

OVERVIEW: The exodus from Egypt and the promise of being shown marvelous things is revealed in the new covenant. The Egyptians were a type of sin that baptism drowned, thereby revealing the mercy of God (AUGUSTINE). The priest of the old covenant ensnared the people by imploring upon them impossible rules and regulations. Christ's ability to take away unrighteousness was foretold by the prophet (CHRYSOSTOM).

In suffering one is not to despair and think that God has abandoned the sufferer. It is the devil who is trying to deceive the believer by

planting grave doubt (AMBROSE). The tunic of salvation must be given to the one who has none, that is those who do not love God (ORIGEN). Baptism is like a floodwater, which washes away sins. Micah spoke of this cleansing as a casting of sins to the bottom of the sea (BASIL).

7:15 The Days of the Exodus

THE EXODUS PREFIGURES BAPTISM. AUGUSTINE: Hear what is even more wonderful, that the hidden and veiled mysteries of the ancient books are in some degree revealed by the ancient prophets. For Micah the prophet spoke thus. "According to the days of your coming out of Egypt will I show unto him marvelous things." . . . Our sins are overwhelmed and extinguished in baptism, just as the Egyptians were drowned in the sea. "He does not retain his anger forever because he delights in steadfast love. . . . You will cast all our sins into the depths of the sea." EXPLANATION OF THE PSALMS 114.5.[1]

7:18 *The Steadfast, Loving God*

GOD ALONE HAS AUTHORITY TO FORGIVE SINS. CHRYSOSTOM: For what was it Jesus' detractors said? "No man can forgive sins, but God alone."[2] Inasmuch then as they themselves laid down this definition, they themselves introduced the rule, they themselves declared the law. He then proceeded to entangle them by means of their own words. "You have confessed," he says in effect, "that forgiveness of sins is an attribute of God alone; my equality therefore is unquestionable." And it is not these men only who declare this but also the prophet Micah, who said, "Who is a God like you?" and then indicating his special attribute he adds, "pardoning iniquity and passing over transgression." HOMILY ON THE PARALYTIC LET DOWN THROUGH THE ROOF 6.[3]

DO NOT ALLOW THE EVIL ONE TO PLANT DOUBTS. AMBROSE: Let us not listen to the devil when we are caught in the troubles of the world, whether the bodily pain or the loss of children or amid other struggles. Let us not listen to the adversary as he says, "So where now is the Lord your God?"[4] When we suffer severe pain we must then beware of his temptations, for he is trying to lead astray the weary soul. Seeing the wonderful works of God, the soul will behold itself already as if in heaven, with the devil creeping around like a snake on the earth. Thus the prophet said, "Who is a God like you, pardoning iniquity and passing over transgression for the remnant of his inheritance?" LETTER 45.[5]

7:19 *Compassion and Forgiveness*

AS GOD FORGIVES, SO WE FORGIVE. ORIGEN: We should give a tunic to one who has none at all. Who is the person who does not have a tunic? It is one who utterly lacks God. Therefore we should divest ourselves and give to one who is naked. One has God; another does not have God at all. We give to the one who does not have God. The prophet in Scripture says, "We should cast our sins into the depths of the sea." John continues, "He who has food should do likewise."[6] Whoever has food should give some to one who has none. He should generously give him not only clothing but also what he can eat. HOMILIES ON THE GOSPEL OF LUKE 23.5.[7]

BAPTISMAL WATERS COVER SINS. BASIL THE GREAT: "The Lord sits enthroned over the flood."[8] A flood is an overflow of water that causes all lying below it to disappear. It cleanses all that was previously filthy. Therefore he calls the grace of baptism a flood, so that the soul, being washed well of its sins and rid of the old person, is suitable henceforth as a dwelling place of God in the Spirit. Further, what is said in the twenty-first psalm agrees with this. For after he has said, "I have acknowledged my sin, and my injustice I have not concealed," and also, "For this shall every one that is holy pray to you," he then said, "And yet in a flood of many waters, they shall not come near him."[9] Indeed, sin shall not come near to one who received baptism for the remission of his transgressions through water and the Spirit. Something akin to this is found in the prophecy of Micah: "Because he delights in mercy, he will turn again and have mercy on us. He will put away our iniquities and will cast them into the bottom of the sea." HOMILIES ON THE PSALMS 28.8.[10]

---

[1]NPNF 1 8:550-51. [2]Mk 2:7. [3]NPNF 1 9:218*. [4]Mic 7:10; Mal 2:17. [5]FC 26:239-40*. [6]Lk 3:11. [7]FC 94:99. [8]Ps 29:10 (28:10 LXX). [9]Cf. Ps 32:5-6 (31:5-6 LXX). [10]FC 46:210-11*.

Nahum

Overview: Nahum (Heb *naḥûm*) is very likely a shorter version of the name Nahumiah, which means "Yahweh comforts." All we know about Nahum is his name. He is called the Elkoshite in reference to a town not mentioned anywhere else in the Scriptures and whose location to this day is unknown. The book is numbered seventh among the Minor Prophets. Nahum 1:2-10 is an incomplete acrostic psalm describing a theophany and judgment of Yahweh. In Nahum 1:11, 13-14 one finds numerous threats made against Assyria followed in contrast to promises to Judah. Nahum 2:1, 3-13 describes the sacking of Nineveh and the ensuing chaos and includes an allusion to the Assyrian conquest of Thebes in Egypt and the failed attempts to prevent the fall of the city. There is scholarly agreement that the book refers to the capture and destruction of Nineveh by the Babylonians and Medes in 612 B.C., culminating a campaign that began in 625 to overthrow the Assyrian Empire. The book seems to be later than 663 B.C., the date of the destruction of Thebes by the Assyrians, but no later than 609 B.C., marking the death of Josiah.

Although Nahum is among the shortest of the Minor Prophets, this fact did not inhibit the church fathers from exploiting its rich content, as did the New Testament writers. There is a direct quote at Romans 10:15 of Nahum 1:15.[1] Also, John's Gospel gives special attention to the activity of the Holy Spirit in relation to his role in the resurrection of Christ and his effect on the twelve apostles.

DIVINE RETRIBUTION TOWARD NINEVEH.

THEODORE OF MOPSUESTIA: While the prophet Jonah reveals the [mercy of God toward Nineveh], Nahum mentions the retribution due to be inflicted in many ways on them for displaying their arrogance against both the Israelites and Jerusalem, as well as against the God of all worshiped in the city. Through this it became obvious to everyone that he would not have allowed the Israelites to suffer this fate at their hands if they themselves had not rendered themselves deserving of such sufferings through their impiety. COMMENTARY ON NAHUM, INTRODUCTION.[2]

---

[1]Cf. Is 52:7. [2]PG 66:400.

1:1-15 GOD'S PUNISHMENT OF NINEVEH

[1]An oracle concerning Nineveh. The book of
the vision of Nahum of Elkosh.
[2]The LORD is a jealous God and avenging,
the LORD is avenging and wrathful;
the LORD takes vengeance on his
adversaries
and keeps wrath for his enemies.
[3]The LORD is slow to anger and of great
might,
and the LORD will by no means clear the
guilty.

His way is in whirlwind and storm,
and the clouds are the dust of his feet.
[4]He rebukes the sea and makes it dry,
he dries up all the rivers;
Bashan and Carmel wither,
the bloom of Lebanon fades.
[5]The mountains quake before him,
the hills melt;
the earth is laid waste before him,
the world and all that dwell therein.

[6]Who can stand before his indignation?
Who can endure the heat of his anger?
His wrath is poured out like fire,
and the rocks are broken asunder by him.
[7]The LORD is good,
a stronghold in the day of trouble;
he knows those who take refuge in him.
[8]But with an overflowing flood
he will make a full end of his
adversaries,[a]
and will pursue his enemies into
darkness.
[9]What do you plot against the LORD?
He will make a full end;
he will not take vengeance[b] twice on his
foes.[c]
[10]Like entangled thorns they are consumed,[d]
like dry stubble.
[11]Did one not[e] come out from you,
who plotted evil against the LORD,
and counseled villainy?

[12]Thus says the LORD,
"Though they be strong and many,[f]
they will be cut off and pass away.
Though I have afflicted you,
I will afflict you no more.
[13]And now I will break his yoke from off you
and will burst your bonds asunder."
[14]The LORD has given commandment about
you:
"No more shall your name be perpetuated;
from the house of your gods I will cut off
the graven image and the molten
image.
I will make your grave, for you are vile."

[15g]Behold, on the mountains the feet of him
who brings good tidings,
who proclaims peace!
Keep your feasts, O Judah,
fulfil your vows,
for never again shall the wicked come
against you,
he is utterly cut off.

a Gk: Heb *her place*   b Gk: Heb *rise up*   c Cn: Heb *distress*   d Heb *are consumed, drunken as with their drink*   e Cn: Heb *fully*   f Heb uncertain   g Ch 2.1 in Heb

OVERVIEW: Nahum's "oracle against Nineveh" is through the grace of the Holy Spirit, who seized the mind of the prophet, revealing hidden things (THEODORE). God's forgiveness is unmerited; therefore there is no room for penitents to pride themselves (JEROME). Out of his patience and lovingkindness, the Lord delays punishment of sinners in an attempt to bring them to repentance. However, if they do not repent, the punishment is certain (THEODORET). The prophet of the Old Testament foresaw the ability of Jesus to walk on water, thereby demonstrating his lordship over all creation. His walking on water was Nahum's rebuke of the sea and making it dry, so to speak, to walk on (TERTULLIAN). God is not unmerciful, contrary to what the heretics assert (ORIGEN). Nahum's prophecy is fulfilled in the Gospels (AUGUSTINE). The exodus is a type of call to celebrate Easter, the new Passover. The admonition of Nahum to keep the feasts is also a call to Christians to celebrate the paschal mystery (ATHANASIUS).

1:1 An Oracle About Nineveh

ORACLES AND VISIONS FROM THE HOLY SPIRIT. THEODORE OF MOPSUESTIA: Something of this kind is the meaning of the word *oracle:* in his wish to give the prophets an insight often productive of rapture, God caused a sudden transformation of their mind so that while in this condition they might receive the knowledge of the future with deeper fear. He calls it "oracle," then, since the grace of the Spirit, as though suddenly taking hold of the prophet's mind, transformed it with a view to the revelation of what was to be made clear. He is saying the same thing here too: "an oracle of Nineveh, a book of the vision of Nahum the Elkoshite," as if to say, the prophet's mind was suddenly seized by the grace of the Spirit and transformed so as to contemplate those things through which he learned of the fate of Nineveh and which he provided to his listeners as instruction in what was shown to him. COMMENTARY ON NAHUM 1.1.[1]

1:3 The Lord Will Not Exonerate the Guilty

DO NOT BOAST EVEN IN FORGIVENESS. JEROME: And again: "I will reestablish my covenant with you, and you shall know that I am Lord, that you may remember and be confounded and may no more open your mouth because of your confusion, when I shall be pacified toward you for all that you have done, says the Lord God."[2] Thus it is clearly indicated by these divine words what was meant in another place by the statement "And though cleansing you he shall not make you innocent."[3] Even the just, being restored to their former state after committing sin, do not dare open their mouth but say with the apostle, "I am not worthy to be called an apostle, because I persecuted the church of God."[4] AGAINST THE PELAGIANS 2.25.[5]

THE LORD DELAYS PUNISHMENT. THEODORET OF CYR: "The Lord is longsuffering, great is his power, and he will certainly not clear the guilty." He does not suddenly and all at once inflict punishment, but only after exercising extreme longsuffering. You Ninevites are witnesses to this, practicing repentance and finding salvation, and then guilty of extreme wickedness and for a time not paying the penalty for it. But after putting up with people's wickedness for a long time, he is accustomed to inflict punishment on the unrepentant (the meaning of "he will certainly not clear the guilty," that is, he will not exempt from retribution the person whose sins deserve punishment). COMMENTARY ON NAHUM 1.3.[6]

1:4 Rivers and Sea Dried Up

WALKING ON WATER PREDICTED. TERTULLIAN: If it is [Marcion's] Christ that is meant, he will not be stronger than the servants of the Creator.[7] I would have been content with the ex-

---

[1]PG 66:404. [2]Ezek 16:62-63. [3]Jerome adds "you" here; it is not found in the Vulgate. [4]1 Cor 15:9. [5]FC 53:339. [6]PG 81:1789-92. [7]That is, the winds and the waves.

amples I have shown you without adding anything further. But here a prediction of [Christ]
walking on the water precedes his advent as
well. The words of the psalm are, in fact, accomplished by Christ's crossing over the lake. "The
Lord," says the psalmist, "is upon many waters."[8] When he scatters its waves, Habakkuk's
words are fulfilled where he says, "scattering the
waters as he walks."[9] When at his rebuke the sea
is calmed, Nahum is also verified: "He rebukes
the sea and makes it dry,"[10] referring to the
winds that had disturbed the sea. AGAINST
MARCION 4.20.[11]

1:9 God Punishes Only Once

**GOD'S MERCY DEFENDED AGAINST HER-
ETICS.** ORIGEN: According to the law, for example, the adulterer and the adulteress were punished with an immediate death. Because of the
fact that he bore the penalty for his sin and paid
punishments which fitted the evil committed,
what will be after this that threatens their souls
with revenge, if they transgressed no more, if
there is not another sin which condemns them,
but they committed only this single fault when
they were punished and bore for this the punishment of the law? "The Lord will not punish twice
for the same thing," for they took their sin and
their penalty for the crime was taken away. And
for this reason, this kind of precept is not found
unmerciful, as the heretics assert, accusing the
law of God and denying that there is human feeling contained in it. But it is full of mercy by virtue of the fact that through this more people
would be cleansed from sins than would be condemned. HOMILIES ON LEVITICUS 11.5.[12]

1:14-15 Cutting Off Idols and Keeping Feasts

**PROPHECY FULFILLED IN THE NEW TESTA-
MENT.** AUGUSTINE: The prophet Nahum (or, better, God speaking through him) says, "I will de-

stroy the graven and molten thing; I will make it
your grave. Behold upon the mountains the feet
of him that brings peace. O Judah, keep your festivals and pay your vows, for it shall no longer be
that they may pass into disuse. It is completed, it
is consumed, it is taken away. He is come up that
breathes into your face and rescues you from tribulation." Anyone who knows the Gospels will
recognize who it was that came up from hell and
breathed the Holy Spirit into the face of Judah,
that is, into the face of his Jewish disciples. The
words about the festivals are, of course, a reference to the New Testament, in which festivals are
so spiritually renewed that they can never "pass
into disuse." The rest of the prophecy too we see
realized in that the gospel brought about the destruction of "graven and molten things," that is,
the idols of the false gods, consigned now to the
oblivion of the grave. CITY OF GOD 18.31.[13]

EASTER CELEBRATION FORETOLD. ATHANA-
SIUS: Once again, dear friends, God has brought
us to the Easter season. By his lovingkindness we
are once more about to assemble for it. The same
God who brought Israel out of Egypt now calls us
to the feast, saying through Moses, "Take note of
the month of new fruits, and keep the Passover to
the Lord your God."[14] And through the prophet
he calls, "Keep your feasts, O Judah; pay your
vows to the Lord." So if God himself loves the
feast and calls us to it, it is not right, brothers and
sisters, to postpone it or to observe it carelessly.
We should come to it eagerly and zealously, so
that with a joyful beginning here we will experience a foretaste of the heavenly feast that is to
come. FESTAL LETTERS 6.[15]

---

[8]Ps 29:3 (28:3 LXX). [9]Hab 3:10 LXX. Tertullian is writing in Latin
before Jerome's Vulgate, which reads *gurges aquarum transiit* (cf. Tertullian's *dispargens inquit aquas itinere*). [10]Old Latin; cf. Tertullian's *commin-
ans, inquit, mari et arefaciens illud* with the Vulgate's *increpans mare et
exsiccans illud*. The meaning is the same; the Vulgate does not differ
from the Hebrew. [11]ANF 3:379. [12]FC 83:214. [13]FC 24:128-29.
[14]Deut 16:1. [15]ARL 100.

2:1—3:19 WOE TO THE CITY OF BLOOD

2 The shatterer has come up against you.*
  Man the ramparts;
watch the road;
  gird your loins;
    collect all your strength.

2(For the LORD is restoring the majesty of
    Jacob
  as the majesty of Israel,
for plunderers have stripped them
  and ruined their branches.)

3The shield of his mighty men is red,
  his soldiers are clothed in scarlet.
The chariots flash like flame^b
  when mustered in array;
  the chargers^i prance.
4The chariots rage in the streets,
  they rush to and fro through the squares;
they gleam like torches,
  they dart like lightning.
5The officers are summoned,
  they stumble as they go,
they hasten to the wall,
  the mantelet is set up.
6The river gates are opened,
  the palace is in dismay;
7its mistress^j is stripped, she is carried off,
  her maidens lamenting,
moaning like doves,
  and beating their breasts.
8Nineveh is like a pool
  whose waters^k run away.
"Halt! Halt!" they cry;
  but none turns back.

9Plunder the silver,
  plunder the gold!
There is no end of treasure,
  or wealth of every precious thing.

10Desolate! Desolation and ruin!
  Hearts faint and knees tremble,
anguish is on all loins,
  all faces grow pale!
11Where is the lions' den,
  the cave^l of the young lions,
where the lion brought his prey,
  where his cubs were, with none to disturb?
12The lion tore enough for his whelps
  and strangled prey for his lionesses;
he filled his caves with prey
  and his dens with torn flesh.

13Behold, I am against you, says the LORD
of hosts, and I will burn your^m chariots in
smoke, and the sword shall devour your young
lions; I will cut off your prey from the earth,
and the voice of your messengers shall no more
be heard.

3 Woe to the bloody city,
  all full of lies and booty—
  no end to the plunder!
2The crack of whip, and rumble of wheel,
  galloping horse and bounding chariot!
3Horsemen charging,
  flashing sword and glittering spear,
hosts of slain,
  heaps of corpses,
dead bodies without end—
  they stumble over the bodies!

⁴And all for the countless harlotries of the
    harlot,
        graceful and of deadly charms,
who betrays nations with her harlotries,
        and peoples with her charms.

⁵Behold, I am against you,
        says the LORD of hosts,
        and will lift up your skirts over your face;
and I will let nations look on your
        nakedness
        and kingdoms on your shame.
⁶I will throw filth at you
        and treat you with contempt,
        and make you a gazingstock.
⁷And all who look on you will shrink from
        you and say,
Wasted is Nineveh; who will bemoan her?
        whence shall I seek comforters for her?ⁿ

⁸Are you better than Thebes^o
        that sat by the Nile,
with water around her,
        her rampart a sea,
        and water her wall?
⁹Ethiopia was her strength,
        Egypt too, and that without limit;
        Put and the Libyans were her^p helpers.

¹⁰Yet she was carried away,
        she went into captivity;
her little ones were dashed in pieces
        at the head of every street;
for her honored men lots were cast,
        and all her great men were bound in chains.
¹¹You also will be drunken,
        you will be dazed;
you will seek
        a refuge from the enemy.

¹²All your fortresses are like fig trees
        with first-ripe figs—
if shaken they fall
        into the mouth of the eater.
¹³Behold, your troops
        are women in your midst.
The gates of your land
        are wide open to your foes;
        fire has devoured your bars.

¹⁴Draw water for the siege,
        strengthen your forts;
go into the clay,
        tread the mortar,
        take hold of the brick mold!
¹⁵There will the fire devour you,
        the sword will cut you off.
        It will devour you like the locust.

Multiply yourselves like the locust,
        multiply like the grasshopper!
¹⁶You increased your merchants
        more than the stars of the heavens.
        The locust spreads its wings and flies away.
¹⁷Your princes are like grasshoppers,
        your scribes^q like clouds of locusts
settling on the fences
        in a day of cold—
when the sun rises, they fly away;
        no one knows where they are.

¹⁸Your shepherds are asleep,
        O king of Assyria;
        your nobles slumber.
Your people are scattered on the
        mountains
        with none to gather them.
¹⁹There is no assuaging your hurt,
        your wound is grievous.

> All who hear the news of you
> clap their hands over you.

> For upon whom has not come
> your unceasing evil?

h Cn: The meaning of the Hebrew word is uncertain   i Cn Compare Gk Syr: Heb *cypresses*   j The meaning of the Hebrew is uncertain   k Cn Compare Gk: Heb *from the days that she has become, and they*   l Cn: Heb *pasture*   m Heb *her*   n Gk: Heb *you*   o Heb *No-amon*   p Gk: Heb *your*   q Or *marshals*   *LXX It is all over with him, he has been removed, one who has been delivered from affliction has come up panting into your presence.*

OVERVIEW: Cyril of Jerusalem refers to Jesus rising from the dead or hell as limbo (CYRIL OF JERUSALEM). Nahum had foretold the breathing of the spirit on the Twelve and the authority to remit sins. "One blowing in your face" is a description of the Holy Spirit, who was operative in vivifying Adam. It is bestowal of the Spirit upon the apostles that perfected Christ's victory over death, which is prefigured by the victory over the Assyrian kingdom (THEODORET). Nahum's reference to substance being revealed is not about money. The mountains removed are things that set themselves above God (AMBROSE). Chrysostom sternly condemns the miserly rich whom Nahum likened to those who build their house on injustice (CHRYSOSTOM).

2:1 Collect Your Strength

BREATH OF THE HOLY SPIRIT FORETOLD.
CYRIL OF JERUSALEM: He imparted the fellowship of this Holy Spirit to the apostles, for it is written, "When he had said that, he breathed upon them, and said to them, 'Receive the Holy Spirit; whose sins you shall forgive, they are forgiven them; and whose sins you shall retain, they are retained.'"[1] This was the second breathing (the first had been impaired by willful sins)[2] to fulfill the Scripture: "One who has been delivered from affliction has come up panting into your presence." He has been delivered from Hades. For it was after his resurrection, according to the gospel, that he breathed on them. He gives the grace at this time, and he will lavish it more abundantly. He says to them, "I am ready to give it to you even now, but the vessel cannot yet hold it. Accept for the time the grace of which you are capable, but look forward to yet more." "But wait here in the

city" of Jerusalem "until you are clothed with power from on high."[3] Receive it in part now; then you will be clad in its fullness. For he who receives often has the gift only in part, but he who is clothed is entirely covered by his garment. Fear not, he says, the weapons and darts of the devil, for you will possess the power of the Holy Spirit. But be mindful of our recent admonition, that the Holy Spirit is not divided, but only the grace he bestows. CATECHETICAL LECTURE 17.12.[4]

THE TYPE OF BESTOWAL OF THE HOLY SPIRIT.
THEODORET OF CYR: "One has come up blowing in your face, rescuing you from tribulation."[5] God is the cause of this for you by his decision as though by some kind of blowing, destroying them but freeing you from their power. Just as by blowing a breath of life into Adam he made him a living being,[6] so he provided you with salvation by the blowing of life. This is also what Christ the Lord gave the sacred apostles after the resurrection. Since Adam lost what he had received by way of image through the divine blowing, it was right that Christ the Lord should renew the image and restore it to the sacred apostles and through them to all the believers, blowing on them and saying, "Receive the Holy Spirit."[7] Since former things are a type of the new, therefore, let us take the Assyrians' kingdom that was destroyed as the devil's tyranny brought to an end through Christ the Lord. COMMENTARY ON NAHUM 2.1.[8]

2:6 All Is in Disarray

---

[1] Jn 20:22-23. [2] Gen 2:7. The first breathing for Cyril was the creation of the soul of Adam by God's breathing upon the man formed from the dust of the earth. [3] Lk 24:49. [4] FC 64:104. [5] Nahum 2:2 LXX. [6] Gen 2:7. [7] Jn 20:22. [8] PG 81:1796.

MOUNTAIN METAPHOR OF THINGS AGAINST GOD. AMBROSE: But is this the only place we read of "substance"? Has it not also been said in another passage: "The gates of the cities are broken down, the mountains are fallen, and his substance is revealed"?[9] What, does the word mean something created here also? Some, I know, are accustomed to say that the substance is substance in money. Then, if you give this meaning to the word, the mountains fell in order that someone's possessions of money might be seen. But let us remember *what* mountains fell, those, namely, of which it has been said, "If you shall have faith as a grain of mustard seed you shall say to this mountain, 'Be removed, and be cast into the sea!' "[10] By mountains, then, are meant high things that exalt themselves.[11] ON THE CHRISTIAN FAITH 3.14.115-16.[12]

3:1 *The Bloody City*

WEEP FOR SINNERS. CHRYSOSTOM: Let us mourn with Nahum and let us say with him, "Woe to him that builds up this house [by injustice]."[13] Or rather let us mourn for them as Christ did in his day, when he said, "Woe to you rich, for you are now having your reward and your comfort."[14] Let us not, I beseech you, cease mourning in this way, and if it is not unbecoming, let us also bewail the apathy of our brothers. Let us not weep loudly for him who is already dead, but let us weep for the robber, the grasping, miserly, greedy man. HOMILIES ON JOHN 64.[15]

---

[9]Nahum 2:8 LXX. [10]Mt 17:20. [11]2 Cor 10:5. [12]NPNF 2 10:258. [13]Actually, the quotation is Jer 22:13; cf. Nah 3:1 for his prophecy of the destruction of Nineveh. [14]Lk 6:24. [15]FC 41:204.

HABAKKUK

OVERVIEW: Habakkuk (Heb *hăbaqqûq*) is designated as the eighth of the minor prophets. Habakkuk is perhaps an Akkadian name that refers to a kind of plant or fruit tree. The book is arranged in the following manner. In Habakkuk 1:1-4, the prophet inveighs against violence and oppression. Habakkuk 1:5-11 predicts the coming of the Chaldean conquerors. Habakkuk 1:12-17 has a further complaint by the prophet against the oppressor. In Habakkuk 2:1-5 the prophet is called a watchman given the task to write his vision where he asserts that the wicked will perish and the just shall live. Habakkuk 2:6-20 is a litany of five woes against enemies; Habakkuk 3:1-19 is a psalm heralding the coming of Yahweh in a theophany to rescue his people from their enemies. If the enemies described in the book are Assyrians, then the book is likely to be dated between 625, when the Chaldeans were the major threat to Assyria, and 612, the date of the fall of Nineveh. However, if the enemies are Chaldeans, then the date shifts to 605 to 600 following the battle of Carchemish.

The book of Habakkuk was valuable to the church fathers for eschatological and christological teaching. The apostle Paul cited Habakkuk 2:4 in Romans 1:17 and Galatians 3:11 to develop his doctrine of justification by faith that became a foundational christological teaching. Furthermore, Habakkuk 2:3-4 is also found in Hebrews 10:35-38 and Habakkuk 1:5 in Acts 13:41.

Augustine, Theodore of Mopsuestia and Cyril of Alexandria are interpreters of Habakkuk. Cyril focused on demonstrating that Jesus was the anticipated Messiah. Numerous Greek and Latin fathers made copious comments to bring out deeper christological meanings of minute details —for example, that the scarab in Habakkuk 2:11 is Christ, who forgave his persecutors as he died on the cross. The book of Habakkuk was a typological, christological litany in the hands of the church fathers.

DIVINE PROVIDENCE. THEODORET OF CYR: There are people who get quite upset at the sight of wrongdoers prospering. Some have doubts as to whether the God of all takes an interest in human beings; others have faith in the talk about providence but are at a loss to explain why God conducts things in this fashion. The remarkable prophet Habakkuk adopted the attitude of the latter, putting the question as though anxious in his own case to learn the reason for what happens and supplying the solution, which the grace of the Spirit provided. He did not, in fact, as some commentators believed, suffer from this complaint; rather, he presents the view of the others and supplies instruction on the questions raised. COMMENTARY ON HABAKKUK, INTRODUCTION.[1]

---

[1]PG 81:1809.

1:1-17 HOW LONG, O LORD?

¹The oracle of God which Habakkuk the prophet saw.
²O LORD, how long shall I cry for help,
and thou wilt not hear?
Or cry to thee "Violence!"
and thou wilt not save?
³Why dost thou make me see wrongs
and look upon trouble?
Destruction and violence are before me;
strife and contention arise.
⁴So the law is slacked
and justice never goes forth.
For the wicked surround the righteous,
so justice goes forth perverted.

⁵Look among the nations, and see;
wonder and be astounded.*
For I am doing a work in your days
that you would not believe if told.
⁶For lo, I am rousing the Chaldeans,
that bitter and hasty nation,
who march through the breadth of the
earth,†
to seize habitations not their own.
⁷Dread and terrible are they;
their justice and dignity proceed from
themselves.
⁸Their horses are swifter than leopards,
more fierce than the evening wolves;
their horsemen press proudly on.
Yea, their horsemen come from afar;
they fly like an eagle swift to devour.
⁹They all come for violence;
terrorᵃ of them goes before them.
They gather captives like sand.

¹⁰At kings they scoff,
and of rulers they make sport.
They laugh at every fortress,
for they heap up earth and take it.
¹¹Then they sweep by like the wind and go
on,
guilty men, whose own might is their god!

¹²Art thou not from everlasting,
O LORD my God, my Holy One?
We shall not die.
O LORD, thou hast ordained them as a
judgment;
and thou, O Rock, hast established them
for chastisement.
¹³Thou who art of purer eyes than to behold
evil
and canst not look on wrong,
why dost thou look on faithless men,
and art silent when the wicked swallows
up
the man more righteous than he?
¹⁴For thou makest men like the fish of the
sea,
like crawling things that have no ruler.
¹⁵He brings all of them up with a hook,
he drags them out with his net,
he gathers them in his seine;
so he rejoices and exults.
¹⁶Therefore he sacrifices to his net
and burns incense to his seine;
for by them he lives in luxury,ᵇ
and his food is rich.
¹⁷Is he then to keep on emptying his net,
and mercilessly slaying nations for ever?

a Cn: Heb uncertain   b Heb his portion is fat   *LXX Look on this, you scoffers, be struck with wonder and disappear.   †LXX cover the breadth of the earth

OVERVIEW: Habakkuk is indignant not against God but against those who cause injustice to the poor (THEODORE). Christ's humble, slavelike revelation is a mystery to behold. The Jews were prophetically told in advance of the humble character of the coming Messiah (CYRIL OF ALEXANDRIA). God is unable to countenance the evils of humanity. He offers grace rather than vengeance. The good do not delight in the punishment of the evil; rather, they show compassion for them. Such sentiments are revealed by the prophets, especially Habakkuk, who pleaded with God to temper his just judgment (CHRYSOSTOM). Those caught up in sin are not bothered by the devil, since he already ensnares them. The saints, however, are continually tormented by the devil, but in the end they will triumph (CAESARIUS). Those who are rich and hold high public positions are in the most danger of destructive pride. Habakkuk saw this when regarding the pride that deludes them into believing that they are self-sufficient (MARTIN).

1:2 God's Vengeance

HABAKKUK'S INDIGNATION IS NOT AGAINST GOD. THEODORE OF MOPSUESTIA: It is not as though bringing a censure against God that the prophet says this. Rather, he speaks this way as it is the custom with people who are in some sort of trouble or who are righteously indignant with those responsible to present the injustice of what is being done under the guise of censure. Blessed David also says in like manner, "Why, O Lord, do you keep your distance? Why do you look down on us in good times and in bad? When the godless act disdainfully, the poor person is inflamed,"[1] and so on, saying this not to censure God but to express indignation with those responsible for it and at a loss as to how they are not quickly called to account. COMMENTARY ON HABAKKUK 1.2.[2]

1:5 Look and See

CHRIST AS SLAVE FORETOLD. CYRIL OF ALEX-ANDRIA: He remained Lord of all things even when he came, for the divine economy, in the form of a slave, and this is why the mystery of Christ is truly wonderful. Indeed God the Father said to the Jews through one of the prophets, "Look on this, you scoffers, be struck with wonder and disappear, for I am doing a work in your days, a work in which you will not believe even if one were to explain it to you."[3] ON THE UNITY OF CHRIST.[4]

1:13 Too Pure to Look on Evil

GOD PROTECTS THE PURE IN HEART. CHRYSOSTOM: "For the Lord does not desire to look upon wrongs, for he, the almighty one, observes all those who perform lawless deeds, and he will save me; and do you plead before him, if you can praise him, as it is possible even now."[5] Not only did the Lord not countenance wrongs, but he did not even wish to see them, as another prophet said: "You who are of purer eyes than to behold evil and cannot look on wrong." You see, what providence, what protection, what comprehension! Even if he does not take vengeance, he nevertheless abhors actions. COMMENTARY ON JOB 35.[6]

1:14 Humans Like Fish Without a Leader

GOD'S PURITY DOES NOT LOOK ON EVIL. CHRYSOSTOM: You see, even if it is the wicked who perish, nevertheless the souls of good people are likely to show compassion when they see people being punished. And you will find each of the good people and the inspired writers making earnest supplication for them, as for example the patriarch did for the Sodomites[7] and the inspired writers all continued to do. One, for instance, said, "Woe is me, Lord; are you wiping out the remnant of Israel?"[8] Another said, "Will you make people like the fish of the sea, deprived of a

---

[1]Ps 11:1 (10:1 LXX). [2]PG 66:428. [3]See also Acts 13:41. [4]OUC 61. [5]Job 35:13-14. [6]WLUA 549. [7]Gen 18:22-23. [8]Ezek 9:8.

leader?" So since without even this the good man was troubled in mind and sick at heart, the Lord, in case the sight of these things should cast Noah into deeper depression, locked him in the ark as though in a prison, lest he have a sight of these events and be terror-struck. In his care for him, therefore, the loving God does not allow him to view the torrent of water or see the disaster occurring that involved the destruction of the world. HOMILIES ON GENESIS 25.12.[9]

1:16 Living in Luxury

SAINTS' VICTORY. CAESARIUS OF ARLES: The entire life of the saints is engaged in this war, for there happens in them what is written: "The flesh lusts against the spirit, and the spirit against the flesh."[10] They, indeed, fight, but they are not overcome. What shall I say about wicked, carnal and dissipated souls who do not struggle but are carried along in subjection? Because they follow willingly, and of their own accord [they] devote themselves to wicked deeds. With such souls the devil does not condescend to fight at all, because they never or only with difficulty oppose his counsels. But with the saints he has daily struggles, because it is written of him, "His food is rich." This, I repeat, is the life of the saints, and in this war people are always in danger until they die. But what are the saints going to say at the end, that is, in the triumph of victory? "O death, where is your victory?"[11] This will be the word of the triumphant. "O death, where is your sting? The sting of death is sin,"[12] and death arises from its consequences. Sin is like a scorpion: it stings us, and we are dead. But when is it that we may say, "O death, where is your victory?"[13] This is not promised to us in this life but at the resurrection. Then it will be granted to the saints neither to wish to sin nor to be able to do so at all. SERMON 177.3.[14]

WARNING ABOUT PRIDE. MARTIN OF BRAGA: Although, in general, this inflation of pride attacks many people, there are none who have to fear it more than those who have reached the perfection of virtues of the spirit or copious riches and highest offices in the flesh. It becomes all the greater in their cases, because the one who shows pride is greater. It is not content to destroy lowly and common people, but it is also present in the wiles of the greatest. The higher their rank, the deeper their fall. Hence Scripture also has this to say about the same spirit of pride: "And his food," it says, "is rich." It attacks people who are select and lofty. It suggests to them that they are great, that they need nothing, that whatever they do, think or say is all due to their wisdom and their prudence. If something turns out well for them under God's direction, they straightaway claim that it was due to their own strength and their own industry, and they shout, "I did this," "I said it," "I thought it," and as if everyone were stunned, they seize the glory of God and offer themselves to be admired in his likeness. By a righteous sentence, God withdraws his protection from them, as the apostle says, "He has given them up to a reprobate sense, so that they do not do or think what is fitting,"[15] because, when they recognize the providence of God in all matters, they do not magnify God or offer thanks, but they boast of themselves and turn aside in their own idle thoughts. Though they claim to be wise, they are foolish; though they boast that they are firm, unconquered, powerful, they are weak, conquered and powerless. ON PRIDE 8.[16]

---

[9]FC 82:133. [10]Gal 5:17. [11]1 Cor 15:55. [12]1 Cor 15:55-56. [13]1 Cor 15:55. [14]FC 47:444*. [15]Rom 1:28. [16]FC 62:47-48.

2:1-3 THE REVELATION AWAITS
AN APPOINTED TIME

¹*I will take my stand to watch,*
    and station myself on the tower,
and look forth to see what he will say to me,
    and what I will answer concerning my complaint.
²*And the* LORD *answered me:*
"Write the vision;
    make it plain upon tablets,
    so he may run who reads it.
³*For still the vision awaits its time;*
    it hastens to the end—it will not lie.
If it seem slow, wait for it;*
    it will surely come, it will not delay.

* LXX *If he tarry, wait*

OVERVIEW: The faithful do not expect to hear from God what they desire, but to desire what they hear (AUGUSTINE). Ascetics of the desert experience the tenacity that is needed to hear God's voice (JOHN CASSIAN). The advent of Christ is that for which Habakkuk was calling to people to be patient (AUGUSTINE). Believers are encouraged to persevere in their trials because God will come (BASIL). Be not double-minded but always ready for God's coming (CLEMENT OF ROME). Habakkuk had foretold Christ's first advent. The Jews did not receive him in the Father's name; rather, they continued to look for another as Messiah (EUSEBIUS). Christians are not to despair, because the Lord keeps faith forever in the way of salvation. Christ secures justice for the oppressed believer, so there is no reason to despair; rather, there is hope for deliverance (JEROME).

2:1 What Will God Say?

HEARING GOD'S VOICE. AUGUSTINE: Where,

then, did I find you in order to learn about you? For you were not already in my memory before I learned of you. Where, then, did I find you in order to learn about you, unless in yourself above me? Yet there is no place. We go backward and we go forward,[1] yet there is no place. O truth, you do preside over all things, even those that take counsel with you, and you do answer in the same time all who consult you, however diverse their questions. You do answer clearly, but all do not hear clearly. All seek counsel concerning what they wish, but they do not always hear what they wish. He serves you best who does not so much expect to hear the thing from you that he himself desires, but rather to desire what he hears from you. CONFESSIONS 10.26.[2]

LISTENING TO GOD. JOHN CASSIAN: If someone perseveres continually in this watchfulness, therefore, he will effectively bring to pass what is quite plainly expressed by the prophet Ha-

[1]Job 23:8. [2]FC 21:296-97.

bakkuk: "I will stand on my watch and go upon my rock, and I will look out to see what he will say to me and what I should reply to him who reproaches me." The laboriousness and difficulty of this is very clearly proved by the experiences of those who dwell in the desert of Calamus or Porphyrion. CONFERENCE 24.4.1.[3]

2:2-3 The Vision Will Surely Come

THE REDEEMER WILL SURELY COME. AUGUSTINE: Of what else than the advent of Christ, who was to come, is Habakkuk understood to say, "And the Lord answered me, and said, 'Write the vision openly on a tablet of boxwood so that the one who reads these things may understand.'" For the vision is yet for a time appointed, and it will arise in the end, and it will not become void. If it delays, wait for it, because it will surely come and will not be delayed. CITY OF GOD 18.31.[4]

HELP IN TRIALS FORETOLD. BASIL THE GREAT: You are perhaps distressed that you are driven outside the walls, but you shall dwell under the protection of the God of heaven. The angel who watches over the church has gone out with you. So they lie down in empty places day by day, bringing upon themselves heavy judgment as seen in the dispersion of the people. And, if in all this there is sorrow to be borne, I trust in the Lord that it will not be without its use to you. Therefore, the more have been your trials, look for a more perfect reward from your last judge. Do not take your present troubles ill. Do not lose hope. Yet a little while and your helper will come to you and will not tarry. LETTER 238.[5]

THE TIME OF GOD'S COMING. CLEMENT OF ROME: The all-merciful and beneficent Father has [a heart for] those who fear him, and kindly and lovingly he bestows his favors upon those who come to him with a simple mind. Therefore let us not be double-minded; neither let our soul be lifted up on account of his exceedingly great and glorious gifts. Far from us be that which is written,

"Wretched are they who are of a double mind and of a doubting heart; who say, 'These things we have heard even in the times of our fathers, but, behold, we have grown old, and none of them has happened unto us.'" You foolish ones! Compare yourselves with a tree; take the vine. First of all, it sheds its leaves, then it buds, next it puts forth leaves, and then it flowers; afterwards comes the sour grape, and then follows the ripened fruit. You perceive how in a little time the fruit of a tree comes to maturity. Of a truth, soon and suddenly shall his will be accomplished, as the Scripture also bears witness, saying, "Speedily will he come, and will not tarry,"[6] and "The Lord shall suddenly come to his temple, even the holy one, for whom you look."[7] 1 CLEMENT 23.[8]

THE VISION AWAITS ITS TIME. EUSEBIUS OF CAESARIA: He is blessed who is named by another prophet, "He that comes," in the passage, "Yet a little while, and he that comes will come and will not tarry,"[9] who also came in the name of the Lord God his Father. And he is the Lord God that appeared for us. For he insists that he has come in the name of his Father when he says to the Jews, "I have come in my Father's name, and you receive me not. If another comes in his own name, you will receive him."[10] He, then, who appeared for us—the Lord God, the blessed, who comes in the name of the Lord—was also the stone that those of old built up on the foundation of the Mosaic teaching, which they set aside and which, though set aside by them, has become the head of the corner of the church of the Gentiles. The oracle says it is wonderful, not to all that look on it but only to the eyes of the prophets, when it says, "And it is wonderful in our eyes." PROOF OF THE GOSPEL 9.18.[11]

THE LORD KEEPS FAITH. JEROME: "[The Lord] who keeps the truth forever."[12] If we are crushed

---

[3]ACW 57:828. [4]NPNF 1 2:377. [5]NPNF 2 8:280. [6]Heb 10:37. [7]Mal 3:1. [8]ANF 9:236*. [9]Heb 10:37. [10]Jn 5:43. [11]POG 2:189*. [12]Ps 146:6 (145:6 LXX).

by falsehood and deceit, let us not grieve over it. The Lord is the guardian of truth for all eternity. Someone has lied against us, and the liar is given more credence than we who are telling the truth. We must not despair. The Lord keeps faith forever. Aptly said, "keeps." He keeps truth and keeps it in his own treasury; he pays back to us what he has stored away for us. "Who keeps truth forever." Christ is truth; let us speak truth, and truth will safeguard truth for us. "[The Lord] secures justice for the oppressed."[13] Even if justice delays its coming, do not give up hope; "it will surely come," and bring salvation, securing justice for the oppressed. May our conscience testify only that we are not suffering on account of our sins and that we are not guilty of the charge brought against us. HOMILIES ON THE PSALMS 55.[14]

---

[13]Ps 146:7 (145:7 LXX). [14]FC 48:395*.

2:4 LIVE BY FAITH

[4]*Behold, he whose soul is not upright in him shall fail,[c]*
    *but the righteous shall live by his faith.[d]***

---

c Cn: Heb *is puffed up*   d Or *faithfulness*   *LXX *the just shall live by my [God's] faithfulness*

OVERVIEW: Pride is contrary to God's justice because it places trust in one's works and not grace. The justice of grace by which the just should live by faith was proclaimed by the prophet (AUGUSTINE). The message of the coming of Jesus as foretold is one harmonious testimony. The just people of the Old Testament are also recipients of God's grace as much as those of the New Testament, because they all rely on faith in God and not in their merits. Perfume was a symbol of justice, and costly nard refers to faith that echoes the prophet's injunction to live by faith in God's grace. Giving to the poor reenacts living for Jesus—anointing his feet and wiping it off with one's hair. Through such deeds Christ is made present on earth. Those lacking sound faith are in turn not among the righteous because the justified live by faith. Heretics and schismatics not justified by faith lack love. They violate the command not to work ill toward a neighbor (AUGUSTINE). Those who follow God live by faith, as did Abraham, whose faith blesses all the nations.

Therefore anyone, Jew or Gentile, can be justified by faith as children of Abraham (CYPRIAN). Godly works are intimately united to faith, as reflected in Tobit. Caring for the poor gives life to the faith that the just live by (LEO). Faith, as trust in divine promises, is the essence of righteousness (THEODORE).

2:4 The Righteous Live by Faith

PRIDE CONTRARY TO GOD'S JUSTICE. AUGUSTINE: Therefore pride is contrary to this justice of God, because it puts its trust in its own works. Thus the psalm continues, "Let not the foot of pride come to me."[1] This justice is the grace of the New Testament, by which the faithful are just, while they live by faith,[2] until, by the perfection of justice, they are brought to the face-to-face vision, as they are also equally brought to immortality of the body itself, by the

---

[1]Ps 36:11 (35:12 LXX). [2]Rom 1:17; Gal 3:11; Heb 10:38.

perfection of salvation. LETTER 140.30.[3]

OLD TESTAMENT SAINTS ARE SAVED TOO.

AUGUSTINE: Those just people also were saved by their salutary faith in him as man and God who, before he came in the flesh, believed that he was to come in the flesh.[4] Our faith is the same as theirs, since they believed that this would be, while we believe that it has come to pass. Hence the apostle Paul says, "But having the same spirit of faith, as it is written: 'I believed for which cause I have spoken,' we also believe for which cause we speak also."[5] If, then, those who foretold that Christ would come in the flesh had the same faith as those who have recorded his coming, these religious mysteries could vary according to the diversity of times, yet all refer most harmoniously to the unity of the same faith. It is written in the Acts of the Apostles that the apostle Peter said, "Now therefore why do you make trial of your God by putting a yoke on the neck of the disciples which neither our fathers nor we have been able to bear? But we believe that we shall be saved through the grace of our Lord Jesus just as they will."[6] If, therefore, they, that is, the fathers, being unable to bear the yoke of the old law, believed that they were saved through grace of the Lord Jesus, it is clear that this grace saved even the just people of old through faith, for "the just man lives by faith."[7] LETTER 190.[8]

THE SUPERFLUITY OF ANOINTED SERVICE.

AUGUSTINE: But "Mary," the other sister of Lazarus, "took a pound of perfume made from costly, pistic, aromatic nard. She anointed Jesus' feet and wiped his feet with her hair, and the house was filled with the ointment fragrance."[9] We have heard what happened; let us search out the hidden meaning. You, whoever wishes to be a faithful soul, together with Mary anoint the Lord's feet with costly perfume. That perfume was justice, and so it was a full pound.[10] However, it was perfume made from costly, pistic, aromatic nard. What does "pistic" mean? We might believe it to

be some place in which this was costly perfume; and yet this is not an idle phrase and is quite well consonant with the mystery. The Greek word means "faith."[11] You were seeking to work justice: "the just man lives by faith."[12] Anoint Jesus' feet by living well. Follow the Lord's footsteps. Wipe with your hair. If you have more than enough, give to the poor, and you have wiped the Lord's feet. For hairs seem to be the body's superfluity. For you they are superfluous, but for the Lord's feet they are necessary. Perhaps on earth the Lord's feet are in need. For about whom except about his members will he say in the end, "When you did it for one of the least of mine, you did it for me"?[13] You spent your superfluity, but you gave service to my feet. TRACTATES ON THE GOSPEL OF JOHN 50.6.[14]

HERETICS HAVE NEITHER FAITH NOR LOVE.

AUGUSTINE: For it is not simply the enduring of such things that is advantageous, but the bearing of such things for the name of Christ not only with a tranquil mind, even with exultation. For many heretics, deceiving souls under the Christian name, endure many such things; but they are excluded from that reward on this account, that it is not said merely, "Blessed are they which endure persecution," but it is added, "for righteousness' sake."[15] Now, where there is not sound faith, there can be no righteousness, for the just man lives by faith.[16] Neither let schismatics promise themselves anything of that reward; for similarly, where there is no love there cannot be right-

---

[3]FC 20:122. [4]Jn 1:7; 1 Jn 4:2. [5]2 Cor 4:13. [6]Acts 15:10-11. [7]Rom 1:17; Gal 3:11; Heb 10:38. [8]FC 30:274-75. [9]Lk 7:38; Jn 11:2; 12:3. [10]The Latin word for "pound," *libra*, also refers to a balance or pair of scales—a symbol for justice. [11]"The Greek adjective describing the perfume, *pistikos*, is simply transliterated in the Latin text [on which this translation from FC is based]. Derived from the Greek verb, *pinō*, it would mean 'liquid.' Augustine gives the word two possible meanings. Following a common early Christian interpretation, he first of all traces the adjective to the Greek noun *pistis*, 'faith,' and gives it the meaning 'faithful,' that is, 'genuine' or 'pure' in its literal application to perfume.... Secondly, Augustine suggests it might refer to the name of the place from which the perfume came" (FC 88:263 n. 8). [12]Cf. Rom 1:17. [13]Mt 25:40. [14]FC 88:263-64. [15]Mt 5:10. [16]Rom 1:17.

eousness, for "love works no ill to his neighbor."[17] And if they had it, they would not tear in pieces Christ's body, which is the church.[18] SERMON ON THE MOUNT 5.13.[19]

TIED TO THE FAITH OF ABRAHAM. CYPRIAN: "And if you will not believe, neither will you understand."[20] Also the Lord in the Gospel: "For if you believe not that I am he, you shall die in your sins."[21] Moreover, righteousness should subsist by faith. In it was life, as predicted in Habakkuk: "Now the just shall live by faith in me." Hence Abraham, the father of the nations, believed. In Genesis "Abraham believed in God, and it was counted to him for righteousness."[22] In like manner Paul wrote to the Galatians: "Abraham 'believed God, and it was reckoned to him as righteousness.' So you see, those of faith are the descendants of Abraham. And the Scripture, foreseeing that God would justify the Gentiles by faith, preached the gospel beforehand to Abraham, saying 'In you shall all the nations be blessed.' So then, those who are people of faith are blessed with Abraham who had faith."[23] THREE BOOKS OF TESTIMONIES AGAINST THE JEWS 12.1.5.[24]

CARE FOR THE POOR GIVES LIFE TO FAITH. LEO THE GREAT: And hence Tobias also, while instructing his son in the precepts of godliness, says, "Give alms of your substance, and turn not your face from any poor man. So shall it come to pass that the face of God shall not be turned from you."[25] This virtue makes all virtues profitable, for by its precepts it gives life to that very faith by which "the just lives" and which is said to be "dead without works."[26] As the reason for works consists in faith, so the strength of faith consists in works. SERMON 10.4.[27]

THE RIGHTEOUS TRUST GOD'S PROMISES. THEODORE OF MOPSUESTIA: "But the righteous one will live from my faith." So even if someone should be uncertain in their trust in the future and doubt if it will really happen, such a one is very much the object of dislike to me, because I define a righteous person as one who trusts in the promises and gets benefit from them. COMMENTARY ON HABAKKUK 2.1-4.[28]

---

[17]Rom 13:10. [18]Col 1:24. [19]NPNF 1 6:7-8. [20]Is 7:9. [21]Jn 8:24. [22]Gen 15:6. [23]Gal 3:6-9. [24]ANF 5:509-10*. [25]Tob 4:7. [26]Jas 2:26. [27]NPNF 2 12:121. [28]PG 66:436.

2:5-20 WOES TO THE WICKED

[5]*Moreover, wine is treacherous;*
the arrogant man shall not abide.[e]
His greed is as wide as Sheol;
like death he has never enough.
He gathers for himself all nations,
and collects as his own all peoples."

[6]*Shall not all these take up their taunt against him, in scoffing derision of him, and say,*[*]

"Woe to him who heaps up what is not his
own—
for how long?—
and loads himself with pledges!"
[7]*Will not your debtors suddenly arise,*
and those awake who will make you
tremble?
Then you will be booty for them.
[8]*Because you have plundered many nations,*

all the remnant of the peoples shall
  plunder you,
for the blood of men and violence to the
  earth,
  to cities and all who dwell therein.

⁹Woe to him who gets evil gain for his house,
  to set his nest on high,
  to be safe from the reach of harm!
¹⁰You have devised shame to your house
  by cutting off many peoples;
  you have forfeited your life.
¹¹For the stone will cry out from the wall,
  and the beam from the woodwork
    respond.

¹²Woe to him who builds a town with blood,
  and founds a city on iniquity!
¹³Behold, is it not from the LORD of hosts
  that peoples labor only for fire,
  and nations weary themselves for
    nought?
¹⁴For the earth will be filled
  with the knowledge of the glory of the
    LORD,
  as the waters cover the sea.

¹⁵Woe to him who makes his neighbors
  drink
  of the cup of his wrath,ᶠ and makes them

drunk,
  to gaze on their shame!
¹⁶You will be sated with contempt instead of
  glory.
  Drink, yourself, and stagger!ᵍ
The cup in the LORD's right hand
  will come around to you,
  and shame will come upon your glory!
¹⁷The violence done to Lebanon will
  overwhelm you;
  the destruction of the beasts will terrify
    you,ʰ
for the blood of men and violence to the
  earth,
  to cities and all who dwell therein.

¹⁸What profit is an idol
  when its maker has shaped it,
  a metal image, a teacher of lies?
For the workman trusts in his own creation
  when he makes dumb idols!
¹⁹Woe to him who says to a wooden thing,
    Awake;
  to a dumb stone, Arise!
  Can this give revelation?
Behold, it is overlaid with gold and silver,
  and there is no breath at all in it.

²⁰But the LORD is in his holy temple;
  let all the earth keep silence before him.

e The Hebrew of these two lines is obscure f Cn: Heb *joining to your wrath* g Cn Compare Gk Syr: Heb *be uncircumcised* h Gk Syr: Heb *them* *LXX *and they shall say*

OVERVIEW: The shepherds of the flock are given the charge to make sure that believers do not become proud by placing false reliance on themselves instead of upon grace (CYPRIAN). We should not become obsessed with the desire for worldly riches. Widows, orphans and neighbors are not to be ignored. Fear of the Lord is the best way to build a city of faith (AMBROSE). Heretics ravage the flock of Christ like wolves, pillaging, bloating and gorging themselves (CYRIL OF ALEXANDRIA). Those who are covetous toward their neighbor and speak ill of them are condemned (APOSTOLIC CONSTITUTIONS). Helena is praised for adoring Christ, who is symbolically identified with a scarab (AMBROSE). Returning to the old Jewish ways is like causing a neighbor to drink from foul water. Instead, believers are to immerse themselves in the teaching and example of Paul (ORIGEN). The birth of Mary was foretold in the Old Testament. Anna is referred to as the holy temple that carried Mary (METHODIUS).

2:5 Greed Wide as Sheol

PRIDE AFFECTS THE FLOCK. CYPRIAN: Since, therefore, the Lord thus threatens such shepherds through whom the sheep of the Lord are neglected and perish, what else ought we to do, dearly beloved brother, but to show full diligence in collecting and restoring the sheep of Christ and to apply the medicine of paternal piety to care for the wounds of the lapsed? The Lord also in the Gospel warns and says, "It is not the healthy who need a physician, but they who are sick."[1] For although we shepherds are many, yet we feed one flock. All of the sheep whom Christ sought by his blood and passion we ought to embrace and to cherish, and not to allow our suppliant and grieving brothers to be cruelly despised and to be trodden under foot by the proud presumption of certain ones, since it is written, "The man, however, who is stiff-necked, boastful of himself, will accomplish nothing at all. His greed is as wide as Sheol." LETTER 68.4.[2]

2:6 Woe to Those Who Accumulate What Is Not Theirs

WARNING AGAINST WEALTH. AMBROSE: Let your people not desire many things, for the reason that few things are many to them. Poverty and riches are names that imply want and satiety. He is not rich who wants anything, nor poor who does not want. Let no one spurn a widow or cheat an orphan or defraud his neighbor. Woe to him who has a fortune amassed by deceit and builds in blood a city, in other words, his soul. For it is this that is built like a city.[3] Greed does not build it but sets it on fire and burns it. Do you wish to

build your city well? "Better is a little with the fear of the Lord than great treasures without fear."[4] The riches of a person ought to work for the redemption of his soul, not to its destruction. Wealth is redemption if one uses it well; so too it is a snare if one does not know how to use it.[5] For what is a person's money if not provision for the journey? LETTER 15.[6]

HERETICS CONDEMNED. CYRIL OF ALEXANDRIA: As for the inventors of impure heresies, those profaners and apostates who have opened their mouths wide against the divine glory, "those who have uttered perverted things,"[7] we could accuse them of having slipped in their madness as low as the foolish pagans. [They have slipped] perhaps even lower, for it would have been better never to have known it than to have turned away from the sacred commandment which was handed on to them. What the book of Proverbs so rightly speaks of has indeed come about: "that the dog has returned to its vomit, and no sooner has it washed than the pig returns to wallow in the slime."[8] They have circulated among themselves blasphemous accusations against Christ and like wild, ferocious wolves ravage the flock for which Christ died. They pillage what is his very own, "bloating themselves on what is not theirs," as it is written, and "stuffing their gorge to the full." How aptly does that saying apply to them, that "they came out from us but were not part of us."[9] ON THE UNITY OF CHRIST.[10]

2:9 Evil Gains

WOE TO HIM WHO GETS EVIL GAIN. APOSTOLIC CONSTITUTIONS: You shall not speak evil; for he says, "Love not to speak evil, lest you be taken away." You shall not be mindful of injuries, for "the ways of those that remember injuries are unto death."[11] You shall not be double-minded or

---

[1]Mt 9:12. [2]FC 51:242-43.* [3]Ps 122:3 (121:3 LXX). [4]Prov 15:16. [5]Prov 13:8. [6]FC 26:80-81. [7]Acts 20:30. [8]Prov 26:11; 2 Pet 2:21-22. [9]1 Jn 2:19. [10]OUC 50. [11]Prov 12:28 LXX.

double-tongued, for "a man's own lips are a strong snare to him,"[12] and "a talkative person shall not be prospered upon the earth."[13] Your words shall not be vain, for "you shall give an account of every idle word."[14] You shall not tell lies, for he says, "You shall destroy all those that speak lies."[15] You shall not be covetous or rapacious, for he says, "Woe to him that is covetous toward his neighbor with an evil covetousness." CONSTITUTIONS OF THE HOLY APOSTLES 7.4.[16]

2:11 The Stone Shall Cry Out of the Wall

THE BEETLE OUT OF THE TIMBER SHALL SPEAK. AMBROSE: Helena[17] adored the king, not the wood [of the cross], indeed, because this is an error of the Gentiles and a vanity of the wicked. But she adored him who hung on the tree, whose name was inscribed in the title; him, I say, as a scarab,[18] cried out to his Father to forgive the sins of his persecutors.[19] The woman eagerly hastened to touch the remedy of immortality, but she feared to trample under the foot the mystery of salvation. Joyful at heart, yet with anxious step, she knew not what she should do. She proceeded, however, to the resting place of truth. The wood shone, and grace flashed forth. And, as before, Christ had visited as woman Mary, so the spirit visited a woman in Helena. He taught her what as a woman she did not know and led her upon a way that no mortal could know. ON THE DEATH OF THEODOSIUS 46.[20]

2:15 Woe to One Who Makes Neighbors Drunk

CALL TO CULTIVATE SEEDS OF SPIRITUALITY. ORIGEN: What then are we to do who received

such instructions about interpretation from Paul, a teacher of the church? Does it not seem right that we apply this kind of rule that was delivered to us in a similar way in other passages? Or as some wish, forsaking these things that such a great apostle taught, should we turn again to "Jewish fables"?[21] It seems to me that if I differ from Paul in these matters I aid the enemies of Christ, and this is what the prophet says, "Woe to him who causes his neighbor to drink for foul subversion!" Let us cultivate, therefore, the seeds of spiritual understanding received from the blessed apostle Paul, insofar as the Lord shall see fit to illuminate us by your prayers. HOMILIES ON EXODUS 5.1.[22]

2:20 The Lord Is in His Holy Temple

MARY'S BIRTH FORETOLD. METHODIUS: "When the time is come, you shall be shown forth."[23] What exposition does this require, if a person diligently direct the eye of the mind to the festival which we are now celebrating? "For then shall you be shown forth," he says, "as upon a kingly charger, by your pure and chaste mother, in the temple, and that in the grace and beauty of the flesh assumed by you." All these things the prophet, summing up for the sake of greater clearness, exclaims in brief: "The Lord is in his holy temple." "Fear before him all the earth."[24] ORATION CONCERNING SIMEON AND ANNA 4.[25]

---

[12]Prov 6:2. [13]Ps 140:11 (139:12 LXX). [14]Mt 12:36; Lev 19:11. [15]Ps 5:6 (5:7 LXX). [16]ANF 7:466*. [17]The mother of Constantine. Ambrose here recounts her pilgrimage to holy sites. [18]Ambrose often uses the scarab as a symbol of Christ. [19]Lk 23:34. [20]FC 22:327-28. [21]Tit 1:14. [22]FC 71:276-77. [23]Cf. Gal 4:4. [24]Ps 96:9 (95:9 LXX). [25]ANF 6:386.

3:1-2 PRAYER OF REPENTANCE AND DOXOLOGY

¹A prayer of Habakkuk the prophet, according to Shigionoth.*
  ²O LORD, I have heard the report of thee,
     and thy work, O LORD, do I fear.
  In the midst of the years renew it;
     in the midst of the years make it known;
     in wrath remember mercy.†

*Vulgate for ignorance †LXX In the midst of the two animals you will be known, you will be acknowledged when the years have drawn close: you will be set forth when the time comes; when my seal is troubles, you will remember your mercy in wrath.

OVERVIEW: Ignorance is a sin in need of repentance, as expressed by the prayer of Habakkuk regarding the need for contrition (JEROME). The two animals (LXX) are the Old and New Testaments, but the "middle" is not to be intended to mean that Christ did not belong fully to either one. Christ was in the middle of the two in a spiritual sense of the two covenants (CAESARIUS). The Lord's reward cannot be fully grasped as well as his vengeance. It is for this reason that Habakkuk expressed great fear for the Lord when he pondered his mercy and wrath (CASSIODORUS). The miracle at Cana and other passages reveal that God's purposes have a very specific timetable. Jesus time and again accomplished his works when the proper hour had arrived in God's providence. The prophet spoke about the timeliness of God's work (IRENAEUS). The prophet's reference to two living things through which divine knowledge is revealed are none other than Christ and the Holy Spirit (ORIGEN). At the transfiguration Moses and Elijah were revealed to be disciples of Jesus. The voice from heaven that confirmed the subservience of Moses and Elijah to Christ was foretold by the prophet (TERTULLIAN).

3:1 Habakkuk's Prayer

WARNED OF IGNORANCE. JEROME: The prophet Habakkuk gives this title to his canticle: "A prayer of Habakkuk the prophet for ignorance."

For he had spoken in a bold manner to the Lord and had said, "How long, O Lord, shall I cry, and you will not hear? Shall I cry to you 'suffering violence,' and you will not save? Why have you shown me iniquity and grievance, to see rapine and injustice before me? Judgment is done against me and opposition is more powerful. Therefore the law is torn to pieces, and judgment comes not to the end, because the wicked prevails against the just; therefore, wrong judgment goes forth."[1] As a reproof to himself for having spoken these words through ignorance, he writes the Canticle of Penance. If ignorance were no sin, it was a futile effort on his part to compose a book of penance, and his desire to express sorrow over an act that was not a sin was an empty gesture. AGAINST THE PELAGIANS 1.39.[2]

3:2 Renew Your Work

TWO TESTAMENTS FORETOLD. CAESARIUS OF ARLES: When the sacred lesson was read just now, we heard that at the time when the twelve spies were sent to view the land of promise, two of them brought back on a lever to the children of Israel a bunch of grapes of wonderful size. Those two men can be understood in many ways, dearly beloved, for they are not unfittingly believed to have signified both the two Testaments and the two precepts

---

[1]Hab 1:2-4. [2]FC 53:291.

whereby God and the neighbor are loved. They can, likewise, be understood both historically and allegorically. That they were a type of the two Testaments we know definitely from the fact that the grapes are read to have been brought between those two men, just as Christ our Lord is clearly recognized in the middle of the two Testaments. According to what is written, "In the middle of the two animals you will be known," that is, between the Old and New Testaments. When we read "in the middle," we are not to understand that Christ was between the New and Old Testaments in such a way that he was contained in neither one. This is not true, beloved brothers, but when it says, "In the middle of the two animals you will be known," we must realize that he is in the midst of the Old and New Testaments, that is, *within* in an interior and spiritual sense. This is not according to the letter, . . . but according to the spirit that vivifies all Christians who have spiritual understanding. Therefore "in the middle of the two animals you will be known" means in the inner sense of the New or Old Testaments. SERMON 107.1.[3]

REBUKE OF ANGER. CASSIODORUS: "For mildness will come upon us, and we shall be corrected. Who knows the power of your anger, or can number your wrath for fear?"[4] He now elaborates on his earlier statement: "the greatest number of them are labor and sorrow."[5] He says that we must not go beyond the precepts of the law, for Jesus Christ, who is mildness perfected, comes upon us and corrects and improves us if we wantonly ignore his Testaments. Since he used the word *corrected*, he prefaced it with "mildness," so that we may realize that all the changes wrought by God in the faithful result from the application of devoted love. Next comes "Who knows the power of your anger or can number your wrath for fear?"[6] Moses, who had experienced the severity of the Lord's response to his errant people when they roused him with incessant grumbling, rightly exclaims that no one's reckoning can measure his vengeance and that the potentialities of angry action open to him cannot be numbered.

Observe in both instances that his boundless power is proclaimed, for just as the Lord's rewards cannot be understood in their fullness, likewise the measure of his vengeance cannot be grasped. He did well to add "for fear;" as another prophet remarks: "I have pondered your works and was afraid." EXPOSITION OF THE PSALMS 89.11.[7]

GOD'S TIMING. IRENAEUS: With him nothing is incomplete or out of due season, just as with the Father there is nothing incongruous. For all these things were foreknown by the Father, but the Son works them out at the proper time in perfect order and sequence. This was the reason why, when Mary was urging on to perform the wonderful miracle of the wine and was desirous before the time to partake of the cup of emblematic significance, the Lord, checking her untimely haste, said, "Woman, what have I to do with you? My hour is not yet come"[8]—waiting for that hour which was foreknown by the Father. This is also the reason why, when men were often desirous to take him, "for the hour of his being taken was not yet to come,"[9] nor the time of his passion, which had been foreknown by the Father; as also says the prophet Habakkuk: "By this you shall be known when the years have drawn close; you shall be set forth when the time comes; because my soul is disturbed by anger, you shall remember your mercy." AGAINST HERESIES 3.16.7.[10]

CHRIST AND THE HOLY SPIRIT LINKED. ORIGEN: And we think that the expression also which occurs in the hymn of Habakkuk, "In the midst either of the two living things, or of the two lives, you will be known," ought to be understood of Christ and the Holy Spirit. For all knowledge of the Father is obtained by revelation of the Son through the Holy Spirit, so that both of these beings which, according to the prophet, are called

---

[3]FC 47:131-32. [4]Ps 90:10-11 (89:10-11 Vulgate). [5]Ps 90:10 (89:10 LXX). [6]Ps 90:11 (89:11 LXX). [7]ACW 52:376. [8]Jn 2:4. [9]Jn 7:30. [10]ANF 1:443.

either "living things" or "lives" exist as the grounds of the knowledge of God the Father. For it is said of the Son that "no one knows the Father but the Son, and he to whom the Son will reveal him."[11] The same also is said by the apostle of the Holy Spirit, when he declares, "God has revealed them to us by his Holy Spirit; for the Spirit searches all things, even the deep things of God."[12] And again in the Gospel, when the Savior speaks of the divine and profounder parts of his teaching, which his disciples were not yet able to receive, he thus addresses them: "I cannot bear them now; but when the Holy Spirit, the Comforter, is come, he will teach you all things, and will bring all things to your remembrance whatsoever I have said unto you."[13] We must understand, therefore, that as the Son, who alone knows the Father, reveals him to whom he will, so the Holy Spirit, who alone searches the deep things of God, reveals God to whom he will: "For the Spirit blows where he lists."[14] We are not, however, to suppose that the Spirit derives his knowledge through revelation from the Son. ON FIRST PRINCIPLES 1.3.4.[15]

TWO TESTAMENTS LINKED, CONTRA MARCION. TERTULLIAN: The Father gave to the Son new disciples after Moses and Elijah had been exhibited along with him in the honor of his glory and had then been dismissed as having fully discharged their duty and office.... But we have the entire structure of this same vision in Habakkuk also, where the spirit in the person of some of the apostles says, "O Lord, I have heard your speech and was afraid." What speech was this, other than the words of the voice from heaven, "This is my beloved Son, hear him"?[16] "I considered your works and was astonished." When could this have better happened than when Peter, on seeing his glory, knew not what he was saying? "In the midst of the two you shall be known"—even Moses and Elijah. AGAINST MARCION 4.12.[17]

---

[11]Lk 10:22. [12]1 Cor 2:10. [13]Jn 14:26; 16:12-13. [14]Jn 3:8. [15]ANF 4:253. [16]Mt 17:5. [17]ANF 3:384-85.

3:3-6 DIVINE ADVENT

[3]*God came from Teman,*
   and the Holy One from Mount Paran.*
His glory covered the heavens,
   and the earth was full of his praise.
                                    Selah
[4]*His brightness was like the light,*
   rays flashed from his hand;
   and there he veiled his power.

[5]*Before him went pestilence,*
   and plague followed close behind.
[6]*He stood and measured the earth;*
   he looked and shook the nations;
then the eternal mountains were scattered,
   the everlasting hills sank low.
   His ways were as of old.

*LXX *the shady mountain*

OVERVIEW: Donatists are rebuked for misinterpreting Habakkuk and thus claiming that Christ came from Africa. It is common knowledge regarding the true earthly origins of Christ and his ascension from the Mount of Olives as recorded in the Gospels (AUGUSTINE). The prophet along with additional testimony proclaimed that Christ would emerge from Judea, Jerusalem and his advent to Bethlehem (IRENAEUS). The prophet makes it clear that Christ came from Judea, thereby endorsed in time and space. The Sabellians deny that Christ is not a Son but Father only, but at the same time they say that he was a mere man (NOVATIAN). The glory of the Lord signifies his glorious ascension that fills the church with praise (AUGUSTINE). Christ is symbolically referred to as a unicorn, the Son of the cross, which the prophet said from whom rays shine forth. Christ's cross emitted fiery flames, which have extinguished the flames of hell (JEROME). God's standing and measuring earth signifies Christ's crucifixion. Furthermore, scattering the mountains and hills, where the pagan altars were located, is a type of Christ's victory over demons (THEODORET).

3:3 God's Coming and Glory

REBUKE OF AFROCENTRIC DONATISTS.

AUGUSTINE: But tell us the other thing you were saying you were going to tell us. "The prophet," says he, "says God 'will come from Afric,'[1] and now of course where the Afric is, there is Africa." Well, there's a fine testimony for you! God will come from the Afric, and from Africa God will come. The heretics are announcing another Christ who is born in Africa and goes through the world. I'm asking what it means, God will come from Africa. If you said, "God has only remained in Africa," you would certainly be saying something shameful enough. But now you also say, "He will come from Africa." We know where Christ was born, where he suffered, where he ascended into heaven, where he sent his disciples from, where he filled them with the Holy Spirit, where he instructed them to evangelize the whole world, and they complied, and the world is filled with the gospel. And you say, "God will come from Africa!" . . .

So how does he come from "the shady mountain"? Read the Gospel once more: it was from the Mount of Olives that Christ ascended into heaven. Continue. And what could be clearer? You hear "from the Afric"; you have heard "from the shady mountain." We recite the law, we recite the Gospel; you have heard "beginning from Jerusalem"; now hear "throughout all the nations." In the same prophet continue with those words that you ignored, those words you left out. . . . "God will come from the Afric, and the Holy One from the shady mountain," that is, from the Mount of Olives, where he ascended into heaven, where he sent his disciples from, where he also said as he was about to ascend, "It is not for you to know the times which the Father has placed in his own power; but you will receive might from on high, and you will be witness to me . . . in Jerusalem, and in Judea and in Samaria, and as far as the whole earth."[2] SERMON 46.38-40.[3]

PLACE OF CHRIST'S COMING FORETOLD. IRENAEUS: And there are also some of them who say, "the Lord has spoken in Zion, and uttered his voice from Jerusalem,"[4] and "in Judah is God known"[5]—these indicated his advent, which took place in Judea. Those, again, who declare that "God comes from the south, and from a mountain thick with foliage," announced his advent at Bethlehem, as I have pointed out in the preceding book. From that place, also, he who rules and who feeds the people of his Father, has come. Those, again, who declare that at his coming "the lame man shall leap as a deer, and the tongue of the dumb shall speak plainly, and the eyes of the blind shall be opened, and the ears of the deaf shall hear,"[6] and that "the hands which hang down, and the feeble knees, shall be strengthened,"[7] and that "the dead which are in the grave shall arise,"[8] and that he himself "shall take our weaknesses, and bear our sorrows"[9]—proclaimed

---

[1]Augustine has *Deus ab Africo veniet*. Following the Hebrew text, LXX has the place name Teman. The Vulgate, however, reads *Deus ab austro* (*austro* from *auster*, meaning "the south wind"). [2]Acts 1:7-8. [3]WSA 3 2:289-91. [4]Joel 3:16. [5]Ps 76:1 (75:1 LXX). [6]Is 35:5-6. [7]Is 33:3. [8]1 Thess 4:16. [9]Is 53:4. .

those works of healing which were accomplished by him. AGAINST HERESIES 4.33.11.[10]

AGAINST SABELLIAN HERESY. NOVATIAN: Habakkuk the prophet says, "God shall come from the south, and the holy one from the dark and dense mountain." Whom would they have come from the south? If they say that God the Father almighty came, then God the Father came from a place; consequently, he is also enclosed by space and contained within the limits of some abode. Thus the sacrilegious heresy of Sabellius, as we said, takes concrete form because of these people who believe that Christ is not the Son but the Father. It is strange how these heretics, while insisting that Christ is a mere man, make an about-face and acknowledge that Christ is the Father, God almighty. ON THE TRINITY 12.7.[11]

CHRIST'S FULLNESS FORETOLD. AUGUSTINE: Where we recognize Christ in what is written: "God will come from the south and the holy one from the shady mountain; his strength will cover the heavens," there we recognize the church in what follows: "And the earth is full of his praise." Jerusalem was settled from Africa, as we read in the book of Joshua, son of Nun; from there the name of Christ was spread abroad; there is the shady mountain, the Mount of Olives, from which he ascended into heaven, so that his strength might cover the heavens and the church might be filled through all the earth with his praise.[12] LETTER 105.[13]

3:4 Brightness Like the Light

POWER OF THE CROSS. JEROME: What does the psalm have to say of the Savior? "As the beloved Son of unicorns."[14] Our beloved Lord and Savior is the Son of the unicorns, the Son of the cross, of whom Habakkuk sings, "Rays shine forth from beside him, where his power is concealed." After this beloved Son was crucified, then, was fulfilled the prophecy of the psalm: "The voice of the Lord strikes fiery flames."[15] For when Christ had been baptized and the entire universe had been purified in his cleansing, the fire of hell was extinguished. ON THE EPIPHANY AND PSALM 28, HOMILY 89.[16]

3:6 The Mountains Scattered

HABAKKUK'S PROPHECY FULFILLED BY CHRIST. THEODORET OF CYR: In all of what he said he conveyed to us the ineffable power of God: action follows his will, and by merely wishing it (the sense of "he took his position and looked down") he moves the earth, undoes human nature, splits open the mountains and melts the hills like wax. In fact, he has not ceased doing such things for people's benefit (by "passing" referring to his doings). Now in what is said he implies also the cross, which is the source of salvation for all people. On it Christ the Lord "took his position," shook the earth, moved and split open the mountains, struck with fear the hordes of demons, and destroyed their shrines on mountains and hills. While it was from the beginning and before the formation of the world that he so decided, it was in the last days that he accomplished it. COMMENTARY ON HABAKKUK 3.6.[17]

---

[10]ANF 1:509-10. [11]FC 67:51*. [12]Josh 15:8, 14, 18; Acts 1:2. [13]FC 18:208. [14]Ps 28:6 LXX. [15]Ps 29:7 (28:7 LXX). [16]FC 57:230. [17]PG 81:1828.

3:7-19 JOY IN THE GOD OF SALVATION

⁷I saw the tents of Cushan* in affliction;
    the curtains of the land of Midian did
      tremble.
⁸Was thy wrath against the rivers, O LORD?
    Was thy anger against the rivers,
    or thy indignation against the sea,
when thou didst ride upon thy horses,
    upon thy chariot of victory?
⁹Thou didst strip the sheath from thy bow,
    and put the arrows to the string.ⁱ
                    Selah
    Thou didst cleave the earth with rivers.
¹⁰The mountains saw thee, and writhed;
    the raging waters swept on;
the deep gave forth its voice,
    it lifted its hands on high.
¹¹The sun and moon stood still in their
    habitationʲ
    at the light of thine arrows as they sped,
    at the flash of thy glittering spear.
¹²Thou didst bestride the earth in fury,
    thou didst trample the nations in anger.
¹³Thou wentest forth for the salvation of thy
    people,
    for the salvation of thy anointed.†
Thou didst crush the head of the wicked,ᵏ
    laying him bare from thigh to neck.ˡ
                    Selah

¹⁴Thou didst pierce with thyᵐ shafts the
    head of his warriors,ⁿ‡
    who came like a whirlwind to scatter me,
    rejoicing as if to devour the poor in secret.
¹⁵Thou didst trample the sea with thy horses,
    the surging of mighty waters.

¹⁶I hear, and my body trembles,
    my lips quiver at the sound;
rottenness enters into my bones,
    my steps totterᵒ beneath me.
I will quietly wait for the day of trouble
    to come upon people who invade us.

¹⁷Though the fig tree do not blossom,
    nor fruit be on the vines,
the produce of the olive fail
    and the fields yield no food,
the flock be cut off from the fold
    and there be no herd in the stalls,
¹⁸yet I will rejoice in the LORD,
    I will joy in the God of my salvation.
¹⁹GOD, the Lord, is my strength;
    he makes my feet like hinds' feet,
    he makes me tread upon my high places.

To the choirmaster: with stringedᵖ
    instruments.§

i Cn: Heb obscure   j Heb uncertain   k Cn: Heb *head from the house of the wicked*   l Heb obscure   m Heb *his*   n Vg Compare Gk Syr: Heb uncertain   o Cn Compare Gk: Heb *I tremble because*   p Heb *my stringed*   *LXX *Ethiopian*   †Old Latin *your christs*   ‡LXX *warriors or dynasties*   §LXX *unto the end* and *that I may conquer in his song*

OVERVIEW: The barbarian calamities are said to have been predicted by the prophet when he spoke of the labors caused by the Ethiopians. Ambrose sees himself encased in the tents of the barbarians [Ethiopians] and dwelling with the Midians (AMBROSE). When the Assyrians threatened Elisha, the Lord sent an army of chariots and horses with no men upon the horses. That is, they were a multitude of angels, and the charioteer was the Lord. Habakkuk had proclaimed their chariots as our salvation. There is also an exhortation for believers to become a horse for the Lord to ride on (JEROME). There are horses and riders of the evil one and there are those who belong to the company of salvation (ORIGEN). The sun and moon, which Habakkuk proclaims, refer to the ascension of Christ and the ecclesiastical order (bishops). Each member of the faith is a sun terrace that receives its light from the sun above (Christ). It is for this reason that Rahab hid the spies in her terrace where the light dwells (FULGENTIUS). Priests and kings are both "christs" as figures of the Lord and Savior of which they are types having been anointed with the saved chrism of oil (BEDE). The name *Christ* is applied not to Emmanuel alone but to others who are anointed, the priests. Scripture testifies to others who are anointed for God's service, such as the prophets and those whom Habakkuk calls the anointed ones (CYRIL OF ALEXANDRIA). Ambrose highlights the horses, which the Lord mounts, and the pious souls, which Christ rides to proclaim salvation (AMBROSE). The trials and tribulation of which the prophets prayed pale in comparison with the eternal rest of the afterlife with the company of saints and Christ (JEROME). Habakkuk's cry for salvation points to Christ as Savior (BEDE).

3:7 Cushan and Midian Afflicted

BARBARIANS FORETOLD. AMBROSE: However, we who are exposed to the outbreaks of barbarians and the storms of war are tossed in the midst of a sea of many troubles and can only infer from these labors and trials more grievous trials in the future. The saying of the prophet seems to be in accord with our condition: "I saw the tents of the Ethiopians for their labors." Having now lived fifty-three years in the body, amid the shadows of this world that obscure the reality of the future perfection, and having already endured such heavy sorrows, am I not encamping in the tents of the Ethiopians and dwelling with the inhabitants of Midian?

They, owing to their knowledge of the works of darkness, fear to be judged even by mortal men. "For the spiritual man judges all things, and he himself is judged by no man."[1] LETTER 29.[2]

3:8 God's Chariot of Victory

HORSE AND CHARIOTS EXPLAINED. JEROME: "Chariots and steeds lay stilled."[3] Let us examine this verse in its tropological significance. At last Pharaoh mounted his steeds, sank into sleep and perished. The Egyptians too had steeds, but they perished. That is the reason for the prescription found in the law[4] that no Hebrew should possess a horse. Solomon, you recall, had no horses from Jerusalem or Judea but bought some from Egypt.[5] Horses are always for sale in Egypt. "Some are strong in chariots; some in horses; but we are strong in the name of the Lord, our God."[6] They, in truth, who mounted horses slumbered and perished. Our Lord has horses too, and he has shining mountains besides, whereas the devil's mountains are full of darkness. Now just as there are bright mountains and dark mountains, there are good horses and again bad horses. We have made a few remarks about bad horses; let us say something about good horses. When horsemen came to Elisha[7] to arrest him and the servant boy went out and saw an army of Assyrians round about the city, Elisha said, "Fear not: for there are more with us than with them." A little further on in Kings it says, "Lord, open the eyes of your servant that he may see." And when his eyes had been opened, he saw chariots and horses. These were helpmates. You notice that it says "chariots and horses." There were no men on the horses, only chariots and horses, in other words a multitude of angels. They were the chariots and they were the horses; the charioteer was the Lord. That is why the prophet Habakkuk sings, "Your chariots are salvation." This is said to God. O, if only we too were God's horses, and God deigned

---

[1]1 Cor 2:15. [2]FC 26:150. [3]Ps 76:6 (75:7 Vg.). [4]Deut 17:16. [5]1 Kings 10:28. [6]Ps 20:7 (19:8 LXX). [7]2 Kings 6:13-17.

to ride us! But those other horses slept their long sleep and their charioteers with them. HOMILIES ON THE PSALMS 9.[8]

HORSES OF GOD, HORSES OF THE DEVIL.
ORIGEN: "He cast forth horse and rider into the sea; he became my helper and protector in salvation."[9] The men who pursue us are horses, and, so to speak, all who have been born in the flesh are figuratively horses. But these have their own riders. There are horses that the Lord mounts, and they go around all the earth, of whom it is said, "And your cavalry is salvation." There are horses, however, who have the devil and his angels as riders. Judas was a horse, but as long as he had the Lord as his rider he was part of the cavalry of salvation. Having been sent with the other apostles indeed, he gave health to the sick and wholeness to the weak.[10]

But when he surrendered himself to the devil —for "after the morsel, Satan entered him"[11]— Satan became his rider, and when he was guided by his reins he began to ride against our Lord and Savior. All, therefore, who persecute the saints, are neighing horses, but they have evil angels as riders by whom they are guided and therefore are wild. If, then, you ever see your persecutor raging very much, know that he is being urged on by a demon as his rider and therefore is fierce and cruel. HOMILIES ON EXODUS 6.2.[12]

3:11 Sun and Moon Stand Still

CHRIST'S ASCENSION. FULGENTIUS OF RUSPE: And the prophet Habakkuk proclaims the ascension of Christ and the strength of the ecclesiastical order under the titles of the sun and the moon: "The sun raised high its hands; the moon stood still in its exalted place." So the heart of each of the faithful is not improperly called a spiritual sun terrace, because it is illumined for its salvation by the rays of that sun above. Therefore Rahab the harlot hid those spies of Joshua on the terrace of her house. That is, she kept them in the upper parts because of the deep love of a heart illumined by spiritual knowledge so that she might sing this prophetic word by the truth of her deed: "I treasure your word in my heart, so that I may not sin against you."[13] To EUTHYMIUS, ON THE FORGIVENESS OF SINS 1.21.4.[14]

3:13 For the Salvation of God's People

CHRIST'S PRIESTLY OFFICE FORETOLD. BEDE: Concerning [his] companions in the anointing, the apostle says, "To each of us grace is given according to the measure of Christ's bestowal."[15] Both the priests and kings are called "christs" in the law, undoubtedly as figures of this king and high priest, our Lord and Savior, and as a type of him they were also anointed with the earthly oil. Not only they, but also the faithful of our own time, as they are called "Christians" from Christ, so also are they rightly called "christs"—from the anointing with the sacred chrism, from the grace of the spirit with which they are consecrated. The prophet testified to this when he said, "You went forth for the salvation of your people, so that you might save your christs."[16] He did indeed go forth for the salvation of his people, so that he might save his christs. "On account of us human beings and on account of our salvation, he descended from heaven and became incarnate" so that he might grant to us who have been thoroughly anointed and healed by spiritual grace to be sharers in his holy name. HOMILIES ON THE GOSPELS 1.16.[17]

PRIESTS AND CHRIST DISTINGUISHED. CYRIL OF ALEXANDRIA: And yet, someone may say, we shall find the name Christ applied not to Emmanuel alone, but also applied to others. For God said somewhere about those chosen and sanctified by the Spirit, "Do not touch my anointed ones, and to my prophets do no harm."[1] The divinely in-

[8]FC 48:64-65. [9]Ex 15:1-2. [10]Mt 10:1. [11]Jn 13:27. [12]FC 71:287. [13]Ps 119:11 (118:11 LXX). [14]FC 95:137. [15]Eph 4:7. [16]Vulgate. [17]CS 110:160-61. [18]Ps 105:15 (104:15 LXX).

spired David calls Saul, who had been anointed as king by God through the hand of Samuel:[19] the "Lord's anointed."[20] And why do I mention this when it is possible for those who desire to look at the matter calmly to see that those who have been justified by faith in Christ and have been sanctified in the Spirit are honored by such a name? And therefore the prophet Habakkuk has foretold the mystery of Christ and salvation through him, saying, "You went forth for the salvation of your people, for the salvation of your anointed ones." Consequently the name Christ would not be applicable exclusively and properly to Emmanuel, as I said, but also to all the rest who may have been anointed with the grace of the Holy Spirit. For the word is derived from the action and the name anointed from the fact of having been anointed. LETTER 1.16-17.[21]

3:15 Trampling the Sea

WE ARE CHRIST'S HORSES. AMBROSE: For the soul at peace swiftly turns and corrects itself, even though it sinned before, and Christ mounts it, rather, and considers it appropriate to guide it. To him it is said, "Mount your horses, and your riding is salvation,"[22] and in another passage, "I have sent your horses into the sea." These are the horses of Christ. Therefore Christ mounts his horses; the Word of God mounts pious souls. ISAAC, OR THE SOUL 8.66.[23]

3:16 Rottenness in the Bones

THIS LIFE AND THE AFTERLIFE CONTRASTED.

JEROME: He who is cautious and wary can avoid sins for a while, but he who is secure in his own justice opposes God, and deprived of his help, he is subject to the snares of the enemy. "Let rottenness," says Habakkuk, "enter into my bones and swarm under me, that I may rest in the day of tribulation, that I may go up to my people that are girded." He prays earnestly for tribulations and trials and affliction of soul so that, in the next world, he may join the company of those who are already reigning with Christ. It is clear from all this that here, in this life, there is strife and contention, and, in the next world, there is victory. AGAINST THE PELAGIANS 2.24.[24]

3:18 Rejoicing in the God of Salvation

CHRIST AS SAVIOR FORESEEN IN THE OLD TESTAMENT. BEDE: "And [Joseph] called his name Jesus."[25] "Jesus" in Hebrew means "saving" or "Savior" in Latin. It is clear that the prophets most certainly call upon his name. Hence these things are sung in great desire for a vision of him: "My soul will exult in the Lord and take delight in his salvation."[26] "My soul pines for your salvation."[27] "I, however, will glory in the Lord; I will rejoice in God my Jesus."[28] And especially that [verse]: "God in your name save me!" as if [the prophet] would say, "You who are called Savior; make bright the glory of your name in me by saving." HOMILIES ON THE GOSPELS 1.5.[29]

---

[19]1 Sam 16:13. [20]1 Sam 24:10. [21]FC 76:19-20. [22]Hab 3:8 LXX. [23]FC 65:54-55. [24]FC 53:335. [25]Mt 1:25. [26]Ps 35:9 (34:9 LXX). [27]Ps 119:81 (118:81 LXX). [28]Old Latin. [29]CS 110:49-50.

ZEPHANIAH

OVERVIEW: Zephaniah is the ninth of the Minor Prophets. The contents of the book are arranged as follows: the title (Zeph 1:1); the day of doom of the world (Zeph 1:2-6, 8-13) and of Jerusalem (Zeph 1:4-6, 8-13); the day of Yahweh (Zeph 1:7, 14-18); an invitation to repentance (Zeph 2:1-3); oracles against foreign nations who are enemies (Zeph 2:4-15): Philistines, Moab and Ammon, Ethiopia and Assyria; threats against Jerusalem (Zeph 3:1-7); judgment of the wicked and deliverance of the remnant (Zeph 3:8-13); and finally the deliverance and glory of Israel (Zeph 3:14-20). Most of the book is attributed to Zephaniah, and it is believed to have been written in the first part of the reign of Josiah (640-609 B.C.). Little is known about the life and person of the prophet, even though the book has a four-generation genealogy at the beginning.

Already in the pre-Christian era, the book of Zephaniah was interpreted as an apocalyptic message with strong messianic overtones. It was nevertheless not a very popular book in either Jewish or Christian circles in the apostolic period. Although Zephaniah is not explicitly quoted in the New Testament, its imagery of the day of judgment endured, as did other motifs. Jerome seems to have been the most prominent exegete who inspired other church fathers to pay attention to this prophet. There was particular focus upon the abolition of the old covenant, which had been exclusively Jewish in the main, and the transition to a new covenant, which included Jews and Gentiles. The most dramatic, visible proof of this transition was the destruction of the temple in A.D. 70. It also proved the decisiveness of the new covenant as interpreter of the old covenant.

1:1-18 THE JUDGMENT
OF THE DAY OF THE LORD

¹The word of the LORD which came to Zephaniah the son of Cushi, son of Gedaliah, son of Amariah, son of Hezekiah, in the days of Josiah the son of Amon, king of Judah.

²"I will utterly sweep away everything
   from the face of the earth," says the LORD.
³"I will sweep away man and beast;
   I will sweep away the birds of the air
   and the fish of the sea.
I will overthrow*a* the wicked;*
   I will cut off mankind
   from the face of the earth," says the LORD.
⁴"I will stretch out my hand against Judah,
   and against all the inhabitants of
      Jerusalem;
and I will cut off from this place the
      remnant of Baal
   and the name of the idolatrous priests;*b*
⁵those who bow down on the roofs
   to the host of the heavens;
those who bow down and swear to the LORD
   and yet swear by Milcom;
⁶those who have turned back from following
      the LORD,
   who do not seek the LORD or inquire of
      him."

⁷Be silent before the Lord GOD!
   For the day of the LORD is at hand;
the LORD has prepared a sacrifice
   and consecrated his guests.
⁸And on the day of the LORD's sacrifice—
"I will punish the officials and the king's

sons†
   and all who array themselves in foreign
      attire.
⁹On that day I will punish
   every one who leaps over the threshold,
and those who fill their master's house
   with violence and fraud."
¹⁰"On that day," says the LORD,
   "a cry will be heard from the Fish Gate,
a wail from the Second Quarter,
   a loud crash from the hills.
¹¹Wail, O inhabitants of the Mortar!
   For all the traders are no more;
   all who weigh out silver are cut off.
¹²At that time I will search Jerusalem with
      lamps,
   and I will punish the men
who are thickening upon their lees,
   those who say in their hearts,
'The LORD will not do good,
   nor will he do ill.'
¹³Their goods shall be plundered,
   and their houses laid waste.
Though they build houses,
   they shall not inhabit them;
though they plant vineyards,
   they shall not drink wine from them."

¹⁴The great day of the LORD is near,
   near and hastening fast;
the sound of the day of the LORD is bitter,
   the mighty man cries aloud there.
¹⁵A day of wrath is that day,
   a day of distress and anguish,

a day of ruin and devastation,
　a day of darkness and gloom,
a day of clouds and thick darkness,
　¹⁶a day of trumpet blast and battle cry
against the fortified cities
　and against the lofty battlements.

¹⁷I will bring distress on men,
　so that they shall walk like the blind,
　because they have sinned against the LORD;

their blood shall be poured out like dust,
　and their flesh like dung.
¹⁸Neither their silver nor their gold
　shall be able to deliver them
　on the day of the wrath of the LORD.
In the fire of his jealous wrath,
　all the earth shall be consumed;
for a full, yea, sudden end
　he will make of all the inhabitants of the
　earth.

a Cn: Heb *the stumbling blocks*　b Compare Gk: Heb *idolatrous priests with the priests*　*LXX *stumbling blocks*　†LXX *sons* is used in the sense of *house*

OVERVIEW: As Zephaniah searched Jerusalem with a lantern, Jesus searched with a lamp but found no rest in the temple because he could find no priests. The darkness that settled in the temple was symbolic of the ignorance of unbelieving Jews. Having searched with lamps in vain in the temple, Jesus then went with the Twelve to Bethany (JEROME). The lust of riches and money was shown by Zephaniah to be vain in light of the coming Lord's day of judgment (CYPRIAN). Penitents are to recall the serious nature of the last judgment, where nothing will be hidden. God, however, offers ample opportunity for repentance (CASSIODORUS). Just as the sun casts light on the created order, so Christ is the light (sun) that enlightens the spiritual realm (ORIGEN). The fenced cities in the prophecy are fallacious minds that think they can escape the last judgment. The lofty corners are insincere hearts that shun the truth. The day of the Lord destroys human hearts that are closed to the truth (GREGORY THE GREAT). The prophet condemned the vanity of external adornments that are of no value in the day of judgment (CLEMENT OF ALEXANDRIA).

1:12 Searching Jerusalem with Lamps

CHRIST THE LAMP. JEROME: The Lord Jesus went into Jerusalem, into the temple. And when he had looked around upon all things, then, as it was already late, he went out to Bethany with the Twelve.[1] The Lord went into Jerusalem and into the temple. He went in, and, having entered, what does he do? He looks about at everything. In the temple of the Jews he was looking for a place to rest his head and found none. "He had looked around upon all things." Why did it say, "He had looked around upon all that was there"? He was looking for the priests; he wanted to be with them, but he could not find them. He always had regard for priests. So he surveyed all that was about him, almost as though he were searching with a lantern; so says the prophet Zephaniah: "I will explore Jerusalem with lamps." In this same way, the Lord too looked around at everything with the light of a lamp. He was searching in the temple, but he did not find what he wanted. When it was already evening, he was still exploring everything; he was looking around upon all things. Even though his search was unfruitful, nevertheless, as long as there was light, he remained in the temple; but when evening had come, when the shades of ignorance had darkened the temple of the Jews, when it was the evening hour, he went out to Bethany with the Twelve. The Savior searched; the apostles searched; in the temple they found nothing, so they left it. HOMILIES ON MARK 82.[2]

1:13-14 The Day of the Lord Draws Near

---

[1]Mk 11:11. [2]FC 57:173.

MONEY AND THINGS TO BE SHUNNED. CYP-RIAN: The lust of possessions and money are not to be sought for. In Solomon, in Ecclesiastes: "He that loves silver shall not be satisfied with silver."[3] Also in Proverbs: "He who holds back the corn is cursed among the people; but blessing is on the head of him that communicates it."[4] Also in Isaiah: "Woe to them who join house to house, and lay field to field, that they may take away something from their neighbor. Will you dwell alone upon the earth?"[5] Also, in Zephaniah: "They shall build houses, and shall not dwell in them; and they shall appoint vineyards, and shall not drink the wine of them, because the Day of the Lord is near." Also in the Gospel according to Luke: "For what does it profit a man to make a gain of the whole world, but that he should lose himself?"[6] To QUIRINUS, TES-TIMONIES AGAINST THE JEWS 12.3.61.[7]

ALWAYS ROOM TO REPENT. CASSIODORUS: With reference to that day the prophet Amos says, "Woe to them that desire the Day of the Lord. To what end is this Day of the Lord for you? The day itself is darkness and not light."[8] The prophet Zephaniah says the same thing: "The voice of the Day of the Lord is grim and bitter." That is why the penitent now introduced before us earnestly supplicates in the ordered divisions of his prayer that he may not be convicted for his deeds on that day of judgment. What is more beneficial and farsighted for the person who could have no hope in his own deserts because of the sins which he has committed than to decide to pray to God's fatherly love while in this world, where there is opportunity for repentance? EXPO-SITION OF THE PSALMS 6.1.[9]

CHRIST IS LIGHT OF THE GREATER SUN. ORI-GEN: But since these are light as perceived by the sense, which are said in Moses to have come into existence on the fourth day, they are not the true light because they enlighten the things on the earth. The Savior, on the other hand, is the light of the spiritual world because he shines on those who are rational and intellectual, that their mind may see its proper visions. Now I mean he is the light of those rational souls which are in the sensible world, of which the Savior teaches us that he is the Maker, being, perhaps its directing and principal part, and, so to speak, the sun of the great Day of the Lord. COMMENTARY ON THE GOSPEL OF JOHN 1.161.[10]

1:15-16 *The Day of Wrath*

FALSE HEARTS REVEALED ON THE DAY OF JUDGMENT. GREGORY THE GREAT: But let them hear how the prophet Zephaniah holds out over them the power of divine rebuke, saying, "Behold, the Day of the Lord comes, great and horrible, the day of wrath, that day; a day of darkness and gloominess, a day of cloud and whirlwind, a day of trumpet and clamor, upon all fenced cities, and upon all lofty corners." For what is expressed by fenced cities but minds suspected and surrounded ever with a fallacious defense; minds which, as often as their fault is attacked, suffer not the darts of truth to reach them? And what is signified by lofty corners (a wall being always double in corners) but insincere hearts; which, while they shun the simplicity of truth, are in a manner doubled back on themselves in the crookedness of duplicity, and, what is worse, from their fault of insincerity lift themselves in their thoughts with the pride of prudence? Therefore the Day of the Lord comes full of vengeance and rebuke upon fenced cities and lofty corners, because the wrath of the last judgment both destroys human hearts that have been closed by defenses against the truth and unfolds such as have been folded up in duplicities. For then the fenced cities fall. For souls that God has not penetrated will be damned. Then the lofty corners tumble, because hearts which erect themselves in the prudence of insincerity are prostrated by the sentence of righteousness. PASTORAL CARE 11.[11]

---

[3]Eccles 5:10. [4]Prov 11:26. [5]Is 5:8. [6]Lk 9:25. [7]ANF 5:550. [8]Amos 5:18. [9]ACW 51:90. [10]FC 80:66. [11]NPNF 2 12:34.

1:18 *Riches Shall Not Save People*

ADORNED WOMEN. CLEMENT OF ALEXANDRIA: I am weary and vexed at enumerating the multitude of ornaments, and I am compelled to wonder how those who bear such a burden are not worried to death. O foolish trouble! O silly craze for display! They squander meretriciously wealth on what is disgraceful and in their love for ostentation disfigure God's gifts, emulating the art of the evil one. The rich man hoarding up in his barns and saying to himself, "You have many goods laid up for many years; eat, drink be merry," the Lord in the Gospels plainly called "fool." "For this night they shall take your soul; whose then shall those things which you have prepared be?"[12]

Apelles, the painter, seeing one of his pupils painting a figure loaded with gold color to represent Helen, said to him, "Boy, being incapable of painting her beautiful, you have made her rich." Such Helens are the ladies of the present day, not truly beautiful but richly got up. To these the Spirit prophesies by Zephaniah: "And their silver and their gold shall not be able to deliver them in the Day of the Lord's anger." But for those women who have been trained under Christ, it is suitable to adorn themselves not with gold but with the Word, through whom alone the gold comes to light. CHRIST THE EDUCATOR 2.13.[13]

---

[12]Lk 12:19-20. [13]ANF 2:269.

2:1-15 PUNISHMENT OF THE PROUD

[1]*Come together and hold assembly,*
    O shameless nation,
[2]*before you are driven away*
    like the drifting chaff,[c]*
before there comes upon you
    the fierce anger of the LORD,
before there comes upon you
    the day of the wrath of the LORD.
[3]*Seek the LORD,[†] all you humble of the land,*
    who do his commands;
seek righteousness, seek humility;
    perhaps you may be hidden
    on the day of the wrath of the LORD.
[4]*For Gaza shall be deserted,*
    and Ashkelon shall become a desolation;
Ashdod's people shall be driven out at noon,
    and Ekron shall be uprooted.
[5]*Woe to you inhabitants of the seacoast,*

you nation of the Cherethites!
The word of the LORD is against you,
    O Canaan, land of the Philistines;
    and I will destroy you till no inhabitant
        is left.
[6]*And you, O seacoast, shall be pastures,*
    meadows for shepherds
    and folds for flocks.
[7]*The seacoast shall become the possession*
    of the remnant of the house of Judah,
    on which they shall pasture,
and in the houses of Ashkelon
    they shall lie down at evening.
For the LORD their God will be mindful of
        them
    and restore their fortunes.[‡]

[8]*"I have heard the taunts of Moab*

and the revilings of the Ammonites,
how they have taunted my people
and made boasts against their territory.
⁹Therefore, as I live," says the LORD of
hosts,
the God of Israel,
"Moab shall become like Sodom,
and the Ammonites like Gomorrah,
a land possessed by nettles§ and salt pits,
and a waste for ever.
The remnant of my people shall plunder
them,
and the survivors of my nation shall
possess them."
¹⁰This shall be their lot in return for their
pride,
because they scoffed and boasted
against the people of the LORD of hosts.
¹¹The LORD will be terrible against them;
yea, he will famish all the gods of the
earth,
and to him shall bow down,
each in its place,
all the lands of the nations.#

¹²You also, O Ethiopians,
shall be slain by my sword.

¹³And he will stretch out his hand against
the north,
and destroy Assyria;
and he will make Nineveh a desolation,
a dry waste like the desert.
¹⁴Herds shall lie down in the midst of
her,
all the beasts of the field;d
the vulturee and the hedgehog
shall lodge in her capitals;
the owlf shall hoot in the window,
the ravengꞬ croak on the threshold;
for her cedar work will be laid bare.
¹⁵This is the exultant city
that dwelt secure,
that said to herself,
"I am and there is none else."**
What a desolation she has become,
a lair for wild beasts!
Every one who passes by her
hisses and shakes his fist.

c Cn Compare Gk Syr: Heb *before a decree is born; like chaff a day has passed away*   d Tg Compare Gk: Heb *nation*   e The meaning of the Hebrew word is uncertain   f Cn: Heb *a voice*   g Gk Vg: Heb *desolation*   *LXX *Be gathered and closely tied together, undisciplined nation, before you become like the flower that passes away.*   †LXX adds *in order that*   ‡LXX *he shall turn away their captivity*   §LXX *and Damascus shall be left as a heap on the threshing floor*   # Vulgate *the islands of the Gentiles*   **LXX *I am, and there is no other with me*

OVERVIEW: The prophet's words about being reunited to God before passing away and perishing are applicable to the unity that is desirable between Christ and the church (CYRIL OF ALEXANDRIA). The scarcity of obedience to parents, lack of chastity, and fallen ascetics, mothers and widows are the result of the lack of genuine mortification (PACHOMIUS). Jeremiah and Zephaniah confirm that the Gentiles—symbolized by the islands—were chosen to come to God through faith in Christ (AUGUSTINE). Although their islands face great storms (persecution), they do not sink, since they have Christ as their foundation (JEROME). The casting out of the gods of the Gentiles by Christ and their coming to the true faith was kept secret by false seers and diviners (AUGUSTINE). Although the Jews rebuilt the temple after the Babylonian captivity, the new covenant made it necessary for it to be destroyed once and for all in order to introduce the worship of the new covenant (CHRYSOSTOM). Worldly habits and behavior are compared with acting like crows and vultures (HORSIESI).

2:1-2 Assemble Together

DIVINITY OF CHRIST DEFENDED. CYRIL OF
ALEXANDRIA: One of the prophets rightly spoke
of this relation to those who had fallen into negligence: "Be gathered again and tied back together,
you undisciplined nation, before you become like
the flower that passes away." A disciple can also
be said to "attach" himself to a teacher in terms of
a love of study, and we too can attach ourselves to
one another not in one fashion only but in many.
In short, when someone assists another in a task,
should we not consider that he has been con-
joined by will to the one who receives his assistance? It seems to us that this is exactly what
these innovators mean by conjunction. You must
have heard how they stupidly maintain that God
the Word assumed a man, as if he were a different
Son to himself, and then proposed him as a kind
of assistant to his designs so that he underwent
the trial and death, came to life again, rose up to
heaven, and even sat upon the throne of the ineffable Godhead? With arguments such as these
have they not completely and utterly proven that
this man is altogether different from the true and
natural son? ON THE UNITY OF CHRIST.[1]

WARNINGS ABOUT LACK OF ASCETICISM.
PACHOMIUS: Struggle, my beloved, for the time is
near and the days have been shortened. There is
no father who instructs his children, there is no
child who obeys his father; good virgins are no
longer; the holy fathers have died on all sides; the
mothers and the widows are no longer, and we
have become like orphans; the humble are
crushed underfoot; and blows are showered upon
the head of the poor. Therefore there is little to
hold back the wrath of God from grieving us,
with no one to console us. All this has befallen us
because we have not practiced mortification.
INSTRUCTIONS 49.[2]

2:11 All the Lands

ISLANDS ARE GENTILES. AUGUSTINE: And nei-

ther will you believe that it was foretold that these
nations would come to some place of God, as it has
been said, "To you the Gentiles shall come from
the ends of the earth."[3] Understand, if you can,
that it is to the God of the Christians, who is supreme and the true God, that the people of these
nations come, not by walking but by believing. For
this same announcement has been made in these
words by another prophet: "The Lord shall be terrible upon them and shall consume all the gods of
the earth, and they shall adore him every man from
his place, all the islands of the Gentiles." One says,
"To you the Gentiles shall come from the ends of
the earth"; the other, "They shall adore him every
man from his own place." Therefore they will not
be required to withdraw from their own place in
coming to him, because they will find him in
whom they believe in their own hearts. ON FAITH
IN THINGS UNSEEN 4.[4]

ISLANDS ARE A TYPE OF THE GENTILES.
JEROME: Let us, however, speak also of the
churches as islands. Moreover, Scripture says in
another place, "Many islands are converted to
me."[5] Would you know that churches are called
islands? The prophet Isaiah says in the name of
the Lord, "Speak to the inhabitants of this isle."[6]
"Let the many isles be glad." Even as islands have
been set in the midst of the sea, churches have
been established in the midst of this world, and
they are beaten and buffeted by different waves of
persecution. Truly these islands are lashed by
waves every day, but they are not submerged.
They are in the midst of the sea, to be sure, but
they have Christ as their foundation, Christ who
cannot be moved. HOMILIES ON THE PSALMS 24.[7]

DEMONS DEFEATED BY TRUTH. AUGUSTINE:
For a long time ... the demons kept silent in their
own temples concerning the things that would
come to pass, although because of the utterances
of the prophets they could not have been unaware

[1]OUC 74. [2]CS 47:36. [3]Jer 16:19. [4]FC 4:463. [5]Is 42:10. [6]Is 20:6.
[7]FC 48:192.

of them. When, later, the events began to draw near, they wished, as it were, to foretell them, so that they might not be deemed ignorant and vanquished. Nevertheless, not to mention other instances for the present, long ago there had been foretold and recorded that which the prophet Zephaniah says: "The Lord shall prevail against them and shall cast out all the gods of the Gentiles of the earth. And they shall adore him every man from his own place, all the islands of the Gentiles." Possibly those gods who were worshiped in the temples of the Gentiles did not believe that those events would occur to them and consequently did not wish them to be noised abroad through their own seers and diviners. ON THE DIVINATION OF DEMONS 7.[8]

THE TEMPLE GONE. CHRYSOSTOM: Despite all this, they still could not raise up a temple and restore the place in which they would be allowed to observe all these rituals according to the law. For the power of Christ, the power which founded the church, has also destroyed that place. The prophet foretold that Christ would come and that he would do these things, even though he would not come until after the captivity. DEMONSTRA-

TIONS AGAINST THE PAGANS 17.5.[9]

2:15 What a Desolation She Has Become

EVERYONE WHO PASSES BY HER HISSES. HORSIESI: Some from the circle of your friendship go out with a made-up face; they wear a bandeau around their face; they put this black thing over their eyes under pretext of illness; they have numberless rings attached to their handkerchief, and on their belt, fringes that flap behind them, like calves frisking about in an enclosure. Often they bathe quite naked without necessity; they wear soft shoes on their feet—"she went out taking pride in the desires of her soul"[10]—they mince along in the assembly; they accost their friend with a boisterous laugh, like the noise of thorny twigs cracking under a cooking pot. They build themselves alcoves; they adopt customs of the crows and vultures of the world, making themselves comparable to them in their food: dead meat and rotted venison. INSTRUCTIONS 7.10.[11]

---

[8]FC 27:433-34. [9]FC 73:259. [10]Jer 2:24 LXX. [11]CS 47:149.

3:1-20 GOD'S PUNISHMENT FOLLOWED BY MERCY

[1]Woe to her that is rebellious* and defiled,
  the oppressing city!
[2]She listens to no voice,
  she accepts no correction.
She does not trust in the LORD,
  she does not draw near to her God.

[3]Her officials within her
  are roaring lions;

her judges are evening wolves
  that leave nothing till the morning.
[4]Her prophets are wanton,
  faithless men;
her priests profane what is sacred,
  they do violence to the law.
[5]The LORD within her is righteous,
  he does no wrong;
every morning he shows forth his justice,

each dawn he does not fail;
   but the unjust knows no shame.
⁶"I have cut off nations;
   their battlements are in ruins;
I have laid waste their streets
   so that none walks in them;
their cities have been made desolate,
   without a man, without an inhabitant.
⁷I said, 'Surely she will fear me,
   she will accept correction;
she will not lose sight^b
   of all that I have enjoined upon her.'
But all the more they were eager
   to make all their deeds corrupt."

⁸"Therefore wait for me," says the LORD,
   "for the day when I arise as a witness.
For my decision is to gather nations,
   to assemble kingdoms,
to pour out upon them my indignation,
   all the heat of my anger;
for in the fire of my jealous wrath
   all the earth shall be consumed.

⁹"Yea, at that time I will change the speech
   of the peoples
   to a pure speech,
that all of them may call on the name of the
   LORD
   and serve him with one accord.†
¹⁰From beyond the rivers of Ethiopia
   my suppliants, the daughter of my
     dispersed ones,‡
   shall bring my offering.
¹¹"On that day you shall not be put to shame
   because of the deeds by which you have
     rebelled against me;
for then I will remove from your midst
   your proudly exultant ones,

and you shall no longer be haughty
   in my holy mountain.
¹²For I will leave in the midst of you
   a people humble and lowly.
They shall seek refuge in the name of the
   LORD,
   ¹³those who are left in Israel;
they shall do no wrong
   and utter no lies,
nor shall there be found in their mouth
   a deceitful tongue.
For they shall pasture and lie down,
   and none shall make them afraid."

¹⁴Sing aloud, O daughter of Zion;
   shout, O Israel!
Rejoice and exult with all your heart,
   O daughter of Jerusalem!
¹⁵The LORD has taken away the judgments
   against you,
   he has cast out your enemies.
The King of Israel, the LORD, is in your
   midst;
   you shall fear evil no more.
¹⁶On that day it shall be said to Jerusalem:
"Do not fear, O Zion;
   let not your hands grow weak.
¹⁷The LORD your God is in your midst,
   a warrior who gives victory;
he will rejoice over you with gladness,
   he will renew you^{i§} in his love;
he will exult over you with loud singing
   ¹⁸as on a day of festival.^{j}
"I will remove disaster^k from you,
   so that you will not bear reproach for it.
¹⁹Behold, at that time I will deal
   with all your oppressors.
And I will save the lame
   and gather the outcast,

and I will change their shame into praise
and renown in all the earth.
²⁰At that time I will bring you home,
at the time when I gather you together;

yea, I will make you renowned and praised
among all the peoples of the earth,
when I restore your fortunes
before your eyes," says the Lord.

h Gk Syr: Heb *and her dwelling will not be cut off*   i Gk Syr: Heb *he will be silent*   j Gk Syr: Heb obscure   k Cn: Heb *they were*   *LXX *glorious and ransomed*   †LXX *yoke,*
Vulgate *shoulder*   ‡Not in LXX   §LXX *and he shall renew you*

Overview: In spite of seeming repentance, Jerusalem remained wicked. Hence Zephaniah is sent to proclaim its annihilation (Theodore). He predicted clearly that spiritual sacrifices would be offered to God the Father and the Son (Fulgentius). The wild hearts are the wild people represented by the Gentiles who would come to worship the true God. The new worship would not be confined to Jerusalem but to wherever one lived (Chrysostom). Worship under the New Testament can now take place anywhere, not just in Jerusalem. The arm and the shoulder refer to the church universal. All should worship in accord with "one shoulder" (Gregory the Great). The reference to the Ethiopian offering sacrifice to God foretold the entry of the Gentiles to the new covenant (Origen). As Redeemer and King of Jerusalem, the Lord grants it peace and joy (Theodore). The new covenant has fulfilled the promise of the washing away of guilt and of judgment for sins committed (Cyril of Jerusalem). Jerusalem shall rejoice even as the church, which knows salvation in Christ (Cyril of Alexandria). The prophecy about redemption was fulfilled in the return from Babylon. However, in a more profound sense, the prophecy concerning restoration was completed through the salvation that is in Christ. Hence the prophecy about deliverance from the captivity of error also applies to the Christians (Theodoret).

3:1-2 The Oppressing City

Jerusalem's Deceitful Repentance. Theodore of Mopsuestia: [Jerusalem] was like this for refusing to the end to hear the word of the prophet sent to it and not accepting in any way

the instruction from that source. Though seeming to undergo a change for a while, once more it went back to its characteristic wickedness; at any rate, it took no account of God's sending the prophet, nor did it make the decision to pay attention to him later, despite having such a remarkable experience. On the contrary, it forsook him completely and declared war on him, attacking Jerusalem after the annihilation of the ten tribes, the city in which the temple of God was to be found. Commentary on Zephaniah 3.1-2.[1]

3:8 "Wait for Me"

Spiritual Sacrifices Foretold. Fulgentius of Ruspe: Nevertheless, lest under the cover of abundance anyone think that we are concealing a lack of defense, we shall bring forward one testimony from the prophets, by which it can clearly be shown that they are holy prophets, divinely inspired. They predicted with a certain and most faithful prophecy that in the time of New Testament, spiritual sacrifices were to be offered not to the Father only but also to the Son by the faithful. For Zephaniah says, "'Therefore wait for me,' says the Lord, 'for the day when I arise as a witness. For my decision is to gather nations, to assemble kingdoms, to pour out on them my indignation, all the heat of my anger; for in the fire of my passion, all the earth shall be consumed. At the time I will change the speech of the peoples to a pure speech, that all of them may call on the name of the Lord and serve him with one accord. From beyond the rivers of Ethiopia, my suppli-

---

[1]PG 66:465.

ants, my scattered ones, shall bring my offering.'" To MONIMUS 2.5.1.[2]

3:9-10 Serving God with One Accord

ALL NATIONS TO WORSHIP. CHRYSOSTOM: Since this text[3] did not literally refer to wild beasts, let the Jews say when this actually happened. For a wolf has never pastured a lamb. If it were to happen that they would pasture together, how would this benefit the human race? The text referred not to wild beasts but to wild people. It referred to Scythians, to Thracians, to Mauretanians, to Indians, to Sarmatians, to Persians. Another prophet made it clear that all these nations would be brought under one yoke when he said, "And they shall serve him under one yoke, and each one shall adore him from his own place."[4] No longer, he said, will people worship him in Jerusalem but everywhere throughout the world. No longer are people bidden to go up to Jerusalem, but each one shall remain in his own home and offer this worship. DEMONSTRATION AGAINST THE PAGANS 6.9.[5]

WORSHIP NOT CONFINED TO JERUSALEM. CHRYSOSTOM: Another prophet again made clear the way God would be worshiped. "They shall each adore him in his own place and serve him under one yoke."[6] And again another prophet said, "The virgin of Israel had fallen. Never more shall she rise."[7] And Daniel explained clearly that everything would be destroyed—the sacrifice, the libation, the anointing, the judgment.[8] DEMONSTRATION AGAINST THE PAGANS 17.7.[9]

METAPHOR OF THE UNIVERSAL CHURCH. GREGORY THE GREAT: "Then let my shoulder fall from its joining and my arm be broken in pieces ailing the bones."[10] Because bodily action is carried on by the shoulder and the arm, when the good things put forth with the lips are not fulfilled in deed, he wants "the shoulder to fall" and "the arm to be broken in pieces."... But if this sentence of a curse is to be referred to a spiritual meaning, it is

no doubt plain that the arm is linked to the body by the shoulders and, as by the arm is meant good practice, so by the shoulder, the knitting together of social life is denoted. So the prophet, regarding the holy peoples of the church universal and that they should serve God in concord, says, "And they shall serve him with one shoulder." MORALS ON THE BOOK OF JOB 4.21.33.[11]

ALL WILL SERVE GOD. ORIGEN: If anyone is able, insofar as he found that Israel is saved "after the full number of pagan nations,"[12] let him consider having passed over by reason the remaining period, when it is that "all serve God under a single yoke," according to what is said in Zephaniah, "And from the ends of Ethiopia they offer sacrifices to him," when, as it is said in the sixty-seventh psalm, "Ethiopia stretches forth its hand to God," and "to the kings of the earth" the word commands, saying, "Sing to the Lord, raise a psalm to the God of Jacob."[13] HOMILIES ON JEREMIAH 5.4.3.[14]

3:14-15 Rejoice, O Daughter of Zion

THE JOY OF THE LORD'S REDEMPTION. THEODORE OF MOPSUESTIA: Live now in utter delight, O Jerusalem, living in complete happiness and satisfaction; for God has removed all your lawless deeds and of necessity has rescued you from the power of the foe, to whom you were subjected in paying the penalty of punishment. The Lord will now be in your midst, showing his kingship by his care for you, so that trouble will no longer be able to approach you. COMMENTARY ON ZEPHANIAH 3.11-15.[15]

NEW TESTAMENT CLEANSING FORETOLD. CYRIL OF JERUSALEM: Take heart, O Jerusalem, the Lord will take away your iniquities. The Lord

---

[2]FC 95:239. [3]Is 11:6. [4]A conflation of Zeph 3:9 with Zeph 2:11. [5]FC 73:214. [6]Zeph 3:9 conflated with Zeph 2:11. [7]Amos 5:2. [8]Dan 9:25-27. [9]FC 73:259-60. [10]Job 31:22. [11]LF 21:541-42*. [12]Rom 11:25. [13]Ps 68:31-32 (67:32-33 LXX). [14]FC 97:46. [15]PG 66:472.

will wash away the filth of his sons and daughters by the spirit of judgment and the spirit of burning.[16] He will pour upon you clean water, and you shall be cleansed from all your sins.[17] Choiring angels shall encircle you, chanting, "Who is it that comes up all white and leaning upon her beloved?"[18] For the soul that was formerly a slave has now accounted its Lord as its kinsman, and he, acknowledging its sincere purpose, will answer, "Ah, you are beautiful, my beloved, ah, you are beautiful . . . your teeth are like a flock of ewes to be shorn"—a sincere confession is a spiritual shearing. And further: "all of them big with twins,"[19] signifying the twofold grace, either that perfected by water and the Spirit or that announced in the Old and in the New Testament. God grant that all of you, your course of fasting finished, mindful of the teaching, fruitful in good works, standing blameless before the spiritual bridegroom, may obtain the remission of your sins from God, in Christ Jesus our Lord, to whom be the glory forever and ever. Amen. CATECHETICAL LECTURE 3.16.[20]

REJOICE IN SALVATION THROUGH CHRIST.
CYRIL OF ALEXANDRIA: As far as the deeper meaning of the passage is concerned, it clearly commands Jerusalem to rejoice exceedingly, to be especially glad, to cheer up wholeheartedly as its trespasses are wiped out, evidently through Christ. The spiritual and holy Zion—that is, the church, the holy multitude of the believers—is justified in Christ and only in him. By him and through him we are also saved as we escape from the harm of the invisible enemies, for we have a Mediator who was incarnated in our form, the king of all, that is, the Word of God the Father. Thanks to him, we do not see evil anymore, for we have been delivered from the powers of evil. He [the Word] is the armor of good will, the peace, the wall, the one who bestows incorruption, the arbiter of the crowns, who shut down the war of the incorporeal Assyrians and made void the schemes of the demons. COMMENTARY ON ZEPHANIAH 43.[21]

3:16-18 Do Not Fear, O Zion

THE PROPHECY ABOUT REDEMPTION. THEODORET OF CYR: I am aware that some commentators understood this [text to apply to] the return from Babylon and the renovation of Jerusalem, and I do not contradict their words: the prophecy applies also to what happened at that time. But you can find a more exact outcome after the incarnation of our Savior: then it was that he healed the oppressed in heart in the washing of regeneration, then it was that he renewed human nature, loving us so much as to give his life for us. After all, "greater love than this no one can show than for one to lay down one's life for one's friend," and again, "God so loved the world as to give his only-begotten Son so that everyone believing in him might not be lost but have eternal life."[22] COMMENTARY ON ZEPHANIAH 3:16-18.[23]

3:19-20 Praised Among the Peoples

THE PROPHECY ABOUT RETURN FROM BABYLON. THEODORET OF CYR: The salvation of human beings rests with divine lovingkindness alone: we do not earn it as the wages of righteousness; rather, it is a gift of divine goodness. Hence the Lord says, "on your behalf I shall save and welcome" and make my own what has become another's, render it conspicuous, make it more famous than all others, free it from its former shame, and from being captives and slaves I shall make them free people and my own. Now, as I have said, this he both made a gift of to those returning from Babylon at that time and also granted to all people later. We who were once in thrall to the devil but are now freed from that harsh captivity and unmindful of the error of polytheism have become God's own, being famous beyond pagans and barbarians, according to the prophecy, and we who were once far off have become near, according to the divine apostle. COMMENTARY ON ZEPHANIAH 3.19-20.[24]

---

[16]Is 4:4. [17]Ezek 36:25. [18]Song 8:5. [19]Song 4:1-2. [20]FC 61:117-18. [21]PG 71:1013-16. [22]Jn 15:13; 3:16. [23]PG 81:1857. [24]PG 81:1860.

HAGGAI

Haggai (Heb *haggay*) may mean "feast," derived from *ḥag*. The book is listed as tenth in the Minor Prophets. Little is known about the prophet, although his name and prophetic office are mentioned in Ezra 5:1. Haggai 1:1-13 contains the exhortation to Zerubbabel and Joshua to finish the completion of the temple begun shortly after 537 B.C. Haggai 2:1-9 promises the glory of the temple. Haggai 2:10-14 is a priestly torah emphasizing the effects of uncleanness and perhaps is directed at the Samaritans as opposed to cleanness. Haggai 2:15-19 promises agricultural fruitfulness and blessings after the completion of the temple. Haggai 2:20-23 is a promise to Zerubbabel that although Yahweh will overturn the nations, he will remain as a signet ring. The messianic dynasty will remain intact through Zerubbabel. The five prophetic oracles are dated from August to December 520 B.C.

Haggai is one of the books among the Minor Prophets that represents the postexilic period. Some of the church fathers focused on the typological meaning of specifically named individuals in Haggai who represented the new covenant. The person of Jehozadak represents Christ's second advent, while Zerubbabel points to Christ and the church. David and Zerubbabel prefigure respectively Elijah and John the Baptist. The signet ring of Zerubbabel reflects the power of Christ the King.

1:1-15 REBUILD THE HOUSE OF THE LORD

^{1}In the second year of Darius the king, in the sixth month, on the first day of the month, the word of the LORD came by* Haggai the prophet to Zerubbabel the son of Shealtiel, governor of Judah, and to Joshua the son of Jehozadak, the high priest, ^{2}"Thus says the LORD of hosts: This people say the time has not yet come to rebuild the house of the LORD." ^{3}Then the word of the LORD came by Haggai the prophet, ^{4}"Is it a time for you yourselves to dwell in your paneled houses, while this house lies in ruins? ^{5}Now therefore thus says the LORD of hosts: Consider how you have fared. ^{6}You have sown much, and harvested little; you eat, but you never have enough; you drink, but you never have your fill; you clothe yourselves, but no one is warm; and he who earns wages earns wages to put them into a bag with holes.

^{7}"Thus says the LORD of hosts: Consider how you have fared. ^{8}Go up to the hills and bring wood† and build the house, that I may take pleasure in it and that I may appear in my glory, says the LORD. ^{9}You have looked for much, and lo,‡ it came to little; and when you brought it home, I blew it away. Why? says the LORD of hosts. Because of my house that lies in ruins, while you busy yourselves each with his own house. ^{10}Therefore the heavens above you have withheld the dew, and the earth has withheld its produce. ^{11}And I have called for a drought§ upon the land and the hills, upon the grain, the new wine, the oil, upon what the ground brings forth, upon men and cattle, and upon all their labors."$^#$

^{12}Then Zerubbabel the son of Shealtiel, and Joshua the son of Jehozadak, the high priest,** with all the remnant of the people, obeyed the voice of the LORD their God, and the words of Haggai the prophet, as the LORD their God had sent him; and the people feared before the LORD. ^{13}Then Haggai, the messenger of the LORD, spoke to the people with the LORD's message, "I am with you, says the LORD." ^{14}And the LORD stirred up the spirit of Zerubbabel the son of Shealtiel, governor of Judah, and the spirit of Joshua the son of Jehozadak, the high priest, and the spirit of all the remnant of the people; and they came and worked on the house of the LORD of hosts, their God, ^{15}on the twenty-fourth day of the month, in the sixth month.

*LXX by the hand of †LXX to strike down ‡LXX and it was §LXX the sword #LXX their hands **LXX adds governor of Judah

OVERVIEW: The Word of God is like a sword that separates truth from false tradition (JEROME). This sword of Christ is double-edged because it contains both Testaments. It separates Jews and Gentiles while it also cuts Christians off from the world, and it now resides in the hands of the saints (CASSIODORUS). Christ overcomes the devil by the good works of those who follow him and not by mere words of mouth. The priestly minis-try is like that of an innkeeper. The priest provides the cup of salvation for thirsty people (JEROME). Lapsed priests, however, follow their own house when they violate their duties from worldliness. The water and wine they mingle is vile and cold (MAXIMUS OF TURIN). Those with monetary abundance are enjoined to keep track not just how much they give but also how much they take in and how. To neglect this is to put one's wealth into a bag of holes (Gregory the Great). Riches out of control are the citadels of evil, and those who covet them run the danger of being excluded from the kingdom (Clement of Alexandria). The temple that Haggai spoke of was not in Jerusalem but the spiritual temple of believers that the Holy Spirit inhabits (Augustine). One speaking the truth without any accompanying works is dead already, even though seemingly alive. This is the manner in which one builds the house of God (Ambrose). The Lord threatens Israel with drought to encourage rebuilding of the temple (Theodore). The Lord does not need the temple; rather, it was the people of the old covenant who needed restoration of the temple (Theodoret). Angels are sometimes called "man" not because of their nature but because of their earthly appearances according to divine providence (Origen).

1:1 The Lord's Word by Haggai

Cutting Through False Tradition.
Jerome: The sword of God, which is the living Word of God, strikes through the things that people of their own accord, without the authority and testimonies of Scripture, invent and think up, pretending that it is apostolic tradition. Commentary on Haggai 1.11.[1]

The Sword of the Spirit Explained. Cassiodorus: "The rejoicings of the Lord are in their throats, and two-edged swords in their hands to execute vengeance upon the nations, chastisements among the people."[2] We must observe how beautiful, how useful these differing expressions are. Earlier he said that the saints rejoice in their beds; now he says that the Lord's rejoicings are set in their throats, the sense being that they never cease to praise, whether in thought or in tongue, him from whom they obtain eternal gifts. He also moves on to explain the power that they wield, with the words "and two-edged swords in their hands." The two-edged sword is the word of the Lord Savior, of which

Christ himself says in the Gospel: "I have come not to send peace to the earth but a sword."[3] It is a two-edged sword because it contains two Testaments. First it separated Jews from Gentiles; subsequently it segregated and cut off Christians from the enticements of the whole world. There is one sword but two ways of cutting that he grants to the chosen peoples at various selected moments of time. So the prophet says that these swords are in their hands, in other words, in the power of the saints, as Scripture has it: "The word of the Lord came to the hand of Haggai the prophet." So the blessed ones will assume this power and pass judgment in company with the Lord. As Scripture says, "You shall sit on twelve seats, judging the twelve tribes of Israel."[4] For note what follows: "To execute vengeance upon the nations, chastisements among the people."[5] This truly takes place when they shall judge in company with the Lord. Exposition of the Psalms 146.6-7.[6]

Good Works Make Christ Present.
Jerome: While you are reflecting upon this thought, meditate upon the mystery that is hidden within it. If we lift up our hands, Jesus triumphs. If we lift up our hands in good works, through our good works, Christ overcomes the devil. Hands, moreover, connote good works, whereupon it is written: "The word of the Lord came by the hand of Haggai"; "the word that came by the hand of Jeremiah the prophet."[7] To be sure, the word of the Lord does not come by the hand but by the mouth, but grasp the mysticism of the Scripture. God does not come because of words but because of good works. Homilies on the Psalms 46.[8]

1:6 Drinking Without Being Filled

Lapsed Priests Condemned. Maximus of Turin: Thus the priestly ministry is a trade.

---

[1]CCL 76A:725. [2]Ps 149:6-7. [3]Mt 10:34. [4]Mt 19:28. [5]Ps 149:7. [6]ACW 53:460*. [7]Hag 1:3 Vg; Jer 37:2, 50:1 Vul. [8]FC 48:345-46.

Hence the prophet says to the children of Israel, "Your innkeepers mix water with their wine."[9] For holy Isaiah is not speaking about the innkeepers who, in the course of their publican ministrations, deceptively mix pure wine with a measure of water. It could hardly be a matter of concern to the blessed man, as if he were a civil judge, that people would dilute tavern vessels to make a less inebriating drink. He is speaking rather about the innkeepers who reside not over taverns but churches. They offer thirsty people a goblet not of wanton desire but of virtue. They do not minister the cup of drunkenness but the Savior's cup. Those innkeepers he censures and rebukes, and he complains that they mix water with wine. This he blames in them—that although they are set over divine functions, they have become followers after human things, as the prophet himself says: "Each of you follows his own house." For if any priest has abandoned the priestly office and delights in worldly pleasures, he mixes water with wine; that is to say, he mingles vile and cold things with holy and warm things. SERMON 28.2.[10]

GENEROSITY ENCOURAGED. GREGORY THE GREAT: And yet, for the most part, such people carefully weigh what is the amount that they give but neglect to consider how much they seize. They count it as a sort of requital but refuse to consider their sins. Let them, therefore, hear what is written: "He that has earned wages put them into a bag with holes." When a bag has holes, the money is indeed seen when it is put in, but it is not seen when it is being lost. They, then, who keep an eye on how much they give, but not on how much they steal, put their wages into a bag with holes because, while piling up [riches], they look to them in the hope that they will be secure but lose them when they are not looking. PASTORAL CARE 3.21.[11]

HOARDING WEALTH CONDEMNED. CLEMENT OF ALEXANDRIA: Generally speaking, riches that are not under complete control are the citadels of evil. If the ordinary people look on them covet-

ously, they will never enter the kingdom of heaven,[12] because they are letting themselves become contaminated by the things of this world and are living above themselves in self-indulgence. Those concerned for their salvation should take this as their first principle, that, although the whole of creation is ours to use, the universe is made for the sake of self-sufficiency, which anyone can acquire by a few things. They who rejoice in the holdings in their storehouses are foolish in their greed. "He that earned wages," Scripture reminds us, "put them into a bag with holes." Such is the man who gathers and stores up his harvest,[13] for by not sharing his wealth with anyone he becomes worse off. CHRIST THE EDUCATOR 2.3.[14]

1:8 Building God's House

A NEW TEMPLE FORETOLD. AUGUSTINE: I believe, brothers, that you remarked and committed to memory the title of this psalm.[15] "The conversion," he said, "of Haggai and Zechariah."[16] These prophets were not as yet in existence when these verses were sung. . . . But both, the one within the year after the other, began to prophesy that which seemed to pertain to the restoration of the temple, as was foretold so long before.[17] . . . "For the temple of God is holy, which temple you are."[18] Whoever therefore converted himself to the work of this building together, and to the hope of a firm and holy edifice, like a living stone from the miserable ruin of this world, understands the title of the psalm, understands "the conversion of Haggai and Zechariah." Let him therefore chant the following verses, not so much with the voice of his tongue as of his life. For the completion of the building will be that ineffable peace of wisdom, the "beginning" of which is the "fear of the Lord."[19] Let him therefore, whom this conversion builds together, begin there. EXPLA-

---

[9]Is 1:22 LXX. [10]ACW 50:68*. [11]ACW 11:162. [12]Mt 19:23. [13]Lk 12:16-21. [14]FC 23:128. [15]Ps 112 (111 Vg.). [16]Title in the Vulgate. [17]Ezra 1:5; Zech 1:16. [18]1 Cor 3:17. [19]Ps 111:10 (110:10 LXX).

NATION OF THE PSALMS 112.1.[20]

LACK OF GOOD WORKS. AMBROSE: The man who dies before his time does not build his tomb, for, although he lives, he is dead.[21] He does not hear the words of Haggai, whose name interpreted the banqueter, for he does not enter the tabernacle of God "with the voice of joy and praise, the noise of one feasting."[22] How does he hear his voice if he does not see his works? If he saw them, he would hear the word which was put within his grasp, he would rejoice in his acts, whereby "he knocked and it was opened to him,"[23] and he would have gone down into his soul that he might feed therein upon the food of sincerity and truth. Because he failed to hear, the word of Haggai again comes, saying: Rise from houses embossed and carved with wickedness, and go up to the mount of heavenly Scriptures and hew the tree of wisdom, the tree of life and the tree of knowledge. Make straight your ways, order your actions so that they may have due order which is necessary and useful for building the house of God.[24] LETTER 80.[25]

1:9-11 God's House in Ruins

DIVINE THREAT AS ENCOURAGEMENT. THEODORE OF MOPSUESTIA: He intends by this to remind them of what they have suffered by neglecting the temple. When you overlooked my house lying in ruins and took an interest in rebuilding your own houses, he is saying, then the rain stopped, the land did not yield its crops, and I destroyed all the crops on the ground as though with a sword, striking many times both people and cattle, and in short ruining the fruit of your labors. In fact, to this exhortation to climb up, cut wood, bring it and give thought to rebuilding, he added these things to cause them fear by the reminder of what had happened lest they receive the command listlessly. COMMEN-

TARY ON HAGGAI 1.9-11.[26]

RESTORATION OF THE TEMPLE. THEODORET OF CYR: Now the God of all made these threats on account of the neglect of the divine house, though not for any need of it: the Maker of all things has no need even of heaven, creating everything out of lovingkindness alone. Rather, it was in his care for them all and his interest in their salvation that he ordered the rebuilding of the temple so that they might observe the law in it and reap the benefit, wanting as he did worship according to the law to be performed until the coming of the heir, according to the divine apostle. After the incarnation of our Savior, you see, when the new covenant was revealed, the old came to an end, and the law, which as a tutor had given us a glimpse of the teacher of great wisdom, yielded pride of place, since those tutored by it had no further need of the basic elements.[27] COMMENTARY ON HAGGAI 1.9-13.[28]

1:13 The Lord with Them

WITH YOU AS AN ANGEL. ORIGEN: In the whole sequence of Scripture, at any one time they are said to be men and at another time angels. But the one who thinks this will say that just as there are angels among those who are admittedly men, as Zechariah, who says, "I am with you as an angel of God, says the Lord almighty," and John, of whom it has been written, "Behold, I send my angel before your face,"[29] so also the angels of God, when they are called "men," are called this because of their work and not because of their nature. COMMENTARY ON THE GOSPEL OF JOHN 2.144-45.[30]

---

[20]NPNF 1 8:546-47*. [21]1 Tim 5:6. [22]Ps 42:4 (41:5 LXX). [23]Mt 7:7. [24]Cf. old Latin. [25]FC 26:450-51*. [26]PG 66:481. [27]See Heb 1:2; Gal 3:24-25. [28]PG 81:1865. [29]Mk 1:2; cf. Mal 3:1. [30]FC 80:133.

1:15 — 2:7 HEAVEN AND EARTH WILL SHAKE

2 [15]*In the second year of Darius the king,* [1]*in the seventh month, on the twenty-first day of the month, the word of the LORD came by Haggai the prophet,* [2]*"Speak now to Zerubbabel the son of Shealtiel, governor of Judah, and to Joshua the son of Jehozadak, the high priest, and to all the remnant of the people, and say,* [3]*'Who is left among you that saw this house in its former glory? How do you see it now? Is it not in your sight as nothing?* [4]*Yet now take courage, O Zerubbabel, says the LORD; take courage, O Joshua, son of Jehozadak, the high priest; take courage, all you people of the land, says the LORD; work, for I am with you, says the LORD of hosts,* [5]*according to the promise that I made you when you came out of Egypt. My Spirit abides among you; fear not.* * [6]*For thus says the LORD of hosts: Once again, in a little while,* † *I will shake the heavens and the earth and the sea and the dry land;* [7]*and I will shake all nations, so that the treasures of all nations shall come in, and I will fill this house with splendor, says the LORD of hosts.*

*LXX *have courage*   †LXX *a little time is it*

OVERVIEW: The prophets anticipated that Christ and the church would be compared to a new Jerusalem building a new temple of God (EUSEBIUS OF CAESAREA). Jesus' second advent garments demonstrate his glory and honor. The son of Jehozadak may be an adumbration of Jesus, yet the former was never clad in other than priestly garments (TERTULLIAN). The abiding presence of the Holy Spirit was confirmed by the prophets, including Haggai (CYRIL OF JERUSALEM). The presence of God's Spirit in Israel signifies divine mercy's favor (THEODORE). The second advent will affect not only the earth but also the entire cosmos, as predicted by Haggai. It will also extend throughout the entire spiritual realm (GREGORY THE GREAT). As there are two covenants, there have also been two shakings of the earth: the first, a transition from idolatry to the law, and the second, from the law to the gospel. A third shaking is also coming: transformation of this present age to a new one (GREGORY OF NAZIANZUS). The earth, which appears immovable in its natural state, is mutable in its spiritual nature according to the free will of God (AMBROSE). The prophet's double prediction has been fulfilled in part by the first advent, and the second awaits the second advent of Christ (AUGUSTINE).

2:2 Speak to Zerubbabel

ZERUBBABEL A TYPE OF CHRIST AND OF THE CHURCH. EUSEBIUS OF CAESAREA: O friends and priests of God, you are clothed with holy robe and heavenly crown of glory, the inspired unction and the priestly raiment of the Holy Spirit. To you, of youthful pride of God's holy temple, honored by God with wisdom that is aged but revealed in choice deeds and works of a flourishing valor that is youthful, God himself, who encompasses the whole world, has given the distinguished honor of building his house on earth and of restoring it for Christ, his only-begotten and his firstborn word, and for his holy and sacred bride.[1] One indeed might wish to call you a new Bezalel,[2] the builder of a divine tabernacle, or a King Solomon,[3] king of a new and far better Jerusalem,[4] or even a new Zerubbabel, who bestowed far greater glory or even a new Zerubbabel on the temple of God. ECCLESIASTICAL HISTORY 10.4.[5]

---

[1]Rev 21:2. [2]Ex 35:30-31. [3]1 Chron 6:32. [4]Rev 21:2. [5]FC 29:244*.

2:4 Take Courage

THE GARMENTS OF THE HIGH PRIEST AND THE GARMENTS OF JESUS. TERTULLIAN: In the next place, he was stripped of his former solid raiment and adorned with a garment down to the foot, and with a turban and a clean miter, that is, [with the garb] of the second advent; since he is demonstrated as having attained "glory and honor." [Since stripped] you will not be able to say that the man [there depicted] is the "son of Jehozadak," who was never clad in a sordid garment but was always adorned with the sacerdotal garment, nor ever deprived of the sacerdotal function. ANSWER TO THE JEWS 14.[6]

TESTIMONY OF THE ENDURING HOLY SPIRIT. CYRIL OF JERUSALEM: Whoever scans all the books of the prophets, both of the twelve and of the others, will find many testimonies regarding the Holy Spirit. Haggai says, "For I am with you, says the Lord of hosts, and my spirit continues in your midst." CATECHETICAL LECTURE 16.29.[7]

2:5 God's Spirit Remains

SPIRIT AS SIGN OF DIVINE GRACE. THEODORE OF MOPSUESTIA: Likewise here too when he says, "My spirit has taken a position in your midst," he means, my grace and my disposition toward you accompanies you, taking a position and providing you with its benefit. In other words, just as he speaks of a soul in reference to God, thus implying not some hypostasis [i.e., separate entity] but his attitude to something—as when he says, "My soul hates your new moons and sabbaths"[8] to refer to the attitude by which he hated what was done by them in their depraved behavior—so too is his mention of the "spirit." COMMENTARY ON HAGGAI 2.1-5.[9]

2:6 Shaking the Heavens and Earth

END TIMES FORETOLD. GREGORY THE GREAT: In truth he comes, who shakes the elements by his coming, in whose sight heaven and earth tremble.

Hence the prophet says, "There is still a little while, and I will move not only the earth but also the sky."[10] He will bring the whole human race to his examination; angels, archangels, thrones, principalities and dominations will obey him, for the punishment of evil and the recompense of the good. Consider, dearly beloved, what terror there will be on that day at the sight of so great a judge. There will be no relief from punishment then. What a shame we will feel in the sight of all human beings and angels because of our own guilt! How we will fear when we see him angry, whom the human mind cannot comprehend even when he is peaceful! FORTY GOSPEL HOMILIES 10.[11]

TWO COVENANTS. GREGORY OF NAZIANZUS: There have been two remarkable transformations of the human way of life in the course of the world's history. These are called two "covenants," and, so famous was the business involved, two "shakings of the earth."[12] The first was the transition from idols to the law;[13] the second, from the law to the gospel.[14] The gospel also tells of the third shaking, the change from this present stage of things to what lies unmoved, unshaken,[15] beyond. An identical feature occurs in both covenants. The feature? There was nothing sudden involved in the first movement to take their transformation in hand. ON THE HOLY SPIRIT, THEOLOGICAL ORATION 5(31)25.[16]

2:7 Shaking All Nations

THE EARTH IMMUTABLE AND MUTABLE. AMBROSE: How the disposition of the earth therefore depends upon the power of God, you may learn also where it is written: "He looks upon the earth and makes it tremble,"[17] and elsewhere: "once again I move the earth." Therefore the earth remains immovable not by its balances, but it is

---

[6]ANF 3:172-73. [7]FC 64:93. [8]Is 1:14. [9]PG 66:485. [10]Heb 12:26. [11]CS 123:72. [12]Heb 12:26; Mt 27:51. [13]Ex 20:3-5. [14]Gal 2:14; Heb 9:3-15. [15]Heb 12:28. [16]FGFR 292-93; NPNF 2 7:325. [17]Ps 104:32 (103:32 LXX).

moved frequently by the nod and free will of God, as Job too says: "The Lord shakes it from its foundations, and its pillars tremble."[18] And elsewhere: "Hell is naked before him, and there is not covering for death. He stretches out the north over the empty space and hangs the earth upon nothing. He binds up the waters in his clouds. The pillars of heaven that fled away are in dread at his rebuke. By his power the seas are calmed, by his wisdom is struck down the sea monster, and the gates of heaven fear him."[19] By the will of God, therefore, the earth remains immovable. "The earth stands forever," according to Ecclesiastes,[20] yet it is moved by nods according to the will of God. It does not therefore continue to exist because it is based on its own foundations. It does not stay stable because of its own props. The Lord established it by the support of his will, because "in his hand are all the ends of the earth."[21] The simplicity of this faith is worth all the proffered proofs. Six Days of Creation 1.6.22.[22]

Two Advents Foretold by Haggai.
Augustine: There remain for discussion the three minor prophets who belong to the closing days of the captivity, namely, Haggai, Zechariah and Malachi. To begin with, Haggai has the following brief but clear prophecy of Christ and the church: "For thus says the Lord of hosts: yet one little while, and I will move the heaven and the earth, and the sea and the dry land. And I will move all the nations, and the desired of all nations shall come." It is obvious that this prediction is, in part, already fulfilled; the rest we may confidently expect at the end of the world. Surely God set the heavens rocking when angels and a star stood as witnesses to the birth of Christ; surely too he moved the earth when he performed the tremendous miracle of giving Christ a virgin birth. Surely he moved the sea and the dry land when he made Christ's name known throughout the whole world, on island and on mainland. For the rest, we ourselves are witnesses of the fact that all nations are being moved to accept the faith. The last part of the text, "and the desired of all nations shall come," refers to Christ's second coming. For before the whole world can await him and desire his coming, it just first believes in him and loves him. City of God 18.35.[23]

---

[18]Job 9:6. [19]Job 9:6; 26:6-11. [20]Eccles 1:4. [21]Ps 95:4 (94:4 LXX). [22]FC 42:22. [23]FC 24:138.

2:8-23 GOD'S BLESSING FOR THE RESTORATION OF THE TEMPLE

[8]*The silver is mine, and the gold is mine, says the* Lord *of hosts.* [9]*The latter splendor of this house shall be greater than the former, says the* Lord *of hosts; and in this place I will give prosperity,* * *says the* Lord *of hosts.' "*

[10]*On the twenty-fourth day of the ninth month, in the second year of Darius, the word of the* Lord *came by Haggai the prophet,* [11]*"Thus says the* Lord *of hosts: Ask the priests to decide this question,* [12]*'If one carries holy flesh in the skirt of his garment, and touches with his skirt bread, or pottage, or wine, or oil, or any kind of food, does it become holy?' " The priests answered, "No."* [13]*Then said Haggai, "If one who is unclean by contact with a dead body touches any of these, does it become unclean?" The priests answered, "It does become unclean."* [14]*Then*

Haggai said, "So is it with this people, and with this nation before me, says the LORD; and so with every work of their hands; and what they offer there is unclean.† ¹⁵Pray now, consider what will come to pass from this day onward.‡ Before a stone was placed upon a stone in the temple of the LORD, ¹⁶how did you fare?ᵃ When one came to a heap of twenty measures, there were but ten; when one came to the winevat to draw fifty measures, there were but twenty. ¹⁷I smote you and all the products of your toil with blight and mildew and hail; yet you did not return to me, says the LORD. ¹⁸Consider from this day onward, from the twenty-fourth day of the ninth month. Since the day that the foundation of the LORD's temple was laid, consider: ¹⁹Is the seed yet in the barn? Do the vine, the fig tree, the pomegranate, and the olive tree still yield nothing? From this day on I will bless you."

²⁰The word of the LORD came a second time to Haggai on the twenty-fourth day of the month, ²¹"Speak to Zerubbabel, governor of Judah, saying, I am about to shake the heavens and the earth, ²²and to overthrow the throne of kingdoms; I am about to destroy the strength of the kingdoms of the nations, and overthrow the chariots and their riders; and the horses and their riders shall go down, every one by the sword of his fellow. ²³On that day, says the LORD of hosts, I will take you, O Zerubbabel my servant, the son of Shealtiel, says the LORD, and make you like a signet ring; for I have chosen you, says the LORD of hosts."

a Gk: Heb *since they were*   *LXX adds *even peace of soul unto preservation to every one that lays foundations to erect this temple.* Jerome considered the addition to be superfluous.   †LXX *And whosoever shall approach them shall be defiled*   ‡LXXB *above;* LXXA *before;* LXX *from this day backward*

OVERVIEW: Gold and silver in themselves are not evil; rather, it is their misuse. Believers show love of God and neighbor by being generous with gold and silver that in the end belong to God. To blame the thing for evil would necessitate condemning virtually all of creation because of idolatry. One would have to blame the sun because the Manichaeans worship and adore it (AUGUSTINE). Riches do not belong to the devil; they belong to God, who creates them. The abuse of riches is blameworthy, but the guilt lies on the person who misuses them. Money when properly used can be a way of blessing (CYRIL OF JERUSALEM). The restoration of Solomon's temple was a prophetic symbol regarding the second Testament. The place that would receive peace is the church. Therefore the glory of the house of the new is greater than that of the old (AUGUSTINE). Priests lacking education do great harm to themselves and to the church. Priests, as the prophet states, must be able to explain the law to believers (JEROME).

The fruits of God's blessing upon his people far surpass the punishment applied in order to correct them. (THEODORET). Just as David was not the later king but Zerubbabel, so John the Baptist was not literally Elijah in the flesh but only in spirit and power (EPHREM). The prophecy about Zerubbabel mystically referred to Christ as symbolized by the signet ring (AMBROSE).

2:8 Silver and Gold Belong to God

SUN WORSHIP OF MANICHAEANS CONDEMNED. AUGUSTINE: But this is not the fault of gold and silver. Let us suppose that someone of tender heart has found a treasure. The kindness of his heart works, does it not, so that hospitality is shown to strangers, the starving are fed, the naked clothed, the needy assisted, captives redeemed, churches are built, the weary are refreshed, the quarrelsome pacified, the shipwrecked set on their feet again, the sick cured—material resources distributed on earth, spiritual ones stored up in heaven? Who does all this? The good and kindhearted person. What does he do it with? Gold and silver. Whom is he serving when he does it? The one who says, "Mine is the gold and mine is the silver." Now, brothers, I think you can see what a great mistake it is, what lunacy indeed, to project onto the things which people misuse the offense of the people who misuse them. If gold and silver, after all, can be blamed simply because people warped by avarice and neglecting the commands of the Creator are carried away by an abominable kind of lust for these things that he brought into being, then let us blame every single creature of God, because, as the apostle says, some perverse people "worshiped and served the creature rather than the Creator, who is blessed forever."[1] Let us also blame this sun, which these same Manichaeans, as we all know, not understanding that it is a creature, never cease to worship and adore as though it were the Creator—or at least some sort of part of him. SERMON 50.7.[2]

MONEY ITSELF IS NOT EVIL. CYRIL OF JERUSALEM: Riches, gold and silver, are not the devil's as some think, for "the whole world of riches is for the faithful man, but for the unfaithful not a farthing."[3] But nothing is more faithless than the devil. God through the prophet says plainly, "Mine is the silver, and mine is the gold." Only use it well and there is nothing blameworthy in silver; but when you abuse a good thing and are then unwilling to blame your own conduct, you impiously put the blame on the Creator. One can even be blessed by money. "I was hungry, and you gave me to eat"[4]—undoubtedly by the use of money; "I was naked and you covered me"[5]—assuredly by the use of money. Consider too that money can be a door to the heavenly kingdom. "Sell," he says, "what you have, and give to the poor, and you shall have treasure in heaven."[6] CATECHETICAL LECTURE 8.6.[7]

THE TESTAMENTS CONTRASTED. AUGUSTINE: Surely the glory of the house of the New Testament is greater than that of the old because it was built of better materials, namely, those living stones that are human beings renewed by faith and grace. Yet precisely because Solomon's temple was renovated—was made new—it was a prophetic symbol of the second Testament which is called the New. Accordingly we must understand the words God spoke by Haggai's mouth, "And I will give peace in that place," as referring to the place for which the temple stood. Since the restored temple signified the church, which Christ was to build, those words can mean only "I will give peace in that place [the church] which this place [the rebuilt temple] prefigures." (All symbols seem in some way to personify the realities of which they are symbols. So, St. Paul says, "The rock was Christ,"[8] because the rock in question symbolized Christ.) Not, however, until the house of the New Testament receives its final consecration will its greater glory in relation to the house of the Old Testament be made perfectly clear. This will take place at the second coming of him whom the Hebrew text calls "the desire of all nations."[9] Obviously his first coming was not desired of all nations, for unbelievers did not even know whom they should desire to come. In the end too, as the Septuagint puts it with equal amount of prophetic meaning, "the chosen of the Lord shall come from all nations." Then, truly, only the chosen shall come, those of whom St. Paul says, even "as he chose us in him before the foundation of the world."[10] CITY OF GOD 18.48.[11]

2:11 Questioning the Priest

PRIESTS SHOULD BE EDUCATED IN THE FAITH. JEROME: He writes to Timothy, who had been trained in the holy writings from a child, exhorting him to study them diligently[12] and not to neglect the gift that was given him with the laying on of the hands of the presbytery.[13] To Titus

---

[1]Rom 1:25. [2]WSA 3 2:347. [3]Prov 17:6 LXX. [4]Mt 25:35. [5]Mt 25:36. [6]Mt 19:21. [7]FC 61:182-83*. [8]1 Cor 10:4. [9]Hag 2:7. [10]Eph 1:4. [11]FC 24:167-68. [12]2 Tim 3:14-15. [13]1 Tim 4:14.

he gives commandment that among a bishop's other virtues (which he briefly describes) he should be careful to seek a knowledge of the Scriptures: "A bishop," he says, must hold fast "the faithful word as he has been taught that he may be able by sound doctrine both to exhort and to convince the gainsayers."[14] In fact, lack of education in a clergyman prevents him from doing well to anyone but himself, and much as the virtue of his life may build up Christ's church, he does it an injury as great by failing to resist those who are trying to pull it down. The prophet Haggai says—or rather the Lord says it by the mouth of Haggai—"ask now the priests concerning the law." For such is the important function of the priesthood to give answers to those who question them concerning the law. LETTER 53.3.[15]

2:18-20 Blessed from This Day On

ABUNDANCE OF GOD'S BLESSING. THEODORET OF CYR: I was inflicting various forms of correction on you—sterility, wind, blight, hail—but in your insensitivity you were unaware of the correction. Be mindful of this, then, and take note of the great prosperity you will enjoy after the commencement of the rebuilding, such being the abundance of necessities I shall provide you, with the result that in the future even the actual measures will have no use on the threshing floor. I shall also supply you with soft fruits as a blessing and provide the crop of the fruit trees. COMMENTARY ON HAGGAI 2.10-22.[16]

2:23 Zerubbabel, God's Servant

ZERUBBABEL AS A DAVIDIC KING. EPHREM THE SYRIAN: "The Jews sent to John and said to him, 'Who are you?' He confessed and said, 'I am not the Messiah.' They said to him, 'Are you Elijah?' He said, 'No.'"[17] But our Lord called him

Elijah, as Scripture attests.[18] However, when they interrogated him, he said, "I am not Elijah." But Scripture does not say that John came in the body of Elijah but "in the spirit and the power of Elijah."[19] Elijah, who was taken up into the heavens, did not return to them, just as it was not David who later became king but Zerubbabel. The Pharisees, however, did not ask John, "Have you come in the spirit of Elijah?" but "Are you Elijah himself?" That is why he said to them, "No." Why should he have needed to be Elijah himself, if the actions of Elijah were to be found present in John? Elisha intervened and stood between John and Elijah, lest John be judged by them, since Elijah was taken up in a sacred chariot,[20] whereas [John's] head was carried away on a dish by a corrupt young girl.[21] COMMENTARY ON TATIAN'S DIATESSARON 3.10.[22]

ZERUBBABEL A TYPE OF CHRIST. AMBROSE: So it is mystically said to him alone: "I will take you, O Zerubbabel, and I will make you as a signet ring, for I have chosen you." For, when our soul becomes so peaceful that it is said to her, "Return, return, O Sulamitess,"[23] which means "peaceful," or to your own name, "Irenic," then she will receive Christ like a signet ring upon her, for she is the image of God. Then she will be according to that image, because heavenly is the heavenly man.[24] And we need to bear the image of the heavenly one, that is, peace. And that we may know that this is true, you have in the Canticles to the soul, now full perfect, what I wish the Lord Jesus may say to you, "Put me as a seal upon your arm."[25] May peace glow in your heart, Christ in your works, and may there be formed in you wisdom and justice and redemption. LETTER 80.[26]

---

[14]Tit 1:9. [15]NPNF 2 6:97. [16]PG 81:1869. [17]Jn 1:19-21. [18]Mt 11:14; 17:12-13. [19]Lk 1:17. [20]2 Kings 2:11-12. [21]Mt 14:11. [22]ECTD 2:78-79. [23]Song 6:13. [24]1 Cor 15:48. [25]Song 8:6. [26]FC 26:454.

ZECHARIAH

OVERVIEW: Zechariah is the eleventh of the Minor Prophets. The book is arranged into two major parts, Zechariah 1—8 and Zechariah 9—14, of which the first is believed to have been written by Zechariah and the other under a pseudonym. Scholars maintain that Zechariah 9—14 dates from the Greek period after the conquests of Alexander the Great. Therefore reference to Egypt means the Ptolemaic era, and Assyria means the kingdom of the Seleucids. Dating the book falls between 520 and 518 B.C., that is, after the return of the Jews to Jerusalem from Babylon and just before the dedication of the temple in 515. Zechariah is identified as the son of Berechiah in Zechariah 1:1, 7, the son of Iddo mentioned in Ezra 5:1 and Ezra 6:14. Most scholars believe that this is the same Zechariah of the priestly family of Iddo mentioned in Nehemiah 12:16. There is a strong current of messianism in the book, most especially in Zechariah 9—14, which incorporates apocalyptic motifs.

Zechariah is one of the lengthiest books among the Minor Prophets and as such provided the church fathers an abundance of material to work with. It is the book among the Minor Prophets most quoted or alluded to in the New Testament. There are twenty-three allusions to Zechariah in Revelation and twelve in the Gospels, along with many others in the New Testament, including Jude 9. Most scholars point out that the distinctive nature of this messianism is the identification of the Messiah with the poor, which may explain the prominence of this book in the New Testament. Jews and Christians made heavy use of Zechariah to support their respective views of the messianic hope. The church fathers had much to build upon to elaborate their christological messianism. Theodore of Mopsuestia of the Antiochene school approached the book more literally and historically, expounding on those specific New Testament passages that were applied to Christ. Given the high number of such texts in the New Testament, Theodore had much to work with. The majority of the church fathers, however, made liberal use of allegory and typology to take Zechariah to greater christological heights, as the pericopes in this volume demonstrate.

1:1-6 THE LORD'S CALL TO REPENTANCE

¹*In the eighth month, in the second year of Darius, the word of the LORD came to Zechariah the son of Berechiah, son of Iddo, the prophet, saying,* ²*"The LORD was very angry with your fathers.* ³*Therefore say to them, Thus says the LORD of hosts:* Return to me, says the LORD of hosts,* and I will return to you, says the LORD of hosts.** ⁴*Be not like your fathers, to whom the former prophets cried out, 'Thus says the LORD of hosts, Return from your evil ways and from your evil deeds.' But they did not hear or heed me, says the LORD.* ⁵*Your fathers, where are they? And the prophets, do they live for ever?* ⁶*But my words and my statutes, which I commanded my servants the prophets, did they not overtake your fathers? So they repented and said, As the LORD of hosts purposed to deal with us for our ways and deeds, so has he dealt with us."*

*In many LXX versions the word *Sebā'ōt* is missing

OVERVIEW: Augustine rejects the Pelagian belief that God's grace is given because of merit. He says that while the prophet is talking about cooperation between free will and grace, it is God who makes the move toward humans (AUGUSTINE). If we cease to sin, God removes the divine punishment we so deserve. This is what the mutual return is about between God and humans (CAESARIUS). God shows his clemency and endurance most especially through sinners. The words of Zechariah are an indication of God's longsuffering with fallen humanity (CHRYSOSTOM). Not everyone receives the same measure of spiritual illumination because not all people are ready to. However, God desires in Christ to take believers to the depths of knowledge. Zechariah understood this in the invitation of God to believers (ORIGEN).

1:3 Return to Me, and I Will Return to You

GOD'S GRACE NOT BASED ON MERITS.
AUGUSTINE: Free will and God's grace are simultaneously commended. When God says, "Turn to me, and I will turn to you," one of these clauses—that which invites our return to God—evidently belongs to our will; while the other, which promises his return to us, belongs to his grace. Here,

possibly, the Pelagians think they have justification for their opinion, which they so prominently advance, that God's grace is given according to our merits. In the east, indeed, that is to say, in the province of Palestine, in which is the city of Jerusalem, Pelagius, when examined in person by the bishop, did not venture to affirm this. For it happened that among the objections which were brought up against him, this in particular was objected, that he maintained that the grace of God is given according to our merits, an opinion which was so diverse from Catholic doctrine and so hostile to the grace of Christ that unless he had anathemized it, as laid to his charge, he himself must have been anathemized on its account. He pronounced, indeed, the required anathema upon the dogm;a, but how insincerely his later books plainly show; for in them he maintains absolutely no other opinion than that the grace of God is given according to our merits. Such passages do they collect out of the Scriptures—like the one which I just now quoted, "Turn to me, and I will turn to you"—as if it were owing to the merits of our turning to God that his grace were given us, wherein he himself even turns to us. Now the persons who hold this opinion fail to observe that unless our turning to God were itself God's gift, it would not be said to him in prayer,

"Turn us again, O God of hosts,"[1] and, "You, O God, will turn and quicken us,"[2] and again, "Turn us, O God of our salvation"[3]—with other passages of similar import, too numerous to mention here. For with respect to our coming to Christ, what else does it mean than our being turned to him by believing? And yet he says, "No man can come to me, except it were given to him of my Father."[4] ON GRACE AND FREE WILL 10.[5]

GOD'S MERCY ALWAYS THERE. CAESARIUS OF ARLES: If we are entirely devoted to God and humbly implore his mercy, through the mercy of God we may deserve to be healed of all our infirmities, rescued from all our sins, set free from the frequent flooding of waters. We ought to believe for certain, dearest brothers, that if our sins cease, the divine mercy will immediately remove the punishments that were due to us. Thus he himself has deigned to promise through the prophet when he said, "Return to me, and I will return to you," and again, "If you groan and return to me, then you shall be saved."[6] Therefore let us turn to a better life while the remedies are still in our power. By our good deeds let us summon to mercy the kind and merciful Lord whom we provoked by our sins. According to his usual practice, he will then deign to keep adversities from us and in his clemency to grant us good fortune. SERMON 207.3.[7]

REPENTANCE IS REWARDED. CHRYSOSTOM: Indeed, God is good to everyone, but he shows his patient endurance especially to those who sin. And if you want to hear a paradoxical statement—paradoxical because it is not customary, but true for the great piety it reveals—listen. God always seems to be severe to the righteous but good to sinners and quick to clemency. He restores the one who sinned and fell and tells him, "Shall not he who falls arise; or he that turns away, shall he not turn back again?"[8] And "Why did that stupid daughter of Judah turn away with a shameless revolting?"[9] And again, "Return to me, and I will return to you."[10] Elsewhere he assures with an oath the salvation from repentance by much clemency. "'As I live,' says the Lord,'I do not desire the death of a sinner, but that he should turn from his way and live.'"[11] To the righteous he says, "If a man achieves every righteousness and truth and later turns from his way and sins, I will not remember his righteousness, but he will die in his sin."[12] O such strictness toward the righteous! O such abundant forgiveness toward the sinner! He finds so many different means, without himself changing, to keep the righteous in check and forgive the sinner, by usefully dividing his rich goodness. HOMILIES ON REPENTANCE AND ALMSGIVING 7.5.[13]

GOD LOVES AND FORGIVES. ORIGEN: All who see are not equally enlightened by Christ, but individuals are enlightened according to the measure in which they are able to receive the power of light. And just as the eyes of our body are not equally enlightened by the sun, but to the extent that one shall have ascended to higher places and contemplated its risings with a gaze from a higher vantage point, to such an extent will he perceive more of both its splendor and heat. So also to the extent that our mind shall have approached Christ in a more exalted and lofty manner and shall have presented itself nearer the splendor of his light, to such an extent will it be made to shine more magnificently and clearly in his light. [This] also he himself says through the prophet: "'Draw near to me, and I shall draw near to you,' says the Lord,"[14] And again he says, "I am God who draws near, and not a God afar off."[15] HOMILIES ON GENESIS 1.7.[16]

---

[1]Ps 80:7 (79:8 LXX). [2]Ps 85:6 (84:7 LXX). [3]Ps 85:4 (84:5 LXX). [4]Jn 6:65. [5]NPNF 1 5:448. [6]Is 30:15. [7]FC 66:85. [8]Jer 8:4. [9]Jer 8:5. [10]Jas 4:8. [11]Ezek 33:11. [12]Ezek 18:24. [13]FC 96:89-90. [14]Jas 4:8. [15]Jer 23:23. [16]FC 71:56.

1:7-21 THE VISIONS CONCERNING JERUSALEM

⁷On the twenty-fourth day of the eleventh month which is the month of Shebat, in the second year of Darius, the word of the LORD came to Zechariah the son of Berechiah, son of Iddo, the prophet; and Zechariah said, ⁸"I saw in the night, and behold, a man riding upon a red horse! He was standing among the myrtle trees* in the glen; and behind him were red, sorrel, and white horses. ⁹Then I said, 'What are these, my lord?' The angel who talked with me said to me, 'I will show you what they are.' ¹⁰So the man who was standing among the myrtle trees answered, 'These are they whom the LORD has sent to patrol the earth.' ¹¹And they answered the angel of the LORD who was standing among the myrtle trees, 'We have patrolled the earth, and behold, all the earth remains at rest.' ¹²Then the angel of the LORD said, "O LORD of hosts, how long wilt thou have no mercy on Jerusalem and the cities of Judah, against which thou hast had indignation these seventy years?' ¹³And the LORD answered gracious and comforting words to the angel who talked with me. ¹⁴So the angel who talked with me said to me, "Cry out, Thus says the LORD of hosts: I am exceedingly jealous for Jerusalem and for Zion. ¹⁵And I am very angry with the nations that are at ease; for while I was angry but a little they furthered the disaster. ¹⁶Therefore, thus says the LORD, I have returned to Jerusalem with compassion; my house shall be built in it, says the LORD of hosts, and the measuring line shall be stretched out over Jerusalem. ¹⁷Cry again, Thus says the LORD of hosts: My cities shall again overflow with prosperity, and the LORD will again comfort Zion and again choose Jerusalem.' "

¹⁸ᵃAnd I lifted my eyes and saw, and behold, four horns! ¹⁹And I said to the angel who talked with me, "What are these?" And he answered me, "These are the horns which have scattered Judah, Israel, and Jerusalem." ²⁰Then the LORD showed me four smiths. ²¹And I said, "What are these coming to do?" He answered, "These are the horns which scattered Judah, so that no man raised his head; and these have come to terrify them, to cast down the horns of the nations who lifted up their horns against the land of Judah to scatter it."

a Ch 2.1 in Heb   *LXX *between overshadowing mountains*

OVERVIEW: The signs shown to the prophet are of profound significance (THEODORE). The spiritual beings that serve the Lord have a variety of shapes and appearances, according to their mission and functions (THEODORET). The angel, who speaks to the heart, is the Lord, who reveals the will of God the Father (JEROME). Angels oftentimes can speak to the hearer's spirit, mind or soul. This is what Zechariah referred to when he spoke of angels communicating to him (AUGUSTINE). The devil, although having rejected sub-

mission to God, is no longer able to do anything without God's expressed approval. The prophet's expression "he came with them" means that he dwells in the world along with the angels, the same way good and evil men are present (CHRYSOSTOM).

1:8 Signs

THE MEANING OF THE SIGNS. THEODORE OF MOPSUESTIA: It is quite clear that all the things shown to the prophet were tokens of certain realities, just as Joseph saw sheaves, sun, moon and stars, each of which carried a clue to some coming event, and the Pharaoh saw ears of corn and oxen, some fat and some skinny,[1] and by these as well other events were signified from what was shown. In exactly the same way the prophet also sees these things by divine revelation, and each of the things shown him contained some sign or indication of a reality. Likewise blessed Peter also saw a cloth let down from heaven, full of various living creatures clean and unclean, and the vision contained a clue to some other things.[2] COMMENTARY ON ZECHARIAH 1.7-10.[3]

THE DIVERSITY OF GOD'S ANGELS. THEODORET OF CYR: It is clear that those who were seen are invisible powers, "sent for service," according to the divine apostle, "for the sake of those who are due to inherit salvation."[4] Their natures are not seen, however, being incorporeal: he who is Lord of them and of everyone else renders them discernible according to need in each case. The divine Scripture clearly teaches us this, giving a glimpse of their different forms: Daniel saw them in one fashion, Ezekiel in another fashion, and Isaiah and Micah in different forms. Not that they have many forms, being naturally incorporeal and spiritual: the Lord of all when need arises gives them a form for discernment. This he did also in the case of Zechariah: he reveals to him the angel who is a leader of the people; St. Michael was this angel. COMMENTARY ON ZECHARIAH 1.8-11.[5]

1:9 The Angel

GOD'S INNER VOICE. JEROME: "I will hear what the Lord God proclaims in me."[6] The prophet is praying for the people and speaks while God is speaking in him: "I will listen to what the Lord God is proclaiming in me." You perceive that God does not speak in the ears but in the heart, as Zechariah says: "The angel who spoke in me answered me." The angel is understood to be our

Lord, who is proclaiming the will of the Father and who, in Isaiah, is called the angel of the great counsel.[7] I will listen to the voice of the Lord God within me; I shall attend with the ear of my heart that I may hear what the Lord God speaks in me. HOMILIES ON THE PSALMS, ALTERNATE SERIES 64.[8]

ANGELIC APPEARANCE EXPLAINED. AUGUSTINE: Likewise, who will tell with what bodies angels appear to people, in such fashion as not to be visible but to be tangible? And again how, not through tangible corporeality but by spiritual power, angels produce certain visions, not to the eyes of the body but to those of the spirit or the mind, or can utter speech, not of the ear from without, but within the soul of humans, being themselves placed there, as is written in the book of the prophets: "And the angel that spoke in me said to me" (for what the prophet says is not "that spoke to me," but "in me")... They appear also in sleep and speak through dreams (for we read in the Gospel:[9] "Behold, an angel of the Lord appeared to him in a dream, saying"). These methods of communication tend to show that the angels have intangible bodies, and make it a very difficult question how the patriarchs could wash the feet of angels,[10] and how Jacob could wrestle with an angel in contact so unmistakable.[11] Asking these questions and answering them with such guesses as we can is not a useless exercise for the mind, if the discussion is kept within bounds and if those who take part avoid the error of thinking they know what they do not know. For what need is there of affirming or denying or making nice distinctions about these and similar matters, when ignorance of them imputes no blame? ENCHIRIDION 15.[12]

1:11 Answering the Angel

ANGELS AND DEMONS CODWELL. CHRYSOSTOM: "And the devil came with them."[13] What are

---

[1]Gen 37:7, 9; 41:17-24. [2]Acts 10:11-12. [3]PG 66:501. [4]Heb 1:14. [5]PG 81:1880. [6]Ps 85:9 (84:10 LXX). [7]Is 9:6 LXX. [8]FC 57:52. [9]Mt 1:20. [10]Gen 18:4; 19:2. [11]Gen 32:24. [12]FC 2:419. [13]Job 1:6.

you saying? "With the angels?" He who rebelled, who dishonored himself? Do not worry, my dear; this is an image, a figure. It is like another passage in the [First] Book of Kings, where it is said, "And there came forth an evil spirit, and the Lord said, 'Who will deceive Ahab?'" And the spirit responded: "I will deceive him,"[14] and he indicates it in such a way. The Scripture often takes on an anthropomorphic character.... The angels came, according to the text, and the devil came with them having compassed the earth and walked around in the subcelestial regions.[15] What do we understand by that? That the earth is filled with demons and angels, and that both are under the power of God; and that the angels present themselves before God, from whom they receive orders; and that the devil can do nothing to please himself, if he has not received permission for it from above. For if he has totally rejected the bridle and is no longer in service to God, he is not in the least held back by fear as by a bit which restrains him from using his own power. But note this: whereas the angels present themselves as servants who render an account to him of their doings, as one can see in Zechariah, the devil has nothing to say to him. Consequently the expression "he came with them"[16] means nothing else but that he too is dependent on God.... What does the expression therefore signify? It signifies that he is with them in the world. In the same way as deceitful people and good people are mixed, so are the angels and the demons. COMMENTARY ON JOB 1.[17]

---

[14]1 Kings 22:22. [15]Job 1:7. [16]Job 1:6. [17]WLUA 27-28.

2:1-13 SYMBOLIC MEASURING OF JERUSALEM

[1]And I lifted my eyes and saw, and behold, a man with a measuring line in his hand! [2]Then I said, "Where are you going?" And he said to me, "To measure Jerusalem, to see what is its breadth and what is its length." [3]And behold, the angel who talked with me came forward, and another angel came forward to meet him, [4]and said to him, "Run, say to that young man, 'Jerusalem shall be inhabited as villages without walls, because of the multitude of men and cattle in it. [5]For I will be to her a wall of fire round about, says the LORD, and I will be the glory within her.'"

[6]Ho! ho! Flee from the land of the north, says the LORD; for I have spread you abroad as the four winds of the heavens, says the LORD. [7]Ho! Escape to Zion, you who dwell with the daughter of Babylon. [8]For thus said the LORD of hosts, after his glory sent me* to the nations who plundered you, for he who touches you touches the apple of his eye: [9]"Behold, I will shake my hand over them, and they shall become plunder for those who served them. Then you will know that the LORD of hosts has sent me. [10]Sing and rejoice, O daughter of Zion; for lo, I come and I will dwell in the midst of you, says the LORD. [11]And many nations shall join themselves to the LORD in that day, and shall be my people; and I will dwell in the midst of you, and you shall know that the LORD of hosts has sent me to you. [12]And the LORD will inherit Judah as his portion in the holy land, and will again choose Jerusalem."

[13]Be silent, all flesh, before the LORD; for he has roused himself from his holy dwelling.

b Ch 2.5 in Heb   *LXX *after the glory sent me*

OVERVIEW: Gregory the Great sees evidence in the prophet's utterance that there exists a hierarchy of angels. Superior-ranked angels send lesser ones to do the bidding of God. The "Almighty" sending the "Almighty" in the prophet anticipates the Father's sending of the Son. It was Christ speaking to the house of Israel in a veiled way (AUGUSTINE). Justin Martyr airs a stern rebuke against the Jews who heaped ridicule upon Christ and his followers (JUSTIN). God promised to send the Messiah to Jews and Gentiles, and true to his word, he accomplished it in Christ (CYRIL OF JERUSALEM).

2:3 The Angels Approach

HOW ANGELS WORK TOGETHER. GREGORY THE GREAT: We have learned from certain places in Scripture that some things are done by cherubim and some by seraphim. Because I have no clear proof, I am unwilling to affirm whether they do these things themselves or accomplish them through bands of angels under their authority, their names, which are greater, being used because the things are done on their authority. But I am certain of this, that to carry out some duty from on high some spirits send others. The prophet Zechariah is our witness: "See," he says, "the angel who talked with me came forward, and another angel came forward to meet him and said to him, 'Run and speak to that boy, saying, "Jerusalem shall be inhabited without a wall."'" When one angel says to another, "Run and speak," there is no doubt that one is sending the other. The lesser ranks are sent; the greater ones do the sending. FORTY GOSPEL HOMILIES 34.[1]

2:8 The Apple of God's Eye

CHRIST SPEAKS THROUGH THE PROPHETS. AUGUSTINE: Another example to prove the same point may be found in a passage of Zechariah where the "Almighty" sends the "Almighty." This can only mean that God the Father sends God the Son. The text runs, "So says the Lord Almighty: 'After the glory he has sent me to the nations that have robbed you; for he that touches you touches the apple of my eye. For behold, I lift up my head upon them, and they shall be a prey to those who served them; and you shall know that the Lord almighty sent me.'" In this case, the Lord almighty says that he is sent by the Lord almighty. How can anyone doubt that it is Christ who is speaking and, in fact, speaking to the lost sheep of the house of Israel? Remember what is said in the Gospel: "I was not sent except to the lost sheep of the house of Israel."[2] The comparison of these lost sheep to the apple of God's eye is explained by the perfection of God's love. And, of course, it was to this flock of sheep that the apostles belonged. "After the glory" of his resurrection—a glory alluded to in the words "Jesus had not yet been glorified"[3]—it was in the person of these apostles that Jesus was sent to the Gentiles. And this was to be the fulfillment of what the psalmist had prophesied: "You will deliver me from the contradictions of the people; you will make me head of the Gentiles."[4] CITY OF GOD 20.30.[5]

JEWS CALLED TO CONVERT. JUSTIN MARTYR: Say no evil thing, my brothers, against him that was crucified, and treat not scornfully the stripes wherewith all may be healed, even as we are healed. For it will be well if, persuaded by the Scriptures, you are circumcised from hardheartedness. This is not that circumcision which you have from the tenets that are put into you; for that was given for a sign, and not for a work of righteousness, as the Scriptures compel you [to admit]. Assent, therefore, and pour no ridicule on the Son of God; do not obey the Pharisaic teachers; and scoff not at the king of Israel, as the rulers of your synagogues teach you to do after your prayers. For if he that touches those that are not pleasing to God is as one that touches the apple of God's eye, how much more so is he that touch-

---

[1]CS 123:292-93. [2]Mt 15:24. [3]Jn 7:39. [4]Ps 18:43 (17:44 LXX). [5]FC 24:332-33*.

es his beloved! And that this is he has been sufficiently demonstrated. DIALOGUE WITH TRYPHO 137.[6]

2:10 God Will Dwell Among Them

NATIONS TO COME TO GOD. CYRIL OF JERUSALEM: The Lord heard the prayer of the prophets. The Father did not despise our race, which was perishing; he sent from heaven his own Son the Lord as our physician. One of the prophets says, "The Lord whom you seek, comes; and he shall come suddenly."[7] Where will he come? "The Lord shall come to his temple,"[8] where you took up stones against him.[9] Another of the prophets, on hearing this, says to him, "In speaking of God's salvation, do you speak softly? In announcing the good tidings of God's coming for salvation, do you speak in secret?" "Go up onto a high mountain, Zion, herald of glad tidings; say to the cities of Judah"—what shall I say?—"Here is your

God! Here comes with power the Lord God."[10] Again the Lord himself has said, "'Behold, I come, and I will dwell in the midst of you,' says the Lord. 'And many nations shall be joined to the Lord.'" The Israelites rejected salvation through me; "I come to gather nations of every language,"[11] for, "he came unto his own, and his own received him not."[12] You come, and what do you bestow upon the nations? "I come to gather nations of every language . . . I will set a sign among them."[13] For from my conflict on the cross I will give to each of my soldiers a royal sign to bear upon his forehead. Still another prophet said, "He inclined the heavens and came down, with dark clouds under his feet."[14] For his coming down from heaven was unknown to humanity. CATECHETICAL LECTURE 12.8.[15]

---

[6]ANF 1:268. [7]Mal 3:1. [8]Mal 3:1. [9]Jn 8:59. [10]Is 40:9-10. [11]Is 66:18. [12]Jn 1:11. [13]Is 66:18-19 LXX. [14]Ps 18:9 (17:10 LXX). [15]FC 61:231-32*.

3:1-2 THE LORD'S REBUKE OF SATAN

[1]*Then he showed me Joshua* the high priest standing before the angel of the LORD, and Satan standing at his right hand to accuse him. [2]And the LORD said to Satan, "The LORD rebuke you, O Satan! The LORD who has chosen Jerusalem rebuke you! Is not this a brand plucked from the fire?"*

*LXX Jesus

OVERVIEW: The great high priest the prophet spoke of was none other than Jesus Christ, who is in the line of the order of Melchizedek, one greater than that of the Levites (GREGORY OF NYSSA). Christ cleanses us from our sins, which accuse us before God. In this manner Jesus fulfills his ministry as high priest, since he is the one clothed with priestly garments and the virtue of salvation on his head (CYPRIAN). It was the devil who guided Adam's hand and caused the fall of

humanity. Jesus, however, took up humanity's fallen condition and set the devil at his right hand. Jesus has conquered our sins. People who are in bondage to sin are not to be hated but prayed for (AMBROSE). Just as God rebuked Satan in defense of Jerusalem, so Jesus has rebuked our sin (the devil) and so believers are to pray with humility that Jesus will rebuke unrepentant sinners (JEROME). The devil at the right hand of Jesus does not stand victorious; rather, Christ vanquishes him. By wearing our filthy garments of sin Jesus has placed the devil behind and under his feet. Jesus is a triumphant high priest who wears the long garment of kingly authority. Joshua the high priest is a type of Jesus, the high priest according to the order of Melchizedek. Satan's opposition to Joshua prefigures Jesus' temptations in the wilderness, as Jesus' ultimate victory over the demons fulfilled Joshua's rebuke of Satan (THEODORET).

3:1 Joshua the High Priest

JESUS THE HIGH PRIEST FORETOLD. GREGORY OF NYSSA: For in that passage too, in giving the name of high priest to him who made with his own blood the priestly propitiation for our sins, he does not by the word *made* declare the first existence of the Only-begotten. But he says "made" with the intention of representing that grace which is commonly spoken of in connection with the appointment of priests. For Jesus, the great high priest (as Zechariah says), who offered up his own lamb, that is, his own body, for the sin of the world; who, by reason of the children who are partakers of flesh and blood, himself also in like manner took part with them in blood.[1] ([This is] not in that he was in the beginning, being the Word and God, and being in the form of God, and equal with God, but in that he emptied himself in the form of a servant, and offered an oblation and sacrifice for us). He, I say, became a high priest many generations later, after the order of Melchizedek.[2] AGAINST EUNOMIUS 4.2.[3]

CHRIST CONQUERED OUR SINS. CYPRIAN: Also in Zechariah: "And the Lord showed me Jesus,[4] that great priest, standing before the face of the angel of the Lord, and the devil was standing at his right hand to oppose him. And Jesus was clothed in filthy garments, and he stood before the face of the angel himself; and he answered them and said to them who were standing before his face, saying,'Take away his filthy garments from him.' And he said to him,'Behold, I

have taken away your iniquities.' And put upon him a priestly garment, and set a fair miter upon his head." Also Paul to the Philippians: "Who being established in the form of God, thought it not robbery that he was equal with God, but emptied himself, taking the form of a servant, and was made in the likeness of men; and being found in fashion as a man, he humbled himself, becoming obedient even unto death, even the death of the cross. Wherefore also God exalted him and gave him a name which is above every name, that in the name of Jesus every knee should bow, of things in heaven, of things in earth, and of infernal things, and every tongue should confess that Jesus Christ is Lord in the glory of God the Father."[5] To QUIRINUS, TESTIMONIES AGAINST THE JEWS 12.2.13.[6]

HOW JESUS CONQUERED THE DEVIL. AMBROSE: But because he forgot God's command and fulfilled the will of the serpent, the devil took hold of his hand and made it to reach out to the tree of the knowledge of good and evil, to pluck things that were forbidden. In him, judgment was passed beforehand on all people, and the adversary began to stand by the right hand of every person. From this, there also came that model of the curse against Judas, "And may the devil stand at his right hand."[7] If that curse is severe, that blessing, whereby the bonds of the harsh curse are undone, is very momentous. For that reason the Lord Jesus, who had taken up humanity's cause and condition, set the devil at his right hand, just as we read in the book of Zechariah. THE PRAYER OF JOB AND DAVID 3.10.37.[8]

3:2 The Lord Rebukes Satan

JESUS CONQUERED THE ACCUSER. JEROME: You can search them out for yourself from sacred Scripture without my help. And it will become clearly

---

[1]Heb 2:14. [2]Heb 7:21. [3]NPNF 2 5:184. [4]The Hebrew *Yĕhôšuaʿ* may be translated "Joshua" or "Jesus" in English. [5]Phil 2:6-11. [6]ANF 5:521. [7]Ps 108:6 (107:7 LXX). [8]FC 65:385.

evident to you that this likely is the age of which it was said, "Believe not in friends and trust not in princes,"[9] and that the prophecy is now being fulfilled: "The leaders of my people have not known me; they are foolish and senseless children. They are wise to do evils, but to do good they have no knowledge."[10] We should rather pity such people than hate them and should rather pray for them than revile them. For we were created to bless and not to revile. Thus also Michael, when he was arguing with the devil over the body of Moses, did not dare to bring an accusation of blasphemy against him even for such a serious offense but said, "May the Lord rebuke you."[11] Even in Zechariah, we read something similar to this. "The Lord rebuke you, O Satan, and the Lord that chose Jerusalem rebuke you." And so we also pray that those who refuse to be rebuked by their friends with humility may be rebuked by the Lord. APOLOGY AGAINST THE BOOKS OF RUFINUS 18.[12]

JESUS IS THE FOUNDATION. JEROME: At the same, the reader should examine carefully that it does not say that the devil was standing triumphantly as a victor, but that he was at a halt in the contest and was being held in the battle line and in uncertainty—no, indeed, he was not victor, since he had not yet begun to fight. As for the words "to accuse him," the devil was his adversary, just as we said, because Jesus was clothed in garments that were filthy with our sins. After Sa-

tan heard the command, "May the Lord who has chosen Jerusalem rebuke you!" he stood no longer on the right but retired behind him and crawled under his feet. Without delay, Jesus the high priest dons the long garment and is clothed in shining raiment, and in harmony with kingly authority—with the hands of Zerubbabel—[he] lays the foundation of the church and erects the spiritual Jerusalem. HOMILIES ON THE PSALMS, ALTERNATE SERIES 61.[13]

JOSHUA A TYPE OF JESUS. THEODORET OF CYR: This is also a type of our situation. Just as the avenging and wicked devil was very opposed to Joshua for being high priest and making intercession to God on behalf of the people, so in turn this same enemy was an opponent of Jesus[14] the great high priest in the order of Melchizedek for taking away the sin of the world[15] and wished to bring him down. It was, however, not Joshua the son of Jehozadak that rebuked him, but Joshua's Lord; when he approached Jesus the Savior of the world, he was rebuked by him, as by his God and Lord, and hears, "Get behind me, Satan."[16] COMMENTARY ON ZECHARIAH 3.1-6.[17]

---

[9]Mic 7:5. [10]Jer 4:22. [11]Jude 9. [12]FC 53:134*. [13]FC 57:31. [14]The two names Joshua and Jesus are rendered with the same word in Greek. Hence Joshua the high priest becomes a type of Jesus the High Priest according to the order of Melchizedek. [15]Cf. Jn 1:29; Heb 5:6. [16]Mt 4:10. [17]PG 81:1892.

3:3-10 SYMBOLIC CLEANSING OF JOSHUA

[3]Now Joshua* was standing before the angel, clothed with filthy garments. [4]And the angel said to those who were standing before him, "Remove the filthy garments from him." And to him he said, "Behold, I have taken your iniquity away from you, and I will clothe you with rich apparel." [5]And I said,† "Let them put a clean turban on his head." So they put a clean turban on his head and clothed him with garments; and the angel of the LORD was standing by.

⁶*And the angel of the* LORD *enjoined Joshua,** ⁷*"Thus says the* LORD *of hosts: If you will walk in my ways and keep my charge, then you shall rule my house and have charge of my courts, and I will give you the right of access among those who are standing here.* ⁸*Hear now, O Joshua** the high priest, you and your friends who sit before you, for they are men of good omen: behold, I will bring my servant the Branch.*‡ ⁹*For behold, upon the stone which I have set before Joshua,** upon a single stone with seven facets, I will engrave its inscription, says the* LORD *of hosts, and I will remove the guilt of this land in a single day.* ¹⁰*In that day, says the* LORD *of hosts, every one of you will invite his neighbor under his vine and under his fig tree."*

*LXX Jesus   †LXX he said   ‡LXX the Orient

OVERVIEW: Through Jesus believers cast off the foul garments of sin. The devil, who is ready to oppose and ensnare believers, can be rebuked by the angel of God, a reference to the power of God (Holy Spirit) sent to the faithful (JUSTIN MARTYR). The eternal priesthood of Christ was promised through the prophet Zechariah. Jesus took the faulty garments of sin upon himself and has given the garments of salvation and the nature of priesthood to believers (LACTANTIUS). The prophet's description of Joshua's replacement of filthy garments with clean ones was a figure of the regeneration of baptism (GREGORY OF NYSSA). The devil standing at the right hand of the son of Jehozadak is a figure of Jesus wearing the filthy garments of our sins (JEROME). Jesus voluntarily became stained with our sins by assuming a human body, contrary to those who deny the incarnation (ORIGEN). Augustine defends the view that uncleanness refers to sin by invoking the words of Zechariah regarding the filthy garments of the high priest Jesus. It is also a refutation of the Manichaean interpretation of flesh and spirit (AUGUSTINE). The prophet spoke of Jesus as the shepherd whose name would be Orient and who wore the sin-soiled garments though being also the Sun of justice (AMBROSE).

3:3 Joshua's Filthy Garments

JESUS REBUKES THE ADVERSARY. JUSTIN MARTYR: To explain more fully the revelation of our holy Jesus Christ, I will continue my discourse by stating that the above quoted revelation [of Zechariah] was given to us who believe in Christ, the high priest and crucified one. For we, who once practiced fornication and every other kind of filthy action, have, through the grace conferred upon us by our Jesus according to the will of his Father, cast off all these foul garments of sin in which we were dressed. Although the devil stands nearby ready to oppose us and anxious to ensnare all of us for himself, the angel of God (namely, the power of God which was sent to us through Jesus Christ) rebukes him, and he departs from us. And we have been, so to speak, snatched from the fire, when we were purified from our former sins and [delivered] from the fiery torment with which the devil and his assistants try us. From such dangers does Jesus, the Son of God, again snatch us. He has also promised, if we obey his commands, to dress us in garments that he has set aside for us and to reward us with an eternal kingdom. DIALOGUE WITH TRYPHO 116.[1]

EVERLASTING PRIEST PROMISED. LACTANTIUS: Now who this one would be to whom God promised an eternal priesthood Zechariah has taught, even giving his name most clearly. For thus he spoke: "And the Lord God showed me Jesus the high priest standing before the face of the angel of the Lord, and the devil stood at his right hand to be his adversary. And the Lord said to the devil, 'May the Lord that chose Jerusalem rule over you,

[1]FC 6:327.

and behold the brand plucked out of the fire!' And Jesus was clothed with filthy garments, and he stood before the face of the angel. And he answered and said to them that stood around before his face, saying, 'Take away the filthy garments from him, and put on him a tunic and sandals, and put a clean miter upon his head.' And they clothed him with garments and put a clean miter upon his head. And the angel of the Lord stood and testified before Jesus, saying, 'Thus says the Lord almighty: If you will walk in my ways and keep my charges, you shall judge my house. And I will give you some of them that are now present to walk with you.' Hear, then, O Jesus, the high priest."[2] EPITOME OF THE DIVINE INSTITUTES 4.14.[3]

BAPTISMAL REMOVAL OF SIN FORETOLD. GREGORY OF NYSSA: Now in this, by that wondrous sacrifice, Elijah clearly proclaimed to us the sacramental rite of baptism that should afterwards be instituted. For the fire was kindled by water thrice poured upon it, so that it is clearly shown that where the mystic water is, there is the kindling, warm and fiery spirit that burns up the ungodly and illuminates the faithful. Yes, and yet again his disciple Elisha, when Naaman the Syrian, who was diseased with leprosy, had come to him as a suppliant, cleanses the sick man by washing him in the Jordan,[4] clearly indicating what should come, both by the use of water generally and by dipping in the river in particular. For the Jordan alone of rivers, receiving in itself the firstfruits of sanctification and benediction, conveyed in its channel to the whole world, as it were from some fount in the type afforded by itself, the grace of baptism. These then are indications in deed and act of regeneration in baptism. Let us for the rest consider the prophecies of it in words and language. Isaiah cried, saying, "Wash you, make you clean, put away evil from your souls,"[5] and David, "Draw nigh to him and be enlightened, and your faces shall not be ashamed."[6] And Ezekiel, writing more clearly and plainly than them both, says, "And I will sprinkle clean water upon you, and you shall be cleansed; from

all your filthiness, and from all your idols, will I cleanse you. A new heart also will I give you, and a new spirit will I give you; and I will take away the stony heart out of your flesh, and I will give you a heart of flesh, and my spirit will I put within you."[7] Most manifestly also does Zechariah prophesy of Joshua, who was clothed with filthy garments (to wit, the flesh of a servant, even ours), and stripping him of his ill-favored raiment, adorns him with the clean and fair apparel, teaching us by the figurative illustration that truly in the baptism of Jesus all we, putting off our sins like some poor and patched garment, are clothed in the holy and most fair garment of regeneration. ON THE BAPTISM OF CHRIST.[8]

JESUS DEFEATS THE EVIL ONE. JEROME: There is much to be said on this subject. In the case of sinners, the devil is standing at the right side, but that is another matter for discussion. Whoever is a sinner has the devil standing at his right hand. Someone is raising the objection: How, then, in Zechariah is the devil said to stand on the right of Jesus [Joshua], the son of Jehozadak?[9] "And Satan stood at his right hand." How in Zechariah is it written that the devil stands at the right hand of the Savior? You appreciate that this is a problem. At the time that the devil stood at the right hand of the Savior, "Jesus," holy Writ says, "was clad in filthy garments." He was wearing our sins; he was wrapped up in the folds of our vices; that is why the devil was standing at his right side. HOMILIES ON THE PSALMS 36.[10]

JESUS BECAME SIN FOR US TO CLEANSE US. ORIGEN: Every soul that has been clothed with a human body has its own stain. But Jesus was stained through his own will, because he had taken on a human body for our salvation. Listen to the prophet Zechariah. He says, "Jesus was clothed with stained garments." Zechariah says

---

[2]Zech 3:1-8 LXX. [3]FC 49:277-78. [4]2 Kings 5. [5]Is 1:16 LXX. [6]Ps 34:5 (33:6 LXX). [7]Ezek 36:25-27 (not exactly as LXX). [8]NPNF 2 5:522-23*. [9]Hag 1:1 LXX. [10]FC 48:275.

this to refute those who deny that our Lord had a human body but say that his body was made of heavenly and spiritual substance.[11] They say this body was made of heavenly matter or, they falsely assert, of sidereal matter, or of some other more sublime and spiritual nature. Let them explain how a spiritual body could be stained, or how they interpret the passage we quoted: "Jesus was clothed with stained garments." If this difficulty drives them to assume that the "stained garment" means the spiritual body, then they should be consistent and say this, that what is said in the prophecies has been fulfilled, that is, "an animal body is sown, a spiritual body rises."[12] Do we thus rise soiled and stained? It is an impiety even to think this, especially when one knows what Scripture says: "The body is sown in corruption but will rise in incorruption; it is sown in weakness but will rise in strength; our animal body is sown, but a spiritual body will rise."[13]

Thus it was fitting that those offerings that, according to the law, customarily cleanse stain should be made. They were made for our Lord and Savior, who had been "clothed with stained garments" and had taken on an earthly body. Christian brothers often ask a question. The passage from Scripture read today encourages me to treat it again. Little children are baptized "for the remission of sins."[14] Whose sins are they? When did they sin? Or how can this explanation of the baptismal washing be maintained in the case of small children, except according to the interpretation we spoke of a little earlier? "No man is clean of stain, not even if his life upon the earth had lasted but a single day."[15] Through the mystery of baptism, the stains of birth are put aside. For this reason, even small children are baptized. For "unless a man be born again of water and spirit, he will not be able to enter into the kingdom of heaven."[16] HOMILIES ON THE GOSPEL OF LUKE 14.4-5.[17]

JESUS CLEAN FROM ALL SIN. AUGUSTINE: Now when he speaks of "uncleanness" here, the mere perusal of the passage is enough to show that he meant "sin" to be understood. It is plain from the words, of what he is speaking. The same phrase and sense occur in the prophet Zechariah, in the place where "the filthy garments" are removed from off the high priest, and it is said to him, "I have taken away your sins." Well now, I rather think that all these passages, and others of like import, which point to the fact that humanity is born in sin and under the curse, are not to be read among the dark recesses of the Manichaeans but in the sunshine of Catholic truth. ON MARRIAGE AND CONCUPISCENCE 2.50.[18]

3:8 The Servant the Branch

JESUS FORETOLD AS "THE ORIENT." AMBROSE: Of him he speaks also through the mouth of Ezekiel, saying, "And I will set up one shepherd over them, and my servant David will rule them, and he will be their shepherd. And I the Lord will be their God, and my servant David the prince in the midst of them."[19] Of course, David the king was already dead, but the true David, the truly humble, the truly meek, the true Son of God, strong of hand, is foretold by this name. He also is pointed out in the book of the prophet Zechariah, God the father saying, "I will bring my servant, the Orient is his name." Although he wore sin-soiled garments, was not the Sun of justice clothed with the splendor of his divinity? LETTER 27.[20]

---

[11]Reference to the Gnostics. [12]1 Cor 15:44. [13]1 Cor 15:43-44. [14]Acts 2:38. [15]Job 14:4-5. [16]Jn 3:5. [17]FC 94:57-58. [18]NPNF 1 5:304. [19]Ezek 34:23-24. [20]FC 26:142.

4:1-14 THE VISIONS OF THE GOLDEN LAMPSTAND AND TWO OLIVE TREES

[1]*And the angel who talked with me came again, and waked me, like a man that is wakened out of his sleep.* [2]*And he said to me, "What do you see?" I said, "I see, and behold, a lampstand all of gold, with a bowl on the top of it, and seven lamps on it, with seven lips on each of the lamps which are on the top of it.* [3]*And there are two olive trees by it, one on the right of the bowl and the other on its left."* [4]*And I said to the angel who talked with me, "What are these, my lord?"* [5]*Then the angel who talked with me answered me, "Do you not know what these are?" I said, "No, my lord."* [6]*Then he said to me, "This is the word of the LORD to Zerubbabel: Not by might, nor by power, but by my Spirit, says the LORD of hosts.* [7]*What are you, O great mountain? Before Zerubbabel you shall become a plain; and he shall bring forward the top stone amid shouts of 'Grace, grace to it!' "* [8]*Moreover the word of the LORD came to me, saying,* [9]*"The hands of Zerubbabel have laid the foundation of this house; his hands shall also complete it. Then you will know that the LORD of hosts has sent me to you.* [10]*For whoever has despised the day of small things shall rejoice, and shall see the plummet in the hand of Zerubbabel.*

"These seven are the eyes of the LORD, which range through the whole earth." [11]*Then I said to him, "What are these two olive trees on the right and the left of the lampstand?"* [12]*And a second time I said to him, "What are these two branches of the olive trees, which are beside the two golden pipes from which the oil[c] is poured out?"* [13]*He said to me, "Do you not know what these are?" I said, "No, my lord."* [14]*Then he said, "These are the two anointed who stand by the Lord of the whole earth."*

c Cn: Heb *gold*

OVERVIEW: The lamp of the seven lips is one of many symbolic references in the Old Testament and New Testament that point to Christ (VICTORINUS). Christ and the Holy Spirit are the authors of the two boughs of the two olives: the Law and the Prophets prepare one to receive the gifts of the new covenant (METHODIUS). God created paradise for humans, where angels and saints rest under the fig tree and the vine (AMBROSE). Zechariah calls the devil a mountain, but through the new covenant faith it can be removed. Being earthly minded is to allow the evil mountain to destroy. It is a mountain that is ruined by its own evil (ORIGEN). The two candlesticks and two olive trees of the Apocalypse were revealed already by Zechariah (VICTORINUS).

4:2 A Golden Lampstand

SEVENS POINT TO CHRIST. VICTORINUS OF PETOVIUM: Behold the seven horns of the lamb,[1] the seven eyes of God[2]—the seven eyes are the seven spirits of the lamb;[3] seven torches burning before the throne of God,[4] seven golden candlesticks,[5] seven young sheep,[6] the seven women in Isaiah,[7] the seven churches in Paul,[8]

---

[1]Rev 5:6. [2]Zech 4:10. [3]Rev 4:5. [4]Rev 4:5. [5]Rev 1:12. [6]Lev 23:18. [7]Is 4:1. [8]Rev 1:4. Victorinus probably means John.

seven deacons,[9] seven angels, seven trumpets,[10] seven seals to the books, seven periods of seven days with which Pentecost is completed, the seven weeks in Daniel,[11] also the forty-three weeks in Daniel;[12] with Noah, seven of all clean things in the ark;[13] seven revenges of Cain,[14] seven years for a debt to be acquitted,[15] the lamp of the seven orifices, seven pillars of wisdom in the house of Solomon. On the Creation of the World.[16]

4:3 Two Olive Trees

Chastity a Path to the Vision of God. Methodius: Zechariah shows that the olive shadows forth the law of Moses, speaking thus: "And the angel that talked with me came again, and waked me, as a man that is wakened out of his sleep, and said to me, 'What do you see?' And I said, 'I have looked, and behold a candlestick all of gold, with a bowl on the top of it, . . . and two olive trees by it, one on the right side of the bowl and the other on its left side.' " And after a few words, the prophet, asking what are the olives on the right and the left of the candlestick and what are the two olive boughs in the hands of the two pipes, the angel answered and said, "These are the two sons of fruitfulness which stand by the Lord of the whole earth." [These signify] the two firstborn virtues that are waiting upon God, which, in his dwelling, supply around the wick, through the boughs, the spiritual oil of God, that humanity may have the light of divine knowledge. But the two boughs of the two olives are the law and the prophets, around, as it were, the lot of the inheritance, of which Christ and the Holy Spirit are the authors. We ourselves, meanwhile, [are] not being able to take the whole fruit and the greatness of these plants, before chastity began to rule the world, but only their boughs—namely, the law and the prophets—did we formerly cultivate, and those moderately, often letting them slip. For who was ever able to receive Christ or the Spirit, unless he first purified himself? For the exercise which prepares

the soul from childhood for desirable and delectable glory, and carries this grace safely there with ease, and from small toils raises up mighty hopes, is chastity, which gives immortality to our bodies. It becomes all people willingly to prefer in honor and to praise above all things; some, that by its means they may be betrothed to the word, practicing virginity; and others, that by it they may be freed from the curse, "Dust you are, and to dust you will return."[17] This, O Arete, is the discourse on virginity which you required of me, accomplished according to my ability; which I pray, O mistress, although it is mediocre and short, that you will receive with kindness from me who was chosen to speak last. Banquet of the Ten Virgins 10.6.[18]

4:4 A Question for the Angel

Angels and Saints Rest Under the Fig Tree. Ambrose: Nevertheless we can find out who was the creator of this paradise. We read in Genesis that God planted a garden to the east, and he put there the man he had formed.[19] Who had the power to create paradise, if not almighty God, who "spoke and they were made"[20] and who was never in want of the thing which he wished to bring into being? He planted, therefore, that paradise of which he says in his wisdom: "Every plant which my Father has not planted will be rooted up."[21] This is a goodly plantation, for angels and saints are said to lie beneath the fig tree and the vine. In this respect they are the type of the angels in that time of peace[22] which is to come. On Paradise 2.[23]

4:7 A Great Mountain

Moving Mountains. Origen: On account of the height of the kingdom he calls Babylon a "mountain" which was "ruined" from idolatry

---

[9]Acts 6:3. [10]Josh 6; Rev 8. [11]Dan 9:25. [12]Dan 9. [13]Gen 7:2. [14]Gen 4:15. [15]Deut 15:1. [16]ANF 7:342-43. [17]Gen 3:19. [18]ANF 6:350. [19]Gen 2:8. [20]Ps 32:9. [21]Mt 15:13. [22]Mk 12:25. [23]FC 42:288.

and unjust works, through which it "destroyed" the others. And it also was the city on high because of the river nearby from which some stairs went up to the city, the city being in two parts and lying close to the river on each bank, with the walls also of the city being very high. And it mentioned a "hand," the avenging power, the same power of his which destroyed something made from "rocks" for security and for watch. And due to the fire having "obliterated" its "stones," they were useless, as there was not a stone to be put together for a firm building. And for the analogical meaning, the devil is named a "mountain," as in the book of Zechariah: "Who are you, a great mountain before the face of Zerubbabel?" And concerning the one who has the "deaf and dumb" demon, the Savior said, "If you have faith as a grain of mustard seed, you will say to this mountain: 'Move away,' and it will move away."[24] Thus the devil is a "mountain" which is "ruined" from his own evil and which "destroys" everyone to the extent they have their mind on what is

earthly. FRAGMENTS ON JEREMIAH 41.[25]

4:14 The Two Anointed

TWO CANDLESTICKS, TWO OLIVE TREES. VICTORINUS OF PETOVIUM: "These are the two candlesticks standing before the Lord of the earth." These two candlesticks and two olive trees he has to this end spoken of, admonished you that if, when you have read of them elsewhere, you have not understood, you may understand here. For in Zechariah, one of the twelve prophets, it is thus written: "These are the two olive trees and two candlesticks which stand in the presence of the Lord of the earth"; that is, they are in paradise. Also, in another sense, standing in the presence of the Lord of the earth, that is, in the presence of the antichrist. Therefore they must be slain by antichrist. COMMENTARY ON THE APOCALYPSE 11.4.[26]

---

[24]Mt 17:20. [25]FC 97:302-3. [26]ANF 7:354.

5:1-11 THE VISIONS OF THE FLYING SCROLL AND THE WOMAN IN THE EPHAH

[1]*Again I lifted my eyes and saw, and behold, a flying scroll!* [2]And he said to me, "What do you see?" I answered, "I see a flying scroll; its length is twenty cubits, and its breadth ten cubits." [3]Then he said to me, "This is the curse that goes out over the face of the whole land; for every one who steals shall be cut off henceforth according to it, and every one who swears falsely shall be cut off henceforth according to it. [4]I will send it forth, says the LORD of hosts, and it shall enter the house of the thief, and the house of him who swears falsely by my name; and it shall abide in his house and consume it, both timber and stones."*

[5]*Then the angel who talked with me came forward and said to me, "Lift your eyes, and see what this is that goes forth." [6]And I said, "What is it?" He said, "This is the ephah that goes forth." And he said, "This is their iniquity[d] in all the land." [7]And behold, the leaden cover[†] was lifted, and there was a woman sitting in the ephah! [8]And he said, "This is Wickedness." And he thrust her*

back into the ephah, and thrust down the leaden weight upon its mouth. ⁹Then I lifted my eyes and saw, and behold, two women coming forward! The wind was in their wings; they had wings like the wings of a stork, and they lifted up the ephah between earth and heaven. ¹⁰Then I said to the angel who talked with me, "Where are they taking the ephah?" ¹¹He said to me, "To the land of Shinar, to build a house for it; and when this is prepared, they will set the ephah down there on its base."

d Gk Compare Syr: Heb *eye* *LXX *sickle* †LXX *talent of lead*

OVERVIEW: The taking of false oaths and the destructive consequences that follow is a playing out of the sickle of divine justice. Regulus and his dealing with the Carthaginians is offered as an example of justice (AUGUSTINE). Sinners who are not sons of Abraham sink like stones. Zechariah's talent of lead is iniquity in every shape and form (ORIGEN). The flying axe and sickle of judgment have already arrived with the first advent. Those who disbelieved Christ have brought calamity upon themselves (CHRYSOSTOM). Virtues are like clouds and doves that fly unimpeded, whereas sin is like lead because it is heavy and drags a person down (GREGORY OF NYSSA). Good and degenerate deeds tip the balance of God's justice. While no one is sinless, through good deeds the weight of sin is lessened. Evil is hard to carry like a heavy lead weight (AMBROSE).

5:1 A Flying Scroll

THE SICKLE IS AN INSTRUMENT OF GOD'S WRATH. AUGUSTINE: As to the suggestion you[1] made in your letter that we should examine together the nature of an oath extorted by force, I beg of you, do not let our discussion turn crystal-clear matters into murky ones. If a servant of God were threatened with certain death, so that he should swear to do something forbidden and wicked, he still ought rather to die than to swear, so as not to commit a crime in fulfilling his oath. But in this case, . . . it was only the persistent shouting of the people that was forcing the man not to any crime but to what could be lawfully done, if it were done. And . . . the only thing to fear was that a few vio-

lent men, mingled with a crowd of mostly good ones, might seize the occasion to start a riot, under pretence of virtuous indignation, and might break out into some accursed disturbance to satisfy their passion for robbery. And when even this fear was unfounded, who would think that perjury could be committed even to avoid certain death, much less loss or some kind of physical injury? That individual called Regulus[2] had never heard what the holy Scriptures say about the wrongfulness of a false oath. He had learned nothing about the sickle of Zechariah, and obviously he had not sworn to the Carthaginians by the sacraments of Christ but by the filthiness of demons. Yet he did not so fear certain torture and a horrible sort of death as to take his oath under compulsion, but he went to meet them to avoid perjuring himself, because he had sworn on oath of his own free will. LETTER 125.[3]

SIN LIKE LEAD SINKS. ORIGEN: "They sank in the depth like a stone."[4] Why "did they sink in the depth like a stone"? Because they were not the kind of "stones which sons of Abraham could be raised up"[5] but the kind which love the depth and desire the liquid element, that is, who seize the bitter and fluid desire of present things. Whence it is said of these: "They sank like lead in very deep water."[6] They are serious sinners. For iniquity is also shown "to sit upon a talent of lead," as Zechariah the prophet says: "I saw a woman sitting upon a talent of lead, and I said, 'Who is this?' And he an-

---

[1]Augustine is writing to Alypius, bishop of Thagaste and close associate of Augustine's throughout their lives. [2]A consul of Rome. [3]FC 18:341-42. [4]Ex 15:5. [5]Mt 3:9. [6]Ex 15:10.

swered, 'Iniquity.' " Hence it is, therefore, that the unjust "sank in the depth, like lead in very deep water."[7] HOMILIES ON EXODUS 6.4.[8]

5:5 Look and See

PURGING THROUGH AXE AND SICKLE. CHRYSOSTOM: "For now," he says, "the axe is laid at the root of the trees."[9] There is nothing more terrible than this turn of his discourse. For it is no longer "a flying sickle,"[10] or "the taking down of a hedge," or "the treading under foot of a vineyard,"[11] but an axe exceedingly sharp, and what is worse, it is even at the roots. For inasmuch as they continually disbelieved the prophets and used to say, "Where is the Day of the Lord?"[12] and "Let the counsel of the holy one of Israel come, that way we may know it,"[13] by reason that it was many years before what they said came to pass; to lead them off from this encouragement also, he sets the terrors close to them. And this he declared by saying "now," and by his putting it to "the root," "for the space between is nothing now," he says, "but it is laid to the very root." And he said not "to the branches" or "to the fruits" but "to the root." Signifying that if they were negligent, they would have incurable horrors to endure, and not have so much as hope of remedy. It being no servant who is now come, as those before him were, but the very Lord of all, bringing on them his fierce and most effectual vengeance. HOMILIES ON THE GOSPEL OF MATTHEW 3:7.4.[14]

5:7 The Lead Cover Lifted

VIRTUE LIKE DOVES, SIN LIKE LEAD. GREGORY OF NYSSA: For virtue is something light and exhilarating. All who live according to it "fly along the clouds," according to Isaiah,[15] and "like doves" with their young, but sin is heavy, seated, as one of the prophets says, upon a "talent of lead." If such an interpretation of Scripture appears to anyone to be forced and unfitting, because he does not think the miracle of the sea[16] was written as an aid to us, let him listen to the apostle saying that he wrote symbolically, both for the people of his own time and "for our correction."[17] ON VIRGINITY 18.[18]

JUDGMENT AND WEIGHT OF SIN LIKE LEAD. AMBROSE: Each one will have the weight of his good deeds hung in the balance, and for a few moments of a good work or a degenerate deed the scale often inclines to this side or that. If evil inclines the scale, alas for me; if good, pardon is ready at hand. No one is free from sin, but when good deeds prevail, the weight of sins is lessened; they are cast into the shadow and covered up. So, in the day of judgment, our works will either succor us or plunge us into the depths, like people weighted down with a millstone. Iniquity is heavy, supported, as it were, on a talent of lead; avarice is hard to carry; so too all pride and appearance of fraud. Urge the people of the Lord to hope more in the Lord, therefore, to abound in the riches of simplicity, in which they may walk without a snare, without hindrance. LETTER 15.[19]

---

[7]Ex 15:5, 10. [8]FC 71:289. [9]Mt 3:10. [10]Zech 5:1 LXX. [11]Is 5:5. [12]Amos 5:18; Jer 17:15; Ezek 12:22, 27. [13]Is 5:19. [14]NPNF 1 10:69-70. [15]Is 60:8. [16]Ex 14:21-31. [17]1 Cor 10:11. [18]FC 58:60. [19]FC 26:83.

6:1-15 VISIONS OF FOUR CHARIOTS
AND THE CROWNING OF JOSHUA

¹*And again I lifted my eyes and saw, and behold, four chariots came out from between two mountains; and the mountains were mountains of bronze. ²The first chariot had red horses, the second black horses, ³the third white horses, and the fourth chariot dappled gray^e horses. ⁴Then I said to the angel who talked with me, "What are these, my lord?" ⁵And the angel answered me, "These are going forth to the four winds of heaven, after presenting themselves before the LORD of all the earth. ⁶The chariot with the black horses goes toward the north country, the white ones go toward the west country,^{f} and the dappled ones go toward the south country." ⁷When the steeds came out, they were impatient to get off and patrol the earth. And he said, "Go, patrol the earth." So they patrolled the earth. ⁸Then he cried to me, "Behold, those who go toward the north country have set my Spirit at rest in the north country."*

⁹*And the word of the LORD came to me: ¹⁰"Take from the exiles Heldai, Tobijah, and Jedaiah, who have arrived from Babylon; and go the same day to the house of Josiah, the son of Zephaniah. ¹¹Take from them silver and gold, and make a crown,^{g} and set it upon the head of Joshua, the son of Jehozadak, the high priest; ¹²and say to him, 'Thus says the LORD of hosts, "Behold, the man whose name is the Branch:* for he shall grow up in his place, and he shall build the temple of the LORD. ¹³It is he who shall build the temple of the LORD, and shall bear royal honor, and shall sit and rule upon his throne. And there shall be a priest by his throne, and peaceful understanding shall be between them both." ' ¹⁴And the crown^h shall be in the temple of the LORD as a reminder to Heldai,^{i} Tobijah, Jedaiah, and Josiah^j the son of Zephaniah.*

¹⁵*"And those who are far off shall come and help to build the temple of the LORD; and you shall know that the LORD of hosts has sent me to you. And this shall come to pass, if you will diligently obey the voice of the LORD your God."*

e Compare Gk: The meaning of the Hebrew word is uncertain   f Cn: Heb *after them*   g Gk Mss: Heb *crowns*   h Gk: Heb *crowns*   i With verse 10: Heb *Helem*
j With verse 10: Heb *Hen*   *LXX *the Orient* or *the east*, i.e., the direction in which the sun rises

OVERVIEW: Chariots are attributed in a mystical sense to heavenly beings, which signify fellowship and unity in the celestial order. The wheels of the chariot typify staying on the straight road of heavenly intelligence and not directed by this world (PSEUDO-DIONYSUS). The writer announces the question as to why the unbelieving Jews are rebuked as Satan and even called sons of Satan for transgressing the commandment (EZNIK). The Orient, which rises from the east to give spiritual light that dispels the ignorance of darkness, is the resurrection of Christ. The resurrection occurred in the dim morning twilight, and he is there daily every morning to help (BASIL). The reference to the octave is a call to accept the transitory nature of time, thus life itself. However, the octave signals that there is a next age to replace the one that now exists. The great day that will rise and whose sun is righteousness is never veiled by the "settings" of this age (GREGORY OF NYSSA). When Judas went out in the night to betray Jesus, he also went into a spiritual night having left "the Sun of justice," Jesus whose name is "Sunrise." Judas is an example of how the darkness did not comprehend the light (ORIGEN).

6:1 Four Chariots

THE CHARIOTS ARE ANGELS. PSEUDO-DIONYSIUS: I must now look at the reason for applying to heavenly beings the title of rivers, wheels and chariots. The rivers of fire[1] signify those divine channels that are forever dispensing their generous and unchecked flow and nourishing with their life-giving fruitfulness. The chariots[2] signify fellowship binding together beings of the same order. As for the winged wheels[3] which go ahead with neither twist nor swerve, these have to do with the power to keep right on along the straight road, directly and without wandering off, and all this because the wheel of their intelligence is guided in a way which has nothing in it of this world. Yet it is possible that the iconography of the wheels of the mind be explained by another uplifting [of the mind from perceptible images to intelligent meanings]. For, as the theologian has pointed out, they are called "Gelgel,"[4] which in Hebrew signifies both "revolving" and "revealing." Those godlike wheels of fire "revolve" about themselves in their ceaseless movement around the Good, and they "reveal" since they expose hidden things, and they lift up the mind from below and carry the most exalted enlightenments down to the lowliest. CELESTIAL HIERARCHY 15.9.[5]

6:11 Joshua, the Son of Jehozadak

JEWS AS SINNERS. EZNIK OF KOLB: And in the days of Joshua, son of Jehozadak, why did an angel say to the adversary who was opposing him, "The Lord rebuke you, O Satan"?[6] And why are the Jews called "sons of Satan" for transgressing the laws, if he [the adversary] perseveres in the command he received and they transgressed the commandment? And why

would he be called utterly a liar,[7] he who remains faithful to the rule? Because that evil comes not from him but from the very one who made him so. And why should he be sent into the "outer darkness"?[8] ON GOD 209.[9]

6:12 The Branch

RESURRECTION FORETOLD. BASIL THE GREAT: Therefore God helps the city, producing in it early morning by his own rising and coming. "Behold a man," it is said, "the Orient is his name." For those upon whom the spiritual light will rise, when the darkness that comes from ignorance and wickedness is destroyed, early morning will be at hand. Since, then, light has come into the world in order that he who walks about in it may not stumble, his help is able to cause the early morning. Or perhaps, since the resurrection was in the dim morning twilight, God will help the city in the morning early, who on the third day, early on the morning of the resurrection gained the victory through death. HOMILIES ON THE PSALMS 45.18.5.[10]

CHRIST IS THE RISING RESURRECTION. GREGORY OF NYSSA: The inscription, "for the octave,"[11] therefore, that we not look to the present time, but that we look toward the "octave." For whenever this transitory and fleeting time ceases, in which one thing comes to be and another is dissolved, and the necessity of coming to be has passed away, and that which is dissolved no longer exists . . . the hebdomad too, which measures time, will by all means halt. Then that "octave," which is the next age, will succeed it. The whole of the latter becomes one day, as one of the prophets says when he calls the life, which is anticipated "the Great Day."[12] For this reason the perceptible sun does not enlighten that day, but

---

[1]Dan 7:10. [2]2 Kings 2:11; 6:17; Ps 104:3 (103:3 LXX). [3]Ezek 1:15-21; 10:1-13; Dan 7:9. [4]Ezek 10:13 LXX. [5]PDCW 189-90. [6]Zech 3:2. [7]Jn 8:44. [8]Mt 8:12. [9]EKOG 126. [10]FC 46:304. [11]E.g., Ps 6; 11. [12]Joel 2:11; Mal 4:1.

"the true light,"[13] the "sun of righteousness,"[14] who is designated "rising" by the prophecy because he is never veiled by the settings. ON THE INSCRIPTIONS OF THE PSALMS 2.5.53.[15]

CHRIST IS SUNRISE. ORIGEN: Nor was there night in Peter when he confessed, "You are the Christ, the Son of the living God,"[16] when the heavenly Father revealed it to him, but there was night in him too at the moment of his denial.[17] And in the present instance, moreover, when Judas received the morsel [and] went out immediately, night was present in him at the same time he went out,[18] for the man whose name is "Sunrise" was not present with him because he left "the Sun of justice"[19] behind when he went out.

And Judas, who was filled with darkness, pursued Jesus; but the darkness and the one who had taken it up did not apprehend the light that was pursued. Wherefore also, when he said as word of justification, "I have sinned because I betrayed just blood"[20] and "went and hanged himself,"[21] Satan, who was in him, led him to the noose and hung him, at which time the devil also touched his soul. For Judas was not such that the Lord could say to the devil on his behalf what he said on Job's behalf, "But touch not his soul."[22] COMMENTARY ON THE GOSPEL OF JOHN 32.315-17.[23]

---

[13]Jn 1:9. [14]Mal 4:2. [15]GNTIP 136-37*. [16]Mt 16:16. [17]Mt 26:69-74. [18]Jn 13:30. [19]Mal 4:2. [20]Mt 27:4. [21]Mt 27:5. [22]Job 1:12; 2:6. [23]FC 89:401.

7:1-14 PROPER FASTING AND REPENTANCE

[1]In the fourth year of King Darius, the word of the LORD came to Zechariah on the fourth day of the ninth month, which is Chislev. [2]Now the people of Bethel had sent Sharezer and Regemmelech and their men, to entreat the favor of the LORD, [3]and to ask the priests of the house of the LORD of hosts and the prophets, "Should I mourn and fast in the fifth month, as I have done for so many years?" [4]Then the word of the LORD of hosts came to me: [5]"Say to all the people of the land and the priests, When you fasted and mourned in the fifth month and in the seventh, for these seventy years, was it for me that you fasted? [6]And when you eat and when you drink, do you not eat for yourselves and drink for yourselves? [7]When Jerusalem was inhabited and in prosperity, with her cities round about her, and the South and the lowland were inhabited, were not these the words which the LORD proclaimed by the former prophets?"

[8]And the word of the LORD came to Zechariah, saying, [9]"Thus says the LORD of hosts, Render true judgments, show kindness and mercy each to his brother, [10]do not oppress the widow, the fatherless, the sojourner, or the poor; and let none of you devise evil against his brother in your heart." [11]But they refused to hearken, and turned a stubborn shoulder, and stopped their ears that they might not hear. [12]They made their hearts like adamant lest they should hear the law and the words which the LORD of hosts had sent by his Spirit through the former prophets. Therefore great wrath came from the LORD of hosts. [13]"As I called, and they would not hear, so they called, and I would not hear," says the LORD of hosts, [14]"and I scattered them with a whirlwind among all the

nations which they had not known. Thus the land they left was desolate, so that no one went to and fro, and the pleasant land was made desolate."

OVERVIEW: Jewish identity, which was based upon the temple and sacrifices, is now confused because of the destruction of the temple by the Romans. Fasting is useless unless it is accompanied by acts of mercy, justice and charity (CHRYSOSTOM). Eating and drinking ritual foods are useless when faith and righteousness are absent. God is pleased only by faith, innocence, truth and virtue that come forth from the soul and not the stomach (NOVATIAN). Just as the fasting of the Jews was made null by the oppression of the slaves, it is now even more so because of their part in the crucifixion of Jesus (CHRYSOSTOM). Caesarius gives a wise caution against judging a person's motive regarding fasting, vigils, alms and abstinence. It is not possible to know the heart of a person. However, in the case of open sin, one is able to render a just judgment (CAESARIUS). The prophet reminds believers that God desires his followers to be just and generous to widows, orphans, the poor and neighbors (IRENAEUS). God expects believers not to plot evil against brother and neighbor (TERTULLIAN).

7:5 Fasting and Mourning

NO TEMPLE, NO WORSHIP FOR THE JEWS. CHRYSOSTOM: Even when they were exiles in Babylon and their captors were trying to force them to sing a sacred hymn, they neither yielded nor obeyed, even though they were captives and slaves to the masters who had conquered them. . . .

And they could not observe the fast. The prophet made this clear when he said, "'Did you keep a fast for me for seventy years?' said the Lord." Nor could they offer sacrifice or pour libations. Listen to the three boys when they said, "We have no prince, prophet or leader, no place to offer firstfruits in your sight and find mercy."[1] The prophet did not say, "We have no priest," because there were priests among the captives. But to make you understand that the whole matter

was a question of the place and that the whole code of laws was bound up with that place, he said, "We have no place." DEMONSTRATION AGAINST THE PAGANS 17.1.3.[2]

FASTING USELESS IF DOING EVIL. CHRYSOSTOM: After all, if the loving Lord said to the hardhearted Jews through the prophet, "Behold those seventy years: surely it was not for me that you kept that fast? And if you eat and drink, is it not for yourselves that you eat and drink? This is what the Lord, mighty ruler, says: 'Deliver just judgments, show mercy and pity each of you to your neighbor, do not oppress widow or orphan, sojourner or poor person, and let none of you plot evil against your brother in your heart.'" In other words, if those people sitting in darkness and caught up in the shadow of error gained no benefit merely from fasting without performing those other good works or expelling from their heart evil intended against their neighbor, what sort of an excuse can we offer of whom more is required—not simply commanded to abstain from that, but even obliged to love our enemies and be kind to them? And why do I say "be kind"? Also to pray for them and beseech the Lord and implore his providence in their behalf. After all, this most of all will be a recommendation for us on that fearful day, and our best insurance against our sins, if we are disposed in this way toward our enemies. I mean, even if the commandment is exceedingly rigorous, provided you keep in mind the prize laid up for those who do right, it will seem nothing at all, even though it is in fact very rigorous. Why is that? Scripture says, "If you do this, you will be like my Father in heaven."[3] To make the point clearer to us it added, "Because he makes his sun rise on the evil

---

[1]Dan 3:38 LXX (Song of the Three Young Men 15). [2]FC 73:257-58.
[3]Mt 5:45.

and the good"; that is, it is saying, you are imitating God as far as human beings can. I mean, just as he makes the sun rise not only on the just but also on those who do evil, and provides rain and seasonal storms not only to the good but also to the evil, so you too, if you love not only those who love you but also those badly disposed to you, are imitating your Lord as far as you can. Homilies on Genesis 4.17.[4]

7:6 Eating and Drinking

Eating and Drinking Are Irrelevant in Relationship with God. Novatian: By righteousness, I say, and by continence and by the rest of the virtues, God is worshiped. For Zechariah also tells us, saying, "If you eat or drink, is it not *you* that eat or drink?" declaring thereby that meat and drink do not pertain to God but to humankind: for neither is God fleshly, so as to be pleased with flesh; nor is he careful for these pleasures, so as to rejoice in our food. God rejoices in our faith alone, in our innocence alone, in our truth alone, in our virtues alone. And these dwell not in our belly but in our soul; and these are acquired for us by divine awe and heavenly fear, not by earthly food. And such the apostle fitly rebuked as "obeying the superstitions of angels, puffed up by their fleshly mind; not holding Christ the head, from whom all the body, joined together by links, and inwoven and grown together by mutual members in the bond of charity, increase to God"[5] but observing those things: "Touch not, taste not, handle not; which indeed seem to have a form of religion, in that the body is not spared."[6] Yet there is no advantage at all of righteousness, while we are recalled by a voluntary slavery to those elements to which by baptism we have died. On Jewish Foods 5.[7]

7:9 Giving True Judgment

Fasting Useless If Quarreling. Chrysostom: [You] should have fasted then, when drunkenness was doing those terrible things to you, when your gluttony was giving birth to your un-

godliness—not now. Now your fasting is untimely and an abomination. Who said so? Isaiah himself when he called out in a loud voice: "'I did not choose this fast,' says the Lord."[8] Why? "You quarrel and squabble when you fast and strike those subject to you with your fists."[9] But if your fasting was an abomination when you were striking your fellow slaves, does it become acceptable now that you have slain your master? How could that be right? Discourses Against Judaizing Christians 1.6.[10]

Caution About Judging. Caesarius of Arles: For this reason, beloved, I am inserting certain headings and notes as to how you ought to understand and receive these matters, so through the goodness of God you can accept and observe them better. In order that the things that I have said may be kept more closely in your hearts, I am briefly repeating what I mentioned. Therefore, in these matters, as I already said above, we judge others dangerously when it is doubtful whether they are acting with a good or bad intention in fasting, keeping vigils, bestowing alms, abstaining or not abstaining from wine and meat, and other similar matters. These things can be done for the sake of God or for human praise, and because we do not know with what motive they are done, we should not judge at all. In matters of this kind the Lord said, "Do not judge, that you may not be judged,"[11] but in a matter of open sin it is said, "Reprove, entreat, rebuke with all patience and teaching."[12] Moreover, there is what we already mentioned: "Render just judgment." Now if we are willing to consider these words carefully, as we believe, brothers, and with God's help to observe them with great solicitude, we are freed from not a little sin. For by the indiscreet judgment, the majority of the human race is proven to be prompt and ready to criticize, although they are not so willing to be judged by others as they are to judge them. Because of this

---

[4]FC 74:62. [5]Col 2:18-19. [6]Col 2:21, 23. [7]ANF 5:649. [8]Is 58:6 LXX. [9]Is 58:4. [10]FC 68:8-9. [11]Mt 7:1. [12]2 Tim 4:2.

fact sacred Scripture admonishes us, saying, "Before investigating, find fault; examine first, then criticize."[13] Every person first wants to be questioned, and then, if he is guilty, he patiently endures reproof. Now since we all want this to happen to us from others, it is just that we strive to fulfill the same thing toward them. Let us first inquire with patience and solicitude. Then, when we have learned something quite certainly, we should be willing to give reproof if it is evil and to defend it if it is good, because of what is written, "All that you wish men to do to you, even so do you also to them in like manner; for this is the law and the prophets."[14] And so let us turn to the Lord and implore his help, so that he himself may deign in his goodness to grant us true discretion and perfect charity: to whom is glory and might together with the Father and the Holy Spirit forever and ever. Amen. SERMON 148.3.[15]

7:10 Do Not Oppress the Disadvantaged

PROTECT THE NEEDY. IRENAEUS: And Zechariah also, among the twelve prophets, pointing out to the people the will of God, says, "These things does the Lord omnipotent declare: 'Execute true judgment, and show mercy and compassion each one to his brother. And oppress not the widow, and the orphan, and the proselyte and the poor; and let none imagine evil against your brother in his heart.'" And again, he says, "'These are the words which you shall utter. Speak the truth every man to his neighbor, and execute peaceful judgment in your gates, and let none of you imagine evil in your heart against his brother, and you shall not love false swearing, for all these things I hate,' says the Lord almighty."[16] Moreover, David also says in like manner: "What man is there who desires life and would long to see good days? Keep your tongue from evil, and your lips that they speak not guile. Shun evil and do good: seek peace, and pursue it."[17] AGAINST HERESIES 4.17.3.[18]

DO NO EVIL TO YOUR NEIGHBOR. TERTULLIAN: And therefore this question must at once be determined, whether the discipline of patience is enjoined by the Creator? When by Zechariah he commanded, "Let none of you imagine evil against his brother," he did not expressly include his "neighbor;" but then in another passage he says, "Let none of you imagine evil in your hearts against his neighbor."[19] He who counseled that an injury should be forgotten was still more likely to counsel the patient endurance of it. AGAINST MARCION 4.16.[20]

---

[13]Sir 11:7. [14]Mt 7:12. [15]FC 47:318-19*. [16]Zech 8:16-17. [17]Ps 34:12-14 (33:13-15 LXX). [18]ANF 1:483-84*. [19]Zech 8:17. [20]ANF 3:370*.

8:1-23 THE FUTURE OF ISRAEL:
LOVE TRUTH, JUSTICE AND PEACE

¹And the word of the LORD of hosts came to me, saying, ²"Thus says the LORD of hosts: I am jealous for Zion with great jealousy, and I am jealous for her with great wrath. ³Thus says the LORD: I will return to Zion, and will dwell in the midst of Jerusalem, and Jerusalem shall be called the faithful city, and the mountain of the LORD of hosts, the holy mountain. ⁴Thus says the LORD of hosts: Old men and old women shall again sit in the streets of Jerusalem, each with staff in hand for very age. ⁵And the streets of the city shall be full of boys and girls playing in its streets. ⁶Thus says the LORD of hosts: If it is marvelous in the sight of the remnant of this people in these days, should it also be marvelous in my sight, says the LORD of hosts? ⁷Thus says the LORD of hosts: Behold, I will save my people from the east country and from the west country; ⁸and I will bring them to dwell in the midst of Jerusalem; and they shall be my people and I will be their God, in faithfulness and in righteousness."

⁹Thus says the LORD of hosts: "Let your hands be strong, you who in these days have been hearing these words from the mouth of the prophets, since the day that the foundation of the house of the LORD of hosts was laid, that the temple might be built. ¹⁰For before those days there was no wage for man or any wage for beast, neither was there any safety from the foe for him who went out or came in; for I set every man against his fellow. ¹¹But now I will not deal with the remnant of this people as in the former days, says the LORD of hosts. ¹²For there shall be a sowing of peace; the vine shall yield its fruit, and the ground shall give its increase, and the heavens shall give their dew; and I will cause the remnant of this people to possess all these things. ¹³And as you have been a byword of cursing among the nations, O house of Judah and house of Israel, so will I save you and you shall be a blessing. Fear not, but let your hands be strong."

¹⁴For thus says the LORD of hosts: "As I purposed to do evil to you, when your fathers provoked me to wrath, and I did not relent, says the LORD of hosts, ¹⁵so again have I purposed in these days to do good to Jerusalem and to the house of Judah; fear not. ¹⁶These are the things that you shall do: Speak the truth to one another, render in your gates judgments that are true and make for peace, ¹⁷do not devise evil in your hearts against one another, and love no false oath, for all these things I hate, says the LORD."

¹⁸And the word of the LORD of hosts came to me, saying, ¹⁹"Thus says the LORD of hosts: The fast of the fourth month, and the fast of the fifth, and the fast of the seventh, and the fast of the tenth, shall be to the house of Judah seasons of joy and gladness, and cheerful feasts; therefore love truth and peace.

²⁰"Thus says the LORD of hosts: Peoples* shall yet come, even the inhabitants of many cities; ²¹the inhabitants of one city shall go to another, saying, 'Let us go at once to entreat the favor of the LORD, and to seek the LORD of hosts; I am going.' ²²Many peoples and strong nations shall come to

seek the LORD of hosts in Jerusalem, and to entreat the favor of the LORD. [23]*Thus says the LORD of hosts: In those days ten men from the nations of every tongue shall take hold of the robe of a Jew, saying, 'Let us go with you, for we have heard that God is with you.'"*

*LXX Many peoples

OVERVIEW: Virginity as a vocation was foretold by the prophet when he spoke about being intoxicated by the spirit (JEROME). God requires Christians to love neighbors and not the burnt offerings and sacrifices of the old covenant (EPISTLE OF BARNABAS). Anger needs to be purged from the heart. To harbor anger leads to torment and grief (CHRYSOSTOM). The feasts of the pagans are worthless, whereas those of the Christians are based upon virtue and temperance, thus fulfilling Zechariah's prophecy regarding their transformation under the New Testament (ATHANASIUS). A good Christian longs to make progress in holiness (AUGUSTINE). The restoration of Israel will result in mass conversion of pagans to the Lord (THEODORE).

8:5 Children Playing in the Streets

THE WINE THAT GIVES BIRTH TO VIRGINITY. JEROME: This is that wine with which, when youths and maidens are intoxicated, they at once thirst for virginity. They are filled with the spirit of chastity, and the prophecy of Zechariah comes to pass, at least if we follow the Hebrew literally, for he prophesied concerning virgins: "And the streets of the city shall be full of boys and girls playing in the streets thereof. For what is his goodness, and what is his beauty, but the corn of the elect, and wine that gives birth to virgins?" They are virgins of whom it is written in the forty-fifth psalm:[1] "She is led to the king, with her virgin companions, her escort, in her train. With joy and gladness they are led along as they enter the palace of the king." AGAINST JOVINIANUS 1.30.[2]

8:16 Virtues Commanded

KEEP A PURE HEART. PSEUDO-BARNABAS:

[Burnt offerings] he accordingly did away with, so that the new law of our Lord Jesus Christ might be without restraining yoke and without manmade offering. Again he says to them, "Did I command your fathers when they came out of the land of Egypt to offer me burnt offerings and sacrifices? Rather I did command them this: Let none of you cherish evil in his heart against his neighbor, and do not love a false oath." We ought therefore to understand, if we are not senseless, the kindly intention of our Father, for he speaks to us, desiring us not to err like them but to seek how to make our offering to him. To us he accordingly speaks thus: "A contrite heart is a sacrifice to the Lord; an odor of sweetness to the Lord is a heart which glorifies its maker."[3] We ought, therefore, to watch carefully after our salvation, brothers, lest the evil one, sneaking in among us deceitfully, push us away from our life. EPISTLE OF BARNABAS 2.[4]

PURGE THE SELF OF ANGER. CHRYSOSTOM: For indeed there is nothing equal to this virtue. Would you learn the power of this virtue? "Though Moses and Samuel stood before me," says God, "my soul would not regard them."[5] Nevertheless those whom Moses and Samuel were not able to snatch away from God's wrath, this precept when observed was able to snatch away. Hence it is that he continually exhorts those to whom he had spoken of these things, saying, "Let none of you revengefully imagine evil against your brother in his heart," and "Let none of you think of his neighbor's malice." It is not said merely, forego wrath; but do not retain it in your mind; do not think of it; part with all your

---

[1]Ps 45:13-15 (44:13-15 LXX). [2]NPNF 2 6:369. [3]Ps 51:17 (50:19 LXX). [4]FC 1:192-93*. [5]Jer 15:1.

resentment; do away with the sore. For you suppose that you are paying him back the injury; but you are first tormenting yourself, and setting up your rage as an executioner within you in every part, and tearing up your own bowels. For what can be more wretched than a person perpetually angry? And just as maniacs never enjoy tranquility, so also one who is resentful and retains an enemy will never have the enjoyment of any peace. Incessantly raging, [such a person] daily increases the tempest of his thoughts, calling to mind his words and his acts, and detesting the very name of one who has aggrieved him. If you but mention his enemy, he becomes furious at once, and sustains great inward anguish; and should he only by chance get a bare glimpse of him, he fears and trembles, as if encountering the worst evils. HOMILIES CONCERNING THE STATUES 20.6.[6]

8:19 *Times of Joy*

CHRISTIAN FEASTS ARE DIFFERENT FROM PAGAN ONES. ATHANASIUS: Therefore, when we come to the feast, we must not treat it as the shadows and pictures that Israel had, for they are fulfilled. Nor should we come to it as we would any ordinary secular feast. Oh, no! Let us go quickly to the Lord, who is himself the feast.[7] We must not look at the feast as a time to delight the appetite and overindulge but as a display of virtue. The feasts of the heathen are made up of laziness and greed. They think idleness is the mark of a feast, and when they feast they do the despica-

ble acts of death and hell. Our feasts, on the other hand, are scenes of virtuous activities and the practice of temperance. The prophetic word says it very clearly, "The fasts of the fourth, fifth, seventh and tenth months shall become feasts of joy and gladness for the house of Judah." FESTAL LETTERS 11.[8]

8:22 *Seek the Lord*

THE ESSENCE OF CHRISTIAN CALLING. AUGUSTINE: The whole life of a good Christian is a holy longing to make progress. SERMONS 4.6.[9]

8:23 *God with You*

MASS CONVERSION TO GOD. THEODORE OF MOPSUESTIA: God will make the return of the remainder so conspicuous that many people who are from different nations and have shared that calamity will perceive God's care for the people. They will lay hold of any one of them and use him as a guide for a return to Jerusalem, since everyone is sufficiently stirred up to that end from the clear realization that God is with them on the basis of the incredible deeds done for them. The phrase "ten men," note, here too refers not to number but has the meaning of many. COMMENTARY ON ZECHARIAH 8.20-23.[10]

---

[6]NPNF 1 9:473-74*. [7]1 Cor 5:7. [8]ARL 180. [9]PMPC 2:392. [10]PG 66:552.

9:1-9 PROPHECY ABOUT THE COMING OF THE MESSIANIC KING OF JERUSALEM

An Oracle

¹The word of the LORD is against the land of
  Hadrach
  and will rest upon Damascus.
For to the LORD belong the cities of Aram,ᵏ*
  even as all the tribes of Israel;
²Hamath also, which borders thereon,
  Tyre and Sidon, though they are very wise.
³Tyre has built herself a rampart,
  and heaped up silver like dust,
  and gold like the mud of the streets.
⁴But lo, the Lord will strip her of her
  possessions
  and hurl her wealth into the sea,
  and she shall be devoured by fire.

⁵Ashkelon shall see it, and be afraid;
  Gaza too, and shall writhe in anguish;
  Ekron also, because its hopes are
  confounded.
The king shall perish from Gaza;

Ashkelon shall be uninhabited;
⁶a mongrel people shall dwell in Ashdod;
  and I will make an end of the pride of
  Philistia.
⁷I will take away its blood from its mouth,
  and its abominations from between its
  teeth;
it too shall be a remnant for our God;
  it shall be like a clan in Judah,
  and Ekron shall be like the Jebusites.
⁸Then I will encamp at my house as a guard,†
  so that none shall march to and fro;
no oppressor shall again overrun them,
  for now I see with my own eyes.
⁹Rejoice greatly, O daughter of Zion!
  Shout aloud, O daughter of Jerusalem!
Lo, your king comes to you;
  triumphant and victorious is he,‡
humble and riding on an ass,
  on a colt the foal of an ass.

k Cn: Heb *the eye of Adam (or man)*   *LXX *Yahweh has an eye for [or on] humanity*   †LXX *against a garrison*   ‡LXX *saving is he*

OVERVIEW: The synagogue has been abandoned by God and is no more efficacious than a theater (CHRYSOSTOM). The prophet predicted that Jesus would ride into Jerusalem on a donkey (JUSTIN MARTYR). The Jews have earned condemnation because they have rejected Jesus, who was foretold by the prophet (IRENAEUS). The specific mention of Christ riding on a young colt is a symbolic reference of humankind's rejuvenation in Christ (CLEMENT OF ALEXANDRIA). The ass that Jesus rode upon was a prefiguring of the salvation of the Gentiles. The ass, which once carried Bal-aam, is the church and now has the privilege to carry Christ (CHRYSOSTOM). The young colt is apparently the Gentiles, and the ass refers to Jews who believe in Christ (CAESARIUS). Jesus is the new grain that God has called out of Egypt. He is the new grain carried by the donkey to bring salvation (AMBROSE).

9:4 Devoured by Fire

JEWS ABANDONED. CHRYSOSTOM: Many, I know, respect the Jews and think that their present way of life is a venerable one. This is why I hasten to uproot and tear out this deadly opinion. I said that the synagogue is no better than a theater, and I bring forward a prophet as my witness. Surely the Jews are not more deserving of belief than their prophets. "You had a harlot's brow; you became shameless before all." Where a harlot has set herself up, that place is a brothel and a theater; it also is a den of robbers and a lodging for wild beasts. Jeremiah said, "Your house has become for me the den of a hyena." He does not simply say "of a wild beast" but "of a filthy wild beast," and again, "I have abandoned my house, I have cast off my inheritance." But when God forsakes a place, that place becomes the dwelling of demons. DISCOURSE AGAINST JUDAIZING CHRISTIANS 1.3.[1]

9:9 The King on an Ass

FOAL REPRESENTS THE GENTILES. JUSTIN MARTYR: Indeed, our Lord Jesus Christ, when he was about to enter Jerusalem, ordered his disciples to get him the ass with its foal, which was tied at a gate of the village of Bethphage, and he rode upon it as he entered Jerusalem. Since it had been explicitly foretold that the Christ would do precisely this, and when he had done it in the sight of all he furnished clear proof that he was the Christ. And yet, even after these things have happened and are proved from the Scriptures, you persist in refusing to believe. Zechariah, one of the twelve prophets, predicted this very event when he said, "Rejoice greatly, O daughter of Zion; shout for joy, O daughter of Jerusalem. Behold, your king will come to you, the just and the Savior; meek and lowly, riding upon an ass, and upon the foal of an ass." The prophetic spirit, as well as the patriarch Jacob, mentioned the ass, an animal accustomed to the yoke, and its foal, which were in his possession. Then he asked his disciples, as I have said before, to lead the beasts to him. This constituted a prediction that both you coming from the synagogue and those who would come from the Gentiles would believe in him. As the unharnessed foal was a figure of the former Gentiles, so the ass, accustomed to the yoke, was a symbol of those coming from among your people. DIALOGUE WITH TRYPHO 53.[2]

JUDGMENT OF THE JEWS. IRENAEUS: A spiritual disciple of this sort truly receiving the spirit of God, who was from the beginning, in all the dispensations of God, present with humankind, and announced things future, revealed things present, and narrated things past—[such a person] does indeed "judge all men but is himself judged by no man." For he judges the Gentiles, "who serve the creature more than the Creator,"[3] and who with a reprobate mind spend all their labor on vanity. And he also judges the Jews, who do not accept the word of liberty nor are willing to go forth free, although they have a deliverer present [with them]. But they pretend, at a time unsuitable [for such conduct], to serve, [with observances] beyond [those required by] the law, God who stands in need of nothing. And [they] do not recognize the advent of Christ, which he accomplished for the salvation of humanity. Nor are [they] willing to understand that all the prophets announced his two advents: the one, indeed, in which he became a man subject to stripes, and knowing what it is to bear infirmity,[4] and sat upon the foal of an ass, and was the stone rejected by the builders,[5] and was led as a sheep to the slaughter,[6] and by the stretching forth of his hands destroyed Amalek.[7] . . . He gathered from the ends of the earth into his father's fold the children who were scattered abroad.[8] . . . [He] remembered his own dead ones who had formerly fallen asleep and came down to them that he might deliver them. But [in the second advent] he will come on the clouds,[9] bringing on the day which burns as a furnace,[10] and striking the earth with the word of his mouth,[11] and judging the im-

---

[1]FC 68:10-11. [2]FC 6:228*. [3]Rom 1:25. [4]Is 53:3, 5. [5]Ps 118:22 (117:22 LXX); 1 Pet 2:6-7. [6]Is 53:7; Acts 8:32. [7]Ex 17:11. [8]Is 11:12. [9]Dan 7:13. [10]Mal 4:1. [11]Is 11:4.

pious with the breath of his lips. Having a fan in his hands, he cleanses his floor, and gathering the wheat indeed into his barn, he burns the chaff with unquenchable fire.[12] AGAINST HERESIES 4.33.1.[13]

THE YOUNG COLT POINTS TO REGENERATION IN CHRIST. CLEMENT OF ALEXANDRIA: At another time, he speaks of us under the figure of a colt. He means by [the colt] that we are unyoked to evil, unsubdued by wickedness, unaffected, high-spirited only with him our Father. We are colts, not stallions, "who whinny lustfully for their neighbor's wife, beasts of burden unrestrained in their lust."[14] Rather, we are free and newly born, joyous in our faith, holding fast to the course of truth, swift in seeking salvation, spurning and trampling upon worldliness. "Rejoice greatly, O daughter of Zion. Shout for joy, O daughter of Jerusalem. Behold, your king comes to you, the just and the Savior, and he is poor and riding upon an ass and upon a young colt." He is not satisfied to say "colt"; he adds "young" to emphasize humankind's rejuvenation in Christ and its unending, eternal youth and simplicity. Our divine Tamer trains such young colts as we little ones. Although the passage speaks of a young ass, it too is a colt. CHRIST THE EDUCATOR 1.5.15.[15]

THE ASS PREFIGURES GENTILES' SALVATION. CHRYSOSTOM: But how, after not walking openly among the Jews and retiring into the wilderness, does Jesus again enter openly? Having quenched their anger by retiring, he comes to them when they were stilled. Moreover, the multitude which went before and which followed after was sufficient to cast them into agony; for no sign attracted the people as that of Lazarus. And another Evangelist says that they strewed their garments under his feet[16] and that "the whole city was moved,"[17] with so great honor did he enter. And this he did, prefiguring one prophecy and fulfilling another; and the same act was the beginning of the one and the end of the other. For "Rejoice, for your king comes unto you meek" belonged to him as fulfilling a prophecy, but the sitting upon the ass was the act of one prefiguring a future event, that he was about to have the impure race of the Gentiles subject to him. HOMILIES ON JOHN 66.1.[18]

JEWISH AND GENTILE BELIEVERS. CAESARIUS OF ARLES: Now since many historical facts have already been mentioned, let us briefly relate some of the allegorical ones at the end. If you see opposing power attacking God's people, you will realize who it is that is sitting upon the ass. If you further consider how people are destroyed by demons, you will understand what the ass is. Indeed, in the Gospel you will recognize Jesus sending his disciples to an ass which was tied and its colt, so that the disciples might loose and bring her for the Lord himself to sit upon her. Perhaps this ass, that is, the church, first carried Balaam and now Christ. She had been loosed by the disciples and released from the bonds that tied for this very purpose, that the Son of God might sit upon her and with her enter the holy and heavenly city of Jerusalem. Then was fulfilled the Scripture which says, "Rejoice, O daughter of Zion, exclaim, O daughter Jerusalem! See, your king comes to you, meek and riding on a beast of burden," that is, an ass (doubtless he is speaking of believers among the Jews) "or young colt" (these apparently are those of the Gentiles who believe in Christ our Lord). SERMON 113.[19]

NEW GRAIN CARRIED BY THE ASS. AMBROSE: The patriarchs had gone at first without Benjamin, and the apostles without Paul. Each came, not as the first, but was summoned by those who were the first, and by his arrival he made the goods of those who were first more plenteous. "There is grain in Egypt"; that is, where the famine is greater, the plenty is greater. There is much

---

[12]Mt 3:12; Lk 3:17. [13]ANF 1:506*. [14]Jer 5:8. [15]FC 23:16*. [16]Mt 21:8. [17]Mt 21:10. [18]NPNF 1 14:245*. [19]FC 47:160.

grain in Egypt. Surely, and God the Father says, "Out of Egypt I called my Son!"[20] Such is the fecundity of that grain, for there could not have been a harvest unless the Egyptians had sown the grain earlier. There is, then, grain which no one earlier believed to exist; the patriarchs engage in negotiations in regard to this grain. And they indeed brought money, but the good Joseph gave them the grain and gave them back the money.[21]

For Christ is not bought with money but with grace; your payment is faith, and with it are bought God's mysteries. Moreover, this grain is carried by the ass,[22] which before was unclean according to the law but now is clean in grace. JOSEPH 8.45.[23]

---

[20]Hos 11:1; Mt 2:15. [21]Gen 42:25-28. [22]Gen 44:3. [23]FC 65:218-19.

9:10-17 ESCHATOLOGICAL KINGDOM OF THE LORD

[10]I will cut off the chariot from Ephraim
  and the war horse from Jerusalem;
and the battle bow shall be cut off,
  and he shall command peace to the
    nations;
his dominion shall be from sea to sea,
  and from the River to the ends of the earth.

[11]As for you also, because of the blood of my
    covenant with you,
  I will set your captives free from the
    waterless pit.
[12]Return to your stronghold, O prisoners of
    hope;
  today I declare that I will restore to you
    double.
[13]For I have bent Judah as my bow;
  I have made Ephraim its arrow.
I will brandish your sons, O Zion,
  over your sons, O Greece,
  and wield you like a warrior's sword.

[14]Then the LORD will appear over them,
  and his arrow go forth like lightning;
the Lord GOD will sound the trumpet,
  and march forth in the whirlwinds of the
    south.
[15]The LORD of hosts will protect them,
  and they shall devour and tread down
    the slingers;[l]
and they shall drink their blood[m] like wine,[*]
  and be full like a bowl,
  drenched like the corners of the altar.

[16]On that day the LORD their God will save
    them
  for they are the flock of his people;
for like the jewels of a crown
  they shall shine on his land.
[17]Yea, how good and how fair it shall be!
  Grain shall make the young men
    flourish,
  and new wine the maidens.

---

l Cn: Heb *the slingstones*   m Gk: Heb *be turbulent*   *LXX *They will drink them as wine*

OVERVIEW: Victory over the evil spiritual power and the passions of the body were foretold by the prophet (AMBROSE). That victory also signifies the eternal peace from the Lord upon Israel (THE-

ODORE). The deliverance from sin and eternal punishment by the resurrection were foretold in the prophet's words regarding the prisoners being saved from the pit (BEDE). The release from death by the resurrection was foretold by Zechariah's prediction that the prisoner would be set free (CYRIL OF JERUSALEM). The tower referred to by Zechariah is Jesus (AUGUSTINE). A holy life is like a wheel that rolls along to higher places of spirituality. Wheels in many other prophets are symbolic of spiritual progress (JEROME). Believers are encouraged that all foods are clean to eat under the new covenant (APOSTOLIC CONSTITUTIONS).

9:10 The Chariot Cut Off from Ephraim

EVIL POWER DESTROYED. AMBROSE: Peace and tranquility of soul are more than all the glory of the house, for peace surpasses all understanding.[1] This is that peace beyond all peace, which will be given after the third moving of heaven, sea, earth and dry land, when he will destroy all the powers and principalities. "Heaven and earth will pass away,"[2] and the whole figure of this world. Every man will rise up against his brother with the sword, that is, with the word that penetrates the marrow of his soul,[3] to destroy what is opposed, namely, the chariot of Ephraim and the horse from Jerusalem, as Zechariah says. And such will be the peace over all the passions of the body which are not in opposition, and over the minds of unbelievers, who are not a hindrance, that Christ will be formed in all and will make an offering of the hearts of all people in submission to his Father. LETTER 80.[4]

END-TIME PEACE OF THE LORD. THEODORE OF MOPSUESTIA: Be glad, therefore, O Jerusalem, since of such a kind is a king appointed for you by God, and he has come to you, capable of saving his own on account of the divine influence accruing to him and justly inflicting total punishment on the adversaries. While he is riding a lowly animal for the reason that he has just arrived back from captivity, he assumes great power through

divine grace, and so from Ephraim and from Jerusalem he will remove all the chariots of the adversaries, every war horse and every battle bow— that is to say, he will drive off all enemies so that there will be no longer any adversary against the country of Judah. He will also wipe out a great multitude of the adversaries and completely deprive them of peace, crushed and destroyed in a war waged by him. COMMENTARY ON ZECHARIAH 9.8-10.[5]

9:11 The Blood of God's Covenant

HELL AND SIN CONQUERED. BEDE: It was fitting that the herald of his resurrection is reported to have been sitting, so that by sitting he might prefigure him who, having triumphed over the author of death, would ascend to his seat in the everlasting kingdom. Concerning this he said a little later, as he appeared to his disciples, "All power in heaven and on earth has been given to me"; and the evangelist Mark says, "The Lord, after he had spoken to them, was taken up into heaven and sat down at God's right hand."[6] [The angel] was sitting upon the stone with which the tomb was closed, but which had been rolled away, to teach that [Christ] had cast down and triumphed over the closed places of the lower world by his power, so that he might lift up to the light and the rest of paradise all of his own whom he found there, according to the prophet's [statement], "You also because of the blood of your covenant, have led your prisoners back from the pit, in which there is no water." HOMILY ON THE GOSPELS 2.7.[7]

TOMBS OPENED. CYRIL OF JERUSALEM: The sun was darkened because of the Sun of justice. The rocks were rent because of "the spiritual rock."[8] Tombs were opened, and the dead arose, because of him who was "free among the dead."[9] He "sent forth his prisoners out of the pit, wherein there is no water." Do not be ashamed, then, of the Cruci-

---

[1]Phil 4:7. [2]Mt 24:35. [3]Heb 4:12. [4]FC 26:453-54. [5]PG 66:556. [6]Mk 16:19. [7]CS 111:62. [8]1 Cor 10:4. [9]Ps 88:5 (87:5 LXX).

fied, but say with confidence, "He bears our sins and carries our sorrows, and by his bruises we are healed."[10] Let us not be ungrateful to our Benefactor. Again, "For the wickedness of my people was he led to death; and I shall give the ungodly for his burial, and the rich for his death." And Paul says clearly "that Christ died for our sins, according to the Scriptures, and that he was buried, and that he rose again the third day, according to the Scriptures."[11] CATECHETICAL LECTURE 13.34.[12]

9:12 Return to the Stronghold

JESUS IS THE TOWER OF SALVATION. AUGUSTINE: "You have led me down, because you have been made my hope: a tower of strength from the face of the enemy."[13] My heart is vexed, says that unity from the ends of the earth, and I toil in the midst of temptations and offenses. The heathen are envious, because they have been conquered. The heretics lie in wait, hidden in the cloak of the Christian name. Within the church itself the wheat suffers violence from the chaff. In the midst of all these things when my heart is vexed, I will cry from the ends of the earth. But there forsakes me not the same that has exalted me upon the rock, in order to lead me down even unto himself, because even if I labor, while the devil through so many places and times and occasions lies in wait against me, he is to me a tower of strength, to whom I shall have fled for refuge. Not only I shall escape the weapons of the enemy, but even against him securely I shall myself hurl whatever darts I shall please. For Christ himself is the tower. He has been made for us a tower from the face of the enemy, who is also the rock upon which the church has been built. Are you taking heed that you not be smitten by the devil? Flee to the tower. The devil's darts will never follow you to that tower. There you will stand protected and fixed. But in what manner shall you flee to the tower? Let not a person, set perhaps in temptation, seek that tower in body, and when he shall not have found

it, be wearied or faint in temptation. The tower is before you. Call Christ to mind, and go into the tower. EXPLANATION OF THE PSALMS 61.4.[14]

9:16 The Jewels of a Crown

THE WHEELS AND STONES ARE THE OLD TESTAMENT AND NEW TESTAMENT. JEROME: We have been speaking in a general way; let us now speak in particular about the interior of a person. A wheel, as you know, rests upon the ground with a very slight base. Nor does it merely rest; it rolls along; it does not stand still but barely touches the ground and passes on. Further, when it rolls onward, it always mounts higher. So the saintly person, because he has a human body, has to give some thought to earthly matters. When it comes to food and clothing and other such matters, he is content[15] with what he has, and merely touching the ground with them, hastens to other things. He who runs in haste to higher things carries within himself your word. We read in the prophet, "Holy stones roll over the land." Notice what he said: "Holy stones roll over the land." Because they are wheels, they speed over the land and on to higher places. Do you want to hear about more wheels? We read, "And one wheel within another";[16] and again in Ezekiel, "The wheels move one within the other." The two wheels are the New and Old Testament; the old moves within the new and the new within the old. And Ezekiel goes on, "Wherever the spirit wished to go, there the wheels went."[17] Ecclesiastes, moreover, says of the end of the world: "And the broken wheel falls into the well."[18] Much more could be said about wheels, but our sermon speeds on to the rest of the psalm. HOMILIES ON THE PSALMS 10.[19]

9:17 Abundance to Make People Flourish

ALL FOOD IS CLEAN. APOSTOLIC CONSTITU-

---

[10]Is 53:4-5. [11]1 Cor 15:3-4. [12]FC 64:27. [13]Ps 61:3 (60:4 LXX). [14]NPNF 1 8:249*. [15]1 Tim 6:8. [16]Ezek 1:16-17. [17]Ezek 1:20. [18]Eccles 12:6. [19]FC 48:75.

TIONS: Now concerning the several sorts of food, the Lord says to you, "You shall eat the good things of the earth,"[20] and "All sorts of flesh shall you eat, as the green herb,"[21] but "You shall pour out the blood."[22] For "not those things that go into the mouth, but those that come out of it, defile a man."[23] "I mean blasphemies, evil speaking, and if there be any other thing like that.[24] But "do you eat the fat of the land with righteousness." For "if anything be pleasant, it is his; and if there be anything good, it is his: wheat for the young men, and wine to cheer the maids." For "who shall eat or who shall drink without him?"[25] Wise Ezra does also admonish you and says, "Go your way, and eat the fat, and drink the sweet, and do not be sorrowful."[26] CONSTITUTIONS OF THE HOLY APOSTLES 7.2.20.[27]

---

[20]Is 1:19. [21]Gen 9:3. [22]Deut 15:23. [23]Mt 15:11. [24]Mk 7:22. [25]Eccles 2:25 LXX. [26]Neh 8:10. [27]ANF 7:469.

10:1-12 WARNING TO THE SHEPHERDS OF ISRAEL

[1]Ask rain from the LORD
   in the season of the spring rain,
from the LORD who makes the storm clouds,
   who gives men showers of rain,
   to every one the vegetation in the field.
[2]For the teraphim utter nonsense,
   and the diviners see lies;
the dreamers tell false dreams,
   and give empty consolation.
Therefore the people wander like sheep;
   they are afflicted for want of a shepherd.

[3]"My anger is hot against the shepherds,
   and I will punish the leaders;"
for the LORD of hosts cares for his flock, the
   house of Judah,
   and will make them like his proud steed
   in battle.
[4]Out of them shall come the cornerstone,
   out of them the tent peg,
out of them the battle bow,
   out of them every ruler.

[5]Together they shall be like mighty men in
   battle,
   trampling the foe in the mud of the streets;
they shall fight because the LORD is with
   them,
   and they shall confound the riders on
   horses.

[6]"I will strengthen the house of Judah,
   and I will save the house of Joseph.
I will bring them back because I have
   compassion on them,
   and they shall be as though I had not
   rejected them;
   for I am the LORD their God and I will
   answer them.
[7]Then Ephraim shall become like a mighty
   warrior,
   and their hearts shall be glad as with
   wine.
Their children shall see it and rejoice,
   their hearts shall exult in the LORD.

8"I will signal for them and gather them in,
    for I have redeemed them,
    and they shall be as many as of old.
9Though I scattered them among the
    nations,
    yet in far countries they shall remember
    me,
    and with their children they shall live
    and return.
10I will bring them home from the land of
    Egypt,
    and gather them from Assyria;

and I will bring them to the land of Gilead
    and to Lebanon,
    till there is no room for them.
11They shall pass through the sea of Egypt,o*
    and the waves of the sea shall be
    smitten,
    and all the depths of the Nile dried up.
The pride of Assyria shall be laid low,
    and the scepter of Egypt shall depart.
12I will make them strong in the LORD
    and they shall gloryp in his name,"
    says the LORD.

n Or he-goats o Cn: Heb distress p Gk: Heb walk *LXX They will pass through

---

OVERVIEW: God shows his goodness as much through blessings as his rejection of sin by chastisement (BASIL). The shepherds are not to overlook sins among believers or reject those who are penitent. To do so is to cause their destruction, which the prophet condemns (APOSTOLIC CONSTITUTION).

10:1 Asking for Rain

GOODNESS AND CHASTISEMENT FROM GOD. BASIL THE GREAT: Let us not, therefore, know God by halves or make his lovingkindness an excuse for our indolence; for this, his thunders, for this, his lightnings—that his goodness may not be held in despite. He who causes the sun to rise[1] also strikes people with blindness.[2] He who sends the rain also causes the rain of fire.[3] By the one he manifests his goodness; by the other, his severity. For the one let us love him, for the other let us fear, that it may not be said also to us, "Or despise you the riches of his goodness and patience and longsuffering? Know you not that the mercy of God leads you to repentance? But according to your hardness and impenitent heart, you treasure up to yourself wrath against the day of wrath."[4] THE LONG RULES, PREFACE.[5]

10:3 God's Anger Against the Shepherds

LAX PRIESTS CONDEMNED. APOSTOLIC CONSTITUTIONS: Observe, you who are our beloved sons, how merciful yet righteous the Lord our God is, how gracious and kind to humankind. And yet most certainly "he will not acquit the guilty,"[6] though he welcomes returning sinners and revives them, leaving no room for suspicion to such as wish to judge sternly and to reject offenders entirely, and to refuse to grant them exhortations which might bring them to repentance. In contradiction to such, God by Isaiah says to the bishops, "Comfort you, comfort you my people, you priests; speak comfortably to Jerusalem."[7] It therefore behooves you, upon hearing those words of his, to encourage those who have offended, and lead them to repentance, and afford them hope, and not vainly to suppose that you shall be partakers of their offenses on account of such your love to them. Receive the penitent with alacrity and rejoice over them, and with mercy and bowels of compassion judge the sinners. For if a person was walking by the side of a river and ready to stumble, and you should push him and

---

[1]Mt 5:45; Rev 21:23. [2]2 Kings 6:18; Acts 9:8. [3]Gen 19:24. [4]Rom 2:4-5. [5]FC 9:230*. [6]Ex 23:7. [7]Is 40:1-2 LXX.

thrust him into the river instead of offering him your hand for his assistance, you would be guilty of the murder of your brother. . . . You ought rather to lend your helping hand as he was ready to fall, lest he perish without remedy, that both the people may take warning and the offender may not utterly perish. It is your duty, O bishop, neither to overlook the sins of the people nor to reject those who are penitent, that you may not unskillfully destroy the Lord's flock or dishonor his new name which is stamped upon his people, and you yourself be reproached as those ancient pastors were, of whom God speaks thus to Jeremiah: "Many shepherds have destroyed my vineyard; they have polluted my heritage."[8] And in another passage, "My anger is waxed hot against the shepherds, and against the lambs shall I have indignation." CONSTITUTIONS OF THE HOLY APOSTLES 2.3.15.[9]

---

[8]Jer 12:10. [9]ANF 7:402*.

11:1-17 WOE TO THE WORTHLESS SHEPHERDS

[1]*Open your doors, O Lebanon,*
  that the fire may devour your cedars!
[2]*Wail, O cypress, for the cedar has fallen,*
  for the glorious trees are ruined!
Wail, oaks of Bashan,
  for the thick forest has been felled!
[3]*Hark, the wail of the shepherds,*
  for their glory is despoiled!
Hark, the roar of the lions,
  for the jungle of the Jordan is laid waste!

[4]*Thus said the* LORD *my God: "Become shepherd of the flock doomed to slaughter.* [5]*Those who buy them slay them and go unpunished; and those who sell them say, 'Blessed be the* LORD, *I have become rich'; and their own shepherds have no pity on them.* [6]*For I will no longer have pity on the inhabitants of this land, says the* LORD. *Lo, I will cause men to fall each into the hand of his shepherd, and each into the hand of his king; and they shall crush the earth, and I will deliver none from their hand."*
[7]*So I became the shepherd of the flock doomed to be slain for those who trafficked in the sheep. And I took two staffs; one I named Grace, the other I named Union. And I tended the sheep.* [8]*In one month I destroyed the three shepherds. But I became impatient with them, and they also detested me.* [9]*So I said, "I will not be your shepherd. What is to die, let it die; what is to be destroyed, let it be destroyed; and let those that are left devour the flesh of one another."* [10]*And I took my staff Grace, and I broke it, annulling the covenant which I had made with all the peoples.* [11]*So it was annulled on that day, and the traffickers in the sheep, who were watching me, knew*

that it was the word of the Lord. [12]*Then I said to them, "If it seems right to you, give me my wages; but if not, keep them." And they weighed out as my wages thirty shekels of silver.* [13]*Then the Lord said to me, "Cast it into the treasury"*[q]*—the lordly price at which I was paid off by them. So I took the thirty shekels of silver and cast them into the treasury*[q] *in the house of the Lord.* [14]*Then I broke my second staff Union, annulling the brotherhood between Judah and Israel.**

[15]*Then the Lord said to me, "Take once more the implements of a worthless shepherd.* [16]*For lo, I am raising up in the land a shepherd who does not care for the perishing, or seek the wandering,*[r] *or heal the maimed, or nourish the sound, but devours the flesh of the fat ones, tearing off even their hoofs.*

[17]*Woe to my worthless shepherd,*
who deserts the flock!
May the sword smite his arm
and his right eye!
Let his arm be wholly withered,
his right eye utterly blinded!"

q Syr: Heb *to the potter* **r** Syr Compare Gk Vg: Heb *the youth* *LXX reads *Jerusalem* instead of *Israel*

Overview: The measure with which the priests failed to show mercy and care to their flock will be meted out to them by the Lord (Gregory of Nazianzus). Moses and Aaron had in common that they did not enter the Promised Land, as well as that entire generation of Jews. The three are symbolically referred to in Zechariah. Christians, on the other hand, have entered the Promised Land through Christ (Jerome). God at times steps back and allows the human race to exercise its own will regardless of disastrous consequences that may result. God's grace, however, is always open to penitents (Theodoret). The payment of thirty pieces of silver, referred to by Zechariah, is a symbol of the ingratitude on the part of sinners for Christ's healing grace. Other prophets confirm the exact amount that Judas paid to betray Christ (Cyril of Jerusalem). Zechariah predicted that the Messiah would be betrayed for thirty pieces of silver as payment for all the good the Messiah had done (Rufinus). The foolish shepherd is a priest who does not counsel his flock with the knowledge of spiritual perfection. Christ the true shepherd brings the entire people of God—flock (laity) and shepherds (clergy)—spotless before God (Gregory of Nazianzus).

11:5 *Shepherds Without Pity*

Lax Shepherds Condemned. Gregory of Nazianzus: Whenever I remember Zechariah, I shudder at the reaping hook[1] and likewise at his testimony against the priests, his hints in reference to the celebrated Joshua, the high priest, whom he represents as stripped of filthy garments and then clothed in rich priestly apparel. As for words and charges to Joshua which he puts into the angel's mouth, let them be treated with silent respect, as referring perhaps to a greater and higher object than those who are many priests.[2] But even at his right hand stood the devil, to resist him, a fact, in my eyes, of no slight significance and demanding no slight fear and watchfulness. Who is so bold and adamant of soul as not to tremble and be abashed at the charges and reproaches deliberately urged against

[1]Zech 5:1 LXX. [2]Heb 7:23.

the rest of the shepherds? A voice, he says, of the howling of the shepherds. A voice of the roaring lions, for this has befallen them. Does he not all but hear the wailing as if close at hand, and himself wail with the afflicted. A little further is a more striking and impassioned strain. Feed, he says, the flock of slaughter, whose possessors slay them without repentance. They sell them saying, "Blessed be the Lord, for we are rich," yet their own shepherds are without feeling for them. Therefore I will no more pity the inhabitants of the land, says the Lord almighty. And again: "Awake, O sword, against the shepherds, and smite the shepherds, and scatter the sheep, and I will turn my hand upon the shepherds";[3] and, "My anger is kindled against the shepherds, and I will visit the lambs,"[4] adding to the threat those who rule over the people. So industriously does he apply himself to his task that he cannot easily free himself from denunciations, and I am afraid that if I referred to the whole series, I should exhaust your patience. This must then suffice for Zechariah. IN DEFENSE OF HIS FLIGHT TO PONTUS, ORATION 2.62-64.[5]

11:8 Shepherds Destroyed

VICTORY IN CHRIST. JEROME: We may understand this historically of Moses and Aaron. Moses—and Aaron also—was conducted to but not inducted into the Promised Land. Jesus took Moses' place. Be sure you grasp the significance of what is written. Moses died in a desert; Aaron died; Mary died; and hear now what is written in the prophet: "In a single month I did away with three shepherds." They died, for they could not enter the Promised Land. They merely looked over toward the land of promise, but enter it they could not. The Jews beheld the Promised Land but could not enter it. They died in the desert, and their dead bodies lie in the wilderness, the corpses of those who died in the desert.[6] We, their children, under the leadership of Jesus, have come to the Jordan and have entered the Promised Land; we have come to Gilgal and have been circumcised with spiritual circumcision and have been cleansed of the reproach of Egypt. Even now Jesus himself, our leader, holds the sword and always goes before us and fights for us and conquers our adversaries. For seven days, we march around the city of Jericho, in other words, this world. We sound the priestly trumpets and march around Jericho, this world, and the walls fall, and we enter and consider ourselves victors. Next we conquer the city Ai; then go to Jebus, to Azor, to other cities; we conquer the enemies that we were unable to vanquish under Moses. HOMILIES ON THE PSALMS 10.[7]

11:9 "Let It Die"

PRAY FOR HELP AGAINST WICKED RULERS. THEODORET OF CYR: We find the God of the universe often giving rein to humanity because of the excess of its wickedness, and he allows the human race to be borne where it will. Of this he has warned us speaking through his prophet to Israel: "And I said, 'I will not tend you. That which dies, let it die, and that which perishes, let it perish; and for the rest let each devour the flesh of his neighbor.'" When wicked rulers are in control, and cruel, harsh masters rule households, then we should implore the one who directs the universe and, by conversion of life and a change in our ways, make supplication, rousing him to help us, fervently begging him to give us better times. ON DIVINE PROVIDENCE 7.38.[8]

11:12 Thirty Shekels of Silver

THIRTY PIECES OF SILVER FORETOLD. CYRIL OF JERUSALEM: Hear now in regard to thirty pieces of silver: "And I will say to them, 'If it seems good to you, give me my wages, or refuse.'" One recompense is due me for curing the blind and the lame, and I receive another; instead of thanksgiving, dishonor, and instead of worship, insult. Do

---

[3]Zech 13:7. [4]Zech 10:3. [5]NPNF 2 7:218*. [6]Heb 3:17. [7]FC 48:77. [8]ACW 49:99.

you see how Scripture foresaw all this? "And they counted out my wages, thirty pieces of silver." O prophetic accuracy! A great and unerring wisdom of the Holy Spirit! For he did not say ten or twenty but thirty, exactly the right amount. Tell also what happened to this payment, O prophet! Does he who received it keep it, or does he give it back? And after its return what becomes of it? The prophet says, "So I took thirty pieces of silver, and I cast them into the house of the Lord, into the foundry." Compare with the prophecy of the Gospel, which says, "Judas repented and flung the pieces of silver into the temple and withdrew."[9] CATECHETICAL LECTURE 13.10.[10]

THE MESSIAH BETRAYED FOR THIRTY PIECES OF SILVER. RUFINUS: You observe that he was appraised by the traitor's covetousness at thirty pieces of silver. Of this also the prophet speaks, "And I said to them, If you think good, give me my price, or if not, forbear"; and "presently, I received from them," he says, "thirty pieces of silver, and I cast them into the house of the Lord, into the foundry." Is not this what is written in the Gospels, that Judas, "repenting of what he had done, brought back the money, and threw it down in the temple and departed"?[11] Well did he call it his price, as though blaming and upbraiding. For he had done so many good works among them, he had given sight to the blind, feet to the lame, the power of walking to the palsied, life also to the dead; for all these good works they paid him death as his price, appraised at thirty pieces of silver. It is related also in the Gospels that he was bound. This also the word of prophecy had foretold by Isaiah, saying, "Woe to their soul, who have devised a most evil device against themselves, saying, 'Let us bind the just one, seeing that he is unprofitable to us.' "[12] COMMENTARY ON THE APOSTLES' CREED 20.[13]

11:15 The Tools of a Worthless Shepherd

CHRIST THE HIGH SHEPHERD. GREGORY OF NAZIANZUS: Such is my defense; its reasonableness I have set forth. And may the God of peace,[14] who made both one[15] and has restored us to each other, who sets kings upon thrones and raises up the poor out of the dust and lifts up the beggar from the dunghill,[16] who chose David his servant and took him away from the sheepfolds,[17] though he was the least and youngest of the sons of Jesse,[18] who gave the word[19] to those who preach the gospel with great power for the perfection of the gospel—may he himself hold me by my right hand. [May he] guide me with his counsel and receive me with glory,[20] who is a Shepherd[21] to shepherds and Guide to guides. [May he guide us] that we may feed his flock with knowledge,[22] not with the instruments of a foolish shepherd, according to the blessing, and not according to the curse pronounced against the men of former days. May he give strength and power to his people[23] and himself present to himself[24] his flock resplendent and spotless and worthy of the fold on high, in the habitation of them that rejoice,[25] in the splendor of the saints,[26] so that in his temple everyone, both flock and shepherds together may say, Glory[27] in Christ Jesus our Lord, to whom be all glory forever and ever. Amen. IN DEFENSE OF HIS FLIGHT TO PONTUS, ORATION 2.117.[28]

---

[9]Mt 27:3, 5. [10]FC 64:11-12. [11]Mt 27:3, 5. [12]Is 3:10 LXX. [13]NPNF 2 3:551. [14]Heb 13:20. [15]Eph 2:14. [16]1 Sam 2:8; Ps 113:7 (112:7 LXX). [17]Ps 78:70 (77:70 LXX). [18]1 Sam 17:14. [19]Ps 147:18 (147:7 LXX). [20]Ps 73:23-24 (72:23-24 LXX). [21]Ezek 34:12. [22]Jer 3:15. [23]Ps 68:35 (67:36 LXX). [24]Eph 5:27. [25]Ps 5:11 (5:12 LXX). [26]Ps 111:3 (110:3 LXX). [27]Ps 29:9 (28:9). [28]NPNF 2 7:227.

12:1-9 OPPRESSION AND SALVATION OF JUDAH

An Oracle

[1]*The word of the LORD concerning Israel: Thus says the LORD, who stretched out the heavens and founded the earth and formed the spirit of man within him:* [2]*"Lo, I am about to make Jerusalem a cup of reeling to all the peoples round about; it will be against Judah also in the siege against Jerusalem.** [3]*On that day I will make Jerusalem a heavy stone for all the peoples; all who lift it shall grievously hurt themselves. And all the nations of the earth will come together against it.* [4]*On that day, says the LORD, I will strike every horse with panic, and its rider with madness. But upon the house of Judah I will open my eyes, when I strike every horse of the peoples with blindness.* [5]*Then the clans of Judah shall say to themselves, 'The inhabitants of Jerusalem have strength† through the LORD of hosts, their God.'*

[6]*"On that day I will make the clans of Judah like a blazing pot in the midst of wood, like a flaming torch among sheaves; and they shall devour to the right and to the left all the peoples round about, while Jerusalem shall still be inhabited in its place, in Jerusalem.*

[7]*"And the LORD will give victory to the tents of Judah first, that the glory of the house of David and the glory of the inhabitants of Jerusalem may not be exalted over that of Judah.* [8]*On that day the LORD will put a shield about the inhabitants of Jerusalem so that the feeblest among them on that day shall be like David, and the house of David shall be like God, like the angel of the LORD, at their head.* [9]*And on that day I will seek to destroy all the nations that come against Jerusalem.*

*LXX and there will be a siege against Jerusalem in Judah   †LXX we shall find for ourselves the inhabitants of Jerusalem

---

OVERVIEW: A person's spirit is his soul insofar as it is endowed with self-determining reason. Jesus, moreover, identified soul with spirit at the crucifixion (AMBROSE). God does not condemn any soul that is not guilty. God's nature is not mutable by virtue of breathing life into people, in opposition to the Manichaeans. The spirit of humans is created as much as the natural created order. The Manichaeans are opposed for holding to the contrary (AUGUSTINE). The spirit has many applications in Scripture, not the least of which is when it refers to the spirit within a human (CYRIL OF JERUSALEM).

12:1 The Spirit Within a Person

GOD CREATES THE SPIRIT. AMBROSE: There-fore he referred the thunders[1] to the words of the Lord, the sound of which went out into all the earth. And we understand the word *spirit* in this place of the soul, which he took endowed with potential reason and perfection. For the Scripture often designates the soul of humankind by the word *spirit*, as you read: "Who creates the spirit of man within him." So too the Lord signified his soul by the word *spirit*, when he said, "Into your hands I commend my spirit."[2] ON THE HOLY SPIRIT 2.4.56.[3]

THE SOUL IS SHAPED BY DOCTRINE. AUGUS-TINE: I do not want anyone to tell me that this view [that God condemns innocent souls] should

---

[1]Job 26:14. [2]Lk 23:46. [3]NPNF 2 10:121-22.

be supported by the passage "who formed the spirit of man in him" and "who made the heart of every one of them."[4] Something supremely strong and invincible is needed to force me to believe that God condemns any souls without any guilt of theirs. It is either as great a thing, or it is, perhaps greater, to create as to form, yet it is written, "Create a clean heart in me, O God."[5] This is no argument for thinking that the soul in this passage prays to be made before it had any being. As, therefore, while now existing, it is created by renewal of its justice, so, while now existing, it is formed by the shaping force of doctrine. LETTER 26.[6]

GOD'S SPIRIT AND THE HUMAN SPIRIT ARE NOT THE SAME. AUGUSTINE: Hence we ought to understand this passage[7] so that we do not take the words "he breathed into him the breath of life, and he became a living soul"[8] to mean that a part, as it were, of the nature of God was turned into the soul of man. Thus we are not forced to say that the nature of God is mutable. It is especially in this error that the truth weighs down upon these Manichaeans. For as pride is the mother of all the heretics, they dared to say that the soul is the nature of God. And thus they are under pressure from us when we say to them, "Then the nature of God errs and is unhappy and is corrupted by the stain of vices and sins, or is, as you say, soiled by the filth of the opposing nature," and other such things that it is wicked to believe about the nature of God. For in another passage Scripture clearly says that the soul was made by almighty God and that it is therefore not a part of God or the nature of God. There the prophet says, "He who formed the spirit for all men made all things,"[9] and in another place it says, "He who formed the spirit of man is in him." These testimonies clearly prove that the spirit of man was made. In Scripture the rational part of man's soul by which he differs from the beasts and rules over them by the law of nature is called the spirit of man. On this the apostle says, "No one knows what pertains to man except the spirit of man which is within him."[10] If these testimonies were not clear proof that the soul of man was made, there would be no lack of those who would say that the spirit of man was not made and who would think that it is the nature of God and say that part of God was changed into it, when there took place that breathing forth by God. Healthy doctrine likewise rejects this, because the spirit of man itself is at times in error and at times thinks wisely; thus it proclaims that it is mutable, and it is in no way permissible to believe this of the nature of God. But there cannot be a greater sign of pride than that the human soul says that it is what God is, while it still groans under such great burdens of vice and unhappiness. ON GENESIS AGAINST THE MANICHAEANS 2.8.11.[11]

MANY FORMS OF SPIRIT. CYRIL OF JERUSALEM: There are many statements of spirit in general in the sacred Scriptures, and a person could easily become confused from ignorance, if he did not know to what sort of spirit the particular text refers; therefore we must be sure of the nature of the Holy Spirit according to Scripture. For example, Aaron is called Christ (anointed), and David also, and Saul and others are called christs, yet there is only one true Christ; similarly, since the name of spirit has been given to many things, we must determine what in particular is called the Holy Spirit. Many things are called spirits; our soul is called spirit; this wind, which is blowing, is called spirit; great valor is called spirit; impure action is called spirit; and a hostile devil is called spirit. Take care, therefore, when you hear such things, not to mistake one for another because of the similarity of the name. Scripture says of the soul, "When his spirit departs, he returns to the earth";[12] and again of the soul: "Who forms the spirit of man within him." CATECHETICAL LECTURE 16.13.[13]

---

[4]Ps 33:15 (32:15 LXX). [5]Ps 51:10 (50:12 LXX). [6]FC 30:29. [7]1 Cor 15:44-46. [8]Gen 2:7. [9]Ps 33:15 (32:15 LXX). [10]1 Cor 2:11. [11]FC 84:106-7. [12]Ps 146:4. [13]FC 64:83.

12:10-14 THE DAY OF MOURNING IN JERUSALEM

[10]"And I will pour out on the house of David and the inhabitants of Jerusalem a spirit of compassion and supplication, so that, when they look on him whom they have pierced, they shall mourn for him, as one mourns for an only child, and weep bitterly over him, as one weeps over a first-born. [11]On that day the mourning in Jerusalem will be as great as the mourning for Hadad-rimmon in the plain of Megiddo.* [12]The land shall mourn, each family by itself; the family of the house of David by itself, and their wives by themselves; the family of the house of Nathan by itself, and their wives by themselves; [13]the family of the house of Levi by itself, and their wives by themselves; the family of the Shimeites by itself, and their wives by themselves; [14]and all the families that are left, each by itself, and their wives by themselves.

*LXX as the mourning for the pomegranate grove bowed down in the Plain

OVERVIEW: The prophet foresees the time when at the last judgment the people will be brought into the presence of Christ. What shall they say and do (JUSTIN)? The appearance of Christ is likened to the building of Zion in the prophets. The Jews and Gentiles will be in confusion for having rejected healthy repentance when it was available. At the last judgment all human flesh will see Christ in his glorified flesh. Christ will return in the same human form with which he ascended. The righteous and the condemned will see Christ in his glorified body. The same body that was struck by a spear will appear to judge all (AUGUSTINE). The Holy Spirit and his gifts are available to all who are open to receive. Among the many graces of the spirit are grace and prayer (BEDE). The devil and his demons will be condemned to eternal punishment and banishment. The Jews too will see Christ in his glory. Jesus will show them the prints of the nails, the wound on the side, the wounds from the crown and his cross. There will be no hope for them; thus will they perish in everlasting punishment (HIPPOLYTUS). Worship of the sun never earned anyone martyrdom, in contrast to those who worship the Son who shines much brighter than the former. The persecution of Christians was described by the prophet as the mourning of the tribes (JUSTIN).

12:10 The One Who Was Pierced

JESUS AND THE SECOND ADVENT OF CHRIST. JUSTIN MARTYR: And what the people of the Jews shall say and do, when they see him coming in glory, has thus been predicted by Zechariah the prophet: "I will command the four winds to gather the scattered children; I will command the north wind to bring them, and the south wind, that it not hold back. And then in Jerusalem there shall be great lamentation, not the lamentation of mouths or of lips but the lamentation of the heart; and they shall not rend their garments but their hearts. Tribe by tribe they shall mourn, and then they shall look on him whom they have pierced; and they shall say, 'Why, O Lord, have you made us to err from your way? The glory which our fathers blessed has for us been turned into shame.'"[1] FIRST APOLOGY 52.[2]

THE CRUCIFIED CHRIST AND THE LAST JUDGMENT. AUGUSTINE: "For the Lord shall build up Zion."[3] This work is going on now. O you living stones, run to the work of the building, not to ruin. Zion is building; beware of the ruined walls. The tower is building, the ark is in building; re-

---

[1]Cf. Is 63:17; 64:11. [2]ANF 1:180. [3]Ps 102:16.

member the deluge. This work is in progress now, but when Zion is built, what will happen? "And he will appear in his glory."[4] That he might build up Zion, that he might be a foundation in Zion, he was seen in Zion, but not in his glory: "We have seen him, and he had no form or comeliness."[5] But truly when he shall have come with his angels to judge,[6] shall they not then look upon him whom they have pierced? And too late they shall [be] put to confusion, who refused confusion in early and healthful repentance. EXPLANATION OF THE PSALMS 102.17.[7]

ALL HUMANS WILL SEE CHRIST AT THE JUDGMENT. AUGUSTINE: And perhaps it is then that the words "all flesh" will become more perfectly fulfilled. Now I mean to say, flesh has seen him, but not all flesh. Then, however, at the judgment, as he comes with his angels to judge the living and the dead, "when all who are in tombs hear his voice and come forth, some to the resurrection of life, others to the resurrection of judgment,"[8] it is not only the just but also the wicked, those on the right, these on the left, who will see that form which he pleased to take on for us. Even those who killed him "will look on the one whom they have pierced."[9] So "all flesh shall see the salvation of God." Body will be seen by body, because he will come to judge him in his real body. But to those placed on the right and sent on into the kingdom of heaven, he is going to show himself in the same way as he could already be seen in the body; and yet he had said, "Whoever loves me shall be loved by my Father; and I will love him, and manifest myself to him."[10] SERMON 277.[11]

CHRIST WILL COME IN HUMAN FORM. AUGUSTINE: Now, indeed, that body is worthy of a heavenly dwelling place, not subject to death, not changeable through the ages [of life]. For as he had grown to that age from infancy, so he does not decline to old age from the age which was young adulthood. He remains as he ascended; he is going to come to those to whom, before he comes, he wanted his word to be preached. So

therefore he will come in a human form. The ungodly too will see this; those placed to the right will see it too; those separate to the left will see it too, as it was written, "They shall see him whom they have pierced."[12] If they will see him whom they have pierced, they will see the same body that they thrust through with a spear, [for] the Word is not struck by a spear. TRACTATES ON THE GOSPEL OF JOHN 21.3.[13]

GIFT OF THE HOLY SPIRIT PROMISED. BEDE: He commanded them, among other things, to pray as follows: "And forgive us our debts as we forgive our debtors."[14] Or [it may be that] he calls his disciples "evil" because in comparison with the divine goodness, every creature is judged to be evil, as the Lord says, "No one is good except God alone."[15] It is only by participation in the divine goodness that a rational creature is recognized as being capable of becoming good. Hence the Lord also bears witness by a benevolent promise that your heavenly Father will "give the Holy Spirit to those who ask him."[16] This is to the point that those who of themselves are evil can become good through receiving the gift of the Spirit. He pledged that his good Spirit would be given by the Father to those asking for him, because whether we desire to secure faith, hope and charity, or any other heavenly goods at all, they are not bestowed upon us otherwise than by the gift of the Holy Spirit. So it is that the same spirit, in Isaiah, is named the spirit of wisdom and understanding, the spirit of counsel and fortitude, the spirit of knowledge and piety, the spirit of the fear of the Lord;[17] and in another place, the spirit of love and peace,[18] [and] the spirit of grace and prayer. Undoubtedly whatever good we truly have, whatever we do well, this we receive from the lavishness of the same Spirit. When a prophet

---

[4]Ps 102:16. [5]Is 53:2. [6]Mt 25:31. [7]NPNF 1 8:499*. [8]Jn 5:28-29. [9]See also Jn 19:37; Rev 1:7. [10]Jn 14:21. [11]WSA 3 8:43-44. [12]Jn 19:37. [13]FC 79:192. [14]Mt 6:12. [15]Mk 10:18. [16]Lk 11:13. [17]Is 11:2-3. [18]2 Cor 13:11.

who understood this was seeking purity of heart, saying, "Create a pure heart in me, O Lord," he immediately added, "Renew an upright spirit in my inmost parts."[19] If the upright spirit of the Lord does not fill our innermost being, we have no pure heart where he may abide. When in his eager longing for and advance in good for his work he had said, "Lord, I have had recourse to you, teach me to do your will,"[20] he at once showed in what way he had to secure this when he went on, "Let your good spirit lead me into the right way."[21] HOMILIES ON THE GOSPELS 2.14.[22]

JEWS WILL REPENT AT SECOND COMING. HIPPOLYTUS: Then shall the son of perdition be brought forward as the accuser, with his demons and with his servants, by angels stern and inexorable. And they shall be given over to the fire that is never quenched, and to the worm that never sleeps, and to the outer darkness. For the crucifiers shall see him in human form, as he appeared to them "when he came" by the holy virgin in the flesh and as they crucified him. And he will show them the "prints of the" nails in his hands and feet, and his side pierced with the spear, and his head crowned with thorns, and his honorable cross. And once for all shall the people of the Hebrews see all these things, and they shall mourn and weep, as the prophet exclaims, "They shall look on him whom they have pierced."[23] ON THE END OF THE WORLD 40.[24]

12:12 Mourning in the Land

PEOPLE WILL MOURN AT THE SECOND COMING. JUSTIN MARTYR: While they remained silent, I continued, "My friends, when Scripture through David speaks of Christ, it says that not 'in his seed' shall the Gentiles be blessed, but 'in him.'" Here are the words: "His name shall endure forever; it shall rise above the sun; and all nations shall be blessed in him."[25] But if all nations are blessed in Christ and we who are from all nations believe in him, then he is the Christ, and we are they who are blessed through him. It is written[26] that God once allowed the sun to be worshiped, and yet you cannot discover anyone who ever suffered death because of his faith in the sun. But you can find people of every nationality who for the name of Jesus have suffered and still suffer all kinds of torments rather than deny their faith in him. For his word of truth and wisdom is more blazing and bright than the might of the sun, and it penetrates the very depths of the heart and mind. Thus Scripture says, "His name shall arise above the sun."[27] And Zechariah affirms, "The East is his name."[28] And again, "They shall mourn tribe by tribe." DIALOGUE WITH TRYPHO 121.[29]

---

[19]Ps 51:10 (50:12 LXX). [20]Ps 143:9-10. [21]Ps 143:10. [22]CS 111:132-33. [23]Cf. Jn 19:37. [24]ANF 5:252*. [25]Ps 72:17. [26]Deut 4:19. [27]Ps 71:17. [28]Zech 6:12 LXX. [29]FC 6:335.

13:1-9 RENEWAL OF THE TESTAMENT
WITH THE REMNANT OF ISRAEL

¹"On that day there shall be a fountain opened for the house of David and the inhabitants of Jerusalem to cleanse them from sin and uncleanness.

²And on that day, says the LORD of hosts, I will cut off the names of the idols from the land, so that they shall be remembered no more; and also I will remove from the land the prophets and the unclean spirit. ³And if any one again appears as a prophet, his father and mother who bore him will say to him, 'You shall not live, for you speak lies in the name of the LORD'; and his father and mother who bore him shall pierce him through when he prophesies. ⁴On that day every prophet will be ashamed of his vision when he prophesies; he will not put on a hairy mantle in order to deceive, ⁵but he will say, 'I am no prophet, I am a tiller of the soil; for the land has been my possession[t] since my youth.' ⁶And if one asks him, 'What are these wounds on your back?' he will say, 'The wounds I received in the house of my friends.' "

⁷"Awake, O sword, against my shepherd,
   against the man who stands next to me,"
                      says the LORD of hosts.
"Strike the shepherd, that the sheep may be scattered;
   I will turn my hand against the little ones.
⁸In the whole land, says the LORD,
   two thirds shall be cut off and perish,
   and one third shall be left alive.
⁹And I will put this third into the fire,
   and refine them as one refines silver,
   and test them as gold is tested.
They will call on my name,
   and I will answer them.
I will say, 'They are my people';
   and they will say, 'The LORD is my God.' "

t Cn: Heb *for man has caused me to possess*

OVERVIEW: The prophets foretold a time when the idols of the world would be abolished in the light of the true revelation of God (AUGUSTINE). The learning and teaching of pagan literature are not one and the same. In the latter, one gives affirmation to idols and gods. A believer, however, is able to learn the pagan literature without giving assent to its idolatry (TERTULLIAN). Christ foretold the consequences of his betrayal by Judas, Peter's denial and the abandonment by the disciples during his arrest. Jesus prayed for the restoration of his disciples (CHRYSOSTOM). The prophet foretold Christ's betrayal and abandonment by the disciples. Later such predictions and fulfillment became a source of great encouragement to the disciples (JUSTIN MARTYR). The believing thief on the cross exhibits a profound faith that God, not an ordinary wrongdoer, was on the cross. The disciples at the moment of Christ's suffering left him, as he was betrayed by Judas (MAXIMUS OF TURIN). The rock, which Moses struck to bring forth water, was Christ. Christ had to be struck (that is, crucified) to bring forth the streams of the New Testament (ORIGEN). A bishop who abandons his flock during persecution is like a shepherd who flees when he sees the wolf come. The prophet minces no words about the condemnation they face from God. Persecution is a time when a person's faith is tested for true loyalty to the Lord. The prophet likens it to gold being purified in the furnace (TERTULLIAN).

13:2 Idols Will Be Removed

IDOLS DESTROYED BY THE TRUE GOD. AUGUSTINE: Hermes Trismegistus[1] lamented these vain, deceptive, pernicious, sacrilegious things because he foresaw that the time was coming when they would be abolished. He was impudent in his grief as imprudent in his prophecy, since the Holy Spirit had made no revelation to him as to the holy prophets, who exultantly proclaimed their inspired visions: "Shall a man make gods to himself, and they are no gods?"[2] and again, "And it shall come to pass in that day, says the Lord of hosts, that I will destroy the names of the idols out of the earth, and they shall be remembered no more." It is relevant to recall that holy Isaiah uttered a particular prophecy concerning Egypt: "And the idols of Egypt shall be moved at his presence, and the heart of Egypt shall melt in the midst thereof,"[3] and the rest. CITY OF GOD 8.23.[4]

DISTINGUISH BETWEEN LEARNING AND TEACHING WORLDLY LITERATURE. TERTULLIAN: Let us see, then, the necessity of literary erudition; let us reflect that partly it cannot be ad-

mitted, partly cannot be avoided. Learning literature is allowable for believers, rather than teaching; for the principle of learning and teaching is different. If a believer teaches literature, while he teaches doubtless he commends, while he delivers he affirms, while he recalls he bears testimony to, the praise of idols interspersed therein. He seals the gods themselves with this name [of gods], whereas the law, as we have said, prohibits "the names of gods to be pronounced"[5] and this name [of God] to be conferred on vanity. Hence the devil gets people's early faith built up from the beginnings of erudition. Inquire whether he who catechizes about idols commits idolatry. But when a believer *learns* these things, if he is already capable of understanding what idolatry is, he neither receives nor allows them; much more if he is not yet capable. Or, when he *begins* to understand, it behooves him first to understand what he has previously learned, that is, touching God and the faith. Therefore he will reject those things and will not receive them; and [the believer] will be as safe as one who knows it not, who knowingly accepts poison but does not drink it. To him necessity is attributed as an excuse, because he has no other way to learn. Moreover, the not teaching literature is as much easier than the not learning, as it is easier too for the pupil not to attend than for the master not to frequent the rest of the defilements incident to the schools from public and scholastic solemnities. ON IDOLATRY 10.[6]

13:7 The Shepherd Stricken, the Sheep Scattered

CHRIST FORETOLD DETAILS OF HIS BETRAYAL. CHRYSOSTOM: Christ spoke of the betrayer; he foretold that all would run away; he predicted his own death. "I shall smite the shepherd, and the sheep will be scattered." He foretold who

---

[1]The Greek name for the Egyptian god Thoth, who was associated with many mystical writings. [2]Jer 16:20. [3]Is 19:1. [4]FC 14:64. [5]Ex 23:13; Josh 23:7; Hos 2:17. [6]ANF 3:66-67*.

was going to deny him, when he would do so, and how many times it would happen. He predicted everything accurately. After he had foretold all these things as a sufficient proof that he possessed knowledge of what was going to happen, he went to a certain place to pray.[7] The heretics say that the prayer is the prayer of the divinity; we say it is the prayer of the plan of redemption. AGAINST THE ANOMOEANS, HOMILY 7.38.[8]

DISCIPLES SCATTERED AND THEN CONVINCED. JUSTIN MARTYR: The same Zechariah foretold that Christ would be struck; after he was crucified, his disciples were dispersed until he rose again from the dead and proved to them that it had been predicted that he would have to suffer. When they were convinced of this, they went out to all the world teaching these things. Thus we are firm in our faith in him and in his doctrine, because our faith is grounded upon both the prophets and those who, openly throughout the world, are worshipers of God in the name of the crucified One. Indeed, Zechariah said, " 'Awake, O sword, against my shepherd, and against the man of my people,' says the Lord of hosts. 'Strike the shepherd, and his sheep shall be scattered.' " DIALOGUE WITH TRYPHO 53.[9]

THE THIEF ON THE CROSS. MAXIMUS OF TURIN: There was, therefore, a great and excellent faith in that thief. Clearly it is great and admirable faith which believed that the crucified Christ was being glorified more than punished. For this is the shape that all salvation takes—that the Savior should be recognized as the Lord of majesty when he is seen to be crucified and subject to humiliation. Hence the apostle says, "If they had known, they would never have crucified the Lord of majesty."[10] This, I say, is an excellent faith, to believe that Christ on the cross is God and not a wrongdoer. Therefore that thief was justified while the Jews insulted the Savior on the gibbet and said to him as if he were a criminal, "Free yourself if you are able."[11] But [the thief], certain of Christ's divinity and sure of his good

will, asks instead to be freed himself. There was a great faith in that thief, I say, and one which was comparable to that of the holy apostles; indeed, it preceded theirs. For he who preceded with respect to devotion preceded with respect to the prize, for the thief came to paradise before the apostles did. Peter follows the Lord, and this man accompanies him. But the Lord gives him a reward according to faith and merit, for, as we read, all the disciples were afraid during the Savior's suffering, and all left him just when he was betrayed. It happened as it was written: "I shall strike the shepherd, and the sheep of the flock will be scattered." SERMON 75.2.[12]

DETAILS OF CHRIST CRUCIFIED. ORIGEN: If there is anyone who, when he reads Moses, murmurs against him, and the law which has been written according to the letter is displeasing to him because it seems incoherent in many things, Moses shows him the rock, which is Christ, and leads him to it that he may drink from it and quench his thirst. But this rock will not give water unless it has been struck; when it has been struck it brings forth streams. For after Christ had been struck and crucified, he brought forth the streams of New Testament. This is why it was said of him, "I will strike the shepherd, and the sheep will be scattered." He had to be struck, therefore, for unless he had been struck and unless "water and blood had gone out from side,"[13] we all would suffer "thirst for the word of God."[14] This therefore is what the apostle also understood when he said, "They all ate the same spiritual food and drank the same spiritual drink. For they drank of the spiritual rock which followed, but the rock was Christ."[15] But note that God said to Moses in this place, "Go before the people, and take with you men advanced in years, that is, the elders of the people."[16] Moses alone does not lead the people to the waters of the rock, but only the elders of the people with him. For

---

[7]Mk 14:32. [8]FC 72:200. [9]FC 6:229. [10]1 Cor 2:8. [11]Mt 27:40. [12]ACW 50:184. [13]Jn 19:34. [14]Amos 8:11. [15]1 Cor 10:3-4. [16]Ex 17:5.

the law alone does not announce Christ, but also the prophets and patriarchs and all "those advanced in years." HOMILIES ON EXODUS 11.2.[17]

CONDEMNATION OF THOSE WHO FLEE PERSECUTION. TERTULLIAN: Besides, Christ himself has confirmed this prefigurement of himself when he said that a shepherd who flees when he sees the wolf and leaves the flock to be devoured is wicked.[18] Such a shepherd will be banished from the farm; his separation pay will be kept from him as compensation for his damage; in fact, he will have to pay back something from his former wages to indemnify the losses of the master. "For to him who has shall be given and from him who does not have even that which he seems to have shall be taken away."[19] Thus Zechariah threatens, "Arise, O sword, against the shepherds, and pluck out the sheep, and I will turn my hand against the shepherds." And against them Ezekiel and Jeremiah thunder with similar recriminations, in that they have not merely battened upon their sheep and fattened themselves but they have themselves dispersed the flock and, without a leader to guide them, left them as prey to all the beasts of the field.[20] For this is what happens when the church is deserted by the clergy in time of persecution. ON FLIGHT IN TIME OF PERSECUTION 11.2.[21]

13:9 A Third Put into the Fire

PERSECUTION AS A PURGING FIRE. TERTULLIAN: These cases occur in persecutions more than at other times (for it is then that we are approved or condemned, humbled or corrected). Their general occurrence is permitted or com-manded by him at whose will they happen even partially; by him, I mean, who says, "I am he who makes peace and creates evil"[22]—that is, war, for that is the antithesis of peace. But what other war has our peace than persecution? If in its issues persecution emphatically brings either life or death, either wounds or healing, you have the author too of this. "I will smite and heal, I will make alive and put to death."[23] "I will burn them," he says, "as gold is burned; and I will try them," he says, "as silver is tried," for when the flame of persecution is consuming us, then the steadfastness of our faith is proved. These will be the fiery darts of the devil, by which faith gets a ministry of burning and kindling; yet by the will of God. As to this I do not know who can doubt, unless it be persons with frivolous and frigid faith, which seizes upon those who with trembling assemble together in the church. For you say, seeing we assemble without order, and assemble at the same time, and flock in large numbers to the church, the heathen are led to make inquiry about us, and we are alarmed lest we awaken their anxieties. Do you not know that God is Lord of all? And if it is God's will, then you shall suffer persecution; but if it is not, the heathen will be still. Believe it most surely, if indeed you believe in that God without whose will not even the sparrow, which a penny can buy, falls to the ground.[24] But we, I think, are better than many sparrows. ON FLIGHT IN TIME OF PERSECUTION 3.[25]

---

[17]FC 71:356-57. [18]Jn 10:12. [19]Lk 8:18. [20]Ezek 34:2; Jer 23:1. [21]FC 40:297. [22]Is 45:7; Job 2:10. [23]Deut 32:39. [24]Mt 10:29. [25]ANF 4:118*.

14:1-21 THE ESCHATOLOGICAL
KINGDOM OF THE LORD

[1]*Behold, a day of the LORD is coming, when the spoil taken from you will be divided in the midst of you.* [2]*For I will gather all the nations against Jerusalem to battle, and the city shall be taken and the houses plundered and the women ravished; half of the city shall go into exile, but the rest of the people shall not be cut off from the city.* [3]*Then the LORD will go forth and fight against those nations as when he fights on a day of battle.* [4]*On that day his feet shall stand on the Mount of Olives which lies before Jerusalem on the east; and the Mount of Olives shall be split in two from east to west by a very wide valley; so that one half of the Mount shall withdraw northward, and the other half southward.* [5]*And the valley of my mountains shall be stopped up, for the valley of the mountains shall touch the side of it; and you shall flee as you fled from the earthquake* in the days of Uzziah king of Judah. Then the LORD your*[u] *God will come, and all the holy ones with him.*[v]

[6]*On that day there shall be neither cold nor frost.*[w†] [7]*And there shall be continuous day (it is known to the LORD), not day and not night, for at evening time there shall be light.*

[8]*On that day living waters shall flow out from Jerusalem, half of them to the eastern sea and half of them to the western sea; it shall continue in summer as in winter.*

[9]*And the LORD will become king over all the earth; on that day the LORD will be one and his name one.*

[10]*The whole land shall be turned into a plain from Geba to Rimmon south of Jerusalem. But Jerusalem shall remain aloft upon its site from the Gate of Benjamin to the place of the former gate, to the Corner Gate, and from the Tower of Hananel to the king's wine presses.* [11]*And it shall be inhabited, for there shall be no more curse;*[x] *Jerusalem shall dwell in security.*

[12]*And this shall be the plague with which the LORD will smite all the peoples that wage war against Jerusalem: their flesh shall rot while they are still on their feet, their eyes shall rot in their sockets, and their tongues shall rot in their mouths.* [13]*And on that day a great panic from the LORD shall fall on them, so that each will lay hold on the hand of his fellow, and the hand of the one will be raised against the hand of the other;* [14]*even Judah will fight against Jerusalem.*[‡] *And the wealth of all the nations round about shall be collected, gold, silver, and garments in great abundance.* [15]*And a plague like this plague shall fall on the horses, the mules, the camels, the asses, and whatever beasts may be in those camps.*

[16]*Then every one that survives of all the nations that have come against Jerusalem shall go up year after year to worship the King, the LORD of hosts, and to keep the feast of booths.* [17]*And if any of the families of the earth do not go up to Jerusalem to worship the King, the LORD of hosts, there will be no rain upon them.* [18]*And if the family of Egypt do not go up and present themselves, then upon them shall*[y] *come the plague with which the LORD afflicts the nations that do not go up to keep the feast of booths.* [19]*This shall be the punishment to Egypt and the punishment to all the*

nations that do not go up to keep the feast of booths.

²⁰*And on that day there shall be inscribed on the bells of the horses, "Holy to the* LORD.*" And the pots in the house of the* LORD *shall be as the bowls before the altar;* ²¹*and every pot in Jerusalem and Judah shall be sacred to the* LORD *of hosts, so that all who sacrifice may come and take of them and boil the flesh of the sacrifice in them. And there shall no longer be a trader in the house of the* LORD *of hosts on that day.*

u Heb *my*   v Gk Syr Vg Tg: Heb *you*   w Compare Gk Syr Vg Tg: Heb uncertain   x Or *ban of utter destruction*   y Gk Syr: Heb *shall not*   *LXX reads *to be stopped up* instead of *to flee*   †LXX *and spirit and frost*   ‡LXX *in Jerusalem*

OVERVIEW: All who rise up against Christ are ultimately destroyed. The unbelieving Jews are the example given, since their rejection of Christ resulted in their destruction by the Romans (EUSEBIUS). The return of Christ to the Mount of Olives is a visible sign for anyone who lives in Jerusalem to recognize (CYRIL OF JERUSALEM). The second advent of Christ with his saints in the end times has been announced by the prophets (AMBROSE). Christ was judged at night when it was cold, and at his crucifixion a darkness prevailed as prophesied by Zechariah (CYRIL OF JERUSALEM). The darkness surrounding the passion of Christ was vividly described by the prophet. The two thieves show in their attitude the response of human beings to the passion. One thief reviles Christ for not delivering them, while the other sees the salvation Christ was effecting and thus obtains redemption (APOSTOLIC CONSTITUTIONS). The living waters of God will bring life to even the Dead Sea. Salvation will come as in ancient times. On that day a great fear will fall on humans. Ephrem offers a mystical meaning for the horse and the bit. All things shall become sacred (EPHREM).

14:2 The Nations Gathered Against Jerusalem

JEWS TO BE PUNISHED FOR CHRIST'S DEATH.
EUSEBIUS OF CAESAREA: And we can see this with our own eyes. For though many have afflicted the word of Christ and are even now contending with it, yet it is lifted above them and become stronger than them all. Yes, truly, the hand of Christ is raised against all that afflicted him, and all his enemies who from time to time rise up against his church are said to be "utterly destroyed." The fulfillment of this also agrees with the passages quoted on the destruction of the whole Jewish race, which came on them after the coming of Christ. For Zechariah writes this prophecy after the return from Babylon, foretelling the final siege of the people by the Romans, through which the whole Jewish race was to become subject to their enemies. He says that only the remnant of the people shall be saved, exactly describing the apostles of our Savior. PROOF OF THE GOSPEL 2.3.50, 53.[1]

14:4 Standing on the Mount of Olives

SECOND COMING ON THE MOUNT OF OLIVES.
CYRIL OF JERUSALEM: But it might happen that he should sit upon a foal; give us rather a sign where the king who enters will stand. Give us a sign not far from the city, that it may not be unknown to us; give us a sign nearby and clearly visible, that being in the city we may behold the place. Again the prophet answers, saying, "That day his feet shall rest upon the Mount of Olives, which is opposite Jerusalem to the east." Is it possible for anyone standing within the city not to behold the place? CATECHETICAL LECTURE 12.11.[2]

14:5-6 The Lord and the Holy Ones Will Come

---

[1]POG 1:97-98. [2]FC 61:233.

SECOND ADVENT FORETOLD. AMBROSE: Yet learn that the Son knows the day of judgment. We read in Zechariah: "And the Lord my God shall come, and all the saints with him. In that day there shall not be light but cold and frost, and it shall be one day, and that day is known to the Lord." This day, then, was known unto the Lord, who shall come with his saints to enlighten us by his second advent. But let us continue the point that we have commenced concerning the Spirit: "He shall glorify me."[3] So then the Spirit glorifies the Son, as the Father also glorifies him, but the Son of God also glorifies the Spirit, as we said. He then is not weak who is the cause of the mutual glory through the unity of the eternal light, nor is he inferior to the Spirit, of whom this is true that he is glorified by the Spirit. ON THE HOLY SPIRIT 2.11.119-20.[4]

THE DARKNESS AND LIGHT OF THE CRUCIFIXION EXPLAINED. CYRIL OF JERUSALEM: Christ, then, was crucified for us; he was judged in the night, when it was cold, and therefore a fire of coal was laid. He was crucified in the third hour, and "from the sixth hour there was darkness until the ninth hour,"[5] but from the ninth hour there was light again. Are these details written down? Let us inquire. Zechariah says, "And it shall come to pass in that day, and there shall be no light but cold and frost through one day (the cold on account of which Peter warmed himself), and that day shall be known to the Lord." (What? Did he not know the other days? There are many days, but "this is the day [of the Lord's patience] the Lord has made.")[6] "And that day shall be known to the Lord, and not day nor night." What dark saying does the prophet utter? That day is neither day nor night. What then shall we call it? The gospel interprets it, telling of the event. It was not day, for the sun did not shine without interruption from rising to setting, but from the sixth hour to the ninth there was darkness. The darkness was interposed, but God called the darkness night. Therefore it was neither all light, so as to be called day, nor all darkness, so as to be

called night; but after the ninth hour the sun shone forth. This also the prophet foretells; for after saying "not day nor night," he adds, "And in the time of the evening there shall be light." Do you see the truth of the events foretold? CATECHETICAL LECTURE 13.24.[7]

14:7 Continuous Day

THE DARKNESS OF THE CRUCIFIXION FORETOLD. APOSTOLIC CONSTITUTIONS: And in another place: "And I was reckoned with the transgressors."[8] Then there was darkness for three hours, from the sixth to the ninth, and again light in the evening; as it is written: "It shall not be day or night, and at the evening there shall be light." All [these] things, when those malefactors saw that they were crucified with him, the one of them reproached him as though he was weak and unable to deliver himself. But the other rebuked the ignorance of his fellow, and turning to the Lord, as being enlightened by him, and acknowledging who he was that suffered, he prayed that he would remember him in his kingdom hereafter.[9] He then presently granted him the forgiveness of his former sins and brought him into paradise to enjoy the mystical good things. He also cried about the ninth hour, and said to his Father, "My God! My God! Why have you forsaken me?"[10] And a little afterward, when he had cried with a loud voice, "Father, forgive them, for they know not what they do,"[11] and had added, "into your hands I commit my spirit," he gave up his spirit[12] and was buried before sunset in a new sepulcher. But when the first day of the week dawned, he arose from the dead and fulfilled those things that before his passion he foretold to us, saying, "The Son of man must continue in the heart of the earth three days and three nights."[13] And when he was risen from the dead, he appeared first to Mary Magdalene and Mary the

---

[3]Jn 16:14. [4]NPNF 2 10:130. [5]Mt 27:45. [6]Ps 118:24. [7]FC 64:20-21. [8]Is 53:12. [9]Lk 23:39-41. [10]Mt 27:46. [11]Lk 23:34. [12]Lk 23:46. [13]Mt 12:40.

mother of James, then to Cleopas in the way, and after that to us his disciples, who had fled away for fear of the Jews but privately were very inquisitive about him.[14] But these things are also written in the Gospels. CONSTITUTIONS OF THE HOLY APOSTLES 5.3.14.[15]

14:8 Living Waters Flow from Jerusalem

THE SPREAD OF THE LIVING WATERS OF GOD. EPHREM THE SYRIAN: On that day living waters shall flow out from Jerusalem, half of them to the eastern sea and half of them to the western sea. After this, from Jerusalem the law of salvation will come. Indeed, as the Lord says, salvation is from the Jews,[16] and it will spread among the neighbor nations. Two seas are proposed as a symbol of the nations: the eastern sea, which Scripture calls Sea of Salt,[17] and the western sea, which is the Great Sea.[18] Again, in a different manner, the prophet calls the eastern sea the people living in the region of light; while by the western sea he indicates the people of Judea, who would not be deprived of the light of the gospel, if they did not want to be. In fact, even though these people are signified through the image of the sunset and the night, nevertheless the living waters of the divine precepts of Christ would not be prevented from constantly flowing to irrigate their hearts, if only they wanted them to come back to their heart. And it shall continue in summer as in winter, as in the ancient times.[19] That is, in the same order and with the same happiness they will flow to the nations who believe as they flowed to our ancestors. COMMENTARY ON ZECHARIAH.[20]

14:9 The Lord Will Rule the Earth

SALVATION TO COME AS IN ANCIENT TIMES. EPHREM THE SYRIAN: It is clear that this passage refers to the glorious time of the Maccabees when, after the idolatry that Antiochus had introduced had been rejected, all of Judea embraced the cult of the one God. At the same time, the things which you see here to be foreshadowed were fulfilled and

perfected by Christ. Therefore the prophet calls summer the very happy time of the manifestation of Christ to the whole world, because Nisan aptly represents the end of the winter month and the beginning of the fruitful summer. On the other hand, he calls winter the night, which constantly oppresses the devil, after the birth of Christ. Again the words "as it was in the ancient times" appear to be suitable to the day, which brought salvation to Moses and the children of Israel. Indeed, it opened a splendid summer for them, whom it carried safe and uninjured through the sea, while it generated a sorrowful winter to the Egyptians by submerging and suffocating their army. On that day the Lord will be one and his name one. What I said to refer to the time of the Maccabees and the dominion of the Jews was brought to its completion all over the world, when, after the promulgation of the gospel of Christ, the whole world believed in him and recognized that he is God and the true king. COMMENTARY ON ZECHARIAH.[21]

14:13 A Great Panic

HOLDING THE OTHER'S HAND IN FEAR. EPHREM THE SYRIAN: On that day a great panic from the Lord shall fall on them, so that each will seize the hand of a neighbor, and the hand of the one will be fastened[22] to the hand of the other. After peace was restored to the Jews, their Greek enemies and those Jews who had abandoned the religion of their fathers fell into a great distress and panic. And therefore it happened that, as is the habit of those who are confounded, they took each other's hand and were not able to let their hold go because of their fear. COMMENTARY ON ZECHARIAH.[23]

14:20 "Holy to the Lord"

---

[14]Mk 16:9, 14; Lk 24:18; Jn 20:11. [15]ANF 7:445*. [16]Jn 4:22. [17]The Dead Sea. [18]The Mediterranean Sea. [19]This phrase is not included in the standard Peshitta or in the Hebrew Bible. [20]ESOO 2:310. [21]ESOO 2:310. [22]The Hebrew reads "will be raised against," but the LXX is very close to the Peshitta. [23]ESOO 2:311.

MYSTICAL MEANING OF THE HORSE AND BIT.
EPHREM THE SYRIAN: On that day there shall be
inscribed on the bit of the horse, "Holy to the
Lord." Not war or wrath but holiness and peace.
Isaiah certainly prophesied this when he said,
"They shall beat their swords into plowshares
and their spears into pruning hooks; nation shall
not lift up sword against nation, neither shall
they learn war any more."[24] Both prophets expected the advent of Christ. In a mystical sense, by
the horse the prophet signifies any servant of
Christ and understands the bit as the divine law,
by which the hearts of the faithful are directed, so
that they may not rush down into vice. The bit
holds the horse in check and obliges it to obey the
horseman, that is, mystically, the Lord. COMMEN-
TARY ON ZECHARIAH.[25]

14:21 Everyday Utensils Sacred to the Lord

ALL THINGS SHALL BECOME SACRED. EPHREM
THE SYRIAN: And the cooking pots in the house
of the Lord shall be as holy as the bowls in front of
the altar; and every cooking pot in Jerusalem and
Judah shall be sacred to the Lord of hosts, so that
all who sacrifice may come and use them to boil
the flesh of the sacrifice. In that veneration the
holy service of the house of the Lord will come, so
that the common cooking pots may be revered by
any foreigner, notwithstanding the fact that you
Jews used to revere the bowls in front of the altar
inside the closure of the house of the Lord. And
not only will there be this honor for the cooking
pots of the house of the Lord and of Jerusalem,
but any cooking pot in the sanctuary as well as in
the holy city and in the whole Jerusalem will be
sanctified to the Lord, so that both the Jews and
Gentiles will revere it as a thing consecrated to
the Lord. The mystical meaning of this prophecy
predicts two things: the honor to be given to the
law of salvation proceeding from Judea and the
conversion of the Jews and the Gentiles, whom
the baptism of Christ received as cooking pots of
flesh and turned into bowls full of perfumes.
COMMENTARY ON ZECHARIAH.[26]

---

[24]Is 2:4. [25]ESOO 2:311. [26]ESOO 2:311.

MALACHI

OVERVIEW: Malachi (Heb *mal'ākî*) means "my messenger." Malachi 1:1 is the title of the book. The election of Israel and the rejection of Edom are heralded in Malachi 1:2-5, while Malachi 1:6—2:9 focuses on priests who failed to carry out their vocation in a faithful and fitting way. Malachi 2:10-16 inveighs against divorce and marriage to foreign wives. Malachi 2:17—3:5 warns about the impending Day of Yahweh with a call to purification, especially of priests, and Malachi 3:6-12 chastises the people for their refusal to pay tithes to the temple. The unbelief of those who envy the prosperity of the wicked, the eventual salvation of the righteous and the punishment of the wicked on judgment day are delineated in Malachi 3:13—4:3 (3:13-21 LXX). Malachi 4:4 (3:22 LXX) exhorts the Jews to be faithful to the law of Moses. Malachi 4:5-6 (3:23-24 LXX) heralds the coming of Elijah to reconcile families before the Day of Yahweh.

Most scholars date the book to after the rebuilding of the temple in 516 B.C., during the Persian period and before the reforms of Nehemiah and Ezra in 432 B.C. The book occupies the last place in the Old Testament and is considered the end of the prophetic canon for those who used the Palestinian and the Septuagint collections. The earliest documentary evidence that we have of its prophetic canonical status is its inclusion in the Septuagint and its appearance in the Qumran scrolls. In all the Jewish and Christian ordering of the Minor Prophets, the book of Malachi is placed at the end of the lists. The New Testament references to Malachi are primarily to define Jesus as the Messiah. The figure of Elijah is used to point to John the Baptist as the last prophetic precursor to the Messiah. This is accomplished by joining Malachi 3:1 and Isaiah 40:3 at Mark 1:2, and Mark 9:11 and Luke 1:17 with Malachi 4:5-6. Paul, in Romans 9:13, saw the reference to Jacob and Esau in Malachi 1:2 as the prophetic election of the Gentiles to replace the limited old covenant. The church fathers made broad use of Malachi to interpret the two covenants, to defend the universality of the gospel and to cite the Eucharist as the new, central sacrament that fulfilled that of Aaron and Melchizedek.

MALACHI, THE LAST OF THE PROPHETS, ANNOUNCED CHRIST'S COMING. THEODORET of Cyr: While Moses the great lawgiver was the first to leave us the divine sayings in writing, the divinely inspired Malachi committed to writing the divine oracles after all the other composers of inspired composition. He did not mention the time like the others, but in his prophecies he indicated that he was accorded this grace after the rebuilding of the divine temple and the people's attainment of peace. In fact, he did not accuse them of indolence in the rebuilding, as did blessed Haggai and Zechariah. He reminds them instead of the divine favors and accuses the priests and the others separately, focusing on the lawless acts committed by them. He announces beforehand the coming of Christ the Lord in the flesh and the salvation the human race enjoyed as a result of it. COMMENTARY ON MALACHI, INTRODUCTION.[1]

---

[1]PG 81:1960-61.

1:1-9 REBUKE OF ISRAEL'S PRIESTHOOD AND SACRIFICE

[1]*The oracle* of the word of the LORD to Israel by Malachi.*[a][†]

[2]*"I have loved you," says the LORD. But you say, "How hast thou loved us?" "Is not Esau Jacob's brother?" says the LORD. "Yet I have loved Jacob* [3]*but I have hated Esau; I have laid waste his hill country*[‡] *and left his heritage to jackals of the desert."* [4]*If Edom says, "We are shattered but we will rebuild the ruins," the LORD of hosts says, "They may build, but I will tear down, till they are called the wicked country, the people with whom the LORD is angry for ever."* [5]*Your own eyes shall see this, and you shall say, "Great is the LORD, beyond the border of Israel!"*

[6]*"A son honors his father, and a servant his master. If then I am a father, where is my honor? And if I am a master, where is my fear? says the LORD of hosts to you, O priests, who despise my name. You say, 'How have we despised thy name?'* [7]*By offering polluted food upon my altar. And you say, 'How have we polluted it?'*[b] *By thinking that the LORD's table may be despised.*[§] [8]*When you offer blind animals in sacrifice, is that no evil? And when you offer those that are lame or sick, is that no evil? Present that to your governor; will he be pleased with you*[#] *or show you favor? says the LORD of hosts.* [9]*And now entreat the favor of God, that he may be gracious to us.'** With such a gift from your hand, will he show favor to any of you?"*[††] *says the LORD of hosts.*

a Or my messenger b Gk: Heb thee *LXX In the hand of the angel [messenger] †LXX Place it upon your heads ‡LXX his borders §LXX adds and the things thereon may be treated with contempt #LXX with it **LXX adds and beseech him ††LXX Shall I accept you?

OVERVIEW: God in his sovereignty metes out justice to the good and evil. God in his sovereignty can choose without any basis of merit that he will bless or curse, as shown from the example of Jacob and Esau (AUGUSTINE). Jacob and Esau reflect Rachel and Leah regarding God's favor or disfavor. Joseph, born of Rachel and a type of Christ, is sold into Egypt. Leah is to be understood as the synagogue, while Rachel is the church. The synagogue filled with jealousy and envy rejected Christ as Lord and Savior (CAESARIUS). God has established in the new covenant a shift away from a relationship of fear and slavery to one of friend and filial relation (JOHN CASSIAN). Bishops and clergy are called to a mutual relationship of love and respect (JEROME). Ungrateful and unworthy people do not acknowledge the kindness of God or know him as Father. Good Christians, however, praise God as Father and express gratitude and honor (MAXIMUS OF TURIN). Clergy are not immune to the judgment of God by virtue of their position if they fail to be faithful to their calling (APOSTOLIC CONSTITUTIONS). In the old covenant God was a master to be revered, not a father to be prayed to, because of the disobedience of the Jews. God desired a fatherly relationship with the Jews, but they made it not possible through their rebellious actions (AUGUSTINE). Inappropriate prayers and impure hearts will result in rejection by God, as happened to Cain and the Israelites (SAHDONA).

1:2 Jacob Loved, Esau Hated

DEFENSE OF GOD'S ELECTION AND GRACE. AUGUSTINE: Furthermore, who would be so impiously foolish as to say that God cannot turn the evil wills of people—as he wills, when he wills and where he wills—toward the good? But when he acts, he acts through mercy; when he does not act, it is through justice. For "he has mercy on whom he wills, and whom he wills, he hardens."[1] Now when the apostle said this, he was commending grace, of which he had just spoken in connection with the twin children in Rebecca's womb: "Before they had yet been born or had done anything good or bad, in order that the electing purpose of God might continue, it was said of them, 'The elder shall serve the younger.'"[2] Accordingly he refers to another prophetic witness, where it is written, "Jacob I loved, but Esau I have hated." Then, realizing how what he said could disturb those whose understanding could not penetrate to this depth of grace, he adds, "What therefore shall we say to this? Is there unrighteousness in God? God forbid!"[3] Yet it does seem unfair that, without any merit derived from good works or bad, God should love the one and hate the other. Now if the apostle had wished us to understand that there were future good deeds of the other—which God, of course, foreknew—he never would have said "not of good works" but rather "of future works." Thus he would have solved the difficulty; or rather he would have left no difficulty to be solved. As it is, however, when he went on to exclaim, "God forbid!" he proceeds immediately to add (to prove that no unfairness in God is involved here), "For he says to Moses, 'I will have mercy on whom I will have mercy, and I will show pity to whom I will show pity.'"[4] Now who but a fool would think God unfair either when he imposes penal judgment on the deserving or when he shows mercy to the undeserving? Finally, the apostle concludes and says, "Therefore it is not a question of him who wills nor of him who runs but of God's showing mercy."[5] ENCHIRIDION 25.98.[6]

GRACE PREDESTINED. AUGUSTINE: Who are these that reply to God, who speaks to Rebecca? She had twin sons of one conception of Isaac our father. "The children were not yet born nor had done any good or evil (that the purpose of God according to election might stand)." The election was of grace, not of merit. It is the election by which he does not find but makes elect—"that it was not of works but of him that calls, that the elder should serve the younger."[7] To this sentence the blessed apostle adds the testimony of a prophet who came along afterward: "Jacob I have loved, but Esau I have hated" to give us to understand plainly by the later utterance what was hidden in the predestination of God by grace before they were born. For what did he love but the free gift of his mercy in Ja-

---

[1]Rom 9:18. [2]Rom 9:11-12. [3]Rom 9:14. [4]Rom 9:15. [5]Rom 9:16. [6]LCC 7:396-97. [7]Rom 9:11.

cob, who had done nothing good before his birth? And what did he hate but original sin in Esau, who had done nothing evil before his birth? Surely he would not have loved in the former a goodness which he had not practiced, nor would he have hated in the latter a nature which he himself had created good. LETTER 194.[8]

LEAH AND RACHEL. CAESARIUS OF ARLES: At the very beginning of the world, of those two sons who were born of Adam, Abel the younger is chosen, while as a figure of the unfaaithful Jews, Cain the older one is condemned. Afterward, in the time of Abraham, the same figure is fulfilled in Sarah and Hagar. Sarah was sterile for a long time as a type of the church, while Hagar as a figure of the synagogue bore a son at once. Hence it is that the younger son Isaac is received into the inheritance, but Ishmael, who was older, is driven away. This fact also seems to have been fulfilled in those two: Jacob the younger was loved by God, while Esau was rejected according to what is written: "I have loved Jacob but hated Esau." This figure is also known to have been fulfilled in those two sisters whom blessed Jacob had as his wives: Rachel, who was the younger, was loved more than Leah the older. In fact, of the former was born Joseph, who was to be sold in Egypt as a type of our Lord and Savior. That Leah was bleary-eyed while Rachel was beautiful in countenance is also significant: in Leah is understood the synagogue; the church is indicated in Rachel. A man whose bodily eyes are afflicted with inflammation cannot look at the brightness of the sun. Similarly the synagogue, which had had the eyes of its heart filled with jealousy and envy against our Lord and Savior as with poisonous floods, could not gaze upon the splendor of Christ, who is "the Sun of justice."[9] SERMON 104.1.[10]

1:6 Fear of God Absent

CHRIST FREES FROM FEAR OF SLAVERY. JOHN CASSIAN: "There is a great distinction, then, between the fear that lacks for nothing, which is the treasure of wisdom and knowledge, and the one that is imperfect, which is called "the beginning of wisdom."[11] This latter has punishment in itself, and it is cast out from the hearts of the perfect upon the advent of the fullness of love. For "there is no fear in love, but perfect loves casts out fear."[12] And in fact, if the beginning of wisdom consists in fear, what but the love of Christ will be its perfection, which contains in itself the fear of perfect love and which is no longer called the beginning but rather the treasure of wisdom and knowledge? Therefore there are two degrees of fear. The one is for beginners—that is, for those who are still under the servile dread. In regard to this it is said, "The slave shall fear his master," and in the Gospel, "I no longer call you servants, because a servant does not know what his master is doing."[13] And consequently he says, "The slave does not remain in the house forever."[14] For he is instructing us to pass from the fear of punishment to the fullest freedom of love and to the confidence of the friends and sons of God. And the blessed apostle, who had long since passed beyond the degree of servile fear, thanks to the power of the Lord's love, disdains lower things and professes that he has been endowed with greater goods. "For," he says, "God has not given us a spirit of fear but of power and love and self-control."[15] Those who burned with perfect love of the heavenly Father and whom, from slaves, the divine adoption had already made sons he also exhorts in these words: "You have not received a spirit of slavery again in fear, but you have received a spirit of adoption, in which we cry out, 'Abba, Father.'"[16] CONFERENCE 11.13.4-6.[17]

CLERGY AS FATHERS IN THE FAITH. JEROME: Be obedient to your bishop and obey him as your spiritual father. Sons love and slaves fear. "If I am a father," he says, "where is my honor? And if I

---

[8]FC 30:323-24*. [9]Mal 4:2. [10]FC 47:113-14. [11]Ps 111:10. [12]1 Jn 4:18. [13]Jn 15:15. [14]Jn 8:35. [15]2 Tim 1:7. [16]Rom 8:15. [17]ACW 57:420-21.

am a master, where is my fear?" In your case one man combines in himself many titles to your respect. He is at once monk, bishop and uncle. But the bishops also should know themselves to be priests, not lords. Let them render to the clergy the honor that is their due that the clergy may offer to them the respect which belongs to bishops. LETTER 52.7.[18]

REVERE GOD AS FATHER. MAXIMUS OF TURIN: Last Sunday I spoke at sufficient length for the correction of those who do not give thanks to the Creator for the divine gifts that they enjoy and who, while benefiting from heavenly kindness, like ungrateful and unworthy persons do not acknowledge the author of kindness. They are ungrateful, I say, who neither fear God as slaves do their master nor honor him as children do their father. God says through the prophets, "If I am a master, where is my fear? If I am a father, where is my love?" That is to say, if you are a slave, render the master service of fear; if you are a son, show your father a reverent love. But when you do not give thanks, you neither love nor fear God; hence you are an insolent slave or a proud son. The good Christian, therefore, ought always to praise his Father and Master and to do all good things with a view of his glory, as the blessed apostle says: "Whether you eat or drink or do anything, do all for the glory of God."[19] SERMON 73.1.[20]

EVIL CLERGY WILL NOT ESCAPE WRATH. APOSTOLIC CONSTITUTIONS: And indeed Balaam the prophet, when he had corrupted Israel by Baal-peor, suffered punishment;[21] and Caiaphas at last was his own murderer; and the sons of Sceva, endeavoring to cast out demons, were wounded by them and fled away in an unseemly manner;[22] and the kings of Israel and of Judah, when they became impious, suffered all sorts of punishments. It is therefore evident how bishops and presbyters, also falsely so called, will not escape the judgment of God. For it will be said to them even now: "O you priests that despise my name, I will deliver you up to the slaughter, as I did Zedekiah and Ahab, whom the king of Babylon fried in a frying pan," as says Jeremiah the prophet.[23] CONSTITUTIONS OF THE HOLY APOSTLES 8.1.2.[24]

"OUR FATHER" NOT IN THE OLD TESTAMENT. AUGUSTINE: We must consider what it is that we have been commanded to pray for—commanded by him from whom we learn to pray for and through whom we obtain what we pray for. He says, "In this manner shall you pray:'Our Father who art in heaven, hallowed be your name. Your kingdom come, your will be done on earth as it is in heaven. Give us this day our daily bread. And forgive us our debts as we forgive our debtors. And lead us not into temptation, but deliver us from evil.'"[25] In every kind of petition we ought first to try to gain the good will of the one we are petitioning. And the praise is usually placed at the beginning of the prayer, where in this instance our Lord has bidden us to say nothing else than "our Father who art in heaven." Praise of God has been expressed in many manners of speech. Anyone can see this as he reads those forms of praise scattered widely here and there throughout the sacred Scriptures. But nowhere is there found any instruction for the people of Israel to say "our Father" or to pray to God as a Father. To them he has been proposed as a master, for they were servants; that is, they were as yet living according to the flesh. When I say this, I am referring to them when they received the commandments of the law which they were ordered to observe, for the prophets frequently point out that this same Lord of ours would have been their father as well, if they did not stray from his commandments. For instance, there are the following expressions: "I have begotten children and exalted them, but they have despised me,"[26] and, "I have said,'You are gods and all of you the sons of the most high,'"[27] and, "If I am a master, where is my fear? And if I am a father, where is

[18]LCC 5:322. [19]1 Cor 10:31. [20]ACW 50:178. [21]Num 25—26. [22]Acts 19:14. [23]Jer 29:22. [24]ANF 7:481. [25]Mt 6:9-13. [26]Is 1:2. [27]Ps 82:6.

my honor?" Even if we were to disregard those prophetic sayings that refer to the fact that there would be a Christian people who would have God as their Father—in accordance with that saying in the Gospel, "He gave them the power of becoming children of God"[28]—there are still many other expressions whereby the Jews are reproved for the fact that by committing sins they refused to be children. The apostle Paul says, "As long as the heir is a little child, he differs in no way from a slave,"[29] but he reminds us that we have received the spirit of adoption, by virtue of which we cry, "Abba, Father."[30] SERMON ON THE MOUNT 2.4.15.[31]

1:8 The Evil of a Deficient Sacrifice

PROPER ATTITUDE IN PRAYER. SAHDONA: Such was the offering of the murderous Cain that was rejected. He had been told by God, "If you act well, I will receive it."[32] Such again were all the offerings of the Israelites that were rejected, whereby they received the curse of the prophet who says, "Cursed is the man who has a ram in his flock, and he vows and sacrifices to the Lord one that is sickly."[33] He rebukes and reproaches them, saying, "Try offering it to your ruler, to see if he will be pleased with it or show you favor; this is what the Lord says." So how will any address made to God during the ministry of prayer that shows any contempt prove acceptable to God—an address that is full of all sorts of distractions, that is sickly and broken up by interruptions? This sort of thing would not be acceptable even to the most insignificant of human beings if he were thus addressed. The offering of turbulent prayer and the ministration of a heart that shows contempt are exactly like the sacrifice of a blemished ram. BOOK OF PERFECTION 18.[34]

---

[28]Jn 1:12. [29]Gal 4:1. [30]Rom 8:15. [31]FC 11:122-23. [32]Gen 4:7. [33]Mal 1:14. [34]CS 101:209-10.

1:10-14 PROPER AND IMPROPER SACRIFICES

[10]*Oh, that there were one among you who would shut the doors, that you might not kindle fire upon my altar in vain! I have no pleasure in you, says the* LORD *of hosts, and I will not accept an offering from your hand.* [11]*For from the rising of the sun to its setting my name is great among the nations, and in every place incense is offered to my name, and a pure offering; for my name is great among the nations, says the* LORD *of hosts.* [12]*But you profane it when you say that the* LORD'S *table is polluted, and the food for* it[c] may be despised.* [13]*'What a weariness this is,' you say, and you sniff at me,[d] says the* LORD *of hosts. You bring what has been taken by violence or is lame or sick, and this you bring as your offering!† Shall I accept that from your hand? says the* LORD. [14]*Cursed be the cheat who has a male in his flock, and vows it, and yet sacrifices to the Lord what is blemished; for I am a great King, says the* LORD *of hosts, and my name is feared among the nations.*

c Heb *its fruit, its food* d Another reading is *it* *LXX *that which is placed upon* †LXX adds *and I will blow against it*

OVERVIEW: The destruction of the temple and its sacrifice were predicted by Malachi to give way to the Gentiles who would honor the true God in all nations (CHRYSOSTOM). The new covenant has destroyed the sacrifice of the temple by replacing it with the eucharistic sacrifice. The celebration of the Eucharist among the Gentiles testifies to the universal nature of the church and reflects God's rejection of the Jews and their worship (AUGUSTINE). God has rejected the Jews and their sacrifices for their having not received Christ and his sacrifice on the cross. The Gentiles now offer true worship to God in the Eucharist. The prophet makes it clear that the old form of Jewish worship would be replaced by the Eucharist and would be found among the Gentiles (CHRYSOSTOM). The flour of the old covenant was a type of the bread of the Eucharist, which purifies from sin (leprosy). The Eucharist has passed on to the Gentiles since the Jews rejected Christ and his sacrifice (JUSTIN).

The Eucharist must be taken only after one is reconciled with one's neighbor if there is a rift present (DIDACHE). Baptism occurs only once, and the priesthood is to be taken from all peoples. The Eucharist has replaced the bloody sacrifices of the temple. Worship is no longer confined to one place; rather, it occurs in every place on earth (APOSTOLIC CONSTITUTIONS). The Catholic church, which is truly universal, unlike the sectarian Donatists, was foreseen by the prophet through the universal offering of sacrifice among the nations of the Gentiles. The universal offering of the Eucharist (i.e., not confined to Jerusalem) was foretold by Malachi. The offerings of Melchizedek to Abraham prefigured the Eucharist and Christ, who is the true high priest (AUGUSTINE). The sacrifices to be offered from the rising to the setting of the sun refer to the New Testament Eucharist offering (JOHN OF DAMASCUS). The celebration of the Eucharist in all places and not specifically in Jerusalem or Mount Gerizim is what Malachi prophesied alone (ORIGEN). Not among the Jews alone, the order of Aaron or even of the order of Melchizedek is the true sacrifice to God to be favored. It is the Eucharist of the church alone, when offered from the "rising of the sun," that became truly universal (AUGUSTINE). Prayers

properly conceived from a pure heart are likened to a pure offering. These are such that saved Noah, healed lameness, conquered armies, divided the sea and revealed mysteries, and many other divine interventions (APHRAHAT). The hands and feet need to be consecrated to God's service in pursuit of the gospel and the prize of eternal life (GREGORY OF NAZIANZUS).

1:10 *Offerings Rejected*

JEWISH RITUALS ABOLISHED. CHRYSOSTOM: The Jews did return from Babylon, they did recover the city, they did rebuild the temple, and they did offer sacrifices. But it was only after all this that Malachi predicted the coming of the present desolation and the abolition of Jewish sacrifices. This is what he said speaking in God's behalf: " 'Shall I for your sakes accept your persons?' says the Lord God almighty. 'For from the rising of the sun, even to its setting, my name is glorified among the nations; and everywhere they bring incense to my name, and a pure offering. But you have profaned it.' "[1] DISCOURSES AGAINST JUDAIZING CHRISTIANS 5.12.3.[2]

THE OLD TESTAMENT REPLACED BY THE NEW TESTAMENT. CHRYSOSTOM: After their captivity in Babylon the Jews did rebuild their temple and restored the place where they were allowed to observe all the rituals according to the law. But now the power of Christ, the power that founded the church, has also destroyed their restored temple. And their prophets foretold this and showed that God would reject Judaism and introduce a new way of worship. DEMONSTRATION AGAINST THE PAGANS 43.[3]

THE NEW SACRIFICE IS PURER. AUGUSTINE: Now I turn to Malachi. This man, prophesying of the church which by Christ's power has now expanded far and wide, takes on the person of God to say to the Jews: " 'I have no pleasure in

---

[1]Mal 1:11-12. [2]FC 68:141. [3]FC 73:176.

you,' says the Lord of hosts, 'and I will not receive a gift from your hand. For from the rising of the sun even to the going down thereof, my name is great among the Gentiles, and in every place there is sacrifice, and there is offered to my name a clean oblation for my name is great among the Gentiles,' says the Lord of hosts." Now if we see that everywhere in our time, "from the rising of the sun to the going down thereof," this sacrifice is being offered by Christ's priests according to the order of Melchizedek, and if the Jews are in no position to deny that their sacrifices, rejected in the first verse, have come to an end—how is it that they can be looking for another Christ? They read the prophecy; they see its fulfillment before their very eyes. Why can they not realize that he must have been the Christ to fulfill it, since nobody else could? CITY OF GOD 18.35.[4]

SACRIFICE IS UNIVERSAL IN THE GENTILES. AUGUSTINE: Lastly, O Jews, if you try to distort these prophetic words into another meaning according to the dictates of your heart, you resist the Son of God against your own salvation. . . . The house of Jacob or Israel is the same people, both called and cast off—not called in respect to some and cast off in respect to others, but the entire house called to walk in the light of the Lord. . . . The reason why the house had been cast off was because its people were not walking in the light of the Lord, or some of the house certainly were called and others cast off in such a way that without any separation having been of the Lord's table as regards the sacrifice of Christ. Both called and cast off were under the same old sacraments, to be sure; both those who walked in the light of the Lord and observed his precepts and those who rejected justice and deserved to be abandoned by it. If you choose to interpret these testimonies in this manner, what are you going to say and how will you interpret another prophet who cuts this reply away entirely, shouting with unmistakable manifestation: " 'I have no pleasure in you,' says the Lord almighty, 'and I will not re-

ceive a gift of your hand. For from the rising of the sun even to the going down my name is great among the Gentiles, and in every place sacrifice is offered in my name, a clean oblation: for my name is great among the Gentiles,' says the Lord almighty." IN ANSWER TO THE JEWS 9.[5]

GOD'S NAME IS GLORIFIED AMONG THE NATIONS. CHRYSOSTOM: Scripture did not pass over in silence the rejection of the Jews. Notice how the prophet Malachi foretold this too. "Behold, among you the doors will be shut, and fire will not be kindled on my altar for anything." He also foretold who would now pay God worship. "From the rising of the sun to its going down, my name has been glorified among the nations." And again he said, "And in every place incense is offered to me and a pure sacrifice." Do you see how he made clear the nobility of worship? How he showed that the new worship had a special honor and differed from the old? Worship will not be confined to a place or a way of sacrifice, nor will it consist in savor or smoke or omens; it will be a different ritual. DEMONSTRATION AGAINST THE PAGANS 7.1.[6]

FLOUR A TYPE OF CHRIST. JUSTIN MARTYR: "And the offering of fine flour, sirs," I said, "which was prescribed to be presented on behalf of those purified from leprosy, was a type of bread of the Eucharist, the celebration of which our Lord Jesus Christ prescribed, in remembrance of the suffering which he endured on behalf of those who are purified in soul from all iniquity. [This was prescribed] in order that we may at the same time thank God for having created the world, with all things therein, for the sake of humankind, and for delivering us from the evil in which we were, and for utterly overthrowing principalities and powers by him who suffered according to his will. Hence God speaks by the mouth of Malachi, one of the twelve [prophets], as I said before, about the sacrifices

---

[4]FC 24:139-40. [5]FC 27:409-10. [6]FC 73:215.

at that time presented by you: "'I will have no pleasure in you,' says the Lord, 'and I will not accept your sacrifices at your hands. From the rising of the sun to the going down of the same, my name has been glorified among the Gentiles, and in every place incense is offered to my name, and a pure offering: for my name is great among the Gentiles,' says the Lord, but you profane it." [So] he then speaks of those Gentiles, namely us, who in every place offer sacrifices to him, that is, the bread of the Eucharist and also the cup of the Eucharist, affirming both that we glorify his name and that you profane [it]. The command of circumcision, again bidding [them] always to circumcise the children on the eighth day, was a type of the true circumcision, by which we are circumcised from deceit and iniquity through him who rose from the dead on the first day after the sabbath, [namely, through] our Lord Jesus Christ. For the first day after the sabbath, remaining the first of all the days, is called, however, the eighth, according to the number of all the days of the cycle, and [yet it] remains the first. DIALOGUE WITH TRYPHO 42.[7]

1:11 God's Name Is Great Among the Nations

EUCHARIST AND RECONCILIATION. DIDACHE: And on the Lord's day, after you have come together, break bread together. Break bread and offer Eucharist, having first confessed your offenses, so that your sacrifice may be pure. But let no one who has quarreled with his neighbor join you until he is reconciled, lest your sacrifice be defiled. For it was said by the Lord, "In every place and time let there be offered to me a clean sacrifice, because I am the great king;" and also, "and my name is wonderful among the Gentiles." DIDACHE 14.[8]

VISIBILITY OF FAITH, THE NEW SACRAMENTS. APOSTOLIC CONSTITUTIONS: He has in several ways changed the baptism ritual of the priesthood and the divine service, which was con-

fined to one place, for instead of daily baptisms he has given only one, which is that into his death.[9] Instead of one tribe, he has pointed out that out of every nation the best should be ordained for the priesthood; and that rather than their bodies, their religion and their lives should be examined for blemishes. Instead of a bloody sacrifice, he has appointed that reasonable and unbloody mystical one of his body and blood, which is performed to represent the death of the Lord by symbols. Instead of the divine service confined to one place, he has commanded and appointed that he should be glorified from sun rising to sun setting in every place of his dominion. CONSTITUTIONS OF THE HOLY APOSTLES 6.4.23.[10]

THE CHURCH IS UNIVERSAL. AUGUSTINE: Whether betrayers of the divine books ordained Caecilian,[11] I do not know; I did not see; I heard it from his enemies; it's not declared to me by the law of God, or by the preaching of the prophets, or by the holy psalms, or by the apostles of Christ or by Christ's words. But the testimonies of the entire Scripture proclaim with one voice that the church, with which the sect of Donatus is not in communion, is indeed spread throughout the entire world. "In your seed shall all the nations of the earth be blessed,"[12] said the law of God. "From the rising of the sun even to the going down, there is offered to my name a clean offering, for my name is great among the Gentiles," said God through the prophet. LETTER 185.5.[13]

BAPTISM AND EUCHARIST ARE SACRAMENTS. AUGUSTINE: You have all just now been born again of water and the spirit, and can see that food and drink upon this table of the Lord in a new light, and receive it with a fresh love and piety. So I am obliged by the duty I have of giving you a sermon and by the anxious care by which I have given you birth, that Christ might be formed in you, to remind you infants of what the mean-

---

[7]ANF 1:215. [8]FC 1:182-83. [9]Cf. Rom 6:3. [10]ANF 7:461. [11]A Donatist. [12]Gen 22:18; 26:24. [13]FC 30:145*.

ing is of such a great and divine sacrament, such a splendid and noble medicine, such a pure and simple sacrifice, which is not offered now just in the one earthly city of Jerusalem, nor into that tabernacle which was constructed by Moses, nor in the temple built by Solomon. These were just "shadows of things to come."[14] But "from the rising of the sun to its setting,"[15] it is offered as the prophets foretold, and as a sacrifice of praise to God, according to the grace of the New Testament. No longer is a victim sought from the flocks for a blood sacrifice, nor is a sheep or a goat any more led to the divine altars, but now the sacrifice of our time is the body and blood of the priest himself. About him, indeed, it was foretold so long ago in the psalms, "You are a priest forever according to the order of Melchizedek."[16] That Melchizedek, priest of God the most high, offered bread and wine when he blessed our father Abraham, we gather from reading about it in the book of Genesis. SERMON 228B.1.[17]

EUCHARIST IS A BLOODLESS SACRIFICE. JOHN OF DAMASCUS: It was with bread and wine that Melchizedek, the priest of the most high God, received Abraham, when he was returning from the slaughter of the alien tribes.[18] That altar prefigured this mystical altar, even as that priest was a type and a figure of the true archpriest, who is Christ. For "you," he says, "are a priest forever according to the order of Melchizedek."[19] This bread was prefigured by the loaves of proposition. This is quite plainly the pure and unbloody sacrifice which the Lord, through the mouth of the prophet, said was to be offered to him from the rising of the sun even to its going down. ORTHODOX FAITH 4.13.[20]

GOD DWELLS WITHIN US IN THE NEW SACRIFICE. ORIGEN: And it is astonishing that Moses is called Moses even among us and each of the prophets is addressed by his own name. For Christ did not change the names in them but the understanding. And he changes it there that now later we might not pay attention "to Jewish fa-

bles"[21] and "endless genealogies,"[22] because "they turn their hearing away from the truth indeed but are turned to fables."[23] He opened, therefore, the wells and taught us, that we might not seek God in some one place but might know that "sacrifice is offered to his name in every land." For it is now that time "when the true worshipers worship the Father neither in Jerusalem nor on Mount Gerizim "but in spirit and truth."[24] God, therefore, dwells in the heart. And if you are seeking the place of God, a pure heart is his place, for he says through the prophet, "'I will dwell in them; and they shall be my people, and I will be their God,' says the Lord."[25] HOMILIES ON GENESIS 13.3.[26]

NEW TESTAMENT SACRIFICE IS BASED ON MELCHIZEDEK. AUGUSTINE: To him it was said, "You are a priest forever, after the order of Melchizedek."[27] For you seek a sacrifice among the Jews; you have none after the order of Aaron. You seek it after the order of Melchizedek, though finding it not among them; but through the whole world it is celebrated in the church: "From the rising of the sun to the setting thereof the name of the Lord is praised." "And they sowed fields and planted vineyards and got fruit of corn,"[28] at which that workman rejoiced who said, "not because I desire a gift, but I seek fruit."[29] "And he blessed them, and they were multiplied exceedingly, and their cattle were not diminished."[30] This stands. For "the foundation of God stands sure, because the Lord knows them that are his."[31] They are called "beasts of burden" and "cattle" that walk simply in the church yet are useful; not deeply learned but full of faith. Therefore, whether spiritual or carnal, "he blessed them." EXPLANATION OF THE PSALMS 108.8.[32]

THE EFFICACY OF PURE PRAYER. APHRAHAT: Purity of heart constitutes prayer more than do all

---

[14]Col 2:17; Heb 10:1. [15]Ps 113:3. [16]Ps 110:4. [17]WSA 3 6:261. [18]Gen 14:18; Heb 7:1. [19]Ps 110:4; Heb 7:17. [20]FC 37:359-60*. [21]Tit 1:14. [22]1 Tim 1:4. [23]2 Tim 4:4. [24]Jn 4:20-23. [25]2 Cor 6:16; Lev 26:12. [26]FC 71:191. [27]Ps 110:4. [28]Ps 107:37. [29]Phil 4:17. [30]Ps 107:38. [31]2 Tim 2:19. [32]NPNF 1 8:535. In modern English translations, it is Ps 107.

the prayers that are uttered out loud, and silence united to a mind that is sincere is better than a loud voice of someone crying out. My beloved, give me now your heart and your thought, and hear about the power of pure prayer; see how our righteous ancestors excelled in their prayer before God and how it served them as a "pure offering." For it was through prayer that offerings were accepted, and it was prayer again that averted the flood from Noah. Prayer has healed barrenness, prayer has overthrown armies, prayer has revealed mysteries, prayer has divided the sea, prayer made a passage through the Jordan. It held back the sun, it made the moon stand still, it destroyed the unclean, it caused fire to descend. Prayer closed up the heaven, prayer raised up from the pit, rescued from the fire and saved from the sea. On Prayer 1.[33]

SERVING CHRIST, NOT EVIL. GREGORY OF NAZIANZUS: And in addition to what has been said, it is good with our head cleansed, as the head which is the workshop of the senses is cleansed, to hold fast the head of Christ,[34] from which the whole body is fitly joined together and compacted, and to cast down our sin that exalted itself, when it would exalt us above our better part. It is good also for the shoulder to be sanctified and purified that it may be able to take up the cross of Christ, which not everyone can easily do.

It is good for the hands to be consecrated, and the feet. [One is consecrated] that they may in every place be lifted up holy and that they may lay hold of the discipline of Christ, lest the Lord at any time be angered; and that the word may gain credence by action, as was the case with that which was given in the hand of a prophet.[35] The other [is consecrated] that they be not too swift to shed blood or to run to evil, but that they be prompt to run to the gospel and the prize[36] of the high calling and to receive Christ who washes and cleanses them. And it would be good if there is also a cleansing of that belly which receives and digests the food of the word. Do not make it a god by luxury and the meat that perishes.[37] Rather, give it all possible cleansing and make it more spare, that it may receive the Word of God at the very heart and grieve honorably over the sins of Israel.[38] I find also the heart and inward parts deemed worthy of honor. David convinces me of this when he prays that a clean heart may be created in him and a right spirit renewed in his inward parts,[39] meaning, I think, the mind and its movements or thoughts. On Holy Baptism, Oration 40.39.[40]

---

[33]CS 101:5. [34]Eph 4:15. [35]Hag 1:1. [36]Phil 3:14. [37]Jn 6:27. [38]Jer 4:19. [39]Ps 51:10. [40]NPNF 2 7:374.

2:1-9 GUILT AND CONDEMNATION OF THE PRIESTS

[1]"And now, O priests, this command is for you. [2]If you will not listen, if you will not lay it to heart to give glory to my name, says the LORD of hosts, then I will send the curse upon you and I will curse your blessings; indeed I have already cursed them,* because you do not lay it to heart. [3]Behold, I will rebuke your offspring,† and spread dung upon your faces, the dung of your offerings, and I will put you out of my presence.ᵉ [4]So shall you know that I have sent this command to you, that my covenant with Levi may hold, says the LORD of hosts. [5]My covenant with him was a cove-

nant of life and peace, and I gave them to him, that he might fear; and he feared me, he stood in awe of my name. ⁶True instruction[f] was in his mouth, and no wrong was found on his lips. He walked with me in peace and uprightness, and he turned many from iniquity. ⁷For the lips of a priest should guard knowledge, and men should seek instruction[f] from his mouth, for he is the messenger of the LORD of hosts. ⁸But you have turned aside from the way; you have caused many to stumble by your instruction;[f] you have corrupted the covenant of Levi, says the LORD of hosts, ⁹and so I make you despised and abased before all the people, inasmuch as you have not kept my ways but have shown partiality in your instruction."[f]

e Cn Compare Gk Syr: Heb *and he shall bear you to it*   f Or *law*   *LXX *indeed I will curse it, and I will scatter blessing, and it will not be among you*   †LXX *the arm*

OVERVIEW: Priests not faithful to their vocations will incur the wrath of God upon themselves and their flock (CYPRIAN). If the sacrifices of the temple have come to an end, how can the Jews possibly look for another Messiah? Christ was also proclaimed reverent because of the good news he brought to humanity (AUGUSTINE). We address ourselves to God through Christ. Likewise, laity come to the clergy for guidance, as was true even in the old covenant (APOSTOLIC CONSTITUTIONS). The burden is upon the priests to have knowledge of divine law and canonical regulations. Not to do so is to imperil the laity, whom the priest is entrusted to teach, with a lack of knowledge (CAESARIUS). Priests are angels in the sense that they are messengers of God who import the gospel through their teaching (CHRYSOSTOM). The priesthood entails becoming a herald of the gospel. A priest is to be a fountain of knowledge to which the faithful can turn for guidance (GREGORY THE GREAT).

2:1-2 Commands for Priests

PRIESTS WARNED TO BE PURE. CYPRIAN: In this place, we must consider, dearly beloved brother, for the sake of the faith and religion of the sacerdotal office which we exercise, whether the account of a bishop of God who asserts and approves and considers acceptable the baptism of blasphemers can be satisfactory when the Lord threatens and says, "'And now, O priests, this commandment is for you. If you do not hear and if

you do not lay it to heart to give glory to my name,' says the Lord God omnipotent, 'I will send a curse upon you, and of your blessing I will make a curse.'" Does he who is in communion with the baptism of Marcion give glory to God? Does he who thinks that the remission of sins is granted among those who blaspheme against God give glory to God? Does he who asserts that sons of God are born of an adulterous and fornicating woman give glory to God? Does he who, not holding the unity and truth coming from the divine law, defends heresies against the church give glory to God? Does he who, as a friend of heretics and an enemy of Christians, thinks that bishops of God protecting the truth of Christ and the unity of the Christ ought to be excommunicated give glory to God? If glory is thus given to God, if the fear and discipline of God are thus preserved by his worshipers and bishops, let us cast aside our arms. Let us surrender into captivity. Let us hand over to the devil the ordination of the gospel, the decree of Christ, the majesty of God. Let the sacraments of the divine welfare be cast aside. Let the standards of the heavenly camp be given up. Let the church succumb and yield to heretics, light to darkness, faith to perfidy, hope to despair, reason to error, immortality to death, love to hatred, truth to lying, Christ to antichrist. LETTER 8.[1]

2:5 A Covenant of Life and Peace

[1]FC 51:290-91.

PRIESTS CARRY GOD'S VOICE. AUGUSTINE: A little further on Malachi speaks of Christ, again in the person of God: "My covenant was with him of life and peace, and I gave him fear; and he feared me, and he was afraid before my name. The law of truth was in his mouth, and iniquity was not found on his lips. He walked with me in peace and equity and turned many away from iniquity. For the lips of the priest shall keep knowledge, and they shall seek the laws at his mouth because he is the angel of the Lord of hosts." No one should be astonished to hear Christ spoken of as "the angel of the Lord of hosts." He was called his servant because he came to humanity in the form of a servant; similarly he was called an angel because of the evangel,[2] which he brought to humankind. CITY OF GOD 18.35.[3]

2:7 A Priest Should Guard Knowledge

PRIESTS REPRESENT GOD TO THE PEOPLE. APOSTOLIC CONSTITUTIONS: For neither may we address ourselves to almighty God, but only by Christ. In the same manner, therefore, let the laity make known all their desires to the bishop by the deacon, and accordingly let them act as he shall direct them. For there was no holy thing offered or done in the temple formerly without the priest. "For the priest's lips shall keep knowledge, and they shall seek the law at his mouth," as the prophet somewhere says, "for he is the messenger of the Lord God almighty." CONSTITUTIONS OF THE HOLY APOSTLES 2.4.28.[4]

WHY PRIESTS SOUND BELLS. CAESARIUS OF ARLES: For this reason we ought to fear lest the harsh rebuke of the prophet be directed toward us: "Dumb dogs are not able to bark."[5] By the barking of dogs and the shepherd's staff the fury of wolves is to be warded off. Now it is certain that priests are not only ordained to be stewards of fields and cultivators of land but also to exercise the spiritual cultivation of souls, that of which the apostle surely spoke when he said, "I have planted, Apollos watered." Again he said,

"We are God's helpers, you are God's tillage."[6] With great fear these facts ought to be considered by all the priests, who cannot be ignorant of the divine law and canonical regulations, according to what the apostle says: "If anyone belongs to the Lord, he knows what I say; but if anyone ignores this, he shall be ignored."[7] For this reason, what the Lord says through the prophet is to be feared exceedingly: "Therefore my people are led away captive, because they had knowledge";[8] moreover, "He that turns away his ears from hearing the law of the Lord, his prayer shall be an abomination";[9] "the lips of the priest shall keep knowledge." Now it is written concerning the garments of priests that when entering the temple they should have gold bells on the edge of their vestments. What else does this mean but that when entering the church all priests of the Lord should not stop shouting, that is, preaching about the last things, namely, the end of the world and the future judgment. By ceaselessly proclaiming the rewards of the just and the punishments of sinners, they may arouse the good to better things and recall the wicked from their sinful actions through fear of the future judgment. SERMON 1.5.[10]

PRIESTS DISPENSE HOLY FOOD. CHRYSOSTOM: See the apostle's wisdom; to obviate the objection that he was prompted by vainglory to applaud his own doctrine, he includes himself also in his anathema. And as they betook themselves to authority, that of James and John, he mentions angels also, saying, "Tell me not of James and John; if one of the most exalted angels of heaven corrupt the gospel, let him be anathema."[11] The phrase "of heaven" is purposely added, because priests are also called angels. "For the priest's lips should keep knowledge, and they should seek the law at his mouth, for he is the messenger angel of the Lord of the hosts." COMMENTARY ON GALATIANS 1.[12]

---

[2]Or "gospel." *Euangelion* (gospel) and *angelos* (angel) have a common root in the Greek, hence the pun. [3]FC 24:140. [4]ANF 7:411. [5]Is 56:10. [6]1 Cor 3:6, 9. [7]1 Cor 14:37-38. [8]Is 5:13. [9]Prov 28:9. [10]FC 31:7. [11]Cf. Gal 1:8-9. [12]NPNF 1 13:8*.

PRIESTS ARE HERALDS OF GOD'S GRACE.
GREGORY THE GREAT: For in sacred language teachers are sometimes called prophets in that, by pointing out how fleeting are present things, they make manifest the things that are to come. And such the divine discourse convinces of seeing false things, because, while fearing to reprove faults, they vainly flatter evildoers by promising security; neither do they at all dissolve the iniquity of sinners, since they refrain their voice from chiding. For the language of reproof is the key of discovery, because by chiding it discloses the fault of which even he who has committed it is often un-

aware. Hence Paul says, "That he may be able by sound doctrine even to convince the gainsayers."[13] Hence through Malachi it is said, "The priest's lips keep knowledge, and they shall seek the law at his mouth." Hence through Isaiah the Lord admonishes, saying, "Cry aloud to spare not, lift up your voice like a trumpet."[14] For it is true that whosoever enters on the priesthood undertakes the office of a herald, so to walk, himself crying aloud, before the coming of the judge who follows terribly. PASTORAL CARE 2.4.[15]

---

[13]Tit 1:9. [14]Is 58:1. [15]NPNF 2 12:11-12.

2:10-17 DIVINE CONDEMNATION OF IDOLATRY AND DIVORCES

[10]Have we not all one father? Has not one God created us? Why then are we faithless to one another, profaning the covenant of our fathers? [11]Judah has been faithless, and abomination has been committed in Israel and in Jerusalem; for Judah has profaned the sanctuary of the LORD, which he loves, and has married the daughter of a foreign god. [12]May the LORD cut off from the tents of Jacob, for the man who does this, any to witness[g] or answer, or to bring an offering to the LORD of hosts!

[13]And this again you do.* You cover the LORD's altar with tears, with weeping and groaning because he no longer regards the offering or accepts it with favor at your hand. [14]You ask, "Why does he not?" Because the LORD was witness to the covenant between you and the wife of your youth, to whom you have been faithless, though she is your companion and your wife by covenant. [15]Has not the one God made[h] and sustained for us the spirit of life?[i] And what does he desire? Godly offspring. So take heed to yourselves, and let none be faithless to the wife of his youth. [16]"For I hate[j] divorce, says the LORD the God of Israel, and covering one's garment with violence, says the LORD of hosts. So take heed to yourselves and do not be faithless."

[17]You have wearied the LORD with your words. Yet you say, "How have we wearied him?" By saying, "Every one who does evil is good in the sight of the LORD, and he delights in them." Or by asking, "Where is the God of justice?"

g Cn Compare Gk: Heb *arouse*   h Or *has he not made one?*   i Cn: Heb *and a remnant of spirit was his*   j Cn: Heb *he hates*   *LXX adds *which I detest*

OVERVIEW: God was initially only Creator, but after the coming of Christ he has opened up the possibility of a filial relationship as Father (ATHANASIUS). God alone is the Cause and Creator of all that exists (IRENAEUS). Remarriage is allowed under only two conditions: that the husband has died or that the woman marries a Christian, not an unbeliever. To do to the contrary is likened to Judah, who intermarried with the Gentile cultures (JEROME). Marriage is a permanent union that cannot be annulled on a whim (TERTULLIAN). Murmuring against God is the result of an unspiritual reading of the law and causes great anguish (AUGUSTINE).

2:10 *All Have One Father*

FROM CREATOR TO FATHER GOD. ATHANASIUS: But this is God's kindness to humanity, that of whom he is the maker, of them according to grace he afterwards becomes Father also. He becomes, that is, when people, his creatures, receive him into their hearts, as the apostle says, "the spirit of his Son, crying, 'Abba, Father.'"[1] And these are they who, having received the word, gained power from him to become sons of God; for they could not become sons, being by nature creatures, otherwise than by receiving the spirit of the natural and true Son. Wherefore, that this might be, "the word became flesh," that he might make humans capable of godhood. This same meaning may be gained from the prophet Malachi, who says, "Has not one God created us? Have we not all one Father?" For first he puts "created" next to "Father" to show, as the other writers, that from the beginning we were creatures by nature. And God is our Creator through the word, but afterwards we were made sons, and thenceforward God the Creator becomes our Father also. FOUR DISCOURSES AGAINST THE ARIANS 2.21.59.[2]

GOD ALONE IS FATHER OF ALL CREATED THINGS. IRENAEUS: The Scripture declares the truth, which says, "First of all believe that there is one God, who has established all things and com-pleted them, and having caused that from what had no being, all things should come into existence":[3] he who contains all things, and is himself contained by no one. Rightly also Malachi said among the prophets: "Is it not one God who has established us?" In accordance with this too does the apostle say, "There is one God, the Father who is above all, and in us all."[4] Likewise does the Lord also say, "All things are delivered to me by my Father,"[5] manifestly by him who made all things; for he did not deliver to him the things of another but his own. AGAINST HERESIES 4.20.2.[6]

2:11 *Faithless Judah*

MIXED MARRIAGES CONDEMNED. JEROME: And if you wish to see more clearly how utterly unlawful it is for a Christian woman to marry a Gentile, consider what the same apostle says, "A wife is bound for so long time as her husband lives. But if the husband be dead, she is freed to be married to whom she will, only in the Lord,"[7] that is, to a Christian. The one who allows second and third marriages in the Lord forbids first marriages with a Gentile. Whence Abraham also makes his servant swear upon his thigh, that is, on Christ, who was to spring from his seed, that he would not bring an alien-born as a wife for his son Isaac.[8] And Ezra checked an offense of this kind against God by making his countrymen put away their wives.[9] And the prophet Malachi thus speaks, "Judah has dealt treacherously, and an abomination is committed in Israel and in Jerusalem; for Judah has profaned the holiness of the Lord which he loves and has married the daughter of a strange god. The Lord will cut off the man that does this, him that teaches and him that learns, out of the tents of Jacob, and him that offers an offering to the Lord of hosts." I have said this that they who compare marriage with virginity may at least know that such marriages as these

---

[1]Gal 4:6. [2]NPNF 2 4:380. [3]*Shepherd* of Hermas, *Mandates* 1, ANF 2:20; cf. Jn 1:3. [4]Eph 4:6. [5]Mt 11:27. [6]ANF 1:488. [7]1 Cor 7:39. [8]Gen 24:1-9. [9]Ezra 10:1-17.

are on a lower level than digamy and trigamy. Against Jovinianus 1.10.[10]

2:15 Faithfulness to the Wife of One's Youth

Permanent Union of Marriage. Tertullian: For in the Gospel of Matthew he says, "Whosoever shall put away his wife, saving for the cause of fornication, causes her to commit adultery."[11] He also is deemed equally guilty of adultery who marries a woman put away by her husband. The Creator, however, except on account of adultery, does not put asunder that which he himself joined together, the same Moses in another passage enacting that he who had married after violence to a damsel should thenceforth not have it in his power to put away his wife.[12] Now if a compulsory marriage contracted after violence shall be permanent, how much rather shall a voluntary one, the result of an agreement! This has the sanction of the prophet: "You shall not forsake the wife of your youth." Thus you have Christ following spontaneously the tracks of the Creator everywhere, both in permitting divorce and in forbidding it. You find him also protecting marriage, in whatever direction you try to escape. He prohibits divorce when he will have the marriage inviolable; he permits divorce when the marriage is spotted with unfaithfulness. You should blush when you refuse to unite those whom even your Christ has united, and repeat the blush when you disunite them without the good reason why your Christ would have them separated. Against Marcion 4.34.[13]

2:17 Wearying the Lord with Words

Murmuring Against God. Augustine: Wherefore now we call the proud people happy, for they that work wickedness are built up.[14] It was such complaints as these that compelled the prophet to anticipate, as it were, the last judgment in which the wicked will be so far from even a pretense of happiness that their misery will be apparent to all, whereas the good, untroubled by even transitory sorrow, will enjoy a manifest and unending blessedness. Malachi had already given a similar illustration of the kind of murmurings that wearied the Lord: "Everyone who does evil is [thought to be] good in the sight of the Lord and as such pleases him." The only point I want to make is that such murmurings against God were the result of an unspiritual interpretation of the law. City of God 20.28.[15]

---

[10]NPNF 2 6:353*. [11]Mt 5:32. [12]Deut 22:28-29. [13]ANF 3:405. [14]Mal 3:14-15. [15]FC 24:328.

3:1 PROPHECY ABOUT THE HERALD OF THE LORD

[1]"*Behold, I send my messenger to prepare the way before me, and the Lord whom you seek will suddenly come to his temple; the messenger of the covenant in whom you delight, behold, he is coming, says the* Lord *of hosts.*

Overview: Malachi foretold both advents by posing the challenge as to who would be able to stand in God's presence on those occasions (Au-gustine). The coming of John the Baptist to herald the Messiah was anticipated in the words of Malachi. The twelve apostles are destined to sit and judge the twelve tribes of Israel. John the Baptist was chosen to announce the new economy of salvation (AUGUSTINE). John the Baptist was in spirit Elijah, the last messenger of God who would announce the coming Messiah (CHRYSOSTOM). John the Baptist was like an Elijah who would bear witness to the true light (Christ) as foretold by the prophet Malachi (IRENAEUS). John the Baptist was like an angel in the sense that he was a messenger of God who proclaimed the Messiah (ORIGEN). In both advents the Messiah acts as a purifying fire to cleanse humans of their fallenness (CYRIL OF JERUSALEM). John the Baptist, who testified about salvation in Christ, fulfilled this prophecy (THEODORE).

3:1 A Messenger to Prepare the Way

FIRST AND SECOND ADVENTS FORETOLD.
AUGUSTINE: Speaking further of Christ in the same vein, Malachi says, "Behold, I send my angel, and he shall prepare the way before my face. And presently the Lord, whom you seek, and the angel of the testament whom you desire, shall come into the temple. Behold, he comes, says the Lord of hosts. And who shall be able to think of the day of his coming? And who shall stand to see him?" In this text he foretells both comings of Christ, the first and the second—the first where he says, "And presently the Lord shall come into his temple." This refers to Christ's body, of which he himself said in the Gospel, "Destroy this temple, and in three days I will raise it up."[1] His second coming is foretold in these words: " 'Behold, he comes,' says the Lord of hosts. 'And who shall be able to think of the day of his coming? And who shall stand to see him?' " CITY OF GOD 18.35.[2]

JOHN THE BAPTIST FORETOLD. AUGUSTINE: "For he whom God has sent speaks the words of God."[3] John said this, of course, about Christ that he might diminish himself from him. Why? Did not God send John himself? And didn't John himself say, "I have been sent before him," and, "He

who sent me to baptize with water,"[4] and about him it was said, "Behold, I send my messenger before you and he will prepare the way"?[5] Does not he too speak the words of God, about whom it was said that he was more than a prophet?[6] Therefore if God also sent John, and he speaks the words of God, how, in regard to the distinction [between himself and Christ], do we know that he said about Christ, "For he whom God has sent speaks the words of God"? TRACTATES ON THE GOSPEL OF JOHN 14.10.1.[7]

JOHN THE BAPTIST IS "THE ANGEL" MESSENGER. AUGUSTINE: Since then it is evident that many are to judge with the Lord but that others are to be judged, not however on equality but according to their deserts, he will come with all his angels.[8] [At the judgment] before him shall be gathered all nations, and among all the angels are to be reckoned those that have been so perfect, that sitting upon twelve thrones they judge the twelve tribes of Israel. For men are called angels; the apostle says of himself, "As an angel of God you received me."[9] Of John the Baptist it is said, "Behold, I send my angel before your face, who shall prepare your way before you."[10] EXPLANATION OF THE PSALMS 1.11.[11]

JOHN IS ELIJAH FORETOLD. CHRYSOSTOM: And what sort of connection may this have with what was said before? Much, assuredly, and in full accord with it. By this topic also he proceeds to urge and press them into faith. At the same time he is speaking in agreement with what had been before said by John. "For if all things are fulfilled even down to John, I am 'he that should come.' "

"For all the prophets," says he, "and the law prophesied until John."[12] For the prophets would not have ceased unless I were come. Expect, therefore, nothing further, and do not wait for anyone else. For that I am he who is manifest both from

---

[1]Jn 2:19. [2]FC 24:140-41. [3]Jn 3:34. [4]Jn 1:33. [5]Mt 11:10. [6]Mt 11:9. [7]FC 79:74. [8]Mt 25:31. [9]Gal 4:14. [10]Mt 11:10. [11]NPNF 1 8:182. [12]Mt 11:13.

the prophets ceasing and from those that every day "take by force" the faith that is in me. For so manifest is it and certain that many even take it by force. Why, who has so taken it? Tell me. All who approach it with earnestness of mind.

Then he states also another infallible sign, saying, "If you will receive it, he is Elijah, who was to come." For "I will send you," it is said, "Elijah the Tishbite, who shall turn the hearts of the fathers to the children."[13] This man then is Elijah, if you attend exactly, says he. For " 'I will send,' says he, 'my messenger before your face.' " And well has he said, "If you will receive it," to show the absence of force. For I do not constrain, says he. And this he said, as requiring a candid mind and showing that John is Elijah, and Elijah John. For both of them received one ministry, and both of them became forerunners. He did not simply say, "This is Elijah," but "If you are willing to receive it, this is he," that is, if with a candid mind you give heed to what is going on. And he did not stop even at this, but to the words "this is Elijah, who was to come" he added, to show that understanding is needed, "he that has ears to hear, let him hear."[14] HOMILIES ON THE GOSPEL OF MATTHEW 37.4.[15]

JOHN IS ELIJAH TO PREPARE THE WAY. IRENAEUS: And that we may not have to ask, of what God was the Word made flesh? He does himself previously teach us, saying, "There was a man sent from God, whose name was John. The same came as a witness, that he might bear witness of that light. He was not that light but [came] that he might testify of the light."[16] By what God, then, was John, the forerunner who testifies of the light, sent [into the world]? Truly it was by him of whom Gabriel is the angel, who also announced glad tidings of his birth: [that God] who also had promised by the prophets that he would send his messenger before the face of his Son, who should prepare his way, that is, that he should bear witness of that light in the spirit and power of Elijah.[17] But, again, of what God was Elijah the servant and the prophet? Of him who

made heaven and earth, as he does himself confess. John therefore, having been sent by the founder and maker of this world, how could he testify of the light, which came down from things unspeakable and invisible? For all the heretics have decided that the demiurge was ignorant of that power above him, whose witness and herald John is found to be. Therefore the Lord said that he deemed him "more than a prophet."[18] For all the other prophets preached the advent of the Father's light and desired to be worthy of seeing him whom they preached. But John both announced [the advent] beforehand, as did the others, and actually saw him when he came, and pointed him out, and persuaded many to believe on him, so that he did himself hold the place of both prophet and apostle. For this is to be more than a prophet, because "first apostles, secondarily prophets,"[19] but all things from one and the same God himself. AGAINST HERESIES 3.11.4.[20]

SPEAKING OF MEN AND ANGELS. ORIGEN: Someone else will appeal to the text, "Let us make man according to our image and likeness," and maintain that whatever is made according to God's image and likeness is man. To support this, numberless instances are adduced to show that in Scripture "man" and "angel" are used indifferently and that the same subject is called both angel and man. This is true of the three who were entertained by Abraham and of the two who came to Sodom. In the whole course of Scripture, persons are styled sometimes men, sometimes angels. Those who hold this view will say that since persons are styled angels who are manifestly men, as when Zechariah says, "The messenger of the Lord, I am with you, says the Lord almighty," and as it is written of John the Baptist, "Behold, I send my messenger before your face,"[21] the angels (messengers) of God are so called on account of their nature. Scripture confirms this view that the names applied to higher powers are not those of

---

[13]Mal 4:5-6. [14]Mt 11:15. [15]NPNF 1 10:245*. [16]Jn 1:6-7. [17]Lk 1:17. [18]Mt 11:9; Lk 7:26. [19]1 Cor 12:28. [20]ANF 1:427. [21]Mk 1:2.

species of living beings but those of the orders, assigned by God to this and to that reasonable being. COMMENTARY ON THE GOSPEL OF JOHN 2.17.[22]

GOD SUDDENLY COMES AND WILL COME.
CYRIL OF JERUSALEM: Of these two comings the prophet Malachi says, "And suddenly there will come to the temple the Lord whom you seek"; that is one coming. Of the second coming he says, "'And the messenger of the covenant whom you desire, yes, he is coming,' says the Lord of hosts. 'But who will endure the day of his coming? And who can stand when he appears? For he is like a refiner's fire or like the fuller's lye. He will sit refining and purifying.'" In what immediately follows the Savior himself says, "I will draw near to you for judgment, and I will be swift to bear witness against sorcerers, adulterers and perjurers."[23] It was with this in view that Paul says in due warning: "But if anyone builds upon this foundation gold, silver, precious stones, wood, hay, straw—the work of each will be made manifest, for the Day of the Lord will declare it, since the day is to be revealed in fire."[24] Paul indicates these two comings also in writing to Titus in these words: "The grace of God our Savior has appeared to all men, instructing us, in order that, rejecting ungodliness and worldly lusts, we may live temperately and justly and piously in this world; looking for the blessed hope and glorious coming of our great God and Savior, Jesus Christ."[25] Do you see how he speaks of a first coming, for which he gives thanks, and of a second we are going to look for? We find the same lesson in the wording of the creed we profess, as delivered to us, that is, to believe in him who "ascended into heaven and sat down on the right of the Father, and is to come in glory to judge the living and dead, of whose kingdom there will be no end." CATECHETICAL LECTURE 15.2.[26]

JOHN TESTIFIED ABOUT SALVATION IN CHRIST. THEODORE OF MOPSUESTIA: I for my part shall come, he is saying, whom you look to as punisher of sins. There will be present also the angel who ministers to the agreements I have often made with you. When you seek him, you will find him punishing the transgression of your agreements with me. While the prophet said this as a consequence of what preceded, it is not surprising that the same verse was cited at the coming of blessed John the Baptist,[27] the statement being fulfilled in actual fact by the coming of blessed John as predetermined forerunner and minister, and by the emergence of Christ the Lord, who came at the same time as he and was testified to by him and in whom the salvation of all people was destined to be achieved. COMMENTARY ON MALACHI 3.1.[28]

---

[22]ANF 9:336. [23]Mal 3:5. [24]1 Cor 3:12-13. [25]Tit 2:11-13. [26]FC 64:54-55. [27]Mt 11:10; Mk 1:2; Lk 1:7; 7:27. [28]PG 66:620*.

3:2-9 COMING JUDGMENT OF THE LORD

²*But who can endure the day of his coming, and who can stand when he appears?*

"For he is like a refiner's fire and like fullers' soap; ³*he will sit as a refiner and purifier of silver, and he will purify the sons of Levi and refine them like gold and silver, till they present right offerings to the* LORD. ⁴*Then the offering of Judah and Jerusalem will be pleasing to the* LORD *as in the days of old and as in former years.*

---

⁵"Then I will draw near to you for judgment; I will be a swift witness against the sorcerers, against the adulterers, against those who swear falsely, against those who oppress the hireling in his wages, the widow and the orphan, against those who thrust aside the sojourner, and do not fear me, says the LORD of hosts.

⁶"For* I the LORD do not change; therefore you, O sons of Jacob, are not consumed. ⁷From the days of your fathers you have turned aside† from my statutes and have not kept them. Return to me, and I will return to you, says the LORD of hosts. But you say, 'How shall we return?' ⁸Will man rob God? Yet you are robbing me. But you say, 'How are we robbing thee?' In your tithes and offerings. ⁹You are cursed with a curse, for you are robbing me; the whole nation of you.

*LXX adds *because*   †LXX *have not departed from the unrighteousness of your fathers*

OVERVIEW: The prophets spoke about the Messiah coming as a judge who would purify sin as a refining fire (CHRYSOSTOM). God is a consuming fire who purges his people of sin to purify them so they can enter into his presence (ORIGEN). Hilary puts forth an argument defending the unchanging nature of God, who does not grow and improve as do humans. In spite of revealing himself in many forms, God does not change (HILARY). God neither increases nor decreases in his nature (NOVATIAN). When God descended from heaven in the incarnation, this did not entail a change in God's nature. God remained unchangeable and was not tainted by evil (ORIGEN). God demonstrates enormous patience in spite of the offenses that humans heap upon him. God's intent for humanity is life not death (CYPRIAN). God desires holiness and cleansing for humanity. He also intends grace and salvation for all, but humans must turn to him with heartfelt repentance (ISAAC OF NINEVEH).

3:2 Who Can Endure God's Coming?

JUDGMENT BY FIRE. CHRYSOSTOM: The same Christ who did all this will hereafter stand before us as our judge. Certainly the prophets did not pass over this but foretold it. Some saw him in that very form which he would stand before us; others predicted this only in words. Daniel was in the midst of the barbarians and the Babylonians when he saw Christ coming in the clouds. Listen to what he said: "I beheld, and lo! One like the Son of man was coming on the clouds. And he advanced to the ancient of days and was presented before him; and to him was given the government and the kingdom, and all the peoples, tribes and languages serve him."[1] And Daniel hinted at God's court and judgment when he said, "The thrones were set, and the books were opened. A river of fire rolled before him. Thousands upon thousands ministered to him, and myriads waited on him."[2] [Daniel not only revealed that, but also he showed the honor that the just would have when he said, "He gave judgment to the holy ones of the most high, and the holy ones possessed the kingdom."][3] And that judgment will come through fire. Malachi said, "He is coming [like the fire of a refiner's furnace, and] like the soap of the fullers." And then the just will enjoy great honor. And Daniel was speaking of the resurrection when he said, "Those lying in the dust shall arise."[4] DEMONSTRATION AGAINST THE PAGANS 11.1-3.[5]

CONSUMING FIRE OF SALVATION. ORIGEN: But as it is in mockery that Celsus says we speak of "God coming down like a torturer bearing fire" and thus compels us unseasonably to investigate words of deeper meaning, we shall make a few remarks, sufficient to enable our hearers to form an idea of the defense which disposes of the ridicule of Celsus against us. And then we shall turn to

[1]Dan 7:13-14. [2]Dan 7:9-10. [3]Dan 7:22. [4]Dan 12:12. [5]FC 73:232-33.

what follows. The divine word says that our God is "a consuming fire"[6] and that "he draws rivers of fire before him."[7] He even enters in as "a refiner's fire and as a fuller's herb," to purify his own people. But when he is said to be a "consuming fire," we inquire what are the things that are appropriate to be consumed by God. And we assert that it is wickedness, and the works which result from it, which are being figuratively called "wood, hay, stubble,"[8] God consumes as a fire. AGAINST CELSUS 4.13.[9]

3:6 The Lord Does Not Change

GOD ETERNALLY THE SAME. HILARY OF POITIERS: He does not need those things that are from him, through him and to him; neither he who is the origin, nor he who is the designer, nor he who embraces all things. He is outside of the things that are within; he is the Creator of those that have been made; and he himself is never in want of his own possessions. Nothing is before him, nothing is from anywhere else, nothing is outside of him. What growth in fullness is therefore wanting to him that God may yet be all in all in the course of time? Or whence shall he procure it outside of whom there is nothing, but nothing in the sense that he always is? And by what kind of an increase is he himself to be made complete who always exists and outside of whom there is nothing? Or by what kind of growth is he to be changed who says, "I am, and I change not," since there is no opportunity for a change or any cause that will enable him to make progress. Nor is there anything prior to eternity or anything else besides God in his relationship with God. Hence God will not be all in all through subjection of the Son, nor will any cause make him perfect from whom, through whom and in whom every cause exists. He remains, therefore, as he is, always God, and he does not stand in need of improvement who is always that which he is from himself and to himself. ON THE TRINITY 11.47.[10]

GOD UNCHANGEABLE. NOVATIAN: He is always

therefore equal to himself; he never changes or transforms himself into other forms, lest through change he should appear to be also mortal. For the modification implied in change from one thing to another involves a share in the death of some sort. Therefore there is never any addition of parts or of glory in him, lest anything should seem to have ever been wanting to the perfect one. Nor can there be any question of diminution in him, for that would imply that some degree of mortality is in him. On the contrary, what he is, he always is; who he is, he always is; such as he is, he always is. For increase in growth indicates a beginning, whereas any wasting away evidences death and destruction. And therefore he says, "I am God and have not changed." He always retains his manner of being, because what is not born is not subject to change. For—whatever that being may be that is God—this must always be true of him, that he always is God, preserving himself by his own powers. And therefore he says, "I am who I am."[11] That which is has this name because it always preserves its same manner of being. Change takes away the name "that which is"; for whatever changes at all is shown to be mortal by the very fact that it changes. It ceases to be what it was and consequently begins to be what it was not. Of necessity, then, God always retains his manner of being, because he is always like unto himself, always equal to himself without any loss arising from change. For that which is not born cannot change, since only those things undergo change which are made or which are begotten; whereas things which at one time were not experience existence by coming into being, and by coming into being they undergo change. On the contrary, things which have neither birth nor maker are exempt from change because they have not a beginning, the cause of change. ON THE TRINITY 4.[12]

CONDESCENSION TO HUMAN FORM DOES NOT CHANGE GOD. ORIGEN: But let us look at

---

[6]Deut 4:24; 9:3. [7]Dan 7:10. [8]1 Cor 3:12. [9]ANF 4:502. [10]NPNF 2 9:217*. [11]Ex 3:14. [12]ANF 5:614*.

what Celsus next with ostentation announces in the following fashion: "And again," he says, "let us resume the subject from the beginning, with a larger array of proofs. And I make no new proofs. And I make no new statement but say what has long been settled. God is good and beautiful and blessed, and that in the best and most beautiful degree. But if he comes down among humanity, he must undergo a change, and a change from good to evil, from virtue to vice, from happiness to misery, and from best to worst. Who, then, would make a choice of such a change? It is the nature of a mortal, indeed, to undergo change and remolding, but of an immortal to remain the same and unaltered. God, then, could not admit such a change." Now it appears to me that the fitting answer has been returned to these objections when I have related what I called in Scripture the "condescension" of God to human affairs. For [this] purpose he did not need to undergo a transformation, as Celsus thinks we assert, nor a change from good to evil, nor from virtue to vice, nor from happiness to misery, nor from best to worst. For, continuing unchangeable in his essence, he condescends to human affairs by the economy of his providence. We show accordingly that the holy Scripture represents God as unchangeable, both by such words as "you are the same"[13] and "I change not." Whereas the gods of Epicurus, being composed of atoms, and, so far as their structure is concerned, capable of dissolution, endeavor to throw off the atoms which contain the elements of destruction. Even the god of the Stoics, as being corporeal, at one time has his whole essence composed of the guiding principle when the conflagration [of the world] takes place; and at another, when a rearrangement of things occurs, he again becomes partly material. For even the Stoics were unable to comprehend distinctly the natural idea of God as a being altogether incorruptible and simple and uncompounded and indivisible. AGAINST CELSUS 4.14.[14]

3:7 "Return to Me, and I Will Return to You"

GOD WILLS LIFE, NOT DEATH. CYPRIAN: And while God is provoked with frequent and continual offenses, he softens his indignation, and in his patience waits for the day of retribution, once for all determined. And although he has revenge in his power, he prefers to keep patience for a long while. [He bears], that is to say, mercifully, and puts off, so that, if it might be possible, the long-protracted mischief may at some time be changed, and humanity, involved in the contagion of errors and crimes, may even though late be converted to God, as he himself warns and says, "I do not will the death of him that dies, so much as that he may return and live."[15] And again, "'Return unto me,' says the Lord." THE ADVANTAGE OF PATIENCE 9.4.[16]

GOD REACHES OUT CONTINUALLY WITH GRACE. ISAAC OF NINEVEH: On account of its great intensity, this reflection is sometimes mingled with wonder. For the heart of those who see the Lord will rejoice.[17] Seek the Lord, O sinners, and be strengthened in your thoughts because of hope. And seek his face through repentance at all times,[18] and you will be sanctified by the holiness of his presence, and you will be purified of your iniquity.[19] Hasten to the Lord, O sinners; he remits iniquity and removes sins. For he has sworn, "I have no pleasure in the death which the sinner dies,"[20] so that the sinner may repent and live. "I have spread out my hands all day toward a quarrelsome and disobedient people."[21] And "Why would you want to die, O house of Jacob?"[22] "Turn to me, and I will turn to you."[23] ASCETICAL HOMILIES 5.76-77.[24]

---

[13]Ps 102:27 (101:28 LXX). [14]ANF 4:502-3. [15]Ezek 18:32. [16]ANF 5:485. [17]Ps 105:3. [18]Ps 105:4. [19]Ezek 36:25. [20]Ezek 33:11. [21]Is 65:2. [22]Ezek 33:11. [23]Also Zech 1:3. [24]INAL 92-93.

3:10-18 JUDGMENT OF THE RIGHTEOUS AND THE WICKED

¹⁰*Bring the full tithes into the storehouse, that there may be food in my house; and thereby put me to the test, says the LORD of hosts, if I will not open the windows of heaven for you and pour down for you an overflowing blessing.* ¹¹*I will rebuke the devourer^k for you, so that it will not destroy the fruits of your soil; and your vine in the field shall not fail to bear, says the LORD of hosts.* ¹²*Then all nations will call you blessed, for you will be a land of delight, says the LORD of hosts.*

¹³*"Your words have been stout against me, says the LORD. Yet you say, 'How have we spoken against thee?'* ¹⁴*You have said, 'It is vain to serve God. What is the good of our keeping his charge or of walking as in mourning before the LORD of hosts?* ¹⁵*Henceforth we deem the arrogant blessed; evildoers not only prosper but when they put God to the test they escape.'"*

¹⁶*Then those who feared the LORD spoke with one another; the LORD heeded and heard them, and a book of remembrance was written before him of those who feared the LORD and thought on his name.* ¹⁷*"They shall be mine, says the LORD of hosts, my special possession on the day when I act, and I will spare them as a man spares his son who serves him.* ¹⁸*Then once more you shall distinguish between the righteous and the wicked, between one who serves God and one who does not serve him.*

k *Or devouring locust*

OVERVIEW: Those who refuse to tithe and give back of their material goods will suffer loss in the long run as they have already done spiritually (CAESARIUS). In the Day of the Lord, God will reveal the true works of individuals as if through a fire. The Old Testament promises are based upon temporal rewards and promises. Those who continue to live in this manner will be judged by the Lord, at the last judgment (AUGUSTINE). Widows who remain chaste are praised for this commitment and are held in high esteem by the Lord, to whom they are now wedded (TERTULLIAN).

3:10-12 *Bringing Full Tithes*

SHARE WEALTH WITH ALMS. CAESARIUS OF ARLES: Listen, then, impious one. You know that everything belongs to God; you will not give the Creator of all things something of his own? The Lord God is not in want; he does not demand rec-

ompense but honor. He does not require you to pay back something of yours. He asks the first-fruits and tithes, and do you refuse? Avaricious one, what would you do if he had taken nine-tenths for himself and left you the tithes? Surely this already happened when the meager harvest failed because rain was withdrawn or when hail struck your vintage or frost killed it. Why does this happen, greedy calculator? The nine-tenths were taken from you because you refused to pay tithes. The fact remains, of course, that you did not give, but God exacted it. This is our Lord's exceedingly just practice. If you deny him the tithes, you are brought down to it. As it is written, "Thus speaks the Lord: 'Tithes of your field and the firstfruits of your land are with you. I see you, and you think you are deceiving me. Within, in your treasure and in your house, there will be plunder.'" You will give to a wicked soldier what you are unwilling to give to the priest. "'Be converted even now,' says the Lord almighty, 'that I may open to you the floodgates of heaven and pour out my blessing to you; and the fruits of your land shall not be spoiled, nor shall the vine in your field grow weak, and all nations shall call you blessed.'" God is always ready to do good, but the wickedness of humanity prevents it, because he wishes that everything can be given him from the Lord God but is unwilling to offer anything of what he seems to possess. Now suppose God should say, "Of course you are mine, man, for I made you. Mine is the earth that you cultivate, mine the seeds you sow. The animals that you work are mine; mine are the rain and showers, the blasts of the winds are mine, mine is the heat of the sun. Since all the elements of life are mine, you who only put your hands to them deserve merely tithes." Now, although almighty God kindly feeds us and gives an ample reward to man for his little labor, he claims only tithes for himself and gives the whole to us. SERMON 33.2.[1]

3:13 Harsh Words Against God

SAVED AND DAMNED COMPARED. AUGUSTINE: Those who are spiritually immature put much stock in temporal promises and serve God with an eye to such remunerations. Then, when the people of evil life prosper, they are very much upset. For their enlightenment, Malachi goes on to differentiate the eternal blessedness of the New Testament, which only the good shall win, from the purely earthly good fortune of the old that as often as not comes to the wicked. He says, "'Your words have been insufferable to me,' says the Lord. And you have said, 'What have we spoken against you?' You have said, 'He labors in vain that serves God, and what profit is it that we have kept ordinances and that we have walked sorrowfully before the Lord of hosts?' Therefore now we call the proud people happy, for they that work wickedness are built up, and they have tempted God and prospered. Then they that feared the Lord spoke everyone with his neighbor, and the Lord gave ear and

heard it, and a book of remembrance was written before him for them that fear the Lord and think of his name." The book in question is, of course, again the New Testament. Now let us hear the rest. "'And they shall be my special possession,' says the Lord of hosts, 'in the day that I do judgment; and I will spare the man as a man spares his son who serves him. And you shall return and shall see the difference between the just and the wicked, and between him that serves God and him that serves not. For behold, the day shall come kindled as a furnace, and all the proud and all that do wickedly shall be as stubble, and the day that comes shall set them on fire,' says the Lord of hosts."[2] That day in question is, of course, the day of the last judgment, concerning which I will have a great deal more to say, God willing, when the proper time comes. CITY OF GOD 28.35.[3]

3:14 "It Is Vain to Serve God"

TEMPORAL PROMISES POINT TO ETERNAL ONES. AUGUSTINE: It was, in fact, of their purely material interpretation of the law and of their failure to perceive that its temporal promises were but symbols of eternal rewards that they broke into such rebellious resentfulness as to say, "He labors in vain that serves God, and what profit is it that we have kept his ordinances and that we have walked sorrowfully before the Lord of hosts? Wherefore now we call the proud people happy, for they that work wickedness are built up." It was such complaints as these that compelled the prophet to anticipate, as it were, the last judgment in which the wicked will be so far from even a pretense of happiness that their misery will be apparent to all, whereas the good, untroubled by even transitory sorrow, will enjoy a manifest and unending beatitude. Malachi has already given similar illustration of the kind of murmurings that wearied the Lord: "every one that does evil is good in the sight of the Lord and

---

[1]FC 31:164-65*. [2]Mal 4:1-3. [3]FC 24:141-42.

such please him."[4] The only point I want to make is that such murmurings against God were the result of an unspiritual interpretation of the law. CITY OF GOD 20.28.[5]

3:16 A Book of Remembrance

WIDOWS AS VIRGINS PRAISED. TERTULLIAN: But by us, who are servants of God, who renounce both voluptuousness and ambition, each is to be repudiated. Fleshly concupiscence claims the functions of adult age, craves after beauty's harvest, rejoices in its own shame, pleads the ne-

cessity of a husband to the female sex as a source of authority and comfort or to render it safe from evil rumors. To meet these counsels, do you apply the examples of sisters of ours whose names are with the Lord—who, when their husbands have preceded them [to glory], give to no opportunity of beauty or of age the precedence over holiness. They prefer to be wedded to God. To God their beauty, to God their youth [is dedicated]. To HIS WIFE 1.4.[6]

---

[4]Mal 2:17. [5]FC 24:328. [6]ANF 4:41.

4:1-3 THE RISE OF THE SUN OF RIGHTEOUSNESS

[1]"*For behold, the day comes, burning like an oven, when all the arrogant and all evildoers will be stubble; the day that comes shall burn them up, says the LORD of hosts, so that it will leave them neither root nor branch. [2]But for you who fear my name the sun of righteousness shall rise, with healing in its wings. You shall go forth leaping like calves from the stall. [3]And you shall tread down the wicked, for they will be ashes under the soles of your feet, on the day when I act, says the LORD of hosts.*

I Ch 4.1-6 are Ch 3.19-24 in the Hebrew

OVERVIEW: The return of Christ is imminent; therefore repentance is urgently enjoined. Christ will judge the living and the dead with a purging fire (PSEUDO-CLEMENT OF ROME). Christians sing of the justice of the Lord, knowing that judgment is coming (VALENTINE). The Son made the sun; hence it is fitting to call him the Sun of justice (AMBROSE). Like sailors on a voyage, believers are to be watchful and alert. The ship they sail on is the Scriptures, and the guide is not the stars but the Sun of justice, who steers the ship (CHRYSOSTOM). If the natural sun is so beneficial, how much more beneficial is the Sun of justice, who

fills all things everywhere with his goodness. Jacob foreshadows Christ in many ways. Jacob's thigh foreshadows the cross through which Christ suffered the numbness of sin. Christ is the Sun of justice foretold by Malachi (AMBROSE). John the Baptist called people to repentance, whereas Christ is the one who cleanses from sin. John lit the lamps while Christ is the Sun of justice (EPHREM). Jesus the Sun of justice has ascended to heaven victorious over sin and death. The Lord's day is a celebration of life over death (JEROME). Christians worship facing the east because Christ is the Sun of justice, and Orient is his name (JOHN OF DAMASCUS). The atonement for sin came from the east, from the one whose name is East (ORIGEN). "Sun of righteousness" signifies the two comings of the Lord. Thus in the first coming he enlightened those who were in darkness, while his second coming, like the rise of the sun, will awaken all, the living and the dead (THEODORET).

4:1 The Day Burns Like an Oven

THE DAY OF JUDGMENT. PSEUDO-CLEMENT OF ROME: So, brothers, having received no slight opportunity to repent, let us, when there is yet time, turn to God who called us, while we still have one who awaits us. For if we bid farewell to these pleasures and overcome our soul by refusing to carry out its evil desires, we shall share in the mercy of Jesus. But you know that "the day" of judgment "is now coming, kindled as a furnace," and "the powers of heaven shall dissolve,"[1] and the whole earth shall be as lead melting in the fire, and then shall the secret and public deeds of people be made known. Almsgiving, therefore, is good as penance for sin; fasting is better than prayer, but almsgiving is better than both; and "charity covers a multitude of sins,"[2] but prayer from a good conscience delivers from death. Blessed is everyone who is found full of these things; for almsgiving relieves the burden of sin. 2 CLEMENT 16.[3]

4:2 The Sun of Righteousnesus

JUDGMENT DAY. VALENTINUS: When we begin to sing justice to the Lord,[4] we shall bear away a reward for our work, because the Lord is merciful and just, compassionate and upright.[5] And, . . . as your holiness teaches us, "We must all be manifested before the judgment seat of Christ, that every one of us may receive the proper things of the body, according as he has done, whether it be good or evil,"[6] because the Lord shall come as a burning furnace and shall burn the wicked like stubble.[7] And to those who fear the name of the Lord, the Sun of justice shall rise, when the wicked shall be punished with the judgment of justice. LETTER 216 (VALENTINE TO AUGUSTINE).[8]

JESUS THE RIGHT CREATOR OF THE SUN. AMBROSE: But in case the evidence presented to your eyes may appear to be scanty, cleanse your ears and apply it to the heavenly oracles: "On the word of two or three witnesses every word is confirmed."[9] Hear God speaking: "Let there be lights made in the firmament of heaven to give light upon the earth."[10] Who says this? God says it. And to whom is he speaking, if not to his Son? Therefore God the Father says, "Let the sun be made," and the Son made the sun, for it was fitting that the Sun of justice should make the sun of the world. He therefore brought it light. He illuminated it and granted it the power of light. Therefore the sun was made. For this reason it is also a subject, since it has been said, "You have founded the earth and it continues. By your ordinance the day goes on, for all things serve you."[11] SIX DAYS OF CREATION 4.2.5.[12]

JESUS GUIDES THE SHIP, THE CHURCH. CHRYSOSTOM: A person who has no knowledge of the sea could not sail in full daylight with such confidence and ease as the helmsman sails in the middle of the night, when the sea shows itself in a more formidable mood. Why is this? The helmsman is wide-awake and quite calm as he puts to practice his skill in sailing. He keeps careful watch not only on the pathways of the sea and the courses of the stars but also on the assaults of the winds. The helmsman's wisdom and knowledge are great. So it is that many a time when the blast of a more violent gale has struck his ship and is about to swamp it, he has the wisdom to make many a quick change in the angle of his sails. He runs before the wind and puts an end to all danger from the gale. By pitting his skill against the

---

[1]Is 34:4. [2]1 Pet 4:8; Prov 10:12. [3]FC 1:75-76*. [4]Ps 100:4. [5]Ps 111:4. [6]2 Cor 5:10. [7]Is 40:10. [8]FC 32:71. [9]Mt 18:16. [10]Gen 1:14. [11]Ps 119:90-91. [12]FC 42:129.

violence of the winds' blasts, he snatches his vessel from the storm. Those sailors voyage over waters we can see and hear and feel. Although they are searching for this world's goods, they continuously keep their minds watchful and alert. All the more must we keep ourselves prepared in the same way they do. Surely the careless person faces a greater danger, while the sober one is more secure. This ship of ours is not constructed of timbers but is joined fast together with the divine Scriptures. The stars in the sky do not guide us on our way, but the Sun of justice steers our ship on its course. As we sit at the tiller, we are not waiting for the blasts of wind. We are waiting for the gentle breath of the Spirit. AGAINST THE ANOMOEANS, HOMILY 7.5-6.[13]

CHRIST IS THE SUN OF JUSTICE. AMBROSE: Do not, therefore, without due consideration put your trust in the sun. It is true that it is the eye of the world, the joy of the day, the beauty of the heavens, the charm of nature and the most conspicuous creation. When you behold it, reflect on its author. When you admire it, give praise to its creator. If the sun as consort of and participant in nature is so pleasing, how much goodness is there to be found in that Sun of justice? If the sun is so swift that in its rapid course by day and night it is able to traverse all things, how great is he who is always and everywhere and fills all things with his majesty![14] If that which is bidden to come forth is deemed worthy of our admiration of whom we read, "Who commands the sun and it rises not!"[15] If the sun which the succession of the seasons advances or recedes is mighty, how mighty must he be also who "when he emptied himself"[16] that we might be able to see him, who "was the true light that enlightens every man who comes into this world!"[17] SIX DAYS OF CREATION 4.1.2.[18]

JACOB FORESHADOWS THE SUN OF JUSTICE. AMBROSE: Because Jacob's faith and devotion were unconquerable, the Lord revealed his hidden mysteries to him by touching the side of his thigh.[19] For it was by descent from him that the Lord Jesus was born to a virgin, and Jesus would be neither unlike nor unequal to God. The numbness in the side of Jacob's thigh foreshadowed the cross of Christ, who would bring salvation to all by spreading forgiveness of sins throughout the whole world and would give resurrection to the departed by the numbness and torpidity of his own body. On this account the sun rose on holy Jacob,[20] for the saving cross of the Lord shone brightly on his lineage, and at the same time the Sun of justice recognizes God, because he is himself the everlasting light. But Jacob limped because of his thigh.[21] "On account of this the children of Israel do not eat the sinew even to the present day."[22] Would that they had eaten it and believed! But because they were not about to do the will of God, therefore they did not eat. There are those too who take the passage in the following sense that Jacob limped from one thigh. Two people flowed from his lineage, and there was then being revealed the numbness which one of them would presently exhibit toward the grace of faith. And so it is the people itself that limped by reason of the numbness of its unbelief. JACOB AND THE HAPPY LIFE 7.30-31.[23]

ELIZABETH AND MARY COMPARED. EPHREM THE SYRIAN: The elderly Elizabeth gave birth to the last of the prophets, and Mary, a young girl, to the Lord of the angels. The daughter of Aaron gave birth to "the voice in the desert"[24] and the daughter of King David to the Word of the heavenly king. The wife of the priest gave birth to "the angel of his face"[25] but the daughter of David to the strong God of the earth. The barren one gave birth to him who remits sins, but the Virgin gave birth to him who takes them away.[26] Elizabeth gave birth to him who reconciled people through repentance, but Mary gave birth to him who purified the lands of unclean-

---

[13]FC 72:186. [14]Ps 72:17-19. [15]Job 9:7. [16]Phil 2:7. [17]Jn 1:9. [18]FC 42:127. [19]Gen 32:25. [20]Gen 32:31. [21]Gen 32:31. [22]Gen 32:32. [23]FC 65:164*. [24]Is 40:3; Mt 3:3. [25]Is 63:9. [26]Jn 1:29.

ness. The elder one lit a lamp in the house of Jacob, his father, for his [lamp] itself was John,[27] while the younger one [lit] "the Sun of justice"[28] for all the nations. The angel announced to Zechariah, so that the slain one would proclaim the crucified one and that the hated one [would proclaim] the envied one. He who was to baptize with water [would proclaim] him who would baptize "with fire and with the Holy Spirit,"[29] and the light which was not obscure [would proclaim] "the Sun of justice." [The one] filled with the Spirit [would proclaim] concerning him who gives the Spirit. The priest calling with the trumpet [would proclaim] concerning the one who is to come at the [sound of] the trumpet at the end. The voice [would proclaim] concerning the Word, and the one who saw the dove [would proclaim] concerning him upon whom the dove rested, like the lightning before the thunder. Commentary on Tatian's Diatessaron.[30]

The Lord's Day Is the Day of the Sun of Justice.

Jerome: "This is the day the Lord has made; let us be glad and rejoice in it."[31] The Lord has made all days, of course, but other days may belong as well to the Jews, and heretics too; they may even belong to the heathens. The Lord's day, however, the day of the resurrection, the day of Christians, is our day. It is called the Lord's day because on this day the Lord ascended to the Father as victor. But when the heathen call it the day of the sun, we are most happy to acknowledge their title, for today has risen "the Sun of justice with its healing wings." Does the sun really have wings? Let the Jews answer, and those who, like them, accept only a literal interpretation of holy Writ. We say, whoever has been under the wings of this sun who has said in the Gospel, "How often would I have gathered the children together, as a hen gathers her young under her wings, but thou would not,"[32] shall be safe from the devil hawk, safe under the great wings of that mighty eagle in Ezekiel,[33] and all the wounds of his sins shall be healed. Homily 94.[34]

Worship to the East Explained.

John of Damascus: It is not without any reason or by any chance that we worship toward the east. On the contrary, since we are composed of a visible and an invisible nature, of an intellectual nature and a sensitive one, that is, we also offer a twofold worship to the Creator. It is just as we also sing both with our mind and our bodily lips, and as we are baptized both in water and in the spirit, and as we are united to the Lord in two ways when we receive the sacrament and the grace of the spirit. And so, since God is spiritual light and Christ in sacred Scripture is called "Sun of justice" and "Orient," the east should be dedicated to his worship. For everything beautiful should be dedicated to God, from whom everything that is good receives its goodness. Also, the divine David says, "Sing to God, you kingdoms of the earth; sing you to the Lord, who mounts above the heaven of heavens, to the east."[35] And still again, Scripture says, "And the Lord had planted a paradise in Eden to the east; wherein he placed man whom he had formed," and whom he cast out, when he had transgressed, "and made him to live over against the paradise of pleasure,"[36] or in the west. Thus when we worship God, we long for our ancient homeland and gaze toward it. The tabernacle of Moses had the veil and the propitiatory altar to the east; and the tribe of Judah, as being the more honorable, pitched their tents on the east; and in the celebrated temple of Solomon the gate of the Lord was set to the east.[37] As a matter of fact, when the Lord was crucified, he looked toward the west, and so we worship gazing toward him. And when he was taken up, he ascended to the east, and thus the apostles worshiped him. And thus he shall come in the same way as they had seen him going into heaven,[38] as the Lord himself said: "As lightning comes out of the east and appears even into the west, so shall also the coming of the Son of man be."[39] And so, while

---

[27]Jn 5:35. [28]Cf. Lk 11:51. [29]Mt 3:11. [30]ECTD 58-59. [31]Ps 118:24. [32]Mt 23:37. [33]Ezek 17:3, 7. [34]FC 57:253. [35]Ps 68:32. [36]Gen 2:8; 3:24 LXX. [37]Num 2:3; Ezek 44:1-2. [38]Acts 1:11. [39]Mt 24:27.

we are awaiting him, we worship toward the east. ORTHODOX FAITH 4.12.[40]

CHRIST THE SUN FROM THE EAST AROSE.
ORIGEN: But do not take the statement that "he sprinkles to the east" as superfluous. From the east came atonement for you; for from there is the man whose name is "East,"[41] who became "a mediator between God and humanity." Therefore you are invited by this to always look "to the east" where "the Sun of Righteousness" arises for you, where a light is born for you; that you may never "walk in darkness" and that that last day does not seize you in darkness. [Therefore may] the night and fog of ignorance not come upon you unawares, but [may] you always be found in the light of knowledge, always have the day of faith and always preserve the light of love and peace. HOMILIES ON LEVITICUS 9.10.2.[42]

A SIGN OF CHRIST'S TWO COMINGS. THEODORET OF CYR: This applies both to the first coming of our Savior and the second: in the first he rose like a kind of sun for us who were seated in darkness and shadow, freed us from sin, gave us a share in righteousness, covered us with spiritual gifts like wings, and provided healing for our souls. In the second coming for those worn out in the present life he will appear either in accord with their will or against it, and as a just judge he will judge justly and provide the promised good things. Just as the material sun in its rising awakens to work those in the grip of sleep, so in his coming he raises up those in the grip of the long sleep of death. COMMENTARY ON MALACHI 4.2.[43]

---

[40]FC 37:352-53. [41]Zech 6:12 LXX. [42]FC 83:199*. [43]PG 81:1984.

4:4-6 ELIJAH'S COMING BEFORE THE DAY OF THE LORD

[4]"*Remember the law of my servant Moses, the statutes and ordinances that I commanded him at Horeb for all Israel.*

[5]"*Behold, I will send you Elijah the prophet* before the great and terrible day of the LORD comes.* [6]*And he will turn the hearts of fathers to their children and the hearts of children to their fathers, lest I come and smite the land with a curse.*"[m]

m Or ban of utter destruction   * LXX adds *the Tishbite*

OVERVIEW: When God warned the Jews about observing the law of Moses, it was a veiled reference to Christ the judge, who alone can judge the good and the evil (AUGUSTINE). Christ's coming fulfills the law of Moses; therefore belief in Christ fulfills the law and obedience to God (THEODORE). Christ, who is the resurrection and the life, has forerunners in the Old Testament: in

particular Elijah, who would proclaim the Messiah, a role fulfilled by John the Baptist (HIPPOLYTUS). When Malachi spoke of Elijah as being the forerunner of the Messiah, he was speaking of John the Baptist. The image of Elijah baptizing refers to John the Baptist, but only Christ baptizes in the Holy Spirit and fire (ORIGEN). The doctrine of reincarnation is refuted. The reference to Elijah being John the Baptist was a spiritual one, not a statement supporting reincarnation (TERTULLIAN). Elijah was the precursor to call people to repentance before the advent of the antichrist (VICTORINUS).

4:4 Remember Moses' Law

THE LAW REVEALS CHRIST. AUGUSTINE: After the prophecy, Malachi says, "Remember the law of Moses my servant, which I commanded him in Horeb for all Israel," and he makes a passing reference to "precepts and judgments." This emphasizes the declaration he had just made about the immense difference there is to be between the observers and the breakers of the law. The prophet's further purpose was that his readers might learn to give a spiritual interpretation to the law, finding in it Christ the judge who is to make the distinction between the good and the wicked. For it was not without reason that Christ said to the Jews, "If you believed Moses, you would believe me also, for he wrote of me."[1] It was, in fact, of their purely material interpretation of the law and of their failure to perceive that its temporal promises were but symbols of eternal rewards that they broke into such rebellious resentfulness as to say, "He labors in vain that serves God, and what profit is it that we have kept his ordinances and that we have walked sorrowful before the Lord of hosts? Wherefore now we call the proud people happy, for they that work wickedness are built up."[2] It was such complaints as these that compelled the prophet to anticipate, as it were, the last judgment in which the wicked will be so far from even a pretense of happiness that their misery will be apparent to all, whereas the good, untroubled by even transitory sorrow, will enjoy a manifest and unending beatitude. Malachi had already given a similar illustration of the kind of murmurings that wearied the Lord: "Every one that does evil is good in the sight of the Lord and such please him."[3] The only point I want to make is that such murmurings against God were the result of an unspiritual interpretation of the law. CITY OF GOD 20.28.[4]

BELIEF IN CHRIST FULFILLS OBEDIENCE TO GOD. THEODORE OF MOPSUESTIA: In addition to all that has been said I transmit this final command to you so that you may keep in mind my law that I gave to the whole of Israel through Moses, having clearly stated that they must observe it in detail. The first token of obedience you will provide, then, will be acceptance of the coming of Christ the Lord, who comes for the salvation of all people. He will bring the law to an end and make clear his own way of perfection. It would therefore be good for you immediately and at the outset to believe in him at his appearance and acknowledge him to be the one that Moses and all the prophets predicted as bringing an end to the law and revealing the salvation of all in common. COMMENTARY ON MALACHI 4.1-2.[5]

4:5 Elijah the Prophet

ELIJAH THE FORERUNNER OF CHRIST. HIPPOLYTUS: But since the Savior was the beginning of the resurrection of all people, it was fitting that the Lord alone should rise from the dead, by whom too the judgment is to enter the whole world, that they who have wrestled worthily may be also crowned worthily by him, by the illustrious Arbiter. [That is, he] himself first accomplished the course, and was received into the heavens, and was set down on the right hand of God the Father, and is to be manifested again at the end of the world as judge. It is a matter of course that his forerunners must appear first, as he says by Malachi and the angel, "I will send to you Elijah the Tishbite before the Day of the Lord, the great and notable day, comes; and he shall turn the hearts of the fathers to the children, and the disobedient to the wisdom of the just, lest I come and smite the earth utterly." These, then, shall come and proclaim the mani-

---

[1]Jn 5:46. [2]Mal 3:14-15. [3]Mal 2:17. [4]FC 24:327-28. [5]PG 66:632.

festation of Christ that is to be from heaven; and they shall also perform signs and wonders; in order that people may be put to shame and turned to repentance for their surpassing wickedness and impiety. On the Antichrist 46.[6]

JOHN AND ELIJAH. ORIGEN: Who of those who hear Jesus say of John, "If you wish to receive it, he is Elijah who is to come,"[7] would not inquire how John says to those who ask, "Are you Elijah?" "I am not"?[8] Will he not also inquire how one ought to consider John himself to be Elijah who is to come, according to Malachi's statement: . . . "And behold, I am sending you Elijah the Tishbite before the great and renewed Day of the Lord comes, who will restore the heart of the father to his son and the heart of a man to his neighbor, lest I come and smite the earth utterly"? COMMENTARY ON THE GOSPEL OF JOHN 6.62.[9]

THE DIFFERENCE BETWEEN JOHN AND JESUS. ORIGEN: And what is the source of your belief that Elijah who is to come will baptize? He did not even baptize the wood on the altar in the times of Ahab, when it needed a bath that it might be burned up when the Lord appeared in the fire.[10] He commanded the priests to do this, and not only once, for he says, "Do it a second time, when also they did it for a second time." And "Do it a third time, when also they did it a third time."[11] How, then, will he who did not baptize at that time but gave the task to others, baptize when he has come in fulfillment of things said by Malachi? Christ therefore does not baptize in water but his disciples.[12] He reserves for himself the act of baptizing with the Holy Spirit and fire.[13] COMMENTARY ON THE GOSPEL OF JOHN 6.125.[14]

REINCARNATION REJECTED. TERTULLIAN: I fully expect these heretics to seize upon the example of Elijah as reincarnated in John the Baptist, and thus they would have become our Lord espousing the doctrine of reincarnation. "Elijah indeed has come, and they knew him not."[15] And again, "And

if you are willing to receive it, here is Elijah who was to come."[16] Was the question of the Jews to John, "Are you Elijah?"[17] to be understood in a Pythagorean sense and not in reference to the divine pronouncement: "Behold, I send you Elijah, the Tishbite"? But their theory of transmigration refers to the recall of a soul that had died long before and to its insertion in some other body. Elijah, however, is to return not after leaving this life by death, not to be returned to his body, since he never left it, but he will come back to the world from which he has been removed. He will return not to take up a life he had left off but for the fulfillment of a prophecy. He will come back as Elijah, with the same name. How, then, could John be Elijah? The voice of the angel tells us: "And he shall go before the people in the spirit and power of Elijah,"[18] not in the soul or body of Elijah. These substances are the specific property of each man, while "spirit and power" are extrinsic gifts conferred by the grace of God, and so they may be transferred to another according to the will of God as happened long ago with respect to the spirit of Moses. On the Soul 36.6.[19]

ELIJAH WILL CALL JEWS TO REPENTANCE IN THE END TIMES. VICTORINUS OF PETOVIUM: "And I saw another angel ascending from the east, having the seal of the living God." He speaks of Elijah the prophet, who is the precursor of the times of the antichrist, for the restoration and establishment of the churches from the great and intolerable persecution. We read that these things are predicted in the opening of the Old Testament and the New Testament, for he says by Malachi, "Lo, I will send to you Elijah the Tishbite, to turn the hearts of the fathers to the children, according to the time of calling, to recall the Jews to the faith of the people that succeed them." COMMENTARY OF THE APOCALYPSE 11.[20]

---

[6]ANF 5:213. [7]Mt 11:14. [8]Jn 1:21. [9]FC 80:185. [10]1 Kings 18:21-38. [11]1 Kings 18:34. [12]Jn 4:2. [13]Mt 3:11; Lk 3:16. [14]FC 80:204. [15]Mt 17:12. [16]Mt 11:14. [17]Jn 1:21. [18]Lk 1:17. [19]FC 10:264-65*. [20]ANF 7:351-52.

Early Christian Writers and the Documents Cited

The following table lists all the early Christian documents cited in this volume by author, if known, or by the title of the work. The English title used in this commentary is followed in parentheses with the Latin designation and, where available, the Thesaurus Linguae Graecae (=TLG) digital reference or Cetedoc Clavis numbers. Printed sources of original language versions may be found in the bibliography of works in original languages.

Ambrose

Concerning Repentance (*De paenitentia*)	Cetedoc 0156
Exposition on the Psalms (*Explanatio psalmorum xii*)	Cetedoc 0140
Flight from the World (*De fuga saeculi*)	Cetedoc 0133
Isaac, or the Soul (*De Isaac vel anima*)	Cetedoc 0128
Jacob and the Happy Life (*De Jacob et vita beata*)	Cetedoc 0130
Joseph (*De Joseph*)	Cetedoc 0131
On Paradise (*De paradiso*)	Cetedoc 0124
On the Christian Faith (*De fide*)	Cetedoc 0150
On the Death of Theodosius (*De obitu Theodosii*)	Cetedoc 0159
On the Holy Spirit (*De Spiritu Sancto*)	Cetedoc 0151
The Prayer of Job and David (*De interpellatione Job et David*)	Cetedoc 0134
Six Days of Creation (*Exameron*)	Cetedoc 0123

Aphrahat

Demonstrations (*Demonstrationes*)	

Athanasius

Festal Letters (*Epistulae festales*)	TLG 2035.014
Four Discourses Against the Arians (spurious) (*Oratio quarta contra Arianos*)	TLG 2035.117
Life of St. Anthony (*Vita sancti Antonii*)	TLG 2035.047

Augustine

Against Julian (*Contra Julianum*)	Cetedoc 0351
Christian Instruction (*De doctrina christiana*)	Cetedoc 0263
City of God (*De civitate Dei*)	Cetedoc 0313
Confessions (*Confessionum libri tredecim*)	Cetedoc 0251
Enchiridion (*Enchiridion de fide, spe et caritate*)	Cetedoc 0295
Explanation of the Psalms (*Enarrationes in Psalmos*)	Cetedoc 0283
In Answer to the Jews (*Adversus Judaeos*)	Cetedoc 0315
Letters (*Epistulae*)	Cetedoc 0262
On Baptism (*De baptismo contra Donatistas*)	Cetedoc 0332

On Faith in Things Unseen (*De fide rerum invisibilium*)	Cetedoc 0292
On Grace and Free Will (*De gratia et libero arbitrio*)	Cetedoc 0352
On Marriage and Concupiscence (*De nuptiis et concupiscentia*)	Cetedoc 0350
On the Divination of Demons (*De divinatione daemonum*)	Cetedoc 0306
Sermon on the Mount (*De sermone domini in monte*)	Cetedoc 0274
Sermons (*Sermones*)	Cetedoc 0284
Tractates on the Gospel of John (*In Johannis evangelium tractatus*)	Cetedoc 0278

Basil the Great

Concerning Baptism (*De baptismo libri duo*)	TLG 2040.052
Homilies on the Hexaemeron (*Homiliae in hexaemeron*)	TLG 2040.001
Homilies on the Psalms (*Homiliae super Psalmos*)	TLG 2040.018
Homily on Mercy and Justice (*Homilia de misericordia et judicio*)	TLG 2040.069
Letters (*Epistulae*)	TLG 2040.004
The Long Rules (*Asceticon magnum sive quaestiones* [*regulae brevius tractatae*])	TLG 2040.050

Bede

Commentary on 1 Peter (*In epistulam septem catholicas*)	Cetedoc 1362
Commentary on the Acts of the Apostles (*Expositio actuum apostolorum*)	Cetedoc 1357
Homilies on the Gospels (*Homiliarum evangelii libri ii*)	Cetedoc 1367
On the Tabernacle (*De tabernaculo et vasis eius ac vestibus sacerdotum libri iii*)	Cetedoc 1345

Braulio of Saragossa

Letters
Life of St. Emilian (*Vita sancti Aemiliani*)

Caesarius of Arles

Sermon (*Sermones*)	Cetedoc 1008

Cassian, John

Conferences (*Collationes*)	Cetedoc 0512

Cassiodorus

Exposition of the Psalms (*Expositio psalmorum*)	Cetedoc 0900

Clement of Alexandria

Christ the Educator (*Paedagogus*)	TLG 0555.002
Exhortation to the Greeks (*Protrepticus*)	TLG 0555.001
Stromateis (*Stromata*)	TLG 0555.004
Who Is the Rich Man That Shall be Saved? (*Quis dives salvetur?*)	TLG 0555.006

Clement of Rome

1 Clement (*Epistula i ad Corinthios*)	TLG 1271.001

Constitutions of the Holy Apostles (*Constitutiones apostolorum*)   TLG 2894.001

Cyprian
The Advantage of Patience (*De bono patientiae*)   Cetedoc 0048
The Lapsed (*De lapsis*)   Cetedoc 0042
Letters (*Epistulae*)   Cetedoc 0050
The Lord's Prayer (*De dominica oratione*)   Cetedoc 0043
To Demetrian (*Ad Demetrianum*)   Cetedoc 0046
To Quirinus: Testimonies Against the Jews (*Ad Quirinum*) Cetedoc 0039

Cyril of Alexandria
Commentary on the Minor Prophets (*Commentarius in xii prophetas minores*)   TLG 4090.001
Letters (see *Concilia oecumenica*)   TLG 5000.001
On the Unity of Christ (*Quod unus sit Christus*)   TLG 4090.027

Cyril of Jeruslaem
Catechetical Lectures (*Catecheses ad illuminandos 1-18*)   TLG 2110.003

Didache (*Didache xii apostolorum*)   TLG 1311.001

Ephrem the Syrian
Commentary on Tatian's Diatessaron (*In Tatiani Diatessaron*)
Commentary on the Minor Prophets

Eugippus
The Life of Saint Severin (*Vita sancti Severini*)

Eusebius of Caesarea
Ecclesiastical History (*Historia ecclesiastica*)   TLG 2018.002
Proof of the Gospel (*Demonstratio evangelica*)   TLG 2018.005

Eznik of Kolb
On God (*De Deo*)

Fulgentius of Ruspe
Letters (*Epistulae*)   Cetedoc 0817
To Euthymius: On the Forgiveness of Sins (*Ad Euthymium de remissione peccatorum libri II*)   Cetedoc 0821
To Monimus (*Ad Monimum libri III*)   Cetedoc 0814

Gregory of Nazianzus
Against the Arians and on Himself, Oration 33 (*Contra Arianos et de seipso*)   TLG 2022.041
In Defense of His Flight to Pontus, Oration 2 (*Apologetica*)   TLG 2022.016
On Basil the Great, Oration 43 (*Funebris oratio in
    laudem Basilii Magni Caesareae in Cappadocia episcopi*)   TLG 2022.006
On His Brother St. Caesarius, Oration 7 (*Funebris in laudem Caesarii fratris oratio*)   TLG 2022.005

On His Father's Silence, Oration 16 (*In patrem tacentem*)	TLG 2022.029
On Holy Baptism, Oration 40 (*In sanctum baptisma*)	TLG 2022.048
On Holy Easter, Oration 45 (*In sanctum pascha*)	TLG 2022.052
On the Arrival of the Egyptians, Oration 34 (*In Aegyptiorum adventum*)	TLG 2022.042
On the Holy Lights, Oration 39 (*In sancta lumina*)	TLG 2022.047
On the Holy Spirit, Theological Oration 5 (31) (*De Spiritu Sancto*)	TLG 2022.011
On the Son, Theological Oration 4 (30) (*De Filio*)	TLG 2022.010

Gregory of Nyssa

Address on Religious Instruction (*Oratio catechetica magna*)	TLG 2017.046
Against Eunomius (*Contra Eunomium*)	TLG 2017.030
On the Baptism of Christ (*In diem luminum* [vulgo *In baptismum Christi oratio*])	TLG 2017.014
On the Inscriptions of the Psalms (*In inscriptiones Psalmorum*)	TLG 2017.027
On Virginity (*De virginitate*)	TLG 2017.043

Gregory Thaumaturgus

On the Annunciation to the Holy Virgin Mary (*In annuntiationem sanctae virginis Mariae*)	TLG 2063.009

Gregory the Great

Forty Gospel Homilies (*Homiliarum xl in evangelia libri duo*)	Cetedoc 1711
Morals on the Book of Job (*Moralia in Job*)	Cetedoc 1708
Pastoral Care (*Regula pastoralis*)	Cetedoc 1712

Hilary of Poitiers

On the Trinity (*De Trinitate*)	Cetedoc 0433

Hippolytus

Against Noetus (*Contra haeresin Noeti*)	TLG 2115.002
On the Antichrist (*De antichristo*)	TLG 2115.003
On the End of the World (spurious) (*De consummatione mundi*)	TLG 2115.029
On the Theophany (dubious) (*De theophania*)	TLG 2115.026

Horsiesi

Instructions

Irenaeus

Against Heresies (*Adversus haereses*)	TLG 1447.002

Isaac of Nineveh

Ascetical Homilies

Isho'dad of Merv

Commentary on the Minor Prophets

Jerome

Against Jovinianus (*Adversus Jovinianum*)	Cetedoc 0610
Against the Pelagians (*Dialogi contra Pelagianos libri iii*)	Cetedoc 0615
Apology Against the Books of Rufinus (*Apologia adversus libros Rufini*)	Cetedoc 0613
Commentary on Ezekiel (*Commentarii in Ezechielem*)	Cetedoc 0587
Commentary on the Minor Prophets (*Commentarii in prophetas minores*)	Cetedoc 0589
Homilies on Mark (*Tractatus in Marci evangelium*)	Cetedoc 0594
Homilies on the Psalms (*Tractatus lix in psalmos*)	Cetedoc 0592
Homilies on the Psalms, Alternate Series (*Tractatuum in psalmos series altera*)	Cetedoc 0593
Homily on the Epiphany and Psalm 28 (*Sermo de die epiphaniorum et de psalmo xxviii*)	Cetedoc 0599
Letters (*Epistulae*)	Cetedoc 0620

John Chrysostom

Against the Anomoeans (*Contra Anomoeos*)	
Homily 4, On the Incomprehensible Nature of God (*De incomprehensibili dei natura*)	TLG 2062.012
Homily 7, On the Consubstantiation (*De consubstantiali*)	TLG 2062.015
Homily 12, On the Divinity of Christ (*De Christi divinitate*)	TLG 2062.020
Commentary on Galatians (*In epistulam ad Galatas commentarius*)	TLG 2062.158
Commentary on Job (*Commentarius in Job*)	TLG 2062.183
Demonstration Against the Pagans (*Contra Judaeos et gentiles quod Christus sit deus*)	TLG 2062.372
Discourses Against Judaizing Christians (*Adversus Judaeos [orationes 1-8]*)	TLG 2062.021
Homilies Concerning the Statues (*Ad populum Antiochenum homiliae [de statuis]*)	TLG 2062.024
Homilies on 2 Corinthians (*In epistulam ii ad Corinthios [homiliae 1-30]*)	TLG 2062.157
Homilies on Genesis (*In Genesim [homiliae 1-67]*)	TLG 2062.112
Homilies on John (*In Joannem [homiliae 1-88]*)	TLG 2062.153
Homilies on Lazarus and the Rich Man (*De Lazaro et divite*)	TLG 2062.244
Homilies on Repentance and Almsgiving	
(*De eleemosyna*)	TLG 2062.075
(*De paenitentia [homiliae 1-9]*)	TLG 2062.027
Homilies on Romans (*In epistulam ad Romanos*)	TLG 2062.155
Homilies on the Acts of the Apostles (*Homiliae in Acta apostolorum [homiliae 1-55]*)	TLG 2062.154
Homilies on the Gospel of Matthew (*In Matthaeum [homiliae 1-90]*)	TLG 2062.152
Homilies on 1 Timothy (*In epistulam I ad Timotheum*)	TLG 2062.164
Homily Against Those Who Say That Demons Govern	
Human Affairs (*Daemones non gubernare mundum*)	TLG 2062.x15
Homily on the Paralytic Let Down Through the Roof (*In paralyticum*	
demissum per tectum)	TLG 2062.063
On the Priesthood (*De sacerdotio*)	TLG 2062.085

John of Antioch

Letter to Cyril of Alexandria (*Concilia Oecumenica*)	TLG 5000.001

John of Damascus

Orthodox Faith (*Expositio fidei*)	TLG 2934.004

Julian of Eclanum
Commentary on Hosea *(Tractatus prophetarum Osee, Johel et Amos)*   Cetedoc 0776

Justin Martyr
Dialogue with Trypho *(Dialogus cum Tryphone)*   TLG 0645.003
First Apology *(Apologia)*   TLG 0645.001

Lactantius
Epitome of the Divine Institutes *(Epitome divinarum institutionum)*   Cetedoc 0086

Leo the Great
Sermons *(Tractatus septem et nonaginta)*   Cetedoc 1657

Martin of Braga
On Pride *(De superbia)*

Martyrius (Sahdona)
Book of Perfection

Maximus of Turin
Commentary on Jonah
Sermons *(Collectio sermonum antiqua)*   Cetedoc 0219a

Methodius
Banquet of the Ten Virgins *(Convivium decem virginum)*
Oration Concerning Simeon and Anna *(De Symeone et Anna)*

Novatian
On Jewish Foods *(De cibis judaicis)*   Cetedoc 0068
On the Trinity *(De Trinitate)*   Cetedoc 0071

Origen
Against Celsus *(Contra Celsum)*   TLG 2042.001
Commentary on the Gospel of John
   (Commentarii in evangelium Joannis [lib. 1, 2, 4, 5, 6, 10, 13])   TLG 2042.005
   (Commentarii in evangelium Joannis [lib. 19, 20, 28, 32])   TLG 2042.079
Commentary on the Gospel of Matthew
   (Commentarium in evangelium Matthaei [lib. 10-11])   TLG 2042.029
   (Commentarium in evangelium Matthaei [lib. 12-17])   TLG 2042.030
Exhortation to Martyrdom *(Exhortatio ad martyrium)*   TLG 2042.007
Fragments on Jeremiah *(Fragmenta in Jeremiam [e Philocalia])*   TLG 2042.084
Fragments on Jeremiah *(Fragmenta in Jeremiam [in catenis])*   TLG 2042.010
Homilies on Exodus *(Homiliae in Exodum)*   TLG 2042.023
Homilies on Genesis *(Homiliae in Genesim)*   TLG 2042.022
Homilies on Jeremiah *(In Jeremiam [homiliae 1-11])*   TLG 2042.009

(*In Jeremiam [homiliae 12-20]*) TLG 2042.021
Homilies on Leviticus (*Homiliae in Leviticum*) TLG 2042.024
Homilies on the Gospel of Luke (*Homiliae in Lucam*) TLG 2042.016
On First Principles (*De principiis*) TLG 2042.002

Pachomius
Instructions (*Catecheses*)
Life of Pachomius (*Vita Pachomii*)

Pacian of Barcelona
On Penitents (*De paenitentibus*)

Paulinus of Nola
Poems (*Carmina*) Cetedoc 0203

Paulus Orosius
Defense Against the Pelagians (*Liber apologeticus contra Pelagianos*) Cetedoc 0572

Peter Chrysologus
Sermons (*Collectio sermonum a Felice episcopo parata*
   sermonibus extravagantibus adjectis) Cetedoc 0227+

Pseudo-Barnabas
Epistle of Barnabas (*Barnabae epistula*) TLG 1216.001

Pseudo-Clement of Rome
2 Clement (*Epistula ii ad Cornithios*) TLG 1271.002

Pseudo-Dionysius
Celestial Hierarchy (*De caelestine hierarchia*) TLG 2798.001

Rufinus
Commentary on the Apostles' Creed

Salvian the Presbyter
Letters
The Governance of God (*De gubernatione Dei*) Cetedoc 0485

Shepherd of Hermas (*Pastor*) TLG 1419.001

Symeon the New Theologian
The Practical and Theological Chapters (*Capita practica et theologica*)

Tertullian
Against Marcion (*Adversus Marcionem*) Cetedoc 0014

An Answer to the Jews *(Adversus Judaeos)* Cetedoc 0033
On Flight in Time of Persecution *(De fuga in perscutione)* Cetedoc 0025
On Idolatry *(De idololatria)* Cetedoc 0023
On Penitence *(De paenitentia)* Cetedoc 0010
On Purity *(De pudicitia)* Cetedoc 0030
On the Resurrection of the Flesh *(De resurrectione mortuorum)* Cetedoc 0019
On the Soul *(De anima)* Cetedoc 0017
To His Wife *(Ad uxorem)* Cetedoc 0012

Theodore of Mopsuestia
Commentary on the Minor Prophets

Theodoret of Cyr
Commentary on the Minor Prophets
Ecclesiastical History *(Historia ecclesiastica)* TLG 4089.003
On Divine Providence *(De providentia orationes decem)* TLG 4089.032

Theodotus the Valentinian
Excerpts of Theodotus (see *Eclogae propheticae*) TLG 0555.005

Theophilus
Letters *(Epistula ad Hieronymum [exc. epist. Augustini] et*
 scripta variorum auctorum) Cetedoc 0620

Theophylact
Commentary on Hosea

Valentinus
Letter to Augustine *(Epistulae ad Augustinum Hipponensem et alios)* Cetedoc 0262°

Victorinus of Petovium
Commentary of the Apocalypse *(Commentarius in apocalypsin)*
On the Creation of the World *(De fabrica mundi)*

BIOGRAPHICAL SKETCHES &
SHORT DESCRIPTIONS
OF SELECT ANONYMOUS WORKS

This listing is cumulative, including all the authors and works cited in this series to date.

Acacius of Caesarea (d. c. 365). Pro-Arian bishop of Caesarea in Palestine, disciple and biographer of Eusebius of Caesarea, the historian. He was a man of great learning and authored a treatise on Ecclesiastes.

Alexander of Alexandria (fl. 312-328). Bishop of Alexandria and predecessor of Athanasius, on whom he exerted considerable theological influence during the rise of Arianism. Alexander excommunicated Arius, whom he had appointed to the parish of Baucalis, in 319. His teaching regarding the eternal generation and divine substantial union of the Son with the Father was eventually confirmed at the Council of Nicaea (325).

Ambrose of Milan (c. 333-397; fl. 374-397). Bishop of Milan and teacher of Augustine who defended the divinity of the Holy Spirit and the perpetual virginity of Mary.

Ambrosiaster (fl. c. 366-384). Name given by Erasmus to the author of a work once thought to have been composed by Ambrose.

Ammonius (c. fifth century). An Aristotelian commentator and teacher in Alexandria, where he was born and of whose school he became head. Also an exegete of Plato, he enjoyed fame among his contemporaries and successors, although modern critics accuse him of pedantry and banality.

Amphilochius of Iconium (b. c. 340-345, d.c. 398-404). An orator at Constantinople before becoming bishop of Iconium in 373. He was a cousin of Gregory of Nazianzus and active in debates against the Macedonians and Messalians.

Andreas (c. seventh century). Monk who collected commentary from earlier writers to form a catena on various biblical books.

Antony (or Anthony) the Great (c. 251-c. 356). An anchorite of the Egyptian desert and founder of Egyptian monasticism. Athanasius regarded him as the ideal of monastic life, and he has become a model for Christian hagiography.

Aphrahat (c. 270-350 fl. 337-345). "The Persian Sage" and first major Syriac writer whose work survives. He is also known by his Greek name Aphraates.

Apollinaris of Laodicea (310-c. 392). Bishop of Laodicea who was attacked by Gregory of Nazianzus, Gregory of Nyssa and Theodore for denying that Christ had a human mind.

Apostolic Constitutions (c. 381-394). Also known as *Constitutions of the Holy Apostles* and thought to be redacted by Julian of Neapolis. The work is divided into eight books, and is primarily a collection of and expansion on previous works such as the *Didache* (c. 140) and the *Apostolic Traditions*.

Book 8 ends with eighty-five canons from various sources and is elsewhere known as the *Apostolic Canons*.

Arius (fl. c. 320). Heretic condemned at the Council of Nicaea (325) for refusing to accept that the Son was not a creature but was God by nature like the Father.

Athanasius of Alexandria (c. 295-373; fl. 325-373). Bishop of Alexandria from 328, though often in exile. He wrote his classic polemics against the Arians while most of the eastern bishops were against him.

Athenagoras (fl. 176-180). Early Christian philosopher and apologist from Athens, whose only authenticated writing, *A Plea Regarding Christians*, is addressed to the emperors Marcus Aurelius and Commodius, and defends Christians from the common accusations of atheism, incest and cannibalism.

Augustine of Hippo (354-430). Bishop of Hippo and a voluminous writer on philosophical, exegetical, theological and ecclesiological topics. He formulated the Western doctrines of predestination and original sin in his writings against the Pelagians.

Babai the Great (d. 628). Syriac monk who founded a monastery and school in his region of Beth Zabday and later served as third superior at the Great Convent of Mount Izla during a period of crisis in the Nestorian church.

Basil the Great (b. c. 330; fl. 357-379). One of the Cappadocian fathers, bishop of Caesarea and champion of the teaching on the Trinity propounded at Nicaea in 325. He was a great administrator and founded a monastic rule.

Basil of Seleucia (fl. 444-468). Bishop of Seleucia in Isauria and ecclesiastical writer. He took part in the Synod of Constantinople in 448 for the condemnation of the Eutychian errors and the deposition of their great champion, Dioscurus of Alexandria.

Basilides (fl. second century). Alexandrian heretic of the early second century who is said to have believed that souls migrate from body to body and that we do not sin if we lie to protect the body from martyrdom.

Bede the Venerable (c. 672/673-735). Born in Northumbria, at the age of seven he was put under the care of the Benedictine monks of Saints Peter and Paul at Jarrow and given a broad classical education in the monastic tradition. Considered one of the most learned men of his age, he is the author of *An Ecclesiastical History of the English People*.

Benedict of Nursia (c. 480-547). Considered the most important figure in the history of Western monasticism. Benedict founded many monasteries, the most notable found at Montecassino, but his lasting influence lay in his famous Rule. The Rule outlines the theological and inspirational foundation of the monastic ideal while also legislating the shape and organization of the cenobitic life.

Book of Steps (c. 400). Written by an anonymous Syriac author, this work consists of thirty homilies or discourses which specifically deal with the more advanced stages of growth in the spiritual life.

Braulio of Saragossa (c. 585-651). Bishop of Saragossa (631-651) and noted writer of the Visigothic renaissance. His *Life* of St. Aemilianus is his crowning literary achievement.

Caesarius of Arles (c. 470-543). Bishop of Arles renowned for his attention to his pastoral duties. Among his surviving works the most important is a collection of some 238 sermons that display an ability to preach Christian doctrine to a variety of audiences.

Callistus of Rome (d. 222). Pope (217-222) who excommunicated Sabellius for heresy. It is very probable that he suffered martyrdom.

Cassia (b. c. 805, d. between 848 and 867). Nun, poet and hymnographer who founded a convent in Constantinople.

Cassian, John (360-432). Author of the *Institutes* and the *Conferences*, works purporting to relay the teachings of the Egyptian monastic fathers on the nature of the spiritual life which were highly influential in the development of Western monasticism.

Cassiodorus (c. 485-c. 580). Founder of the monastery of Vivarium, Calabria, where monks transcribed classic sacred and profane texts, Greek and Latin, preserving them for the Western tradition.

Chromatius (fl. 400). Bishop of Aquileia, friend of Rufinus and Jerome and author of tracts and sermons.

Clement of Alexandria (c. 150-215). A highly educated Christian convert from paganism, head of the catechetical school in Alexandria and pioneer of Christian scholarship. His major works, *Protrepticus, Paedagogus* and the *Stromata*, bring Christian doctrine face to face with the ideas and achievements of his time.

Clement of Rome (fl. c. 92-101). Pope whose *Epistle to the Corinthians* is one of the most important documents of subapostolic times.

Commodian (probably third or possibly fifth century). Latin poet of unknown origin (possibly Syrian?) whose two surviving works suggest chiliast and patripassionist tendencies.

Constitutions of the Holy Apostles. *See Apostolic Constitutions.*

Cyprian of Carthage (fl. 248-258). Martyred bishop of Carthage who maintained that those baptized by schismatics and heretics had no share in the blessings of the church.

Cyril of Alexandria (375-444; fl. 412-444). Patriarch of Alexandria whose extensive exegesis, characterized especially by a strong espousal of the unity of Christ, led to the condemnation of Nestorius in 431.

Cyril of Jerusalem (c. 315-386; fl. c. 348). Bishop of Jerusalem after 350 and author of *Catechetical Homilies*.

Cyril of Scythopolis (b. c. 525; d. after 557). Palestinian monk and author of biographies of famous Palestinian monks. Because of him we have precise knowledge of monastic life in the fifth and sixth centuries and a description of the Origenist crisis and its suppression in the mid-sixth century.

Diadochus of Photice (c. 400-474). Antimonophysite bishop of Epirus Vetus whose work *Discourse on the Ascension of Our Lord Jesus Christ* exerted influence in both the East and West through its Chalcedonian Christology. He is also the subject of the mystical *Vision of St. Diadochus Bishop of Photice in Epirus.*

Didache (c. 140). Of unknown authorship, this text intertwines Jewish ethics with Christian liturgical practice to form a whole discourse on the "way of life." It exerted an enormous amount of influence in the patristic period and was especially used in the training of catechumen.

Didymus the Blind (c. 313-398). Alexandrian exegete who was much influenced by Origen and admired by Jerome.

Diodore of Tarsus (d. c. 394). Bishop of Tarsus and Antiochene theologian. He authored a great scope of exegetical, doctrinal and apologetic works, which come to us mostly in fragments because of his condemnation as the predecessor of Nestorianism. Diodore was a teacher of John Chrysostom and Theodore of Mopsuestia.

Dionysius of Alexandria (d. c. 264). Bishop of Alexandria and student of Origen. Dionysius actively engaged in the theological disputes of his day, opposed Sabellianism, defended himself against accusations of tritheism and wrote the earliest extant Christian refutation of Epicureanism. His writings have survived mainly in extracts preserved by other early Christian authors.

Dorotheus of Gaza (fl. c. 525-540). Member of Abbot Seridos's monastery and later leader of a monastery where he wrote *Spiritual Instructions*. He also wrote a work on traditions of Palestinian monasticism.

Epiphanius of Salamis (c. 315-403). Bishop of Salamis in Cyprus, author of a refutation of eighty heresies (the *Panarion*) and instrumental in the condemnation of Origen.

Epiphanius the Latin. Author of the late fifth-century or early sixth century Latin text *Interpretation of the Gospels*, with constant references to early patristic commentators. He was possibly a bishop of Benevento or Seville.

Epistle of Barnabas. *See Letter of Barnabas.*

Ephrem the Syrian (b. c. 306; fl. 363-373). Syrian writer of commentaries and devotional hymns which are sometimes regarded as the greatest specimens of Christian poetry prior to Dante.

Eucherius of Lyons (fl. 420-449). Bishop of Lyons c. 435-449. Born into an aristocratic family, he, along with his wife and sons, joined the monastery at Lérins soon after its founding. He explained difficult Scripture passages by means of a threefold reading of the text: literal, moral and spiritual.

Eugippius (b. 460). Disciple of Severinus and third abbot of the monastic community at Castrum Lucullanum, which was made up of those fleeing from Noricum during the barbarian invasions.

Eunomius (d. 393). Bishop of Cyzicyus who was attacked by Basil and Gregory of Nyssa for maintaining that the Father and the Son were of different natures, one ingenerate, one generate.

Eusebius of Caesarea (c. 260/263-340). Bishop of Caesarea, partisan of the Emperor Constantine and first historian of the Christian church. He argued that the truth of the gospel had been foreshadowed in pagan writings but had to defend his own doctrine against suspicion of Arian sympathies.

Eusebius of Emesa (c. 300-c. 359). Bishop of Emesa from c. 339. A biblical exegete and writer on doctrinal subjects, he displays some semi-Arian tendencies of his mentor Eusebius of Caesarea.

Eusebius of Vercelli (fl. c. 360). Bishop of Vercelli who supported the trinitarian teaching of Nicaea (325) when it was being undermined by compromise in the West.

Euthymius (377-473). A native of Melitene and influential monk. He was educated by Bishop Otreius of Melitene, who ordained him priest and placed him in charge of all the monasteries in his diocese. When the Council of Chalcedon (451) condemned the errors of Eutyches, it was greatly due to the authority of Euthymius that most of the Eastern recluses accepted its decrees. The empress Eudoxia returned to Chalcedonian orthodoxy through his efforts.

Evagrius of Pontus (c. 345-399). Disciple and teacher of ascetic life who astutely absorbed and creatively transmitted the spirituality of Egyptian and Palestinian monasticism of the late fourth century. Although Origenist elements of his writings were formally condemned by the Fifth Ecumenical Council (Constantinople II, A.D. 553), his literary corpus continued to influence the tradition of the church.

Eznik of Kolb (early fifth century). A disciple of Mesrob who translated Greek Scriptures into Armenian, so as to become the model of the classical Armenian language. As bishop, he participated in the synod of Astisat (449).

Fastidius (c. fourth-fifth centuries). British author of *On the Christian Life*. He is believed to have written some works attributed to Pelagius.

Faustinus (fl. 380). A priest in Rome and supporter of Lucifer and author of a treatise on the Trinity.

The Festal Menaion. Orthodox liturgical text containing the variable parts of the service, including hymns, for fixed days of celebration of the life of Jesus and Mary.

Filastrius (fl. 380). Bishop of Brescia and author of a compilation against all heresies.

Fulgentius of Ruspe (c. 467-532). Bishop of Ruspe and author of many orthodox sermons and tracts under the influence of Augustine.

Gaudentius of Brescia (fl. 395). Successor of Filastrius as bishop of Brescia and author of twenty-one Eucharistic sermons.

Gennadius of Constantinople (d. 471). Patriarch of Constantinople, author of numerous commentaries and an opponent of the Christology of Cyril of Alexandria.

Gnostics. Name now given generally to followers of Basilides, Marcion, Valentinus, Mani and others. The characteristic belief is that matter is a prison made for the spirit by an evil or ignorant creator, and that redemption depends on fate, not on free will.

Gregory of Elvira (fl. 359-385). Bishop of Elvira who wrote allegorical treatises in the style of Origen and defended the Nicene faith against the Arians.

Gregory of Nazianzus (b. 329/330; fl. 372-389). Cappadocian father, bishop of Constantinople, friend of Basil the Great and Gregory of Nyssa, and author of theological orations, sermons and poetry.

Gregory of Nyssa (c. 335-394). Bishop of Nyssa and brother of Basil the Great. A Cappadocian father and author of catechetical orations, he was a philosophical theologian of great originality.

Gregory Thaumaturgus (fl. c. 248-264). Bishop of Neocaesarea and a disciple of Origen. There are at least five legendary *Lives* that recount the events and miracles which led to his being called "the wonder worker." His most important work was the *Address of Thanks to Origen*, which is a rhetorically structured panegyric to Origen and an outline of his teaching.

Gregory the Great (c. 540-604). Pope from 590, the fourth and last of the Latin "Doctors of the Church." He was a prolific author and a powerful unifying force within the Latin Church, initiating the liturgical reform that brought about the Gregorian Sacramentary and Gregorian chant.

Hesychius of Jerusalem (fl. 412-450). Presbyter and exegete, thought to have commented on the whole of Scripture.

Hilary of Arles (c. 401-449). Archbishop of Arles and leader of the Semi-Pelagian party. Hilary incurred the wrath of Pope Leo I when he removed a bishop from his see and appointed a new bishop. Leo demoted Arles from a metropolitan see to a bishopric to assert papal power over the church in Gaul.

Hilary of Poitiers (c. 315-367). Bishop of Poitiers and called the "Athanasius of the West" because of his defense (against the Arians) of the common nature of Father and Son.

Hippolytus (fl. 222-245). Recent scholarship places Hippolytus in a Palestinian context, personally familiar with Origen. Though he is known chiefly for *The Refutation of All Heresies*, he was primarily a commentator on Scripture (especially the Old Testament) employing typological exegesis.

Horsiesi (c. 305-c. 390). Pachomius's second successor, after Petronius, as a leader of cenobitic monasticism in Southern Egypt.

Ignatius of Antioch (c. 35-107/112). Bishop of Antioch who wrote several letters to local churches while being taken from Antioch to Rome to be martyred. In the letters, which warn against heresy, he stresses orthodox Christology, the centrality of the Eucharist and unique role of the bishop in preserving the unity of the church.

Irenaeus of Lyons (c. 135-c. 202). Bishop of Lyons who published the most famous and influential refutation of Gnostic thought.

Isaac of Nineveh (d. c. 700). Also known as Isaac the Syrian or Isaac Syrus, this monastic writer served for a short while as bishop of Nineveh before retiring to live a secluded monastic life. His writings on ascetic subjects survive in the form of numerous homilies.

Isho'dad of Merv (fl. c. 850). Nestorian bishop of Hedatta. He wrote commentaries on parts of the Old Testament and all of the New Testament, frequently quoting Syriac fathers.

Isidore of Seville (c. 560-636). Youngest of a family of monks and clerics, including sister Florentina and brothers Leander and Fulgentius. He was an erudite author of comprehensive scale in matters both religious and sacred, including his encyclopedic *Etymologies*.

Jacob of Nisibis (d. 338). Bishop of Nisibis. He was present at the council of Nicaea in 325 and took an active part in the opposition to Arius.

Jacob of Sarug (c. 450-c. 520). Syriac ecclesiastical writer. Jacob received his education at Edessa. At the end of his life he was ordained bishop of Sarug. His principal writing was a long series of metrical homilies, earning him the title "The Flute of the Holy Spirit."

Jerome (c. 347-420). Gifted exegete and exponent of a classical Latin style, now best known as the translator of the Latin Vulgate. He defended the perpetual virginity of Mary, attacked Origen and Pelagius and supported extreme ascetic practices.

John Chrysostom (344/354-407; fl. 386-407). Bishop of Constantinople who was noted for his orthodoxy, his eloquence and his attacks on Christian laxity in high places.

John of Damascus (c. 650-750). Arab monastic and theologian whose writings enjoyed great influence in both the Eastern and Western

Churches. His most influential writing was the *Orthodox Faith*.

John the Elder (c. eighth century). A Syriac author who belonged to monastic circles of the Church of the East and lived in the region of Mount Qardu (northern Iraq). His most important writings are twenty-two homilies and a collection of fifty-one short letters in which he describes the mystical life as an anticipatory experience of the resurrection life, the fruit of the sacraments of baptism and the Eucharist.

John the Monk. Traditional name found in *The Festal Menaion*, believed to refer to John of Damascus. *See* John of Damascus.

Josephus, Flavius (c. 37-c. 101). Jewish historian from a distinguished priestly family. Acquainted with the Essenes and Sadducees, he himself became a Pharisee. He joined the great Jewish revolt that broke out in 66 and was chosen by the Sanhedrin at Jerusalem to be commander-in-chief in Galilee. Showing great shrewdness to ingratiate himself with Vespasian by foretelling his elevation and that of his son Titus to the imperial dignity, Josephus was restored his liberty after 69 when Vespasian became emperor.

Julian of Eclanum (c. 385-450). Bishop of Eclanum in 416/417 who was removed from office and exiled in 419 for not officially opposing Pelagianism. In exile, he was accepted by Theodore of Mopsuestia, whose Antiochene exegetical style he followed. Although he was never able to regain his ecclesiastical position, Julian taught in Sicily until his death. His works include commentaries on Job and parts of the Minor Prophets, a translation of Theodore of Mopsuestia's commentary on the Psalms, and various letters. Sympathetic to Pelagius, Julian applied his intellectual acumen and rhetorical training to argue against Augustine on matters such as free will, desire and the locus of evil.

Justin Martyr (c. 100/110-165; fl. c. 148-161). Palestinian philosopher who was converted to Christianity, "the only sure and worthy philosophy." He traveled to Rome where he wrote several apologies against both pagans and Jews, combining Greek philosophy and Christian theology; he was eventually martyred.

Lactantius (c. 260-c. 330). Christian apologist removed from his post as teacher of rhetoric at Nicomedia upon his conversion to Christianity. He was tutor to the son of Constantine and author of *The Divine Institutes*.

Leander (c. 545-c. 600). Latin ecclesiastical writer, of whose works only two survive. He was instrumental in spreading Christianity among the Visigoths, gaining significant historical influence in Spain in his time.

Leo the Great (regn. 440-461). Bishop of Rome whose *Tome to Flavian* helped to strike a balance between Nestorian and Cyrilline positions at the Council of Chalcedon in 451.

Letter of Barnabas (c. 130). An allegorical and typological interpretation of the Old Testament with a decidedly anti-Jewish tone. It was included with other New Testament works as a "Catholic epistle" at least until Eusebius of Caesarea (c. 260/263-340) questioned its authenticity.

Letter to Diognetus (c. third century). A refutation of paganism and an exposition of the Christian life and faith. The author of this letter is unknown, and the exact identity of its recipient, Diognetus, continues to elude patristic scholars.

Lucifer (d. 370/371). Bishop of Cagliari and vigorous supporter of Athanasius and the Nicene Creed. In conflict with the emperor Constantius, he was banished to Palestine and later to Thebaid (Egypt).

Luculentius (fifth century). Unknown author of a group of short commentaries on the New Testament, especially Pauline passages. His exegesis is mainly literal and relies mostly on earlier authors such as Jerome and Augustine. The content of his writing may place it in the fifth century.

Macarius of Egypt (c. 300-c. 390). One of the Desert Fathers. Accused of supporting Athanasius, Macarius was exiled c. 374 to an island in the Nile by Lucius, the Arian successor of Athanasius. Macarius continued his teaching of monastic theology at Wadi Natrun.

Macrina the Younger (c. 327-379). The elder sister of Basil the Great and Gregory of Nyssa, she is known as "the Younger" to distinguish her from her paternal grandmother. She had a powerful influence on her younger brothers, especially on Gregory, who called her his teacher and relates her teaching in *On the Soul and the Resurrection*.

Manichaeans. A religious movement that originated circa 241 in Persia under the leadership of Mani but was apparently of complex Christian origin. It is said to have denied free will and the universal sovereignty of God, teaching that kingdoms of light and darkness are coeternal and that the redeemed are particles of a spiritual man of light held captive in the darkness of matter (*see* Gnostics).

Marcion (fl. 144). Heretic of the mid-second century who rejected the Old Testament and much of the New Testament, claiming that the Father of Jesus Christ was other than the Old Testament God (*see* Gnostics).

Marius Victorinus (b. c. 280/285; fl. c. 355-363). Grammarian of African origin who taught rhetoric at Rome and translated works of Platonists. After his conversion (c. 355), he wrote against the Arians and commentaries on Paul's letters.

Mark the Hermit (c. sixth century). Monk who lived near Tarsus and produced works on ascetic practices as well as christological issues.

Martin of Braga (fl. c. 568-579). Anti-Arian metropolitan of Braga on the Iberian peninsula. He was highly educated and presided over the provincial council of Braga in 572.

Martyrius. *See* Sahdona.

Maximus of Turin (d. 408/423). Bishop of Turin. Over one hundred of his sermons survive on Christian festivals, saints and martyrs.

Maximus the Confessor (c. 580-662). Palestinian-born theologian and ascetic writer. Fleeing the Arab invasion of Jerusalem in 614, he took refuge in Constantinople and later Africa. He died near the Black Sea after imprisonment and severe suffering, having his tongue cut off and his right hand mutilated. He taught total preference for God and detachment from all things.

Methodius of Olympus (d. 311). Bishop of

Olympus who celebrated virginity in a *Symposium* partly modeled on Plato's dialogue of that name.

Minucius Felix (second or third century). Christian apologist who was an advocate in Rome. His *Octavius* agrees at numerous points with the *Apologeticum* of Tertullian. His birthplace is believed to be in Africa.

Montanist Oracles. Montanism was an apocalyptic and strictly ascetic movement begun in the latter half of the second century by a certain Montanus in Phrygia, who, along with certain of his followers, uttered oracles they claimed were inspired by the Holy Spirit. Little of the authentic oracles remains and most of what is known of Montanism comes from the authors who wrote against the movement. Montanism was formally condemned as a heresy before by Asiatic synods.

Nemesius of Emesa (fl. late fourth century). Bishop of Emesa in Syria whose most important work, *Of the Nature of Man*, draws on several theological and philosophical sources and is the first exposition of a Christian anthropology.

Nestorius (c. 381-c. 451). Patriarch of Constantinople (428-431) who founded the heresy which says that there are two persons, divine and human, rather than one person truly united in the incarnate Christ. He resisted the teaching of *theotokos*, causing Nestorian churches to separate from Constantinople.

Nicetas of Remesiana (fl. second half of fourth century). Bishop of Remesiana in Serbia, whose works affirm the consubstantiality of the Son and the deity of the Holy Spirit.

Novatian of Rome (fl. 235-258). Roman theologian, otherwise orthodox, who formed a schismatic church after failing to become pope. His treatise on the Trinity states the classic western doctrine.

Oecumenius (sixth century). Called the Rhetor or the Philosopher, Oecumenius wrote the earliest extant Greek commentary on Revelation. Scholia by Oecumenius on some of John Chrysostom's commentaries on the Pauline Epistles are still extant.

Origen of Alexandria (b. 185; fl. c. 200-254). Influential exegete and systematic theologian. He was condemned (perhaps unfairly) for maintaining the preexistence of souls while purportedly denying the resurrection of the body. His extensive works of exegesis focus on the spiritual meaning of the text.

Pachomius (c. 292-347). Founder of cenobitic monasticism. A gifted group leader and author of a set of rules, he was defended after his death by Athanasius of Alexandria.

Pacian of Barcelona (c. fourth century). Bishop of Barcelona whose writings polemicize against popular pagan festivals as well as Novatian schismatics.

Palladius of Helenopolis (c. 363/364-c. 431). Bishop of Helenopolis in Bithynia (400-417) and then Aspuna in Galatia. A disciple of Evagrius of Pontus and admirer of Origen, Palladius became a zealous adherent of John Chrysostom and shared his troubles in 403. His *Lausaic History* is the leading source for the history of early monasticism, stressing the spiritual value of the life of the desert.

Paschasius of Dumium (c. 515-c. 580). Translator of sentences of the Desert Fathers from Greek into Latin while a monk in Dumium.

Paterius (c. sixth-seventh century). Disciple of Gregory the Great who is primarily responsible for the transmission of Gregory's works to many later medieval authors.

Paulinus of Nola (355-431). Roman senator and distinguished Latin poet whose frequent encounters with Ambrose of Milan (c. 333-397) led to his eventual conversion and baptism in 389. He eventually renounced his wealth and influential position and took up his pen to write poetry in service of Christ. He also wrote many letters to, among others, Augustine, Jerome and Rufinus.

Paulus Orosius (b. c. 380). An outspoken critic of Pelagius, mentored by Augustine. His *Seven Books of History Against the Pagans* was perhaps the first history of Christianity.

Pelagius (c. 354-c. 420). Contemporary of Augustine whose followers were condemned in 418 and 431 for maintaining that even before Christ these were people who lived wholly without sin and that salvation depended on free will.

Peter of Alexandria (d. c. 311). Bishop of Alexandria. He marked (and very probably initiated) the reaction at Alexandria against extreme doctrines of Origen. During the persecution of Christians in Alexandria, Peter was arrested and beheaded by Roman officials. Eusebius of Caesarea described him as "a model bishop, remarkable for his virtuous life and his ardent study of the Scriptures."

Peter Chrysologus (c. 380-450). Latin archbishop of Ravenna whose teachings included arguments for adherence in matters of faith to the Roman see, and the relationship between grace and Christian living.

Philo of Alexandria (c. 20 B.C.-c. A.D. 50). Jewish-born exegete who greatly influenced Christian patristic interpretation of the Old Testament. Born to a rich family in Alexandria, Philo was a contemporary of Jesus and lived an ascetic and contemplative life that makes some believe he was a rabbi. His interpretation of Scripture based the spiritual sense on the literal. Although influenced by Hellenism, Philo's theology remains thoroughly Jewish.

Philoxenus of Mabbug (c. 440-523). Bishop of Mabbug (Hierapolis) and a leading thinker in the early Syrian Orthodox Church. His extensive writings in Syriac include a set of thirteen *Discourses on the Christian Life*, several works on the incarnation and a number of exegetical works.

Poemen (c. fifth century). One-seventh of the sayings in the *Sayings of the Desert Fathers* are attributed to Poemen, which is Greek for shepherd. Poemen was a common title among early Egyptian desert ascetics, and it is unknown whether all of the sayings come from one person.

Polycarp of Smyrna (c. 69-155). Bishop of Smyrna who vigorously fought heretics such as the Marcionites and Valentinians. He was the leading Christian figure in Roman Asia in the middle of the second century.

Potamius of Lisbon (fl. c. 350-360). Bishop of Lisbon who joined the Arian party in 357, but later returned to the Catholic faith (c. 359?). His works from both periods are concerned with the larger Trinitarian debates of his time.

Procopius of Gaza (c. 465-c. 530). A Christian exegete educated in Alexandria. He wrote numerous theological works and commentaries on Scripture (particularly the Hebrew Bible), the latter marked by the allegorical exegesis for which the Alexandrian school was known.

Prudentius (c. 348-c. 410). Latin poet and hymn-writer who devoted his later life to Christian writing. He wrote didactic poems on the theology of the incarnation, against the heretic Marcion and against the resurgence of paganism.

Pseudo-Dionysius the Areopagite (fl. c. 500). Author who assumed the name of Dionysius the Areopagite mentioned in Acts 17:34, and who composed the works known as the *Corpus Areopagiticum* (or *Dionysiacum*). These writings were the foundation of the apophatic school of mysticism in their denial that anything can be truly predicated of God.

Pseudo-Macarius (fl. c. 390). An anonymous writer and ascetic (from Mesopotamia?) active in Antioch whose badly edited works were attributed to Macarius of Egypt. He had keen insight into human nature, prayer and the inner life. His work includes some one hundred discourses and homilies.

Quodvultdeus (fl. 430). Carthaginian bishop and friend of Augustine who endeavored to show at length how the New Testament fulfilled the Old Testament.

Rufinus of Aquileia (c. 345-411). Orthodox Christian thinker and historian who nonetheless translated and preserved the works of Origen, and defended him against the strictures of Jerome and Epiphanius. He lived the ascetic life in Rome, Egypt and Jerusalem (the Mount of Olives).

Sabellius (fl. 200). Allegedly the author of the heresy which maintains that the Father and Son are a single person. The patripassian variant of this heresy states that the Father suffered on the cross.

Sahdona (fl. 635-640). Known in Greek as Martyrius, this Syriac author was bishop of Beth Garmai. He studied in Nisibis and was exiled for his christological ideas. His most important work is the deeply scriptural *Book of Perfection* which ranks as one of the masterpieces of Syriac monastic literature.

Salvian the Presbyter of Marseilles (c. 400-c. 480). An important author for the history of his own time. He saw the fall of Roman civilization to the barbarians as a consequence of the reprehensible conduct of Roman Christians. In *The Governance of God* he developed the theme of divine providence.

Second Letter of Clement (c. 150). The so-called *Second Letter of Clement* is an early Christian sermon probably written by a Corinthian author, though some scholars have assigned it to a Roman or Alexandrian author.

Severian of Gabala (fl. c. 400). A contemporary of John Chrysostom, he was a highly regarded preacher in Constantinople, particularly at the imperial court, and ultimately sided with Chrysostom's accusers. He wrote homilies on Genesis.

Severus of Antioch (fl. 488-538). A monophysite theologian, consecrated bishop of Antioch in 522. Born in Pisidia, he studied in Alexandria and Beirut, taught in Constantinople and was exiled to Egypt.

***Shepherd* of Hermas** (second century). Divided into five *Visions*, twelve *Mandates* and ten *Similitudes*, this Christian apocalypse was written by a former slave and named for the form of the second angel said to have granted him his visions. This work was highly esteemed for its moral value and was used as a textbook for catechumens in the early church.

Sulpicius Severus (c. 360-c. 420). An ecclesiastical writer from Bordeaux born of noble parents. Devoting himself to monastic retirement, he became a personal friend and enthusiastic disciple of St. Martin of Tours.

Symeon the New Theologian (c. 949-1022). Compassionate spiritual leader known for his strict rule. He believed that the divine light could be perceived and received through the practice of mental prayer.

Tertullian of Carthage (c. 155/160-225/250; fl. c. 197-222). Brilliant Carthaginian apologist and polemicist who laid the foundations of Christology and trinitarian orthodoxy in the West, though he himself was later estranged from the catholic tradition due to its laxity.

Theodore of Heraclea (d. c. 355). An anti-Nicene bishop of Thrace. He was part of a team seeking reconciliation between Eastern and Western Christianity. In 343 he was excommunicated at the council of Sardica. His writings focus on a literal interpretation of Scripture.

Theodore of Mopsuestia (c. 350-428). Bishop of Mopsuestia, founder of the Antiochene, or literalistic, school of exegesis. A great man in his day, he was later condemned as a precursor of Nestorius.

Theodoret of Cyr (c. 393-466). Bishop of Cyr (Cyrrhus), he was an opponent of Cyril who commented extensively on Old Testament texts as a lucid exponent of Antiochene exegesis.

Theodotus the Valentinian (second century). Likely a Montanist who may have been related to the Alexandrian school. Extracts of his work are known through writings of Clement of Alexandria.

Theophanes (775-845). Hymnographer and bishop of Nicaea (842-845). He was persecuted during the second iconoclastic period for his support of the Seventh Council (Second Council of Nicaea, 787). He wrote many hymns in the tradition of the monastery of Mar Sabbas that were used in the *Paraklitiki*.

Theophilus of Antioch (late second century). Bishop of Antioch. His only surviving work is *Ad Autholycum*, where we find the first Christian commentary on Genesis and the first use of the term *Trinity*. Theophilus's apologetic literary heritage had influence on Irenaeus and possibly Tertullian.

Theophylact of Ohrid (c. 1050-c. 1108). Byzantine archbishop of Ohrid (or Achrida) in what is now Bulgaria. Drawing on earlier works, he wrote commentaries on several Old Testament books and all of the New Testament except for Revelation.

Valentinus (fl. c. 140). Alexandrian heretic of the mid-second century who taught that the material world was created by the transgression of God's Wisdom, or Sophia (*see* Gnostics).

Valerian of Cimiez (fl. c. 422-439). Bishop of Cimiez. He participated in the councils of Riez (439) and Vaison (422) with a view to strengthening church discipline. He supported Hilary of Arles in quarrels with Pope Leo I.

Victorinus of Petovium (d. c. 304). Latin biblical exegete. With multiple works attributed to him, his sole surviving work is the *Commentary on the Apocalypse* and perhaps some fragments from *Commentary on Matthew*. Victorinus expressed strong millenarianism in his writing, though his was less materialistic than the millenarianism of Papias or Irenaeus. In his allegorical approach he could be called a spiritual disciple of Origen. Victorinus died during the first year of Diocletian's persecution, probably in 304.

Vincent of Lérins (d. before 450). Monk who has exerted considerable influence through his writings on orthodox dogmatic theological method, as contrasted with the theological methodologies of the heresies.

Timeline of Writers of the Patristic Period

Location / Period	British Isles	Gaul	Spain, Portugal	Rome* and Italy	Carthage and Northern Africa
2nd century				Clement of Rome, fl. c. 92-101 (Greek)	
				Shepherd of Hermas, c. 140 (Greek)	
				Justin Martyr (Ephesus, Rome), c. 100/110-165 (Greek)	
		Irenaeus of Lyons, c. 135-c. 202 (Greek)		Valentinus the Gnostic (Rome), fl. c. 140 (Greek)	
				Marcion (Rome), fl. 144 (Greek)	
3rd century				Callistus of Rome, regn. 217-222 (Latin)	Tertullian of Carthage, c. 155/160-c. 225 (Latin)
				Minucius Felix of Rome, fl. 218-235 (Latin)	
				Hippolytus (Rome, Palestine?), fl. 222-235/245 (Greek)	Cyprian of Carthage, fl. 248-258 (Latin)
				Novatian of Rome, fl. 235-258 (Latin)	
				Victorinus of Petovium, 230-304 (Latin)	
4th century				Marius Victorinus (Rome), fl. 355-363 (Latin)	
		Lactantius, c. 260-330 (Latin)		Eusebius of Vercelli, fl. c. 360 (Latin)	
				Lucifer of Cagliari (Sardinia), d. 370/371 (Latin)	
		Hilary of Poitiers, c. 315-367 (Latin)	Hosius of Cordova, d. 357 (Latin)	Faustinus (Rome), fl. 380 (Latin)	
			Potamius of Lisbon, fl. c. 350-360 (Latin)	Filastrius of Brescia, fl. 380 (Latin)	
				Ambrosiaster (Italy?), fl. c. 366-384 (Latin)	
			Gregory of Elvira, fl. 359-385 (Latin)	Gaudentius of Brescia, fl. 395 (Latin)	
			Prudentius, c. 348-c. 410 (Latin)	Ambrose of Milan, c. 333-397; fl. 374-397 (Latin)	
			Pacian of Barcelona, 4th cent. (Latin)	Rufinus (Aquileia, Rome), c. 345-411 (Latin)	Paulus Orosius, b. c. 380 (Latin)

*One of the five ancient patriarchates

Alexandria* and Egypt	Constantinople* and Asia Minor, Greece	Antioch* and Syria	Mesopotamia, Persia	Jerusalem* and Palestine	Location Unknown
Philo of Alexandria, c. 20 B.C. – c. A.D. 50 (Greek)				Flavius Josephus (Rome), c. 37-c. 101 (Greek)	
Basilides (Alexandria), 2nd cent. (Greek)	Polycarp of Smyrna, c. 69-155 (Greek)	*Didache* (Egypt?), c. 100 (Greek)			*Second Letter of Clement* (spurious; Corinth, Rome, Alexandria?) (Greek), c. 150
Letter of Barnabas (Syria?), c. 130 (Greek)	Athenagoras (Greece), fl. 176-180 (Greek)	Ignatius of Antioch, c. 35–107/112 (Greek)			
Theodotus the Valentinian, 2nd cent. (Greek)	*Montanist Oracles*, late 2nd cent. (Greek)				
		Theophilus of Antioch, c. late 2nd cent. (Greek)			
Clement of Alexandria, c. 150-215 (Greek)	Gregory Thaumaturgus (Neocaesarea), fl. c. 248-264 (Greek)		Mani (Manichaeans), c. 216-276		
Sabellius (Egypt), 2nd–3rd cent. (Greek)					
Letter to Diognetus, 3rd cent. (Greek)					
Origen (Alexandria, Caesarea of Palestine), 185-254 (Greek)					
Dionysius of Alexandria, d. 264/5 (Greek)	Methodius of Olympus (Lycia), d. c. 311 (Greek)				
Anthony, c. 251-355 (Coptic/Greek)	Theodore of Heraclea (Thrace), fl. c. 330-355 (Greek)	Eusebius of Emesa, c. 300-c. 359 (Greek)	Aphrahat (Persia) c. 270-350; fl. 337-345 (Syriac)	Eusebius of Caesarea (Palestine), c. 260/263-340 (Greek)	Commodius, c. 3rd or 5th cent. (Latin)
Peter of Alexandria, d. c. 311 (Greek)	Epiphanius of Salamis (Cyprus), c. 315-403 (Greek)	Ephrem the Syrian, c. 306-373 (Syriac)	Jacob of Nisibis, fl. 308-325 (Syriac)	Acacius of Caesarea (Palestine), d. c. 365 (Greek)	
Arius (Alexandria), fl. c. 320 (Greek)	Basil (the Great) of Caesarea, b. c. 330; fl. 357-379 (Greek)	Nemesius of Emesa (Syria), fl. late 4th cent. (Greek)		Cyril of Jerusalem, c. 315-386 (Greek)	
Alexander of Alexandria, fl. 312-328 (Greek)	Macrina the Younger, c. 327-379 (Greek)	Diodore of Tarsus, d. c. 394 (Greek)			
Pachomius, c. 292-347 (Coptic/Greek?)	Apollinaris of Laodicea, 310-c. 392 (Greek)	John Chrysostom (Constantinople), 344/354-407 (Greek)			
Horsiesi, c. 305-390 (Coptic/Greek)	Gregory of Nazianzus, b. 329/330; fl. 372-389 (Greek)	*Apostolic Constitutions*, c. 375-400 (Greek)			
Athanasius of Alexandria, c. 295-373; fl. 325-373 (Greek)	Gregory of Nyssa, c. 335-394 (Greek)	*Didascalia*, 4th cent. (Syriac)			
Macarius of Egypt, c. 300-c. 390 (Greek)	Amphilochius of Iconium, c. 340/345- c. 398/404 (Greek)	Theodore of Mopsuestia, c. 350-428 (Greek)			
Didymus (the Blind) of Alexandria, 313-398 (Greek)	Evagrius of Pontus, 345-399 (Greek)			Diodore of Tarsus, d. c. 394 (Greek)	
	Eunomius of Cyzicus, fl. 360-394 (Greek)			Jerome (Rome, Antioch, Bethlehem), c. 347-420 (Latin)	
	Pseudo-Macarius (Mesopotamia?), late 4th cent. (Greek)				
	Nicetas of Remesiana, d. c. 414 (Latin)				

Timeline of Writers of the Patristic Period

Location / Period	British Isles	Gaul	Spain, Portugal	Rome* and Italy	Carthage and Northern Africa
5th century	Fastidius (Britain), c. 4th-5th cent. (Latin)	Sulpicius Severus (Bordeaux), c. 360-c. 420/425 (Latin)		Chromatius (Aquileia), fl. 400 (Latin)	Quodvultdeus (Carthage), fl. 430 (Latin)
		John Cassian (Palestine, Egypt, Constantinople, Rome, Marseilles), 360-432 (Latin)		Pelagius (Britain, Rome), c. 354-c. 420 (Greek)	Augustine of Hippo, 354-430 (Latin)
		Vincent of Lérins, d. 435 (Latin)		Maximus of Turin, d. 408/423 (Latin)	Luculentius, 5th cent. (Latin)
		Valerian of Cimiez, fl. c. 422-449 (Latin)		Paulinus of Nola, 355-431 (Latin)	
		Eucherius of Lyons, fl. 420-449 (Latin)		Peter Chrysologus (Ravenna), c. 380-450 (Latin)	
		Hilary of Arles, c. 401-449 (Latin)		Julian of Eclanum, 386-454 (Latin)	
		Prosper of Aquitaine, d. after 455 (Latin)		Leo the Great (Rome), regn. 440-461 (Latin)	
		Salvian the Presbyter of Marseilles, c. 400-c. 480 (Latin)			
		Gennadius of Marseilles, d. after 496 (Latin)			
6th century		Caesarius of Arles, c. 470-543 (Latin)	Paschasius of Dumium (Portugal), c. 515-c. 580 (Latin)	Epiphanius the Latin, late 5th–early 6th cent. (Latin)	Fulgentius of Ruspe, c. 467-532 (Latin)
			Leander of Seville, c. 545-c. 600 (Latin)	Eugippius, c. 460- c. 533 (Latin)	
			Martin of Braga, fl. 568-579 (Latin)	Benedict of Nursia, c. 480-547 (Latin)	
				Cassiodorus (Calabria), c. 485-c. 540 (Latin)	
				Gregory the Great (Rome), c. 540-604 (Latin)	
				Gregory of Agrigentium, d. 592 (Greek)	
7th century			Isidore of Seville, c. 560-636 (Latin)	Paterius, 6th/7th cent. (Latin)	
			Braulio of Saragossa, c. 585-651 (Latin)		
8th century	Bede the Venerable, c. 672/673-735 (Latin)				

*One of the five ancient patriarchates

Alexandria* and Egypt	Constantinople* and Asia Minor, Greece	Antioch* and Syria	Mesopotamia, Persia	Jerusalem* and Palestine	Location Unknown
Palladius of Helenopolis (Egypt), c. 365-425 (Greek)	Nestorius (Constantinople), c. 381-c. 451 (Greek)	Book of Steps, c. 400 (Syriac)	Eznik of Kolb, fl. 430-450 (Armenian)	Jerome (Rome, Antioch, Bethlehem), c. 347-419 (Latin)	
Cyril of Alexandria, 375-444 (Greek)	Basil of Seleucia, fl. 440-468 (Greek)	Severian of Gabala, fl. c. 400 (Greek)		Hesychius of Jerusalem, fl. 412-450 (Greek)	
Ammonius of Alexandria, c. 460 (Greek)	Diadochus of Photice (Macedonia), 400-474 (Greek)	Theodoret of Cyr, c. 393-466 (Greek)		Euthymius (Palestine), 377-473 (Greek)	
Poemen, 5th cent. (Greek)	Gennadius of Constantinople, d. 471 (Greek)	Pseudo-Victor of Antioch, 5th cent. (Greek)			
	Oecumenius (Isauria), 6th cent. (Greek)	Philoxenus of Mabbug (Syria), c. 440-523 (Syriac)	Jacob of Sarug, c. 450-520 (Syriac)	Procopius of Gaza (Palestine), c. 465-530 (Greek)	Pseudo-Dionysius the Areopagite, fl. c. 500 (Greek)
		Severus of Antioch, c. 465-538 (Greek)	Babai the Great, c. 550-628 (Syriac)	Dorotheus of Gaza, fl. 525-540 (Greek)	
		Mark the Hermit (Tarsus), c. 6th cent. (4th cent.?) (Greek)		Cyril of Scythopolis, b. c. 525; d. after 557 (Greek)	
	Maximus the Confessor (Constantinople), c. 580-662 (Greek)	Sahdona/Martyrius, fl. 635-640 (Syriac)	Isaac of Nineveh, d. c. 700 (Syriac)		(Pseudo-) Constantius, before 7th cent.? (Greek)
					Andreas, c. 7th cent. (Greek)
	Theophanes (Nicaea), 775-845 (Greek)	John of Damascus (John the Monk), c. 650-750 (Greek)	John the Elder of Qardu (north Iraq), 8th cent. (Syriac)		
	Cassia (Constantinople), c. 805-c. 848/867 (Greek)		Isho'dad of Merv, d. after 852 (Syriac)		
	Symeon the New Theologian (Constantinople), 949-1022 (Greek)				
	Theophylact of Ohrid (Bulgaria), 1050-1126 (Greek)				

Bibliography of Works
in Original Languages

This bibliography refers readers to original language sources and supplies Thesaurus Linguae Graecae (=TLG) or Cetedoc Clavis (=Cl.) numbers where available. The edition listed in this bibliography may in some cases differ from the edition found in TLG or Cetedoc databases.

Ambrose. "De fide." In *Sancti Ambrosii opera*. Edited by O. Faller. CSEL 78, pp. 3-307. Vienna, Austria: F. Tempsky; Leipzig, Germany: G. Freytag, 1962. Cl. 0150.

———. "De fuga saeculi." In *Sancti Ambrosii opera*. Edited by Karl Schenkl. CSEL 32, pt. 2, pp. 163-207. Vienna, Austria: F. Tempsky; Leipzig, Germany: G. Freytag, 1897. Cl. 0133.

———. "De interpellatione Job et David." In *Sancti Ambrosii opera*. Edited by Karl Shenkl. CSEL 32, pt. 2, pp. 211-96. Vienna, Austria: F. Tempsky; Leipzig, Germany: G. Freytag, 1897. Cl. 0134.

———. "De Isaac vel anima." In *Sancti Ambrosii opera*. Edited by Karl Schenkl. CSEL 32, pt. 1, pp. 641-700. Vienna, Austria: F. Tempsky; Leipzig, Germany: G. Freytag, 1896. Cl. 0128.

———. "De Jacob et vita beata." In *Sancti Ambrosii opera*. Edited by Karl Schenkl. CSEL 32, pt. 2, pp. 3-70. Vienna, Austria: F. Tempsky; Leipzig, Germany: G. Freytag, 1897. Cl. 0130.

———. "De Joseph." In *Sancti Ambrosii opera*. Edited by Karl Schenkl. CSEL 32, pt. 2, pp. 73-122. Vienna, Austria: F. Tempsky; Leipzig, Germany: G. Freytag, 1897. Cl. 0131.

———. "De obitu Theodosii." In *Sancti Ambrosii opera*. Edited by O. Faller. CSEL 73, pp. 371-401. Turnhout, Belgium: Brepols, 1955. Cl. 0159.

———. *De paenitentia*. Edited by R. Gryson. SC 179. Paris: Éditions du Cerf, 1971. Cl. 0156.

———. "De paradiso." In *Sancti Ambrosii opera*. Edited by Karl Schenkl. CSEL 32, pt. 1, pp. 263-336. Vienne, Austria: F. Tempsky; Leipzig, Germany: G. Freytag, 1897. Cl. 0124.

———. "De Spiritu Sancto." In *De Spirito Sancto libri tres; De incarnationis Dominicae sacramento*. Edited by O. Faller. CSEL 79, pp. 7-222. Vienna, Austria: F. Tempsky; Leipzig, Germany: G. Freytag, 1962. Cl. 0151.

———. "Exameron." In *Sancti Ambrosii opera*. Edited by O. Faller. CSEL 32, pt. 1, pp. 3-261. Vienna, Austria: F. Tempsky; Leipzig, Germany: G. Freytag, 1897. Cl. 0123.

———. *Explanatio psalmorum xii*. Edited by M. Petschenig. CSEL 64. Vienna, Austria: F. Tempsky; Leipzig, Germany: G. Freytag, 1919. Cl. 0140.

Aphrahat. "Demonstrationes (IV)." In *Opera omnia*. Edited by R. Graffin. Patrologia Syriaca 1, cols. 137-82. Paris: Firmin-Didot, 1910.

Athanasius. "Epistulae festales." In *Cosmas Indicopleustès. Topographie chrétienne*, vol.3. Edited by W. Wolska-Conus. SC 197, pp. 241-53. Paris: Cerf, 1973. TLG 2035.x01.

———. "Oratio quarta contra Arianos [Sp.]." In *Die pseudoathanasianische 'IVte Rede gegen die Arianer' als* 'κατὰ Ἀρειανῶν λόγος' *ein Apollinarisgut*, pp. 43-87. Edited by A. Stegmann. Rottenburg: Bader, 1917. TLG 2035.117.

———. "Vita sancti Antonii." In *Opera omnia*. Edited by J.-P. Migne. PG 26, cols. 835-976. Paris: Migne, 1887. TLG 2035.047.

Augustine. "Adversus Judaeos." In *Opera omnia*. Edited by J.-P. Migne. PL 42, cols. 51-64. Paris, Migne,

1861. Cl. 0315.

———. *Confessionum libri tredecim.* Edited by L. Verheijen. CCL 27. Turnhout, Belgium: Brepols, 1981. Cl. 0251.

———. "Contra Julianum." In *Opera omnia.* Edited by J.-P. Migne. PL 44, cols. 641-874. Paris: Migne, 1861. Cl. 0351.

———."De baptismo contra Donatistas." In *Sancti Aureli Augustini Scripta contra donatistas*, vols 2. Edited by M. Petschenig. CSEL 51, pp. 145-375. Cl. 0332.

———. *De civitate Dei.* Edited by B. Dombart and A. Kalb. CCL 47-48. Turnhout, Belgium: Brepols, 1955. Cl. 0313.

———."De divinatione daemonum." In *Sancti Aureli Augustini opera.* Edited by J. Zycha. CSEL 41, pp. 599-618. Vienna, Austria: F. Tempsky; Leipzig, Germany: G. Freytag, 1900. Cl. 0306.

———. "De doctrina christiana." In *Opera.* Edited by J. Martin. CCL 32, cols. 1-167. Turnhout, Belgium: Brepols, 1962. Cl. 0263.

———. "De fide rerum invisibilium." In *Sancti Aureli Augustini opera.* Edited by M. P. J. van den Hout. CCL 46, pp. 1-19. Turnhout, Belgium: Brepols, 1969. Cl. 0292.

———. "De gratia et libero arbitrio." In *Opera omnia.* Edited by J.-P. Migne. PL 44, cols. 881-912. Paris: Migne, 1845. Cl. 0352.

———."De nuptiis et concupiscentia." In *Sancti Aureli Augustini opera.* Edited by C. F. Verba and J. Zycha. CSEL 42, pp. 211-319. Vienna, Austria: F. Tempsky; Leipzig, Germany: G. Freytag, 1902. Cl. 0350.

———."De sermone Domini in monte." In *Sancti Aureli Augustini opera.* Edited by A Mutzenbecher. CCL 35, pp. 1-188. Turnhout, Belgium: Brepols, 1967. Cl. 0274.

———."Enchiridion de fide, spe et caritate." In *Sancti Aureli Augustini opera.* Edited by E. Evans. CCL 46, pp. 49-114. Turnhout, Belgium: Brepols, 1969. Cl. 0295.

———. *Enarrationes in Psalmos*, 3 vols. Edited by E. Dekkers and J. Fraipont. CCL 38, 39 and 40. Turnhout, Belgium: Brepols, 1956. Cl. 0283.

———. "Epistulae." In *Sancti Aureli Augustini opera.* Edited by A. Goldbacher. CCL 34, pts. 1, 2; 44; 57; 58. Vienna, Austria: F. Tempsky, 1895-1898. Cl. 0262.

———. *In Johannis evangelium tractatus.* Edited by R. Willems. CCL 36. Turnhout, Belgium: Brepols, 1954. Cl. 0278.

———. *Sermones.* Edited by J.-P. Migne. PL 38 and 39. Paris: Migne, 1844-1864. Cl. 0284.

Basil the Great. "Asceticon magnum sive Quaestiones [regulae brevius tractatae]." In *Opera omnia.* Edited by J.-P. Migne. PG 31, cols. 1052-1305. Paris: Migne, 1885. TLG 2040.050.

———. "De baptismo libri duo." In *Opera omnia.* Edited by J.-P. Migne. PG 31, cols. 1513-1628. Paris: Migne, 1885. TLG 2040.052.

———. "Epistulae." In *Saint Basile: Lettres*, vol. 2, pp. 101-218; vol. 3, pp. 1-229. Edited by Y. Courtonne. Paris: Les Belles Lettres, 1961-1966. TLG 2040.004.

———. "Homilia de misericordia et judicio." In *Opera omnia.* Edited by J.-P. Migne. PG 31, cols. 1705-14. Paris: Migne, 1885. TLG 2040.069.

———. "Homiliae super Psalmos." In *Opera omnia.* Edited by J.-P. Migne. PG 29, cols. 209-494. Paris: Migne, 1886. TLG 2040.018.

———. "Prologus 4 [prooemium in asceticum magnum]." In *Opera omnia.* Edited by J.-P. Migne. PG 31, cols. 889-901. Paris: Migne, 1885. TLG 2040.047.

Bede. "De tabernaculo et vasis eius ac vestibus sacerdotum libri iii." In *Bedae Venerabilis opera.* Edited by D. Hurst. CCL 119A, pp. 5-139. Turnhout, Belgium: Brepols, 1969. Cl. 1345.

———. "Expositio actuum apostolorum." In *Bedae Venerabilis opera*, pp. 3-99. Edited by D. Hurst. CCL

121. Turnhout, Belgium: Brepols, 1953. Cl. 1357.

————. "Homiliarum evangelii libri ii." In *Bedae Venerabilis opera*. Edited by D. Hurst. CCL 122, pp. 1-378. Turnhout, Belgium: Brepols, 1956. Cl. 1367.

————. "In epistulam septem catholicas." In *Bedae Venerabilis opera*, pp. 181-342. Edited by D. Hurst. CCL 121. Turnhout, Belgium: Brepols, 1953. Cl. 1362.

Braulio of Saragossa. "Epistolae." In *Opera omnia*. Edited by J.-P. Migne. PL 80, cols. 639-700. Paris: Migne, 1863.

————. "Vita s. Aemiliani confessoris." In *Opera omnia*. Edited by J.-P. Migne. PL 80, cols. 699-714. Paris: Migne, 1863.

Caesarius of Arles. *Sermones*. Edited by G. Morin. CCSL 103 and 104. Turnhout, Belgium: Brepols, 1953. Cl. 1008.

Cassian, John. *Collationes*. Edited by M. Petscheig. CSEL 13. Vienna, Austria: F. Tempsky; Leipzig, Germany: G. Freytag, 1886. Cl. 0512.

Cassiodorus. *Expositio psalmorum*. Edited by M. Adriaen. 2 vols. CCL 97 and 98. Turnhout: Brepols, 1958. Cl. 0900.

Clement of Alexandria.

————. "Paedagogus." In *Le pédagogue [par] Clement d'Alexandrie*. 3 vols. Edited by M. Harl, H. Marrou, C. Matray and C. Mondésert. SC 70, pp. 108-294; SC 108, pp. 10-242; SC 158, pp. 12-190. Paris: Cerf, 1960-1970. TLG 0555.002.

————. "Protrepticus." In *Clément d'Alexandrie. Le protreptique*. 2nd ed. Edited by C. Mondésert. SC 2, pp, 52-193. Paris: Cerf, 1949. TLG 0555.001.

————. "Quis dives salvetur" In *Clemens Alexandrinus*, vol. 3. 2nd ed. Edited by O. Stählin, L. Früchtel and U. Treu. GCS 17, pp. 159-91. Berlin: Akademie-Verlag, 1970. TLG 0555.006.

————. "Stromata." In *Clemens Alexandrinus*, vol. 2. (3rd ed.); vol. 3. (2nd ed.). Edited by O. Stählin, L. Früchtel and U. Treu. GCS 15, pp. 3-518; GCS 17, pp. 3-102. Berlin: Akademie-Verlag, 1960-1970. TLG 0555.004.

Clement of Rome. "Epistula i ad Corinthios." In *Clément de Rome: Épître aux Corinthiens*. Edited by A. Jaubert. SC 167, pp. 98-204. Paris: Cerf, 1971. TLG 1271.001.

Constitutions of the Holy Apostles. ("Constitutiones apostolorum"). In *Les constitutions apostoliques*. 3 vols. Edited by M. Metzger. SC 320, pp. 100-338; SC 329, pp. 116-394; SC 336, pp. 18-310. Paris: Cerf, 1985-1987. TLG 2894.001.

Cyprian. "Ad Demetrianum." In *Sancti Cypriani episcopi opera: Pars II*. Edited by M. Simonetti. CCL 3A, pp. 35-51. Turnhout, Belgium: Brepols, 1976. Cl. 0046.

————. "Ad Quirinum." In *Sancti Cypriani episcopi opera: Pars I*. Edited by R. Weber and M. Bévenot. CCL 3, pp. 3-179. Turnhout, Belgium: Brepols, 1972. Cl. 0039.

————. "De bono patientiae." In *Sancti Cypriani episcopi opera: Pars II*. Edited by M. Simonetti and C. Moreschini. CCL 3A, pp. 118-33. Turnhout, Belgium: Brepols, 1976. Cl. 0048.

————. "De dominica oratione." In *Sancti Cypriani episcopi opera: Pars II*. Edited by M. Simonetti and C. Moreschini. CCL 3A, pp. 87-113. Turnhout, Belgium: Brepols, 1976. Cl. 0043.

————. "De lapsis." In *Sancti Cypriani episcopi opera: Pars I*. Edited by R. Weber and M. Bévenot. CCL 3, pp. 221-42. Turnhout, Belgium: Brepols, 1972. Cl. 0042.

————. "Epistulae." In *Sancti Cypriani episcopi opera: Pars III:1-2*. Edited by G. F. Diercks. CCL 3B, 3C. Turnhout, Belgium: Brepols, 1994-1996. Cl. 0050.

Cyril of Alexandria. "Commentarius in xii prophetas minores." In *Sancti patris nostri Cyrilli archiepiscopi Alexandrini in xii prophetas*, vol. 1, pp. 1-740; vol. 2, pp. 1-626. Edited by P. E. Pusey. 2 vols. Oxford: Clarendon Press, 1868. Reprint, Brussels: Culture et Civilisation, 1965. TLG 4090. 001.

———. "Epistulae." In *Concilium universale Ephesenum*. Edited by E. Schwartz. Berlin: Walter De Gruyter, 1927. TLG 5000.001.

———. "Quod unus sit Christus." In *Cyrille d'Alexandrie. Deux dialogues christologiques*. Edited by G. M. de Durand. SC 97, pp. 302-514. Paris: Cerf, 1964. TLG 4090.027.

Cyril of Jeruslaem. "Catecheses ad illuminandos 1-18." In *Cyrilli Hierosolymorum archiepiscopi opera quae supersunt omnia*, vol. 1, pp. 28-320; vol. 2, pp. 2-342. 2 vols. Edited by W. C. Reischl and J. Rupp. Munich, Germany: Lentner, 1860 (repr. Hildesheim: Olms, 1967). TLG 2110.003.

Didache. In *Instructions des Apôtres*, pp. 226-242. Edited by J. P. Audet. Paris: Lecoffre, 1958. "Didache xii apostolorum." TLG 1311.001.

Ephrem the Syrian. "In Tatiani Diatessaron." In *Saint Éphrem: Commentaire de l'Evangile Concordant—Text Syriaque, (Ms Chester-Beatty 709), Folios Additionnels*. Edited by L. Leloir. Leuven and Paris, 1990.

———. Commentary on the Minor Prophets. In *Sancti patris nostri Ephraem Syri opera omnia*. Edited by J. A. Assemani. Rome, 1737.

Eugippus. *Vita sancti Severini*. Edited by P. Knöll. CSEL 9. Vienna, Austria: F. Tempsky; Leipzig, Germany: G. Freytag, 1886. Reprint, New York: Johnson Reprint, 1967.

Eusebius of Caesarea. "Demonstratio evangelica." In *Eusebius Werke, Band 6: Die Demonstratio evangelica*. Edited by I. A. Heikel. GCS 23, pp. 493-96. Leipzig, Germany: Hinrichs, 1913. TLG 2018.005.

———. "Historia ecclesiastica." In *Eusèbe de Césarée. Histoire ecclésiastique*. 3 vols. Edited by G. Bardy. SC 31, pp. 3-215; SC 41, pp. 4-231; SC 55, pp. 3-120. Paris: Èditions du Cerf, 1952-1958. TLG 2018.002.

Eznik of Kolb. *De Deo*. Traduction française, notes et tables par L. Mariès and Ch. Mercier. PO 28.3-4. Paris: Firmin-Didot, 1959.

Fulgentius of Ruspe. "Ad Euthymium de remissione peccatorum libri II." In *Sancti Fulgentii episcopi Ruspensis opera*. Edited by J. Fraipont. CCL 91A, pp. 649-707. Turnhout, Belgium: Brepols, 1968. Cl. 0821.

———. "Ad Monimum libri III." In *Sancti Fulgentii episcopi Ruspensis opera*. Edited by J. Fraipont. CCL 91, pp. 1-64. Turnhout, Belgium: Brepols, 1968. Cl. 0814.

———. *Epistulae XVIII*. In *Sancti Fulgentii episcopi Ruspensis opera*. 2 vols. Edited by J. Fraipont. CCL 91, pp. 189-273, 362-81, 387-444; and CCL 91A, 447-57, 563-624. Turnhout, Belgium: Brepols, 1968. Cl. 0817.

Gregory of Nazianzus. "Apologetica [orat. 2]." In *Opera omnia*. Edited by J.-P. Migne. PG 35, cols. 408-513. Paris: Migne, 1885. TLG 2022.016.

———. "Contra Arianos et de seipso [orat. 33]." In *Opera omnia*. Edited by J.-P. Migne. PG 36, cols. 213-37. Paris: Migne, 1886. TLG 2022.041.

———. "De filio [orat. 30]." In *Gregor von Nazianz. Die fünf theologischen Reden*, pp. 170-216. Edited by J. Barbel. Düsseldorf, Germany: Patmos-Verlag, 1963. TLG 2022.010.

———. "De spiritu sancto [orat. 31]." In *Gregor von Nazianz. Die fünf theologischen Reden*, pp. 218-76. Edited by J. Barbel. Düsseldorf, Germany: Patmos-Verlag, 1963. TLG 2022.011.

———. "Funebris oratio in laudem Basilii Magni Caesareae in Cappadocia episcopi [orat. 43]." In *Grégoire de Nazianze. Discours funèbres en l'honneur de son frère Césaire et de Basile de Césarée*, pp. 58-230. Edited by F. Boulenger. Paris: Picard, 1908. TLG 2022.006.

———. "Funebris in laudem Caesarii fratris oratio [orat. 7]." In *Grégoire de Nazianze. Discours funèbres en l'honneur de son frère Césaire et de Basile de Césarée*, pp. 2-56. Edited by F. Boulenger. Paris: Picard, 1908. TLG 2022.005.

———. "In Aegyptiorum adventum [orat. 34]." In *Opera omnia*. Edited by J.-P. Migne. PG 36, cols. 241-56. Paris: Migne, 1886. TLG 2022.042.

———. "In patrem tacentem [orat. 16]." In *Opera omnia*. Edited by J.-P. Migne. PG 35, cols. 933-64.

Paris: Migne, 1885. TLG 2022.029.

———. "In sanctum baptisma [orat. 40]." In *Opera omnia*. Edited by J.-P. Migne. PG 36, cols. 360-425. Paris: Migne, 1886. TLG 2022.048.

———. "In sancta lumina [orat. 39]." In *Opera omnia*. Edited by J.-P. Migne. PG 36, cols. 336-60. Paris: Migne, 1886. TLG 2022.047.

———. "In sanctum pascha [orat. 45]." In *Opera omnia*. Edited by J.-P. Migne. PG 36, cols. 624-64. Paris: Migne, 1886. TLG 2022.052.

Gregory of Nyssa. "Contra Eunomium." In *Gregorii Nysseni opera*, vol. 1.1, pp. 3-409; vol. 2.2, pp. 3-311. Edited by W. Jaeger. 2 vols. Leiden: Brill, 1960. TLG 2017.030.

———. "De virginitate." In *Grégoire de Nysse. Traité de la virginité*. Edited by M. Aubineau. SC 119, pp. 246-560. Paris: Cerf, 1966. TLG 2017.043.

———. "In diem luminum [*vulgo* In baptismum Christi oratio]." In *Gregorii Nysseni opera*, vol. 9.1, pp. 221-42. Edited by E. Gebhardt. Leiden: Brill, 1967. TLG 2017.014.

———. "In inscriptiones Psalmorum." In *Gregorii Nysseni opera*, vol. 5, pp. 24-175. Edited by J. McDonough. Leiden: Brill, 1962. TLG 2017.027.

———. "Oratio catechetica magna." In *The Catechetical Oration of Gregory of Nyssa*, pp. 1-164. Edited by J. Srawley. Cambridge: Cambridge University Press, 1903. Reprint, 1956. TLG 2017.046.

Gregory Thaumaturgus. "In annuntiationem sanctae virginis Mariae [homiliae 1-2]." In *Opera omnia*. Edited by J.-P. Migne. PG 10, cols. 1145-69. Paris: Migne, 1857. TLG 2063.009.

Gregory the Great. "Homiliarum xl in evangelica." In *Opera omnia*. Edited by J.-P. Migne. PL 76, cols 1075-1312. Paris: Migne, 1857. Cl. 1711.

———. *Moralia in Job*. Edited by D. Norbery. CCL 143A and 143B. Turnhout, Belgium: Typographi Brepols Editores Pontificii, 1953. Cl. 1708.

———. *Regula pastoralis*. Edited by F. Rommel and R. W. Clement. CCL 141. Turnhout, Belgium: Typographi Brepols Editores Pontificii, 1953. Cl. 1712.

Hilary of Poitiers. *De trinitate*. Edited by P. Smulders. CCL 62 and 62A. Turnhout, Belgium: Brepols, 1979-1980. Cl. 0433.

Hippolytus. "Contra haeresin Noeti." In *Hippolytus of Rome. Contra Noetum*, pp. 43-93. Edited by R. Butterworth. London: Heythrop College (University of London), 1977. TLG 2115.002.

———. "De antichristo." In *Hippolyt's kleinere exegetische und homiletische Schriften*. Edited by H. Achelis. GCS 1.2, pp. 1-47. Leipzig: Hinrichs, 1897. TLG 2115.003.

———. "De consummatione mundi." In *Hippolyt's kleinere exegetische und homiletische Schriften*. Edited by H. Achelis. GCS 1.2, pp. 289-309. Leipzig: Hinrichs, 1897. TLG 2115.029.

———. "De theophania." In *Hippolyt's kleinere exegetische und homiletische Schriften*. Edited by H. Achelis. GCS 1.2, pp. 257-63. Leipzig: Hinrichs, 1897. TLG 2115.026.

Horsiesi (Horsiesios). "Instructions." In *Oeuvres de s. Pachôme et de ses disciples*. Edited by L. T. Lefort. CSCO 159, pp. 66-79. Louvain: Durbecq, 1956.

Irenaeus. "Adversus haereses [liber 3]." In *Irénée de Lyon. Contre les hérésies, livre 3*, vol. 2. Edited by A. Rousseau and L. Doutreleau. SC 211, pp. 22-436. Paris: Cerf, 1974. TLG 1447.002.

Isaac of Nineveh. "Asketica." In *Mar Isaacus Ninivita. De perfectione religiosa*, pp. 1-99. Edited by P. Bedjan. Paris, 1966.

Isho'dad of Merv. *Isô'dâdh's Stellung in der Auslegungsgeschichte des Alten Testamentes an seinen Commentaren zu Hosea, Joel, Jona, Sacharja 9-14 und einigen angehängten Psalmen*. Edited by G. Diettrich. Giessen: J. Ricker, 1902.

Jerome. "Adversus Jovinianum." In *Opera omnia*. Edited by J.-P. Migne. PL 23, cols. 221-352. Paris: Migne, 1845. Cl. 0610.

———. "Apologia adversus libros Rufini." In *Contra Rufinum*. Edited by P. Lardet. CCL 79, pp. 1-72. Turnhout, Belgium: Brepols, 1982. Cl. 0613.

———. "Commentarii in Ezechielem." In *Commentariorum in Hiezechielem libri XIV; Commentariorum in Danielem libri III*. Edited by F. Glorie. CCL 75, pp. 3-743. Cl. 0587.

———. *Commentarii in prophetas minores*. 2 vols. Edited by M. Adriaen. CCL 76 and 76A. Turnhout, Belgium: 1969-1970. Cl. 0589.

———. *Dialogi contra Pelagianos libri iii*. Edited by C. Moreschini. CCL 80. Turnhout, Belgium: Brepols, 1990. Cl. 0615.

———. *Epistulae, Pars 1-3*. Edited by I. Hilberg. CSEL 54, 55 and 56. Vienna, Austria: F. Tempsky; Leipzig, Germany: G.F. Freytag, 1910-1918. Cl. 0620.

———. "Sermo de die epiphaniorum et de psalmo xxviii." In *S. Hieronymi presbyteri opera, Pars 1*. Edited by B. Capelle. CCL 78, pp. 530-32. Turnhout, Belgium: Brepols, 1958. Cl. 0599.

———. "Tractatus in librum psalmorum." In *S. Hieronymi presbyteri opera, Pars 2*. Edited by G. Morin. CCL 78, pp. 3-352. Turnhout, Belgium: Brepols, 1958. Cl. 0592.

———. "Tractatus in Marci evangelium." In *S. Hieronymi presbyteri opera, Pars 2*. Edited by G. Morin. CCL 78, pp. 449-500. Turnhout, Belgium: Brepols, 1958. Cl. 0594.

———. "Tractatuum in psalmos series altera." In *S. Hieronymi presbyteri opera, Pars 2*. Edited by G. Morin. CCL 78, pp. 355-446. Turnhout, Belgium: Brepols, 1958. Cl. 0593.

John Chrysostom. "Ad populam Antiochenum [homiliae 1-21]." In *Opera omnia*. Edited by J.-P. Migne. PG 49, cols. 15-222. Paris: Migne, 1862. TLG 2062.024.

———. "Adversus Judaeos [orationes 1-8]." In *Opera omnia*. Edited by J.-P. Migne. PG 48, cols. 843-942. Paris: Migne, 1859. TLG 2062.021.

———. "Commentarius in Job [prooemium tantum]." In *Opera omnia*. Edited by J.-P. Migne. PG 64, cols. 504-6. Paris: Migne, 1862. TLG 2062.183.

———. "Contra Anomoeos [homiliae 1-5]: De incomprehensibili dei natura." In *Jean Chrysostome. Sur l'incompréhensibilité de Dieu*. Edited by F. Cavallera, J. Daniélou and R. Flaceliere. SC 28, pp. 92-322. Paris: Cerf, 1951. TLG 2062.012.

———. "Contra Anomoeos [homilia 7]: De consubstantiali." In *Opera omnia*. Edited by J.-P. Migne. PG 48, cols. 755-68. Paris: Migne, 1859. TLG 2062.015.

———. "Contra Anomoeos [homilia 12]: De Christi divinitate." In *Opera omnia*. Edited by J.-P. Migne. PG 48, cols. 801-12. Paris: Migne, 1859. TLG 2062.020.

———. "Daemones non gubernare mundum." In *Georgii monachi chronicon*, vol.1, pp. 108-12. Edited by C. de Boor. Leipzig: Teubner, 1904. Reprint, Stuttgart: Wirth, 1978. TLG 2062.x15.

———. "De Lazaro et divite [sp.]." In *Opera omnia*. Edited by J.-P. Migne. PG 59, cols. 591-96. Paris: Migne, 1859. TLG 2062.244.

———. "De paenitentia [homiliae 1-9]." In *Opera omnia*. Edited by J.-P. Migne. PG 49, cols. 277-350. Paris: Migne, 1862. TLG 2062.027.

———. "De sacerdotio." In *Jean Chrysostome. Sur le sacerdoce*. Edited by A.-M. Malingrey. SC 272, pp. 60-372. Paris: Cerf, 1980. TLG 2062.085.

———. "In Acta apostolorum [homiliae 1-55]." In *Opera omnia*. Edited by J.-P. Migne. PG 60, pp. 13-384. Paris: Migne, 1862. TLG 2062.154.

———. "In epistulam ad Galatas commentarius." In *Opera omnia*. Edited by J.-P. Migne. PG 61, cols. 611-82. Paris: Migne, 1859. TLG 2062.158.

———. "In epistulam ii ad Corinthios [homiliae 1-30]." In *Opera omnia*. Edited by J.-P. Migne. PG 61, cols. 381-610. Paris: Migne, 1859. TLG 2062.157.

———. "In epistulam ad Romanos." In *Opera omnia*. Edited by J.-P. Migne. PG 60, cols. 391-682. Paris:

Migne, 1862. TLG 2062.155.

———. "In epistulam i ad Timotheum [homiliae 1-18]." In *Opera omnia*. Edited by J.-P. Migne. PG 62, cols. 501-600. Paris: Migne, 1862. TLG 2062.164.

———. "In Genesim [homiliae 1-67]." In *Opera omnia*. Edited by J.-P. Migne. PG 53, cols. 21-385; PG 54, cols. 385-580. Paris: Migne, 1862. TLG 2062.112.

———. "In Joannem [homiliae 1-88]." In *Opera omnia*. Edited by J.-P. Migne. PG 59, cols. 23-482. Paris: Migne, 1859. TLG 2062.153.

———. "In Matthaeum [homiliae 1-90]." In *Opera omnia*. Edited by J.-P. Migne. PG 57, cols. 13-472; PG 58, cols. 471-794. Paris: Migne, 1862. TLG 2062.152.

———. "In paralyticum demissum per tectum" In *Opera omnia*. Edited by J.-P. Migne. PG 51, cols. 47-64. Paris: Migne, 1859. TLG 2062.063.

John of Antioch. "Epistulae." In *Acta conciliorum oecumenicorum*, vol. 1, pp. 151-52. Edited by E. Schwartz. Berlin and Leipzig: de Gruyter, 1914. TLG 5000.001.

John of Damascus. "Expositio fidei." In *Die Schriften des Johannes von Damaskos*, vol. 2, pp. 3-239. Edited by B. Kotter. Patristische Texte und Studien 12. Berlin: De Gruyter, 1973. TLG 2934.004.

Julian of Eclanum. "Tractatus prophetarum Osee." In *Expositio libri Job : Tractatus prophetarum Osee, Johel et Amos : accedunt operum deperditorum fragmenta post Albertum Bruckner denuo collecta aucta ordinata*. Edited by L. De Coninck. CCL 88, pp. 115-329. Turnhout: Brepols, 1977. Cl. 0776.

Justin Martyr. "Apologia." In *Die ältesten Apologeten*, pp. 26-77. Edited by E.J. Goodspeed. Göttingen, Germany: Vandenhoeck & Ruprecht, 1915. TLG 0645.001.

———. "Dialogus cum Tryphone" In *Die ältesten Apologeten*, pp. 90-265. Edited by E.J. Goodspeed. Göttingen, Germany: Vandenhoeck & Ruprecht, 1915. TLG 0645.003.

Lactantius. "Epitome divinarum institutionum." In *L. Caeli Firmiani Lactanti Opera omnia*. Edited by S. Brandt. CSEL 19, pp. 675-761. Vienna, Austria: F. Tempsky; Leipzig, Germany: G. Freytag, 1890. Cl. 0086.

Leo the Great. *Tractatus septem et nonaginta*. Edited by A. Chavasse. CCL 138 and 138A. Turnhout, Belgium: Brepols, 1973. Cl. 1657.

Martin of Braga. "Item de superbia." In *Martini episcopi Bracarensis Opera omnia*, pp. 69-73. Edited by C.W. Barlow. Papers and Monographs of the American Academy in Rome, 12. New Haven, Yale University Press, 1950.

Martyrius [Sahdona]. "Liber de perfectione." In *Martyrius (Sahdona): Oeuvres spirituelles*, part 3. Edited by A. de Halleux. CSCO 252 (Scriptores Syri 110). Louvain, Belgium: Secrétariat du Corpus Scriptorum Christianorum Orientalium, 1965.

Maximus of Turin. "Collectio sermonum antiqua." In *Maximi episcopi Taurinensis sermons*. Edited by Almut Mutzenbecher. CCL 23, pp. 1-364. Turnhout, Belgium: Brepols, 1962. Cl. 0219a.

Methodius. "Convivium decem virginum." In *Opera omnia*. Edited by J.-P. Migne. PG 18, cols. 27-220. Paris: Migne, 1857.

———. "De Symeone et Anna." In *Opera omnia*. Edited by J.-P. Migne. PG 18, cols. 347-82. Paris: Migne, 1857.

Novatian. "De cibis judaicis." In *Opera*. Edited by G. F. Diercks. CCL 4, pp. 89-101. Turnhout, Belgium: Brepols, 1972. Cl. 0068.

———. "De Trinitate." In *Opera*. Edited by G. F. Diercks. CCL 4, pp. 11-78. Turnhout, Belgium: Brepols, 1972. Cl. 0071.

Origen. "Commentarii in evangelium Joannis [lib. 19, 20, 28, 32]." In *Origenes Werke*, vol. 4. Edited by E. Preuschen. GCS 10, pp. 298-480. TLG 2042.079.

———. "Commentarium in evangelium Matthaei [lib.10-11]." In *Origène. Commentaire sur l'évangile selon*

Matthieu, vol. 1. Edited by R. Girod. SC 162, pp. 140-386. Paris: Cerf, 1970. TLG 2042.029.

———. "Commentarium in evangelium Matthaei [lib.12-17]." In *Origenes Werke*, vols. 10.1 and 10.2. Edited by E. Klostermann. GCS 40.1, pp. 69-304; GCS 40.2, pp. 305-703. Leipzig: Teubner, 1935-1937. TLG 2042.030.

———. "Contra Celsum." In *Origène Contre Celse*, 4 vols. Edited by M. Borret. SC 132, pp. 64-476; SC 136, pp. 14-434; SC 147, pp. 14-382; SC 150, pp. 14-352. Paris: Éditions du Cerf, 1967-1969. TLG 2042.001.

———. "De principiis." In *Origenes vier Bücher von den Prinzipien*, pp. 462-560, 668-764. Edited by H. Görgemanns and H. Karpp. Darmstadt, Germany: Wissenschaftliche Buchgesellschaft, 1967. TLG 2042.002.

———. "Exhortatio ad martyrium." In *Origenes Werke*, vol. 1. Edited by P. Koetschau. GCS 2, pp. 3-47. Leipzig, Germany: Hinrichs, 1899. TLG 2042.007.

———. "Fragmenta in Jeremiam." In *Origenes Werke*, vol. 3. Edited by E. Klostermann. GCS 6, pp. 195-98. Berlin: Akademie-Verlag, 1901. TLG 2042.084.

———. "Fragmenta ex commentariis in evangelium Matthaei." In *Origenes Werke*, vol. 12. Edited by E. Klostermann and E. Benz. GCS 41.1, pp. 3-235. Leipzig: Teubner, 1941. TLG 2042.031.

———. "Homiliae in Exodum." In *Origenes Werke*, vol. 6. Edited by W. A. Baehrens. GCS 29, pp. 217-18, 221-30. Leipzig: Teubner, 1920. TLG 2042.023.

———. "Homiliae in Genesim [fragmenta]." In *Origenes Werke*, vol. 6. Edited by W. A. Baehrens. GCS 29, pp. 23-30. Leipzig: Teubner, 1920. TLG 2042.022.

———. "Homiliae in Leviticum." In *Origenes Werke*, vol. 6. Edited by W. A. Baehrens. GCS 29, pp. 332-34, 395, 402-7, 409-16 Leipzig: Teubner, 1920. TLG 2042.024.

———. "Homiliae in Lucam." In *Opera omnia*. Edited by J.-P. Migne. PG 13, cols. 1799-1902. Paris: Migne, 1862. TLG 2042.016.

———. "In Jeremiam [homiliae 12-20]." In *Origenes Werke*, vol. 3. Edited by E. Klostermann. GCS 6, pp. 85-194. Berlin: Akademie-Verlag, 1901. TLG 2042.021.

Pachomius. "Catecheses." In *Oeuvres de s. Pachôme et de ses disciples*. Edited by L. T. Lefort. CSCO 159, pp. 1-26. Louvain: Imprimerie Orientaliste, 1956.

———. "Vita Pachomii." *Le corpus athénien de saint Pachome*, pp. 11-72. Edited by F. Halkin. Cahiers d'Orientalisme 2. Genève: Cramer, 1982.

Pacian of Barcelona. "De paenitentibus." In *Opera omnia*. Edited by J.-P. Migne. PL 13, cols. 1081-88. Paris: Migne, 1849.

Paulinus of Nola. "Carmina." In *S. Pontii Meropii Paulini Nolani opera*. Edited by W. Hartel. CSEL 30, pp. 1-3, 7-329. Vienna: F. Tempsky, 1894. Cl. 0203.

Paulus Orosius. "Liber apologeticus contra Pelagianos." In *Sancti Paulus Orosius opera*. Edited by C. Zangemeister. CSEL 5, pp. 603-64. Vienna: F. Tempsky, 1882. Cl. 0572.

Peter Chrysologus. *Sermonum collectio a Felice episcopo parata, sermonibus extravagantibus adiectis*, 3 vols. Edited by A. Olivar. CCL 24, 24A and 24B. Turnhout: Brepols, 1975-1982. Cl. 0227.

Pseudo-Barnabas. "Barnabasbrief." In *Die apostolieschen Väter*, pp. 10-34. Edited by K. Bihlmeyer. Tübingen: J. C. B. Mohr, 1924.

Pseudo-Clement of Rome. "Sog. zweiter Klemensbrief." In *Die apostolischen Väter*, pp. 71-81. Edited by K. Bihlmeyer. Tübingen: J .C. B. Mohr, 1924.

Pseudo-Dionysius. "De caelesti hierarchia." In *Denys l' Aréopagite: La hiérarchie céleste*. Edited by R. Roques, G. Heil and M. de Gandillac. SC 58, pp. 70-225. Paris: Éditions du Cerf, 1958. Reprint, 1970. TLG 2798.001

Rufinus. "Commentarius in symbolum apostolorum." In *Opera omnia*. Edited by J.-P. Migne. PL 21, cols.

335-86. Paris: Migne, 1849.

Salvian the Presbyter. "De gubernatione Dei." In *Ouvres*, vol. 2. Edited by G. LaGarrigue. SC 220, pp. 96-527. Paris: Éditions du Cerf, 1975. Cl. 0485.

———. "Epistolae." In *Salviani presbyteri massiliensis*. Edited by F. Pauly. CSEL 8, pp. 201-23. Vienna, Austria: F. Tempsky; Leipzig, Germany: G. Freytag, 1883. Reprint, New York: Johnson Reprint, 1983.

Symeon the New Theologian. "Capita practica et theologica." In *Opera Symeonis Junioris*. Edited by J.-P. Migne. PG 120, col. 604. Paris: Migne, 1864.

Tertullian. "Ad uxorem." In *Opera*, vol. 1 Edited by E. Kroymann. CCL 1, pp. 373-94. Turnhout, Belgium: Brepols, 1954. Cl. 0012.

———. "Adversus Judaeos." In *Opera*, vol. 2. Edited by E. Kroymann. CCL 2, pp. 1339-96. Turnhout, Belgium: Brepols, 1954. Cl. 0033.

———. "Adversus Marcionem." In *Opera*, vol. 1. Edited by E. Kroymann. CCL 1, pp. 441-726. Turnhout, Belgium: Brepols, 1954. 0014.

———. "De anima." In *Opera*. Edited by J. H. Waszink. CCL 2, pp. 781-869. Turnhout, Belgium: Brepols, 1954. Cl. 0017.

———. "De fuga in persecutione." In *Opera*, vol. 2 Edited by J. J. Thierry. CCL 2, pp. 1135-55. Turnhout, Belgium: Brepols, 1954. Cl. 0025.

———. "De idololatria" In *Opera*, vol. 2. Edited by A. Reifferscheid and G. Wissowa. CCL 2, pp. 1101-24. Turnhout, Belgium: Brepols, 1954. Cl. 0023.

———. "De paenitentia." In *Opera*, vol. 1. Edited by J. G. P. Borleffs. CCL 1, pp. 321-40. Turnhout, Belgium: Brepols, 1954. Cl. 0010.

———. "De pudicitia." In *Opera*, vol. 2. Edited by E. Dekkers. CCL 2, pp. 1281-330. Turnhout, Belgium: Brepols, 1954. Cl. 0030.

———. "De resurrectione mortuorum." In *Opera*, vol. 2. Edited by J. G. P. Borleffs. CCL 2, pp. 921-1012. Turnhout, Belgium: Brepols, 1954. Cl. 0019.

Theodore of Mopsuestia. "Explanatio in XII prophetas minores." In *Opera omnia*. Edited by J.-P. Migne. PG 81, cols. 1546-1988. Paris: Migne, 1864.

Theodoret of Cyr. "De providentia orationes decem." In *Opera omnia*. Edited by J.-P. Migne. PG 83, cols. 556-773. Paris: Migne: 1864. TLG 4089.032.

———. "Explanatio in XII prophetas minores." In *Opera omnia*. Edited by J.-P. Migne. PG 81, cols. 1546-1988. Paris: Migne, 1864.

———. "Historia ecclesiastica." In *Theodoret. Kirchengeschichte*. 2nd ed. Edited by L. Parmentier and F. Scheidweiler. GCS 44, pp. 1-349. Berlin: Akademie-Verlag, 1954. TLG 4089.003.

Theodotus the Valentinian. "Excerpta ex Theodoto." In *Eclogae propheticae*. Edited by Stählin, Früchtel and Treu. GCS 3, pp. 137-155. Berlin: Akademie-Verlag, 1970. TLG 0555.005.

Theophilus. "Epistula ad Hieronymum [exc. epist. Augustini] et scripta variorum auctorum." In *Sancti Eusebii Hieronymi Epistulae*. Edited by I. Hilberg. CSEL 55, p. 140. Vienna, Austria: F. Tempsky; Leipzig, Germany: G. Freytag, 1915. Cl. 0620°.

Theophylact. "Expositio in Oseam prophetam." In *Opera omnia*. Edited by J.-P. Migne. PG 126, cols. 575-818. Paris: Migne, 1864.

Valentinus. "Epistulae ad Augustinum Hipponensem et alios." In *S. Aureli Augustini Hipponiensis episcopi Epistulae*. Edited by A. Goldbacher. CSEL 57, p. 396-402. Cl. 0262°.

Victorinus of Petovium. "Fragmentum de fabrica mundi." *In Opera omnia*. Edited by J.-P Migne. PL 5, cols. 301-16. Paris: Migne, 1844.

———. "Scholia in Apocalypsin Joannis." In *Opera omnia*. Edited by J.-P Migne. PL 5, cols. 317-44. Paris: Migne, 1844.

Bibliography of Works
in English Translation

Ambrose. *Funeral Orations*. Translated by Leo P. McCauley et al. FC 22. Washington, D.C.: The Catholic University of America Press, 1953.

———. *Hexameron, Paradise, and Cain and Abel*. Translated by John J. Savage. FC 42. Washington, D.C.: The Catholic University of America Press, 1961.

———. *Letters*. Translated by Mary Melchior Beyenka. FC 26. Washington, D.C.: The Catholic University of America Press, 1954.

———. *The Minor Prophets: A Commentary*. Vol. 2. Edited by E. B. Pusey. Grand Rapids, Mich.: Baker, 1972.

———. *Select Works and Letters*, pp. 327-60. Translated by H. De Romestin. NPNF 10. Series 2. Edited by Philip Schaff and Henry Wace. 14 vols. 1886-1900. Reprint, Peabody, Mass.: Hendrickson, 1994.

———. *Seven Exegetical Works*. Translated by Michael P. McHugh. FC 65. Washington, D.C.: The Catholic University of America Press, 1972.

Aphrahat. "Demonstration 4." In *The Syriac Fathers on Prayer and the Spiritual Life*, pp. 1-28. Translated by Sebastian Brock. CS 101. Kalamazoo, Mich.: Cistercian Publications, 1987.

———. "Select Demonstrations." In *Gregory the Great, Ephraim Syrus, Aphrahat*, pp. 345-412. Translated by James Barmby. NPNF 13. Series 2. Edited by Philip Schaff and Henry Wace. 14 vols. 1886-1900. Reprint, Peabody, Mass.: Hendrickson, 1994.

[Apostolic Constitutions]. "Constitutions of the Holy Apostles." In *Lactantius, Venantius, Asterius, Victorinus, Dionysius, Apostolic Teaching and Constitutions, 2 Clement, Early Liturgies*, pp. 391-505. Edited with notes by James Donaldson. ANF 7. Edited by Alexander Roberts and James Donaldson. 10 vols. 1885-1887. Reprint, Peabody, Mass.: Hendrickson, 1994.

Athanasius. "Life of St. Anthony." In *Early Christian Biographies*, pp. 133-216. Edited by Roy J. Deferrari. FC 15. Washington, D.C.: The Catholic University of America Press, 1952.

———. *The Resurrection Letters*. Paraphrased and introduced by Jack N. Sparks. Nashville: Thomas Nelson, 1979.

———. *Selected Works and Letters*. Translated by Archibald Robertson. NPNF 4. Series 2. Edited by Philip Schaff and Henry Wace. 14 vols. 1886-1900. Reprint, Peabody, Mass.: Hendrickson, 1994.

Augustine. *Against Julian*. Translated by Matthew A. Schumacher. FC 35. Washington, D.C.: The Catholic University of America Press, 1957.

———. *Anti-Pelagian Works*. Translated by Peter Holmes and Robert Ernest Wallis. NPNF 5. Series 1. Edited by Philip Schaff. 14 vols. 1886-1889. Reprint, Peabody, Mass.: Hendrickson, 1994.

———. *The City of God*. Translated by Marcus Dods. NPNF 2. Series 1. Edited by Philip Schaff. 14 vols. 1886-1889. Reprint, Peabody, Mass.: Hendrickson, 1994.

———. *The City of God: Books VIII-XVI*. Translated by Gerald G. Walsh and Grace Monahan. FC 14. Washington, D.C.: The Catholic University of America Press, 1952.

———. *The City of God: Books XVII-XXII*. Translated by Gerald G. Walsh and Daniel J. Honan. FC 24. Washington, D.C.: The Catholic University of America Press, 1954.

———. *Commentary on the Lord's Sermon on the Mount with Seventeen Related Sermons*. Translated by Denis

J. Kavanagh. FC 11. Washington, D.C.: The Catholic University of America Press, 1951.

———. *Confessions*. Translated by Vernon J. Bourke. FC 21. Washington, D.C.: The Catholic University of America Press, 1953.

———. *Confessions and Enchiridion*. Translated and edited by Albert C. Outler. LCC 7. London: SCM Press, 1955.

———. *The Confessions of Augustine in Modern English*. Translated and abridged by Sherwood E. Wirt. Clarion Classics. Grand Rapids, Mich.: Zondervan, 1971.

———. "Enchiridion." In *Christian Instruction; Admonition and Grace; The Christian Combat; Faith, Hope and Charity*, pp. 369-472. Translated by Bernard M. Peebles. FC 2. Washington, D.C.: The Catholic University of America Press, 1947.

———. *Exposition of the Psalms, 33-50*. Translated by Maria Boulding. WSA 16. Part 3. Edited by John E. Rotelle. New York: New City Press, 2000.

———. *Expositions on the Book of Psalms*. Edited and annotated by A. Cleveland Coxe. NPNF 8. Series 1. Edited by Philip Schaff. 14 vols. 1886-1889. Reprint, Peabody, Mass.: Hendrickson, 1994.

———. *Letters*. Translated by Sister Wilfrid Parsons. FC 18, 20 and 30. 3 vols. Washington, D.C.: The Catholic University of America Press, 1953-1955.

———. "On Baptism." In *The Writings Against the Manichaeans, and Against the Donatists*, pp. 411-514. Translated by J. R. King. NPNF 4. Series 1. Edited by Philip Schaff. 14 vols. 1886-1889. Reprint, Peabody, Mass.: Hendrickson, 1994.

———. *On Christian Doctrine*. Translated by D. W. Robertson Jr. Library of Liberal Arts. Indianapolis: Bobbs-Merrill, 1958.

———. "On Faith in Things Unseen." In *The Immortality of the Soul; The Magnitude of the Soul; On Music; The Advantage of Believing; On Faith in Things Unseen*, pp. 451-69. Translated by Roy Joseph Deferrari. FC 4. Washington, D.C.: The Catholic University of America Press, 1947.

———. *Sermon on the Mount, Harmony of the Gospel, Homilies on the Gospels*. Translated by David Schley Schaff et al. NPNF 6 Series 1. Edited by Philip Schaff. 14 vols. 1886-1889. Reprint, Peabody, Mass.: Hendrickson, 1994.

———. *Sermons*. Translated by Edmund Hill. 4 vols. WSA 2, 4, 6 and 10. Part 3. Edited by John E. Rotelle. New York: New City Press, 1990-1995.

———. *Tractates on the Gospel of John 11-54*. Translated by John W. Rettig. 2 vols. FC 79 and 88. Washington, D.C.: The Catholic University of America Press, 1988, 1993.

———. *Treatises on Marriage and Other Subjects*. Translated by Charles T. Wilcox et al. FC 27. Washington, D.C.: The Catholic University of America, 1955.

Basil the Great. *Ascetic Works*. Translated by M. Monica Wagner. FC 9. New York: Fathers of the Church, Inc., 1950.

———. *Exegetic Homilies*. Translated by Agnes C. Way. FC 46. Washington, D.C.: The Catholic University of America Press, 1963.

———. *Letters*. Translated by Agnes C. Way. 2 vols. FC 13 and 28. Washington, D.C.: The Catholic University of America Press, 1951, 1955.

———. *Letters and Select Works*. Translated by Blomfield Jackson. NPNF 8. Series 2. Edited by Philip Schaff and Henry Wace. 14 vols. 1886-1900. Reprint, Peabody, Mass.: Hendrickson, 1994.

Bede. *Commentary on the Acts of the Apostles*. Translated with an introduction and notes by Lawrence T. Martin. CS 117. Kalamazoo, Mich.: Cistercian Publications, 1989.

———. *Commentary on the Seven Catholic Epistles*. Translated by David Hurst. CS 82. Kalamazoo, Mich.: Cistercian Publications, 1985.

———. *Homilies on the Gospels: Book One*. Translated by Lawrence T. Martin and David Hurst. CS 110.

Kalamazoo, Mich.: Cistercian Publications, 1991.

———. *On the Tabernacle*. Translated with notes and introduction by Arthur G. Holder. TTH 18. Liverpool: Liverpool University Press, 1994.

Braulio of Saragossa. "Braulio of Saragossa." In *Iberian Fathers. Volume 2: Braulio of Saragossa, Fructuosus of Braga*, pp. 3-142. Translated by Claude W. Barlow. FC 63. Washington, D.C.: The Catholic University of America Press, 1969.

Caesarius of Arles. *Sermons*. Translated by Mary Magdeleine Mueller. 3 vols. FC 31, 47 and 66. Washington, D.C.: The Catholic University of America Press, 1956-1973.

Cassian, John. "Conferences." In *Western Asceticism*, pp. 190-289. Translated by Owen Chadwick. LCC 12. Philadelphia: Westminster Press, 1958.

———. *The Conferences*. Translated and annotated by Boniface Ramsey. ACW 57. New York: Paulist, 1997.

Cassiodorus. *Explanation of the Psalms*. Translated by P. G. Walsh. 3 vols. ACW 51, 52 and 53. New York: Paulist, 1990-1991.

Clement of Alexandria. *Christ the Educator*. Translated by Simon P. Wood. FC 23. Washington, D.C.: The Catholic University of America Press, 1954.

———. *Stromateis: Books 1-3*. Translated by John Ferguson. FC 85. Washington, D.C.: The Catholic University of America Press, 1991.

[Clement of Alexandria]. *Fathers of the Second Century: Hermas, Tatian, Athenagoras, Theophilus, and Clement of Alexandria*. Translated by F. Crombie et al. ANF 2. Edited by Alexander Roberts and James Donaldson. 10 vols. 1885-1887. Reprint, Peabody, Mass.: Hendrickson, 1994.

Clement of Rome. "First Letter to the Corinthians." In *The Apostolic Fathers*, pp. 9-58. Translated by Francis X. Glimm et al. FC 1. New York: Christian Heritage, 1947.

[Clement of Rome]. "1 Clement." In *Gospel of Peter, Diatessaron, Testament of Abraham, Epistles of Clement, Origen, Miscellaneous Works*, pp. 227-56. Translated by John Keith. ANF 9. Edited by Allan Menzies. 10 vols. 1885-1887. Reprint, Peabody, Mass.: Hendrickson, 1994.

Cyprian. *Letters 1-81*. Translated by Rose Bernard Donna. FC 51. Washington, D.C.: The Catholic University of America Press, 1964.

———. *Treatises*. Translated and edited by Roy J. Deferrari. FC 36. Washington, D.C.: The Catholic University of America Press, 1958.

[Cyprian]. "Cyprian." In *Fathers of the Third Century: Hippolytus, Cyprian, Caius, Novatian, Appendix*, pp. 267-596. Translated by Ernest Wallis. ANF 5. Edited by Alexander Roberts and James Donaldson. 10 vols. 1885-1887. 10 vols. Reprint, Peabody, Mass.: Hendrickson, 1994.

Cyril of Alexandria. *Letters 1-50*. Translated by John I. McEnerney. FC 76. Washington, D.C.: The Catholic University of America Press, 1985.

———. *Long-Suffering Love: A Commentary on Hosea with Patristic Annotations*. Translated by Eugen J. Pentiuc. Brookline, Mass.: Holy Cross Orthodox Press, 2002.

———. *The Minor Prophets: A Commentary*. Edited by E. B. Pusey. 2 vols. Grand Rapids, Mich.: Baker, 1971-1972.

———. *On the Unity of Christ*. Translated by Catharine P. Roth. New York: St. Vladimir's Seminary Press, 1984.

Cyril of Jerusalem. "Catechetical Lectures." In *Cyril of Jerusalem and Nemesius of Emesa*, pp. 64-199. Edited by William Telfer. LCC 4. Philadelphia: Westminster Press, 1955.

———. "Catechetical Lectures." In *S. Cyril of Jerusalem, S. Gregory Nazianzen*, pp. 1-202. Translated by Edward Hamilton Gifford et al. NPNF 7. Series 2. Edited by Philip Schaff and Henry Wace. 14 vols. 1886-1900. Reprint, Peabody, Mass.: Hendrickson, 1994.

[Cyril of Jerusalem]. *The Works of Saint Cyril of Jerusalem*. Translated by Leo P. McCauley and Anthony A. Stephenson. 2 vols. FC 61 and 64. Washington, D.C.: The Catholic University of America Press, 1969-1970.

Didache. In The Apostolic Fathers, pp. 171-84. Translated by Francis X. Glimm et al. FC 1. New York: Christian Heritage, Inc., 1947.

[Ephrem the Syrian]. *Saint Ephrem's Commentary on Tatian's Diatessaron*. Translated by Carmel McCarthy. Journal of Semitic Studies Supplement 2. Oxford: Oxford University Press, 1993.

Epistle of Barnabas. In *The Apostolic Fathers*, pp. 191-222. Translated by Francis X. Glimm et al. FC 1. New York: Christian Heritage, 1947.

Eugippius. *The Life of St. Severin*. Translated by Ludwig Bieler. FC 55. Washington, D.C.: The Catholic University of America Press, 1965.

Eusebius of Caesaria. *Ecclesiastical History (Books 6-10)*. Translated by Roy J. Deferrari. FC 29. Washington, D.C.: The Catholic University of America Press, 1955.

———. *Proof of the Gospel*. Translated by W. J. Ferrar. London: SPCK, 1920. Reprint, Grand Rapids, Mich.: Baker, 1981.

[Eznik of Kolb]. *A Treatise on God Written in Armenian by Eznik of Kolb*. Translated by Monica J. Blanchard and Robin Darling Young. Leuven: Peeters, 1998.

Fulgentius of Ruspe. *Selected Works*. Translated by Robert B. Eno. FC 95. Washington, D.C.: The Catholic University of America Press, 1997.

Gregory of Nazianzus. "Orations." In *Cyril of Jerusalem, Gregory of Nazianzen*. Translated by Charles Gordon Browne et al. NPNF 7. Series 2. Edited by Philip Schaff and Henry Wace. 14 vols. 1886-1900. Reprint, Peabody, Mass.: Hendrickson, 1994.

———. "Orations." In *Funeral Orations by Saint Gregory Nazianzen and Saint Ambrose*, pp. 5-156. Translated by Leo P. McCauley et al. FC 22. Washington, D.C.: The Catholic University of America Press, 1953.

[Gregory of Nazianzus]. *Faith Gives Fullness to Reasoning: The Five Theological Orations of Gregory Nazianzen*. Translated by Lionel Wickham and Frederick Williams, with introduction and commentary by Frederick W. Norris. Leiden: E.J. Brill, 1991.

Gregory of Nyssa. *Ascetical Works*. Translated by Virginia Woods Callahan. FC 58. Washington, D.C.: The Catholic University of America Press, 1967.

———. "Address on Religious Instruction." In *Christology of the Later Fathers*, pp. 268-325. Edited and translated by Cyril C. Richardson. LCC 3. Philadelphia: Westminster Press, 1954.

[Gregory of Nyssa]. *Gregory of Nyssa's Treatise on the Inscriptions of the Psalms*. Translated by Ronald E. Heine. Oxford Early Christian Studies. Oxford: Clarendon Press, 1995.

———. *Select Writings and Letters of Gregory, Bishop of Nyssa*. Translated by William Moore and Henry Austin Wilson. NPNF 5. Series 2. Edited by Philip Schaff and Henry Wace. 14 vols. 1886-1900. Reprint, Peabody, Mass.: Hendrickson, 1994.

Gregory Thaumaturgus. "On the Annunciation of the Holy Virgin Mary." In *Gregory Thaumaturgus, Dionysius the Great, Julius Africanus, Anatolius and Minor Writers, Methodius, Arnobius*, pp. 7-79. Translated by S. D. F. Salmond. ANF 6. Edited by Alexander Roberts and James Donaldson. 10 vols. 1885-1887. Reprint, Peabody, Mass.: Hendrickson, 1994.

Gregory the Great. *Forty Gospel Homilies*. Translated by David Hurst. CS 123. Kalamazoo, Mich.: Cistercian Publications, 1990.

———. *Morals on the Book of Job*. Translated by Members of the English Church. LF 18, 21 and 23. 3 vols. Oxford: John Henry Parker, 1844-1850.

———. *Pastoral Care*. Translated and annotated by Henry Davis. ACW 11. New York: Paulist, 1978.

———. *Pastoral Rule and Selected Epistles*. Translated by James Barmby. NPNF 12. Series 2. Edited by

Philip Schaff and Henry Wace. 14 vols. 1886-1900. Reprint, Peabody, Mass.: Hendrickson, 1994.

Hilary of Poitiers. *The Trinity*. Translated by Stephen McKenna. FC 25. Washington, D.C.: The Catholic University of America Press, 1954.

———. *Select Works*. Translated by E. W. Watson et al. NPNF 9. Series 2. Edited by Philip Schaff and Henry Wace. 14 vols. 1886-1900. Reprint, Peabody, Mass.: Hendrickson, 1994.

[Hippolytus]. "Hippolytus." In *Fathers of the Third Century: Hippolytus, Cyprian, Caius, Novatian, Appendix*, pp. 9-266. Translated by J.H. MacMahon et al. ANF 5. Edited by Alexander Roberts and James Donaldson. 10 vols. 1885-1887. Reprint, Peabody, Mass.: Hendrickson, 1994.

Horsiesi (Horsiesios). "Instructions." In *Pachonian Koinonia: Volume Three*, pp. 135-52. Translated with an introduction by Armand Veilleux. CS 47. Kalamazoo, Mich.: Cistercian Publications, 1982.

Irenaeus. "Against Heresies." In *The Apostolic Fathers, Justin Martyr, Irenaeus*, pp. 315-567. ANF 1. Translated by M. Dods. Edited by Alexander Roberts and James Donaldson. 10 vols. 1885-1887. Reprint, Peabody, Mass.: Hendrickson, 1994.

———. "Against Heresies." In *Long-Suffering Love: A Commentary on Hosea with Patristic Annotation*. Translated by Eugen J. Pentiuc. Brookline, Mass.: Holy Cross Orthodox Press, 2002.

Isaac of Nineveh. *On Ascetical Life*. Translated by Mary Hansbury. Crestwood, N.Y.: St. Vladimir's Seminary Press, 1989.

Jerome. "Commentary on Hosea." In *Long-Suffering Love: A Commentary on Hosea with Patristic Annotations*. Translated by Eugen J. Pentiuc. Brookline, Mass.: Holy Cross Orthodox Press, 2002.

———. *Dogmatic and Polemical Works*. Translated by John N. Hritzu. FC 53. Washington, D.C.: The Catholic University of America Press, 1965.

———. "Letters." In *Early Latin Theology: Selections from Tertullian, Cyprian, Ambrose and Jerome*, pp 290-389. Translated by S. L. Greenslade. LCC 5. Philadelphia: Westminster Press, 1956.

———. *Letters and Select Works*. Translated by W. H. Fremantle. NPNF 6. Series 2. Edited by Philip Schaff and Henry Wace. 14 vols. 1886-1900. Reprint, Peabody, Mass.: Hendrickson, 1994.

———. *The Minor Prophets: A Commentary*. Edited by E.B. Pusey. 2 vols. Grand Rapids, Mich.: Baker, 1971, 1972.

[Jerome]. *The Homilies of Saint Jerome*. Translated by Marie Liguori Ewald. FC 48 and 57. 2 vols. Washington, D.C.: The Catholic University of America Press, 1964, 1966.

John Chrysostom. *Apologist*. Translated by Margaret A. Schatkin and Paul W. Harkins. FC 73. Washington, D.C.: The Catholic University of America Press, 1985.

———. *Commentary on Saint John the Apostle and Evangelist: Homilies 1-47*. Translated by Thomas Aquinas Goggin. FC 33. Washington, D.C.: The Catholic University of America Press, 1957.

———. *Discourses Against Judaizing Christians*. Translated by Paul W. Harkins. FC 68. Washington, D.C.: The Catholic University of America Press, 1979.

———. *Homilies on Galatians, Ephesians, Philippians, Colossians, Thessalonians, Timothy, Titus, and Philemon*. Translated by Gross Alexander et al. NPNF 13. Series 1. Edited by Philip Schaff. 14 vols. 1886-1889. Reprint, Peabody, Mass.: Hendrickson, 1994.

———. *Homilies on Genesis*. Translated by Robert C. Hill. FC 74, 82 and 87. 3 vols. Washington, D.C.: The Catholic University of America Press, 1986-1992.

———. *Homilies on the Acts of the Apostles and the Epistle to the Romans*. Translated by J. Walker, J. Sheppard and H. Browne. NPNF 11. Series 1. Edited by Philip Schaff. 14 vols. 1886-1889. Reprint, Peabody, Mass.: Hendrickson, 1994.

———. *Homilies on the Epistles of Paul to the Corinthians*. Translated by Talbot W. Chambers. NPNF 12. Series 1. Edited by Philip Schaff. 14 vols. 1886-1889. Reprint, Peabody, Mass.: Hendrickson, 1994.

———. *Homilies on the Gospel of Saint John and the Epistle to the Hebrews*. The Oxford translation edited and revised by Philip Schaff and Frederic Gardiner. NPNF 14. Series 1. Edited by Philip Schaff. 14 vols. 1886-1889. Reprint, Peabody, Mass.: Hendrickson, 1994.

―――. *Homilies on the Gospel of Saint Matthew.* The Oxford Translation. NPNF 10. Series 1. Edited by Philip Schaff. 14 vols. 1886-1889. Reprint, Peabody, Mass.: Hendrickson, 1994.

―――. *On Repentance and Almsgiving.* Translated by Gus George Christo. FC 96. Washington, D.C.: The Catholic University of America Press, 1998.

―――. *On the Incomprehensible Nature of God.* Translated by Paul W. Harkins. FC 72. Washington, D.C.: The Catholic University of America Press, 1984.

―――. *On the Priesthood, Ascetic Treatises, Select Homilies and Letters, Homilies on the Statues.* Translated by W. R. W. Stephens et al. NPNF 9. Series 1. Edited by Philip Schaff. 14 vols. 1886-1889. Reprint, Peabody, Mass.: Hendrickson, 1994.

―――. *On Wealth and Poverty.* Translated by Catharine P. Roth. New York: St. Vladimir's Seminary Press, 1984.

―――. *Six Books on the Priesthood.* Translated by Graham Neville. Crestwood, N.Y.: St. Vladimir's Seminary Press, 1977.

―――. *Wisdom. Let Us Attend: Job, the Fathers and the Old Testament.* Edited by Johanna Manley. Menlo Park, Calif.: Monastery Books, 1997.

John of Antioch. "Letter to Cyril of Alexandria." In *St. Cyril of Alexandria: Letters 51-110*, pp. 184-87. Translated by John I. McEnerney. FC 77. Washington, D.C.: The Catholic University of America Press, 1987.

John of Damascus. *Writings.* Translated by Frederic H. Chase. FC 37. Washington, D.C.: The Catholic University of America Press, 1958.

Julian of Eclanum. "Commentary on Hosea." In *Long-Suffering Love: A Commentary on Hosea with Patristic Annotations.* Translated by Eugen J. Pentiuc. Brookline, Mass.: Holy Cross Orthodox Press, 2002.

Justin Martyr. "Dialogue with Trypho." In *The Apostolic Fathers with Justin Martyr and Irenaeus*, pp. 194-270. Arranged by A. Cleveland Coxe. ANF 1. Edited by Alexander Roberts and James Donaldson. 10 vols. 1885-1887. Reprint, Peabody, Mass.: Hendrickson, 1994.

―――. "First Apology." In *Early Christian Fathers*, pp. 242-89. Translated by Edward Rochie Hardy. LCC 1. Edited by Cyril C. Richardson. Philadelphia: Westminster Press, 1953.

―――. "First Apology." In *The Apostolic Fathers with Justin Martyr and Irenaeus*, pp. 163-87. Arranged by A. Cleveland Coxe. ANF 1. Edited by Alexander Roberts and James Donaldson. 10 vols. 1885-1887. Reprint, Peabody, Mass.: Hendrickson, 1994.

[Justin Martyr]. *Writings of Saint Justin Martyr.* Translated by Thomas B. Falls. FC 6. New York: Christian Heritage, 1948.

Lactantius. *The Divine Institutes: Books I-VII.* Translated by Mary Francis McDonald. FC 49. Washington, D.C.: The Catholic University of America Press, 1964.

Leo the Great. "Sermons." In *Leo the Great, Gregory the Great*, pp. 115-205. Translated by Charles Lett Feltoe. NPNF 12. Series 2. Edited by Philip Schaff and Henry Wace. 14 vols. 1886-1900. Reprint, Peabody, Mass.: Hendrickson, 1994.

―――. *Sermons.* Translated by Jane P. Freeland and Agnes J. Conway. FC 93. Washington, D.C.: The Catholic University of America Press, 1996.

Martin of Braga. "On Pride." In *Iberian Fathers (Volume 1): Martin of Braga, Paschasius of Dumium, Leander of Seville*, pp. 43-50. Translated by Claude W. Barlow. FC 62. Washington, D.C.: The Catholic University of America Press, 1969.

Martyrius. *See* Sahdona.

Maximus of Turin. "Commentary on Jonah." In *The Minor Prophets: A Commentary*, vol. 1. Edited by E. B.

Pusey. Grand Rapids, Mich.: Baker, 1971.

[Maximus of Turin]. *The Sermons of St. Maximus of Turin*. Translated and annotated by Boniface Ramsey. ACW 50. New York: Newman Press, 1989.

[Methodius]. "Methodius." In *Gregory Thaumaturgus, Dionysius the Great, Julius Africanus, Anatolius and Minor Writers, Methodius, Arnobius*, pp. 309-412. Translated by William R. Clark. ANF 6. Edited by Alexander Roberts and James Donaldson. 10 vols. 1885-1887. Reprint, Peabody, Mass.: Hendrickson, 1994.

[Novatian]. "Novatian." In *Fathers of the Third Century: Hippolytus, Cyprian, Caius, Novatian, Appendix*," pp. 611-50. Translated by Robert Ernest Wallis. ANF 5. Edited by Alexander Roberts and James Donaldson. 10 vols. 1885-1887. Reprint, Peabody, Mass.: Hendrickson, 1994.

———. *Novatian: The Trinity, the Spectacles, Jewish Foods, in Praise of Purity, Letters*. Translated by Russell J. DeSimone. FC 67. Washington, D.C.: The Catholic University of America Press, 1974.

Origen. *An Exhortation to Martyrdom, Prayer and Selected Works*. Translated by Rowan A. Greer. The Classics of Western Spirituality. New York: Paulist, 1979.

———. *Commentary on the Gospel According to John Books 1-10 and 13-32*. Translated by Ronald E. Heine. FC 80 and 89. 2 vols. Washington, D.C.: The Catholic University of America Press, 1989, 1993.

———. "Commentary on the Gospel of John." In *The Gospel of Peter, The Diatessaron of Tatian, The Apocalypse of Peter, The Vision of Paul, The Apocalypse of the Virgin and Sedrach, the Testament of Abraham, The Acts of Xanthippe and Polyxena, The Narrative of Zosimus, The Apology of Aristides, The Epistles of Clement, Origen's Commentary on John (Books 1-10), and Commentary on Matthew (Books 1, 2, and 10-14)*," pp. 297-408. Translated by Allan Menzies. ANF 9. Edited by Alexander Roberts and James Donaldson. 10 vols. 1885-1887. Reprint, Peabody, Mass.: Hendrickson, 1994.

———. *Homilies on Genesis and Exodus*. Translated by Ronald E. Heine. FC 71. Washington, D.C.: The Catholic University of America Press, 1982.

———. *Homilies on Jeremiah, Homilies on 1 Kings 28*. Translated by John Clark Smith. FC 97. Washington, D.C.: The Catholic University of America Press, 1998.

———. *Homilies on Leviticus: 1-16*. Translated by Gary Wayne Barkley. FC 83. Washington, D.C.: The Catholic University of America Press, 1990.

———. *Homilies on Luke; Fragments on Luke*. Translated by Joseph T. Lienhard. FC 94. Washington, D.C.: The Catholic University of America Press, 1996.

[Origen]. "Origen." In *Tertullian (IV); Minucius Felix; Commodian; Origen (I and III)*, pp. 221-669. Translated by Frederick Crombie. ANF 4. Edited by Alexander Roberts and James Donaldson. 10 vols. 1885-1887. Reprint, Peabody, Mass.: Hendrickson, 1994.

Pachomius. *Pachomian Koinonia: Volumes One and Three*. Translated by Armand Veilleux. CS 45 and 47. 2 vols. Kalamazoo, Mich.: Cistercian Publications, 1980, 1982.

[Paulinus of Nola]. *The Poems of St. Paulinus of Nola*. Translated and annotated by P. G. Walsh. ACW 40. Edited by Johannes Quasten, Walter J. Burghardt and Thomas Comerford Lawler. New York: Newman Press, 1975.

[Paulus Oriosus]. "Orosius of Braga." In *Iberian Fathers (Volume 3): Pacian of Barcelona, Orosius of Braga*, pp. 97-174. Translated by Craig L. Hanson. FC 99. Washington, D.C.: The Catholic University of America Press, 1999.

Peter Chrysologus. "Sermons." In *Saint Peter Chrysologus: Selected Sermons and Saint Valerian: Homilies*, pp. 25-282. Translated by George E. Ganss. FC 17. New York: Father of the Church, Inc., 1953.

[Pseudo-Barnabas]. *Epistle of Barnabas*. In *The Apostolic Fathers*, pp. 191-222. Translated by Francis X. Glimm. FC 1. New York: Christian Heritage, 1947.

[Pseudo-Clement of Rome]. "2 Clement." In *The Apostolic Fathers*, pp. 65-85. Translated by Francis X.

Glimm. FC 1. New York: Christian Heritage, 1947.

[Pseudo-Dionysius]. *The Complete Works*. Translated by Colm Luibheid. The Classics of Western Spirituality. New York: Paulist, 1980.

Rufinus of Aquileia. "Commentary on the Apostles' Creed." In *Theodoret, Jerome, Gennadius, Rufinus: Historical Writings, etc.*, pp. 541-63. Translated by William Henry Fremantle. NPNF 3. Series 2. Edited by Philip Schaff and Henry Wace. 14 vols. 1886-1900. Reprint, Peabody, Mass.: Hendrickson, 1994.

[Sahdona (Martyrius)]. "Martyrius (Sahdona)." In *The Syriac Fathers on Prayer and the Spiritual Life*, pp. 197-239. Translated by Sebastian Brock. CS 101. Kalamazoo, Mich.: Cistercian Publications, 1987.

[Salvian the Presbyter]. *The Writings of Salvian the Presbyter*. Translated by Jermiah F. O'Sullivan. FC 3. Washington, D.C.: The Catholic University of America Press, 1962.

Shepherd of Hermas. In The Apostolic Fathers, pp. 235-352. Translated by Joseph M.-F. Marique. FC 1. New York: Christian Heritage, 1947.

Symeon the New Theologian. *The Practical and Theological Chapters and the Three Theological Discourses*. Translated by Paul McGuckin. CS 41. Kalamazoo, Mich.: Cistercian Publications, 1982.

Tertullian. *Disciplinary, Moral and Ascetical Works*. Translated by Rudolph Arbesmann, Emily Joseph Daly and Edwin A Quain. FC 40. Washington, D.C.: The Catholic University of America Press, 1959.

———. "On the Soul." In *Tertullian: Apologetical Works, and Minucius Felix: Octavius*, pp. 179-309. Translated by Edwin A. Quain. FC 10. Washington, D.C.: The Catholic University of America Press, 1950.

———. *Treatises on Penance: On Penitence and on Purity*. Translated and annotated by William P. Le Saint. ACW 28. New York: Newman Press, 1959.

———. "Tertullian." In *Tertullian (IV); Minucius Felix; Commodian; Origen (I and III)*, pp. 5-166. Translated by S. Thelwall. ANF 4. Edited by Alexander Roberts and James Donaldson. 10 vols. 1885-1887. Reprint, Peabody, Mass.: Hendrickson, 1994.

[Tertullian]. *Latin Christianity: Its Founder, Tertullian*. Translated by S. Thelwall et al. ANF 3. Edited by Alexander Roberts and James Donaldson. 10 vols. 1885-1887. Reprint, Peabody, Mass.: Hendrickson, 1994.

Theodore of Mopsuestia. "Commentary on Hosea." In *Long-Suffering Love: A Commentary on Hosea with Patristic Annotations*. Translated by Eugen J. Pentiuc. Brookline, Mass.: Holy Cross Orthodox Press, 2002.

———. *Commentary on the Twelve Prophets*. Translated by Robert C. Hill. FC 108. Washington, D.C.: The Catholic University of America Press, 2004 (forthcoming).

Theodoret of Cyr. "Commentary on Hosea." In *Long-Suffering Love: A Commentary on Hosea with Patristic Annotations*. Translated by Eugen J. Pentiuc. Brookline, Mass.: Holy Cross Orthodox Press, 2002.

———. "Ecclesiastical History." In *Theodoret, Jerome, Gennadius, Rufinus: Historical Writings, etc.*, pp. 33-160. Translated by Blomfield Jackson. NPNF 3. Series 2. Edited by Philip Schaff and Henry Wace. 14 vols. 1886-1900. Reprint, Peabody, Mass.: Hendrickson, 1994.

———. *On Divine Providence*. Translated and annotated by Thomas Halton. ACW 49. New York: Newman Press, 1988.

[Theodotus the Valentinian]. "Excerpts of Theodotus." In *The Twelve Patriarchs, Excerpts and Epistles, The Clementina, Apocrypha, Decretals, Memories of Edessa and Syriac Documents, Remains of the First Ages*, pp. 43-50. Translated by William Wilson. ANF 8. Edited by Alexander Roberts and James Donaldson. 10 vols. 1885-1887. Reprint, Peabody, Mass.: Hendrickson, 1994.

Theophilus. "Letters." In *Jerome: Letters and Select Works*, p. 184. Translated by W. H. Fremantle. NPNF 6. Series 2. Edited by Philip Schaff and Henry Wace. 14 vols. 1886-1900. Reprint, Peabody, Mass.: Hendrickson, 1994.

Theophylact. "Commentary on Hosea." In *Long-Suffering Love: A Commentary on Hosea with Patristic Anno-tations*. Translated by Eugen J. Pentiuc. Brookline, Mass.: Holy Cross Orthodox Press, 2002.

Valentinus. "Letter to Augustine." In *Saint Augustine: Letters (Volume V: 204-270)*, pp. 68-73. Translated by Wilfrid Parsons. FC 32. Washington, D.C.: The Catholic University of America Press, 1956.

[Victorinus of Petovium]. "Victorinus." In *Lactantius, Venantius, Asterius, Victorinus, Dionysius, Apostolic Teaching and Constitutions, 2 Clement, Early Liturgies*, pp. 341-60. Translated by Robert Ernest Wallis. ANF 7. Edited by Alexander Roberts and James Donaldson. 10 vols. 1885-1887. Reprint, Peabody, Mass.: Hendrickson, 1994.

Subject Index

Aaron, xxv, 89, 168, 170, 266, 267, 270, 283, 289, 292, 309
Abel, 154, 173, 174, 286
abomination of desolation, 154
Abraham, 45, 154, 164, 165, 166, 192, 194, 246, 286, 289, 292, 297, 300
abstinence, 89, 109, 251
Achan, 10
Adam, 27, 39, 142, 184, 237
adamant, 108
admonition, 42, 70, 134, 142-43, 184. *See also* correction
adoption, 5, 10-11, 55, 99-100, 112, 286, 288
adornment, 211, 214
adultery, 4, 9, 17, 20, 22, 31, 37, 51, 89, 92, 98, 145, 174, 298
advent, first
    Jews and, xxi
    mildness of, 64
    nations and, 228
    prophecy of, 201, 283-84, 299, 302
    signs of, 311
advent, second
    Jesus and, 271
    Jesus' garment represents, 225
    judgment and, xxii, 64, 258-59
    Old and New Testaments and, 228
    prophecy of, xxi, xxiv, 191, 200-202, 226, 280, 299, 301
    signs of, 311
    See also return of Christ; second coming
adversity, 8-9, 137, 166. *See also* persecution; trials; tribulations
Africa, 201-2
afterlife, 206

Agatho, 82
Ahab, 123, 170, 235, 287, 313
Ahaz, 85, 149, 151
Ahijah, 104
Alexandrian exegesis, xviii n, 117
almsgiving, xxiv, 61, 305, 308
Amaziah, 83, 110, 124
Ambrose, 74
Amos, xxii, 83-84, 107-10, 117, 119, 120
angel of God, 240, 295, 299
angel(s)
    appearance of, 234
    demons and, 234-35
    diversity of, 234
    in the fiery furnace, 55
    hierarchy of, 236
    horses, chariots and, 204, 249
    as inner voice of God, 234
    John the Baptist as, 299-300
    men as, 223, 299-300
    in paradise, 162
    saints and, 244
    work of, 223
anger, 24, 144, 146-47, 199, 255-56
anointing, 193
Anthony, 21, 32
antichrist, xxiii-xxiv, 53, 245, 294, 313
Antiochene exegesis, xviii n
Antiochus, 281
anvil, 109
Apelles, 211
apostasy, xxii, 126
apostates, 78, 126
apostles, 160-61
Apostles' Creed, xxiii
Aquila, 154
Araratites, 72
Archelaus, 41
Arzanites, 72
asceticism, lack of, 213
ass, 259
Assyrians
    defeat of, 184, 218
    as "the northerner," 72
    oppressors of Israel, 83-84, 123, 129, 130, 132, 161, 167
Athanasius, 82, 157
axe, 175, 247
Baal, 126
Baal-peor, 38, 287
Babylon, 244-45

Babylonians, 2, 72, 83-84, 118, 125, 161, 163, 178
Balaam, 130, 259, 287
Balak, 170
baldness, 152
baptism
    of blasphemers, 294
    into death, 27-28, 252
    the exodus represents, 176
    Holy Spirit and, 74
    of infants, 242
    of Jesus, 241
    prophets and, 241
    Red Sea represents, xxiii, 177
    regeneration and, 25, 65, 174-75, 241
    as a sacrament, 291-92
    sin and, 176-77, 241
    of water, fire and spirit, 313
barbarians, 204
Basil, 137
Basilla, 102
Belial, 21
belief and obedience to God, 312
believers, Jewish and Gentile, 259
Benjamin, 125, 259
Bethlehem
    Messiah prophesied from, 40-41, 163-68
    prophecies regarding, xviii, xxiii, 160, 201
betrayal, 275-76
betrothal, 12
Bez'alel, 224
bishop(s), 42, 70, 286-87. *See also* priest(hood)
blessing, 99, 229
boasting, 180
body, 39, 53, 75, 170, 217, 262
bread, 15, 32, 38, 45, 95, 112, 113, 290-91, 292
Caesar Augustus, 166
Caiaphas, 287
Cain, 45, 89, 154 n, 174, 244, 286, 288
calamity, 62
calf, golden, 22, 24
calling, 6, 13, 129-30, 256
canon, xix, xxi-xxii
captivity. *See* exile
carelessness, 9, 42
catastrophes, natural, 91-92, 143
celestial bodies, 65, 77. *See also* sun worship

chaff, 125, 173-74
Chaldeans, 122-23
change, 142, 303-4
chariots, 204, 248-49
chastisement, 25, 44, 264
chastity, 12-13, 52, 244
cheek, 44, 64, 165
Chemosh, 38
child of God, 175
Christ, Jesus. *See* Jesus Christ
christ, title of, 205, 270
Christian calling, 256
christology, 202
church
    ass represents, 259
    Gilead represents, 86
    islands represent, 213
    Jerusalem represents, xxiii
    Jesus and, 3, 11 n, 308-9
    Mount Esau represents, xxiii, 126
    Mount Zion represents, xxiii, 123
    new Israel as, xxi
    the old covenant and, xvii
    prophecy and/of, xx-xxv, 13-14, 202
    Rachel represents, 286
    struggles of, 3
    temple restored represents, 228
    universality of, 217, 291
circumcision, 267, 291
    of the heart, 236
city, the bloody, 185
clergy, 286-87. *See also* bishop(s); priest(hood); spiritual leaders
commandment, the greatest, 29, 171-72
community of faith, 6
compassion, 12, 29, 45, 68, 93, 108, 141, 144, 170, 171, 177, 188-89, 253, 264
complacency, condemnation of 103-7
condescension, 4, 9, 48, 49, 304
confession of faith, xxii, 68, 86, 161, 218
conversion, xx, 32, 236-37, 256
cornerstone, 109
correction, 22, 42, 69
covenant
    baptism and, 149
    church and, xvii
    forgiveness of, 70-71
    fulfillment of the new, xxiii
    inclusiveness of the new,

Scripture Index